The Blackwell Guide to the
Musical Theatre on Record

by

Kurt Gänzl

Blackwell Reference

First published 1990

Basil Blackwell Ltd
108 Cowley Road, Oxford, OX4 1JF, UK

Basil Blackwell Inc.
3 Cambridge Center, Cambridge, MA 02142, USA

British Library Cataloguing in Publication Data
Gänzl, Kurt 1946–
The Blackwell guide to the musical theatre on record.
(Blackwell guides)
1. Musical shows
I. Title
782.14
ISBN 0–631–16517–7

Library of Congress Cataloging-in-Publication Data
Gänzl, Kurt.
The Blackwell guide to the musical theatre on record
by Kurt Gänzl.
p. cm.
ISBN 0–631–16517–7
1. Musical theater—Reviews. 2. Sound recordings—Reviews.
3. Musical theater—Discography. I. Title.
ML156.9.G36 1990
782.1'4'0266—dc20 89–78226 CIP MN

Typeset by Opus, Oxford
Printed in Great Britain by
T.J. Press Ltd, Padstow, Cornwall

This book was written with assistance from the Authors' Foundation.

CONTENTS

Introduction by Gerald Bordman   ix

Author's Preface   xi

1   From *Opéra-bouffe* to *Opérette*   1

2   Victorian and Edwardian Musical Comedy in Britain   53

3   Vienna's Golden Age   87

4   LPs of America's Pre-LP Days   153

5   Britain Between the Great War and the LP   214

6   The Continental Musical from Supremacy to Oblivion   241

7   Bonanza on Broadway: the first part   311

8   Bonanza on Broadway: the second part   384

9   Thirty Years of British Musicals, 1950–1980   431

10   The 1980s   476

Index   518

INTRODUCTION

'I sing of songs and a man.'

The songs are the songs composed for the Western world's most popular stages – for the rococo operetta houses of Central Europe, for the multi-tiered, guilded boulevard auditoriums of Paris, for the cramped, inelegant theatres of the West End and Broadway. Such show music is a genre apart and seems to have been so from early on. To one side are the honky-tonk outpourings of Tin Pan Alley, Denmark Street and their Paris and Berlin equivalents. On the other side are art songs and opera. For many, show tunes fall so comfortably in between: not too cheap, not too lofty – just right. They are the melodies generation after generation have whistled carelessly while walking down the street. They are the songs to which, until recently, everyone danced, dined and rode elevators. For more than a century they have been part and parcel of our lives. Sad to say, in recent years great new show tunes have become increasingly rare. There were decades when one musical after another each provided three, four or five – occasionally more – standards. Today a whole decade can pass without leaving behind more than the most meagre handful of durable favourites. A generation has come of age nurtured on fast food and rock and roll, and has known little about and cared even less for our older traditions. Are we simply in a slump? Or are we about to close the book on a truly popular, creative and memorable musical stage? If so, we can at least be grateful that the advent and development of recorded sound followed with such reasonable swiftness the birth and growth of modern musical theatre. And we are doubly fortunate that the appearance of the LP (and now of the CD) often allowed virtually a show's entire score to be imprinted on a single, relatively imperishable disc. This book examines most of those discs.

Then there's the man who does the examining. Kurt Gänzl effortlessly transcends the parochialism of all too many theatrical historians – Germans whose knowledge extends no farther than Austria and Hungary, Frenchmen whose world is confined to the city limits of Paris, English and American writers who think themselves renaissance men because they know a mite about each others' musicals. He's a man for all theatrical seasons, a man of the theatrical world. He has been a performer, an agent, a casting director and a librettist. He is fluent in French, not thrown for a loss by German, and, since he was born and raised in New Zealand, speaks English almost like a native. Kurt is as much at home with *Les P'tites Michu* as with *Li'l Abner*; he will just as soon hum something from *The Beggar's Opera* as from *Der Bettelstudent*. As a result, readers will find material here on practically every musical they are curious about – from the most celebrated to the most neglected – so long as it has been put on LP or CD. (He has overlooked *Ankles Aweigh* and *Seventh Heaven*, but nobody's perfect.) Kurt is so knowledgeable and so well connected that he has even heard tapes of unreleased material; perhaps after some record company reads his mouth-watering description of the Smithsonian's as yet unpublished *Rose Marie* they will rush it into print.

There's one additional bonus. Kurt is not a stolid, dry-as-dust scholar. You'll find that reading this book is every bit as delightful as listening to the records he recommends.

Gerald Bordman

AUTHOR'S PREFACE

The purpose of this book is to gather in review the bulk of the many recordings of British, American, French, German, Austrian and Hungarian operettas and musicals made over the forty odd years since the introduction of the long-playing record, and to extract from this vast mass of material a representative selection of one hundred of the very best recordings which might make up a small but all-embracing collection for someone starting out as a collector of show recordings.

The book falls naturally into two parts. In the earlier chapters, those dealing with the French, Austrian, German and Hungarian operettas of the nineteenth and twentieth centuries, with the Gilbert and Sullivan era and with those of the pre-war musicals of Britain and America that have been given modern recordings, I have first been concerned to let the reader know what actually exists. Often it is very little, and when this is the case I have simply tried to show just what recorded coverage has been given to the show in question; when there are two or three recordings I have attempted to compare the attractions of each version and perhaps come out with a recommendation. But sometimes it is a tidal wave: such pieces as *Die Fledermaus* and *Die lustige Witwe*, for example, have been recorded in every size, shape and language imaginable, and over and over again. In such instances, as I had no intention of giving over thirty or forty pages to endless reviews of little selections from one operetta, I have limited myself to dealing with the more complete recordings on the reasoning that, since these pieces are so famous and popular, any collection should include a full-scale recording rather than one disc of snippets.

In these early chapters, however, I have attempted to mention and, to a lesser or greater extent, deal with each and every show from the period which has appeared on a record under its own title. That is to say, I have not gone so far as to track down every individual number from an otherwise unrecorded show which may appear on a concert or recital disc, but have been concerned largely with such shows as have a record or part record to themselves, even if it be only a 45 EP.

The second part of the book, the part that covers the recordings of shows from the LP era itself, had to be dealt with differently. Whereas, by and large, the shows from earlier days which now appear on record represent only the best and most long-lived of the thousands that were produced, in more recent years we have seen the advent of the so-called original cast recording and the confiding to disc, at some periods in time, of virtually every show that appeared on the stage – large, small, good, bad, indifferent, long-running, closed-before-opening or, sometimes, never produced. The mass of modern show material on disc is vast and, under these circumstances, it was necessary to be more selective. Although, in dealing with the shows of the LP age, I have covered wide areas of the musical theatre of the last forty years, it has not been possible to mention or to discuss every one of these thousands of recordings; whilst always looking at things from a broad standpoint, I have limited myself to those which are, in my opinion, the most important and the most interesting. Thus, rather than dig deeply into the umpteenth and unsuccessful work by a composer or writer with many successes to his or her name, I have preferred to look at perhaps equally unsuccessful pieces by authors who are not so heavily represented. After all, anyone who wants to own records of every show of Richard Rodgers, for example, only need look in the catalogues. Here, I limit myself to the large body of his best and most successful work, and move on to deal with lesser-known composers.

For these later chapters, I have, again, when the number of recordings of an individual piece has become extravagant, limited myself to dealing with original and revival cast recordings in preference to studio cast recordings – except on occasions where one of the last is of a particular interest or standard. I have, however, always included any foreign-language recordings – which, in the case of such pieces as *My Fair Lady*, involved almost a week of listening to cover the vast list of *Mi bella dama*s and suchlike which have been issued over the years.

There are two ways of approaching all these recordings. Often, with the many works which are not well-known classics of the musical stage, it is necessary to review the material that makes up the show with equal or even more consideration than the way in which it is performed. In these cases it is the show itself which will be of prime interest to the listener. On the other hand, it is scarcely necessary to summarize the content of *The Mikado*, *Die Fledermaus* or *Oklahoma!* – here we are concerned as to which gives us the best performance of the show.

This, of course, involves opinions, and what you will read in this book are simply my opinions. Like everyone else, I have tastes and prejudices insofar as shows are concerned, though I flatter myself that I have a wide taste in music; I am equally at home with rock opera and Gilbert and Sullivan, and I have always loved and enjoyed musical theatre of all kinds. I also, equally naturally, have preferences and prejudices where performers and performances are concerned, preferences which only grew and were confirmed over my hectic years as a casting director for the West End musical theatre, and I judge by these criteria in selecting my favourite discs. Somewhere in this world there may be people who like hooty, wobbly sopranos, bottled-up baritones and constipated tenors with a passion for oversinging, performers who howl and bellow rather than sing, those who are unable to keep in tune, or those who give such an effect of effort that it is impossible to enjoy their mincing of the music. There must be, because people who fit these descriptions turn up time and time again on record. I don't enjoy listening to them, so you will not find them amongst the discs I recommend.

The hundred selected discs – ten from each of the ten chapters – have been backed up by a further list of enjoyable and/or interesting recordings, so that anyone finding particular pleasure in one area or another may be able to expand his or her collection more widely in that particular sphere. Some of this may take doing, for I have not confined myself to recordings that are currently on release. I have covered all those recordings issued since the mid-1940s, of which the largest part are now to be found only by diligent searching in the many very fine specialist second-hand record shops of the world – a type of establishment that must now just about outnumber the serious new-record shops. Apart from being great fun, these searches can yield all sorts of enjoyable discoveries.

The coming of the compact disc has been a blessing, as it has resulted in the reissue of a good number of the best performances of the past which had virtually disappeared as black vinyl records. There are still many such, of course, and not only from the smaller record companies, which have not reappeared – for example, the outstanding French EMI operetta series begun in the 1950s – and there have also been reissues of some of the worst recordings known to man's ears. But in spite of the fact that the sound quality of a reissue is not the same as that of a made-for-CD recording, the new medium may yet prove to be a safety-line for the preservation of the great recordings of the past. Let us hope that it is.

'Sound quality' is not something that you will hear me talk about very much in this book. I am not a hi-fi expert, and unless the sound on a recording is of such a kind as either to spoil my pleasure or to make me sit up and drool (in the way some modern CDs do), you will not find me lingering amongst the woofers and tweeters. If the performance and the show come through clearly and unaffectedly, that is all I ask.

There is a handful of recordings which I know exist and which, despite serious searching, I have unfortunately never been able to find, and they are passed over, obviously, without comment in this book; it is perhaps only right that what would seem to be unfindable rarities are not evaluated. By and large, the records (and issue numbers) of which I speak are those in my own collection, supplemented by some borrowings from my friends Ian Bevan, Rexton S. Bunnett and Andrew Lamb. Although I think I and they know of every musical theatre disc that has been issued on LP, it is always possible there is the odd one, particularly from Europe or South America, which has escaped us. If so, I'd be delighted to hear about them (c/o Basil Blackwell, 108 Cowley Road, Oxford OX4 1JF, England).

In the same way, whilst there have been original cast recordings of contemporary musicals from Italy, Scandinavia, Australia, Russia, Lebanon, Israel, East Germany, the Netherlands and many other countries, they do not appear in these pages. Few of them have been successful and even fewer have had any sort of significant life outside their own countries, and their recordings, of which there

are a considerable number, are normally sought only by collectors whose care is
to be as complete as possible.

Wishing you happy hunting and happy listening,

KURT GÄNZL
St Paul de Vence, 1990

CHAPTER 1

From *opéra-bouffe* to *opérette*

The world-wide flowering of the modern light musical theatre began in the 1850s with the vast international popularity of the French *opéra-bouffe*, that delicious combination of burlesque humour and superbly joyful music initiated and most successfully practised by the composers Jacques Offenbach and Hervé and their librettists. Although first the German and Austrian operetta and then the British comic opera and musical comedy came to challenge and, for certain periods, eclipse the subsequent products of French authors and composers in the later nineteenth and early twentieth centuries, France continued, through more than half a century, to supply a steady stream of fine works not only to its own stages but also to, particularly, the English and German-speaking theatres of the world, which it had so thoroughly dominated in the middle of the nineteenth century. The great French comic playwrights of the era teamed with such composers as Charles Lecocq, Robert Planquette, Edmond Audran and André Messager to produce a body of works which became the classic core of the French musical stage repertoire – works which were restaged regularly both at home and abroad for many decades.

France has rarely received the products of the British and American musical theatre with any enthusiasm and, although the Viennese operetta became the rage on French stages in the years before the Great War, it, too, left only a minor imprint on the basic repertoire of the French theatre. *Rose-Marie, No, No, Nanette, Le Chant du désert* and, in more recent years, *Hello, Dolly!, Un Violon sur le toit (Fiddler on the Roof)* and *La Mélodie de bonheur (The Sound of Music)* have won and still win performances in French theatres, *Balalaika*, thoroughly dead in Britain, has been known to surface in the provinces, whilst *Der Zigeunerbaron, Ein Walzertraum, Das Dreimäderlhaus, Walzer aus Wien, Im weissen Rössl, Die Csárdásfürstin, Drei Walzer, Das Land des Lächelns* and *Die lustige Witwe* remain to represent the heyday of the Viennese theatre. But, although *L'Auberge du Cheval Blanc* and *Le Pays de sourire* rate amongst the most frequently performed works and *Les Trois valses* is infinitely more popular in France than in its native Germany, by and large, the French theatre prefers, and has almost always preferred, its own shows.

Since the second war, however, the French tradition has been in decline. Whilst the light musical theatre as a spectator sport has gone from one strength to another in Britain and America, and whilst the musical houses of the other European countries have, until very recently, plunged happily on with a repertoire of mainly old favourites, the *opérette*, as the French happily call virtually all light musical theatre, has become unpopular, scorned even (nay, particularly) by the sophisticated folk of Paris. With the odd notable exception, the few French attempts at new pieces in recent years have been sadly limp, the periodic revivals of past glories – usually brought from one of the more enterprising provincial theatres which now seem to constitute the last living and growing heart of the French musical theatre – under-appreciated, and the imports mostly ignored.

One of the results of this decline, which was becoming reasonably well defined in the 1950s, is that the original cast recording has never held in France the position it established on Broadway and in London in the post-war years. There was little in the way of successful new shows to put on to the increasingly popular long-playing record and it was probably partly as a result of this that the record companies looked back to the great shows of the old-established standard repertoire which were still, at that date, played in Paris and even more frequently in the provinces.

Unlike Britain and America which, with plenty of new works to promote, largely failed at this time to look back to shows of the pre-LP era for new recordings, France has done well by the works of its classic repertoire. The coverage may be a little patchy and the choices of works recorded sometimes a little eccentric, but at least there is a substantial coverage and the modern listener has access, both in the current catalogue and in deletions which are still not too difficult to find, to a splendid selection of recordings of the most outstanding shows of the great days of the French musical theatre.

For this, we have two record companies, in particular, to thank. The first is Pathé-Marconi (now EMI-Pathé) and the second Decca. From the early 1950s, these two firms began to issue, variously, so-called full-length (*intégrale*) versions, where the score was tied together with usually potted stretches of dialogue, and vocal selections from the principal favourites of the *opérette* repertoire. Most of these recordings, added to during the 1960s and very occasionally in the early 1970s, have been liberally reissued and maintained in the catalogue virtually ever since. Other labels, notably Festival, Véga and CBS, took a similar route, but usually only with a few of the most popular pieces, and Pathé's list of more than forty shows and the Decca list of thirty plus remained, and remain, the significant part of the discs available.

We also have to thank the French radio (ORTF), which at the same period recorded and broadcast practically the entire principal repertoire of light musical theatre – native and foreign – as played in France in the post-war years. These recordings have been safely enshrined in the Institut National de l'Audiovisuel (INA – the French have a mania for acronyms) in Paris, from where, in the 1980s, a number of splendidly made examples have been plucked and released on disc and subsequently on compact disc by various record companies.

Fortunately, the period of all these recordings was one especially rich in outstanding French *opérette* performers, and the Pathé set, in particular, is almost always impeccably cast. Performers such as the cool, clear high baritone Michel Dens, the delightfully light-hearted and true-voiced soprano Liliane Berton and the fine comedian Duvaleix appear on many of these recordings alongside a *brochette* of soaring and sweet-voiced tenors such as a producer would give his left speaker for in these deprived days. This series is a fine example of how intelligent and knowledgeable casting of what are not theatrical but studio cast recordings can give a set a continued and highly appreciated life even when considered in competition with later, technically more advanced versions of the same material.

The most important part of the later recordings are, once again, the work of EMI. Whereas Decca issued a large number of complete or quasi-complete recordings in its early listings, the original Pathé issues were almost entirely excerpts discs. Over the last decade or so, EMI have gradually brought out new, complete versions of a number of the most popular works. By and large, the performances do not go anywhere near equalling those on the older series, and there is a tendency – in line with modern fashions – to more operatic singing and heavier and more thickly recorded orchestral playing; however, improved sound techniques and a tardy conversion to the inclusion of the libretto (or of the cut-up version recorded) and detailed sleeve notes instead of the minimal information given on most French recordings are significant plusses.

The Decca and EMI sets cover the entire first hundred years of the French musical theatre but, although they give a very fair general overview of that century's shows, they rarely include lesser-known works and cannot and do not cover each composer's work in any depth. For that, one has to look elsewhere and, alas, generally without luck. Only one composer, Offenbach, has been systematically recorded and released, on the Bourg label, in an excellent series taken from the radio broadcasts of the 1960s, but after an initial spurt of a dozen or so records which, fortunately, included several of the otherwise unavailable titles, this series, which has appeared on CD as well as on disc, seems sadly to have ceased.

Outside their two or three favourite works, Hervé, Lecocq, Planquette and Audran are not represented on disc, and only Messager, thanks to Pathé, gets anything like a deeper representation. Regrettably, but understandably, record producers, like theatre producers, have always found it safer to issue yet another *Les Cloches de Corneville*, *La Vie parisienne* or *La Fille de Madame Angot* rather than risk filling in one or two of the historical and musical gaps. In the operatic field this stage has been reached and passed and, in the 1980s, recording companies have varied their output marvellously with a mixture of well-known and very much less known works. Perhaps one day the light musical theatre will get the same consideration.

Opéra bouffe: Offenbach

The *opéra-bouffe*, which set so much in motion during the brief period in which it reigned supreme, is relatively well represented on record but, as noted, almost entirely in the shape of the works of Offenbach. *Orphée aux enfers*, *La Belle Hélène*, and *La Grande-Duchesse de Gérolstein*, which are all still regularly performed in the opera and operetta houses of the world, can be found in a variety of recordings, as can *La Périchole* and *La Vie parisienne* which, in spite of their authors' description, cannot be regarded as *opéra-bouffe* in the true burlesque sense of the term.

The splendid *Geneviève de Brabant*, *Barbe-Bleue* and *Le Pont des soupirs*, all in more or less complete versions with dialogue, and a selection from *Les Brigands* (under the Milan label) are amongst the Bourg issues, along with an appreciable series of the composer's shorter pieces, including *La Chanson de Fortunio*, *Croquefer*, *Ba-ta-Clan*, *Les Deux Aveugles*, *Le Violoneux*, *La Rose de Saint-Flour*, *Les Deux Pêcheurs*, *Lischen et Fritzchen*, *Pomme d'api* and *Le Leçon de chant*. Elsewhere, *Les Bavards* appears on the Erato DUE label, twinned with *Ba-ta-Clan*, which has also been the subject of a recent recording on Pluriel; *Monsieur Choufleuri restera chez lui le . . .* has been issued on Gallo and again on EMI in a three-record box set with *Mesdames de la Halle* and *Pomme d'api* (the result of a successful theatre production of this triple bill in 1983), while *L'Ile de Tulipatan* and *Tromb-al-ca-zar* have been produced on the gallant TLP label, whose enthusiasm to put Mlle Claudine Granger on record in as large a variety of roles as possible has led to one or two hitherto unavailable works appearing unexpectedly on disc. Recordings of *La Boulangère a des écus* and *Le Château à Toto* were issued on the Golden Age label and several other records bootlegged from radio broadcasts have also emerged but, unlike the discs listed above, these are not readily available. Some of the shorter works have, like the major Offenbach shows, also appeared in languages other than the original French.

The three long-lived and lively staples of the *opéra-bouffe* repertoire have been given regular attention by the world of the gramophone record, both in the original French and in other languages.

Orphée aux enfers

Orphée aux enfers has, on the whole, come out the best of the three. Although Decca saw fit to bypass *Orphée* (and, by and large, Offenbach in general) in its series, Musidisc Festival in 1952 and Pathé in 1953 were both quick off the mark with very enjoyable complete and excerpt recordings respectively. Both these *Orphée*s are well cast and well performed and both gain much from the presence of Claudine Collart (disappointingly little recorded otherwise) as a joyfully petulant and girlish Eurydice.

The Festival two-record set, regularly re-released and for a long time the standard recording of the work, represents the original 1858 version of *Orphée*, as played in two acts. Collart, whose beautifully sweet, light soprano carries a delicious giggle and whose piquantly squeaky acting is full of *bouffe*, is delicious at the head of affairs, making Eurydice into a poutingly sexy ancient Greek schoolgirl. Her Hymn to Bacchus has none of the abandoned lushery of some Eurydices – this is a wide-eyed, naughty little girl who knows more about wine and men than she ought.

She is equipped with two fine leading tenors – Jean Mollien as a virile Orpheus and André Dran a winsome Pluto. There is also a Jupiter (Bernard Demigny) who bites into his dialogue vigorously and a charming Diana (Janine Lindenfelder) who makes the most of her hunting couplets, and, even if some of the lesser members of the pantheon are less sure vocally than the leading players, the overall standard of solo and choral singing is fine. René Leibowitz, at the helm, moves things along at a good vigorous clip most, but annoyingly not all, of the time, and it is not difficult to see why this more than competent recording remained for so long the unchallenged *intégrale* version of *Orphée aux enfers*.

The Pathé excerpts disc, however, has the advantage over its contemporary in two important areas. The first is in the extremely spirited swing of its performance under the direction of the admirable Jules Gressier, and the second in its very superior casting. Mlle Collart's *confrères* on this occasion are Claude Devos (Orphée) and Aimé Doniat (Pluton), and the only reason I can imagine for casting them that way round is the fact that there is much more of Orphée's music on this selection than there is of Pluton's. Devos's seductive tones, along with some winning violin playing, make this flibberty-gibbet of a Eurydice seem a horribly ungrateful little wife. When a husband sings and plays as enticingly as do Devos and the first violinist of the Concerts Lamoureux in the deliciously performed concerto scene, it seems simply perverse of the girl to go gallivanting off with even the most handsome of shepherds. However, although the palm for beautiful singing amongst the men indubitably goes to Devos, both tenors are splendid and, with Michel Roux as a briskly characterful and true-voiced Jupiter and Liliane Berton enticingly pouting out her sad story of parental interference as a crystalline Diana at the head of a fine selection of immortals (Andrée Grandjean, Deva Dassy, Huguette Prudhon, Pierre Germain), this recording leaves little to be desired on the level of performance.

It does, however, have one grave disadvantage. A one-record *Orphée* simply cannot fit in all the favourite highlights of this most continuously melodious and sparkling show, and the pieces chosen for the Pathé recording omit some important sections of the score. The concerto scene, the awakening of the gods and Diana's couplets, the Transformation Rondo and the finale represent the first act; the Fly Duet, the Hymn to Bacchus, and the minuet and galop leading to the dénouement are included from the second. Eurydice's beautiful opening song, 'La Femme dont le coeur rêve', Aristeus' entrance solo ('Je suis Aristée'), Eurydice's death ('La Mort m'apparaît souriante') and the song of John Styx ('Quand j'étais roi de Béotie') are all missing. The chuckle-voiced singing comedian Duvaleix was at this time a part of the Pathé team, and his version of the pathologically gloomy song of the Boeotian King would have been worth hearing.

All these missing pieces turn up on another very fine selection record, but this one is in English. The 1960 recording of the memorable Sadler's Wells Theatre production in its superbly humorous and atmospheric translation by Geoffrey Dunn is equally memorable on disc. Alexander Faris zips through the score with such Gallic glee that, in spite of including a lengthy overture, only the opening of the second act and the last finale of the pieces included in the Pathé selection have to be omitted to make space for the rest of the best of the bon-bons.

The star of the recording, as of the production, is the Australian soprano June Bronhill as Eurydice. Like Liliane Berton in France, Miss Bronhill proved to be the outstanding recording artist in the operetta and musical comedy area in Britain in the 1960s, her straight, clear and wide-ranging soprano voice coupled with a fine sense of humour and of characterization making the most of a series of rôles – of which this is certainly one of the very best – under the HMV label and producer Norman Newell. Both these artists will recur time and again through the pages which follow, infallibly giving glorious performances of a range of musical theatre rôles. The recording legacy of the 1960s would be very much poorer without them.

Kevin Miller is a nicely stiff-necked Orpheus with a clean tenor voice, who battles against his wife's sour imitations of his violin playing through the concerto scene with all the evidence of wounded dignity. This time it is quite evident to the ears that Eurydice is right in thinking she is going to have much more fun being dead with the dapper Aristaeus/Pluto of Jon Weaving. Eric Shilling (Jupiter) lets himself go with a sizzling set of 'buzzes' in the Fly Duet, Alan Crofoot sings a rich and suitably flat-faced 'King of the Boeotians' and Suzanne Steele gives a slightly staid version of Diana's couplets, but it is clearly Miss Bronhill's show and Miss Bronhill's record. Her opening number, her attack on her husband and his music, her beautifully rich and flowing Invocation to Death, her proud, self-confident Hymn to Bacchus, and her sparky and technically triumphant contribution to the Fly Duet (try singing 'zzzz' on the notes she takes here without bursting something) are each and every one a joy.

All three of these fine recordings have much to recommend them: the first has its completeness, the second its superb cast, and the third the fine combination of a comprehensive selection and an outstanding star performance, and it was undoubtedly these superior qualities which long dissuaded record companies from trying to challenge the existing sets. It was not until 1979, some thirty years after the first, that a new and complete French *Orphée* was issued.

This version, on EMI, follows the text of the revised and enlarged 1874 *Orphée*, including large expanses of ballet music, and, as a result, stretches to three records. It is one of the better modern EMI sets, going less far in the currently popular direction of heavy playing and singing than some others. However, a tendency to a potentially comedy-killing large sound can be forgiven in this case, when it is considered that this expanded version of the most twinkling of *opéras-bouffes* was expressly produced by Offenbach and his collaborators to be an *Orphée* on a grand scale.

Oddly, Mady Mesplé, the most widely recorded French operetta soprano of recent years, is not at her very best in a rôle which would seem perfect for her as a silvery-voiced but uneven Eurydice in the classic style, but her Orphée (Michel Sénéchal) is impeccable in singing and in broadly pompous comedy, and her Aristée (Charles Burles) is highly enjoyable in both dialogue and singing except when he bursts very dubiously into ugly falsetto. Jane Rhodes is a superbly fearsome Public Opinion – easily the best available – yodelling out the Monster's commands like a bibulous Brunnhilde, and Michel Trempont is a stentorian Jupiter at the head of a full-voiced set of lesser deities. The additional numbers tacked into the new *Orphée* give André Mallabrera, as a nimble Mercury, and Jane Berbié, as a Cupid who sounds like Venus' mother rather than her son, rather more to do than we are used to.

This recording is certainly interesting as a document but, although they may have been the excuse for much magnificence on the stage, the additions Offenbach made to his original score really do little more than water down the string of gems which made up *Orphée* Mark 1 and, from a happy listening point of view, the four-act *Orphée* is not as incessantly enjoyable as the two-act version. Since the performance, whilst mostly more than respectable and occasionally (as in the case of Mlle Rhodes) simply grand, is not overall as appreciable as those on earlier discs, the only reason to prefer this set would be to have the only complete recording of *Orphée* Mark 2, or to have the show, in its original language, on CD – for neither the Festival Musidisc set nor the Pathé selection have, for the moment at least, been transferred to that medium.

Amongst the other *Orphée*s there are several German-language versions, on record and CD, including a complete 1978 set on EMI which provides practically all that could be asked for anyone seeking a good two-act *Orpheus in der Unterwelt*. It has one or two drawbacks – an occasional lack of gaiety and a few draggy tempi on the recording and the most curious and horribly translated booklet of notes with it – but by and large it is a well-sung, well-acted, well-played version of this uncredited German version. Highlights include a richly roguish Jupiter from Benno Kusche, the most lovely, fresh singing from Brigitte Lindner as a Cupid who really sounds young, and a lip-smacking performance from Ferry Gruber who plays Aristée in flute-like tones and makes melodramatic mincemeat of Pluto's lines. Adolf Dallapozza is a nicely pompous Orphée (with a running joke of musical quotes from *Die lustige Witwe* to *Fidelio*), Anneliese Rothenberger sings as impeccably as ever as Eurydice without ever convincing you that she is the sexpot who set the Styx on fire, Gisela Litz is a strict, motherly Public Opinion and Theo Lingen a repulsive Styx with an unfunnily rewritten song.

There is no full-scale English *Orphée*, but in 1987 That's Entertainment Records produced a cast recording of the newest English version, based on the four-act *Orphée*, written by Snoo Wilson and staged at the English National Opera in 1985. A timely reissue of the Sadler's Wells recording by EMI, however, served only to emphasize the large superiority both of the Geoffrey Dunn text (based on the two-act original) and the performances of the earlier production and record.

La Belle Hélène

Offenbach's other great burlesque of classical antiquity, *La Belle Hélène*, is more substantially represented by five double-record versions and two other recordings of excerpts. As in the case of *Orphée*, it is the earliest records that prove to be the most appreciable.

The Musidisc Festival complete recording of 1952 features Linda Felder, alias Janine Linda (who is surely, in any case, the Janine Lindenfelder of the *Orphée* set), as Hélène and André Dran as Paris. Under the happily smooth baton of René Leibowitz both artists give very sweetly sung and cheerfully played burlesque performances. She is piquant in her scenes and charmingly pretty in her singing, and he floats and waltzes through his rôle, opening up the voice only when necessary. There is lively and well-sung support from the boyish sounding Loly Valdarnini as Orestes and from a competent bunch of kings, headed by Jean Mollien's fine Achilles, on a clean, crisp mono set which certainly equals its equivalent *Orphée*, like which it remained, for many years, the standard recording of the work.

However, had Pathé chosen to extend their 1952 excerpts disc into a full-length recording there is little doubt that this would have been a very serious rival. This one-disc *Belle Hélène* omits Orestes' 'Au cabaret du labyrinthe', the Snakes-and-Ladders sequence of the second act and the Menelaos/Helen duet of the last act of the principal music, and gives only part of the second-act finale but, of course, it forgoes the dialogue included on the double-disc set. It is a recording with rather more gusto and personality than the Festival one. Both the orchestra, under Jules Gressier, and the cast seem to be having a lot of fun with the piece without ever overstepping the limits of *opéra-bouffe* style. It yields to the Festival recording in only one area, but that area is a particularly important one – its Helen. This is the beginning of a downward trend in Helens – not necessarily in quality but in voice. Deva Dassy is a vigorous and amusing Helen, but the actual vocal sound she produces is a heavier soprano than that of Mlle Felder and neither as attractive nor as joyously free.

The cast is otherwise as perfect as one could wish. Claude Devos as Paris sails through Offenbach's gloriously lilting version of the famous tale of the Judgement of Paris ('Au Mont Ida trois déesses') with an amazing ease and clarity on a track which I find myself putting this record on just to have the pleasure of listening to once again; Duvaleix gives a genuine comedian's performance as the cuckolded Menelaos, in contrast to the more straightly sung versions of most other recordings; Willy Clément is a rich tenor Agamemnon and Michel Roux a sonorous and globally ideal Calchas. The small rôle of the second Ajax is taken by no less a performer than Aimé Doniat, and what little remains of Orestes' music is sung with sopranic sparkle by Liliane Berton (who would have been a delicious Helen). It all goes to make up a really splendid recording that only just misses being quite perfect.

The later recordings, in stereo instead of the mono of these early discs, and issued both on record and CD, fall into two groups. Two are studio cast recordings and two are records of French stage productions. Both the former sets are from EMI, one dating from 1970 and the other from 1985.

The first set gathers together the *fine fleur* of contemporary French male singers and adds a splendid orchestra and chorus and the liveliest and most sympathetic of conductors in Jean-Pierre Marty. Here is a recording on which Michel Dens, Charles Burles, Jean-Christophe Benoît, Michel Hamel and Bernard Sinclair – all top-billers in their own right at various times – are brought together, some in quite small rôles, to make up a first-class phalanx of ancient Greeks. Having assembled them all, I'm not sure that EMI and René Challan have given them the right rôles. Michel 'the voice' Dens is not a particularly comical Agamemnon, and Benoît would probably have been happier in that rôle, which would have allowed Hamel to be upped from the few lines of Ajax 1er to Menelaos. This would have avoided the rather confused sound of three baritones singing the patriotic trio – for, unusually, Calchas (Luis Masson) is also a baritone, albeit a slightly heavier one.

The piece of casting which works the best is that of Burles as Paris. I always find this singer-actor a pleasure. It may not be the most superlative voice in the world – his stronger tenor never achieves the marvellous easy purity of Amade or Devos – but, apart from what I find an occasional overuse of falsetto, he really knows how to tackle both music and text. The voice is a no-nonsense one, sweet and masculine, and the sense of humour delightful. He makes an admirable job of the Judgement of Paris and the Tyrolienne (where his falsetto is put to good use) and generally lights things up when he is on.

Bernadette Antoine, as a mezzo-soprano Orestes, makes a pleasantly lilting middle-weight boy, and Sylvia Paule in the tiny role of Bacchis shows up a nimble soprano which makes you wish she had been cast as Hélène for, alas, this set falls wholly and horribly apart on the casting of its title rôle. Not only has Challan gone for a mezzo-soprano, but Danièle Millet, the mezzo he has chosen, has a hefty, ugly voice which lives somewhere up near her uvula, shows not a spark of fun nor of *opéra-bouffe* sense, and hoots and wobbles her way through this delicious soubrette role like a gorgon on tranquilizers. It is quite horrible. Ah! Who will deliver me from yodelling Helens?

But the trend continues. Reaction to the 1985 recording must largely depend on what the listener thinks of the curious idea of casting the American operatic soprano Jessye Norman as Helen. She is, at least, a soprano, but I fear that it is an idea which, on the whole, misfires. The diva's glorious rich tones never get the opportunity to soar into their favourite orbit and she sometimes sounds ponderous and/or inhibited as she negotiates the flippant intricacies of Offenbach's melodies. Naturally, she sings tastefully throughout, shaping the petulant 'Dis-moi, Vénus' attractively, gliding creamily through the lovely duet 'C'est une rêve' in counterpoint to the pleasant voice of her Paris (John Aler) and in fine form when it is a case of a spot of operatic burlesque, but the coquettish moments come hard and the dialogue ever harder. I was never comfortable with the performance but, as one who prefers his Offenbach sung by the bright and bubbling voice of a Berton or a Bronhill, I might have known in advance that I would not be.

Aler's Judgement of Paris isn't very exciting, though he is more fun later on and yodels out the Tyrolienne in fine style, Colette Alliot-Lugaz as another mezzo Orestes sounds less youthful than her soprano predecessors and Jean-Philippe

Lafont is operatic in song and speech as Calchas, but all three suffer in comparison with their Pathé predecessors. On the other hand, Charles Burles, moved across to be a splendid singing and acting Menelaos in a vein totally different to that mined by Duvaleix, and a fine pompous Agamemnon by Gabriel Bacquier help to make the comic patriotic trio 'Lorsque la Grèce est un champ de carnage' the most enjoyable moment of a generally tidy version, which I find, simply, lacking in gaiety and *bouffonerie*. This is, perhaps, a *Belle Hélène* for opera fans rather than lovers of *opéra-bouffe*.

The two recordings made in the 1970s based on stage performances are not very satisfactory. The 1976 Bouffes-Parisiens production recorded on Véga with Nicky Nancel and André Battedou suffers, apart from anything else, from being reorchestrated for a small piano-based ensemble, and the *intégrale* 1977 Opéra du Rhin performance on Barclay is often on the borders of being plain embarrassing. Its Helen (Jane Rhodes) alternates between some very campy pantomime acting and hooty singing which sometimes sounds like a man fooling about in falsetto, its Paris (Rémy Corazza) sounds decidedly worn; and its orchestra, perhaps in the image of its conductor, who has got himself billed on the back of the sleeve in larger type than any of the singers – or Offenbach – is too often obtrusive.

The 1963 Sadler's Wells production of the only recorded English-language version by Geoffrey Dunn was put down on HMV with Joyce Blackham and Kevin Miller starring, but the translator does not quite reach the admittedly lofty heights of his *Orpheus in the Underworld*, and the performances, although well sung, almost entirely lack the bubbling vivacity found on the companion disc.

Once again, Germany has issued several versions of the piece, as *Die schöne Helena*, in which the incomprehensible alterations made to Offenbach's score in the original Ernst Dohm German version – the horrifying elimination of the patriotic trio and the addition of a showy new piece for Helen ('Es war ein Traum') amongst them – are enshrined. EMI's Germanic version features Anneliese Rothenberger and Nicolai Gedda.

La Grande-Duchesse de Gérolstein

La Grande-Duchesse, with its marvellous mixture of martial burlesque and romantic excesses, has fared least well of the 'big three' Offenbach *opéras-bouffes* on record. As on the stage, it has suffered all too often in the casting of its determinedly nubile twenty-year-old heroine with heavy-handed sub-operatic *grandes dames* whose ideas of burlesque and, indeed, comedy are minimal; they seem only to want to show off their best hooty notes in the two great vocal showpieces of the rôle, the celebrated Sabre Song, 'Voici le sabre de mon père', and the smoothly suggestive 'Dites-lui'. All three of the double-disc recordings of *La Grande-Duchesse* in the original language fall more or less into this prima donna trap.

Decca, who issued (and have regularly reissued) a set based on the 1966 stage performance given by the often-recorded Suzanne Lafaye, fell perhaps the least far, but Lafaye's occasionally humourless mezzo-soprano performance of this most outrageously sexy and comic juvenile rôle reminds me a little of the Renata Tebaldi recording of *Madama Butterfly*, in which the star declaims that she is fifteen years old before issuing a Wagnerian giggle that sounds as if it came from a particularly lusty grandmother.

Try as Mlle Lafaye may (and she does), the mezzo-soprano quality of her voice needfully makes the quicker portions of such sung phrases as the impudent, rippling 'J'ai-me les mi-li-tair-es' a bit of a race against the orchestra and also suggests, notably in speech, a maturity which is quite at odds with the real requirements of the rôle. Perhaps because of this excessive vocal colour, she somehow doesn't succeed in making a major moment of 'Voici le sabre de mon père', in spite of the help from a good, lusty chorus, but she is much more at home with the more measured waltz melody of 'Dites-lui', where her warm, strong lowest notes have a chance to glow.

Elsewhere on this set, Jean Aubert makes a pretty, natural tenor Fritz, with a fluid, unforced voice that clips through his Act 2 rondo splendidly and a really nifty hand for the dialogue, and Henri Bédex splutters out an enjoyably emphatic and flamboyant General Boum, a regular fire-eater in both song and speech. He is sometimes confusingly indistinguishable from René Terrasson's rich Baron Puck, but when the two come together with Grog (Marcel Robert) and Népomuc (Jean Mollien) in the show's comical plotting scenes, they produce some of this set's most enjoyable moments.

There is a rather silly-aristocrat performance of Prince Paul from Christian Asse and a regular soprano Wanda (Michèle Raynaud) to complete the star cast. However, the centre-piece of a *Grande-Duchesse* is its title performer and, since Mlle Lafaye's attempt at the rôle – whilst in advance of anything achieved on the other two major sets – is not in the ideal class, there must be some reservations hanging over this recording.

There is very little but reservations over the set, featuring Eugenia Zareska, issued on Saga and Urania outside France. It fails not only in its Duchess but on practically every other count as well. It is very poorly recorded and almost everywhere performed with no feeling for the material at all. Zareska oversings horribly, the usually attractive tenor André Dran pushes himself to unpleasant excesses, the General Boum bellows and René Leibowitz and his orchestra compound their sins. Amazingly, a selection disc taken from this set still appears in the catalogue and, usually priced very cheaply, in the shops. Even at the minimum price, it is robbery.

EMI has not, to date, chosen to re-record *La Grande-Duchesse* in a complete version and it was left to CBS to produce the *La Grande-Duchesse* of the 1980s, with the most successful of France's operatic vocalists of recent years, Régine Crespin, as the Duchess. For much the same reasons as the Decca version, but more so, the result is not entirely happy. Mme Crespin gives a vigorous enough rendering of the show's spoken text, but her weighty, richly coloured singing is often strangely lifeless, particularly in the two highlight numbers, and she too falls very definitely into the mature category – neither her tone of voice nor her turn of phrase have anything of the randy young noblewoman about them.

Otherwise EMI have assembled a fine and fitting cast. Charles Burles is a rich and smooth Prince Paul – and why shouldn't he be? After all, he gets the girl in the end – giving his 'Chronique de la gazette de Hollande' with rueful charm, which is a most agreeable alternative to the usual vacuous creaking. Alain Vanzo makes a virile Fritz, Mady Mesplé turns in her usual sharply sweet and appreciable performance as Wanda, and Robert Massard invests General Boum not only with humour but with very much more in the way of genuine vocal values than is normal in this comedy rôle.

This recording does have another drawback. The snipping practised by record producers in order to fit shows onto two records has normally, in the sets discussed, been done with a relaxed and seamless skill. The results here are less happy and there are some unnecessarily lumpy joins which could have been aided by a little connecting narration. This problem shows up all the more because EMI have been good enough to include in the boxed set not only three different sets of fine notes, in French, German and English, but also a version of their libretto. At several stages, this does not tally with what is on the record and, also, chopped about as it is, it makes awkward reading as a representation of the original libretto.

Pathé chose soprano Eliane Lublin to play the Grand Duchess on their regular selection recording, and this is a casting which seems, on paper at least, as if it ought to be more suitable than any of those on the full sets. This version is all the more inviting in that it has cast that most limpid of tenors Raymond Amade as Fritz, but I am left to my hunger as, in spite of the fact that this recording has been several times reissued over the last thirty years, I have not been able to lay hands on a copy. Piles of Pathé operetta discs appear in every new and second-hand French record shop – but *La Grande-Duchesse* is never there. However, I understand that it is included in a 1980 EMI-Pathé boxed set entitled 'Offenbach: 6 Opérettes', a truly magnificent set which also includes all of the very best of Pathé's 1950s Offenbach selections – *La Fille du tambour-major, La Belle Hélène, Orphée aux enfers, La Vie parisienne, La Périchole* – in one coffret.

There is also, apparently, an EMI recording of *La Grande-Duchesse* with Jane Rhodes cast as the Duchess. After her monstrously overcooked *Belle Hélène*, I can't say I really want to find this one.

There is no English-language recording of *La Grande-Duchesse*, but there are German versions, the most recent of which stars Henriqueta Tarrès in the title rôle. Since I remember this lady as a marvellous Covent Garden Chrysothemis to Amy Shuard's Elektra in 1968, I have fears that Offenbach's teenage temptress is in for another very big sing. Others may love all these vastly operatic *opéra-bouffe* heroines – if so there are plenty of *Grande-Duchesse*s for you. I am looking forward to the day when the part is recorded by a Fabienne Guyon or a Sophie Marin – a really young and electric soprano comedienne.

Although the best of these recordings of *Orphée, La Belle Hélène* and *La Grande-Duchesse*, with their incessant flow of the choicest of Offenbachian melody and the familiarity of their best-known songs and ensembles, may make the most obvious *opéra-bouffe* easy-listening, some of the composer's less played *opéras-bouffes* repay consideration both as fine, melodious and comical pieces and also as outstanding examples of exactly what *opéra-bouffe* was. The excellent Bourg recordings – now also issued on CD – of *Geneviève de Brabant*, *Barbe-Bleue* and *Le Pont des soupirs*, in particular, merit considerable attention.

Geneviève de Brabant

The complete recording of *Geneviève de Brabant* illustrates better than any other the comedy and the burlesque nature of *opéra-bouffe*. Here, in one show, are gathered not only the general parody of medieval times and of the contemporary theatrical and literary pieces which dealt, oh so seriously, with that period, but also particular parodies. The villain is too villainous for words, the crusading heroics of the knightly heroes of the piece are set to music of a ridiculously high-flown kind, the lofty monarch of Brabant breaks into a song of utter silliness, and everywhere almost-serious music is set to words of such total buffoonery as to create an outrageously comic juxtaposition. Antique French heroes like Charles Martel, Renaud de Montauban and Saladin are reduced to anachronistic carousers, a jack-in-the-box hermit who lives in a tree trunk and utters his dicta in recitative invades the stage in a parody of the famous Wolf's Glen scene from Weber's *Der Freischütz*, and an incidental pair of *gens d'armes*, equipped with the famous duet which has been the generally surviving part of this show and with a knockabout low comedy scene of the kind beloved by modern pantomime comedy duos, stop the show to do what is little more than a turn.

Alongside this broad comedy and the humorous and satirical songs and music which are the lot of the male members of the cast, however, Offenbach placed some truly lovely musical pieces. The first-act chorus of maids of honour, the Couplets de la toilette, the charming Trio de la main et de la barbe and the delicious second-act storm trio all make beautiful use of varying combinations of female voices. Thus, far from being all low jinks and debunking, the piece holds a balance between humour and charm which makes it a model of the genre.

The Bourg recording of *Geneviève* consists of a neatly filleted libretto and nearly all of the score of Offenbach's first revised version of 1867. Only the Tyrolienne and ballet of Act 2 – often omitted in performance – and the third-act Hunting Quartet are missing. It is honestly if unstarrily cast, with Monique Stiot as a suitably boyish page in the leading travesty role of Drogan, Annick Simon as a pretty, persecuted Geneviève and Huguette Hennetier particularly good as the maid, Brigitte, who is mainly around to make up the ladies' trios. The men, led by Bernard Plantey (Sifroy) and René Terrasson (Golo), go heavily for the comedy, perhaps sometimes a touch too heavily, but they have the courage to prefer the fun to beautiful notes in the comic songs, and the result is well and truly in the spirit of the thing.

Barbe-Bleue

The *Geneviève de Brabant* recording, made in 1970, is a mono one, but Bourg's *Barbe-Bleue*, also taken from the archives of L'Institut National de l'Audiovisuel, and made three years earlier, is in stereo. Don't ask me why. For breadth of sound, therefore, it is noticeably superior, and this is welcome as *Barbe-Bleue* contains more music that requires fine singing than does its more barefacedly comical predecessor.

Whereas *Orphée* and *La Belle Hélène* burlesqued classical Greece and *La Grande-Duchesse* took a pot-shot at things military and political, *Barbe-Bleue* has its fun at the expense of the pastoral and *féerie* conventions. The murderous Bluebeard stalks through Arcadian villages and the court of his overlord, King Bobèche, selecting and disposing of new candidates for his seigneurial hand in the broad style of a comical melodrama villain, but in the happy ending, when everyone turns out to be alive, he is sent away with a flea in his ear and a termagant wife. In true burlesque style the piece is loaded with topical jokes and anachronisms and, in true Offenbach style, with some splendid music, the bulk of which falls to the tenor Bluebeard himself and to the soprano, Boulotte, the pushy peasant girl who is his last wife.

On the Bourg record, these rôles are taken with equal skill in song and dialogue by the really vigorous tenor Henri Legay – splendidly ringing in his 'Légende de Barbe-Bleue' with its famous refrain 'Je suis Barbe-Bleue, o gué, Jamais veuf ne fut si gai' – and by Lina Dachary, a highly experienced recording artist with a fine soprano voice, attractive and even through all its registers. The ubiquitous Aimé Doniat as Popolani, the villain's private astrologer, gives a splendid comedy performance, and one can note Linda Felder, the star of the early Festival recordings, now reduced to the tiny rôle of one of Bluebeard's earlier wives.

The adaptation for disc has been excellently done, although the sleeve lists a couple of sections which in fact do not appear on the record and one or two other numbers have been shortened. The recording, however, still lasts very little under two hours and is both an excellent display of the piece and a listening pleasure from beginning to end.

Le Pont des soupirs

Le Pont des soupirs is another extravagant burlesque, probably nearest to *Geneviève de Brabant* in style with its crazy parody of melodrama and grand opera, full of durable social satire and including no less than twenty-seven musical pieces. The score is perhaps a mite less exciting than those of Offenbach's very best works, but many of the ensembles in particular are delightful – the multiple serenade 'Catarina, je chante', the murder-to-music Quatuor des poignards, the bouncy and ridiculous recounting of the Doge's defeat at sea in the Complainte de Cornarino, the burlesque mad scene staged by the

Doge's wife to escape the clutches of the lecherous usurper, the second-act finale with its send-up of a triumphal march, and the two duos in disguise (Spur Duet, Swashbucklers' Duet) which make up the heart of the third-act Interrogation before the Council of Ten – and the solos are always tuneful and mostly short.

Le Pont des soupirs loses just a little of its point and fun on disc – the contrast of the magnificent Venetian settings and other such operatic excesses with the loony plot and dialogue is basic to the piece – but the 1968 INA recording, released on Bourg, once again fillets the book into a neat mixture of narrative and dialogue, making sure that as much of the spirit of the show is retained as is possible. The score gets a good performance too, with two fine singing actors in Michel Hamel (Malatromba) and Aimé Doniat (Cornarino) taking the lead rôles, alongside Claudine Collart as Catarina Cornarino and Monique Stiot as the page, Amoroso. The ladies are a touch less reliable than the men, but they have the right sort of voices for the material and their Swashbucklers' Duet is a delight. The supporting cast, chorus and orchestra under Jean Doussard are all fine, and the set provides a good and enjoyable audio version of a show which really needs to have been seen to be enjoyed to its fullest.

Les Brigands

The Bourg-Milan *Les Brigands* is not, unfortunately, taken from the same series of radio recordings as the three previous sets. It is a recording of a production abortively planned for the Théâtre Mogador in 1980 and consists only of a one-disc selection, which bills its stars, Danièle Perriers (Fiametta) and Robert Manuel (Falsacappa) heavily. Although it has a false air of authenticity about it, with its orchestra (which the sleeve insists has twenty-two players) sounding like a Victorian seaside band and performers who mash up their material and spit it out with more regard for big comic performances than musical values, it is not a very satisfactory version. Only Mlle Perriers, who has been a fine *Rosenkavalier* Sophie in her time, and Jean Kriff, in a brief appearance as Campotasso, are vocally adequate. Manuel makes the brigand chief into a large-theatre buffoon, the mezzo-soprano rôle of Fragoletto is distastefully entrusted to an effeminate sounding tenor, and the musical direction of Daniel Mourruau is sometimes worryingly wayward.

On the whole, the 1970 soundtrack of ORTF's less authentic television broadcast is preferable. The selection here is rather different, with most of the second-act music, including the Trio des marmitons, the Couplets de l'ambassade and the Couplets des Espagnoles, all of which are found on the Bourg disc, omitted in favour of a full-scale twelve minutes plus of the first-act finale, with its celebrated chorus 'Ce sont les bottes des carabiniers' and Fragoletto's attractive opening song; both the performances and the recording, however, are of a much more pleasant standard. Jean Doussard's orchestra firmly supports the singers, led by Dominique Tirmont (Falsacappa), who loses none of the rôle's comedy in giving it some good rich baritone singing, and the smoothly attractive Eliane Manchet as Fiametta. Fragoletto is unfortunately given to a tenor again, but Michaël Pietri is much more vigorous than his counterpart on the Bourg disc. It is not by any means an ideal record of the piece, but it is a fair forty minutes' compression of a very attractive score which will do very well as a taster of *Les Brigands* until EMI's planned full-scale recording sees the light of day.

In the meanwhile, Offenbach's score can be heard in full on the very acceptable complete *Die Banditen* issued in 1981 by RCA, a set which must be the only French *opéra-bouffe* or *opérette* ever recorded whole in a foreign language while unavailable in the original. I don't know the whys and wherefores of its production, but the recording comes from Cologne where, over the years, the forces of the Kölner Rundfunk and RCA have given uneven but welcome exposure to some of the less obvious parts of the German and Austrian operetta repertoire, and this is probably the best of all their efforts.

It is a two-disc set, including only the musical score – no dialogue or narration – and sung in the original German translation made by Ernst Dohm for the Vienna première in 1870. It has two peculiarities: the first (which is sadly becoming the norm) is, yet again, the casting of a male Fragoletto, and the second – even more startling – a female Antonio. This minor culture shock is mitigated by the fact that both artists are first rate, as, indeed, are not only the whole cast of this highly enjoyable set, but also the crisp and humorously dramaticky orchestra and chorus under Pinchas Steinberg, who do more than their share in making this a genuinely happy *opéra-bouffe* performance.

The three star performances are all very fine – which makes it sad and unfair that someone has seen fit to bill on the cover better-known artists playing minor rôles. Hubert Möhler is an attractively virile tenor Falsacappa, and Eva Csapó a very appealing Fiorella who moulds the phrases of her lovely music beautifully and makes a particularly delicious, caring job of her second-act solo, tastefully diffusing what is clearly a big voice with delicacy and, when necessary, humour. It is, however, Jean van Ree, as Fragoletto, who is the star of this show. He has an easy, light tenor voice with an almost feminine (but not effeminate) sweetness to it which is ideally suited to Offenbach's mezzo-soprano music; he flips trippingly through his delicious saltarello in a way that usually only the most mobile of feminine voices can, and takes part very effectively in the many delightfully accurate and pointedly performed ensemble portions of the show.

Amongst the rest of the cast, Evelyn Künneke sounds suitably mannish in her splendidly comical *diseuse* portrayal of the Caissier's rôle, actor Gerd Vespermann makes the Prince a jolly fellow in his third-act number, supported by two comically overblown operatic ladies (one of whom is the ageing opera star Martha Mödl) as his courtly paramours, and the banditti and contadine of the chorus are all happily sung, making up a performance which I find –

in spite of its being sung in the unfamiliar German – well in the spirit of the piece.

Hervé

Le Petit Faust

Outside the works of Offenbach, the *opéra-bouffe* is represented on record only by two different versions of Hervé's *Le Petit Faust*. The first is issued on the Clio label in a version taken, once again, from the archives of L'Institut National de l'Audiovisuel. Like the broadcasts issued on Bourg, it is a magnificent recording, putting in evidence not only the marvellously extravagant comedy of the piece but also its considerable musical values. The title rôle is taken by Michel Hamel, who copes equally well, in both song and dialogue, with the creakingly aged Faust of the first act and the sweet-voiced and naïve young Faust of the second. He is partnered by Lina Dachary as a petulant Marguerite and a superbly comical Gaston Rey as the military Valentin, whose burlesque soldier song is one of the highlights of the show. The mezzo-soprano Agnès Disney is slightly less light-handed in the travesty part of Méphisto, but she joins Dachary and Hamel in a fine rendition of another of the piece's choice moments, the nonsensical 'Trio de Vaterland'.

Le Petit Faust has also been issued on Rare Recorded Editions, whose products, true to their title, are often fairly difficult to find. The cast advertised as being on this edition – Dachary, Aimé Doniat and Liliane Berton – has always seemed a truly tempting one to me, but having finally located and played this set I insist very firmly that Liliane Berton is not on this recording. It may just be Dachary singing Marguerite (though I wouldn't have guessed it) and the Faust very probably is Doniat, but the Méphisto is certainly not Berton by any stretch of the imagination.

I assume that this recording, with pretty much the same virtually full score plus narration and dialogue as is contained on the Clio issue, is also the result of a radio broadcast, and, even if it has not been transferred to disc with quite the sonic clarity of its rival, it has other advantages. The first and foremost of these is its Méphisto. Whoever she is, she is a real bobby-dazzler. A strong, high mezzo with bags and bags of dash and temperament, she throws off her opening rondo ('Je suis Méphisto') with devilish style, makes mincemeat of her burlesque of the Song of the Flea ('La Satrape et la puce') and tops her lively third-act couplets with the most infernal laugh I have ever heard from a feminine throat. It is a marvellous performance, and I just wish I knew to whom it should be credited.

If the Marguerite is Dachary, it is Dachary being distinctly fruitier and less sprightly than usual, but the lady in question sings well and acts her frivolous rôle vigorously. The Faust doesn't achieve quite the distinction between the old and the young which Hamel does; the same voice can clearly be heard behind both, especially when it comes to singing, but that voice is first rate and the singing is splendidly virile and characterful. Jean-Christophe Benoît is credited with the grand, ghostly Valentin, and, since it is the original version of *Le Petit Faust* which is being played here, the role of Siebel which was much enlarged for the first major revival is limited to only a few lines. As on the other recording, this mezzo-soprano role is played by a man.

To make a choice between these two thoroughly enjoyable sets is difficult. If you are particularly keen on up-to-date sound, it is perhaps best to stick with the Clio set. On the other hand, the performance of the mystery Méphisto on RRE is one I wouldn't happily give up. Then again, finding either without going to the manufacturers is quite a trudge, so I'd say take either one if you can find it. *Le Petit Faust* is an *opéra-bouffe* joy and it has been done proud in its recordings. For the record, RRE's version takes up only three and a half discs and the fourth side is filled up with transfers of some early 78s of Hervé and Audran material. It is interesting stuff, but very difficult to judge or to enjoy under the hairy, distant sound of elderly 78s.

The quality of the performances on these radio reissues makes me wonder longingly just what other treasures lie lurking in the Institut's archives. If there were a recording of Hervé's *Chilpéric* or *L'Oeil crevé*, of Offenbach's *La Princesse de Trébizonde* and one or two of his *opéras-bouffes féeries* such as *Le Roi Carotte* and *Le Voyage dans la lune*, or maybe even Jonas's *Le Canard à trois becs*, what a fine selection of the best of *opéra-bouffe* we could have. Nevertheless, what exists is already appreciable, and all the more so in that so many of the recordings, in particular these radio *intégrale* versions and the EMI-Pathé excerpt discs, are of such a high standard.

Offenbach: from *opéra-bouffe* to *opéra-comique*

Undiluted burlesque is a variety of entertainment which must, eventually, pall, and the heyday of the *opéra-bouffe* soon gave way to a less frenetic style of comic opera. Offenbach himself foreshadowed the change in his *La Périchole*, which, although labelled *opéra-bouffe*, was not written in the full burlesque manner but, with its contrasting moments of genuine pathos and textual and musical sentiment, was much more an example of what would soon be called, in the old style, *opéra-comique*. Similarly, another of his greatest successes, *La Vie parisienne*, written for the actors of the Palais-Royal rather than for the singers of the Bouffes-Parisiens, and also designated *opéra-bouffe*, was rather a musical comedy of manners. But *opéra-bouffe* was the fashionable term of the moment, and so *opéras-bouffes* they were duly called on their first production.

Offenbach's later works found, on the whole, less success than his true *opéras-bouffes*, but amongst them came two triumphant *opéras-comiques*, *Madame Favart* and *La Fille du tambour-major*. This pair stood up proudly alongside the flourishing works of the new brigade of musical theatre composers and alongside *La Périchole* and *La Vie parisienne* to make up the nucleus of his non-burlesque works. All four of these major works are represented on both double and single-disc recordings.

La Vie parisienne

La Vie parisienne, by its nature, really needs to be listened to in its entirety. The play, in this case, is every bit as important as the music and one without the other is rather like a half-baked cake. Unfortunately, it cannot be said that there is as yet any recording which manages to marry happily the comedy and the music.

On the one hand there is the actors' version – a very full single-disc recording made from the performances given at the Palais-Royal by the Madeleine Renaud/Jean-Louis Barrault company in 1958, which urges on its sleeve that we remember that the piece was created for actors who sang. Perhaps in the theatre the fact of having the comedy finely performed can overcome vocal deficiencies, but on a record it isn't so. Pitch and timing go astray all over the place, unpleasant noises are manifold and, surprisingly enough, even the text doesn't get an expert treatment. Then, in the midst of all the sputtering and creaking, comes a real performance. Suzy Delair (Métella), who can both sing and act, gives a magnificent rendition of the the actress's gamut-running letter scene which makes the whole recording almost worthwhile.

Then there is the singers' version – the 1976 EMI two-record set, conducted by Michel Plasson and featuring Michel Sénéchal (Gardefeu), Michel Trempont (Bobinet), Mady Mesplé (Gabrielle) and Régine Crespin (Métella). As usual, the 'singers' act much better than the 'actors' sing, but this recording falls into precisely the opposite end of the musical comedy quicksands. The musical part sounds as if it is being accompanied by an orchestra of hundreds and a vast chorus, and the whole thing is rendered with such an overblown hand as to strip it of all the tongue-in-cheek verve which is its *raison d'être*. Sénéchal and Trempont, veterans of many good recordings, have all the singing and acting qualities necessary to be perfect as the two gay Parisians, Mesplé skips predictably charmingly through Gabrielle's music and Crespin makes a thoroughly *grande dame* of Métella, again more happy in the dialogue than in the oversung music, but the atmosphere is more *Aïda* than *ésprit de boulevard* and the whole overcooked thing quickly ends up becoming wearisome.

The right spirit can be found on a third version, which marries the acting and singing requirements better than either of these, a 1974 recording on Carrère of a production by the Compagnie Nationale de l'Opérette as played at the Opéra-Comique. Alas, the spirit may be right here but the text is lacking. For some incomprehensible reason, *La Vie parisienne* has been chopped up and chopped around many a time, since Offenbach's days, to produce 'new versions', and this is one of those times. This one was probably a fun show – its layout demonstrates that it had much more opportunity for spectacle than the original; the new and enormously lively orchestral arrangements are splendid if anything but authentic, and many of the performances are right on the nail, but for all that it is not the real *La Vie parisienne* as she was writ. That has yet to be recorded.

There are selections available which include Liliane Berton (Pathé) and June Bronhill (HMV, in English) amongst their cast, as well as a French Philips excerpts disc conducted by Marcel Cariven, and an Ariola-Eurodisc version in German (*Pariser Leben*) with Lisa della Casa featured, all of which have their moments. The Philips (otherwise Epic) disc is an acceptable one. It omits all of the first-act opening up to the trio 'Jamais, foi de cicérone', as well as the first part of Act 3, but otherwise manages to include the large part of the score. It is played and sung efficiently – especially played, witness the fact that Marcel Cariven's lively, generous-toned orchestra won him a Grand Prix du Disque for this recording – even if there is some hectic singing in places and no single outstanding performance.

Pathé's selection contains much of the same material, but includes the Pauline/Gondremarck duet and the complete finale from Act 3 in preference to Frick's solo, Gabrielle's description of 'frou-frou', 'Fermons les yeux' and Métella's final number. It also has a splendid, virtually all-Pathé-star cast, even if some of the rôles are rather oddly distributed. Liliane Berton (who would surely have been a superb Gabrielle) is the comedy maid, Pauline; Nadine Renaux, whom I would have expected to see as Métella (actually played by Deva Dassy, who is surely Pauline material), is Gabrielle and the fourth feminine rôle of the Baronne de Gondremarck goes to Lina Dachary. In spite of my preconceptions, all four are excellent – Dassy being notably better here than as *La Belle Hélène*, if still not the equal of Delair, Renaux making some simply glorious sounds in her solos and Berton turning her little duet with Roux into a thing of perhaps unnecessary loveliness. The men are equally top drawer, with Michel Hamel a bouncing Gardefeu, Michel Roux (Gondremarck) richly declaring, at the sight of Paris's varying delights, 'Je veux m'en fourrer jusqu'à la!' (I want to stuff myself up to there!) and Willy Clément having heavily accented fun with the famous song of the Brésilien ('Ye suis Brésilien, Y'ai de l'or').

The English version, from Sadler's Wells, has the virtue of a good Geoffrey Dunn translation, a superlative Gabrielle from Bronhill and several handfuls of competent character performances from such as Jon Weaving, Eric Shilling, John Fryatt and Anna Pollak as a contralto Baronne, but it is – Bronhill apart – of little use as a record of *La Vie parisienne*. Although it manages to include fifteen numbers and an overture, it inexplicably omits Métella's showpiece Letter Song. What can Norman Newell have been thinking of?

Ariola Eurodisc's *Pariser Leben* selection (there was, at one stage, an *intégrale* of this) is a first-class singers' version, large in orchestra and chorus and with impeccably musical solo vocals. Like *Die schöne Helena*, the German version of *La Vie parisienne* also contains a few national alterations. Gabrielle's 'frou-frou' song is given to Pauline (the lustily soubretty Dorothea Chryst), and the last-act rondo for the Baroness (Margit Schramm) (a relic of the original five-act version, which is seemingly the one the Germans do) is restored. The highlight of this recording comes from Gerhard Unger (a marvellously sparky Frick) and Ingeborg Hallstein (Gabrielle), in outstanding form, who give a delicious rendering of their bootmaker and *gantière* duo. Lisa della Casa sings Métella's Letter Song with lovely tone, Schramm makes a merry mouthful of her rondo and Peter Alexander is an enjoyably brisk Bobinet. Ferry Gruber's Gardefeu gets little exposure, as the big first-act trio is omitted from this selection, and Rudolf Schock, who ought to be a smashingly extravagant Brazilian, is hamstrung by a laborious tempo in his main number. This, however, is a small quibble in what is a fine recording. It would be preferable, with such omissions as the trio, to find that elusive double-disc version of this performance, for, given its alterations and the fact of hearing this essentially French piece sung in German, this *La Vie parisienne* is as good as any.

It is certainly much better than the 1977 'bande originale du film', a very curious affair, the sleeve of which puts you immediately *en garde* when you see 'Adaption et musiques additionelles: Pierre Porte' and 'Adaption et textes additionels: Jacques Emmanuel'. M Porte is clearly a disciple of Mantovani with a passion for harps, and M Emmanuel apparently believes he can improve Meilhac and Halévy's script by putting the end at the beginning and chopping the songs up in little bits. And I mean little bits, for rare is the musical section on this pair of discs which runs beyond two minutes. There is nothing wrong with the performances that half a ton less echo wouldn't cure, and the photos on the gate-fold show that this was obviously a lushly decorative film, but it would have been a better recording without the aid of Messieurs Porte and Emmanuel.

Although I remain convinced that in an ideal world *La Vie parisienne* needs to be taken whole, and preferably in French, I find that, in the absence of a wholly satisfying full-scale recording, I'm happier with the Pathé selection or even the German disc. And I add, with more hope than confidence in this age of operaticky recording, 'in the meantime'.

La Périchole

La Périchole has been issued in a choice of three original-language sets – an early Pathé version, another on Erato, and the most recent, in 1982, by EMI who have, nevertheless, maintained the earlier Pathé recording in the catalogue. There seems to be an idea current amongst record producers that the title rôle of *La Périchole*, like that of *La Grande-Duchesse*, is meat for an altogether weightier performer than that of the other Offenbach operas. Pathé chose Suzanne Lafaye in 1958, Erato recorded with Crespin in 1977 and EMI with another mezzo-soprano, Teresa Berganza. The only English-language recording, from the Metropolitan Opera, features their Patrice Munsel. There is no doubt that Périchole is a part which can take a more richly coloured voice than a Hélène or a Eurydice, but I remain to be convinced that any of these big-voiced castings are truly on the right lines. However, since there is, at the moment, no choice it is either a big French Périchole or none. Both Crespin and, particularly, Lafaye are considerably more at home here than on their *Grande-Duchesse* recordings, but as a whole it is the Pathé set, conducted in a delightfully bright manner by Igor Markevitch (another conductor who takes billing larger than the composer and the artists) which comes out quite clearly as the superior recording of the two.

The Erato set, another production from the Opéra du Rhin, does not include dialogue but instead relies on a linking narration from author and broadcaster Alain Decaux to carry the story forward. Although this is done effectively enough, the mixture of narration and dialogue on the Pathé rcording is much livelier and succeeds in creating an atmosphere which is altogether lacking on the Erato version.

Crespin sings the rôle of the little street singer with expansive power and the supporting cast of the Opéra du Rhin, headed by Alain Vanzo as Piquillo, is a more than capable one. However, the Pathé version wins out on casting as well, with Lafaye finding more of both the humanity and the comedy in Périchole and using her not-too-weighty mezzo voice effectively and occasionally prettily, a thoroughly superb Piquillo from Raymond Amade and a richly comic Don Andrès from basso Louis Noguera. Amade clips through his solos with a clear tenor tone and an easy articulation that are a joy to listen to, and helps bounce the mezzo-soprano tones of his partner through the famous refrain 'Il grandira car il est Espagnol' in a memorable fashion in a performance which I cannot imagine bettered.

Even the smallest parts – the trio of harmonizing cousins (Janette Vivalda, Monique Linval, Denise Monteil) and a pair of comical notaries (Christian Asse and Jacques Pruvost) – are all very well taken, and there is no doubt that this *Périchole*, with its sustained gaiety and picturesque performances is, from all angles, the most satisfying of those readily available.

The new EMI set is a rather different *Périchole*. As with their new *Orphée aux enfers*, the producers have chosen to record the expanded version which Offenbach prepared for a later revival. The expansion is considerable, as the 1874 rewrite turned the show from a two-act to a three-act piece, largely beefing up the roles of Périchole, Piquillo and Don Andrès for the three original stars of the show, Mlle Schneider, Dupuis and Grenier, with broadly comic scenes and a mass of musical numbers. Although the revival had less success than the blown-up *Orphée*, the new style *Périchole* is the better-made work. Instead of letting in a tuck here and there as in *Orphée*, the authors have simply inserted a whole new turning in the plot, strengthening the slightly perfunctory final part of the original. Offenbach's new numbers include some delightful pieces – two courtiers leering over poor Piquillo in his dungeon for troublesome husbands ('Les Maris courbaient la tête'), a jolly trio with the Viceroy disguised as a jailer ('Je suis le joli géolier') and Périchole's love song 'Je t'aime, brigand', as well as a replacement for the lovers' final duet.

The recording itself is in the style nowadays favoured by EMI and conductor Michel Plasson – rich layers of orchestral and choral sound, warm recording quality, and a principal cast with operatic leanings. Teresa Berganza's Périchole ranges from the first rate to the not quite. She lightens off her big mezzo voice most effectively in the delicately played drunk scene ('Ah, quel diner!'), points her 'Mon Dieu, que les hommes sont bêtes' marvellously, and gets in some deft comical touches, but there are times when the voice cannot be held in check, and the famous Letter Song soliloquy, for example, is not as convincingly played as the lighter moments.

José Carreras as Piquillo unfortunately misses the fun of the piece altogether and, although he sings with lyrical strength and only occasional effort, there is none of the joyous vulnerability that is so effectively found in Amade's performance on the earlier set. Gabriel Bacquier, on the other hand, is quite perfect as Don Andrès, matching acting and singing talents impeccably and taking to the style of the piece in a way which the two real Spaniards do not. He gets fine support from Michel Sénéchal and Michel Trempont as his courtiers. When these splendid veterans of the French *opéra-comique* are on, the sparkle which too often lacks in the playing on this set comes back.

This seems to be the result of a question of attitude, an attitude typified by the performance of Pierrette Delange in the small rôle of Guadalena. On the French cast recording of *Hello, Dolly!* this artist sings with an adorably sweet, piquant tone as Irene Molloy; here she is clearly putting on her opera voice and she shouldn't have bothered. She was much more effective when less pretentious and, anyway, *La Périchole* is not *Les Troyens*. Like the Plasson *Belle Hélène*, this is perhaps a *Périchole* for opera buffs and, of course, for those who are interested in the expanded version.

The only foreign-language set of which I know is a pair of Russian discs on the Melodiya label, which I suspect the cover says dates from 1948 and which combines narration, dialogue and music with perhaps a little less spoken material than the standard text-heavy Melodiya proportions. These are the moments where I wish I spoke Russian for, both musically and in spirit, I think this is the happiest *Périchole* of all. Things get under way merrily with an overture which has more French gaiety than most French efforts. It is followed up by what is clearly a truly vivacious performance of a version (with many a variant) of the enlarged *Périchole* in which the two stars give super performances. G. Polyakov is a perfect Piquillo, rather like a Russian Raymond Amade with an ounce more edge, and S. Galemba is an attractive medium-weight soprano Périchole with a bright, easy acting style, who succeeds in making a much merrier character of the show's heroine than her French counterparts. She also sings extremely well. The two of them rattle through their seguidilla with energetic flair: she produces lovely tone in her uncomplicated Letter Song, goes cleverly through a dignified drunk scene which ends up in a fit of the giggles and gives a piquant 'Je t'adore, brigand', whilst he sings and acts with impeccable brightness throughout, making up with his third-act aria for having lost the one in the previous act. The comedy rôles are played with comic effect by the usual efficiently rich Russian character voices, and even the minor ones – three middle-aged wobbly sounding Cousines, two nicely tipsy notaries – are well taken on a set which, in spite of its musical lacunae and variations, is lively and likeable.

The single-disc Metropolitan opera version, the only English-language *Périchole*, is little more than a choppy series of musical snippets in an unexceptional translation with a rather embarrassing narration. For some reason, it has an operatic baritone Piquillo (Theodore Uppman) and Cyril Ritchard is a twee Don Andrès who doesn't sound as if anything could have interested him in the charms of Patrice Munsel's Périchole. This is one to be avoided.

Madame Favart

There is less choice when it comes to Offenbach's later successes, *Madame Favart* and *La Fille du tambour-major*. *Madame Favart* has been issued on a double-disc set by the elusive Rare Recorded Editions, with a radio cast apparently headed by Mlles Dachary and Felder, Doniat and Bernard Plantey, which on casting evidence ought to be good, but the more readily available set is a second performance taken from the radio and issued on the Discoreale label. Yet another recording from the archives of the INA, it features Suzanne Lafaye in the large, showy and protean rôle of the famous actress who, in the course of the evening, goes through a fanciful series of disguises in order to escape the attentions of a lecherous and vengeful nobleman amongst a proliferation of plotlines.

This is not the best of these transfers. Chivot and Duru's excellent libretto has not been adapted for record as well as some of the others, perhaps because it is such a very incident-packed one, and several chunks of the show have disappeared in the process. The actual recording has been transferred less happily than on the similar discs later issued by Bourg and Clio, and the sound quality is consequently not as good as it might be. Identifying the billed singers from their other performances is a risky business, but it is the only way to do so as, although the boxed set includes a fine historical note on the show, it gives only the cast from the piece's original performance and not the casting of the record!

From the cover billing and from, by now, long acquaintance, Mlle Lafaye is readily recognizable in the rôle written for the soprano Juliette Simon-Girard and, once again, one can only ask, 'Why?' She makes a very reasonable fist of it, although the tessitura sometimes catches her out, but there were plenty of fine soprano actresses about in 1960. One of them, Lina Dachary, is a lovely *jeune première* Suzanne. Camille Maurane plays Favart and Joseph Peyron pairs with Mlle Dachary as Hector. This recording – which is not bad, merely imperfect – only proves that this superb *opéra-comique* deserves another and long look from those in recording power.

The RRE edition manages to fit in more of the show. In fact, it starts off very promisingly, delivering music and only a slightly thinned text through the first act; it is only when you realize that at that rate there is no way the whole thing will fit on four sides that you start to worry. Sure enough, the cuts come thick and fast later, and in the final act, sadly, two important musical numbers – Suzanne's 'Le Peril que court ma vertu' and the big duo for Favart and his wife, 'Je tremble, je tremble' – bite the dust.

I am puzzled by the sound of this recording, for it cannot be the fact that it is just a bit imperfect that makes neither Linda Felder (who I presume is the Mme Favart) nor Dachary sound like themselves. Both perform their rôles acceptably, if very surprisingly a bit shrilly at times, but the shrillness (which may be the fault of the recording) is preferable to taking a mezzo-soprano Mme Favart. Felder (?) is light on characterization – of her impersonations, only the moments spent in the character of the elderly Countess get a really noticeable change of voice – but she is bright and brisk and, in her serving-wench disguise, delivers a fine version of the mock-rustic 'Ma mère aux vignes m'envoyit'. The Hector is good and there is a lot of standard buffo bumbling from the character men playing Cotignac and Pontsablé, but the best performance comes from the baritone (who may or may not be the advertised Plantey or Benoît) playing the rôle of Favart, who performs with an attractive ease and brightness. Like the Discoreale set, this one has its faults and its favours, and there is very little to choose between them.

La Fille du tambour-major

Decca, which has been sparing in its Offenbach recordings, is responsible for the only allegedly *intégrale La Fille du tambour-major*, and even it cannot correctly be called 'complete'. The dialogue has been trimmed to a tiny proportion of its original length, giving little idea of the real fun of the libretto and, even so, several numbers, including the delightfully comical 'J'ai ma migraine' have been omitted. Like others of this series, it is a broadly acted and energetically sung recording of sometimes less than perfect technical quality. It has some fine moments, notably a jewel of a performance from André Mallabrera, whose rendition of the pretty song of the lovesick tailor, Griolet, is a model one, a lusty vivandière from Monique de Pondeau and some splendidly martial ensemble singing and playing, but it cannot compare with the first-rate performance that this most delightful of Offenbach's late works gets on its 1966 Pathé excerpts recording.

This may have slightly less than perfect sound, by modern standards, and its tracks cut off drily in a manner which suggests that the selected pieces have come from a larger recording. If they did, please may we have it, for this is a beauty of a performance. Gem follows gem as the lively Liliane Chatel as the piquant Stella of the title goes from schoolgirl in the tomboyish 'Légende de la fruit défendu' to rebel in the patriotic 'Petit Français, brave Français' and vivandière in the vigorous 'Chanson de la fille du tambour-major'. Nadine Sautereau as the real vivandière, Claudine, sings hoydenishly of her donkey in the brilliant, braying Chanson de l'âne, Michel Dens as the heroine's rich baritone lover switches from the soldierly to the serenading with equal skill, and tenor Rémy Corazza sighs comically but gracefully over the lass with the ass. Suzanne Lafaye, cleverly cast in a rôle which at last allows her her head, is quite perfect as the loopy, mismarried Duchess who is the cause of all the trouble, as she teams humorously – while avoiding the low comedy excesses of their Decca counterparts – with Dominique Tirmont as her long-lost husband in the 'confession' scene which finally brings Stella's real family back together again, or gasps vacuously 'J'ai ma migraine'.

The overall strength of the soloists on this recording gives additional shine to the show's many ensembles – the marvellous Quattuor du billet de Logement

(Corazza/Dens/Tirmont/Thierry Peyron) is a real winner – whilst some lusty chorus singing and enthusiastic playing by the Orchestre de la Société des Concerts du Conservatoire under Félix Nuovolone both help to make a thoroughly Offenbachian record in which there is never a dull moment.

La Créole

The only other of Offenbach's full-length works generally available in *intégrale* is the 1875 *opérette La Créole*. Bourg's two-record set of a 1969 ORTF broadcast, however, is based on the 1934 Théâtre Marigny revival, when the not very successful original show was reworked by Albert Willemetz and Georges Delance in order to feature the black revue star Josephine Baker in the title rôle created by a tinted Judic.

The score of *La Créole* hasn't the dazzling brilliance of the favourite Offenbach works, but there are some attractive items in a light opera style, such as the wistfully pretty duo 'A la Jamaïque', the long and lilting Duo de l'amitié and the splendidly silly ensemble 'La Poularde', with its reminiscences of *opéra-bouffe*.

The leading rôles are taken with their usual fine combination of vocal quality and humour by tenors Aimé Doniat and Michel Hamel and soprano Lina Dachary. Only the adorably characterful Huguette Boulangeot, who sounds occasionally less than happy with the tessitura of the rôle of the créole – which must have sounded odd sung by la Baker – is not entirely at home with her musical material. Monique Stiot gives a nice cutesy performance as the kookie black nurse Crême Fouettée and Gaston Rey blusters away in good heavy-father style as the heavy father of this rather conventional tale. Marcel Cariven is in musical command, which ensures tasteful and spirited playing – and in this piece the tasteful gets more use than the spirited. The whole recording is well done, but, enjoyable though *La Créole* may be, this is not really the very best of Offenbach.

Ba-ta-Clan

The 'chinoiserie musicale' *Ba-ta-Clan* is a great little piece of utter *bouffonerie*, full of extravagant craziness, and its eight or nine numbers (depending how you count them) which, even with narration, still make up a rather short record, are a fine example of *opéra-bouffe* at its most loonily liberated. The Chinese Quartet, all nonsensical noises and incoherent foreign-sounding words, is a magnificent burlesque; Italian operatic styles get a good and tuneful sending-up in the splendid basso/tenor Italian duet condemnation to 'Morto!' and in the elongated setting of the simplest words to florid harmonized phrases in the trio 'Je suis français'; and operatic parody rises to the most splendid heights in the show's finale, where regular big singing is mixed with utter sung silliness.

The 1966 Erato recording of *Ba-ta-Clan* is a good one. The narrative, spoken by Jean Desailly, is clear and useful, and the four performers cast in the piece's unprintably named rôles all seem to enjoy its extravagances roundly. Raymond

Amade is particularly impressive in the light, high tenor music and Rémy Corazza makes a ringing job of the top line of Italian duet with a very pompous and constipated-sounding René Terrasson. Huguette Boulangeot, as what passes for a heroine in this piece, holds up the feminine end of things more than adequately, coping nippily with the crazy extravagances of the soprano lines. Apart from anything else, Amade deserves the Thierry le Luron medal for impersonations for his hilarious trombone imitations (presumably done with the aid of comb) in the final 'Le Chapeau chinois, le trombone'. It is all the most splendid fun.

The Milan recording, of a performance given in Paris in 1980, is accompanied only by a couple of rumty-tum and not very well synchronized duo pianos, narrated by an irritatingly giggly Chinee, and amateurishly done in comparison with that on Erato. The artists themselves are a competent if not brilliant group, worthy, in any case, of a better back-up, the best singing coming from Anne-Marie Sanial, who attacks her music with particular gusto. There is no musical director or conductor credited on this disc. If there had been one, the ensembles might have stuck together better and the basso might have kept more in tune. In a word, this *Ba-ta-Clan* is not a patch on the earlier one.

Like so many recordings in France, the disc of the 1987–8 production from Normandy, which appeared at the Théâtre Dejazet for a season, sneaked out quietly and quickly disappeared. It has now reappeared in CD form, which the Erato one has not, and so it has at least the opportunity to be the best in that particular area – which it is. It is not a wonderful *Ba-ta-Clan*, for it has neither the unloosed kind of craziness needed in its script nor the galloping ease in its singing which the Erato performers achieve. It is honestly sung, with Michel Hubert in the bass rôle the most enjoyable of the four vocalists and Maryse Castets in the soprano part doing some nice things with the less tripping bits of the music, but after Amade's seamless, rippling performance, Vincent Vittoz in the top tenor rôle sounds effortful and raw, and the lightness of vocal touch which characterized the Erato recording is somehow absent. The best marks must go to the Ensemble Instrumental de Basse-Normandie, whose fourteen pieces provide an adept and very funny accompaniment in a spirited orchestration by Alain Mabit.

Les Bavards

The reissue of the Erato *Ba-ta-Clan* on the double-disc cheap-label DUE series paired it with a more substantial recording of the two-act version of Offenbach's delightful 1863 piece *Les Bavards*. This countrified little musical comedy, in line of descent from *Les Noces de Jeannette* and Offenbach's successful *Le Mariage aux lanternes*, is full of the same kind of personality which characterizes those two most successful short musicals. All of it is retained on this recording, which allows large portions of dialogue in between the show's dozen numbers, and which is left here in the hands of the vivacious if rather overlarge ORTF orchestra and chorus and a fine set of soloists.

The two chatterboxes of the title are outstandingly played by Lina Dachary (Béatrix), who makes a gloriously gabbling job of her rôle and particularly of the demanding first-act song, and by Aimé Doniat, who takes on what should really be another soprano rôle as Roland, the young suitor for the hand of Béatrix's niece who is set on the garrulous woman by her exhausted husband to out-talk her. He trips gaily through his opening song, but in his splendidly sung duo *bouffe* with René Terrasson, in the rôle of the father, it is nevertheless clear that a soprano voice would lie better.

There are many grand musical moments among the dozen songs and ensembles in *Les Bavards*, beginning with the songs for Roland and Béatrix, and peaking in the ensembles which end the first act with their skittering patter sections and the languorous waltz (a predecessor to 'Too Darn Hot') declaring 'La chaleur est accablante'. The second act continues with the splendid tea-table ensemble, its 6/8 song for Roland and his hilarious non-stop chatter-patter, marvellously performed by Doniat, and a dazzling trio for three female voices. Here, alas, this is done by two females and one male, but with such finesse and fine singing that it is (almost) impossible to grouch about it. All in all, this is a splendid recording, which comes as a fine surprise when you have it 'thrown in', so to speak, when buying the best of the *Ba-ta-Clan*s.

Offenbach's shorter pieces fall into two basic categories: those which, like *Ba-ta-Clan*, belong to the outrageously nonsensical burlesque genre, and those which follow the style of the often rural comic love stories, as in *Les Bavards*. The first group is represented on record by *Croquefer* (1857), *Tromb-al-ca-zar* (1855) and *L'Ile de Tulipatan* (1868), and they make up a very uneven little group of recordings.

Croquefer

The Bourg recording of *Croquefer*, a piece of hugely foolish medieval warfare in the extravagantly grotesque-historic *Bombastes Furioso* vein, is, unfortunately, of the same family as the *Ba-ta-Clan* of its brother Milan company. This time, instead of the two pianos there is a small, clumsy, wind-based ensemble assisted by some obtrusively silly and modern-sounding percussion. By the end of the long overture, you are wondering why anyone should have wanted to put such a performance on record. When the singing starts, things are a bit better, for this time the cast keeps largely in time and in tune. Jean Kriff makes a reasonable job of the title rôle and Chantal Reyjal sings effectively as the Princess Fleur-de-Soufre, but there is little of the crazy *bouffonerie* that such a piece needs and none of the zany zip of the Erato *Ba-ta-Clan*. The awful arrangements sabotage practically everything. The mock-operatic quintet (with the bass who has had his tongue cut out barking the bottom line!) gets a good big sing, but every time the singers stop for breath, and the thin, silly 'orchestra' pipes up, all their efforts go for little.

The best thing about this record is that it contains a reproduction of the original libretto, in spite of the fact that none of the dialogue is included on what are two rather short sides, and is thus a useful reference.

Tromb-al-ca-zar

TLP's recording of *Tromb-al-ca-zar* would have been more comprehensible (although these things are scarcely meant to be comprehensible) with a libretto, but this time dialogue is included alongside the music, and we can follow the story of the wicked innkeeper frightened into repentance by a trio of extravagantly melodramatic actors, if not necessarily the lyrics of their seven operatic burlesque songs.

This recording is in a different league to the preceding one. It is professionally accompanied by the large Orchestre de Chambre de la RTBF, Brussels, which establishes the tone of affairs in the long (and rather un-merry) overture, the largest drawback of which, in 1989, is that it has distractingly borrowed the principal phrase of *Aspects of Love*'s 'Love Changes Everything'. There are plenty of other reminiscences – intentional of course – in the score (helpfully pointed out in the notes supplied), including one very obvious one from Suppé's *Leicht Kavallerie* which hadn't yet been written.

Tromb-al-ca-zar is a jolly little piece with its farcical, high-spirited scenes and its gipsy boléro, its silly Trio du jambon de Bayonne and its opera-within-an-opera quartet, topped, for good measure, by a really swinging waltz. It is performed throughout this recording with a suitably broad and brazen over-the-top acting style and capably sung by a quartet of vocalists (Albert Voli, Yerry Mertz, Claudine Granger, Jacques Legrand) who are not stretched by its admittedly undemanding musical range and who switch nimbly between song and speech through the three-quarters of an hour of the piece.

L'Ile de Tulipatan

The most complete of these three pieces is *L'Ile de Tulipatan*, a bouncy little *bouffonerie* whose hero is a girl and whose heroine is a boy. And that is just the beginning of the nonsensical ins-and-outs of this topsy-turvy little piece of tuneful nonsense. There is not a lot more to say – the libretto is hilariously ridiculous and the score bright, bubbling Offenbach throughout, ranging from the deliciously 'straight' sounding Humming Bird Waltz ('J'ai perdu mon ami') sung by the young prince(ss) to the crazy un-Venetian barcarolle ('Dans Venezia la belle'), yodelled out energetically by the whole cast, or the Duke's punning entrance song.

TLP's recording gives the piece *in toto*, which means that, apart from the dozen brief and light-hearted musical pieces involved, there is a good deal of dialogue. It is splendidly funny stuff, but obviously a bit much to take if the French language means nothing to you. If it does, this is without doubt the pick of the recordings of Offenbach's most *bouffe* short *opéras-bouffes*.

Apart from the qualities of the show, which are not in doubt, the qualities of the recording are also many. The piece is accompanied neither by a tacky little group nor a huge orchestra like its companions, but by a fine ensemble called Les Solistes de Liège, who give the music exactly the right light-hearted, middle-weight expression that it calls for. It is played by a lively cast, up-front but not vulgar, in which Yerry Mertz as the Duke (who thinks he has a son), Stéfano Memma as the Chamberlain's daughter (who is actually a boy) and Marcelle Rieu as his culpable mama are outstanding, and sung brightly and unpretentiously all round.

Such recordings of Offenbach's more 'normal' short works as exist are mainly courtesy of Bourg. They are a spotty lot, some being recorded with the minimum of resources, others getting a more professional treatment.

Les Deux aveugles/Le Violoneux

Les Deux aveugles (1855), one of Offenbach's greatest successes in the field of the comic musical playlet, is a two-handed little festival of humorous acting but, unfortunately, Bourg's recording – in spite of filling only about half of the side of the record – gives none of the dialogue. It simply puts down the four little musical numbers which make up the score, performed by two acceptable vocalists who sing the notes but who give no idea of the fun of the piece. This recording, by the way, has also suffered under the hand of the same Louis-Vincent Bruère who 're-orchestrated' *Croquefer*: this time the tinny little group which accompanies the piece sounds like the pit band from a particularly poor provincial theatre or pierrot show. It is less harmful here, given the nature of the piece, but to deprive us of Offenbach's musical battle between the mandolin and the trombone is going too far.

The other side of this skimpy disc is taken up by the music (but only a fragment of the text) from the sentimental *opérette Le Violoneux* (1855), which includes a sweet duettino ('J'sais bien que ce n'est pas l'usage'), but the music is again feebly rearranged and not particularly well sung. As with *Croquefer*, the best part of this package is the facsimile libretti provided with the disc. This pair have been issued, along with the *Croquefer*, on CD – why, I can't imagine.

Les Deux pêcheurs/La Rose de Saint-Flour

Les Deux pêcheurs (1857), a palpable follow-up to *Les Deux aveugles*, is another two-handed piece of musical comedy which, this time, is recorded *in toto*. The dialogue and five happy little musical numbers get a jolly, pantomime broad performance from Jean Kriff and François Salez assisted by a two-piano accompaniment which is wholly preferable to the mimsy mini-arrangements of the other record.

The rest of the first side and all of the second on this disc are taken up by a performance of the immensely likeable one-act *La Rose de Saint-Flour* (better known to Victorian English theatre-goers as *The Rose of the Auvergne*), in which the pianos get the reinforcement of an occasional flute and the two men are joined by Françoise Bidault in a little tale of Auvergnat country love and jealousy. Their performance is at least adequate, if neither particularly endearing nor exciting, and what this recording gains in its playing it loses by not giving us the text to follow (and once the rural accents and 'character' voices start coming, you need it!).

Lischen et Fritzchen/La Chanson de Fortunio

With this pairing, things get rather more professional. Both pieces are INA archive recordings of broadcasts, from 1970 and 1973 respectively, cast with first-rate singers and accompanied by the ORTF orchestra. And there are libretti, too.

Lischen et Fritzchen (1864) is another little rural piece, one in which the accents of its protagonists are the moving influence of the whole plot. Sadly, only the musical numbers are recorded, but they are done in proper style. After the previous recordings it is a real relief to be in the presence of such singers as the delicious Lina Dachary and the accomplished Joseph Peyron, and the massed forces of the ORTF orchestra succeed in sounding much lighter, brighter and more frivolous than the plonky pianos or whining bands ever did. The two characters of the piece, joining in the apparently Alsatian duo (it sounds just like a Tyrolean Schuhplatter to me), are both charming and comical, and, even if the sound leaves a little to be desired, this recording is in a different class to the others.

La Chanson de Fortunio (1861), another light-hearted piece woven around a tale of love and jealousy, has one of the most delightful scores of all Offenbach's short works. Beginning with a really dashing song for the heroine of the piece ('Prenez-garde'), sung here with every ounce of *entrain* needed by Lina Dachary, it gallops happily through some glittering songs for the young men of the cast, ranging from a lilting drinking song – about water – to a rhapsodic 'Je l'aime' and some lovely ensembles, to the show's most famous number, the Chanson de Fortunio, meltingly sung by André Mallabrera in the very best French fashion. It is a shame that the text could not have been included – it seems by one or two of the clippings of the music as if it were there originally – but at least the enclosed libretto enables you to fill in the story between the songs.

Le Leçon de chant electromagnétique

The *Chanson de Fortunio/Lischen et Fritzchen* pairing is reissued on CD in tandem with Bourg's brief one-side recording of this fantastical little two-handed piece (1867) about an excessively Italian singing teacher who can turn 'un crétino' into a *primo tenore* with the aid of his electro-magnetic instruments. The subject matter has given someone the idea of backing the 1983 recording with a synthesizer accompaniment (repeated without voices on side 2 of the record so that you can have your own singing lesson!), over which Jean Kriff metamorphoses from his favourite silly voice to a budding vocalist with one lively, showy duo to share with his teacher (Jacomo Zanetti).

Pomme d'api/Mesdames de la Halle/Monsieur Choufleuri

Bourg's 1983 issue of Offenbach's much later *Pomme d'api* (1873), another little rural love tale with a pretty if politish score, has the plus of an accompaniment by the Solistes de Liège, and the minus of not letting us have the libretto even though the text is included on the recording. It gets a fair performance. Claudine Granger in the title rôle is best when lightest (i.e. not at the top of the voice), and Jacques Ducros – a tenor in yet another travesti rôle – makes her lover less effortful than André Payol as the heavyish uncle.

Pomme d'api received a second and generally better recording as a part of a triple bill, played several times in Paris during the early 1980s and subsequently put on record by EMI with its Parisian cast, with Mady Mesplé replacing the leading ladies of not only *Pomme d'api* but of the other two pieces, *Mesdames de la Halle* (1858) and *Monsieur Choufleuri* (1861). Manuel Rosenthal and the Monte Carlo Philharmonic supply a mostly well-judged musical performance, and all three singers in the *Pomme d'api* are superior to their Bourg equivalents. Léonard Pezzino has an attractive light tenor, which he uses delicately, Mady Mesplé has just the right innocent glitters in her voice for the character of the determined Cathérine, Jean-Philippe Lafont is not too extravagant with the baritone rôle, and all three have a good time with the slightly shorter variant of the text (rearranged by Robert Dhéry, who has also had a go at the other two pieces) used here.

Mesdames de la Halle is a larger-scale affair, with half a dozen principal players and a chorus – a genuine short full-scale *opérette bouffe*. The subject matter, another bundle of love affairs, gains much of its *bouffonerie* from the fact that the three ageing ladies of the title, all falling ludicrously over their sagging charms to gain the notice of the pretty kitchen-boy, are played by men. The kitchen-boy is played by a girl, and he, of course, ends up with the only girl who is played by a real girl. She has a brilliant soprano aria and, just for good measure, turns out to be the daughter of the impecunious and ageing Drum Major who has been chatting up the three ladies in search of a dowry. And so forth.

This recording is splendidly cast and played. Mady Mesplé is the heroine, lickety-splitting through her coloratura and making the same perfect little ingénue she has been making for twenty years and more. The three market ladies, very cleverly played by Lafont, Michel Trempont and Michel Hamel, are never camped up into boring parodies but turned into genuinely comical characters, and Charles Burles is first rate (if eternally young and handsome-sounding) as the prospecting Raflafla, the Drum Major.

Alas, with half the parody casting right, the effect is then spoiled by Croûte-au-Pot, the kitchen-boy, being cast not with a soprano, but a tenor. Pezzino is, again, very fine, but a duo for two female voices becomes an ordinary male/female number and the vocal balance in the superb long final burlesque septet and ensembles are upset. Otherwise there is little to quarrel with in this recording.

Monsieur Choufleuri restera chez lui le 24 Janvier 1833 is a marvellous little charade in which the silly friends of pretentious M Choufleuri get entertained by his daughter and her lover, instead of Sontag and Rubini, and don't know the difference. It mainly gives the opportunity to the two artists playing those rôles to join M Choufleuri in indulging in a jolly and very particular burlesque of Italian opera singers and a lively boléro, and for everyone concerned to take the Michel out of the social-climbing bourgeoisie. Mesplé is in her element as young Ernestine, who spends a fair amount of her time in the leger lines above the stave, and Burles, replacing the soprano intended as her beloved Babylas, echoes her happily right up to the top Cs. Their pieces together are precisely sung, and comically first rate. Lafont (Choufleuri), Trempont (the Belgian butler) and Hamel (Balandard, the guest) are all excellent and the piece gets as good a representation as could be wished.

This little musical comedy was the subject of another recording, on the Gallo label in 1981 (billed as 'première mondiale sur disque'), with the soloists accompanied by the attractive Ensemble Instrumental de Grenoble. It, too, is an enjoyable recording, which remembers its burlesque character well in the dialogue (particularly when the guests are concerned) if sometimes less so in the musical sections. Danielle Borst (Ernestine) sings so beautifully in the andante section of the burlesque operatic trio and takes her runs with such smooth clarity (even though she skips to top D), that you have to remind yourself that this is not the real thing. Serge Maurer (another tenor Babylas) and Charles Ossola (Choufleuri) may be a bit less accomplished but sound funnier. A little more extravagance all round from the singers (the actors have it splendidly) would have been welcome, but this recording is nevertheless a well-made one which represents the piece effectively.

Le Mariage aux lanternes

The delightful *Le Mariage aux lanternes*, one of the prettiest of Offenbach's rural romantic comedies, does not seem to have had a proper French recording. The only one I have discovered in the original language is an ineffectual version sung by a children's group from Monaco. There is, apparently, an English-language recording on Magic Tone, but this is a rarity which I have not succeeded in winkling out.

Offenbach extras

Various Offenbach works have appeared on bootleg discs and some not otherwise available, including his last full-length *opérette Belle Lurette*, apparently, in Russian and East German versions. These are, needless to say, also rarities. I hope they are good, and I look forward one day to finding out.

Amongst the other regular Offenbach discs which are more available, reference ought to be made to two pieces which really fall outside the terms of reference of this work. Since they are by Offenbach, however, it seems pertinent to point them out. Both, oddly enough, are of British origin and are the result of some enterprising work by the group Opera Rara and its guiding lights Patric Schmid and Don White. The first is a complete 1980 recording of the 1867 *Robinson Crusoe*, one of Offenbach's attempts to get his work played at the Opéra-Comique and, thus, a consciously 'proper' light opera. Even the extremely neat and singable English version written by White cannot disguise the fact that this is Offenbach, given little help from his librettists, Crémieux and Cormon, striving to do something that doesn't come naturally. The piece has some tuneful moments but none of the sparkle of the favourite works and, compounded by several pedestrian performances, it comes out as a rather self-conscious affair.

Opera Rara's other production was an *opéra-bouffe*, *Christopher Columbus*, cleverly constructed by White around melodies from some of the lesser known Offenbach works. The libretto burlesqued the Christopher Columbus story, having its trigamist hero hustled off to adventures in the West by a sex-mad Queen Isabella, and its score was a splendidly sewn patchwork of pretty melodies, including one or two gems, which often gained from the change of lyrics. A piece from *La Boulangère* was transformed into an exceedingly comic jewel song which has since found its way into the repertoire of many a soprano who is looking for an alternative to 'Glitter and Be Gay'. The recording, on three discs, is by and large well performed, with Maurice Arthur in the title rôle displaying a first-rate *opéra-bouffe* tenor, Anna Dawson combining the lowest of comedy with the highest of notes as Isabella, and such artists as Marilyn Hill Smith and Alan Opie in support. Some brighter conducting and orchestral playing would have been an advantage, but on the whole the set is an enjoyable record of a worthwhile venture.

Charles Lecocq

The man who headed the movement from *opéra-bouffe* to the less zany areas of *opéra-comique* was Charles Lecocq, and the work which set the seal on this change in direction was his acknowledged masterpiece *La Fille de Madame Angot*. *La Fille de Madame Angot* has duly been recorded several times over, but it is dispiriting to notice that the work of Lecocq, the composer of a massive list of outstanding pieces of musical theatre, and as highly regarded as Offenbach in his time, has otherwise been poorly treated by posterity and the recording companies. His beautiful *Le Petit Duc*, arguably his most outstanding lyric piece, even though it lacks some of the more obvious and vigorous attractions of *Angot*, has reached both Decca and Pathé, but the marvellous *Giroflé-Girofla* exists only on an East German recording transferred to the not-so-readily available Urania label; *La Camargo* is to be found with difficulty on Rare Recorded Editions, and such works as *Les Cent Vièrges*, *Le Coeur et la main* and *Le Jour et la nuit* are represented only by the occasional number on a recital disc.

La Fille de Madame Angot

La Fille de Madame Angot is not one of those works that merely throws up two or three popular pieces from a score that is otherwise just pleasant. It is a finely constructed series of comedy, drama and musical pieces, solos and ensembles, in which virtually every scene is dramatically substantial and every musical section both significant and delightful. There are half a dozen 'hit numbers', ranging from the celebrated Conspirators' Chorus to the Quarrelling Duet, and several solos which swept the world during the nineteenth century and which are still outstanding examples of the *opéra-comique* composer's craft.

Over the years, *La Fille de Madame Angot* has suffered from some changing ideas over the playing of two of its three principal characters. The original Belgian production, and the many other productions throughout the world in the years that followed, cast the leading male rôle of the political satirist, Ange Pitou, with a tenor and that of the actress, Mademoiselle Lange, with a soprano. Some time during the twentieth century, it became fashionable to exchange this casting for a baritone/mezzo pairing, possibly to contrast better with the ingénue soprano rôle of Clairette and the comedy tenor part of Pomponnet. As a result, the recordings that exist exhibit some rather noticeable variations of performance. I, myself, strongly prefer the soprano/tenor coupling, and it is noticeable that even Gabriel Bacquier and Michel Dens, probably the two most outstanding high baritones of the French *opérette* scene, get into difficulty with the highest notes of Ange Pitou's opening 'Certainement j'aimais Clairette', while the mezzo Langes, impressive in the dramatic scenes, are inclined to be less happy with the fast-moving passages of 'Les Soldats d'Augereau sont des hommes'.

There are two double-disc recordings of *La Fille de Madame Angot*: a Decca version dating from 1958 and an EMI one made in 1973. The former uses the baritone/mezzo pairing of Bacquier and Suzanne Lafaye, the latter the almost-tenor of Bernard Sinclair and the sort-of soprano Christiane Stutzmann and, given my predilections, it is just my luck that the former is by far the better of the two.

The EMI recording is a very patchy one both in sound and performance. It is recorded in such a way that, if it is played to bring out the best in the solo voices, the chorus and orchestra blast your ears out but, since the soloists are almost uniformly not-so-impressive, it bears playing down. Many of the show's most famous pieces simply miss the mark: the rousing market-woman's song 'Marchande de Marée' goes for very little, Sinclair sounds more uncomfortable than most in his lovely opening song, Mady Mesplé as Clairette gives a surprisingly unenthusiastic rendering of the initial 'Je vous dois tout' and Stutzmann's 'Les Soldats d'Augereau' goes sadly astray. Things improve a bit later, particularly when Pomponnet (Charles Burles) is in evidence, but, apart from anything else, the voices match poorly and the whole effect is just plain unimpressive.

The Decca version gives better value. Georgette Spanellys gives more gusto and accuracy to 'Marchande de Marée', Bernard Alvi is a delightful light comedy Pomponnet, Gabriel Bacquier – in spite of the high notes – is as perfect a baritone Pitou as could be wished and Lafaye negotiates 'Les Soldats d'Augereau' smoothly and the rest of the rôle with a pleasing tone. As Clairette, Colette Riedinger chooses to adopt an agressive, hectic manner which, while it fits well with the last scenes of the show, becomes a little monotonous elsewhere. It is a true-voiced and gutsy performance, but I prefer my Clairettes a little less hectoring. The daughter of the outrageous Madame Angot she may be, but it is better for the coherence of the play that she does not show her true colours until the final act.

There are three excerpts recordings of *La Fille de Madame Angot* in existence, two of which are very fine. One is on Pathé and the other on Philips, and the only complaint I have with either is that they are not double-disc recordings, as I enjoy both better than either of the full sets. The Pathé version pairs a perfect Clairette in Lina Dachary with a splendid mezzo Lange (Solange Michel) and with Michel Dens who, if one has to have a baritone Pitou, could not be bettered. The smaller rôles are finely taken and, under the baton of Jules Gressier, there are some superb moments here, particularly the second-act finale, with its Conspirators' Chorus and its marvellous rolling waltz ('Tournez, tournez'), and the celebrated Quarrelling Duet scene. Unfortunately, since this selection chooses to include these two lengthy sections in full, several of the well-loved solos have had to be omitted. There is no 'Je vous dois tout', and the Duo des Deux Forts, the Pitou/Clairette duet 'Pour être fort', and the charming Lange/Clairette duo 'Jours fortunés' are all missing as well.

The Philips disc squeezes in all of these except the Deux Forts, at the price of reducing the finales and omitting an overture. This is a finely performed version, under Jésus Etcheverry, with Claudine Collart as a sweet Clairette – about as different from Riedinger as could be – Mathilde Casadesus walloping into 'Marchande de Marée' like a real fishwife, Henri Legay as a fine tenor Pitou and Lyne Cumia as a soprano Lange, thus assembling, alone of the four versions, the voices of the original production. For this reason, I find it perhaps more satisfying than the others, but, as is so often the case, all the virtues don't find themselves on the same recording and it is the EMI-Pathé version and its marvellous rendition of the great waltz tune to which I generally find myself turning when I go to listen to an *Angot*.

Le Petit Duc

Le Petit Duc is less well served in quantity – just one *intégrale* (Decca) and one selection disc (Pathé). In spite of some attractive singing by André Jobin in the title rôle, however, the former is an absolute non-starter for me. The part of the teenaged Duc de Parthenay was written for a soprano and the duets between the little Duke and his little Duchess are some of the most lovely female ensemble music in all *opérette*. Sung by a tenor and the indifferent Eliane Thibault as the Duchess they simply sound awkward and ordinary. The comedy rôles on this set are well enough played, but nothing can make up for this strange and unnecessary switch of sex in the casting.

Regret is tempered by the fact that the Pathé excerpts disc, under the baton of Jules Gressier, is one of the very best of all of that famous series. Of course, it is sad that this mono recording, dating from 1953, can include only a portion of the show's score. However, the choice has been well made and, although some of the Duke's music has had to be omitted, all three finales are included along with the principal showpieces for both the comedians, the Duo de l'idylle for Frimousse (René Herent) and the Couplets and Chanson du petit bossu for the military Montlandry (Willy Clément). Above all, there are superb performances of the two romantic rôles by the sopranos Nadine Renaux (Duc) and Liliane Berton (Duchesse), joining together as if by nature intended in their glorious duet 'C'est pourtant bien doux'/'Je t'aime' and the scarcely less delightful 'Ah! qu'on est bien'.

The completeness of Lecocq as a composer can be seen by comparing this uplifting sentimental music and the delicacy of the little pages' chorus with the buffoonery of the Idylle Duet, in which the foolish schoolmaster woos a phoney country maiden, the military vigour of the first-act finale ('Mon Colonel') and Montlandry's music, and with the swirling dancing tunes and musical conflicts of *La Fille de Madame Angot*. *Le Petit Duc* is a model of an *opérette* and this recording a model representation of it.

Robert Planquette

Les Cloches de Corneville

The piece which shared with *La Fille de Madame Angot* the international spotlight of many years was Robert Planquette's *Les Cloches de Corneville*. Planquette, though briefly classically trained, was as much a man of the popular song as of the *opéra-comique*, and his first score for the theatre reflected that background in its memorable tunefulness as it turned itself into one of the classic musicals of all time. Although he had plenty of success thereafter, particularly in Britain, where his *Rip van Winkle*, *Paul Jones* and *The Old Guard* were long-lived successes, Planquette never succeeded in equalling his first great hit and, of his other works, only *Rip!*, as it was titled in France, became part of the general repertoire and won itself a place in the Pathé canon.

It is perhaps owing to the immense singability of Planquette's music (and this is not to say that it is in any way undemanding) that, in contrast to *La Grande-Duchesse* or *La Vie parisienne*, there doesn't seem to be a bad recording of *Les Cloches de Corneville* amongst the half dozen or so made to date. There are two double-disc recordings, once again from Decca and EMI. The Decca set, dating from 1955, has a very agreeable cast, all of whom are in fine voice – Huguette Boulangeot as a charming Germaine, Colette Riedinger as a truly shrewish Serpolette, Ernest Blanc as a ringing Henri and Jean Giraudeau as a smooth and sweet Grenicheux. The two important acting rôles of the miser, Gaspard, and the old Bailli naturally show up to less effect on a recording than do the predominantly singing roles, but Louis Musy (Gaspard) makes a fine job of his big set-pieces: he succeeds in being both amusing and pathetic in the famous second-act finale, where he is surprised amongst his stolen gold, and in his last-act mad scene and confession. This set contains a good deal of spoken material, including narration, genuine dialogue and dialogue fabricated to fill in the story and, because of this, it omits a couple of musical pieces which it would have been preferable to have included.

Nevertheless, it is a lively and enjoyable recording which compares favourably with the later EMI set.

This latter, dating from 1974, features much the same team as was responsible for the poor *La Fille de Madame Angot* but they are uniformly and unrecognizably in better form here. Burles is splendid as the loutish Grenicheux, more virile and less beautiful in tone than some others and right on line with his comedy, Mesplé is a crisp and attractive Germaine and Bernard Sinclair is much more at home as Henri than in the more tenorish heights of Ange Pitou. There are a singing Gaspard (J-C. Benoît) and Bailli (the same Jean Giraudeau who nineteen years earlier recorded Grenicheux) and their big acting set-pieces thus show up less prominently than on the recordings which feature 'star' Gaspards. Only Stutzmann, who speaks perfectly well but seems to put on a funny voice lodged somewhere near the back of her neck to sing, is less than comfortable as Serpolette, a lapse which sadly prevents this set being thoroughly enjoyable. Nevertheless, it has some fine moments and the big orchestral and choral sound which is so wrong for some works comes into its own here in the dramatic moments of the second act.

The selection discs are an equally pleasant group. Pathé, having recorded the show with a notable cast including Martha Angelici, Nadine Renaux and Michel Dens in the 1950s, replaced this version with a newer one also featuring Dens, alongside Nicole Broissin, Janine Micheau and Michel Sénéchal, in 1961. The earlier disc is now practically unfindable but the later one makes me long to hear it, for it is obvious that the rôle of Henri really fits Michel Dens with all the splendour of a good pair of tights. But whatever he did with the part in the 1950s, here he is still in marvellous form. The recording does not allow him to soar with quite the operatic splendour that he might in the big Ancestors Ensemble, but his beauty of tone and crisp delivery make the lyric moments of the score quite outstanding. He is supported by a really sparky Serpolette (Mlle Broissin) and a fine lyrical Grenicheux (Sénéchal), a Bailli (Pierre Germain) who can sing and who also makes the character rather more human than some of his more obviously comical *confrères*, and a pretty but not quite first-class Germaine in Janine Micheau. The selection omits totally the character of Gaspard and his set-pieces in favour of the lyrical music and five minutes of overture, which tilts this recording the opposite way from most of the other excerpt discs, but it does have the advantage of allowing a particularly good version of the trio 'Fermons les yeux' and the Henri/Germaine Act 3 duo to be included alongside the more obvious bon-bons.

Philips issued a good full selection sung by a staunchly operatic group under Jésus Etcheverry, in which Fernand Ledoux is given large billing on the cover and plenty of space on the recording to play his three big scenes as Gaspard alongside a cast in which René Coulon's Grenicheux and Lyne Cumia's Germaine are as enjoyable as any. Odéon/CBS issued France's Mr and Mrs Musical, Marcel Merkès and Paulette Merval, in a selection that would probably be the choice of their many fans. As with all recordings by this couple, I find his baritone impeccably masculine if unexciting and her soprano uncomfortably nasal and prefer to shop elsewhere, but I hasten to add that thousands of record buyers and theatre-goers would disagree with me.

The best I have kept to last. It's a real surprise – one of those recordings from an unexpected label which suddenly gets simply everything dead right. Even sitting with your critic's hat on and waiting for the first fault, the first infelicity, you suddenly find that you have got to the end of the first side and you have a silly grin on your face. I picked up Véga's 1962 *Cloches de Corneville* in the Marché aux Puces in Nice for 20 francs and I don't think I ever spent a better 20 francs. It's a little beauty. Jean-Claude Hartemann at the head of the ubiquitous Orchestra and Chorus of Raymond Saint-Paul heads a cast where, once again, the Gaspard (Daniel Sorano) gets star billing but, although he gives a splendid performance of the miser's three scenes and their songs, the outstanding performance on this disc is surely that of baritone Robert Massard as the Marquis. Where other baritones negotiate the high notes of the popular 'J'ai fait trois fois le tour du monde', Massard sails through them effortlessly; when he comes to the stirring ending to the second act, where the Marquis, disguised in the ghostly armour of his ancestors, leads the massed forces of his friends in upon the guilty miser, his rendition of 'Sous des armures à leur taille' is nothing short of thrilling. It is as if the Conte di Luna had unexpectedly marched in from *Il Trovatore*, and nothing could be more suitable or more exciting.

Aimé Doniat is the Grenicheux, always tuneful and comical when required, Lina Dachary is an ideal Germaine, and Suzy Deilhes (whom I haven't encountered elsewhere) a sparky Serpolette with a fine voice, whilst Serge Clin as the Bailli is funny without indulging the excesses of characterization sometimes used. This is one of those rare recordings which sound effortless in every way – a total joy.

Rip!

Rip! was by no means another *Cloches de Corneville* – Planquette would never write one, and few other composers approached it. It was a piece in a different style – more dramatic and spectacular, less merry and romantic – and this style was compounded when the show was rewritten for its French production. The title rôle of Rip van Winkle, originally written for the English singing comedian Fred Leslie, was made over as a strong light opera baritone leading part with rather more dramatic overtones than comic ones.

On the Pathé recording, this overwhelming star rôle is taken by Michel Dens and the result is predictably impressive. He gambols through the anti-hero's carefree 'Vive la paresse', the show's big tune, with rich insouciance, launches gloriously into the piratical Legend of the Katskills and his dramatic dream meeting with the ghostly crew of Captain Henrik Hudson's ship (Chanson à boire), covers the wide range of the Air de jeunesse (interpolated for the French version) with ease, joins delightfully with the two little children in the trio 'Mes enfants, sachez qu'en ménage', and almost loosens into comedy in the nervous Echo Song, sung by the benighted hunter fleeing his persecutors in the depths of the mountains. It is as fine a performance of the French Rip as one could ask for, and my only quibble is that I prefer the more light-hearted English Rip van Winkle.

No one but the star gets to do much in this show, but Liliane Berton as Mrs van Winkle does her usual lovely job in the little waltz 'Pour marcher dans la nuit obscure' and some bits of obbligato, and Jean-Christophe Benoît and Monique Linval are particularly good as the comic relief, mixing humour and delightful singing in the duo 'L'avenir avec ses féeries'. This recording is an excellent representation of a dramatically and musically interesting work which, preferably in its original form, would probably appeal to today's theatrical tastes.

The Pathé-Marconi series, for all its glories, has one consistent fault. It has suffered over the years from sadly inadequate sleeve material, and the *Rip!* sleeve sees it at its poorest. Jacques Slyper's very brief plot synopsis gives an unfortunately inaccurate idea of the show's story, one character's name is misspelt, one song wrongly attributed, and the first performance misdated. When this definitive series is released again (preferably in its entirety), EMI owe it to themselves to supply definitive sleeves.

Edmond Audran

The third member of the leading triumvirate of the mid- to late nineteenth-century musical theatre in France was Edmond Audran. Like Lecocq and like Planquette, his biggest success came early in his career, with the delightful, tuneful *La Mascotte*, another piece which has duly found its way into both *intégrale* and excerpt recordings. But, as in the case of Lecocq, Audran's other considerable stage successes – *La Cigale et la fourmi*, *Les Noces d'Olivette*, *Le Grand Mogol*, *Miss Helyett* and *La Poupée* – have unfortunately not been considered as recordings.

La Mascotte

La Mascotte has been issued twice in double-record sets, in 1956 by Decca and again in 1985, on Clio, in a version taken from the INA files. The Clio recording, featuring mezzo-soprano Freda Betti in the star rôle, did the French trick. It came out, was everywhere for a few months, and then vanished so utterly that I have not been able to find a copy. If it is as good as the Clio *Le Petit Faust* it is worth chasing, but the idea of a mezzo Bettina is not encouraging.

Such a chase is not really necessary, for the earlier recording is a splendid, lively piece of theatre. The lengthy libretto is slimmed down into fine and funny linking text which is given a very broad and big comic performance by all its participants. Lucien Baroux, as the madcap monarch who spends the evening trying to steal Bettina, the luck-bringing turkey girl, for himself, gives an hilarious performance both in speech and in song in the central comedy rôle, and he is supported by a set of rich-voiced artists who give Audran's score a really grand sing. Robert Massard lends his broad baritone to the rôle of the heroine's lover, Pippo – usually taken by a much less thoroughly splendid voice – and Geneviève Moïzan is a lusty wench of a Bettina whose heavy but mobile soprano makes a proper prima donna part of the title rôle. Their famous Turkey Duet with its clucking, gurgling and bleating noises gets a rather more operatic treatment than usual.

Bernard Alvi is splendid in the tenor rôle of Fritellini, immaculate in his spun-out 'Je ne sais quoi', and Denise Cauchard is a lively Princess Fiametta, tossing off her comical Song of the Orang Outang with glee. It is a set which will appeal particularly to those who like their light musical theatre thoroughly sung.

Pathé's 1954 selections disc is a very differently conceived one. Conductor Jules Gressier, the soloists and the Raymond Saint-Paul choir take the piece in a much lighter and less pretentious style and the result is a recording which gives the show quite another spirit. I suppose neither is 'right' – it just depends how you prefer your *Mascotte* played. Certainly, in its particular style, this couldn't be better done. The casting is perfect. Nadine Renaux is a warm, charming Bettina, producing some beautiful notes in her singing; Michel Dens gives Pippo a softer edge than Massard and a likeable character as well as his invariably fine singing, Liliane Berton is a silvery, rippling Fiametta, Claude Devos a seamlessly sweet Fritellini and Duvaleix a comical Laurent. My only complaint with this recording is that its short length means again that several of the show's loveliest pages have had to be omitted. Two of Bettina's songs are missing, along with Fritellini's third-act number and the big quartet leading to the evening's dénouement. All are sadly missed. Nevertheless, this is an adorable record of an adorable show and, for my money, more enjoyable in spite of its lacunae than the more roundly sung and more complete Decca one.

Louis Varney

Les Mousquetaires au couvent

Another nineteenth-century composer whose reputation survives today on one work is Louis Varney, whose *Les Mousquetaires au couvent* has remained a strong favourite throughout the years. Regularly revived on French stages, it is a charming combination of a slim but cleverly plotted story about two soldiers trying to carry off a pair of noble schoolgirls from their convent and a scoreful of lively songs and choruses that caught the popular ear and earned the show a place amongst the standards of its era.

Some of the musical pieces of *Les Mousquetaires* are indeed amongst the most enjoyable of their kind: the lilting male trio 'Parle! explique-toi', the droll duo 'Nous venons de la Palestine', intoned by the soldiers disguised as mendicant priests, the pretty soubrette Rondo de la Curieuse and, in contrast, the heroine's romance 'Que votre volonté se fasse' and its mocking reply, the giggling Pensionnaires' Chorus.

Les Mousquetaires au couvent suffered from the nineteenth-century star system when two cheery and very obviously vocal songs were added to the score for the baritone Morlet to enlarge the rôle of the hero's best friend (the one who gets the soubrette in the end). Add to this the introduction of an incidental serving maid into the first act to sing three equally incidental pieces to make up for the fact that the girls of the piece don't enter until Act 2, and you are left with a score which, without its libretto (and even with it) doesn't truly represent the main outlines of the work. The baritone Brissac and the mezzo-soprano or sometimes soprano Simonne force the more interesting characters into a musical corner and, in consequence, excerpt discs include a lot of what are really incidental songs. They are, however, perfectly happy pieces and don't seem to have harmed the work's reputation. I, personally, prefer the comedy of the plotworthy Abbé Bridaine and the songs of the tenor hero, his soprano sweetheart and her soubrette sister, but I'm clearly in a minority.

Les Mousquetaires has earned two full-scale recordings, one on Decca dating from 1957 and the other, on EMI, from 1979. The Decca version has some sound problems – the transitions between the spoken and sung sections are not easy – and it also suffers from some hefty botching of the text, much of which is far from the original, to fit it on to two records. On the credit side, however, it is a really lusty and enthusiastic performance which fairly gallops along headed by Gabriel Bacquier as Brissac. He makes a royally rich job of his Musketeer's Song and his drunken scene, the voice ringing out with all the authority of the future Don Giovanni and Scarpia he was to become, and yet, at the same time, he doesn't allow the rather irritating side of the character to show up too strongly. Colette Riedinger is well cast as the aggressive Simonne, grabbing extra top notes whenever possible, there is a delightful soubrette Louise (Mireille Lacoste), and Pierre Blanc (Gontran) and Louis Musy (Bridaine) are fine in the other leading rôles. There is even a treat for the nostalgic in the casting of two famous veterans, Gabrielle Ristori and Pauline Carton, as the chief nuns. I find, perhaps, that all the relentlessly vigorous singing and very theatrical acting on this set is at the expense of a certain lightness and sparkle but, all round, it is certainly one of the best of the Decca series.

The EMI recording, which also takes in all the extra pieces of music and has its own ideas about the book, is made more in the fashion of recent years. It is richly played and sung, in a rather serious fashion, with a vast chorus (which sounds quite nonsensical as a class of schoolgirls, and too many to fill Simonne's inn) and a large and lustrous orchestra. All of the principals sing strongly and mostly well – Michel Trempont making a fine, masculine Brissac, Charles Burles a romantic Gontran, producing a *fil de voce* in the big trio and caressing his heartbroken 'Il serait vrai' tenderly, Jules Bastin a friendly, robust Bridaine, more sung then comicked, and Mady Mesplé (Marie) her usual effectively unsoppy ingénue self, handicapped only by the excessively slow tempo of her little prayer. The ever-intrusive Simonne gets a very lusty operatic sing from Michèle Command, who shows a rich mezzo top in her best pieces, but goes oddly limp in the first-act chanson and lacks genuine gaiety elsewhere. The surprise for me, and a very pleasant one, comes in a delightful performance from Christiane Château – an artist new to me – as a bright as a button Louise whose Rondo de la Curieuse is a real pleasure. It also sounds, when one or two neat-voiced girls emerge from the serried ranks of the chorus, as if there may be more like her coming up behind. I hope so. A good soubrette in these oh-so-serious days is hard to find.

Alongside these two sets, there are the usual selection discs, headed, as always, by a Pathé version which is even more impeccable than usual. This recording, which manages to include all the highlights of the score (although leaving out the pretty second-act quartet 'Je voudrais qu'approchant'), has a dream cast: Raymond Amade at his most limpid as the tenor hero, Michel Dens as his sidekick (equipped with all his extra material), Lina Dachary as the somewhat underparted heroine, Liliane Berton as her more prominent soubrette sister and Duvaleix as the comical Abbé. All are in superb form and the first-act trio, the Monk's Duo, the Pensionnaires' Chorus and the third-act Ladder Quintet are quite beautifully sung (and balanced) examples of ensemble performance to set alongside a bouquet of charming solos ranging from Duvaleix's irresistibly bouncing introduction of 'L'Abbé Bridaine' to the soulful tones of Marie's romance and the piquant soubrette rondo. Dens and Nadine Renaux sing the more extraneous music splendidly, making up a thoroughly enjoyable disc.

The Philips recording, which does include the missing quartet at the expense of some of the choral music, doesn't reach the same heights either in its recording or in its performance. Rosine Bredy (Louise) and Michel Hamel (Gontran) catch the *opérette* spirit of the piece better than Mlles Cumia (Marie) and Doria (Simonne) and Lucien Huberty is a suitably relaxed Brissac, but the character of the Pathé recording is missing.

The Return of Hervé

Mam'zelle Nitouche

One cannot leave the early years of the French musical without mentioning the remarkable return of old Hervé who, fourteen years after *Chilpéric* and *Le Petit Faust*, came up with the adorable score for the comedy musical *Mam'zelle Nitouche*. Like *La Vie parisienne*, *Mam'zelle Nitouche* is a triumphant combination of play and music which, by virtue of its outstanding comic merits, still finds its way regularly to the stage and has also made several appearances on the screen. Being, as it is, more in a line of descent from the *vaudeville* than the *opéra-comique*, this show's score consists almost entirely of light comedy numbers, and by far the largest part of these are for the title character. The tenor hero gets a couple of brief moments but nary a chance to wax too lyrical, and the principal comedian (who is, in this style of work, the leading man) sings but little. Vocally and, thus, for recording purposes, it is Nitouche's show.

The two recordings that exist both enshrine well-known performances. The figures speak for themselves. Pathé chose to feature Germaine Roger – on the stage in as far back as the late 1920s and a Nitouche in 1945 (and 1960!) – in the rôle of the romp-of-the-convent schoolgirl on its recording from the 1950s, while Decca starred the famous comedian Fernandel, who had appeared as the double-living music master Célestin in the 1953 film, on its 1968 set when he had passed fifty.

Given these facts, the performance of Mme Roger, floating up to the highest notes and throwing herself energetically into the schoolgirl foolery of the rôle, is quite remarkable, but she cannot really capture the girlish gaiety and youthful tone of the character and, although the feat has to be admired, the result is in the end unsatisfactory. Duvaleix makes as much as he can of the little music alloted to the comedian, but, for some reason, Claude Devos – he of the ultimate romantic tenor voice – is cast in what should be the very low comedy rôle of Loriot and is singularly unfunny in that character's one song. For once, Pathé got its casting wrong.

The Decca set is much better. Fernandel, who had practically no singing voice by this time, is pretty embarrassing in his few musical pieces, but you take the comedy and remember that you are listening to a legend. Eliane Thibault is a hundred times happier here than as Lecocq's Little Duchess and gives a really snappy and sparkly version of the title rôle, while Aimé Doniat is as fine as ever as her love interest, and Christian Asse is a Loriot who makes perfect crock-voiced fun of his foolish number. Add to all this a much bouncier, happy-go-lucky orchestral sound from André Grassi and his orchestra than is evident from Marcel Cariven's Pathé team, and you have a very fair representation of Hervé's comedy with songs.

Emmanuel Chabrier

L'Etoile

One final work of this period has also won its way on to record. Chabrier's 1877 piece L'Etoile, a soi-disant opéra-bouffe, was taken into the repertoire of the choosy (dare one say snooty) Opéra-Comique at a time when little of Offenbach, and none of most other light theatrical composers' works, was considered sufficiently legitimate. It remained there through infrequent performances, failed in bad adaptations overseas, and has become one of those works which certain scholars and cognoscenti have persisted in claiming as a masterpiece. It was broadcast, played in the provinces and recorded both on PLM with Liliane Berton, Jane Berbié and Jean-Christophe Benoît and by MRF Records in 1981 on a three-disc set featuring Isabelle Garcisanz, Anne-Marie Blanzat and Michel Sénéchal. Both of these sets disappeared pretty quickly and completely, but then a 1984 revival, originating at the Opéra de Lyon, reached Paris, allowing modern theatre-goers there to judge the piece for themselves, and

EMI's well-circulated recording of that production allows us to make up our own minds.

There is no doubt that the composer of *L'Etoile* was a very fine musician. The score which is attached to Vanloo and Leterrier's cheerfully nonsensical libretto is a classy affair, elegant and musically inventive, using the scope of voices and instruments and avoiding the obvious in its turn of phrase and its orchestration. Even when at its most operatic in construction it always maintains the flavour of the light musical theatre, whether with charm, as in the Kissing Quartet ('Quand on veut ranimer sa belle'), or with a certain humour, as in the drunken duo 'Chartreuse verte'. It is easy to see why the music of *L'Etoile* should attract the scholarly. It is also easy to see why it has less general appeal. In spite of its qualities it lacks the more common catchiness of an Offenbach or a Planquette.

EMI's recording does the piece full justice musically. The five lead rôles are all finely and freshly sung, with the sopranos Colette Alliot-Lugaz (Lazuli), Ghyslaine Raphanel (Laoula) and Magali Damonte (Aloès) each distinctive enough in tone to be comfortably distinguished, Georges Gautier (Ouf) producing a beautiful clear tenor sound but rather little comedy in what is theoretically the principal comic rôle, and Gabriel Bacquier (Siroco), now labelled a bass, adept in both vocal and humorous areas.

The Lyon orchestra under John Eliot Gardiner is equally felicitous in a production which took some liberties with libretto, but which maintained in full the score. The latter is, on the whole, the better served of the two elements. The chopped down version of the script made for the recording is patchy and occasionally incoherent, but the artists fling themselves into it with vigour and the general direction of things is maintained. The set is accompanied by a booklet containing the text of what appears on the discs, some attractive production photos and, as might have been expected, a rather hefty set of notes (by Roger Delage) which stress the admiration paid to Chabrier's work by the likes of Duparc and Reynaldo Hahn and drop the name of Wagner rather a lot.

The MRF set, which features the very massed forces of the New Philharmonia Orchestra and French Radio Chorus under Jacques Mercier, is taken from a 1981 radio broadcast (with live audience) under the auspices of the Service Lyrique de Radio-France, and it is a rather different, and perhaps more satisfactory, version textually. It is, in fact, a more than acceptable recording all round, both dramatically and musically, with top-notch performances in the two lead rôles by Michel Sénéchal as a fine, comical King Ouf, displaying his strong, unpretentious tenor voice to fine effect, and Isabelle Garcisanz a very convincingly boyish Lazuli, with a strong mezzo-soprano which is most attractive when least covered.

Anne-Marie Blanzat (Laoula) suffers a bit from the over-operatics, so that pieces like the Tickling Trio, which pairs her with two other heavyish voices, become a little more turgid than twinkling, but that is the way the piece is done – this is a big *Etoile*. Still, the show has plenty of largely played comedy scenes and it can take equally large musical moments. In many ways, I prefer this version to the Lyon one, particularly as its third record devotes its spare side to a selection from the score of Chabrier's one-act *opérette Fisch-ton-kan*, otherwise unrecorded. However, since it is so difficult to find, and the EMI, alterations and all, is a perfectly good and enjoyable rendering of the score, it seems simpler to stick with that one.

André Messager

The French musical theatre had passed its prime period by the early part of the twentieth century and its colours were kept at the front largely by one man, André Messager. Messager's range of theatre work covered a wide field from opera and ballet and to the light musical theatre, where he was responsible for several pieces that hold their own with the work of the nineteenth-century masters.

Pathé has done Messager proud, issuing (or rather, assembling and reissuing) in 1980 a box set of their full-record selections from five of his best works. Two of these, *La Basoche* and *Fortunio*, linger on the borders of the land of light opera, but the other three, *Véronique, Les P'tites Michu* and *Monsieur Beaucaire*, are the three *chefs d'oeuvre* of the period in the *opérette* genre.

Véronique

Véronique has always been the most generally popular of Messager's works, successful both in France and overseas in its original productions and a constant candidate for revival in its home country. Its famous swing song and the Duo de l'âne, better known to the English-language duettists of my youth as 'Trot Here, Trot There', are *opérette* standards. *Véronique* has been the subject of two complete recordings, the first from 1955 in the Decca series with Géori Boué in the title rôle and the second, featuring Mady Mesplé and Michel Dens, on a 1969 EMI pairing.

The Decca set is not very satisfactory. Virtually all the music is there, and the slimming of the book has been neatly done, but the performance is a dreary one. Pierre Devaux and his orchestra and chorus never lift the piece off the ground, and they are not helped by featured artists who range from the just-all-right to the simply unattractive. Mlle Boué ('Véronique') and Geneviève Moïzan (Agathe) in the two largest female rôles give attacking performances which sometimes verge on the shrill, and Mary Marquet is a droll, chesty Ermerance with a limited range, but they are preferable to the men. These include an uncomfortable Florestan (Roger Bourdin), a clumsy Loustot (Max de Rieux), and a twee Coquenard (Marcel Carpentier) who, like several of the minor players, indulges in an unnecessarily silly voice. On the whole, the big numbers come off fairly well, but the whole thing lacks any kind of sparkle and is simply not as enjoyable as this piece ought to be.

EMI's set, an equally deftly filleted version, has rather more gaiety to it. The piece bounces along fairly well and the players of the Concerts Lamoureux under Jean-Claude Hartemann only rarely confuse gusto and loudness. The important members of the cast, too, are happier in their rôles here, with Mady Mesplé, a really adorable 'Véronique', sweet and flighty and utterly sure of her silvery voice, giving one of her best recorded performances, and Michel Dens infallibly smooth and solid, if a little stolid, as that gay young blade Florestan. Their Donkey Duet is a nicely intimate little affair, the Swing Song barely less so and their ending happy. The supporting rôles are all adequately if not excitingly taken.

There seem to be some odd sound levels and unecessarily effortful attempts at stereo effects (or is this maybe only on the World Record Club transfer?) on what is not a top-class *Véronique*, but rather one whose leading performance gives it a clear edge over its only competitor.

Turning to the selection discs, there is immediately better to be found. Pathé's 1953 recording builds itself securely around the music of the two leading characters, allowing space for Ermerance's Romance and a couple of Agathe's little pieces, but omitting Loustot's song and the two quartets and snipping out just Florestan's letter ('Adieu, je pars') from the second-act finale. A good two-thirds of the score is here however, and it is given a beautifully light-handed treatment by conductor Jules Gressier and a free-voiced, clearly articulated cast headed by Martha Angelici as a pretty Hélène/Véronique.

Both the Decca and EMI sets follow the original casting of Florestan (Jean Périer) as a *baryton-ténorisant*, and this recording chooses Camille Maurane, at the very lowest surely a *ténor-barytonisant* (though he gets billed as a baritone), whose flowing singing is more enjoyable than the necessarily effortful high phrases of even the best of the heavier baritones. He and Mlle Angelici make a particularly happy job of the final 'A Véronique je dirai' and of the tripping Duo de l'âne, except that the lady indulges in a laugh which sounds more like the donkey than a teenage girl. It's the Tebaldi syndrome again. Why can't sopranos laugh naturally on recordings instead of stage-projecting such almighty chuckles down the microphone? Freda Betti is a splendidly robust Ermerance and Nadine Renaux a lovely, bright Agathe, but such top artists as Claude Devos (Loustot), Aimé Doniat (Séraphin) and Michel Roux (Coquenard) have unfortunately very little to do.

There is also a selection record of *Véronique* on CBS with Merkès and Merval for those who admire this pair.

Les P'tites Michu

Whilst enjoying *Véronique*, I have always had a preference for *Les P'tites Michu*, and this may not be unconnected with the fact that my first experience of this delightful piece was through the 1954 Pathé recording on which Liliane Berton and Nadine Renaux, repeating their pairing of the lovely *Le Petit Duc* recording, appear as the two little mixed-up (in the physical sense) Michu sisters. This disc is a treasure. Listening to these two glorious voices rollicking sweetly through the harmonies of their introductory duet 'Blanche-Marie et Marie-Blanche' in blatant mono makes you wonder why stereo and digital and compact had to be invented. It also makes you wonder why *Les P'tites Michu* has been so largely overlooked, as this outstanding moment is by no means the only gem in the score and on the recording. There are two delightful trios for the sisters and the General's son (Camille Maurane) whom one of them – but we don't know which – is destined to marry, the second of which ('C'est la fille du Général') is surrounded by two versions of the girls' pretty harmonized 'Prière à St Nicolas', the first praying that each isn't the one chosen and the second – after they've seen him – praying that she is! Blanche-Marie's wistful waltz 'Ah! Soeurette', Marie-Blanche's saucy Ronde des Halles, the jolly entrance song of Mme Michu (Gisèle Desmoutiers) and the tenor solos of the bemused Aristide (Claude Devos), unable to decide which of the girls he wants to wed and thoroughly relieved at having his choice made for him, are all delightful moments. Messager's score is unfailingly charming and musical, bubbling with a gentle tunefulness of the most refined kind, sweetly seductive, never vulgar, fitting its story and its characters beautifully, and this recording serves it quite perfectly.

I suppose I've already said everything I need to about Mlles Berton and Renaux, but it does need to be said that here, in rôles very different to those they played in *Le Petit Duc*, they succeed utterly both in character and in voice, both individually and, particularly, as a pair. Their sympathetic, light yet heartfelt performance of the beautiful 'Blanche-Marie et Marie-Blanche' is a track reserved for my compilation disc of all-time joys. Maurane gives a warm tenor performance of seamless effortlessness as the sexy soldier, contrasting with the lighter and even more seamless tones of Devos as the simple shopboy, and there are fine comic performances from Mlle Desmoutiers, Duvaleix (Michu) and Lucien Lovano (General), whilst Jules Gressier at the head of the orchestra and chorus shows again that he has a special sympathy with Messager's music.

Monsieur Beaucaire

Monsieur Beaucaire is, strictly speaking, not a French show, nor a show which fits within the parameters of this chapter. It was written for the British stage, to a libretto by Frederick Lonsdale and lyrics by the doyen of British lyricists Adrian Ross, and it was produced, with the British soprano Maggie Teyte and the American baritone Marion Green in its leading rôles, at London's Princes Theatre as late as 1919. However, Messager belongs more to this period and to France than to post-war Britain, and I use Pathé's boxing of this disc with four of his earlier works in the set already referred to as an excuse to include it here.

It is a fine score, providing large rôles for its star soprano and baritone and a few sparkling songs for its soubrette couple, with the waltz song 'Philomel' proving perhaps the bon-bon of the show. The original cast recordings by Teyte and Green have been gathered on LP by Opal/Pearl and, whilst applauding the initiative of this enterprise, one cannot truly enjoy the result. It is kindest to say, perhaps, that Teyte suffered less from 1919 recording techniques than did Green, who must have sung better than this sounds to have had any career at all, much less play opposite the not undemanding Miss Teyte.

Pathé come to the rescue with a 1952 French-language version headed by Martha Angelici and Michel Dens. Dens, with his unpretentiously heroic baritone, is perfectly cast in the title rôle of this 'romantic opera'. He makes the French versions of 'Red Rose' and 'Under the Moon' sound magnificent, and quite steals the show. Mlle Angelici's warm, attractive soprano makes much of the music written for Maggie Teyte, from the light operatic solos and duets with their adept period flavour to the more frankly popular 'Philomel' ('Rossignol' in the French), which she negotiates with particular flair, and she proves a thoroughly worthy partner. Most of the comedy of the piece is the preserve of the non-singing characters, but there are two splendid light duets for the soubrette pair (Liliane Berton and René Lenoty), who also are given the task of speaking one of Pierre Hiégel's sillier linking narratives. A little more of the music and a little less of the chat would have been preferable, but this is still an appreciable record of a show which compares very favourably with such nearly contemporary costume pieces as *The Vagabond King* but which has regrettably vanished from the English-language stage.

Louis Ganne

The only other French composer of this period to have won the graces of the recording companies is Louis Ganne, whose *Les Saltimbanques* and *Hans le joueur de flûte* are both available, the former on several labels, and the latter on Pathé alone.

Les Saltimbanques

Les Saltimbanques, a great success on its production in 1899, has survived revival after revival and a clutch of recordings with a vigour which I can only think is due to its colourful circus-based story and scenic possibilities. It surely cannot be because of its book which, in contrast to the majority of French libretti of the times, is a garbled mass of clichés, nor to its pretty but generally unremarkable score. Whatever the reason, this piece has been accorded much more attention than many other and, I think, more worthy pieces, as both Decca and EMI have recorded it in full, while Pathé and Odéon have provided selections discs.

The two complete versions have, of course, to cope with the libretto, and it must be said that adaptation for record purposes doesn't improve it any except in reducing its length. Musically, there is not very much to choose between them. Both are well played and well sung, with Ganne's march music (circus as well as military) showing up well alongside the nicely tailored sentimental music and the occasional bit of humour. The Decca set has, perhaps, the edge insofar as the male performers are concerned: Robert Massard's rendition of the march song 'Va, gentil soldat' is really splendid (which is not to say that Claude Calès on the EMI disc isn't also extremely good), Michel Roux is a warm-voiced Grand

Pingouin, and Raymond Amade, who plays the Jack-Pointy Paillasse on both sets, is in fresher form on the earlier Decca recording.

In its turn, the EMI set comes out a little ahead on the feminine side, with Mady Mesplé's sweet and simple Suzon proving more appealing than the fuller-voiced version by Janine Micheau, and Eliane Lublin more lively in the soubrette role than the slightly oversung interpretation of Geneviève Moïzan. If you like full-sized singing in your operetta, then go for the Decca set, but if, like me, you like your artists to sound something like the characters they are playing, it is less easy to choose.

Probably the easiest thing to do is skip both and go for one of the single-disc versions, which start off with the advantage of little or no text. The Odeon recording actually has more than a little, for it is a novelty disc – a potted show with fragments of text and fragments of songs, which certainly dates from well before the LP age as it features Robert Jysor (André) and Henri Laverne (Paillasse), both of whom appeared in the show at the Gaîté-Lyrique in the very early 1920s.

Pathé's 1953 recording has, like so many of its series, the biggest advantage of all – some superbly suitable singers. The one-and-only Liliane Berton is Suzon and Devos is Paillasse, deprived of his solo 'La Nature a pour ses élus', Freda Betti an energetic, fruity Marion, and Guy Godin a fine tenor André who sails through his 'Va, gentil soldat' with more shine but less thunder than the baritones. With Jules Gressier's orchestra attacking the rhythms of Ganne's music energetically, this tip-top team perform the selection very happily and, unless you really yearn for *Les Saltimbanques* in its entirety, this recording, including most of the show's best bits, is far and away the happiest available.

Hans le joueur de flûte

I rate *Hans le joueur de flûte* a far better work than *Les Saltimbanques*. A version of the Pied Piper story with a trenchant message demanding subsidy for the arts (which ought to make it a natural for a production at London's Royal Shakespeare Company or English National Opera), it has both a charming libretto and a delightful score which ranges from ballad to march music and from burlesque humour to memorable melody. No sooner have proceedings begun than there is a delightfully comic chorus of the night watch, a group of officials about as inefficient as Offenbach's carabiniers, whilst the first act finishes on a desperate tutti as the whole town mourns, to a sweeping melody worthy of a great love duet, the sabotage of their cat population in the face of a plague of mice ('Adieu, petits minets, petits minous'). The piper himself leads the praise of his flute in one of the most splendid marches in all musical theatre ('C'est la flûte qui mena le monde'), the heroine sweetly regrets to a sparkling tune that 'mon petit père est un commerçant' ('poor, dear daddy's in trade'), and the tenor poet apostrophizes the arts-conscious past with a Tristanic passion

('Vous n'êtes plus, pauvres poupées') as tune follows tune and one satiric twist follows another.

Compared with its gaudier fellow, *Hans le joueur de flûte* has had a less expansive career (except in Hungary!), but some wise person at Pathé selected it for their series and, even more wisely, cast Michel Dens as Hans the piper, Liliane Berton as the heroine Lisbeth and André Mallabrera as the poet Yoris. They, and the splendid orchestra and chorus under Jean-Pierre Marty, give the piece a fine performance, bringing out all the enjoyments of a show which deserves a regular hearing. As you may have guessed from my little rash of adjectives, this is one which I myself play much more often than some of its better-known contemporaries.

My Ten Essential Records

ORPHEUS IN THE UNDERWORLD: selection in English, with June Bronhill and Jon Weaving (HMV CSD 1316/ CLP 1885); reissued (EMI CFP 4539)

GENEVIEVE DE BRABANT: complete, with Monique Stiot, Annick Simon, Bernard Plantey and René Terrasson (2 records, Bourg BG2012–3); CD (Bourg BGC 10–11)

LA BELLE HELENE: selection, with Deva Dassy and Claude Devos (EMI-Pathé 057.10852); also included in 'Offenbach: 6 Opérettes' (EMI boxed set)

LE PETIT FAUST: complete, with Aimé Doniat and Lina Dachary (2 records, Rare Recorded Editions 176–7); or complete, with Michel Hamel and Lina Dachary (2 records, Clio 004–005)

LA FILLE DE MADAME ANGOT: selection, with Lina Dachary and Solange Michel (EMI-Pathé 057.12085)

LES CLOCHES DE CORNEVILLE: selection, with Robert Massard, Lina Dachary and Suzy Deilhes (Véga 30LT13043)

LE PETIT DUC: selection, with Liliane Berton and Nadine Renaux (EMI-Pathé 057.12107)

LA FILLE DU TAMBOUR-MAJOR: selection, with Michel Dens and Liliane Chatel (EMI-Pathé 057.12192)

LES MOUSQUETAIRES AU COUVENT: selection, with Michel Dens and Duvaleix (EMI-Pathé 057.10848 or 50)

LES P'TITES MICHU: selection, with Liliane Berton and Nadine Renaux (Pathé DTX 149); also included in 'André Messager: 5 Opérettes' (EMI boxed set)

Other Recommended Records:

L'Ile de Tulipatan: with Yerry Mertz and Marcelle Rieu (TLP 95001); also issued on CD

Ba-ta-Clan: with Huguette Boulangeot and Rémy Corazza, b/w Les Bavards, with Lina Dachary and Aimé Doniat (2 records, Erato DUE 20240)

Tromb-al-ca-zar: with Yerry Mertz, Albert Voli and Claudine Granger (TLP 95003); CD (Adès C35003)

Mesdames de la Halle/Pomme d'api/Monsieur Choufleuri ... : with Mady Mesplé, Michel Hamel and Michel Trempont (2 records, EMI 1C 157 SLS); CD (EMI 7493612)

Lischen et Fritzchen/La Chanson de Fortunio: (Bourg 2007); CD with *Le Leçon de chant electromagnétique* (Bourg BCG 14)

Orphée aux enfers: complete, with Claudine Collart and André Dran (2 records, Musidisc Festival 261)

Le Pont des soupirs: complete, with Claudine Collart, Michel Hamel and Aimé Doniat (2 records, Bourg 2008–9); also issued on CD

La Belle Hélène: complete, with Linda Felder and André Dran (2 records, Musidisc Festival 253/Nixa PLP 206–1 and 2)

Barbe-Bleue: complete, with Henri Legay, René Lenoty and Lina Dachary (2 records, Bourg BG2005–6); CD (Bourg BCG 2–3)

La Vie parisienne: selection, with Nadine Renaux, Willy Clément, Michel Hamel and Liliane Berton (Pathé 057.10851); also included in 'Offenbach: 6 Opérettes' (EMI boxed set)

La Grande-Duchesse de Gérolstein: complete, with Suzanne Lafaye, Jean Aubert and Henri Bédex (2 records, Decca SKL 30.176–7)

La Périchole: complete, with Suzanne Lafaye and Raymond Amade (2 records, EMI-Pathé CO53–10669–70); CD (EMI CDM 7698442)

Les Brigands: complete, in German (*Die Banditen*) (2 records, RCA RL 30474)

La Créole: complete, with Huguette Boulangeot (2 records, Bourg 2014–5); CD (Bourg BGC 12–13)

La Fille de Madame Angot: complete, with Colette Riedinger and Suzanne Lafaye (Decca 40.234–5)

Les Cloches de Corneville: complete, with Colette Riedinger and Huguette Boulangeot (Decca 115.182–3)

L'Etoile: complete, with Colette Alliot-Lugaz and René Hérent (2 records, EMI 270086–7); CD (EMI CDS 7 47889 8)

Madame Favart: complete, with Suzanne Lafaye and Lina Dachary (2 records, Discoreale 10010–11)

La Mascotte: selection, with Nadine Renaux (EMI-Pathé 057.10843); or complete, with Robert Massard and Geneviève Moïzan (Decca SSL 40.223–4)

Mam'zelle Nitouche: complete, with Fernandel and Eliane Thibault (2 records, Decca 115.063–4)

Véronique: selection, with Martha Angelici and Camille Maurane (EMI-Pathé 057.10841); also included in 'André Messager: 5 Opérettes' (EMI boxed set)

Les Saltimbanques: selection, with Liliane Berton and Claude Devos (EMI-Pathé 057.10842)

Hans le joueur de flûte: selection, with Liliane Berton and Michel Dens (EMI-Pathé 057.12194)

Monsieur Beaucaire: selection, with Michel Dens and Martha Angelici (EMI-Pathé 057.12086); also included in 'André Messager: 5 Opérettes' (EMI boxed set)

Rip!: selection, with Michel Dens (EMI-Pathé 2C 057.12899)

CHAPTER 2

Victorian and Edwardian Musical Comedy in Britain

Whilst *opéra-bouffe* was in its first fine flourishing in France, the British musical theatre began putting out the initial shoots of its own development in the fields of both musical burlesque and comic opera. Led by composers such as Arthur Sullivan, Edward Solomon, Frederic Clay, Meyer Lutz and Edward Jakobowski, and with significant contributions from a whole range of French musicians including Offenbach, Emil Jonas, Hervé, Gaston Serpette and Planquette, the writers and producers of London's theatres began to set in motion the first great period of Britain's light musical theatre.

Although they achieved considerable successes in their own time, few works from this period – beginning with Frank Musgrave's *Windsor Castle* and Sullivan's *Cox and Box* in the 1860s, through the quarter of a century up to the development of the so-called musical comedy – survived in production beyond the nineteenth century. The odd song from pieces like the triumphant *Erminie*, the most successful legitimate musical of *fin de siècle* America, or the famous Gaiety burlesques worked its way into the standard repertoire and even, in some cases, onto early recordings, but only one group of shows won a significant and lasting future, and that was the Gilbert and Sullivan canon, the Savoy operas.

Gilbert and Sullivan

These shows, beginning with the earliest Sullivan one-acter, *Cox and Box*, passing through the twelve full-length works of the famous partnership, and ending thirty-five years later with the last works of Sullivan, *The Rose of Persia* and *The Emerald Isle*, again written without Gilbert, is comprehensively represented on record. From the days of the 78 rpm recording onwards, the D'Oyly Carte Opera Company, which, until the expiry of the copyright on Gilbert and Sullivan's work held a firm dominion over the Savoy works, appeared regularly on recordings. Made first with a mixture of company members and guests and later wholly by the company, the majority of recordings which have been available over the years have had the seal of the official purveyors of Gilbert and Sullivan upon them.

The earliest of these available to modern listeners on LP are the transfers of the set of recordings made from 1928 onwards under the musical direction of Malcolm

Sargent and featuring such well-known D'Oyly Carte company members as Henry Lytton, Bertha Lewis, Winifred Lawson, George Baker and Derek Oldham. Three of these reconstituted shows were released in Britain on HMV, but the full series was taken up by the American Arabesque label and issued in finely decorated boxed sets with accompanying booklets containing both lyrics and well-culled notes. Some of them were then put out in Britain by World Records, although from all evidence not in great numbers. They have, however, now been issued by Arabesque on CD.

The first made-for-LP recordings began almost as soon as the long-playing record made its first appearance in Britain. From 1949, under the supervision of Bridget D'Oyly Carte, the grand-daughter of Gilbert and Sullivan's producer, the company systematically recorded the musical sections of *Trial by Jury* and the ten principal operas (*The Grand Duke* and *Utopia Limited* being ignored), so that, by 1955, the set was complete. A number of the principals of the company remained the same over the largest part of this period, and the sopranos Muriel Harding and Margaret Mitchell, contraltos Ella Halman and later Ann Drummond-Grant, tenor Leonard Osborn, a group of more or less durable baritones and comedian Martyn Green (succeeded for the last two operas by Peter Pratt) take the featured roles in all or most of these recordings.

In 1955, the reissues of the company's old 78 rpm *Trial by Jury* from 1928, the 1930 *HMS Pinafore* and the 1936 *Mikado*, referred to above, were released before, in 1958, the whole process was started for a second time. In the following decade the same eleven works plus *Cox and Box* were again recorded and, although the personnel were not as stable as in the earlier set, performers such as tenor Thomas Round, comedian John Reed, contralto Gillian Knight and baritone Donald Adams are regulars. Thereafter, a number of the staple shows were recorded yet again, some with dialogue for the first time, and the D'Oyly Carte Company also took the occasion to put on record some of the less popular and infrequently recorded parts of the Gilbert and/or Sullivan repertoire.

Parallel to these three sets of Decca D'Oyly Carte releases, a series of recordings was made by HMV, conducted once again by the now Sir Malcolm Sargent, with the Pro Arte Orchestra, the Glyndebourne Festival Opera Chorus and a team of singers which featured Richard Lewis, Elsie Morison, Monica Sinclair, John Cameron, Owen Brannigan, Geraint Evans and the now veteran vocalist George Baker (who had performed on the earliest 78 rpm recordings made under Rupert D'Oyly Carte's supervision immediately after the Great War). This series included *Trial by Jury* but, curiously, omitted *The Sorcerer* as well as *Princess Ida* and the two late shows.

Alongside these substantial sets, which were, and which have largely remained, the basic recordings of the Gilbert and Sullivan repertoire on LP, various other records appeared. These included a whole set on BASF, reissued subsequently on Pye, a goodly number of isolated selection recordings, largely on cheaper labels, and several cast recordings of non-D'Oyly Carte productions, ranging from the

Sadler's Wells Opera productions of the 1960s to English National Opera and New Sadler's Wells versions of the 1980s.

Most Gilbert and Sullivan devotees have a firmly ingrained preference for one or other of the principal groups of recordings – the transferred discs of the 1930s, the first D'Oyly Carte group of LPs, the second D'Oyly Carte group, the with-dialogue recordings, or the later Malcolm Sargent series. Having grown up with the sounds of Ella Halman and Muriel Harding ringing in my ears, I remember having always been very fond of the performances on the oft-reissued discs of the early 1950s. Over the years, I never saw any need to replace them in my own collection with their D'Oyly Carte successors and, without quite knowing why – maybe simply because they were not 'real' D'Oyly Carte recordings – I quite frankly scorned the HMV Sargent discs.

For the purposes of this work, however, it was time for me to listen again to each of these groups, as well as to their less widely diffused competitors, musical by musical. The result was not at all what I had expected. Not only did my old favourites often fail to live up to fond memories, but no one group proved to be consistently the best through the whole range of the Gilbert and Sullivan canon. Although the repertoire system existed solidly in the D'Oyly Carte company during the recording years, as it had done more or less since its inception, performers given a traditional 'line' of rôles often proved much happier in some of their parts than others, and the same singers and musicians who give a fine performance of one musical sometimes prove unsatisfying in another.

Trial by Jury

Trial by Jury, a satirical little sung-through piece telling the tongue-in-cheek tale of a breach-of-promise suit brought by the sweetly innocent but very money-wise Angelina against the man who proposed to her but later changed his mind, is a musical and comical delight. Given its nature as a half-hour or so of comic cantata, it has always been recorded whole, but curiously it ranges on disc from one lengthy side of an LP to two skimpy sides or, in one case, one and-a-half sides, topped up with other Gilbert and Sullivan material. The five recorded versions I have gathered together (there is a sixth which I don't have) give an interesting look at the limited progression of playing style in the Savoy operas through half a century as although, beginning with a transfer of the 1928 recording, they have been made at regular intervals in time up to 1975, all largely retain the same performance conventions.

Each of the five recordings, sadly, also concentrates very much more on the cantata than the comic and none enters truly into the happy burlesque spirit of the work, but this rather earnest fashion of interpretation was the manner which the venerable D'Oyly Carte company adopted not only with this piece but with its more substantial fellows as they became encrusted with traditional emphases and mannerisms over the years. All the recordings have their strong points, but this sometimes desperate lack of humour means that, in spite of some enjoyable performances, none is entirely ideal. We will have to wait a bit longer for a *Trial by Jury* which really has fun with the show and, in the meantime, look for one with good singing and only a twinkle of burlesque.

The LP transfer of the 1928 discs has very square orchestral playing and the inevitable taken-from-78 rpm tone to it, a tone which affects particularly the soprano sound of the charming Winifred Lawson as the Plaintiff. There is so little attempt at humour that the plummy Derek Oldham as the Defendant sounds more like a genuinely puffed-up Victorian parlour singer than a burlesque of the same type, whilst Leo Sheffield, who was a legitimate baritone before becoming a comic, shows the remnants of his voice handily, though allowing himself only the occasional extravagance in the chief comic rôle of the Judge. The crisp, bright female chorus and George Baker's declamatory Usher come across the best in what is certainly an unobjectionable recording, but not one to enthuse over.

The 1949 version, spread over two sides of its disc, is more than a little less po-faced and a lot better in sound, and, in place of the tartly smart parody the piece requires, we get at least a very agreeably sung and merrily played *Trial by Jury*. Richard Watson is the Judge, combining a richly unfussy bass voice with an appealingly roguish delivery in good comic opera style, warming to his task splendidly as the piece progresses and seemingly spurred at half-way by the appearance and song of Leslie Rands, in the rôle of the Plaintiff's Counsel, who gets nearest of all to combining first-rate singing with a nicely clipped and clear sense of comic style. Plaintiff (Muriel Harding) and Defendant (Leonard Osborn) both have such ideal voices for their material, light and clear and effortlessly enunciated, that it is a real shame that she attempts no characterization of the slyly coquettish abandoned bride at all, and he shies away from any passion or extravagance in his performance. Chorus and orchestra are both fine, and the only real let-down is an uncomfortably irregular performance from Radley Flynn as the Usher.

The Sargent version of 1958 is another two-side affair. Its chief advantages come in a strong, clear chorus and an attractive orchestral sound, a splendid performance as the Counsel for the Prosecution from John Cameron, a pleasant Defendant (Richard Lewis) and some superior sleeve notes by Arthur Jacobs. Amongst its disadvantages is George Baker's Judge – thirty years on he does not have the voice to sing the rôle through the way he tries, and, even if his style of playing is in word-of-mouth descent from Gilbert's direction, his comedy isn't very funny. There is also an overly operatic and dullish Plaintiff (Elsie Morison) and a rather approximate Usher (Owen Brannigan), who does, however, at least attempt some comedy on a recording where, once again, the fun is generally lacking.

By the time of the 1964 D'Oyly Carte recording, the orchestra and chorus seem to have grown to Bayreuthian proportions. This trial seems to have more members on its jury than is permitted even in comic opera, and the massed orchestra of the Royal Opera House provides an accompaniment which often seems too strong-armed for such a light piece. This mass of sound is probably partly to blame for the fact that most of the chorus lyrics are indecipherable. The words, however, are given their due thoroughly in Thomas Round's splendid performance of the Defendant and by John Reed's crisply delivered light baritone Judge, which would have been even more enjoyable had he not bowed himself to performing the part with its received mannerisms. The rest of the cast sing perfectly well, but Ann Hood's mezzo-soprano sound is unsuited to the very soubrette rôle of the Plaintiff and the Usher (Donald Adams) often sounds as if he is on the other side of the room swallowing oysters. One way and another, this is a *Trial by Jury* musically rather overdone.

The 1975 D'Oyly Carte version is the one which has so far eluded me, but another 1970s performance by a company including several former D'Oyly Carte members, Round and Adams amongst them, is issued on PRT. It is, curiously, the only one to pair *Trial by Jury* with the other most famous Sullivan one-acter, *Cox and Box*, but it is a very indifferent recording, with surprisingly mediocre singing and very little presence – perhaps only to be expected of a disc whose sleeve names the librettist as 'Winston Schwenck Gilbert'.

Cox and Box and *The Zoo*

If the *Trial by Jury* discs fail to throw up a really exceptional *opéra-bouffe* recording, Sullivan has come out rather better with two of his other short-form works, *Cox and Box* (to a libretto by F. C. Burnand) and *The Zoo*, written with Charlie Stephenson, author of the century's biggest hit, *Dorothy*. These delightful one-acters are paired on a 1978 Decca set made by then current members of the D'Oyly Carte company, and the result is a recording that not only successfully captures the flavour of the very light-hearted Victorian genre of which these litle pieces are superior examples, but also one that features some fine singing and – less expectedly – acting.

Cox and Box, a charmingly funny musicalization of the famous farce about a doubly let apartment, is the better of the two, both as a piece and as a performance, a performance which follows the shortened version of the show made by the authors after the work's first season and thereafter generally played. It includes nine musical items, as well as some portions of the dialogue, in a happy adaptation that heightens the comedy and enhances the characters admirably, and allows the songs, set in context, to be far more intelligible and amusing than would otherwise have been the case.

It is a delight to find two performers like baritone Gareth Jones (Cox) and tenor Geoffrey Shovelton (Box) who are capable not only of turning out first-rate comedy performances in the dialogue, stylishly pitched at just the right level of tongue-in-cheek burlesque, but also of performing their songs and duets in a splendidly articulated manner without ever detracting from the clean and rich light operatic tone of their singing voices. There is barely a modified vowel or a gargled note on the whole recording.

It is a shame that these two performers could not have been included in the cast of the little burlesque *The Zoo* which, as a sung-through piece, is played *in toto* on the reverse. Shovelton, in fact, is given the job of narrating this foolishly funny tale of amorous shenanigans amongst the animal cages and, after a slightly sticky start, he helps keep the tone of the affair in a suitably silly key. He is less missed than he might have been as a performer, thanks to the casting of another excellent tenor, Meston Reid, as the lovesick apothecary whose attempts to kill himself by rope (in a burlesque of *La Périchole*) or by jumping into the bear-pit fortunately fail just long enough for him to be happily united with his Laetitia (Julia Goss). Jones is more missed, for the baritone rôle in this piece – a duke in mufti out in search of true love who ends up with the lady from the zoo's refreshment stall – gets a rather hit-and-miss performance from veteran Kenneth Sandford. This is a minor quibble, however, in what is a splendidly played (by the Royal Philharmonic under Royston Nash), happily sung version of a snippet of musical theatre. It makes one regret both the passing of the curtain-raiser and that a wider area of Gilbert and Sullivan works were not recorded with this group of perfomers.

An earlier D'Oyly Carte *Cox and Box* recording featuring Joseph Riordan, Alan Styler and Donald Adams was issued in 1961, making up the sixth side of the three-disc set of *The Gondoliers*, and it has been subsequently reissued. This is surprising as it is a comparatively run-of-the-mill version, stuffy and stagey, which does not come up to the later recording either in its presentation or in its performance. The same may be said for the PRT recording mentioned above. This is performed, as was the original, with only a piano for accompaniment, and it, too, features Adams as Bouncer. He is not at his best here, and neither are his partners, Thomas Round and Thomas Hemsley.

The Sorcerer

The Sorcerer, Gilbert and Sullivan's first full-length collaboration, tells the trippingly terrible tale of what happens when a love potion is administered to the inhabitants of a picture-book English village, in the delicately ridiculous comic opera style which the writers were to develop into the craze of a century. This show has been, most unfairly, given lesser coverage over the years, both on stage and on disc, than its fellows. The D'Oyly Carte company has seen to it that it has had two full-scale recordings but that is all. Perhaps, compared with the authors' later works, it is a little less joyfully eccentric, a little less colourful, a little more genteel in the manner of the Victorian drawing room operetta, but if its jokes – both musical and textual – are of a more subtly classic breed, they are nonetheless quite delightful and, properly played and pointed, equally as merry as their more extravagant successors.

Unfortunately, the two recordings don't seem to have discovered this. They are genteel all right, but the humour is often hard to find. The later set, made in 1966, takes half an hour before you realize that the singers aren't practising for a Handel oratorio with half a dozen deaths in it. There is nice rounded tone, careful counting of the beats, and not a hint of the comic element of this comic opera to be heard until contralto Christene Palmer (Sangazure) starts to edge a bit of 'oomph' into the burlesque duet she shares with a stodgy Donald Adams

(Marmaduke). It carries on in much the same way, with Miss Palmer and tenor David Palmer (Alexis) showing the most spirit, John Reed articulating his comedy patter song 'My Name Is John Wellington Wells' actively, and Valerie Masterson (Aline) showing off an energetic soprano in rather a vacuum.

The earlier set, made in 1953, takes much the same attitude. The piece is carefully and tastefully played and sung, but rare are the moments when the fun is allowed to intrude. Nevertheless, given that this is the way the company was determined to play *The Sorcerer*, there are some finely sung (if barely acted) performances and the ensembles and choruses in particular are well served. Peter Pratt makes a pleasingly common little fellow of the dubious John Wellington Wells, turning the tale of the unpredictable love potion into something rather like a shopkeeper's problem with faulty goods. The best comic moment of the set comes when he gets entangled in duet with the amorous Lady Sangazure, whom Anne Drummond-Grant plays with splendidly rich tones and more bite than anyone else around, she pursuing him boomingly and he resisting with frantic fibs about his marital status. Muriel Harding, producing that sweet-toned sound which characterizes all her performances, suits the rôle of the pale English Aline better than she does some of Gilbert's more energetic heroines; Yvonne Dean makes a lovely sound as the droopy, lovelorn ingénue Constance, and Jeffrey Skitch delivers Dr Daly's charming song 'I Was a Pale Young Curate Then' with a strong simplicity and some amusingly clerical vowels. The other rôles are adequately taken, and there would be really very little to complain about in this set were it not that genuine burlesque gaiety is unfortunately absent.

HMS Pinafore

HMS Pinafore, the first great international hit of the Gilbert and Sullivan partnership, and one of the comic masterpieces of the light musical theatre, has rarely been absent from the world's stages since its first performance well over a century ago. Its catchphrases ('Never? Well, hardly ever!') became part of the English language and its songs – most particularly the First Lord of the Admirality's description of how he 'polished up the handle of the big front door' – classics of their kind. *HMS Pinafore* has been regularly recorded, although comparatively little given its century of mega-popularity, and half a dozen complete versions and several less sizeable (and usually less worthwhile) selections have found their way on to the market.

The earliest, once again, is the transfer from 78 rpm discs of the 1930 version made by the D'Oyly Carte company and featuring several famous D'Oyly Carte names, including Henry Lytton as Sir Joseph Porter, the Admiral of the fleet who has never been to sea. It is, of course, interesting to hear such artists from an archive point of view, but although the transfer to LP is remarkably well done, inevitably the orchestral sound and soprano Elsie Griffin suffer more, and other artists less, from the change in sound values. Unless you are adept at switching your ears to ignore these conditions, the recording has to be to a certain, if small, degree unsatisfying. This is a shame, for tenor Charles Goulding (Ralph), George Baker (Corcoran), the crystal-clear Lytton and Bertha Lewis as a magnificently unwoofy, down-to-earth Buttercup give what were clearly top-notch performances.

The first made-for-LP version was the 1949 set featuring Martyn Green in the lead comedy rôle. On listening critically to this recording, although I realize it is not as perfect as I thought in my youth, I can see why I then deemed it so superior. On the debit side there is the usual D'Oyly Carte lack of humour on disc and there are one or two little vocal accidents, but on the credit side we find an all-round clear, crisp sound, a happy chorus and orchestra and, above all, a group of attractive, unpretentious made-for-comic-opera solo voices. The sweet soprano of Muriel Harding – delicious in her tightly laced dilemma in 'The Hours Creep on Apace' – the virile yet vulnerable tenor of Leonard Osborn, Darrell Fancourt's glutinous Dick Deadeye and a languorously lofty Sir Joseph Porter from Green all give Sullivan's music and, more often than not, Gilbert's words the type of treatment they were intended to have. Ella Halman, happier in the more aristocratic rôles of the G & S opus, is neverthless an effective contralto Buttercup with a rumbling admission of her 'remorse' at getting the plot going by mixing up the babies entrusted to her care, and Leslie Rands completes the principal team with a competent Corcoran. There are, as always, moments where one would like things to be a touch brighter – this is, and how many times will I longingly repeat it, comic opera – but this set is by no means alone in taking an 'English opera' approach to the work.

The HMV–Sargent set does the same with a vengeance. There is no doubt that this recording contains the most proficient singing and playing of the *Pinafore* score available. The show is given a very straight, clean performance, coolly controlled, with every word clearly enunciated and every note neatly sung and played. Richard Lewis (Ralph) displays a splendid English tenor, Monica Sinclair is a rich and rosy Buttercup, John Cameron a fine, straightforward Corcoran and Elsie Morison an accomplished Josephine, while George Baker gets in all the words of Sir Joseph's comic part, albeit with apparently little enthusiasm. But, given all the pretty singing, you long for a touch of temperament, of spirit, for a dash of the satire and parody inherent in the work. Alas, it emerges only in the tiniest flashes, and, in spite of such fine musical moments as the 'British Tar' madrigal with its first-class male voices and a lot of very agreeable solo and choral work, the set suffers, even more than the D'Oyly Carte version, from a lack of a sense of enjoyment.

There is more life to be found in the 1959 D'Oyly Carte recording, but again only in parts. There is more comic potential here, because with this set the company for the first time recorded one of the Gilbert and Sullivan pieces integrally – music and text – and Gilbert's arch and wordful witticisms add immeasurably to the fun of the affair. They would add more, however, if they had been given a more generally accomplished performance. There seems to have been oddly little attempt to impose a style here – not even the style which has become known to us as standard D'Oyly Carte, and which appears in its ossified glory on other discs. On the one hand, Jeffrey Skitch as Corcoran gives a really stylish actor's performance, pointing his lines delicately and cleverly and singing with the same elegant ease, John Reed (Porter) and Jean Hindmarsh (Josephine) work well in the same style, and Thomas Round is a refreshing, natural Ralph in song and speech. On the other, there are some heavy burlesque performances from some of the lesser players and there are one or two who don't seem to be able to cope with the dialogue too well at all. So, whereas this recording has a very solid heart, with four stars who perform the whole of their rôles extremely well, it is really too uneven as a whole to be thoroughly satisfying.

Pinafore was recorded again by the D'Oyly Carte company, in 1971, and maybe by that time a little more comic style had found its way into the show. I don't know, because it is a recording which has defied my many attempts to dig it up in any one of a hundred second-hand record shops.

With the general loosening-up in the approach to the Gilbert and Sullivan musicals in recent years, some lively, unclassical productions have been seen, one of which, the New Sadler's Wells Opera Company's production of 1987, has made its way onto the TER label. It is, unfortunately, a real disappointment. Nonsensically billed in large letters as 'the first complete recording of the authentic version' on the grounds that it has fiddled about with some extraneous fragments and, in the fashion of this 'scholarly' age, tacked them back in when authors and stage performance had decided (on the evidence, rightly) that they were better omitted, it also achieves the unlikely distinction of making this delicious show really dull. Lazy conducting, which threatens on occasion to drive the whole show to a halt, mediocre and even boring performances and an utter lack of feeling for the material make this set a dreary experience. Quite why TER chose to record this performance instead of the joyously comical and splendidly sung Irish production which appeared at the same time is a mystery to me. It is our loss. Hopefully the 1990s will bring us a bright, modern comic opera *Pinafore* on disc, and, until then, I will stick with my old love – the forty year-old D'Oyly Carte recording.

The Pirates of Penzance

My happy memories of Decca's 1950 *Pirates of Penzance* prove to be less reliable than I had hoped. A cast substantially similar to the one which recorded *HMS Pinafore* are simply less at home with the lusty melodramatic burlesque of its successor, and only Martyn Green, in top form with his effortlessly upper-class performance of the famously pattering Major General Stanley, does anything much more than sing the notes. Muriel Harding produces her usual lovely tone and risky moments and Leonard Osborn is a capable Frederic, but the recording sadly lacks character.

Something of the same criticism can be levelled at the 1933 HMV version, but this recording, extremely well transferred to LP, comes out, on the singing side, ahead of the later discs, with Peter Dawson as a particularly virile Pirate King, Dorothy Gill a splendid Ruth and Derek Oldham a fine Frederic, even though George Baker's Major General cannot compare with Green's for pure characterfulness. The sound on this set is, of course, necessarily an 'old' sound and this recording – a perfectly good one – is once again only for those who are at home with such quality.

George Baker returns as the Major General on the Malcolm Sargent recording of 1961 and, all in all, this set is a bit more fun than the D'Oyly Carte ones, even though I'm not quite sure that it was actually intended to be. The operatic singers chosen for the cast light into this music with more gusto than they do in their *HMS Pinafore*, and the result is something that borders on the operatic burlesque which so much of this piece was intended to be. Elsie Morison tackles 'Poor Wandering One' as if it were a Bellini mad scene, Monica Sinclair acts and sings Ruth with magnificent aplomb, Richard Lewis is an heroic Frederic, and the orchestra and chorus are as truly fine as on the other sets of this series. Amongst this, Baker's distinctly ordinary Major General is rather a low spot, but the effect of the whole is enjoyably on the edge of parody. I'd like to be wholly sure that it was meant to be so, but the result is there.

There is no doubt about the intentions of the most recent *Pirates of Penzance* disc, taken from the modernized Broadway production of 1981. This one is burlesque and fun through and through; on the stage, its colourful foolery was hugely enjoyable and its combination of up-to-date musical arrangements and modern song and dance styles really refreshing. It transfers rather less well to record, however, as only Rex Smith as a pop-singing Frederic, equipped with an Elvis Presley cadenza, really has sufficient voice to do justice to the music and to make its jokes come off.

Popular singer Linda Ronstadt's Mabel is a novelty performance of some versatility, but the painfulness of the key change just before 'Poor Wandering One' to allow her to sing the piece in a lower key is as unbearable to anyone familiar with the work as is the ridiculous interpolation of pieces of *Pinafore* and *Ruddigore* to allow the lady more to sing. George Rose is a jolly Major General, Kevin Kline happier in speech than song as the Pirate King, and the girls' chorus adept at switching from chesty 'belt' to legitimate singing, but on the whole, although this set scores high points on the humour side, it falls down just too much on the vocal side to make it really acceptable. It is a souvenir of a great evening in the theatre rather than a *Pirates of Penzance* for the record player.

There is more of the traditional Gilbert and Sullivan type of fun in the last of the D'Oyly Carte *Pirates of Penzance* recordings, made in 1968 and including not only the music but also the text of the show. Far from the colloquial tones of the updated *Pirates*, this one is delivered in the artificial, obvious style to which we have today become accustomed when Gilbert's works are played, the well-articulated archness which has become accepted as Victorian comic opera delivery and enshrined in D'Oyly Carte productions.

The cast take to it with a will. They also produce some very fine vocal performances, and the wonderfully ingenuous Philip Potter (Frederic) with his fluent, sweet tenor and Valerie Masterson (Mabel), her voice noticeably more substantial than in the *Princess Ida* recording of three years earlier, yet prettily gentle in the celebrated 'farmyard noises' of the coloratura chorus of 'Poor Wandering One', turn in some truly lovely singing. John Reed is an agreeably cheerful Major General and Donald Adams a Pirate King who clearly enjoys lavishing his chunky bass-baritone on the masculine music and mock-piratical sentiments of his rôle, and if the minor players do not quite come up to the same standard I suppose that is why they are minor players. This set is an enjoyable and faithful reproduction of the show as played in the latter days of D'Oyly Carte Opera Company, and it is clearly the choice for anyone wanting to listen the show as a whole.

For those who want only the music, the D'Oyly Carte's previous recording, made in 1958, would seem the best choice. There isn't a great deal of acting or of obvious fun in evidence, but the piece is regularly and uncomplicatedly played (once the endless and indifferent overture is over) by orchestra and chorus under Isidore Godfrey, and neatly sung by a very attractive collection of light operatic vocalists. Thomas Round as an unusually energetic and bright-voiced Frederic, who performs his rôle rather than just singing it, and Jean Hindmarsh as a sometimes meltingly sweet and always impressively accurate Mabel are especially enjoyable. Ann Drummond-Grant's easy mezzo-contralto ensures the clarity of Ruth's lines in a way many heftier contraltos find impossible; Peter Pratt is a fluent, unexaggerated and masculine Major General; and Donald Adams is already at home in the rôle of the 'pie-rayte' king. Several of the numbers – the Frederic/Ruth scene in Act 1, 'Away, Away, My Heart's on Fire', 'Stay Frederic Stay' – get a treatment it would be hard to better, and the set is never less than perfectly competent.

Patience

Patience, a pointed satire on the Aesthetic movement as represented to modern mind by the fake medieval affectations of Oscar Wilde, is a piece which not unexpectedly depends a lot on its textual and visual sides to make it work, and it is no real surprise to me that most of its recordings – and there are fewer of them than of the two preceding operas – are just a little spiceless.

The first of the three existing D'Oyly Carte recordings, made in 1930, is noticeably less good than its contemporary *Pinafore* and *Pirates* sets. Pretty Winifred Lawson (Patience) sounds almost too soubrette-like (if such a thing is possible) in this lightest of Gilbert and Sullivan soprano rôles and, while George Baker as the pseudo-Wildean poet Bunthorne and the remarkably deep-voiced Bertha Lewis as his massively devoted disciple Lady Jane fulfil their parts well, the rest of the principal artists incline to the dull.

Oddly enough, these same two rôles come out best on the 1952 recording, in which Martyn Green puts his very personal mark on Bunthorne and Ella Halman hoots imperiously through Lady Jane's music. Margaret Mitchell, in the title rôle, has clearly decided, like Emilie Petrelli who had played Mabel in the first *Pirates* but turned down the part of Patience in the original production of this show, that she doesn't want to be a soubrette. She oversings her music to the point of destroying the contrast between the artlessly innocent little milkmaid, who wins the men that the entire chorus covet, and the determinedly sophisticated and sub-operatic lady followers of the fashionable poet. The sound is more modern on this recording than on that of twenty years earlier, but the result is little if any better all round.

If anyone were going to oversing the rôle of Patience, you would expect it to be HMV's Elsie Morison, who would seem wholly unsuitably cast as the sweetly ingenuous milkmaid in the 1958 Sargent recording. In fact, she makes a very brave stab at lightening off her voice for the occasion, but nature and years of singing lessons win out and she cannot stop herself launching into the occasional full-throated sounds, particularly at the top of her voice – once, unfortunately, just after she has been referred to as 'pretty child'. As usual, the Glyndebourne chorus and Pro Arte orchestra are excellent and the lovesick maidens who drape themselves over the two aesthetic heroes of the show are particularly classy, including as they do two future *prime donne* in Heather Harper and Elizabeth Harwood. There are other fine voices, too, in John Cameron (Grosvenor), Monica Sinclair, as a Jane who makes much more of the words of her burlesque song of ageing – accompanied on the sawing violoncello – than her predecessors, and John Shaw (Calverly), but George Baker in the key rôle of Bunthorne had by this stage simply lost too much of his vocal capital to be comfortable in the part he had held for so long, and even his comedy is routine. This is particularly unfortunate in that, Ms Sinclair's splendidly grotesque *roucoulements* apart, there isn't much in the way of laughs anywhere else in a recording of a show which is, above all, a comedy.

Fortunately, the last D'Oyly Carte recording of *Patience* is an integral one and it is quickly evident just how much extra vivacity and appeal is given to the delectable score of this particular piece when it is played in combination with Gilbert's gimlet-like dialogue and scenes of satire. Fortunately, also, most of the rôles are taken here by performers who are as happy in speech as in song, and, although there are a few dialogue lapses, notably from a very stilted group of lovesick maidens, the cast rattle through the parody of the excesses of the aesthetic movement with precise but rarely overdone burlesque style and produce a thoroughly enjoyable performance.

John Reed (Bunthorne) and Kenneth Sandford (Grosvenor) play the pair of posing poets who are rivals for the attentions of the milkmaid who hasn't quite grasped the dictionary meaning of the verb 'to love', and they make a comical pair – Reed acidulous, crisp and dry and Sandford ping-ponging splendidly between the languid and the extravagant – successful most particularly in the dialogue scenes. Their Patience is Mary Sansom, a delightful light soprano who performs the rôle with just the right simplicity and brightness, clear and happy in her singing and suitably unpretentious in her speech.

There are other fine performances, too – Philip Potter lights up the show (after a slightly slow beginning) with his endearing, foppish portrait of the Duke of Dunstable and, in contrast, Donald Adams chews up the rôle of Colonel Calverley with blatant extravagance, turning the leader of the picturesque but jilted Dragoons into a real fire-eater. Gillian Knight, as Lady Jane, is a little at sea when she attempts the Bertha Lewis baritone boom, particularly in the dialogue, but she sings her burlesque ballad, 'Silvered Is the Raven Hair', with all the creamy tone of a Victorian parlour singer.

Iolanthe

If *Patience* is by its nature not the best suited of the Gilbert and Sullivan works to record, the opposite can be said of *Iolanthe*, with its gentle humour, its charmingly tongue-in-cheek fairy music, and its unusual moments of genuine sentiment. *Iolanthe* needs to be lovingly played and prettily sung, and its crisp and classy comedy requires few of the energetic burlesque effects found in the three previous operas. In other words, it needs all of the things that the D'Oyly Carte company on record are traditionally good at and not the one thing – bold satirical fun – which they so blatantly lack. Just to point this rule of thumb, it is notable that on every single *Iolanthe* recording the one piece of real burlesque, Lord Mountararat's blustery parody of a patriotic song, 'When Britain Really Ruled the Waves', is sung not for satire but for real. But, by and large, the other smiling moments are better judged and more amusingly played than usual.

The 1929–30 recording of *Iolanthe* is a splendid one, perhaps the best of all this particular group, and it is a great shame that on the Arabesque transfer (or, hopefully, only my copy of it) the final portion of the set seems to have been taken from a less than perfect original. Practically everything else is beautifully done. The orchestra takes the chance it is given to shine in one of the best of the Savoy overtures (one which was written by Sullivan himself, as it happens, and not by one of his assistants) and continues to play with sparkle and smoothness throughout, never ever allowing the music to drag, whilst the ladies' chorus makes a crocodile of Joyce Grenfell schoolgirls out of Gilbert's peculiar fairies and the Peers sound like a very well-bred male voice choir in some fine, straight singing.

The company are almost all very happy in their rôles here, with Bertha Lewis as a wondrously deep-voiced Fairy Queen giving what is to me one of the best single Gilbert and Sullivan performances on any disc. Whether sonorously summoning Iolanthe from her deep exile, quelling the impertinent Lord Chancellor with a baritonic blast or lambasting her foolish fays for their feminine weakness, she is a model of the genre. Winifred Lawson is a deliciously girlish soubrette Phyllis, Derek Oldham's posh warbling is splendidly suited to the utterances of the blue-blooded Lord Tolloller, and soprano Nellie Briercliffe as a young, ingenuous Iolanthe brings a sweet, sensitive pathos to a rôle which is too often trampled over by a hefty mezzo. Leslie Rands's Strephon, half-fairy and half-mortal, sounds wholly effete Englishman and – a touch of the Marie Antoinettes – just the sort of po-vowelled fellow that an aristocrat might have imagined an Arcadian shepherd would be. George Baker's Lord Chancellor is the one rôle that lacks something in its presentation. It takes him quite a while to get going, and for the first part of the show we have to make do with just neat singing and clear diction until, in the first-act finale, he starts to enjoy himself a bit. Moment after moment of this recording is quite definitive, and some pieces, like Iolanthe's moving final apostrophe, are simply lovely.

The 1952 version, in spite of its superior recorded sound, cannot equal its predecessor in performance. It has good orchestral and choral values, but of the principal performances only Martyn Green's Lord Chancellor, mixing sung and spoken lines with expertise and projecting a quirky, aristocratic character of much more individual delineation than Baker's, comes up to the standard of the earlier set. The performance elsewhere is all too often too earnest, with Margaret Mitchell doing her 'I'm-not-a-soubrette' routine as Phyllis, Ann Drummond-Grant giving a well-sung but very heavy Iolanthe, Eric Thornton bullocking his way through Mountararat's music and, worst of all, a Strephon (Alan Styler) of such numbing unsubtlety and dreariness as to send any self-respecting soubrette running for the nearest Peer in pure self-defence.

It is not so much earnestness as dullness that afflicts a lot of the last of the D'Oyly Carte *Iolanthe*s, a 1960 set including dialogue. John Reed is an accurate and acidulous Chancellor, at his best when most relaxed and/or under full steam, Mary Sansom sings prettily as Phyllis without equalling her Patience, Thomas Round boasts of his 'Blue Blood' quite nicely and Kenneth Sandford richly resists the permanent inclination of Private Willises to oversing his one number, but much of the dialogue is delivered with such uncomprehending one-syllable-after-another deliberateness ('But-io-lanthe-did-n't-die') as to be risible, and even long stretches of the music seem to have been affected by the same plodding tendencies. The singing voices are worthy, but Gillian Knight (Fairy Queen) is too light and mannered in speech and in song for this most voluminous of contralto rôles, Yvonne Newman's mezzo-soprano Iolanthe is more careful than affecting, and although Styler improves his Strephon significantly it is still not a performance of choice.

The HMV Sargent recording of 1959 is a very beautiful one. The piece is played and sung with all the grace and charm of the Victorian fairy operas that Gilbert was gently parodying. Long, soulful tones and sonorous playing are the order of the day, and the chorus of fairies sounds as if it has taken the day off from the Carl Rosa Opera Company to join in the proceedings. Monica Sinclair as the Fairy Queen is wholly un-grotesque, singing her opening invocation with a lovely warm tone and a smooth sincerity and depositing her curses on the naughty House of Lords with all the dignity of a headmistress giving out detentions. Elsie Morison (Phyllis) almost turns herself into a soubrette, and pairs effectively with John Cameron (Strephon) in their pretty pastoral moments, whilst Marjorie Thomas (Iolanthe), Ian Wallace (Mountararat) and Alexander Young (Tolloller) all maintain the high level of vocal quality, the last even getting a touch of humour into his 'Spurn Not the Nobly Born'. The humour is largely the province of George Baker, again cast as the Lord Chancellor, and he grasps his rôle on this recording with more immediate enjoyment than on the older disc. This is probably his best incarnation on the HMV series, traditionally mannered but crisp and light-hearted, giving welcome light relief to what is otherwise a very lovely but not enormously lively *Iolanthe*.

The Sadler's Wells company, which produced such a splendid *Mikado* recording, did rather less well with a very light-opera excerpts disc of *Iolanthe*. The blissful brightness of Studholme and the comicalities of Revill are sadly missed. They are not replaced by Eric Shilling (Chancellor), who rather hacks out his Nightmare Song in a very sung, though unquestionably clear, performance, and Elizabeth Harwood, who is an unsoubrettish Phyllis with rolling Rs and sings uncomfortable things like 'thine the beeellow'. There is quite a lot of warbling on this recording – the Private Willis (Leon Greene) and dark mezzo Iolanthe (Patricia Kern, who was such a good Pitti-Sing) being the principal oversingers. The best moments come from a really soaring Tolloller (Stanley Bevan), a securely contralto Fairy Queen (Heather Begg), who attempts to put some spirit into her rôle, and a marvellously sung and almost bouncy 'Faint Heart Never Won Fair Lady' from Shilling, Bevan and Denis Dowling, but too often this is a droopy *Iolanthe* – all voice and no heart.

Every Gilbert and Sullivan collection ought to have a record which displays the best of Bertha Lewis, and since her Fairy Queen is arguably her most splendid incarnation, it is really worth going to the trouble to track down a copy of the fine Arabesque or World Records *Iolanthe*. Its transfer to CD should have at last made this easier. But if you can't, it is probably best to settle for the HMV set and the fine singing it contains.

Princess Ida

Princess Ida has always been one of the lesser-loved of the Gilbert and Sullivan works and it is not difficult to see why. It lacks the crazy gaiety of the more favoured works both in its text and in its music, with the slightly ponderous old-fashioned measures and rearranged lines of Gilbert's original made-over burlesque, *The Princess*, suiting themselves less well to the lines of Sullivan's music than the freer, later lyrical style. There are instances when Gilbert breaks out into something like his favourite manner, such as in the two patter songs for the comedy rôle of King Gama, and there are instances when Sullivan grasps a more serious moment to enjoy himself with some light operatic strains, both in solo and in the many attractive ensemble passages of this most atypical of the Savoy operas, but there are also *longueurs* and a frustrating lack of brilliance and of lively fun.

The show has, however, been given its due recordings. The first, dating from 1932, takes up two and a half sides of an Arabesque set, paired with a selection from a contemporary *Pirates of Penzance*. It isn't one of the better of these sets, although it is interesting to hear the sixty-five-year-old Henry Lytton giving his crabbily stagey version of King Gama's songs. It is also interesting to hear Muriel Dickson give a straightforward light soprano Ida in contrast to the more dramatic voices which, although the rôle was originally intended for none other than the distinctly unweighty American star Lillian Russell, later became popular. There are some good performances from the sweet tenor Charles Goulding (Cyril), the neat and clear George Baker (Florian), the characterful Richard Watson (Hildebrand) and Nellie Briercliffe (Melissa), some less good elsewhere, and some, like Dorothy Gill's Lady Blanche, deprived of her solo, who have little chance. Some of the ensembles sound suitably sonorous, but the final effect is an indifferent one.

The 1955 Decca *Princess Ida*, containing the same material and also omitting Blanche's solo, stretches to cover four sides. It is a rather more enjoyable production, even though it is occasionally a little unevenly performed, but it still fails to reach the heights of the recordings of its fellow operas. Victoria Sladen is a bigger-voiced Ida, Peter Pratt follows faithfully in Lytton's style in Gama's numbers, and Thomas Round (Hilarion) and Ann Drummond-Grant (Blanche) are particularly good in a cast where one or two people are tempted to perform in 'I-really-wanted-to-be-in-grand-opera-but-didn't-quite-make-it' style, but, in spite of a faithfully conducted performance by Isidore Godfrey, I still get a feeling that I'd like to grab the handle of the barrel-organ and wind it faster.

All in all, the 1965 Decca version comes out on top. The Royal Philharmonic Orchestra and Sir Malcolm Sargent attack the piece with something that sounds like real enthusiasm, and the contrasts amongst the light-hearted pieces of the score, the various musical burlesques, and the larger lyrical sections are well established. Among the cast, there is particular pleasure to be found in Philip Potter's Hilarion – a real lollipop tenor this, sweet, clear things tumbling out on every breath – and in Valerie Masterson's deliciously girlish Melissa, pleading irresistibly with the invading enemy 'Please you, do not hurt us'. Elizabeth Harwood is Ida, and she succeeds by taking a middle line, singing with a clear, full, medium-weight voice and unpretentious diction into which only the odd operatic vowel or consonant ('Minerva, hearrrr me') creeps when she feels the need to push things a bit. When she joins with Potter and his two fine friends (Jeffrey Skitch and David Palmer) in the lovely 'The World Is But a Broken Toy', the effect is melting. Donald Adams is a suitably pompous Arac, gleefully delivering his mock-Handelian piece like a provincial oratorio singer, Christene Palmer dives into the depths of Lady Blanche's rôle effectively (still without 'O, Mighty Must', which seems to have been permanently banned from the piece), John Reed attacks King Gama's patter energetically and Ann Hood is a neat if unadventurous Psyche. Only a rather lifeless Hildebrand (Kenneth Sandford) is below par, and since he hasn't too much to do – a fact to which Rutland Barrington, who created the rôle, modestly attributed the comparative failure of the show – that cannot mar an effective recording.

Ruddigore

The more wholeheartedly burlesque nature of the words and music of the tale of *Ruddigore*, with its wicked uncles and melodramatic moments, may be a reason why this comparatively overlooked Gilbert and Sullivan work is more successful on record than such a piece as *Patience*, which has always been preferred to it in the theatre. Certainly the 1950 recording by the D'Oyly Carte company is one of the best of the series recorded around that time, having both fine singing performances and that very energy and humour which is too often missing in the other recordings.

Here, the cast positively seem to be enjoying themselves under the leadership of a splendidly characterful Richard Watson as the temporarily evil Sir Despard Murgatroyd, an energetic and masculine Leonard Osborn (Richard) and a lustily loopy Anne Drummond-Grant (Mad Margaret) all in top form. Martyn Green is as excellent as ever, singing smoothly as the bad baronet disguised as a 'pure and blameless peasant'. He is more at home once he becomes an aristocrat – the peasant is a bit of an effort for him, but then it probably was for the bad baronet, too. Margaret Mitchell as the ingenuous Rose Maybud is a mite happier here than in *Patience* and, together with the rest of the cast, she winds up into a magnificent first-act finale of operatic burlesque proportions. The orchestra and chorus seem to have caught the prevailing intent to enjoyment as well, and the whole performance – in spite of the odd blooper here and there – is just the great kind of fun it should be.

Sir Malcolm Sargent's team also let themselves go nicely in their *Ruddigore*. Monica Sinclair (Dame Hannah) sets the ball rolling with a suitably melodramatic telling of the legend of Ruddigore – rather as if Azucena had pushed old Ferrando out of the way and was having a go at the opening of *Il Trovatore* – and Owen Brannigan is at his villainous best as Sir Despard, lashing his way through the chorus with unprintable noises. Joseph Rouleau, supported by a helpful echo, makes a spectral job of the rolling basso solo 'The Ghosts' High Noon' and Pamela Bowden gives a well-considered, if slightly polite, rendering of Margaret's burlesque mad scene. Richard Lewis (Richard) is another who stands back a little from giving a good, vulgar performance, but he is always in fine voice.

Not all goes quite as well, however. Unfortunately, this is not Elsie Morison's best recording of the series and George Baker is simply too old-sounding for the young hero of the piece, so, as in the *Patience* recording, although it is in the main an enjoyable set, the strong right arm of this walloping work has a bit of a limp wrist.

A second D'Oyly Carte set was issued in 1962 and this one, which prides itself on using 'the original overture', is also good. It has a particularly charming Rose in Jean Hindmarsh, Thomas Round in ringingly bright form as Richard and Kenneth Sandford in his best recorded characterization as a rich-voiced Sir Despard, whilst Jean Allister sings splendidly in Margaret's mad scene and John Reed is a crisp and believable juvenile leading man as Robin-cum-Ruthven. The whole affair is a wee bit gentlemanly here and there – a touch more transpontine acting wouldn't have hurt – and this unnecessary gentility makes me prefer the older version. But apart from the fact that it is just a little lacking in presence, it cannot actually be faulted. It is merely a matter of preference.

Incidentally, like the Arabesque reissues of the HMV material, this set uses a very attractive piece of nineteenth-century advertising material as its cover design. Sadly, it isn't credited or explained, even though there is space on the sleeve to tell us that the cover is 'laminated with *Clarifoil* made by British Celanese Ltd'. And whilst I'm complaining about the sleeve, this set also falls into the irritating pattern familiar on Gilbert and Sullivan discs: it fails to list the songs, either separately or in the potted plot. I know the whole world is supposed to know them – but it is nice to have them there for when you forget.

The latest *Ruddigore* recording is a TER set made in 1988 for the centenary of the original production. Unfortunately, this suffers from most of the same defects as the companion *Pinafore* set: silly claims on the cover ('first complete recording of the original version'), material cut by the authors shovelled tastelessly back in, bland sound, dreary conducting and much mediocre casting. It does have the advantage of the presence of Marilyn Hill Smith as Rose, but even this usually spunky soprano seems to have been affected by her surroundings and is not at her brilliant best. It seems a shame that, when a company equipped with the most modern techniques is found willing to invest in new recordings of this repertoire, more care cannot be taken over the personnel involved. Or is it, perhaps, those modern techniques themselves which are, at least partly, to blame? I don't pretend to know. I only know that for some reason the Gilbert and Sullivan recordings made in 1949 and 1950 sound so much better.

The Mikado

The Mikado is certainly the most popular and possibly, if it is necessary to make comparative judgement, the best of the Gilbert and Sullivan musicals (though I think that my vote, if I could have only one, would be for *HMS Pinafore*). It has, indubitably, over the years received the most attention from stage and record producers, both in its original state and in a whole series of variant versions, for it is a piece that lends itself most willingly to variation. I have thirteen different *Mikado*s and *Mikado* derivatives on my record shelf (and there are probably more which I don't have), ranging from the transfers of the 1936 D'Oyly Carte recording through 'Hot', 'Cool' and 'Black' *Mikado*s up to the latest *Boy Friend*-age version staged at the English National Opera in 1986. It must be said that they are an unpredictable lot.

I should have expected that this most Gilbert and Sullivan of Gilbert and Sullivan shows would have had a joyfully definitive recording from its crucible, the D'Oyly Carte Opera Company, but it turns out that their four recordings are mostly strangely disappointing. Both the transfers of the 1936 company's recording and the 1950 version find Martyn Green far from his supreme performances as Sir Joseph Porter and the Major General; Ko-Ko doesn't seem (record-wise, at least) to suit him half so well. The 1936 version seems to have fallen in an interregnum between top D'Oyly Carte performers and, with Derek Oldham (Nanki-Poo), wreathed in pompous vowels and unfortunate notes, also failing to come up to his best, this ranks as one of the least good of the early recordings. Leonard Osborn, on the 1950 disc, also catches the same disease. He is quite out of form as Nanki-Poo, but he is not alone. There are disappointing performances from other trusted favourites like Richard Watson, and even Ella Halman, trumpeting regally as Katisha, lacks any sort of involvement.

The most recent D'Oyly Carte version of *The Mikado*, made in 1973, is technically very competent but simply not a very enjoyable listen. There is some appreciable singing from the clear-voiced Colin Wright (Nanki-Poo) and the fresh and rarely gusty Valerie Masterson (Yum-Yum), but the rest of the performances range from the effortful and the creaky to, in the cases of the Mikado and Katisha, the plain unpleasant. There are, incidentally, several examples of notation here which I don't recollect having heard before and which jar somewhat.

The best of the four D'Oyly Carte *Mikado*s is the 1958 version. This is played with vigour and, particularly in the case of Thomas Round as a fine, energetic Nanki-Poo and Jean Hindmarsh as his sweet-voiced Yum-Yum, sung with distinction. They are supported by some pleasingly girlish little maids (Beryl Dixon, Jennifer Toye), a fluent Ko-Ko (Peter Pratt) and a commanding Katisha (Anne Drummond-Grant) and, although other rôles are less convincingly cast, there is enough here to add up to a perfectly pleasant performance.

The other companies which have recorded *The Mikado* have suffered various fortunes. Sargent's HMV version of 1956, in the full-scale series, is not one of its better efforts. It has its usual fine orchestral and choral values and much accomplished singing – particularly from Richard Lewis who, unlike most other Nanki-Poos, actually gets up to all of the rôle's notes in a nice relaxed style, and from John Cameron's Pish-Tush – but ultimately it lacks character. The accomplished singing is one of the main problems: there is just too much of it and it all sounds the same. When you have a barrage of big-voiced baritones (Cameron, Geraint Evans, Ian Wallace, Owen Brannigan) all making round about the same nice noise, dramatic comprehension 'flies out through the flies. As for the women, they are simply not as good as elswhere: Elsie Morison sounds as if she's had enough of it all, and Monica Sinclair – so energetic and gutsy elsewhere – seems to be having comedy troubles. This is not the famous Duchess of Krakenthorp (*The Daughter of the Regiment*) beloved of collectors of operatic curiosities.

However, after this wreath of not-quite-satisfactory *Mikado*s, rescue is at hand. The TER recording of the English National Opera production is, after the unpleasantness of the same label's *Pinafore* and *Ruddigore*, a royally pleasant surprise. It has infinitely more life than its fellows, the performances are in a different league, and, as a *bonne bouche*, it makes no pompous claims on its cover, which has just a good, concise note, enjoyable photos and a vast list of credits. But, wouldn't you know it, whereas the other two TER Gilbert and Sullivan efforts were deemed worth a double-disc recording, this infinitely superior one is limited to just a single record.

I have to admit that, irritated by the scenic shift of this production from Japan to Victorian England, I did not go to see it in the theatre. I maintain my reservation (with a little less conviction than before), but I give whole-hearted full marks to the director, Jonathan Miller, for his choice of singers – the record is a hoot and a joy, and its artists are almost without exception very cleverly picked for their rôles. After having spent an entire day listening to all these *Mikado*s, in chronological order, and getting more and more depressed, this recording came as a very big ray of sunshine.

I was a little dubious when it started. That sexless digital sound seemed to intrude, Nanki-Poo (soon followed intermittently by everyone else) was putting on what came dangerously near to qualifying as a silly voice, and the Ko-Ko couldn't sing. Further irritations lurked – the lyrics to the Little List song had been rewritten not quite well enough, and the Mikado's song had been tampered with too – but although all these objections popped up momentarily they were popped down again straight away by pure enjoyment. How can you resist a Nanki-Poo (Bonaventura Bottone) with a soaringly lovely operetta voice and a splendid sense of comedy timing (oh, rare combination)? What does it matter if Ko-Ko (Eric Idle) can't sing much if he can wring your withers with the simplicity of his 'Tit Willow'? And you can't see (except on the cover) how big the three little maids are when they launch into their utterly charming girlish trio. As for the silly voices, I (who really loathe such things) have to admit that they sometimes actually push the words forward so you can hear exactly what's going on, for a change.

Many a time, as I've watched *Aida* in the theatre, I've felt that it should be called *Amneris* – she's so clearly the most interesting person. After listening to this record, I think that *The Mikado* should really be called *Katisha*. Felicity Palmer, in that rôle, is the supreme gorgon. She turns the Act 1 finale into a brilliant operatic burlesque and – even though she can't resist singing her big solo 'Alone, and Yet Alive' for real – she is the comic and musical treat of the recording. She is run a close second both by Bottone and by Lesley Garrett's clear, lovely Yum-Yum and, if the effect of these three performances is to shift the emphasis of the piece away a bit from the classic Ko-Ko and comedy axis, that seems to me only to improve it.

The supporting performances are mostly fine – a pompous Mikado with a cold in the nose (Richard Angas), a fruity Pooh-Bah (Richard van Allan), a vigorous Pish-Tush (Mark Richardson) and a sonorous if perhaps rather unfunny Pitti-Sing (Jean Rigby) do their bit to make up a recorded *Mikado* for today which is, quite simply, preferable to all of the many *Mikado*s on disc of yesterday. More of the same, please.

This is, of course, not a disc for those who prefer their Gilbert untampered with and their Sullivan complete, but the same company, a quarter of a century earlier, produced one of the first non-D'Oyly Carte productions of *The Mikado* at Sadler's Wells Theatre, and the resultant recording is the most appealing of the full sets. Here, the Gilbert is as it was written, and the Sullivan all in place, but the first moments of the first side of the first record produce a little bit of a shock. The overture has been reorchestrated. It's only after you've got your breath back that you realize that it has been reorchestrated (by one named Dodgson) with a delectably light hand and, with Alexander Faris conducting the theatre's orchestra with a joyously spirited touch, you are zipped along into the frivolous high spirits of the show in a very helpful way.

What follows is equally pleasant. Opera company or no, virtually no one in the cast oversings or yodels his words, and several of the performances are quite outstanding. At the top of the list comes the finest Ko-Ko on disc, Clive Revill. He acts his rôle with beautifully timed humour – just to hear him helplessly give up his bride with a gulping 'Take her, she's yours', a line usually thrown away for nothing, is a joy. Bright and utterly coherent, he combines just enough clear, accurate singing voice with his comedy and creates a joyfully ridiculous little character quite free of received mannerisms. On the feminine side, Marion Studholme (Yum-Yum) also gives an utterly delightful performance, artlessly producing a voice that really deserves that tired old comparison with ornithologia.

In first-rate support, there are a smoothly articulate Pooh-Bah (Denis Dowling), an attractive Pitti-Sing (Patricia Kern), who swoops down to the low notes of her 'cervical ver-ertebrae' with glorious ease, and a pompous walrus of a Mikado (John Holmes). The Katisha (Jean Allister) sounds more like a jilted housewife than Ms Palmer's glorious gorgon, but Ms Palmer is pretty impossible to equal, and John Wakefield (Nanki-Poo) shows a stylish tenor when not pushed, rounding off a fine cast and a fine recording which only lacks the inspired, lunatic qualities of the best and most extravagant moments of the newer disc.

The most eye-catching *Mikado* sleeve is undoubtedly that on the CBS television soundtrack recording. What is eye-catching is not any pictorial or design content, but the big, big names – Groucho Marx (in letters twice as big as Gilbert and Sullivan), Dennis King, Helen Traubel, Robert Rounseville, Stanley Holloway . . . the promise of such a starry recording is immense. Sadly, for all the performers can do, it remains just a promise. This is a 'Bell Telephone Hour' production, and the meaningful word in that title is 'Hour'. The recording is a potted *Mikado*, a nonsensically clipped and chopped mixture of dialogue and music which delivers nearly nothing unmangled, and drives you mad as it hops and skips from one familiar fragment to the next. It is truly a shame, for the casting – unlike most of these star casting exercises – has been ingeniously done. Robert Rounseville with his manly, ringing tenor is a superb Nanki-Poo, Dennis King is the zaniest of Mikados, Groucho Marx a jolly, colloquial, almost non-singing Ko-Ko, Stanley Holloway a comical Pooh-Bah with more vocal power than you might expect, and Helen Traubel a richly impressive Katisha who deserves better than to have her part shorn of its tempestuous first-act finale. But they can do nothing to make this patchwork of pieces of *The Mikado* presentable.

The Yeomen of the Guard

The Yeomen of the Guard stands alone amongst the works of Gilbert and Sullivan as the one piece which cannot be called – and was not called – a comic opera. It is a light romantic piece more in the tradition of the mid-ninetenth-century operas of Balfe and of Wallace, whose *Maritana* its plot much resembles, without the elements of burlesque and paradoxical behaviour usually present in Gilbert's libretti. Sullivan's music reflected this difference in style, and *The Yeomen of the Guard* has become regarded alternatively as either the most musically satisfactory (by the young and serious and those who find the comic element degrading) or the least purely enjoyable (by the non-operatic). Wherever between these extremes the truth lies, it is certain that, if it is more restrained in its comic conceits, *The Yeomen of the Guard* offers much in the way of vocal opportunity to its singers, particularly in the way of ensemble music, which is liable to make an appreciable recording.

Thus, it turns out that all the three complete recordings that have been made of *The Yeomen of the Guard* for LP have much to recommend them. The earliest is the 1950 D'Oyly Carte set, which features the usual team of Martyn Green, Muriel Harding and Leonard Osborn in its principal rôles. This is a very enjoyable recording, and much credit must be given to the recording company and its engineer for the particular success of the technical side of affairs. As on others of these Decca recordings of the early 1950s, the sound is a clean, bright one, with the voices firmly to the front – exposed, of course, which is probably why one notices the odd vocal bloomer, but so attractive to listen to. The chorus sounds clear and brilliant and the orchestra is always supportive and never obtrusive. If this could be done thirty years ago and more, why, I ask plaintively, don't all recordings do it?

As it happens, on this set, each of the three principals is in good form. Green makes Jack Point a lugubrious fellow; he's a victim right from the start, which probably stops you from feeling overly sorry for him at the end (no bad thing). Osborn and Miss Harding, with their open, occasionally risky voices, bring off their big moments splendidly and add their valuable presence to the ensembles, which are one of the principal highlights of the show and the recording. The only number which comes off less than well is 'I Have a Song to Sing, O' which lacks any sort of showmanship – but Jack and Elsie were probably pretty rotten buskers anyhow. Amongst the rest of the cast, Ella Halman's authoritative hoot is in its element as the domineering Dame Carruthers and Ann Drummond-Grant is a strong and simple Phoebe with an outstanding beefy mezzo, whilst Richard Watson is as much fun as ever as Shadbolt. Some of the lesser rôles are less safely sung, but when everyone comes together in the show's big moments, the sound is quite splendid.

In Sargent's 1958 set, quite the opposite stands good. The casting of the show's secondary rôles is absolutely marvellous: Denis Dowling as Cholmondeley, Alexander Young as Leonard, John Carol Case as Meryll and John Cameron in the tiny part of the 2nd Yeoman, singing his few lovely lines with a beauty that makes one gulp. Higher up the bill, Richard Lewis is a perfect Fairfax, mixing splendid lyrical lines with both lighter and more dramatic moments, whilst the casting of Geraint Evans as Point, if against tradition, proves perfectly acceptable. A lusty, unmannered, Welsh Jack is just as possible as a lugubrious and traditional English one and, since in this show the other middle voices are less prominent, one doesn't have the feeling of being swamped in baritones.

The ladies come out of it a little less well. I'm sure that Elsie Morison (Elsie), Monica Sinclair (Carruthers) and the nice, unpretentious Marjorie Thomas (Phoebe) are singing perfectly well, but somehow their performances are a bit damp. They seem to have acquired a sort of soft-grained touch which mixes them with the orchestra rather than sitting them up in front of it. It is a tendency which I have noticed before on this series, but it is particularly obvious when listening to this set directly after the Decca one with its up-front sound, and it certainly gets in the way of my enjoyment.

The second D'Oyly Carte set, dating from 1964 and also under the baton of Sargent, has different qualities to the first. It is certainly a more thoughtful performance, with tempi and light and shade more varied and with not too much in the way of mannerisms; it also takes a very different line on the voices used. John Reed employs his usual dryly precise delivery as Point, but he makes the jester an altogether perkier chappie than his predecessor and 'I Have A Song' gains notably, even though brightness is the most notable quality lacking in Elizabeth Harwood's assured and smoothly sung Elsie. The singing of Philip Potter, a lovely easy lyric tenor, as Fairfax is something else altogether. It is a performance that lacks the attack of Osborn, but the sweetness and smoothness of Potter's delivery is beautifully suited to Fairfax's two songs. After listening to the contralto voices of Halman and Sinclair, one cannot help feeling that mezzo-soprano Gillian Knight had not at this stage the weight for Carruthers. She at times leaves the feeling that she would have made a lovely Phoebe. On the whole, the piece is well played and sung but I do not feel that it is ideally cast, and, in spite of obvious attempts to be interesting, it does not come up to the older set for simple on-the-spot pleasure.

The Gondoliers

The Gondoliers has always been a Gilbert and Sullivan favourite and, looking at it academically, it is a model of the genre. There is light-hearted foolishness in abundance, charming music, low and less low comedy, cockeyed romance and an absurdly logical conclusion. There are comic scenes for several groups of characters including one set, the impoverished ducal Plaza Toro family, who have become models of their kind. There are songs and ensembles of all the standard types from the clever and attractive opening burlesque of comic opera Italians to the famous revamping of the oft-used cowardly commander song ('In Enterprise of Martial Kind'), the celebrated tenor solo 'Take a Pair of Sparkling Eyes' and the bouncy cachuca and, taken one by one, all the individual pieces of the successful comic opera are there. Yet, as a whole, *The Gondoliers*, alone amongst the successful Gilbert and Sullivan operas, always leaves me a little bit indifferent.

Perhaps it is the rather boring subsidiary plot featuring the semi-blighted romance of the wet drummer, Luis, and the otherwise betrothed Signorina di Plaza Toro, which stretches the show out to what seems unnecessary lengths? For this work, in spite of fitting musically on to four sides of long-playing record, always seems rather longer than the rest. However, whatever your thoughts on it, there is no reason to complain about the variety of recordings that have been made. They are all perfectly competent, if not exciting, with each, as usual, having its individual advantages and disadvantages.

The earliest, the Arabesque 1927 version under Harry Norris, has the usual slight sound problem and an exceptionally boring Luis (most of the Luises seem pretty pompous and boring and I am going to assume it is the fault of the rôle), but on the credit side it features a definitive pair of Plaza Toroi in Henry Lytton, urgently birdlike and crisply accurate, and Bertha Lewis, who almost equals her *Iolanthe* Fairy Queen with a performance of unmatchable booming hauteur whilst still getting out the words of a very briskly played 'On the Day that I Was Wedded'. It also has an enjoyably lightweight Don Alhambra (Leo Sheffield) rather than the now popular buffo bass, and a soubrette Tessa (Aileen Davies) rather than the now usual squelchy mezzo, both of whom help to lend a nice air of lightness to the proceedings. However, the juvenile men (Derek Oldham, George Baker and Arthur Hosking as the dreaded Luis) are, unfortunately, more than a little bit stolid, which cancels out the ladies' advantage. Norris keeps the orchestra and chorus going with an appreciable vigour throughout and, on the whole, there is more to like about this recording than not.

The same goes for the 1950 set, for although by this time a fairly buffo Don Alhambra (Richard Watson) and a not overly hefty mezzo Tessa (Yvonne Dean) have arrived, the men (Leonard Osborn, Alan Styler and Henry Goodier as a marginally less boring Luis) are rather less pompous sounding and more relaxed in their singing, and Muriel Harding finds the rôle of Gianetta one of the parts most suited to her delightfully bright soprano. Martyn Green is a rather more aristocratic-sounding Duke than Lytton, making a fine pairing with the Duchess of Ella Halman and her owl-like tones without equalling the outstanding combination of the earlier discs, and Margaret Mitchell's rich tones are more at home in Casilda's pining legato music than in some of the more lively rôles of the repertoire. The chorus and orchestra under Isidore Godfrey perform with their usual efficiency and, while it is not a set to raise great enthusiasms, there is little that you can actually dislike about it.

The 1961 recording, which includes dialogue, stretches the piece to five sides (*Cox and Box* makes up the sixth). This is a very light *Gondoliers* and, to my way of thinking, none the worse for it. The long musical opening scene, which too often displays a handful of choristers going over the top in their one chance at solo work, gets things off in dancing mood with a lively band of fresh-voiced featured players, and the principals who follow on behind are in the same mould – Thomas Round (Marco) and Alan Styler (Giuseppe) are pleasant and energetic, Mary Sansom (Gianetta) and Joyce Wright (Tessa) light and bright. The ducal band, too, are a lightweight lot, with John Reed lofty, precise and pertinent at their head and a splendidly pouting Casilda (Jennifer Toye) and classy Luis (Jeffrey Skitch) using their skill in dialogue to liven up their characters in between their moments of musical melancholia. If some of the voices are a little less impressive than on other recordings, the cast make up for this with a brightness in their performance of text and music which is too often lacking.

The HMV–Sargent *Gondoliers* recording is the poorest of that series. Even when this group is not at its most attractive, it is always well nigh impeccable in its singing and playing, but this time there are chinks even in that wall. Some of the music seems dreadfully turgid in its tempi and there is a lot of legato in the singing where levity would be more in order. Amongst the performers, the HMV regulars turn in reliable if not particularly vibrant performances, with Geraint Evans and Monica Sinclair giving a stately, well sung and perfectly enunciated Duke and Duchess, Richard Lewis politely correct in 'Take a Pair of Sparkling Eyes', John Cameron a little more vigorous as Giuseppe, and Elsie Morison (Gianetta) producing more brightness than Marjorie Thomas (Tessa), who is a rather un-merry maiden in her solo number. Alexander Young makes a nippy-voiced tenor Luis, altogether less lugubrious than the baritones, but his Casilda has caught the drears instead, so little is gained in their duets. The biggest let down, however, is in the supporting cast. Some very weak contadine get the show off to a feeble start and it never gets going as it needs to thereafter.

Utopia (Limited)

Left in the doldrums for many years by the professional Gilbert and Sullivan purveyors, *Utopia (Limited)* nevertheless found its way onto record in productions by two American companies, the Blue Hill Troupe of New York and Washington's Lyric Theatre Company, which went to the extreme of privately putting down both two- and three-disc versions, the second of which was re-released in England on the Pearl label.

The D'Oyly Carte Company finally got around to tackling *Utopia (Limited)* properly in 1976, putting down a two-disc version of the score (without dialogue) on Decca with members of their company, with whom *Utopia* had been recently brought back into the repertoire. It is a very efficient recording and, if it doesn't glitter with textual fun and musical jollity in the way of the best Gilbert and Sullivan works, that is, at least partly, quite simply because it is not one of the best Gilbert and Sullivan works.

There seem, however, to be a few cases of miscasting which don't help – Judi Merri's mezzo-soprano Kalyba sounds more fifty than fifteen years old – and several of the players just never succeed in raising a sparkle. Lyndsie Holland is so busy making a plummy contralto sound in Lady Sophy's comedy waltz that she forgets the comedy, veteran Kenneth Sandford in the main comic rôle of King Paramount is inexplicably dreary, and the Flowers of Progress are a fairly uninteresting lot.

When John Reed (why wasn't he given the King's rôle?) and John Ayldon, as the conniving wise men, appear on the scene, things liven up considerably, but Pamela Field's delicious Princess Zara and her bright-as-a-battleaxe Life Guards

Captain, as played by the very appreciably tenor Meston Reid, are responsible for all the best moments of this set both vocally and dramatically. Reid has one of the score's comedy highlights in the tale of 'A Tenor All Others Above', which he sings both robustly and with humour, but the other, Gilbert's bitterly witty 'Seven Men Form an Association', debunking Company Law, gets a damply proficient performance. *Utopia (Limited)* may not be the funniest or the most tuneful piece, but it needs, in the words of the song, to be 'done justice' in all its parts and not just some.

The Grand Duke

Like *Utopia (Limited)*, *The Grand Duke* for many years owed its only LP recordings to amateur societies, both from America (Lyric Theatre of Washington) and Britain (Cheam Operatic Society on Pearl), until it, too, received its full-scale recording from the D'Oyly Carte Company in 1976. That recording has now become scarce enough that I was not able to find a copy to review here, but I can only assume that it is better than the two previously mentioned.

Sullivan without Gilbert

The works written by Gilbert during the period of his estrangement from Sullivan (*The Mountebanks* with Cellier, *His Excellency* with Osmond Carr and *Haste to the Wedding* with George Grossmith) have unfortunately not reached the LP, but Sullivan's five full-length Gilbertless works have all been preserved on disc in more or less complete musical form, thanks to various groups of modern enthusiasts. The Sawston Light Opera Group has recorded a poorly revised version of the early *The Chieftain* (*The Contrabandista*), the Cheam Operatic Society a less tampered-with *Haddon Hall*, and the St Albans Operatic Society *The Rose of Persia*, whilst the Prince Consort feature in both *The Beauty Stone* and *The Emerald Isle*. Each recording includes some good singing and/or playing as well as some less acceptable performances, but all five are welcome as the sole existing version of these historically interesting pieces.

Unfortunately, the Rare Recorded Editions *The Rose of Persia*, by far the best work of the five integrally, is the least well recorded. It is apparently a transfer from a taped live performance, including both dialogue and music, made in 1963, and the quality is commensurate. The fact that no one is credited on the sleeve, except Gilbert and Sullivan guru Dr Terence Rees who provides the notes, also suggests that it is a bootleg recording. However, it is just good enough to allow us to hear the quality of this, the most undeservedly forgotten of Sullivan's scores. It has beautiful ensembles and some fine lyric and comic songs, in which Basil Hood's splendid lyrical contribution clearly encouraged the composer back to something like the style he had employed so successfully in his collaboration with Gilbert.

Sullivan was less happy in his teamings with playwrights Sydney Grundy and Arthur Pinero. Neither of these was a writer in the burlesque-comic style of Gilbert or Hood and the works that the composer turned out in his collaborations with them are correspondingly less lively. *Haddon Hall* is an old-fashioned light opera which could have been written twenty years earlier or more, and *The Beauty Stone*, for all its use of Gilbert's favourite 'lozenge' plot, is nearer to *Ivanhoe* than *The Sorcerer* in flavour. Neither makes particularly jolly listening. The *Haddon Hall* disc is nicely recorded on the Pearl label. Soprano Elsie Broadbent does a good job as the heroine Dorothy Vernon, but the cast, like their composer, take the whole thing rather earnestly and what you get is a rather stolid parade of Victorian music which only occasionally shows signs of having been written by the composer of *The Mikado*.

The Beauty Stone, totally unfrivolous and intentionally so, gets a similar treatment on the same label, even to the extent of casting the rôle of the Devil, originally played by comedian Walter Passmore, with a rather woofy and unfunny baritone. The high spot of the recording is Margaret Aronson's performance as the jealous Saida, powering up to the dramatic high notes of her 'Mine, Mine at Last' in a way that has equally little to do with the light musical theatre. This piece of music is one of the few times when the show takes off, and it is not too hard to see why *The Beauty Stone* survived only fifty performances on the stage.

The Contrabandista was Sullivan's first full-length work for the stage, written to a text by journalist and burlesque-writer F. C. Burnand, and it is extremely interesting in that it shows the first flourishings of several elements, dramatic and musical, which would later flourish in the Gilbert and Sullivan shows. It was later rewritten by the authors as *The Chieftain* but, unfortunately, the version captured by Rare Recorded Editions is one rearranged by a gentleman from the Sawston amateur society who, convinced of what he calls 'the inferior quality of the libretto', has provided new text and lyrics of his own which are of very inferior quality instead. If you feel so inclined, you can tape the real numbers, omitting the fabricated ones, and end up with a fairish version of *The Chieftain* – otherwise, this is one to avoid.

Sullivan's posthumous *The Emerald Isle*, completed by Edward German, was, like *The Rose of Persia*, written to a libretto by Basil Hood and, as a result, although it is not a return to the gaiety of Gilbert days, its humorous content is much higher than that of *Haddon Hall* and *The Beauty Stone*. If it does not quite come up to the earlier collaboration as an entire piece, *The Emerald Isle* contains much that is both charming and whimsical, from the fairy music of the first-act finale and German's pretty soprano ballad 'Oh, Setting Sun' to the comicalities of the odd-ball Professor Bunn's description of how to be 'A Typical Irish Pat'. Pearl's double-disc recording of this score is taken live from a concert performance of 1982 and it has some of the disadvantages of non-studio recordings, including the occasional bits of scratchy playing and singing and some balance problems. With the exception of Mary Timmons as a fine leading lady, the performances are only honourable, but the all-round combination of score, performance and adequate recording makes this the most likely bit of listening amongst the non-professional Sullivan discs.

Edward German

Merrie England

Edward German's success with *The Emerald Isle* led to his continuing at the Savoy Theatre, where he worked with Hood on *A Princess of Kensington* and on his most successful show, *Merrie England*. Successfully revived on several occasions, *Merrie England* and its most popular songs 'The Yeomen of England', 'The English Rose' and the waltz 'Who Shall Say that Love Is Cruel?' were plentifully recorded, including on two complete sets of 78s under the direction of the composer himself, in 1918 and 1931. The big songs continued to feature on recital discs, but the only full-scale modern recording of *Merrie England* was the result of a revival at Sadler's Wells Opera in 1960.

Unfortunately, this production was another 'revised version', in which the adapter, Dennis Arundell, had seen fit to fiddle with the plot and introduce several earnestly historical characters into Hood's joyously unhistorical period burlesque, but the recording is a different matter. Though Arthur Jacobs tactfully nods towards what he calls Arundell's 'improved' libretto on the sleeve, Norman Newell's recording of German's score is based squarely on the real *Merrie England* and, even if it sometimes has a sound to it that is more 1960 than 1902, a wholly splendid recording it is both in its technical values and in its performances.

The principal rôles are without exception well cast and performed in a clear, comic opera style, without affectation or pretentiousness. June Bronhill, at the peak of her powers, plays Bessie Throckmorton, the lady-in-waiting love of Sir Walter Raleigh; she delivers her showpiece waltz with an admirable brilliance and clarity as well as leading many of the show's superb ensembles in an impeccable style which has everything to do with keeping the unaccompanied portions smack in tune. Her Raleigh is the strong-voiced William McAlpine, perhaps more at home in his drinking songs than in the more gentle, lovelorn moments of 'The English Rose', but clearly a match for the machinating Essex (Peter Glossop), whose rich, clear baritone is just made for 'The Yeomen of England'. Patricia Kern's dark mezzo makes Jill-All-Alone a very cultured witch, but she adds a wicked mystery to her apostrophe to her cat in the second-act opening, and Monica Sinclair is a really regal Queen Elizabeth, rolling out her 'O Peaceful England' with true contralto tone.

The principal comedy rôle of Wilkins, originally played by Walter Passmore, is here given to the bass Howell Glynne, and a splendid job he makes of it, never allowing the weight of his voice to get in the way of its agility as he gambols his way through Hood's delightfully funny lyrics. This part loses nothing by being properly sung instead of skittered through in the style of the standard Gilbert and Sullivan comedian, as long as it is not oversung, and Glynne never does that. When he and Charles Young celebrate 'The Big Brass Band', or when he splatters out a tongue-twisting list of fish in 'King Neptune Sat on his Lonely Throne', the result is both musical and amusing. Eric Wilson-Hyde and Neil Howlett perform the foresters' duet 'We Are Two Proper Men' with rich masculinity but, for some inexplicable reason, they are not allowed to maintain these rôles through the whole recording. The same treatment is given to the part of Wilkins, whose music is shared by two minor singers. This is a pity as, although the dramatic significance is not great, some of the theatricality in this, admittedly, rather untheatrical recording is lost.

Although the individual songs and performances are of singular importance and popularity, I have always found the heart of *Merrie England*'s music to be in the ensembles which make up such a large part of the score: the lovely quintet 'Love Is Meant to Make us Glad', the quartets 'In England, Merrie England' and 'When Cupid First this Old World Trod', the all-male 'When a Man Is a Lover' and 'Two Merry Men a-Drinking', the Arcady Duet, the splendid Robin Hood Pageant and the dramatic first-act finale. It is one of the greatest merits of this recording that the singers have the art of ensemble singing beautifully mastered and, doubtless with the aid of Newell's intelligent producing hand, the balance of the voices amongst themselves and with the orchestra is unfailingly well-organized. You can hear any line you want to, or none, and that is surely the art in question. The Williams Singers who supply the chorus are clear, bright and unplummy (although I think I detect the odd bit of 1960s crooning) and Michael Collins and his orchestra provide a lively backing (and I'm sure I didn't really hear a bit of BBC arranging somewhere), both adding their bit to a very superior and enjoyable recording which has been reissued several times since its original pressing and has justly become a classic.

Tom Jones

1967 saw the issue of a selection disc from German's other most successful work, *Tom Jones*. Although another period piece, *Tom Jones* is as unlike *Merrie England* as could be. Where the latter piece is squarely in the comic opera mould, tightly and wittily moulded by its librettist into something between a burlesque and a romantic light opera, *Tom Jones*, written to a book by Alexander M. Thompson, is an out-and-out comedy opera, tumbling from one picaresque adventure to the next and from a lusty song or chorus to soprano solo or soubrette number with joyful vigour. There are no queens and knights here; this is Elizabethan middle-to-low life, lived with some of the rampant rawness of Fielding's novel.

The two principal rôles of Tom Jones and his Sophia, originally played by the picturesque baritone Hayden Coffin and operetta soprano Ruth Vincent, have the lion's share of the solo singing, and on this recording Frederick Harvey and Cynthia Glover are even more prominent than in the show; apart from the two soubrette songs belonging to the rôle of Honour (Shirley Minty) and the one solo of Squire Trelawney, which is nabbed by Harvey, only the numbers in which the two stars take part are included. Gone is the music for the comedians – the patter-singing 'person of parts', Benjamin Partridge, and Honour's yokel lover, Gregory – and the recording thus presents a rather lopsided view of the show.

However, what is there is so well done that it would be ungrateful to complain. Frederick Harvey (who was fifty-seven when this recording was made and died shortly after) has one of those beautifully straight, unforced baritone voices that England used to be famous for, and he sounds all of twenty-one as he attacks 'West Country Lad', 'A Soldier's Scarlet Coat' and 'If Love's Content' with a virile lilt. Miss Glover is equally good, delicately tiptoeing through the adventures of 'Dream o' Day Jill' and launching sweetly and securely into the coloratura of the famous waltz song 'For Tonight'.

To cast a mezzo in the very spritely rôle of Honour seems an odd choice, but it grows on you, and would grow more if the colour of Miss Minty's voice didn't mean the loss of many of the words of the soubrette's flirtatious 'Green Ribbon' number. The several choruses and dance music which makes up the disc frame the solos nicely, but I think it would have been worth the extra wage to have had a singer in to record Benjamin Partridge's number instead of including the substantial opening orchestral track.

The Nigel Brooks Chorus and Gilbert Vinter's orchestra perform well, lilting into the music in such a way that makes one realize what an awful shame it was that, after his unfortunate collaboration with Gilbert on *Fallen Fairies* in 1909, German wrote no more for the musical stage. His melodies give the promise of splendid operettas to come and his shows could and should have been there alongside the romantic works of Romberg and Friml on post-war stages – not to mention films. Lawrence Tibbett and Grace Moore could have had a great time with what Edward German had to offer. But it didn't happen, and this disc of *Tom Jones* is about all there is to witness to what might have been.

Sidney Jones

The Geisha

The operetta king of the turn of the English century was undoubtedly Sidney Jones. Jones was responsible for the scores of the most outstanding series of musical shows of the 1890s, ranging from *A Gaiety Girl* and *An Artist's Model* through *The Geisha*, *A Greek Slave* and *San Toy*, all played at Daly's Theatre under the management of George Edwardes, up to the innovative *The King of Cadonia* in 1908. Vastly recorded in their time, revived around the world for many decades, virtually none of Jones's works have made it onto LP and not one has been systematically recorded in Britain. Ironically, the most famous, *The Geisha*, has been recorded both in Italy and in Germany, where it has remained in the repertoire with considerable vigour over the years, proving, until the coming of the 1980s wave of internationally produced British musicals, the most popular British work on Continental stages, well ahead of its only challenger, *The Mikado*.

The principal German recording, made by Decca in the 1950s and issued in Britain on one side of a ten-inch disc paired with *Im weissen Rössl*, is one of those pot-pourris so beloved of the Germans. It takes a chorus here and a few lines there from the show's most popular songs and blends them together in a twenty-minute sampler of what the musical in question has to offer. It is an infuriating formula, as you are just starting to enjoy a song when it switches, unannounced, into another one, which you have just time to begin to digest when it, in its turn, is replaced by yet another. I suppose that it could be a plot in league with the music publishers – you are so frantic to know or remember what comes next that you rush out and buy the vocal score.

Here, in one side of a ten-inch record, you are tempted by so many glorious fragments of songs that it is quite dispiriting that you can't somewhere find the whole thing. There is a little bit of Sonja Schöner singing about 'Der verliebte Goldfisch' (The Amorous Goldfish) and a chunk of the glorious waltz songs 'Lieb, lieb, so wundersüss' ('Love, Love') and 'O tanz', du kleine Geisha' ('A Geisha's Life'); Werner Schöne gives his comical version of 'Chin-Chin-Chinaman' (which is the same in any language); and Jean Löhe makes the most of the tenor moments of the first-act finale ('Perle des Orients, Mächen mein') supported by some truly splendid orchestral arrangements and playing and a first-rate choir. The odd liberty is taken with Jones's score – particularly in the realm of extra high notes – but it is all done in such a magnificently sweeping way that you can't possibly object. There is only one objection – the usual one – there just isn't enough of this recording.

There is a little more, or apparently more, on another, scarcer *Geisha* recording (backed with *Viktoria und ihr Husar*) put out in 1954 on Polydor. This one manages to cram fragments of no less than sixteen numbers onto its ten-inch side and, once again, though infuriating, it is a joyful display. The Polydor team of singers (Ilse Hübener, Gretl Schorg, Rosl Schwaiger, Franz Fehringer, Willy Hoffmann etc) sing the material without the slightest reverence for its age, giving a thoroughly 1940s performance, backed by 'the Sunshine Singers' with some croony period harmonies. A 'hit-parade' version of 'Boshafter Papagei' ('The Interfering Parrot') is followed by a lovely coloratura bit of 'Lieb, Lieb', a straight baritone 'Traum, o mein Liebling' ('Star of my Soul') and an MGM finale, and the score not only takes the treatment but takes it very happily.

The twelve-inch Italian Cetra disc put out in 1974 has a little more space again, even though this, too, devotes only one side of a record (backed with the Italian musical *L'Acqua cheta*) to the music from *The Geisha*. It's a slightly strange selection – the 'Pescolino Innamorato' gets in, along with the soubrette's 'Chon Kina', the hero's 'Jack's the Boy' and the Italian version of 'Chin-Chin-Chinaman', but the Italians have clearly been worried by the fact that the minor tenor rôle has only a few lines to sing (the hero was the baritone) and they have fabricated a very Italianate aria for him by joining up his two passages in the first-act finale with the soprano music in between and tagging on an ending with a high note. It is very impressive and, well sung by Carlo Pierangeli, enjoyable, but scarcely genuine *Geisha*.

The soprano makes herself a big moment, too, by taking the tragi-comical saga of the goldfish at half speed in throbbing legato tones, endowing it with an operatic variation that verges on coloratura, and generally turning it into quite another song than that which Marie Tempest twinkled out at her audience in 1896. *In toto*, this disc gives us six numbers, one piece of finale-turned-aria and a massive opening chorus. The best moment is Armando Sorbara's giggling 'Chin-Chin-Chinaman', but the whole thing doesn't have the dash and joyously operetta feel of the German records. Nevertheless, if you aren't able to track down the now rather rarely seen German recordings, this is certainly an acceptable substitute. Any *Geisha* is better than no Sidney Jones at all.

Howard Talbot and Lionel Monckton

The Arcadians

Some of the additional light numbers for Jones's Daly's Theatre shows were written by the young composer Lionel Monckton, who simultaneously collaborated with Ivan Caryll on the music for the concurrent series of musical comedies at the Gaiety Theatre, also under the management of George Edwardes. In spite of a large number of successes under the Edwardes banner, it was not until comparatively late in his career that Monckton turned out his biggest hit for producer Robert Courtneidge. This time his collaborator was Howard Talbot, composer of the record-breaking *A Chinese Honeymoon*, and the show was *The Arcadians*, the greatest of all Edwardian musicals. *The Arcadians*, which was revived as recently as 1984 to delighted noises from critics and public, was put on record in 1968 by Columbia and the Norman Newell/June Bronhill combination. The result is everything that could be hoped for.

1968 is not the bloom of Bronhill years, but the star makes a model job of the music allotted to the soprano role of Sombra – the famous 'Pipes of Pan', 'Arcady Is Ever Young' and 'The Joy of Life' – supported by a splendid orchestra and a fine choir under the baton of Vilem Tausky. The other rôles, too, are well cast. Ann Howard, improbably allotted the Phyllis Dare soubrette role, shows how it is possible to mix a weighty mezzo and a pert personality. She comes up with a 'Girl With a Brogue' that is not only convincing but positively endearing, and joins in her light-hearted duets ('Charming Weather', 'Half Past Two') with the delightful baritone of Peter Egan with great success. Andy Cole gives a happily relaxed rendering of the chief comedian's songs, including the well-known 'All Down Piccadilly', and Jon Pertwee puts over the show's comedy hit 'My Motter' with all the required lugubriousness.

The undoubted highlight of the recording, however, is the massed performance of the Act 1 finale, beautifully sung, splendidly balanced and, like all the rest, as clear and true in sound as could be wished. There is, of course, plenty more music in *The Arcadians*, but this selection is well and wisely made, with only 'I Like London' of the featured numbers being omitted along with some of the show's attractive choral music.

'I Like London' is actually included on the Music for Pleasure recording which was issued the following year. This, however, is about the only advantage that this disc has over its predecessor. The selection is a shorter one and omits the entire Act 1 finale, the song 'Somewhere' and the ensemble 'Truth Is So Beautiful', which are all included on the Columbia recording. Although Cynthia Glover is a pretty Sombra, neither the performance nor the recording quality on this version is equivalent to the other.

Sadly, apart from *The Geisha* and *The Arcadians*, none of the great successes of the Victorian and Edwardian era of British musicals has been comprehensively recorded. An enthusiast gathered together a bundle of the 78 rpm recordings of another of the most famous shows of the time, *Florodora*, which were transferred to LP and released on the Opal label, but the quality of the turn-of-the-century recordings is dismal and the record is of value only for archive purposes. A number of other, more successful, transfers have been made by other archival labels, but these are basically of single numbers taken from here and there and gathered into thematic collections. The World Record Club devoted a disc to the Gaiety star Gertie Millar, which includes songs from Lionel Monckton's *The Quaker Girl*, whilst another entitled 'Singing Actresses' includes Evie Greene's versions of the songs she introduced in the same composer's *A Country Girl*. Of the works of Ivan Caryll (apart from an American *Pink Lady* recording), Leslie Stuart, Walter Slaughter, Meyer Lutz, Osmond Carr and their fellows, who dazzled the world of the musical theatre for the last of Victoria's days, there is nothing to show. It is a pity, for the tiny handful of shows which have been paid attention by the LP age show us enticingly what we are missing.

My Ten Essential Records

COX AND BOX/THE ZOO: D'Oyly Carte Opera Company, 1978, with Gareth Jones and Geoffrey Shovelton (Decca TXS 128)

THE PIRATES OF PENZANCE: complete, with dialogue, D'Oyly Carte Opera Company, 1968, with Valerie Masterson and Philip Potter (2 records, Decca LK/SKL 4925–6); CD (London 414 286–2)

RUDDIGORE: complete, D'Oyly Carte Opera Company, 1950, with Martyn Green and Margaret Mitchell (2 records, Decca LK 4027–8)

THE MIKADO: selection, English National Opera cast, 1986 (TER 1121); CD (CDTER 1121)

IOLANTHE: complete, with George Baker and Bertha Lewis (2 records, Arabesque 9066–2/World Records SHB 64); CD (Arabesque Z8066–2)

THE YEOMEN OF THE GUARD: complete, D'Oyly Carte Opera Company, 1950, with Martyn Green and Muriel Harding (Decca LK2029–30)

THE GEISHA: selection (b/w *Im weissen Rössl*), in German, with Sonja Schöner, Jean Löhe and Werner Schöne (10-inch, Decca LW5049)

MERRIE ENGLAND: complete, with June Bronhill, William McAlpine and Howell Glynne (2 records, EMI Double-Up DUO121, reissued EMI CFPD 4710); CD (CD-CFPD 4710; CDB 7 62778–2)

TOM JONES: selection, with Frederick Harvey and Cynthia Glover (EMI CSD 3628)

THE ARCADIANS: selection, with June Bronhill, Ann Howard and Peter Regan (Columbia/EMI TWO 233)

Other Recommended Records

Trial by Jury: complete, D'Oyly Carte Opera Company, 1949, with Richard Watson, Muriel Harding and Leonard Osborn (Decca LK 4001)

The Sorcerer: complete, D'Oyly Carte Opera Company, 1953, with Peter Pratt, Muriel Harding and David Palmer (2 records, Decca LK 4070–1)

HMS Pinafore: complete, D'Oyly Carte Opera Company, 1949, with Muriel Harding, Leonard Osborn and Martyn Green (2 records, Decca LK4002–3)

The Pirates of Penzance: complete, D'Oyly Carte Opera Company, 1958, with Thomas Round, Jean Hindmarsh and Peter Pratt (2 records, Decca SKL 4038–9)

Patience: complete, with dialogue, D'Oyly Carte Opera Company, with Mary Sansom, John Reed and Kenneth Sandford (2 records, Decca LK 4414–5 / SKL 4146–7)

Princess Ida: complete, D'Oyly Carte Opera Company, 1965, with Elizabeth Harwood and Philip Potter (2 records, Decca LK/SKL 4708–9)

The Mikado: complete, Sadler's Wells Opera Company, 1962, with Clive Revill and Marion Studholme (2 records, HMV CSD 1458–9; reissued on HMV Greensleeves ESDW 1077183)

The Gondoliers: complete, with dialogue, D'Oyly Carte Opera Company, 1961, (3 records, with Cox and Box, Decca LK4402–4)

Utopia Ltd: complete, D'Oyly Carte Opera Company, 1976, with Pamela Field, Meston Reid and Kenneth Sandford (Decca 414 359–1)

The Emerald Isle: complete, The Prince Consort (2 records, Pearl SHE 574–5)

CHAPTER 3

Vienna's Golden Age

Hard on the heels of Offenbach's and Hervé's first great successes, Austria and Germany began to develop a native comedy opera tradition of their own and, within a decade, the foundations for what has cavalierly become known as the Golden Age of operetta had been laid by a group of productive librettists and composers. Led by such memorable musicians as Franz von Suppé, Johann Strauss and Carl Millöcker, they developed a distinctive 'Viennese' operetta style which happily complemented the successful French and British works then playing on the stages of the world's light musical theatres.

Golden though it might have been, the reputation of this period of operetta rests today on a surprisingly slim number of works, and this is reflected in the recordings of such pieces produced over the thirty-year history of the long-playing record. In spite of his 'saleable' name, Strauss is represented, in complete recordings of his original operettas, only by *Die Fledermaus*, *Eine Nacht in Venedig* and *Der Zigeunerbaron*, and in full-disc selections by *Der lustige Krieg*, *Karneval in Rom* and a hashed-up *Cagliostro in Wien*. However a number of the operettas compiled from his music by other hands (*Wiener Blut*, *Walzer aus Wien*, *Tausend und eine Nacht*, *Casanova*, *Die Tänzerin Fanny Elssler*) have also had the honours of recording in various degrees.

Suppé survives, apart from endless recordings of his overtures (doesn't it ever occur to anyone to look into what they were overtures to?), largely through his enduringly popular short operetta *Die schöne Galathee* and the full-length *Boccaccio*; and Millöcker through *Der Bettelstudent* and *Gasparone*. These, along with Zeller's *Der Vogelhändler*, are the only other pieces from this era to have been recorded complete and, as in so many other cases and in other countries, record producers have preferred almost entirely to turn out repeated new discs of these same few works rather than to look at other operettas from the same composers or, indeed, others of the era.

Johann Strauss

Die Fledermaus

In the latter half of the twentieth century, Strauss's *Die Fledermaus* has become the most popular of all Viennese operettas, outdoing in prominence even Lehár's

Die lustige Witwe – with which it shares, in the world's consciousness, the position of being the distillation of everything that the words 'Viennese operetta' mean. New productions have proliferated throughout the subsidized opera houses of the world since they began to take into their repertoires a narrow selection of the classic operettas (no longer commercially viable in the general theatre), and every decade since the beginning of the long-playing record industry has seen several new full-scale recordings of the piece. I make the total at the time of writing sixteen, mostly in the original German, but including versions in English, Russian, Hungarian and French.

The first of these, which includes the music but no dialogue, was put out in 1950–1 by Decca, and it is a reference for all subsequent recordings. Clemens Krauss held the baton for the occasion, directing the Vienna Philharmonic, the Vienna State Opera Chorus, and a superlative group of soloists on what is a simply delightful pair of records. Conductor, orchestra, chorus and principals all have the temperature of the piece perfectly. From the first bars of the celebrated overture to the last chords of the equally famous champagne-filled finale, the score trips along vivaciously, played with an unselfconscious sparkle and gaiety, and chorused as crisply and lightly as if the same choir had never sung *Die Walküre*.

All the leading performances are very fine, effortlessly accurate and unforcedly comedic, but it is Julius Patzak in the musically comparatively unshowy rôle of the tentatively philandering Eisenstein who makes the most enduring impression with his flippant, characterful performance. He sings in an easy, conversational tenor, which is so natural that it makes it sound perfectly normal for a man to hold a conversation to music, yet he shows himself capable of rising to any and all of the rôle's lyrical phrases, and his final indignant disposal of his disguise is played and sung with unstrained clarity and character.

I have often been glad to see a howling tenor Alfred dragged off to prison at the end of Act 1, but it is really sad that this Alfred (Anton Dermota) couldn't have been invited to the Act 2 party for a couple of numbers. His sweet tenor serenade would make any girl's ears prick up, and his lilting contribution to the intimate *souper à deux* with Frau Eisenstein ('Trincke, liebchen, trincke schnell') is splendidly seductive. Hilde Güden as the lady in question gives as good as she gets. Poised and charming, her silky soprano glides provocatively through her masked seduction of her own husband ('Dieser Anstand'), and she makes a stylish light lunch of her showpiece csárdás ('Kläng die Heimat') – smoked salmon to certain other sopranos' richer *filet à foie gras* – in a number which Krauss does not forget is a dance.

The other ladies are equally attractive. Wilma Lipp is a perfect operetta soubrette who tosses off the flittering coloratura phrases of the rôle of Adele deliciously. Pouting and piquant in turn, she sounds almost computerised in the showiest phrases of her two big numbers, both of which she performs splendidly. The done-to-death 'Mein Herr Marquis' (Laughing Song) gets a refreshingly straightforward performance with no party piece tricks, while the Audition Song ('Spiel ich die Unschuld vom Lande') is rather more characterful. And why not?

– Adele has been at the party all night too, and has undoubtedly been at the champagne which Prince Orlofsky (Sieglinde Wagner, singing her number in an uncomplicated, creamy mezzo) has been dispensing so liberally.

Alfred Poell (Falke) and Kurt Preger (Frank) keep or are kept happily in the same style, mixing good singing and some nice comic touches – the tipsy counting of the 6 a.m. chimes, and Frank's ever-so-slightly out-of-tune homeward whistling – on a set where all the many well-loved songs and ensembles get a truly first-rate performance.

I can find only a couple of peripheral faults, things which could be confusing for those not familiar with the score. The tracks are so close together that it is sometimes hard to tell where one piece of music stops and another begins, and, in the absence of dialogue, the synopsis on the sleeve doesn't show you where the songs fit in.

The next recording, made by Walter Legge for EMI in 1955, is also an extremely finely sung one, with an equally outstanding group of performers in the leading rôles – Elizabeth Schwarzkopf (Rosalinde), Rita Streich (Adele), Nicolai Gedda (Eisenstein), Erich Kunz (Falke) – and the Philharmonia Orchestra and Chorus conducted by Herbert von Karajan. It is slightly differently laid out to the earlier recording, as it includes fragments of linking dialogue between the musical numbers, and there are vast chunks of low comedy material for Frosch included in Act 3 in preference to the second-act dance music. It also quite unnecessarily casts a tenor in the mezzo-soprano rôle of Prince Orlofsky.

The chief joy of this recording is Schwarzkopf's beautifully performed Rosalinde. Her deliciously modulated soprano gives her lyrical music all the shapely care that she would give to a Richard Strauss Lied, yet she can launch with equal skill and charm into moments of twinkling humour (witness the marvellous 'Dieser Anstand' with Gedda) or the more vigorous fun of the third-act denouement. Her big csárdás is quite simply a triumph. This Rosalinde never lets you forget that she is a phoney Hungarian. The opening lines are sung with an unbounded Magyar emotion – which nevertheless never impedes the glorious tone – and she soars spiritedly and powerfully to the song's climax with all the dazzling and dashing bravura of the genre. And, no matter what she is doing, that endless flow of superb voice, which never seems to take time off to snatch a breath, is curling peerlessly around the musical phrases. It is sheer beauty.

Streich is a model Adele, her two big numbers sung with crystalline accuracy and fine control. She ventures a few giggles in 'Mein Herr Marquis' which risk qualifying her for at least the semi-finals of the Renata Tebaldi Prize for Unfortunate Laughter, but the singing is impeccable. The men, with fewer showy opportunities, make the most of their moments, Gedda in fine voice and having plenty of fun with his impersonation of the stuttering old lawyer, Kunz using his cool, smooth baritone – a sweeter and less lusty sound than Poell – to the best of effect in the very prettiest of 'Brüderlein's, and Helmut Krebs making a prettily bumptious Alfred. There is also a deliberately mannered Rudolf Christ as Orlofsky, cruising all around the notes in a curious and unsatisfying spoken-sung performance. He makes the Prince bored, as per the text, but also, alas, rather boring. And when Orlofsky is boring, the second act sags not just once but twice.

In spite of all the outstanding performances on this set, however, I still remain overall marginally in favour of the first recording. It waltzes along with just that little more élan than its successor and its cast are more evenly excellent.

Many of the stars of these two superb sets appear again in later recordings. The third original-language set, issued by Columbia in 1959, uses Dermota, Lipp and Kunz (as Frosch!) alongside Karl Terkal (Eisenstein) and Gerda Scheyrer (Rosalinde), while Decca's extended 1960 set features Güden opposite Waldemar Kmentt and Erika Köth. Kunz is Frosch again here, but for RCA's 1964 set (Eberhard Wächter/Adele Leigh/Anneliese Rothenberger) he switches to the rôle of Frank. Ariola-Eurodisc (1966) does another switch by using Lipp as Rosalinde along with their inevitable Rudolf Schock (Eisenstein) and Renate Holm (Adele, for the first of three times). Gedda repeats his Eisenstein alongside Rothenberger and Holm on EMI as late as 1972, and in 1974 on Decca's third set, Kunz is Frank again, with Wächter, Holm and Gundula Janowitz. However, for my money, none of these later recordings, fine though some of them are, comes up to the two earliest sets for pure, all-round enjoyment.

The Columbia set, in stereo, is an unexceptional one. Terkal is a high-energy Eisenstein with an enjoyably incisive tenor but, although Scheyrer has some attractive moments, her occasionally gusty performance cannot compare with those of Schwarzkopf or Güden. Dermota repeats more happily than Lipp, there is a sibilant, friendly Falke (Walter Berry), a very idiosyncratic Orlofsky (Christa Ludwig), and an accompaniment which is more still wine than champagne. This recording is, however, much preferable to an odd 1960 set issued as *Il Pipistrello* in Italy by a branch of Warner Communications and thus obviously not as pirated as it sounds. It has been recorded very live and very badly in Vienna on New Year's Eve with the Vienna Philharmonic and Staatsoper Chorus under von Karajan and a longwinded 'gala concert' with a series of items by Giuseppe di Stefano interpolated into the party scene, which is responsible for making this into a three-record set.

A large number of the cast of this misguided recording were given a better chance when Decca recorded the show properly, in the Sophiensaal, around the same time. Once again, this was a three-record set, equipped with all the ballet music and a 'gala concert' of operatic celebrities singing unlikely pieces, of which Simionato and Bastianini's heavily accented 'Anything You Can Do' became the disc jockeys' novelty favourite. The recording was also, sensibly, issued in a two-disc set without the extras.

From a singing point of view, the cast is very fine. Güden repeats her top-class Rosalinde, Waldemar Kmentt puts a lot of beautiful notes and phrases into Eisenstein's rôle, Erika Köth is an Adele who bears comparison with (if she is not herself) the very best, and the baritones make a lovely noise. Giuseppe Zampieri (Alfred) sounds just like a tenor called Giuseppe Zampieri should be programmed to sound, and Regina Resnik as Orlofsky is very low, very laid-back, very unyouthful and rather rewritten. There are, in fact, a number of moments here which don't seem to be very Zell and Genée to me, but no one is credited with extra (unfunny) bits. The unfunniness goes as far as calling an amateurish extra 'Omar Godknow'.

Mr Godknow apart, this is an efficient recording with several fine (and mostly feminine) highspots. But at times I feel that it lacks dash and sparkle in its playing, and there are times, for all that this is a real, Viennese recording, when it doesn't seem very 'Viennese' either.

The RCA set has a baritone Eisenstein – a folly, as with Falke and Frank also going to the ball it all becomes a bit like baritones' night out and, anyway, it just sounds wrong, unnecessary and even confusing. It also leaves out Frosch's stand-up comedy scene. Its principal asset is its Adele, Anneliese Rothenberger, whose rôle is expanded with a party piece in mini-imitation of the Decca episode. Another fine Adele, Renate Holm, is the most enjoyable part of the otherwise unexceptional Ariola-Eurodisc version.

Shortly after these two issues, Rothenberger and Holm came together in HMV's 1972 recording, the first straightforward *Fledermaus* to come near the two staple versions in quality. The forces of the Vienna Staatsoper, under Willi Boskovsky, are put to fine use this time in a *Fledermaus* which twinkles along very happily. Rothenberger is now cast as Rosalinde, and the rôle suits her splendidly. The music is no trouble – she can be sweetly confidential or as bravura as you like, as witness her csárdás, and she gives the character the aura of being what can only be called 'a lovely lady'. Sympathy is well and truly on her side and against her rakish husband. Gedda is, predictably, less fresh than in his recording of seventeen years earlier, but the assurance he has developed makes up for any little diminution in vocal elegance and, in fact, is not unsuited to the character, which he plays with enjoyably raffish style. Holm is a vigorous Adele, not one of the computerized brigade, who rattles off her two big numbers energetically, speaks her lines effectively . . . and can laugh!

For those who have only previously heard him in Lieder and opera, Dietrich Fischer-Dieskau (Falke) gives a surprisingly relaxed and, of course, warmly sung Falke, and in deference to his status gets a rather nice extra bit of solo in the party. Brigitte Fassbänder is quite the best Orlofsky I have heard, splendidly androgynous in speech and with a dark blue mezzo-soprano that surges easily through her song with none of the specious effects or overacting the rôle sometimes attracts; Adolf Dallapozza is a good Alfred, and Otto Schenk does quietly comical things with Frosch's scene.

All the dialogue on this set is, in fact, played intelligently for recording rather than in imitation of stage delivery. When there are conversations it is conversational, soliloquy is soliloquized, and only when someone is addressing a roomful of people is projection put into operation. It is a very pleasant convention and easy on the ear, but one which does not, of course, carry through into the music of what is, all in all, a highly enjoyable set.

The 1974 Decca version goes in for both a baritone Eisenstein and a tenor Orlofsky, and DGG plungers even lower (in pitch) in casting Hermann Prey as Eisenstein. I'm sure he would play the part splendidly on stage, but it seems a little perverse as record casting.

If anything, the 'playing safe' of the record companies seems to have increased in recent years. In spite of the backlog of *Fledermice* still readily available and now, in many cases, transferred to CD, the 1980s have produced three more complete sets to add to the pile.

The first of these comes from the Vienna Volksoper and is one of a group of live performance recordings made by the company in Japan in 1982. It has all the usual live recording attributes, including applause and laughter (brought up and down artificially), a lot of clomping and knocking, biggish theatrical acting and some uneven sound balancing amongst voices, but it also has a good degree of vivacity and humour in the execution of both music and text. The performances, headed by Mirjana Irosch (Rosalinde), Waldemar Kmentt (Eisenstein), Melanie Holliday (Adele), Robert Granzer (Falke) and Ryszard Karczykowski (Alfred), are all at least honourable, and there is no doubt that, for a live recording, this is streets ahead of the 1960 one. Curiosities here include the interpolation of the 'Thunder and Lightning Polka' and the 'Blue Danube' waltz as dance music and an adept, fairly low comedy Orlofsky from the operetta and musical comedy soprano Dagmar Koller.

EMI's 1986 recording gives top billing to Placido Domingo, who, fortunately, is not cast as Eisenstein but instead somehow doubles as Alfred and conductor of the Münchner Rundfunkorchester and also pops in 'Ach wie so herrlich' from *Eine Nacht in Venedig* as a party piece during the second act. As a conductor he does a fine if occasionally rather broad job, assisted by a very, very richly recorded orchestra which shows off energetically in the interpolated 'Donner und Blitzen'. As Alfred he is, predictably, quite incomparably lush and Italianate as well as comical, and he performs his interpolated number to a crowd of what sounds like squealing pop fans with both romantic vigour and an enjoyable liveliness.

The other principal performances on this recording are also first rate. Lucia Popp is a splendid Rosalinde, amusingly melodramatic or piquant as required in the comedy of the first act, joining tit-for-tat with Domingo in their supper-table duo and the subsequent scene in the creamiest tones, and alternately seductive and sprightly alongside Peter Seiffert's dashingly enthusiastic and clear-voiced Eisenstein in their 'Dieser Anstand'. Her big csárdás is played and sung straight and strong and, like Domingo and the other stars, she gets an extra showpiece with the insertion of the Dompfaff Duo from *Der Zigeunerbaron*, which she and Sieffert sing beautifully if a little self-indulgently.

Eva Lind performs Adele's music (plus the bonus 'Il Bacio') with less lightsome glitter than my favourites, allowing many of her notes to tell lingeringly rather than dancing over them *en pointe*, but Agnes Baltsa's Orlofsky is in the very top class, even if the soft baritone speaking voice and the vibrant mezzo singing are a little incompatible. Her party piece is a stirring, stalking version of the nominally soprano 'Habet Acht' (*Der Zigeunerbaron*), and it is a stunner which even Domingo, who follows her in the concert, cannot top. Both Falke (Wolfgang Brendel) and Frank (Kurt Rydl) are strong, fulsome baritones, and the chorus are both vigorous and full-voiced on a set which is very much a *Fledermaus* with all the sauces in the book.

Technically the recording is very fine, with a full, rich sound throughout and a delightful party atmosphere in Act 2. The piece is neatly arranged in its dialogue to keep the story clipping along without going into longueurs, managing to fit everything onto four unfull sides even with the addition of all the interpolations. It is perhaps less perfect than elsewhere in just one way. On a number of occasions the orchestra is brought up to such an extent as to swamp the singers, and on others a performer (poor Dr Blind is one example) suffers from being rather pushed into the background in a scene or ensemble.

After the production of this rather glamorous recording, I wonder why Teldec felt it necessary to follow up the very next year with another *Fledermaus* which has nothing but stretches of ballet music in addition and, in every other area, considerably less to offer. This version, recorded in Amsterdam with the Concertgebouw Orchestra under Nikolaus Harnoncourt (in large billing) concentrates on the music of the score, omitting the dialogue (which is replaced with some foolish fragments of Frosch), and concentrates so hard that it wholly forgets that *Die Fledermaus* is supposed to be enjoyable. This is an earnest, tasteful *Fledermaus*, so damned tasteful that is quite, quite boring. Give me the extrovert 'showbizzyness' of the EMI set or the lusty out-front playing of Volksoper, but not this pale, unfeeling sort of thing. Werner Hollweg (Eisenstein) makes the most effort to escape the wreck of the *Fledermaus*, but mostly, he, like Edita Gruberova (Rosalinde), Barbara Bonney (Adele) and Josef Protschka (Alfred) only gets to be tasteful.

And now that we have had every kind of *Fledermaus* possible – with and without dialogue, with and without interpolated concerts, with and without taste/vigour/colour and with and without superb singing, can the show be taken off the record companies' schedules for at least one decade to allow them to produce other operettas?

This proliferation has not happened in other countries, which have made do with just one full *Fledermaus* apiece. Each of the existing complete recordings in a foreign language is at least two decades old, beginning with the American CBS set of 1950 starring Ljuba Welitch and Charles Kuhlman, following up in 1955 with the Russian set, and in 1967 with Polydor's *La Chauve-Souris* from France, featuring a fine pairing of André Mallabrera and Nicole Broissin, and a Hungarian Qualiton set (*Denever*) with Tibor Udvardy and Karola Agay. The only English disc is a Sadler's Wells selection from 1959 with Victoria Elliott, Alexander Young and Marion Studholme featured.

Unless you have a particular wish for a translated *Fledermaus* (and I cannot see why anyone should), the very fine best of the original-language discs – the textless 1950 Decca version (which would be a much better bet for them on CD than their most recent one), EMI's early Schwarzkopf–Gedda set or their most recent pair of Domingo discs with all its extravagant extras (both already on CD) – should, according to taste, give you all you could ever want in the way of a *Fledermaus*.

Der Zigeunerbaron

After *Die Fledermaus*, the most generally popular of Strauss's stage works is *Der Zigeunerbaron* (*The Gipsy Baron*), a deliciously melodious mishmash of romance, comedy, treasure-hunting, gipsies, petty politics and pig-farming, which, shed of its harum scarum plot, makes up into a particularly fine recording of quite a different character to the frothy, Frenchified comedy of *Die Fledermaus* – a strong red wine to the champagne of the earlier piece. The score, in line with its heterogeneous story, mixes the lushly almost-operatic with Hungarian gipsy strains, bubbling waltzes and full-blooded choruses, and is full of memorable numbers, ranging from the comic-heroic waltz melody of the hero's well-known 'Als flotter Geist' (you may think you don't know it, but wait till you hear the tune) to the striking soprano gipsy song 'Habet Acht!', the gentle, charming little Dompfaff love duet 'Wer uns getraut' (recognizable to the profane as 'One Day When We Were Young'), the ringing baritone Recruitment Song and the lovely waltz 'So voll Frölichkeit'.

Although it has received less recording attention than its famous brother work, *Der Zigeunerbaron* has nevertheless been given more regard than almost any other operetta, to the extent of nine full-scale recordings (one in Russian) as well as a wide-ranging list of selections. Unfortunately the size of the score means that, even taking in little or no linking dialogue, it has been, until the advent of the compact disc at least, necessary to omit a good half an additional side of music to fit it on two records. It is the lesser characters' music that usually gets the hook: Mirabella's 'Just sind er vierundzwanzig Jahre', her Morality Commission duo with Carnero, Arsena's 'Ein Mädchen hat es gar nicht gut' and the third-act opening chorus leading up to it, but other pieces are more or less tactfully slimmed from time to time.

Like *Die Fledermaus*, *Der Zigeunerbaron* received its first double-disc treatment from Decca in a 1951 set with Patzak featured in the heroic tenor title rôle of Sándor Barinkay, Hilde Zadek as his soprano gipsy baroness and Kurt Preger at the head of the comedy as the pig-farmer Zsupán. Four years later, Columbia-EMI (Gedda/Schwarzkopf/Kunz) and Philips (Kmentt/Scheyrer/Preger) put out rival recordings. Capitol-EMI followed in 1958 with Karl Terkal, Hilde Güden and Kunz starring, while Ariola-Eurodisc (1965) paired resident tenor Rudolf Schock with Erszébet Házy and Benno Kusche. In the 1970s the so-called Grosses-Operetten Ensemble with Martin Ritzmann and Elisabeth Ebert were recorded on the Fontana label, and EMI subsequently issued two further recordings, one with Gedda again, this time sharing the billing with Grace Bumbry and Kurt Böhme, and in 1987 the most recent of *Zigeunerbaron*s, featuring Josef Protschka, Julia Varady and Walter Berry.

I have never been able to find copies of the earliest Decca and Philips recordings – a shame, as I would like to hear Patzak's Barinkay, if nothing else – but I am happy to say that their relative scarcity seems to be due to the fact that the excellent Columbia-EMI set with Gedda and Schwarzkopf, conducted by Otto Ackermann, simply sent them scurrying into oblivion.

It is not difficult to see why. In every department this *Zigeunerbaron* is quite splendid. The Philharmonia Orchestra and Chorus are in fine form, attacking the gipsy music with plenty of fire and the lyrical moments with due soulfulness, on a recording that puts the passion and colour of the show before the comic content. Gedda's glorious tenor is suited superbly to the rôle of Barinkay. He doesn't – as some Barinkays do – barge his way bullock-like through the big singing moments in the manner of an ambitious baritone, but soars along on top of the music with all the graceful bravado of the well-bred mountebank that the 'gipsy baron' is. His big solo 'Als flotter Geist' is performed with plenty of personality in the comic verses and with beautiful flowing tone in the waltz chorus – here is a man who can actually be flamboyant and elegant at the same time. His reaction to his first meeting with Arsena is unmodified rapture, his part in the Bullfinch Duet delicately lyrical and his blending with the soprano and mezzo in the tripping Treasure Waltz and Trio faultless. It is a classy and lovely performance.

I never saw Schwarzkopf in the theatre, but I have always thought of her as a very beautiful lady – Marschallin, Rosalinde, Hanna Glawari, Lisa – not quite the passionate gipsy-cum-Pasha's daughter of *Der Zigeunerbaron*. But this recording shows you what a really consummate artist can do even with a rôle that mightn't be the most obvious for her. Saffi's showpiece solo, the demanding, driving, awkwardly lying csárdás 'Habet Acht', is magnificently done – perfectly paced and majestically sung, with richly ringing sounds in the much solicited upper register where too many performers manage only shrill shrieks. But, impressive though this is, Schwarzkopf is always at her best when she turns on that meltingly lovely tone of voice which was her speciality and, in moments like the soaring Bullfinch (Dompfaff) Duet, she can give you those little spinal tingles that mean 'extra special'.

The character rôles on this recording are performed with more restraint than is normal, particularly in the theatre. The part of pig-farmer Zsupán, writ large for star comic Girardi, is sung characterfully but without the usual walloping vulgarity by Erich Kunz, while the old gipsy Czipra, instead of being made into a cackling crone, gets an almost straight performance from the very attractive sounding mezzo-contralto Gertrud Burgsthaler-Schuster. It is perhaps habit that makes me look for just a touch more of the traditional comedy buffo in Zsupán – there is no reason for him to be a grunting grotesque.

The supporting rôles are very well taken. Erika Köth is a lovely young Arsena who makes an impression from the first moments of her entrance song and she is prettily paired with the equally young-sounding Josef Schmidinger as her beloved Ottokar. Hermann Prey (Homonay) gives a masculine and martial ring to his Recruiting Song, Willy Ferenz is the sonorous rather than comical Carnero and Monica Sinclair is wasted in what is left of the sung part of the rôle of Mirabella (the spoken lines being done by the former operetta diva Lea Seidl). Every member of the well-chosen cast contributes to what is a very superior and desirable recording.

The Capitol *Zigeunerbaron*, accompanied by Heinrich Hollreiser and the Vienna Philharmonic, is another highly enjoyable recording if not, perhaps, one which reaches out and grabs you. Of the performances, I particularly like Karl Terkal's Barinkay, accurately sung with a vigorous flair but without histrionics, saving the really big singing for such dramatic moments as the discovery of the treasure ('Ha, der Schatz!'). Hilde Güden's Saffi also avoids excesses of passion, her 'Habet Acht' being less dashing than some, but she comes into her own in the lyrical passages of the king-size first-act finale (CD at last permits us to have this finale in one piece without having to change records) and in the second-act duets with Terkal.

Anneliese Rothenberger sings beautifully as Arsena, though she does not have the contrasting girlish tones Köth produces, and she is happily partnered by Kurt Esquiluz (Ottokar). Erich Kunz repeats his unexaggerated Zsupán and Hilde Rössl-Majdan sings Czipra's music with a smoothly attractive mezzo-soprano that fits well with Terkal and Güden in their second-act trio. These performances are in the same vein as those of the two leading players – long on finely controlled and on-the-button singing, a little shorter on showiness.

Although everyone on it performs correctly, the Ariola-Eurodisc recording doesn't have the same class as either of the previous two recordings. Schock attacks 'Als flotter Geist' like a party piece and carries on from there in the same vein; the jam he lays on so thickly unfortunately also has one or two pips in it, particularly when he approaches the upper reaches. Erszébet Házy is a rather hectic Saffi and Benno Kusche comes out by far the best on this set as a very jolly Zsupán.

The Fontana set and the Gedda/Bumbry version have proved to be as difficult to locate nowadays as the earliest *Zigeunerbaron*s, but in the current EMI *Zigeunerbaron* we have a version that has all the most up-to-date advantages: a triple digital, custom-made for CD recording with a breadth of design which allows almost all of the score to be included. This time we have Mirabella's delightful first-act saga of her escape from the embraces of a Turkish Pasha, which is such fun that you wonder why on earth it kept getting left off in tighter days. If the same doesn't go for Arsena's lyrically limp final number, it is still nice to have the chance to hear it. Only the Carnero/Mirabella Morality Commission number is still omitted; it is sad, since there appears to be plenty of space on CD number two at least, that it could not have been included if just for completeness' sake. There is some dialogue – not too much, and not very elegant – but it clarifies the story very efficiently, particularly with the help of a much better translation than usual.

The performance of the piece is respectful. There is a lot of beautiful playing from the Munich Radio Orchestra and very choral singing from the Bavarian Radio Chorus but, under Willi Boskovsky's experienced hand, surprisingly little 'oomph'. The singers can virtually all be covered by this same comment. They make some glorious noises in their music, technically and vocally admirable, but this is a set (and I don't think digital sound is to blame) where atmosphere, acting and passion are not in evidence.

Julia Varady's Saffi is the principal example. She makes a clear, rich and very legato sound, impressively accurate in the most difficult bits of a 'Habet Acht', which hasn't an ounce of temperament in it. She comes into her own in the lyrical moments – the Dompfaff Duet and the Treasure Trio – but she is never a gipsy or a Pasha's daughter. Her Barinkay, Josef Protschka, is in the same league, his attractive tenor flowing through the lyrical moments and occasionally opening up a little, but for the most an unheroic hero.

There is particularly lovely singing from the other women – Hanna Schwarz as a very young-sounding mezzo Czipra with a strong top, Ilse Gramatzki making Mirabella's music sound quite beautiful if not very funny, and Brigitte Lindner as a fresh, creamy Arsena, but without any of the gay brilliance of an Erika Köth. It really sounds as if this dignified style has been purposely imposed. The men do a little more. Fischer-Dieskau puts some energy into the Recruiting Song – it is almost impossible not to – and Martin Finke shows his usual liveliness as Ottokar, but Walter Berry's Zsupán mistakes some hefty, emphatic playing for comedy. If I make this recording sound unattractive, I should hastily add that it is not; it is just that, in the image of a chorus which sings 'Freuet euch' (Rejoice!) like an invitation to tea, it is not very exciting.

The two *Gypsy Baron* recordings in English are both excerpts discs, a necessarily short American one as part of the twelve-disc Reader's Digest set (William Lewis/Jeannette Scovotti), and a larger one by the Sadler's Wells company which performed Geoffrey Dunn's translation in 1964. 'Larger' is relative here, for Derek Hammond-Stroud's Zsupán unfortunately doesn't get a look in, and it is a really dashing Nigel Douglas (Barinkay), June Bronhill (Saffi) and the chorus who are the most prominently displayed. All three are in top form, singing gloriously, although Bronhill's brilliant vocal quality and style are surely more suited to Arsena than to the darker gypsy music. As it happens, Jennifer Eddy is delicious in the little bit of Arsena's rôle that is heard and Ann Howard (Czipra) and James Hawthorne, singing Homonay's Song without the often prevalent 'woofiness', keep up the general level in a very fine, if extremely English, performance.

There are four oldish French *Baron Tzigane* recordings, but all are now rare enough that I have not been able to find them. Tibor Udvardy and Erzsébet Házy have recorded a selection in Hungarian, but the most substantial foreign-language recording is the two-disc Russian Melodiya set, another which is not easily come by but which, going by the usual high vocal standards of the label and given the very suitable style of the gipsy material to Russian performance, should be a particularly interesting one.

It is odd that when, over the years, I have succeeded in locating and listening to so many musical theatre recordings, including many which are very rarely found, that my *Der Zigeunerbaron* collection should have such gaps in it. But I cannot repine too much, for the old EMI set is so enjoyable that I cannot really mind doing without any or all of the other eight.

Eine Nacht in Venedig

Unlike the two top Strauss works, *Eine Nacht in Venedig* has had a rocky career through its nevertheless continual stream of productions over the years. Its original libretto came in for much criticism and it was subsequently rearranged and rewritten by so many different 'improving' hands that to attempt now to say what is the 'real' *Eine Nacht in Venedig* is a bit hopeless. Certainly none of the adaptations I have encountered seem to be much, if any, of an advance on the original book.

From a recording point of view this would not matter very much had not these adaptors, notably Erich Korngold (who was something of a specialist at doing over other people's music), also decided on improving and rearranging the much-loved score. The most far-reaching alteration was the switch of the focus of the piece away from the Figaro-like comedy rôle of Caramello (played in Vienna by Girardi) to the benefit of the principal tenor, the mashing Duke of Urbino (created in Korngold's version by Tauber), by padding his part with one pilfered soprano melody and with a second solo fabricated from music taken from another Strauss operetta. These two romantic bon-bons ('Sei mir gegrüsst, du holdes Venezia!' and 'Treu sein – das liegt mir nicht'), needless to say, made the Duke's rôle more attractive to star tenors and thus encouraged both the survival of the work and its repeated recording.

The first substantial (but not musically complete) recording of *Eine Nacht in Venedig* was made for LP by participants in the 1951 Bregenz Festival production of *Der Zigeunerbaron* under Anton Paulik. It did not use the Korngold adaptation, and listening to it does rather lend weight to the arguments in favour of popping a couple of showy solos into the score. The jolly quartet 'Alle maskiert', the pretty 'Ninana', the catchy Carnival March, the comic's serenade 'Komm in die Gondel' and the sweet soprano sounds of 'Die Tauben von San Marco' make up the most enjoyable part of a score which needs more help than the popular Lagunen-Walzer alone can give to come anywhere near *Die Fledermaus* or *Der Zigeunerbaron* in appeal. Unfortunately, this well-meant recording is simply dull. The cast, all with competent voices, seem to find little enjoyment in the score, and it remains of interest only as the most substantial generally available recording of the version of *Eine Nacht in Venedig* as played during the first forty years of its existence.

The other, less common, recordings which follow, in varying degrees, the pre-Korngold *Eine Nacht in Venedig* are a transfer of a 1938 German radio broadcast and a 1976 CBS set which, like most recordings which trumpet that they are 'the first recording of the original version', is anything but.

Korngold's version, or variations of it, has been the subject of two full recordings, both on EMI. The first, recorded on HMV, dates from 1954, the second from 1968, and both feature Nicolai Gedda as the Duke. The first of these has a fine, starry cast which includes Schwarzkopf (Annina), Emmy Loose (Ciboletta) and Kunz as a baritone Caramello. It incorporates a small amount of dialogue, enough just to keep the wobbly wheels of the plot turning, and, although basically Korngold musically, it makes, probably on account of its casting, some notable alterations to his standard score. Firstly, Kunz, who has to take the key of the Lagunen-Walzer down, gives up 'Komm in die Gondel' to Gedda. This makes total nonsense of the plot, but the plot in *Eine Nacht in Venedig*, it has to be agreed, has been made sufficient nonsense of already as to deserve minimal consideration. For once, I counsel, just listen to the music.

Gedda, having hogged 'Komm in die Gondel' and won 'Sie mir gegrüsst', himself gives up 'Treu sein', which goes back to being a soprano song and gets re-added to Schwarzkopf's rôle, which makes up for the fact that she has, thanks to Korngold, lost her Act 3 song. Since 'Was mir der Zufall gab' sounds better sung by a soprano than by a tenor, this is a gain. I am not so sure about a rich, baritone Lagunen-Walzer, though. It doesn't soar along in quite the same fashion even with Kunz at the wheel. Otherwise, what you get here is what has mostly been played in the theatre for the last half-century.

The star of the recording, without question, is Schwarzkopf. After turning herself surprisingly successfully into a lusty gipsy for *Zigeunerbaron* she now, whole-heartedly and both vocally and dramatically, becomes perky, bristling little Annina the Venetian fish-seller. In a rôle that hardly ever gives the voice a moment to linger gloriously in the best Schwarzkopfian manner, she pulls out a whole other bank of artillery, clipping her way briskly, laughingly through her entrance number as she cries her wares – 'Frutti di mare!' – and keeping a gay glitter in her voice as she vamps her way saucily through the second act, whether whispering out her line in 'Ninana' or letting rip in 'Was mir der Zufall gab'. It is both a great piece of singing and a great piece of vocal characterization.

Kunz ought to be fine for Caramello. He has the light-heartedness needed for the rôle, but surprisingly not the range so, in the end, he is a little disappointing. On the other hand, both Gedda and Loose are first rate. Gedda is fresh and unforced in his singing and suitably cavalier in his style, and Loose is such a pretty soubrette that one longs to hear more of her. Peter Klein is an acceptable Pappacoda and Hanna Ludwig sings the little contralto piece given to one of the senators' wives at the opening of the second act well, but Karl Dönch makes Senator Delacqua into a hundred-year-old idiot, which seems unlikely. On the orchestral side, all goes along as would seem intended . . . though, as with everything about this work, I'm not quite sure what is or was intended.

The EMI-Electrola set also uses the Marischka/Korngold adaptation as the basis for an adaptation of its own. The Duke (Gedda) has both his arias, but gives 'Komm in die Gondel' back to the tenor Caramello (Cesare Curzi) and, instead, apparently reclaims the Lagunen-Walzer (which was originally his in *Venedig* Mark very number one) and gets a half-share in an interpolated duet. Annina (Rita Streich) loses 'Was mir der Zufall gab' and gets nothing in return, because the recording has been stuffed full of extraneous numbers for the once tiny rôle of Enrico and the practically non-existent one of senator's wife Constantia Testuccio, which have been beefed up to allow Hermann Prey and Anneliese Rothenberger to be included.

The songs 'Stadt der Liebe, Stadt der Freuden' and 'In Hispaniens heissem Sonnenland' (here become 'Italy's sunny land' instead of 'Spain's', although the castanets remain in the accompaniment), from the Strauss pasticcio *Casanova*, and 'Die Karneval heut' die Stunde regiert', from *Karneval in Rom*, are more than sufficient to make Prey's rôle ringingly prominent, whilst Rothenberger gets the other half-share (with Gedda) in the *Casanova* duet 'Ich hab' dich lieb' and a song from the same piece, 'Sul mare luccica'. The result of all this interpolating is a recording of a sort of *Eine Nacht in Venedig/Casanova* hybrid which is, frankly, a lot more fun than the other versions.

Franz Allers and the Graunke Symphony are full of vivacity and sparkle, and the soloists give their all to what, with its basketful of added bon-bons, becomes something like a Johann Strauss all-star pop concert. If there is no single performance that arouses the admiration due to Schwarzkopf's Annina on the earlier set, the general level of singing and playing is of an even high standard and bristles with an energy which sweeps you along very happily.

Curzi's Caramello displays immediately how much better the part works when sung by a tenor. He is bright and incisive, light and flippant, without ever losing vocal quality, and his 'Komm in die Gondel' rings out with splendidly comic over-heroics and unnecessary top notes. Gedda's Duke is in his 'later' style – less pure and fresh, more characterful and, in this case, more attractively raffish than his earlier version; his performance of 'Treu sein' is so fetching as almost to make me reverse my feelings about the number being more suitable for a woman's voice. Prey's interpolated numbers are dashingly delivered in an enjoyably dark baritone – a voice which rarely gets a really good sing in works of this kind – that contrasts agreeably with the higher and less chesty tones of Hans-Günther Grimm as a properly baritonal Pappacoda. Rita Streich sings with a fluid accuracy as Annina – the voice and style are quite impeccable although you miss something of the light-hearted fun of the madcap fishergirl – but there is plenty of liveliness in Christine Görner's happy, bright Ciboletta. Rothenberger has to take a supporting place to Gedda in what is a very tenor-orientated duet, but she sings her *Casanova* song well enough, if not perhaps her very best. All in all, it is a jolly, swinging recording of a version which has just as much right to call itself *Eine Nacht in Venedig* as any of the others.

The usual range of selection discs include one, on EMI-Electrola, that features Fritz Wunderlich and Rudolf Schock. Another pairs Schock, as Caramello, with Curzi taking a turn as the Duke to equally good effect as he did previously with the comic rôle. But, putting aside any consideration of coherence – and the exerpts discs obviously have little – the happy spirits and good singing of the *Eine Nacht in Venedig/Casanova* mélange still come out on top.

Eine Nacht in Venedig has not had a lot of attention outside Austria and Germany, and the only foreign-language discs of which I know are in English or, more specifically, in American. A vast spectacle was built around a version of *A Night in Venice* at the Jones Beach Marine Theatre in 1952 and some of the resulting score put on to disc by Everest. It is a fairly horrid affair, with the story and characters muddled about into a much worse mess than they were before, the score needlessly fiddled with, some very average lyrics, and a lot of hearty singing and heavily-accented, by-numbers acting in fragments of linking material of the 'oh look, here comes the Duke' kind. The sleeve notes are of the type where everyone and everything is 'the foremost' or 'unequalled', and the very ordinary sound is claimed to be 'revolutionary'. It has too much hype and not enough delivery. Unfortunately there is little more joy for anyone intent on an English-language *A Night in Venice* in the shorter selection included in the Readers' Digest boxed set. Its nine numbers are again a hashed-up affair in stilted English, often strenuously (the tenors) or even drearily sung, and a lively Cibroletta (*sic*) from Jeanette Scovotti and some intermittently bright conducting cannot compensate.

Der lustige Krieg

For pure pleasure, I must admit that I would much rather listen to (and hopefully, one day, see) *Der lustige Krieg* in preference to the same authorial team's *Eine Nacht in Venedig*. Nineteenth-century theatre-goers felt the same, and this delightfully cock-eyed Ruritanian comic operetta was played regularly for many years while the later piece was largely ignored. Its score has no obvious flavouring like the Venetian tints of *Eine Nacht*, the gipsy strains of *Zigeunerbaron* or the champagne taste of *Fledermaus*; it is simply a glittering piece of light, comic musical theatre full of delightfully bright rhythms and gliding melodies, and including some of Strauss's prettiest and undeservedly little-known numbers.

The charming scene of the little Dutch lady bewailing her fate at having strayed into a war and lost her husband on the way, to the accompaniment of Strauss's lovely music for 'Durch Wald und Feld'; her duet with her silly husband, wondering touchingly when they will ever escape from this farrago and see their children again ('Zwei Monat sind es schon'); the glittering and tuneful soprano music lavished on the jaunty leading lady's rôle – the coloratura polka 'Für dieses Kriegeszugs Wohl und Wehe bring' ich die schwersten Opfer doch' and the march strains of 'Es war ein lustig Abenteuer'- and the show's comic-tenor hit tune 'Nur für Natur' are all marvellous moments.

Sadly, the piece has not ranked high in the recording popularity stakes and, apart from an elderly, rare and tempting selection on Philips which I do not have, only one recording exists. Originally put out on Vox, it turned up some years later on a disc issued on the Summit label by a firm called CMS Records of New York. It was clad in a sleeve which credited none of the artists but simply called them the Operetta Ensemble of the City Theater, Salzburg; listed a selection of numbers which bore little relation to what was on the disc; and paraded some half-cocked notes (plus one of the most irrelevant and ugly covers about) and a warning forbidding reproduction of the disc FOR ANY REASON WHATSOEVER without the express permission of Mr Louis C. Duncan. There has to be a story in all that somewhere, but, whatever it may be, at least there is, as a result, a reasonable recording of *Der lustige Krieg* generally available.

The disc contains eleven of the show's twenty musical numbers (some slimmed) plus an entr'acte, with the songs for the Violetta (Elisabeth Roon), Balthasar Groot (Georg Oeggl) and Else (Gerda Scheyrer) getting most prominence. Roon flings herself bravely and fairly successfully into the considerable vocalizing perils of the prima donna rôle, Oeggl is suitably lugubriously baritonal as the gormless Dutchman, and the famous 'Nur für Natur' gets a sweeping waltz treatment from Rudi Kreuzberger (Sebastiani), but the honours go to Scheyrer, who spins out her 'Durch Wald und Feld' quite beautifully. The performance in general isn't out of the very top drawer, but it is good enough to allow you to enjoy a reasonable selection from a lovely score.

Karneval in Rom

I'm not well enough acquainted with the original score of Strauss's early work *Karneval in Rom* to know how much of it has been included as it was originally written on the RCA transfer from a 1950 German radio broadcast. The sleeve admits that Franz Marszalek's 1936–7 version, conducted here by the adapter, fabricated the big duet 'Wenn der Nachtwind rauscht' and the heroine's solo 'O wie ist das Leben schön' from Strauss themes, but tells us no more. Whatever the truth is, the recording is a very enjoyable pot-pourri of lively melodies finely sung. You even get a shock touch of the reverse of the usual borrowing process when the impressive duet 'Wieviel Frau'n hast du geküsst' turns out to be the original of one of the most beautiful Johann Strauss II themes reused by Oscar Straus in *Drei Walzer*.

This duet is probably the outstanding piece of the score, and it gets thoroughly sung by the very appreciable Liselotte Losch and by Peter Anders, but there is a recordful of wholly enjoyable bright numbers, including some tripping, light-hearted ones for the delightful soubrette Ruth Zillger and her happy partner Willy Hoffman, before everyone ends up celebrating carnival to what sounds like the strains of a can-can.

The recording is a slightly awkward one in that it is untracked and the numbers follow on one behind the other without pause for breath. Particularly when a series of sung scenes, rather than songs, occurs this really makes separation difficult unless you are listening very hard. Still, this is a minor quibble over a recording which is finely done, historically interesting and very pleasant listening.

More Strauss

Unfortunately, the same cannot be said for the 1986 cast recording of a selection from a version of *Cagliostro in Wien*. This time the 'bearbeitung' – that warning word in the credits that tells you someone has been having a go at the book and even the score – has got out of hand and the show is a thin, would-be-modern travesty of Straussian remnants, sort of sung by a group of people, most of whom sound like leftovers from the auditions for the chorus of *Hair*. Maybe there was a point in this exercise in the theatre, but there seems none in putting it on record unless to allow the adapter to have four photos of himself conducting plastered down the middle of the cover. For a taste of *Cagliostro* it is a matter of tracking down the elusive Philips disc which this work shares with *Der lustige Krieg*.

A glimpse of the eminently successful *Das Spitzentuch des Königin* – long a favourite in America as *The Queen's Lace Handkerchief* – is even harder to get. You might find the odd track, such as Heinz Hoppe's version of 'Du Märchenstadt in Donautel', on a recital record, and the melodies of 'Stets kommt mir wieder in den Sinn' and 'Wo die wilde Rosen erblüht' are now well known (with no small thanks to the BBC) as part of the celebrated waltz 'Roses from the South'. As for *Prinz Methusalem, Simplicius, Fürstin Ninetta* and the others, only by a diligent dissection of the pasticcio Strauss operettas concocted by others will you find their traces.

1001 Nacht

Indigo und die vierzig Räuber, Strauss's first work, does the best in this kind of musical hide-and-seeking as, stripped of the Ali Baba story around which it was created, much of its score was pasted on to another Arabian Nights tale under the title *1001 Nacht*. The resultant operetta, produced in 1906, has been played in recent decades, recorded, and issued on Urania and Classics Club both in a two-disc set and a single excerpts record.

I have only heard the excerpts disc, which, I assume, contains the best bits of the show, and it shows up a pleasant rather than a remarkable score with only one big featured solo – the tenor waltz 'Nun lachst du mir wieder, du flüchtiges Gluck' – and a number of attractive ensembles. The first-act finale includes the hit of the original show, 'Ja, so singt man in der Stadt wo ich geboren', sung by the soubrette, and the second act ends with a flow of billowing melody that carries the dream sequence which makes up the body of the show into its epilogue.

The performance is only fair. Most of the cast seem to be infected with the quivers, particularly the insecure leading lady, Ilse Mentzel, but also the unsteady soubrette, Rosl Seegers, and the comic tenor, Adi Appelt, who sometimes shakes himself right off the note. The bulk of the big music, however, falls on the hero of the piece in a double rôle of *Prisoner of Zenda* proportions as both Prince and fisherman. Herbert Ernst Groh does some stirring singing, which doesn't become strenuous too often, making the most of his waltz song, but he is afflicted by the predilection of the cast as a whole for soap opera acting. It is not entirely his fault: if he had had to gasp 'Leila!' throatily one more time, there would not have been another tone left in which to do it.

Strauss by Other Hands

Of the barrowful of Strauss pasticcios that have been trundled out over the years, it is undoubtedly the fictionalized biography *Walzer aus Wien* (1930), with its Korngold-Strauss score, which has won the most success world-wide. A staple of the repertoire in France (*Valses de Vienne*), it has been the subject of half a dozen French-language recordings, while in English it has had stage and film success in varying versions as *The Great Waltz* and *Waltzes from Vienna*. However, in Austria and Germany there has always been a marked preference over this piece for the 1899 *Wiener Blut*, which is played and recorded liberally there while being largely ignored overseas. Italy has shown her preference over both these for the 1934 *Die Tänzerin Fanny Elssler*, which has surfaced on disc in a short selection on the treasure trove of an RAI (EDM) series, but the best-known single number comes from yet another 'scissors and paste' job, the 1928 *Casanova* with its celebrated and well-recorded Nun's Chorus. None of these compilations is the equal of the marvellous *Drei Walzer*, but Strauss Jr can claim only the music for one act of this 1935 piece, the other two acts being made up of selections from Strauss Sr (Act 1) and original material by the *éminence grise* of the affair, Oscar Straus.

Wiener Blut

The most substantially recorded of these pasticcio works is clearly *Wiener Blut*, which has, amazingly, been the subject of no less than five double-disc recordings, and a large armful of selections. I say 'amazingly' because it is a piece which does not appeal to me at all. As with many manufactured musicals, it lacks character and identity. The score is a sort of wishy-washy Strauss purée which, when it finds an effective tune, is inclined to bring it back once too often; elsewhere it wanders along in repetitive dance-time through its routine story of mistaken identity and sexual musical beds, only occasionally coming to effective musical life in such pieces as the title waltz.

There have been recordings with Rita Streich (Urania), Schock and Hilde Güden (Ariola-Eurodisc), and a recent one from the live-performance series made by the Vienna Volksoper in Japan with Adolf Dallapozza and Sigrid Martikke featured. EMI has, again, two sets to its credit, both with Nicolai Gedda in the lead tenor rôle as yet another philandering count. The first, from 1954, is an odd effort covering three sides and including some dialogue but omitting a half-dozen of the lesser musical numbers. It is performed under Otto Ackermann's baton in a very cultured way, and Elisabeth Schwarzkopf (Gabriele), Erika Köth (Franzi) and Emmy Loose (Pepi) are well contrasted as the three women in the Count's life alongside a Gedda in impeccable voice. It does, however, rather lack the vigour needed to lift these arrangements into a more interesting listen.

The later 1976 set, conducted by Willi Boskovsky and pairing Gedda with the flowing Anneliese Rothenberger, the now rather rich soubrette voice of Renate Holm and the charming lighter soprano of Gabriele Fuchs, is perhaps less perfect in terms of pure vocal quality but it does have much more that feeling of attack. It also puts back the numbers not used in the earlier set and enough extra dialogue to make up a full four sides.

Walzer aus Wien

Walzer aus Wien has been sufficiently more obviously put together than *Wiener Blut* to include the 'Blue Danube' waltz and the Radetzky March prominently in the musical mincemeat used for its score. It has a much more straightforward appeal than the earlier piece, an appeal which is quite simply helped by the appearance of these familiar melodies and also such gems as, in prelude to Act 2, the waltz melody used for Yvonne Printemps's big solo 'Te souvient-il' in *Drei Walzer*. *Walzer aus Wien* is apparently unrecorded as such in its original German, but it has been recorded liberally in France in the variant version that is still popular on the French provincial circuits.

EMI put out a two-disc set of *Valses de Vienne*, music and linking dialogue, in 1972. Bernard Sinclair is an all-stops-out romantic high baritone Strauss, Mady Mesplé a sparky soprano girlfriend Rési and Christiane Stutzmann a lusty, tuppence-coloured Countess Olga (the 'other woman'), who joins Sinclair throb for throb in the show's big duet 'Une fée a passé'. There is also a particularly enjoyable comedy couple in Arta Verlen (Pépi) and Philippe Gaudin (Léopold). It is an agreeable enough set, but the various selection discs which have been put out manage to take in most of the score (including sometimes the additional number 'Quand l'amour nous ensorcelle'), and the most successful of these, those from Pathé-Marconi (1957) and RCA Victor (1963), feature notable casts.

The Pathé disc, regularly reissued, has Michel Dens as Strauss and Mado Robin, the coloratura soprano who held for many years the curious distinction of having sung the highest note recorded, as Rési. Both magnificent singers, they don't make an entirely comfortable pair. He is at his most operatic (which is not excessively) and she, with her very individual forward soprano tone, while dazzling in 'Tout est soleil', doesn't always sound as if she is in the same duet when it is time for a duet. The less striking but heftier soprano of Vivienne Barthelemy (Olga) matches more happily with Dens's baritone in 'Une fée a passé' and Michel Sénéchal (Léopold) and Huguette Boulangeot (Pépi) complete the team delightfully.

There is little to choose between this disc and the RCA one, which is rather less easy to find. The Strauss here is Gabriel Bacquier, singing richly and stylishly, and yet warm and gentle when required in the duets with his Rési, as played by the deliciously girlish sounding Janine Ervil with a piquancy and point (and without Mlle Robin's extra top note). Colette Riedinger who, like Ervil, had appeared in more than one Châtelet revival of the show, is ideally cast as the Countess, and Arlette Poirier, another Châtelet performer, is a very musical comedy Pépi on a fine recording which omits choruses and preludes and, in consequence, is able to include Rési's sometimes omitted solo 'Je ne suis plus de votre rang'.

Franz von Suppé

Die schöne Galathee

Suppé's continuously popular one-act burlesque operetta *Die schöne Galathee*, the first German-language work to make a significant international mark, is a natural for recording, as its delightful short score, full of both lyrical beauty and catchy comedy, makes up neatly into one short long-playing record. From the lovely overture, with its combination of varying rhythms, its picturesque dawn music and its superb principal waltz melody, through the comical posturings of the art critic ('Meinem Vater Gordios'), Pygmalion's mock-operatic prayer to Venus ('Zum Altar zieht die Schaar') and the resulting awakening of an *opéra-bouffe* statue with a taste for coloratura ('Was sagst du!'), a topical Greek number ('Wir Griechen'), a tipsy Offenbachian drinking song ('Hell im Glas'), a splendid Jewel Trio ('Seht den Schmuck') and Galatea's tunefully amorous attack on young Ganymede ('Ach mich zieht's zu dir') up to the tiny finale, every number is happily melodious and amusing.

Over the years, endless attempts have been made to 'improve' the show either to spread it into a full evening's entertainment, to swell one rôle or another into a star vehicle, or simply to alter the humour to someone's contemporary idea of what is funny. Evidence of such tampering can be seen on the Telefunken recording in the Goldene Operette series, where a certain Herbert Küster has not only had a go at the lyrics, but also fabricated new numbers. The results are, in any case, sung by some fairly mediocre singers and, as there are other recordings which deliver the show attractively in something more or less like its original condition, this one can safely be disregarded.

The 1977 RCA recording not only gives the best representation of the show's text, it also has the advantages of good singing and a comic operatic burlesque spirit. The casting of the very substantial voices of tenor René Kollo (Pygmalion) and soprano Anna Moffo (Galatea), both of whom join in the fun of the piece with a will, helps the essential burlesque nature of the piece and, as they are supported by the lively Ferry Gruber as the art critic and Rose Wagemann as a purposeful, bouncy mezzo boy servant, the music is all well served – the Jewel Trio, the Drinking Song and the final Love Duet being particularly successful.

It is shame that the 1976 Saga recording, which also takes in the full score and nothing but the score, is not so faithful to the composer's intentions elsewhere. A bass has no business singing the mezzo-soprano rôle. This alteration upsets the flavour of the score as a whole and, most particularly, the entire vocal construction of the three ensemble pieces that build up to the show's climax: the Jewel Trio, the Drinking Song and the Kiss Duet. Elisabeth Roon, with a much lighter voice than Moffo, scatters coloratura coquettishly all over her vigorous Pygmalion (Kurt Preger) who, in spite of what the sleeve says, certainly doesn't sound much like a baritone, and their big duet comes off very successfully, but then on comes that wretched basso Ganymede and ruins everything.

A second RCA disc was issued in 1979, apparently taken from a Cologne radio broadcast. No one but Suppé and his lyricist are given credits, but someone has again been fiddling with the words and the opening chorus and Ganymede's first solo, 'Zieht in Frieden', have been curiously pushed into the middle of the show. Although the musical numbers otherwise remain more or less in the right order, spaced out with considerable dialogue, and the Drinking Trio, Galatea's romance and 'Hinaus! O weh!' have at least kept their titles, 'Meinem Vater Gordios' has been rechristened 'Bin der grösste Kunstmäzen', and the text of every other number revamped for modern times. Reinhold Bartel and Renate Holm sing well in the principal parts, and Ferry Gruber shifts across to the mezzo rôle of Ganymede, leaving Midas to the rather approximate Kurt Grosskurth.

Boccaccio

Boccaccio has suffered much less from the hands of 'improvers' than *Die schöne Galathee*, but, over the years, it has been what one can only call rather operaticized. There have, in fact, been several attempts to perform *Boccaccio* in all-out operatic style, and a version of the piece patched up with bits of other Suppé works was even staged in 1931 at the Metropolitan Opera House. Admittedly *Boccaccio* is not as consistently gay and frothy in its music as the *opéras-bouffes* of Offenbach and Hervé, or even *Die schöne Galathee*. There are plenty of occasions, particularly in the least lively opening act, when the composer takes on more of the more formal tones of Rossini or Mozart comic opera than of the joyously frivolous French masters or, indeed, of Viennese popular music. But when he bursts into the joyous waltz measures of the third-act duet 'Florenz hat schöne Frauen' or the lovely Letter Trio ('Wonnevolle Kunde, neu belebend'), or skips along infectiously in the liveliest parts of his finales or the marvellous third-act March Septet ('Ihr Toren, ihr wollt hassen mich'), there is no doubt that you are in the presence of a master of the light musical theatre whose music needs to be performed with all the lightness and comic sense of operetta.

Another alteration that has become standard in this show is the infuriating switch of voices for the title rôle. Like Ganymede in *Die schöne Galathee*, the part of Boccaccio was conceived for a travesti (mezzo-)soprano. The music is written in consequence of this setting, and, as in Lecocq's *Le Petit Duc* (and all those other shows where I have made the same bitter complaint) in which similar ravages have been wrought, it is quite wrong and even unpleasant to have the young hero's vocal range replaced by a baritone or a tenor. Such a substitution means that duets intended for two female voices are given a different texture, with vocal lines which fit together less attractively, and a trio for one female and two male voices becomes instead a grumbly all-male affair. Brightness, lightness, and the sense of comicality which travesti casting always adds to a piece are all diminished. Unfortunately, all three principal recordings of *Boccaccio*, including the only existing two-disc set on EMI-Electrola, choose to go with a male star, so it is a case of making do with the best of not really genuine *Boccaccio*s.

The 1975 EMI set, conducted by Willi Boskovsky, is a first-rate recording, even if it lingers on the verge of being culpable on the 'operatic' side. The cast gathered together is a superb one, full of well-loved stars such as Hermann Prey (Boccaccio), Anneliese Rothenberger (Fiametta), Walter Berry (Leonetto), Kurt Böhme (Scalza), Edda Moser (Beatrice) and Adolf Dallapozza (Lotteringhi). Each and every one of them is in such impeccably beautiful voice that is seems churlish to long for a touch more of the *jeune fille* in Rothenberger's Fiametta, and even just a little more lightness from Prey, from Moser and, in particular, from the Bavarian State Opera Chorus and Symphony Orchestra, both of which sound so vast and so operatic (the chorus do 'gasp' acting in unison) that some of the spirit and fun in the choral music is inevitably crowded out.

On the credit side, however, the use of such fine singers adds vastly to the effect of the ensembles – Rothenberger, Moser and Gisela Litz, singing the Letter Trio, blend gloriously – and the long and large concerted finales get every ounce of musicality poured into their many-parted music. The lovely second-act serenade ('Ein Stern zu sein'), the charming duo 'Nur ein Wort' and the show's big tune 'Florenz hat schöne Frauen' are amongst the numbers which lose from being sung by the wrong sex, but, given that is how it must be in these sexually unimaginative times, they are splendidly done. Dallapozza's comical Cooper's Song ('Tagtäglich zankt mein Weib') with its ridiculous 'bumpti rapata' chorus is another highlight.

Boccaccio is in three acts, getting happier and happier as it bubbles along, but they are three substantial acts and the full score cannot be fitted onto two discs without wiping the potted dialogue that helpfully links the numbers. In consequence, this fairly complete recording omits several pieces, including the second-act 'Um die Spannung zu erhöh'n' and 'So oft man mich nach Neuem fragt' and the third-act opening, and makes cuts in others.

Much of the musical content of the EMI set has been reproduced on a single selection record. The principal losses here are the extended second-act finale, Lotteringhi's appealing first-act comic serenade and the delightful 'Ein Stern zu sein', which are sufficient to make it worthwhile to opt for the set, unless you are unsupportably bored by foreign-language dialogue. The other two main *Boccaccio*s are also one-record selections, one on Eurodisc with Rudolf Schock as a tenor Boccaccio and Renate Holm, the other on the Philips label with Waldemar Kmentt and Elisabeth Roon.

The second of these is the harder to find and the happier to listen to. It manages to fit a good amount of the score onto its one full and one less full side – omitting the same numbers as are left out of the two-record set plus 'Ein Stern zu sein' and Lambertuccio's 'Um des Fürsten Zorn zu meiden', but including the comedy serenade. Kmennt is a clear, masculine leading man who sings with style and without vulgarity and, if you have to have a male Boccaccio, this is the kind of performance that is most acceptable. Gerda Scheyrer is a punchy Beatrice and

Elisabeth Roon a pretty, unforced Fiametta, making the same happy contrast they did in the *Der lustige Krieg* recording. The comedy rôles are vigorously taken by a more than competent team in Kurt Preger, Kurt Esquiluz, Laszlo Szemere and Walter Berry.

Fatinitza

The general disappearance of Suppé's once popular *Fatinitza* is a sad loss judged by the one brief existing modern recording of some of its score. It isn't a recording that allows you to appreciate the music at leisure – a handful of numbers crammed onto a flimsy 45 EP on the Amiga label with a light, high and occasionally risky tenor in the title rôle (which was, once again, written for a female voice) sharing the forefront with a good comedy tenor and an under-used leading lady. But the lively march trio 'Vorwärts mit Frisches Mut', the pretty 'Silberglöcken rufen helle', the comic 'Ein bissel aufrischen' and the chattery harem girls' chorus combine to provide a varied and very attractive sampler of Suppé's score which makes you want to hear more.

Apart from those ubiquitous overtures, which also make you want to hear what came after them, the rest of Suppé's works have gone the same way as *Fatinitza* and, although I suspect that there is a Russian recording of *Donna Juanita* lurking somewhere (it apparently remains popular in Russia), they remain unrecorded.

Carl Millöcker

Der Bettelstudent

Carl Millöcker's *Der Bettelstudent* – a comic operetta with an intelligent and staunchly dramatic heart – followed its 1882 Vienna production by becoming a world-wide success and, if it is now less well known outside the German-speaking countries, it still remains a bulwark of the operetta repertoire there. Its score is a particularly enjoyable one, a string of delightful, dancing melodies, both lively and delicate, if perhaps not so immediately and obviously catchy as some other popular works, and including some particularly charming ensemble and part-writing. The proven gems include the classic 'Ach ich hab' sie nur auf die Schulter geküsst', in which the show's bass-baritone villain gets an unusual chance to launch into a rich waltz refrain, the tenor hero's lilting praise of Polish women ('Ich knüpfte manche zarte Bande'), and the principal lovers' lovely waltz duet ('Ich setz' den Fall'), but there is a whole panoply of other fine musical numbers, solo and ensemble, which makes *Der Bettelstudent*, even shorn of its top-class libretto, an ideal recording proposition.

The show is, indeed, well represented on record. There have been three virtually musically complete, two-record sets and some dozen larger or lesser selection records. The first double-disc recording was produced on the Amadeo label with the Vienna State Opera forces under Anton Paulik and featuring a cast including Kurt Preger, Eberhard Wächter, Rudolf Christ and Wilma Lipp. It is a splendidly played and well-sung recording with barely a musical hiccup from start to finish. Rudolf Christ (Symon) and Eberhard Wächter (Jan) as the beggar students present a tenor/baritone pairing instead of the usual two tenors, but they blend together beautifully and, with Christ producing an attractively strong, compact tone that spreads very little on the top, and Wächter a warm, smooth baritone that powers with minimal audible effort up to the top notes of the rôle, separately make a fine job of their solo music.

There is another untraditional (though by no means unprecedented) and highly successful bit of casting in the choice of tenor Kurt Preger instead of a richer voice as nasty Colonel Ollendorf. Preger gives us a sneeringly haughty Colonel, effectively squeezing his tenor tones into a nastily superior mode with great effect in his entrance waltz and going for oleaginous low comedy in later scenes. Wilma Lipp is an impeccable leading lady who sings clearly and expressively throughout her range, and she is ably seconded by Esther Réthy (Bronislawa). Karl Dönch avoids making the small but important rôle of the gaoler into a caricature, leaving the excesses to Rosette Anday (Palmatica), who galumphs through the 'older lady' rôle like a superannuated seal.

Ariola-Eurodisc's set, with Robert Stolz at the head of the Berlin Symphony Orchestra and Opera Chorus, is also a good one. Fritz Ollendorf makes his namesake, the conniving Colonel, the star of the show, delivering his famous song with a splendid full basso ring and well-tempered comic style. Tenors Rudolf Schock and Peter Minich (although the former is not a hundred percent happy at the top of his voice) are well paired as the two young men picked by the Count to trick proud Laura into a lowly marriage, Hilde Güden is warmly attractive as the lady in question, and Lotte Schädle a pretty partner for Minich.

However, this set in particular is outpointed in almost every area by EMI's 1968 issue. Here Franz Allers conducts the Symphonie-Orchester Graunke and the Chor des Bayerischen Rundfunks in a merrily played, vivaciously spoken and superbly sung performance which is both happily atmospheric and musically splendid.

Colonel Ollendorf is played here neither by a tenor nor a bass, but by the very baritone Hermann Prey, who looks so handsome on the cover and sounds so seductively smooth in his singing that you would think that Laura ought to have her eyes and ears tested for turning his propositions down. He performs his big number with a silky vigour, and proves in his second-act comedy song that it is possible to sing superbly and still make all the comic points as strongly as necessary without graunching about making odd swoops, growls and other noises. It is a fine, dashing, unorthodox performance of a rôle often confided to a portly and often overacting comic – more Count di Luna than Doctor Bartolo.

Symon, the poor student (with a marvellous tenor voice) who is sent to woo

Laura, sings opposite her and, ultimately, genuinely wins her, is played by Nicolai Gedda. Almost every time I listen to another Gedda recording, particularly the ones from around this period, I find myself thinking, 'This is a rôle that really suits him.' The feeling is particularly strong here. He is a magnificent Symon, soaring excitingly into his opening duet ('Doch einmal ich noch nicht verlor') with fellow 'student' Jan (Gerhard Unger), singing his praise of Polish women stylishly and without the tendency towards rather vulgar rubati and throbs of some others, swinging martially into his third-act solo ('Ich hab' kein Geld') complete with an uncalled-for top D, which can be wholly forgiven because it is so sizzlingly taken, and pairing beautifully with Rita Streich's Laura in their big duet.

Streich is a charming Laura, clear and classy in her solos and duet music and blending beautifully with an impeccable Renate Holm (Bronislawa) and Gisela Litz (Palmatica) – a contralto who shuns all that is campy and sings with accuracy and warmth – in both the twinkling Shopping Trio which is their first appearance and in their second-act ensemble. The spoken rôles are energetically played, and the scenes well directed by someone unnamed, and there are indeed very few faults to be found with what is a first-rate set. The almost always tiny slimmings and cuts in the music are so insignificant as to make me wonder why they were done – perhaps they have become normal? There is a touch of over-stretched stereo, a touch of heavy echo, and a bit of unnecessary silly voice acting in the character music allotted to the prison warder (unfortunately this opens the show), but these little imperfections stand out in what is one of the most enjoyable of all EMI's sets only because everything else is so spot on. And that without Schwarzkopf who, sadly, doesn't seem ever to have recorded Laura.

Several other well-known stars have tackled a selection of *Der Bettelstudent* music – Tauber and Fritz Wunderlich can be heard on Asco and EMI respectively – and there was also once a selection in Hungarian on the Qualiton label, but there seems to me to be no need to look beyond this splendid *Bettelstudent* for content or quality.

Gasparone

Millöcker's swashbuckling *Gasparone* is another piece still popular – often, admittedly, in severely souped-up versions – in German and Austrian houses, even though it has had a very limited overseas career and has not ever, to my knowledge, been played in Britain or France. Its recordings were for a long time limited ones – half or even a quarter of a full-sized record, or sometimes an EP to itself – usually enough to allow the dashing hero of the affair – a sort of Germano-Italian Red Shadow – to perform the waltzing 'Dunkelrote Rosen', the popular song hit of the revised 1932 version of the show, and the heroic 'O, dass ich doch der Räuber wär'.

Like all the selections, large and small, that I have encountered, the most substantial of the excerpts records, RCA's rather tightly concentrated transfer of sixteen pieces from a Cologne broadcast conducted by Franz Marszalek, follows the lines laid down by the drastic 1932 Paul Knepler/Ernst Steffan rearrangement of the show, which has become the basis for all subsequent rearrangements. The three-quarters of the score which make it onto this record feature Josef Metternich as a rich baritone leading man. It does make a nice change to have a baritone hero after all those tenors, and the new *Gasparone* gives its hero plenty of chances for some big singing. It also lays him the trap of oversung pomposity but, although Metternich is rather a serious performer and his 'Dunkelrote Rosen' is definitely earnest in tone, he avoids this pitfall. He is paired with a fine soprano in Anny Schlemm (Carlotta) who copes well with both the charm of her entrance song and her lusty love music, but there is plenty of more lighthearted material, and Willy Hoffmann in the comic tenor rôle of Benozzo, originated by Girardi, has one of the most attractive and catching pieces of the show in his bouncy third-act waltz duo, 'Er soll dein Herr sein', with Sora (Herta Talmar). Benno Kusche is, as usual, immaculate in the two basso waltz songs which try gallantly to repeat the success of the great comedy waltz hit of *Der Bettelstudent*.

The other one-record *Gasparone* is Telefunken's recording in its Goldene Operette series, which gives its version of the revised version in ten musical pieces linked by a brisk narrative. Wilfried Badorek is a lusty, heroic tenor Gasparone who pours heart and voice into a richly passionate 'Dunkelrote Rosen', Sári Bárabás gives a splendidly characterful and beautifully sung account of the heroine's solo, 'Im dunklen Wald', and the two join effectively in their expansive duet 'Hüten sie sich vor dem Räuberpaar'. Telefunken's regular comic, Hans-Maria Lins (Nasoni, featured here at the expense of Benozzo), disguises a strong singing voice under a heavy character performance. Rita Bartos (Sora) trips out the tarantella of the first-act finale in a piquant soprano, and the nippy Ernst Schütz (Benozzo) has to make to do with a share of the comic ensemble 'Stockfinster war die Nacht' as, although 'Er soll dein Herr sein' is billed as a number on the sleeve, it appears only as a jolly finale to the recording.

There is more of the show to be heard on the RCA recording, but in spite of this, and in spite of the bit of filleting which seems to have been practised on the music of this much rearranged show, the less comprehensive Telefunken recording under Carl Michalski's vivacious musical direction is the more enjoyable listen of the two.

In 1982 EMI produced a complete recording of the score of the 1932 version of *Gasparone*. The music is joined up by some sketchy dialogue which lets you see what Knepler's replacement plot is all about, and what shows up immediately is how much weaker it is than the original! Some of the songs fit very uneasily in their situations and, all in all, the show as it stands is a bit of a mess. However – and it is surely this however that has led people to keep revamping and producing this piece – there are some splendid melodies to be heard in the musical portions, and the rewrite has definitely made *Gasparone* into the kind of big-sing operetta fashionable in the 1980s.

The leading rôles of the Stranger (who isn't the robber Gasparone at all but the

Governor in disguise) and the Countess Carlotta (whom he pretends to rob so that her mercenary fiancé will renounce her) have a good deal of strong, lyrical music to deliver, beyond their principal solos, and it is they rather than the comedians who now form the backbone of the show. On this set they are played by Hermann Prey and Anneliese Rothenberger. Both perform with their usual warmth and willingness of voice and personality, but I can't say that this is my favourite recording of either singer. Prey gives every ounce of his darkly coloured baritone in the many romantic moments of his rôle and bites into the phoney swashbuckling of 'Nur Gold will ich haben' incisively, but I can only remember the easy grace and effortless tones of his *Bettelstudent* on the one hand and Badorek's blithely bravura tenor *Gasparone* on the other. I like them both better. Rothenberger, too, just isn't quite wholly comfortable. Of course, even at not quite best both these artists have the edge on almost all the competition, but . . . well, maybe it is the show that is to blame?

The rest of the cast, led by a jolly Benozzo (Martin Finke) and Sora (Gabriele Fuchs), are fine, but the outstanding performance on this set by a swarthy head and a pair of very large shoulders comes from Günter Wewel as Nasoni, the plotting father of the fiancé. A marvellously dark, freely rumbling bass – both in song and speech – he gets hold of the two comedy waltzes – 'Der verdammte Gasparone' and 'Auch ich war einst ein junger Mann' – and he quite simply makes them sound as if they really are as good as the hit of *Der Bettelstudent*. It is a performance of staggeringly impressive vocal colouring and fine comic playing, the value of which can best be judged when it is put alongside the interpretations of such top-rank players as Kusche and Lins. Truly one for the hit parade of 'best ever' appearances on an operetta disc.

Which *Gasparone* you choose really depends on how much of it you want. The EMI set is the only one which gives you the show (1932 brand) in its musical entirety, in the correct order and with some attempt to connect it up with a story, but for all that it is a rather incoherent affair, particularly in its early stages, and its dialogue is truly corny and functional. RCA does without either version of the story and gives a compressed gallop through much of the rearranged score, and Telefunken displays just the best bits . . . except for Benozzo and Sora's sprightly duet. But then the Telefunken has Badorek . . . and the EMI has Wewel.

Die Dubarry

Millöcker's *Gräfin Dubarry* (1879) underwent even heftier revision than *Gasparone* in order to get itself a second life. Its score was so thoroughly revamped as to leave it only just recognizable, but the result included some pretty solos and duets, mostly for the benefit of the soprano in the title rôle, but also for the tenor playing the part of René, the true love whom she leaves to devote herself to a royal lover, and for the secondary pair. The amount of usable material in *Die Dubarry* has not led to its being offered more than one side of a selection record, but oddly enough two of the three of these I have encountered do take in noticeably different material.

Jeanne's two big songs 'Ich schenk mein Herz' and the showpiece 'Ja, so ist sie, die Dubarry' are common to both, as is René's most popular solo 'Wie schön ist alles', but the other numbers are different, and the duets for the lighter, secondary couple are quite simply omitted in what are really duo recital discs of the *Dubarry* romantic plums.

Of these two, there is better value in the Ariola-Eurodisc recording (backed with a second-best selection from Leo Fall's *Die Rose von Stambul*) – even if the label does credit *Die Dubarry* to Fall as well. Erika Köth is an agile, sweet-voiced Jeanne, particularly at home in the stratospheric cadenza of her Dubarry song, and her partner, Horst Wilhelm, if a little uneasy in the stronger moments, is a fair enough René. They have the edge on Melitta Muszely (who takes a less adventurous cadenza) and Rudolf Schock, who make rather a hectic pair in their telescoped EMI-Electrola selection. However, this latter recording has the advantage of sharing a disc with the only LP selection from Fall's *Madame Pompadour*, so it is probably the better bet for those with a first-best *Rose von Stambul* already on their shelves.

The third *Dubarry* disc, however, is easily the most substantial. Fontana's recording (backed with *Gasparone*) includes not only the three basic numbers but also practically everything else the two other discs have (the duo 'Ich denk zurück' on the Ariola and 'Goldener Mondschein' on EMI are the exceptions), as well as the two light duets. It is only on this recording that you can see how very much *Die Dubarry* was recomposed for its revival. Those two light duets are energetically, almost viciously, swung by the hugely enjoyable Christine Spierenburg and Karl Weber in a way that the 1870s could never even have imagined. The fun-folk have no chance, however, of stealing the show here. Else Liebesberg as the Dubarry has no less energy than they, and she lights into the demanding music of her rôle with passion and a full-blooded soprano. She has a harder job than Köth, with her lighter tones, in making it up and down to all those leger lines, but she makes it every time. Her René is Karl Terkal, ringing royally through his 'Wie schön ist alles' in a truly classic style that quite outclasses the tenors on the other two recordings.

The *Gasparone* selection paired with this *Dubarry* is another variant, credited to Paul Burkhard and E. Rogati, which doesn't stop it from incorporating 'Dunkelrote Rosen' from the usual variant version. It is sung in a jolly fashion by a cast including Hans Strohbauer (Erminio), Lotte Rysanek (Carlotta), Herta Staal (a sweet Sora) and Horst Heinrich Braun (Benozzo).

An alternative to all this *Dubbary*ing is to unearth – which I have not been able to do – the Vienna Disc, which spreads a record among *Die Dubarry*, Zeller's *Der Vogelhändler* and his even less recorded *Der Obersteiger*, although from this three-onto-two share-out it would not seem that the content of the Fontana disc is equalled.

Several numbers from Millöcker's *Der arme Jonathan* appear on another Vienna Disc compilation alongside numbers from more popular operettas, but the composer's many other works, from *Drei Paar Schuhe* to *Der Feldprediger* and *Der Viceadmiral*, successful in their day in both Europe and America but now mostly forgotten, are to be found only in dusty scores.

Carl Zeller

Der Vogelhändler

Carl Zeller's exquisite, folksy-flavoured operetta *Der Vogelhändler* is another work whose popularity has endured almost entirely in German-speaking countries, where it is still freely played and hugely enjoyed. The soubrette's ingenuous little song 'Ich bin der Christel von der Post' has, in particular, lasted more than a century as a favourite vehicle for perky sopranos – and as much of a terror for competition judges as 'I Feel Pretty' in English-speaking areas.

However, the-mistress's little song is not the only enduring highlight of a marvellously melodious score that swings along with an endless and infectious jollity, giving splendid opportunities to all its players. The star comic part – another rôle made for Girardi – is blessed with a splendid first-act entrance ('Grüss enk Gott') and a delightfully lazy second-act waltz song ('Wie mein Ahnl zwanzig Jahr'), as well as the popular highlight of the show, the beautiful waltz 'Schenkt man sich Rosen in Tirol' in the lively and tuneful first-act finale (where you can also hear a tiny reminiscence of *The Sound of Music*); there is a crisply funny duo for two loony professors, a sweet female trio, two sweeping solos for the soprano and some effectively merry ensemble writing.

Available in any number of selection discs of various sizes over the years, *Der Vogelhändler* has also won two full recordings, the first on Philips in the 1950s, with Julius Patzak starring in the title rôle as Adam the birdseller, and the second by EMI twenty years later, with Adolf Dallapozza taking the lead. Neither is musically utterly complete, although the earlier set, which takes only tucks here and there, goes much closer than the more recent one. This latter, in order to include dialogue (which the Philips set does not), omits both the opening of Act 3 and Adam's delightful little final song, reducing the last act to very minor proportions.

The Philips set is just about the ideal *Vogelhändler*, for it is played and sung with an unshowy simplicity that is absolutely right for this most unpretentious of musical comedies. And the performance that gives it its very big heart is, rightly, that of Patzak, stealing the show as the ingenuous little Tyrolean bird-seller whose straightforward love-life starts getting in a tangle when folks from the 'big' world interfere in rural matters. His Adam is a gentle comedy performance of great charm, from the moment his youthful tones are heard, matter-of-factly lilting out the famous 'Flix, flux, flax, Florian!' of his opening number, through his boyish tantrums and honest homesickness, up to the happy ending. Vocally, he is entrancing. There is no big singing, no beautiful singing with a capital B, just lovely, straightforward singing, which has its highlights in the adorable slow waltz of the Act 2 finale ('Wie mein Ahnl zwanzig Jahr'), a 'Schenkt man sich Rosen in Tirol' of melting simplicity, and that last, longing 'Kam ih iazt wieder ham'.

He is happily partnered by the cutest of Christels in Wilma Lipp who, like Patzak, keeps everything uncomplicated. She makes the prettiest job of her pop solo on her first appearance, and pairs quite perfectly with her man thereafter. Just to make things even better, the rôle of Stanislaus (who provides the straight tenor singing against Adam's character comedy) is taken by Karl Terkal, singing with all his usual brio and accuracy and not at all averse to some fun, as witness his rollicking duet with Kurt Preger, who gives a good clean comic baritone performance as the culpable Baron Weps. Erich Majkut and Eberhard Wächter add to the fun with a fine comic turn, as per the script, as the two zany examiners.

The one disappointment (and this is where the 'just about' qualification comes in) is Hilde Zadek's singing of the lyric soprano rôle of Princess Marie – the 'other woman' in the story. Her entrance song, 'Fröhlich Pfalz', is admittedly a throatful, and she tackles it with a bright but heavily vibratoed voice which never sounds properly secure or even attractive, and which goes through several uncomfortable periods during the course of her performance.

The second *Vogelhändler* is, in the style of these times, a heavier one. The voices are more weighty, the orchestra and chorus sound bigger – it is all built for a much larger theatre than the earlier version. It also, as mentioned, has dialogue. I miss the pleasing naturalness of the Philips set, but that is not to say that this is not a fine recording, and Willi Boskovsky and the Vienna Philharmonic and Staatsoper Chorus (both of which also appeared on the first set) are in first-rate form behind a top-flight set of soloists.

One of the outstanding pieces of casting is, ironically, that of Princess Marie with Anneliese Rothenberger. It is a rôle that fits her perfectly, and when you listen to her well-oiled 'Fröhlich Pfalz', and the voice gliding up in one and the same warm colour through the number's wide range to wonderful effect, you can see just what is wrong with Zadek's version. Renate Holm is a hugely accomplished, spunky Christel, but the other big success of the recording is Gerhard Unger's Stanislaus. The voice is quite beautiful, with comedy bubbling always at hand, and it is hard to believe that this very youthful performance is coming from a man who, according to the sleeve, was nearly sixty years of age at the time. Walter Berry is a much heavier Weps than Preger, a hairy comic baritone voice where the other is a bald one, and the Professors' Duo (which has never been known to miss) gets a duly vigorous and daft performance from Jürgen Förster and Karl Dönch.

That leaves Adam, and here this set is less happy. There is no doubting that Adolf Dallapozza has a fine voice, but he doesn't seem to have the measure of this rôle. Not only does he give it an unsuitably 'big sing', tense and weighty, but he does not in any case seem to be in top form here. The effortful, the uncomfortable and even the dubiously pitched all peep in as he pushes the music about in an almost Italianate way. It is too often simply overcooked and, listening to him straight after the pleasures of Patzak, there is simply no comparison.

Thus, there are two mostly excellent, almost-whole *Vogelhändler*s. You have to decide whether to have Patzak and the extra music, or Rothenberger and Unger and the dialogue. And, if you go for the former, you then have the not very easy task of tracking it down for, alas, Philips have let this one go well and truly out of print.

Of the selection discs, the fullest are Ariola-Eurodisc's Rudolf Schock/Erika Köth/Renate Holm recording and Telefunken's 1971 version in the Goldene Operette series, featuring Peter Minich, Hilde Güden and Lotte Schädle in fourteen pieces. This latter is an especially enjoyable recording, more extrovert than the Philips set, but without the tendency to overweightiness of EMI's. Minich is a hearty, ringing Adam – much more the lusty country lad than Patzak's simple peasant – singing 'Schenkt man sich Rosen in Tirol' with a bright and happy voice, walloping merrily into his 'Flix, flux, flax, Florian', and waltzing confidently through 'Wie mein Ahnl zwanzig Jahr' without mannerism and with friendly warmth. Hilde Güden, like Rothenberger, is well suited to the rôle of Princess Marie, Schädle is a delightfully bouncy Christel – perhaps even the best on record – carolling out her 'Christel von der Post' with joyous carelessness, and Karl Terkal repeats his splendid Stanislaus. With the comedy rôles taken by Benno Kusche (Weps), Martha Mödl (Adelaide) and Hans-Maria Lins, giving his usual extravagant characterization as both the mayor and one of the two professors, there is not a weak link in the cast. Carl Michalski's orchestra plays with a lively vigour and, although there have been a few bits of slimming practised on the music, notably in extracting pieces from the finales, and the Weps/Stanislaus duet and Adam's third-act song are missing, this selection, with one melodious highlight tumbling over the next, is a happy cavalcade through a very happy show.

A smaller selection of just seven pieces from the show which was recorded by Philips in 1970 and has been reissued on CD is another very attractive bit of *Vogelhändler*. Adolf Dallapozza proves that he can handle Adam's rôle much better than he does on the fuller recording, but the triumphs of this version come from the women – a royally ringing Teresa Stratas as Princess Marie and a wholly magnificent Christel from Lucia Popp. But it is only seven pieces, and it is backed with excerpts from a rather nasty, souped-up *Dollarprinzessin*.

Der Obersteiger

Zeller's other principal success was *Der Obersteiger* (1894). This contained its composer's best-known show tune, the Obersteiger waltz 'Sei nicht bös' (otherwise 'Don't be Cross'), the joy of sopranos world-wide in spite of the fact that it was written for a comic tenor – the ubiquitous Girardi who had to have a big waltz song written for him in each of his rôles – and that in Germany and Austria the tenors still sing it. Apart from the little miscellany referred to in connection with *Die Dubarry*, the only *Obersteiger* selection I know of is on that same Amiga label which did the honours with *Fatinitza*, and it is in the form of one of those medleys which squeeze fragments of thirteen pieces into twelve and a half minutes of a 45 EP. It is sufficient to show another happy, tuneful score which tries quite blatantly to repeat every element of the success of *Der Vogelhändler*. If it doesn't quite make that very lofty level, it is obviously a thoroughly delightful score and its fragments are well sung here, especially by the friendly, unpretentious and unidentified artist in the Girardi rôle. I have a feeling, however, that 'Sei nicht bös' is not supposed to go quite so greedily slowly, and that Zeller would not have approved of the Leipzig Rundfunkchor's linking bits of disembodied 'ah-ah-ing'.

Other Bits of Vienna Gold

Carl Michael Ziehrer's *Der Fremdenführer* (1901) has maintained some popularity and has been played recently at the Volksoper, but it has fared poorly on record, as have Ziehrer's stage works in general. Although the odd number from *Der Landstreicher* pops up from time to time, the only real sampler can be found on a Philips recording from 1979 where Ziehrer's works share a disc with *Die lustige Witwe*. The record is called *Die lustige Witwe* and you have to look closely to see in smaller print that 'die schönsten Melodien von Carl Michael Ziehrer' are on side two. It is a very pleasant selection – three pieces of *Fremdenführer* and one each from *Der Landstreicher*, *Der Schatzmeister* and *Ball bei Hof* – nicely sung by Harald Serafin and Mirjana Irosch. She has a big, showy time with the prima donna's 'Töne Liedchen, Töne' (*Fremdenführer*) and then joins Serafin in a simply sung version of a light duet from the same show, whilst he puts across his numbers in a pleasantly relaxed and very Viennese style which is more than a little helped by some 'Vienna as she is played' backing from Herbert Mogg and the Wiener Hofburgorchester.

Another and much more continuously popular piece which has also had a poor time from the recording world is Richard Heuberger's one big operetta success *Der Opernball* (1898). This, like *Der Obersteiger*, has donated an operetta classic to the recital world in the form of the delicious 'Geh'n wir in's Chambre séparée'. There are umpteen recordings of the one song and several short selections – a 45 from Ariola-Eurodisc (with Margit Schramm but without Rudolf Schock!), a part of a Philips disc with *Die Dubarry*, and one, with Elisabeth Roon and Hans Löffler, taking up a whole record, all of which are elusive.

The Berlin Operetta

With the best 'Golden Age' works firmly in the past, Berlin began to rival Vienna as a source of new works, and several attractive and internationally played musical shows emerged from Germany round the turn of the century, written by composers such as Paul Lincke, Walter Kollo and Jean Gilbert. Lincke became best known outside Germany for the little Glow-worm Song from his operetta *Lysistrata*, which travelled extensively without the rest of the operetta, but by far his most successful stage work, particularly at home, was the one act spectacular-burlesque-fantastic-operetta *Frau Luna* (1899).

Frau Luna

As that description might suggest, there is not much link between Lincke's little show and the classic operettas of Strauss and Suppé. *Frau Luna* is musical comedy on contemporary British lines, a derivative of the German musical farce tradition rather than of Viennese operetta, mixing music hall-type songs for a bunch of jolly, comical people with some lyrical numbers for a soprano leading lady in a musical layout more likely to throw up single song hits than to combine in a coherent score. There is little concerted music and a lot of bounce and vigour and marked rhythms, from waltz to march and back. The popular songs duly emerged, headed by the title rôle's lively 'Lasst den Kopf nicht hängen' and the pretty 'Schlösser, die im Monde liegen'.

Several smaller selections from this revusical show, whose revised and expanded version – revised this time by the composer himelf – boasted a fine additional hit in the singalong 'Das macht die Berliner Luft', have been recorded, but its most substantial recording is another of the RCA radio transfers. This devotes a full record to eighteen (sometimes brief) portions of the score, including several pieces interpolated in the 1929 rewrite and some others – mainly extending the romantic tenor/soprano area at the expense of the original basic comedy – from even later.

It is a more than slightly odd record, as the show has been given a modern musical reworking that drags in some Hollywoodian light orchestral and choral moments, a vibraphone and a peskily insistent brushed drum, making some of the songs sound very 1950s. In the musical comedy style of the time, the comedy characters aren't required to sing much, but merely to bounce broadly through their numbers, which the performers here do effectively. Ingeborg Hallstein as Frau Luna deploys her clear soprano prettily in the lioness's share of the regular sung music, with Willi Brokmeier as Prince Sternschnuppe (Shooting Star) making the most of the additional opportunities given to his rôle, notably in a big, obvious waltz duo ('Frohe munt're Lieder') and a pretty 'In deiner Augen steht es geschrieben'.

The light comedy pair (Beate Granzow and Harald Juhnke) have the catchiest tune in 'Schenk mir doch ein kleines bisschen Liebe' – another 1929 addition – which they perform brightly and without pretentiousness. It is jolly, unsophisticated stuff, and interesting as an isolated recording of the other side of the German-language musical theatre of the late nineteenth and early twentieth century, but not in any way what might be called 'authentic'.

For more vaguely genuine Lincke, you can go to one of the two half-records – Telefunken's or Polydor's (both backed with *Die Csárdásfürstin*) – or to Eurodisc's recording, originally an EP, from which the a few numbers (but not as many as the sleeve would have you believe) are included on a Lincke compilation disc

('Schlösser, die im Monde liegen'), mashed up along with bits of other operettas and some of the composer's famous Viennese songs. Unfortunately I do not have the Telefunken recording, but the Polydor – one of those medleys so beloved of that firm – is a really jolly affair. The lively Herta Talmar and the agreeably uncomplicated tenor Franz Fehringer head a group of singers in a parade of songs which still sound, no little thanks to the heavenly voices and harmonizing of the Günter Kallmann Choir, more 1950s in style than turn of the century. I wonder for what element Messrs Neumann and Schönfeld, whose names are joined to the original credits here, are actually responsible? Presumably for the interpolation of the Glühwürmchen-Idyll, at least. The best moment is a rich run-through of 'Lose, muntre Lieder' sung properly as a solo by baritone Willy Schneider.

The Eurodisc compilation, like the Polydor one, simply treats Lincke's songs as bits of movable melody and doesn't make any reference to the original show to decide who sings what or mind how much of it they sing. Amongst the snatches of this and that, Margit Schramm takes the prima donna's 'Von Sternem umgeben' with silvery assurance and what was, at one stage, the leading man's 'Schlösser, die im Monde liegen'. Brigitte Mira (who also appears on the Polydor disc) again gives Frau Pusebach's bumpity waltz 'Theophil, O Theophil', but she also grabs a couple of lines of 'Lasst den Kopf nicht hängen', which are confusingly tacked onto a couple more lines from 'Das macht die Berliner Luft'. The other numbers included are given similarly as fragments of orchestral and choral material in a recording which, by trying to fit in too many bits of all sorts of Lincke's work, ends up by being an irritating hotch-potch. Ah, well. Perhaps Telefunken have been able to record the piece as it was written.

No Lincke operetta other than *Frau Luna* has had a disc devoted wholly to it, but his remaining works have won rather more attention than those of other composers. Apart from the pasteurized Eurodisc compilation already mentioned, EMI Electrola have included selections from both *Lysistrata* – the glow-worm included – and *Im Reiche des Indras* along with pieces of *Frau Luna* on a further recital disc.

Wie einst im Mai

Although Kollo had some success in London at the height of the fashion for German operetta with *The Girl on the Film*, his name is remembered today partly through the success of his grandson, the tenor René Kollo, and partly through his musical comedy *Wie einst im Mai* (1913), an early example of the three-generations musical play later successfully followed in *Drei Walzer*, *Perchance to Dream* and the Americanization of the work (without Kollo's music) as *Maytime*. Inevitably, the show has not survived in its original state. In 1943 Kollo's son Willi reorganized the score and added numbers of his own and some songs of his father's taken from elsewhere, and this version was again revamped for a 1966 revival. It is the score for this revival, performed by the cast from the Theater des Westens which, with a couple of interpolations by grandson René taken from Kollo's *Derfflinger* and *Mariette*, has been preserved, like *Frau Luna*, on the enterprising RCA series.

Only half a dozen numbers from the original show make it into this version, including the very attractive 'Es war in Schöneberg im Monat Mai' and two of the four parts of the charming 'Heissgeliebtes Firlefänzchen', which supply respectively the romantic and comic links between the play's various eras. Also included are the (here) raunchy cabaret song 'Die Männer sind aller Verbrecher' and the dreamy might-have-been 'Grossmamma, Grossmamma', but these do not get the most attractive performance from a sometimes rather vulgar heroine and a vocally pale and unsophisticated hero who, unfortunately for him, has to put up with the juxtaposition of the two interpolated songs (recorded separately and much better) ringingly sung by the splendid René Kollo. Kollo's performance, in spite of an hilariously syrupy orchestra, puts in evidence the considerable attractions of his grandfather's music better than either the Berlin cast or the brief orchestral pot-pourri of his better-known melodies interpolated in the first act.

In his heyday Jean Gilbert was by far the most internationally successful of the Berlin writers. His *Die keusche Susanne* was a huge hit in London as *The Girl in the Taxi* and in France as *La chaste Suzanne*, and he had further world-wide successes with such pieces as *Die Kinokönigin*, *Die Frau im Hermelin* and *Katja, die Tänzerin*. In spite of having his most productive period handicapped by anti-German wartime sentiments, Gilbert was better known outside his own country, and whereas the best works of Lincke and Kollo have been given notice in the LP age, Gilbert is almost entirely ignored. To find his music, you have to go back to the many foreign 78 rpm recordings, mainly British, made of his works at the height of their success.

Franz Lehár

The Golden Age of operetta had scarcely time to recognize that its credentials were wearing rather thin before the relief had well and truly arrived, headed by Franz Lehár and *Die lustige Witwe* (*The Merry Widow*) (1905), which played the same part in launching the new wave of musical shows – neatly referred to in this day and age as the Silver Age of operetta – which *Die Fledermaus* had played in setting the first fine flush in action.

Lehár followed the immense international success of *The Merry Widow* with more pre-war successes in *Der Graf von Luxemburg* (1909), *Zigeunerliebe* (1910) and *Eva* (1911), each of which established itself both at home and abroad. Operetta flourished in Austria and Hungary in the first decades of the new century as it had never done before, with delightful new works coming regularly from such internationally successful composers as Leo Fall, Oscar Straus, Emmerich Kálmán and Victor Jacobi.

Die lustige Witwe

I would imagine that *Die lustige Witwe/The Merry Widow* is the most frequently played of all Viennese operettas. It is certainly the most widely recorded. Nine complete sets – including Italian and Russian versions – may be less than the total expended on *Die Fledermaus*, but the flood of world-wide excerpt recordings – some twenty in English, a good half-dozen in French (*La Veuve joyeuse*), *La vedova allegra* in Italian, *A vig özvegy* in Hungarian, *Glada änken* in Swedish, and so forth – as well as a regular supply, beginning with transfers of recordings of the original cast stars, in the original language, more than make up the difference.

The seven German-language sets provide the opportunity for several of the regular in-house stars of the various recording companies to appear in the rôle of the widow – Schwarzkopf recorded it twice for EMI, Margit Schramm for Ariola-Eurodisc, Hilde Güden for Decca – as well as the less forseeable Elizabeth Harwood (Deutsche Grammaphon) and Edda Moser (EMI), and Mirjana Irosch, star of the Volksoper, in the latest (live) recording on Denon. They are equipped with leading men whose Count Danilos range from the resolutely tenor (Schock, Kollo, Minich) to the definitely baritone (Kunz, Wächter, Prey).

Polemic has long raged over whether the rôle of Danilo should be played by a tenor or a baritone, amongst those who rage about such things, and it will undoubtedly continue to rage until the unforseeable time when *Die lustige Witwe* has ceased to be. It is a little more than a simple choice of voice colour, in this case, for the baritones and the tenors take noticeably different notation in several places in the score – the latter, obviously, choosing more showy options. For once, I have no firm opinion on the question. Danilo was, to all evidence, first played by what would now politely be called a 'light baritone' of limited vocal capacity and a certain amount of raffish charm and, now that the show has gone upmarket and operawards and such a thing is no longer permissible, some sort of a compromise seems the most sensible. Clearly, the voice in question should not be too like that used for the lyric tenor part of Camille, but apart from that I'd say give the rôle to the most dashing and charming fellow regardless of which set of notes he sings.

The other irregularity on *lustige Witwe* recordings concerns, as usual, what goes in and what gets left out. The usual casualty, apart from some orchestral and reprise material, is the very lovely but definitely *de trop* 'Ja was? Ein trautes Zimmerlein' ('Zauber der Hauslichkeit'), one of no less than three duets for the secondary, lyrical pair of Camille (tenor) and Valencienne (soprano). There have been many efforts to salvage this piece by turning it into something more useful – the original British version made it a solo for Camille, the later one transformed it into a duet for Danilo and Hanna – but, more often than not, it ends up getting left out. On stage it is intrusive; on a record, however, it would seem to do no harm and give much pleasure.

EMI is the one firm to have more than a single double-disc *Die lustige Witwe* to its name, for it has inherited both the 1953 and 1962 HMV recordings on which Schwarzkopf starred, and also produced its own version in 1980. The inheritance in question is a particularly fine one, for the 1953 recording, with Otto Ackermann and the Philharmonia Orchestra and Chorus, and a group of leading players who seem born to their rôles, is quite simply a classic.

Schwarzkopf's performance as Hanna Glawari is one that calls forth a rash of superlatives. From the moment she makes her first entrance, with a little catch of breath, a gentle laugh, full of amused self-confidence in the face of the foolish gentlemen rushing to fawn on her, and answering them with a ravishingly pure and secure cascade of sung greeting, she has the rôle apparently effortlessly under control. She can turn to vigorous, dashing singing – as in her vengeful description of the delights of Paris – and she can produce sheer soprano beauty in her lingering delivery of the Merry Widow Waltz. She can also take the character established in song through into the short sections of dialogue that link the musical parts of the show together into a cohesive and forward-going whole.

Erich Kunz is her Danilo, and it is a long way into the recording before you even stop to think whether this is a tenor Danilo or a baritone Danilo. He just *is* Danilo. He has a splendidly easy masculine style and an attractively unshowy personality, never oversings (although when an opportunity comes to let his angora baritone tell he lets it tell with dark brown warmth), and he doesn't try to make the man into a chocolate box operetta hero. When the 'low options' in the vocal line come along, you don't even consider that the tenor alternatives might be a possibility. It is just right – even to someone such as myself who was brought up on the tenor version of Danilo.

Emmy Loose is an ideal Valencienne, not a skittish girl, but a married woman who declares with flattered firmness and a fine soprano 'Ich bin eine anständige Frau' (I'm a respectable married woman) when confronted by the enthusiastic passion of the young Camille de Rosillon (Nicolai Gedda). Gedda, in the fresh bloom of youthful voice, gets the impulsive passion of Camille splendidly, and then turns out such a bon-bon of a 'Wie eine Rosenknospe' as to leave you breathless.

The rest of the cast are all adequate, with a low-key non-buffo Baron Zeta (Anton Niessner) and a competent bundle of men to make up the numbers for the March Septet, and all the other values are very fine. This made me all the more surprised to find, on the 1988 CD reissue of this version, a notice in three languages apologizing for the 'old' quality of the sound. I have news for EMI. Digitally remastered or not digitally remastered, the sound on this set and its contemporaries has a theatricality and character that someone might like to spend millions on finding how to get *back* into many modern recordings.

EMI decided to remake the piece in 1962 in stereo (with more dialogue and orchestral music but still no 'Zauber der Hauslichkeit'), but I can't say I notice much difference as far as sound is concerned. In fact on my newly purchased direct-metal-mastered French pressing there is some rather nasty distortion which I assume wasn't there on the original. Caveat emptor.

Schwarzkopf and Gedda both return to their rôles and both are, once again, splendid. Schwarzkopf's performance is perhaps a little bigger but still just as beautiful, and Gedda, now utterly assured, cruises along through his rôle in a model of operettic performance which is, naturally, a little less excitingly young-sounding than before. Hanny Steffek is a simply delightful Valencienne, sprightly and clear in voice and piquant in character. You could not ask for better.

The Danilo on this recording is Eberhard Wächter, a definitely baritone Danilo who does everything a Danilo should do and does it with conviction and energy and an appreciable, smooth baritone which is only sometimes a touch swallowed. For my money, however, he is not in the same class as Kunz. Where Kunz's personality bounces off the earlier recording, you can hear Wächter acting. And he makes such a meal of the first-act finale you would think you were in *Pagliacci*.

The modern EMI recording, which takes in the entire score, simply cannot compare with either of these in any way. This is an ill-judged, welterweight *Widow* which takes the modern preference for large voices in light music just that much too far. The dazzling gaiety of Lehár's score gets plunged into a turgid mass of throaty, unsuitable singing and comes out as a soggy mess. It is hardly the fault of the performers. Edda Moser as Hanna and Herman Prey as Danilo do their best to make up for the fact that they are vocally miscast with some lively, characterful dialogue, but since the major part of *Die lustige Witwe* is music they have little chance. She is quite simply all over the place, sounding desperately ill at ease, singing with so much vibrato at one stage that it sounds as if she is incessantly trilling, and plunging into an almost comically melodramatic 'Vilja-Lied'. He sounds, at times, as if he will choke under the effort to hold back his rich bass-baritone and give it the flippant light-heartedness he knows the rôle needs. The budding Heldentenor Siegfried Jerusalem (Camille) succeeds a little better and occasionally gets the voice gliding, and Helen Donath is just a respectable Valencienne. Benno Kusche's cracking Zeta is the only moment of relief on a badly misconceived set.

Decca's recording, which dates from 1958, is much less pretentious and much more successful. It starts off badly, with a very long, soupy, modern-sounding overture (what was wrong with the usual one?), but it very soon looks up as Robert Stolz launches the forces of the Vienna State Opera into a merrily played opening scene and then, one by one, the principals put in their appearance. Emmy Loose, again a charmingly pretty Valencienne, flirts prohibitively with a tidy, slightly hard-voiced Camille (Waldemar Kmentt) before Hilde Güden (Hanna) arrives with a splendidly casual, laughing entrance song, all gaiety and effortless singing, and Per Grunden (Danilo) tosses off his opening lines with tenor ease.

With such a sure-handed lead team and such a solid back-up, an enjoyable, light-hearted, unlanguishing set is ensured. Grunden sails agreeably casually through his 'Ballsirenen' waltz, Güden tells the little folktale of the 'Vilja' with a lightsome touch and some very lovely, gently-spun musical phrases, before they come together in a pretty 'Dummer Reitersmann' and a moody 'Lippen Schweigen' in which her melting tone vanquishes even the odd rough high note on his part. The second pair make more than acceptable work of their other two duets (both are there), with Kmentt – who really sounds more of a Danilo than a Camille – warming up nicely through his big 'Rosenknospe' solo. The infallible 'Weiben' March Septet, headed by Karl Dönch as a lightweight Baron Zeta, gets a particularly lusty rendering which sounds, in the middle, more like a 'twenty-septet'. This is – with just the odd incomprehensible lapse – a good, straightforward rather than an extra special *lustige Witwe*, accorded extra sheen by Güden's gracious, light-handed Hanna; but given recordings like the previous one, a good, straightforward presentation is something devoutly to be given thanks for.

Ariola-Eurodisc's 1965 set is another fairly unobjectionable and utterly unpretentious *lustige Witwe*. Once again, it is conducted by Robert Stolz, which means lots of jollity and no messing about with lingering tempi, but this time it is cast and played in a rather more 'popular' way. As with virtually all the Ariola series, Rudolf Schock is given the lead rôle. You would have thought that for this operetta, with its almost laid-back leading man, they might have found someone else, someone less 'crowd-pleasing', but no. It is Schock. The result is predictable and not a little amusing. Danilo will never be quite the same man again.

The rest of the recording, however, is cast and played in a strong, basic operetta fashion. Margit Schramm is a needle-bright, almost mocking Hanna, convincing and sharply attractive, and wholly different to Güden's 'lovely lady'. She chips out her music with a lively, incisive tone and a total lack of sentimentality and makes the merry widow into a very self-possessed woman. Dorothea Chryst is a sweetly sung and characterful Valencienne, paired in all three duos with Jerry J. Jennings as a very acceptable, secure Camille, and Benno Kusche repeats his Baron Zeta with unshakeable skill. If you can take the matinée-idol-on-skates Danilo, this is a brisk version of the show which may not please the purists but which does nothing wrong.

Deutsche Grammophon's 1972 set doesn't seem to work on my record players. It goes from vastly loud to unhearable in a few bars and requires incessant fiddling with the knobs to get a proper listen. It also doesn't seem to work in other ways. When you can hear it as it must have been sung, it seems to have been miscast. Teresa Stratas as Valencienne has the brightness, power and temperament for a very fine Hanna, while Elizabeth Harwood's smooth, cool and even dispassionate delivery in Hanna's music makes it seem as if she might have made a nice Valencienne. Neither is in any way lacking vocally, but they don't fit my preconceptions and don't seem to make the piece take off in the way that even the 'basic' *lustige Witwe*s do. Werner Hollweg is a very fine if unadventurous Camille (deprived of his third duet), René Kollo an uncriticizable, very definite and tenorish Danilo, Zoltan Kelemen an unexceptional Zeta, and Herbert von Karajan a correct and rather straight conductor. All those names ought to have produced something more than this very efficient but ultimately unsparkly *lustige Witwe*.

From 1972 (and forgetting, for peace of mind's sake, the 1980 EMI set) we move to 1982 and Japan for the most recent *Witwe*, from the live-performance Wiener Volksoper series. As with the others of this series, there are here both jokey, theatrical acting performances and an absolutely infectious vivacity as well as some awkward balances in the sound department. Unfortunately, the performances, if lively and sometimes distinctly original in their lines, are musically run-of-the-mill. Mirjana Irosch is a capable but not very recordworthy Hanna, Peter Minich (why do they applaud his entrance in Japan?) a harsh Danilo, and neither a hectic Ryszard Karczykowski (Camille) nor a rather vibrating Dagmar Koller (Valencienne) is as successful as in the rather better companion *Fledermaus* set.

It is possible to fit almost all of the *lustige Witwe* score onto a decent-sized single disc, and this possibly explains the proliferation of such recordings compared with the limited array of double-disc sets. Excerpts taken from most of the sets have been issued, and the Decca version, shorn of its objectionable overture but still equipped with an unnecessary reprise of 'Lippen schweigen', is a good example. Of the sung music it leaves out entirely only the 'Zauber in Häuslichkeit' duet, although it tops the first-act finale of its 'Damenwahl!' section, drops the duetting leading into 'Wie eine Rosenknospe' and makes cuts in several other items. On what is otherwise a fine recording, I find these fiddly cuts very irritating. It would surely be better simply to do without the dance music from the second-act opening, but even that would probably not be sufficient to allow the reopening of all the cuts, and there is really little else in the solid mass of gems that makes up this score that one could dare to leave out. Ariola-Eurodisc's one-disc, fifty-one minute reduction of the score, however, keeps the dance and, taking its courage and its scissors in hand, simply and drastically wipes the whole second-act finale, a solution which is not really a solution at all.

The need to get rid of a few minutes of music from somewhere has led to some odd operations being practised on the *lustige Witwe* score for one-record consumption and this, for me, spoils some of what should be the best single-disc versions. It is a problem that will undoubtedly be solvable with the advent of the compact disc, but for the moment those CD selections available are merely copies of the recordings of the past decades, and the cuts are included. The most obvious such recording is EMI-Electrola's 1967 single, which features Anneliese Rothenberger as a predictably delightful Hanna and Gedda as an older but still first-class Danilo. It also has Erika Köth (Valencienne), Róbert Ilosfálvy (Camille) and a good handful of those wretched nips and tucks.

Foreign-language recordings of *Die lustige Witwe* have almost always limited themselves to one disc. Only the ever-substantial Melodiya with its Russian version and Italy's double disc *Vedova allegra* go further, with results that I have not been able to hear. In the one-record sphere, it is the English and Americans who have been the most prolific, both with cast and studio recordings, and there has been a vast list of *Merry Widow*s recorded in both countries.

Amongst the more significant of these, one of the earliest, made in America in 1950, gives a short selection in Adrian Ross's long standard translation (ten of the fourteen sung numbers) centred on the Hanna/Danilo axis. Its main significance is that it features a very fine, light-hearted, lightish-baritone Danilo in Wilbur Evans, who plays and sings the rôle splendidly in its pre-operatic style and proves how very much better for the music that style was. His Hanna (now become Sonia), Kitty Carlisle, is enjoyably natural, transposed down and without top notes, which matters less than you would suspect, in a very pleasantly musical comedy version of *The Merry Widow*.

The Ross translation is used on several other early American LP recordings, including one from 1952 which apparently (I have not heard it) includes 'Butterflies', an additional dance/chorus number written by Lehár for Countess Mabel Russell (later MP for Berwick-on-Tweed), as a grisette, in the London production.

The Sadler's Wells Opera Company abandoned the Adrian Ross translation for one by Christopher Hassall, which turned 'Zauber der Häuslichkeit' into a sparky duet for the two stars. This gets record space on the 1958 album made of their production and, to make room for it, the 'Dummer Reitersmann' duet goes. June Bronhill is a magnificent widow (called Anna here). Her bright, forward tone gives the character the kind of sparkling, tempting attractiveness which wouldn't need any twenty millions to attract an embassy full of men, and her easy, clear-voiced encompassing of the music is a joy to listen to. She knocks off her entrance song with glittering gaiety and points the tale of the 'Vilja' with a smoothness and clarity and an unquenchable brightness of the voice. Bright, forward and clear are adjectives which apply equally to Thomas Round's very tenor Danilo as well and, if he is marginally less rock solid than she, it is nevertheless a lively and enjoyable performance.

Alongside these two well-judged operetta performances, and the splendidly lively chorus and orchestra under William Reid, the rest of the cast tend more to the operatic. William McAlpine and Marion Lowe sing their two remaining duets firmly and Howell Glynne is a buffo Zeta. It is sad about the 'Dummer Reitersmann', but this is nevertheless a very happy recording which has been often reissued on disc and now on CD.

Miss Bronhill recorded the rôle and the translation again, in 1968, in one of her collaborations with Norman Newell. This time the 'new' duet is omitted, along with the Act 3 ending, and there are a few bits of musical jiggery-pokery elsewhere, but 'Jogging in a one-horse Gig' (as 'Dummer Reitersmann' has become) is back. Bronhill sings now with less of that very forward glitter, but with no less ebullient character and effortless grace, in what is an extremely brightly played and recorded version. Jeremy Brett is a very natural sounding, actorish light baritone Danilo who carefully replaces any high notes he doesn't fancy. Apart from that, he doesn't sound too out of place alongside the stronger vocalists and he pairs intelligently with Bronhill in their duets.

The pairing of a Schock-ish tenor in David Hughes and a mezzo-soprano (!) Valencienne (Ann Howard) is a little unusual, but she keeps such a bright unplummy tone going to match his slightly hectic bravura that their duets don't ever bog down. Leslie Fyson plays Zeta as a Hooray Heinrich and something goes odd in the top tenor line in 'Women', but, all in all, this is another merry *Merry Widow*.

Another Hassall *Widow* was recorded by Scottish Opera in 1977 and issued on Music for Pleasure. This one lacks the show's opening scene, but includes the cake-walk from the Act 3 dance music. It also utterly lacks the brightness and temperament of the two previous recordings. Catherine Wilson's Anna has a lovely voice, used in an endless legato, which ultimately becomes as unexciting as Jonny Blanc's rather dull tenorish Danilo, whilst David Hillman and Patricia Hay sing accurately and glumly through their duets. It is all there notewise, but it is not much fun.

The same remark might apply to another operatic *Merry Widow* put together in 1977 with Joan Sutherland at its head. This is semi-Hassall, but takes in the comic 'Quite Parisian', the other one of the two additional numbers Lehár wrote for the original London production, and does more than the regulation amount of fiddling with the score.

Amongst the other versions is an American one by Merl Puffer and Deena Cavalieri (with reminiscences of both the earlier translations), which was recorded on a very likeable CBS disc in 1962. It has an attractive Hanna in Lisa della Casa, who mixes a smoothly accomplished voice and a certain amount of sprightliness, while Charles K. Davis and Laurel Hurley sing their duets (two only) in shiny, attractive middle-weight voices, but this recording's biggest plus is its Danilo. John Reardon is what I imagine as the perfect Danilo – a relaxed and charming *baryton-ténorisant* without a strained note in his repertoire who also acts the rôle with an easy, youthful flair. Since all the other values are well cared for, from a clear-voiced group of rather young-sounding Pontevedrian diplomats to an agreeably unforced orchestra under Franz Allers, this comes out as one of the most accomplished of the English-language recordings.

A more theatrical version is the cast recording made from the New York Lincoln Center revival of 1964, also under the musical direction of Allers. This one is 'based on the version by Edwin Lester', but seems to have some bits of Hassall floating around in it, calls the widow Sonia as per Ross and uses the whole of his 'Vilja' translation. It includes a long and very musical overture (apparently Lehár's original one) and, as a result, drops 'Zauber der Häuslichkeit' (which is replaced in Act 1 by the 'Dummer Reitersmann' as 'Riding on a Carousel'), the dance music and the last little finale and does some funny things to the first-act opening.

There are some shocks in store, too, when the widow makes her first entrance. Patrice Munsel mixes some semi-spoken lines which sound more like Mae West than Merry Widow with a lusty, true soprano in a performance that may not be kosher but is really effective. She comes up with all that could be required in the legitimate line when she tackles 'Vilja' with a warm, straight voice. She also goes so slowly as to need the odd breath where a breath doesn't really fit, but her real presence holds the performance together effortlessly. Bob Wright's Danilo sounds a little mature, but it is a fine, dashing portrayal in the healthy American line of unplummy baritone heroes. Frank Poretta and Joan Weldon do their duets well, and the 'Women' team performs lustily. This is not by any means everyone's cup of Lehár, but it is a jolly, uninhibited *Merry Widow* which must have been a lot of fun in the theatre.

Another American cast recording, issued by EMI in 1978 and which had its provenance in the New York City Opera, is 'straighter' but less satisfying. It has no overture, omits the show's opening and the usual duet, and has an Anna in Beverley Sills who wobbles more than is safe for the ears. The other three principals have attractive, ringing voices which get pushed just a tiny bit much, but the best point of this recording seems to be an easily flowing new translation by Sheldon Harnick.

One more translation, by Nigel Douglas, appears on the most recent *Merry Widow*, from the New Sadler's Wells Company on TER, but this rather earnestly sung and played version has neither character nor the best of musical values to lift it above the distinctly so-so.

There are seven *Veuve joyeuse*s around (all in the one-and-only de Flers and de Caillavet translation), of which I have five. One of these is an early Merkès/Merval record (for fans only), another is a TLP affair, and the others, on Decca, EMI and the Guilde Internationale de Disque respectively, don't really throw up a thoroughly top-notch *Veuve*.

Decca's disc features Colette Riedinger as a very aggressive Missia Palmieri (the widow changes her name every time she is translated) and Réda Caire as a tough tenor Prince (!) Danilo. Both have strong, edgy voices and their relationship is a real battle. Camille (Bernard Alvi) and Nadia (Marthe Amour) are a more compatible sounding pair who make a nice job of 'Zauber der Häuslichkeit', which trips along very merrily in French. The feature of the disc, however, is his excellent performance of the Rose solo in the Pavilion Duet (ex-'Wie eine Rosenknospe').

EMI-Pathé's record (no spare duet, no 'Dummer Reitersmann', no grisettes, all the Act 2 dances) has a delightful Missia in Janette Vivalda, piquant and punchy with a strong soprano, and a baritone Danilo (Michel Dens) who is fine when relaxed but who gets very hefty when the pitch rises. It also has a useful second pair in Monique Linval and Raymond Amade. Their music sounds so very right sung French, but Amade, who ought to be the ideal Camille, is a little thin and disappointing in the Pavilion Song. I should dearly love to hear it tackled by Claude Devos, who played the rôle on EMI's alternate recording with Jacques Jansen and Denise Duval, a disc apparently suppressed in favour of this one.

The last recording, which calls itself a 'version de concert', is an untidily played affair with some dragging tempi, but it is redeemed by the performance of Lina Dachary, who is the best Missia on these records. Aimé Doniat is another good Camille and Pierre Mollet a more relaxed and light baritone Danilo than elsewhere – and both cheat into falsetto rather than bleat at peak moments. The 'version de concert' gets in the phantom first-act duet, about which the French seem to have less qualms than the rest of the world, but its personnel doesn't run to seven male soloists, which means the March Septet is left out! It also chops off the beginnings of the first two finales and ignores the third.

All these are, however, preferable to Philips's 1967 Swedish live performance *Glada änken*, which suffers from poor sound quality and some awful rearrangements by Gert-Ove Andersson. A particularly pretty Valencienne (Gunnel Eklund) deserves better, but the rest of the cast actually don't. But Sweden has a Per Grunden/Sonia Sternquist disc which is assuredly better. As for the Russian, Spanish, Hungarian and Italian widows . . . who knows?

Der Graf von Luxemburg

Der Graf von Luxemburg is another bubbling *belle époque* operetta with a score at least partially in the same light and bright vein as *Die lustige Witwe*. The big difference comes in the character of the leading man. Whereas Count Danilo in *Die lustige Witwe* is an attractively diffident fellow with an unpretentious light baritone, René, Count of Luxembourg, is a full-blooded, dashing tenor leading man equipped with all the emotions and high notes of the genre. As a result, the secondary couple, instead of being the lyrical tenor/soprano combination of the earlier show, are more the standard light comedy pair. Although *Der Graf von Luxemburg* has a happy ending, there are already signs of the shape and the line-up of Lehár's more romantic post-war works coming to the fore.

Der Graf von Luxemburg was a popular follow-up to its blockbusting predecessor and it has maintained its place in the affections of the theatres of its native land through three-quarters of a century, even though foreign productions have now become infrequent. The show's highlights have won a wide selection of recordings through the years in German, French, English, Italian and even Spanish. The soaring first-act solo 'Heut' noch werd' ich Ehefrau' for star soprano Angèle, her showy second-act entrance and duet with its big waltz tune ('Sind sie von Sinnen') with René, the soubrette's lovely 'Denn doppelt schmeckt's dem Bübchen', her cute duet 'Mädel klein, Mädel fein', and the tuneful waltzes of the first-act finale are all first-rate fodder for an extracts disc, but the rest of the score includes many equally attractive passages, which makes it odd that only one full-scale set has been put out, a 1969 EMI one with Nicolai Gedda in the title rôle.

This is a well-sung and played recording, with every rôle being given full vocal value, and, if it lacks a bit of the real vivacity I would enjoy, I think that the artists are probably not to blame. *Der Graf von Luxemburg* doesn't sparkle quite in the same way as *Die lustige Witwe* does on any of its many recordings, and the dialogue which is given here doesn't help, as most of it is more romantic or declamatory than light-hearted. Gedda gives his usual soaring, strong-voiced performance, achieving a dramatic lift-off in the second-act 'Es duftet nach Trèfle incarnat', but I can't say that the rather unsympathetic René is one of my favourites from his repertoire, even though the character has some splendid waltz tunes and some well-fabricated dramatic moments in which to place his big singing and his high notes, all of which is duly and superbly done.

Lucia Popp, excellently cast as Angèle, sings her rather more grateful rôle beautifully, producing lovely tone and a degree of excitement in turn, able to encompass the vocal and dramatic extremes of her big numbers without oversinging. Willi Brokmeier and Renate Holm are fine in the secondary parts, and the celebrated basso Kurt Böhme, cast as the fall guy of the piece, plays and sings his rôle for a fortunately not too exaggerated buffo comedy. This part of Prince Basil seems always to be treated comically, but given the temperature of the piece and the playing of the star rôles, it surely requires a Hermann Prey or Erich Kunz. If you're going to play and sing your big romantic love scenes for real, where is the triumph in filching the girl from a silly, fat old comic-opera rival?

Willy Mattes is at the head of the Symphonie-Orchester Graunke and the Bavarian State Opera Chorus, performing as usual to full effect, and the show is given all the performance values it could require. Any reservations that I may have are not, I think, about the disc but about the piece which, though much loved by many operetta fans, simply isn't one of my own favourites.

The most considerable of the more easily available German-language selection discs both feature Rudolf Schock as René, paired with Erika Köth on EMI-Electrola and with Margit Schramm on Ariola-Eurodisc. Schock's performance is in both cases much as usual, energetically crowd-pleasing and out-front, bordering on the over-the-top, and Köth comes out the better of the two Angèles. There is a recording, on Intercord, which features Karl Terkal and Friedl Loor which ought to repay tracking down, but the majority of discs, including the Telefunken selection with Sonja Schöner and Heinz Hoppe, devote only one side of a pairing to Der Graf von Luxemburg.

The French go in for baritone Renés, making the rôle less aggressively showy. I think this works well, but there are only two selection discs in French, the better of which, on Decca, has Gabriel Bacquier paired with Colette Riedinger as a nicely tough Angèle.

As for the English language recordings (which incline to lighter but firmly tenor Renés), the earlier (1969) featuring June Bronhill is just that – it is a short selection centred on its female star performing the best bits of both Angèle and Juliette, alongside a feeble René shorn of all his best bits and an otherwise mostly insufficient cast. It is worth a listen to hear Miss Bronhill soaring seamlessly through the sections other sopranos change gear in, but skip the rest of the tracks. The more recent and more representative New Sadler's Wells Opera version on TER (1983) also has an outstanding Angèle in Marilyn Hill Smith. She is well supported by a pleasantly unforced René (Neil Jenkins), and particularly by a delightful soubrette Juliette (Vivien Tierney), on a competent but rather unexciting recording, where the excellent diction shows up a nastyish Eric Maschwitz translation clipping through clearly in spite of someone's passion for excess echo.

Zigeunerliebe

Lehár's Zigeunerliebe (1910), another show to win world-wide productions, has lasted less prominently than Der Graf von Luxemburg, but it has been preserved on several recordings, the most substantial of which are unfortunately very difficult to lay hands on. The most readily available is the only one-disc selection recording, on Ariola-Eurodisc, with Margit Schramm and Rudolf Schock.

Zigeunerliebe is a remarkable piece. This time the champagne jollity of *Die lustige Witwe* is a whole world away, for this story of storms and passions in the Romanian gipsy wilds is no comic operetta. Lehár himself called it a romantic operetta; I would call it at least a passionate operetta. A version of the show has, in fact, been played in Hungary as an opera and, though the idea of some of the heftier Hungarian voices tackling this music doesn't appeal to me, I can see why they did it. Lehár's score is a perfect whirlwind of emotion, from the first moments of the heroine's entrance, like some Weberian thing, wild and flower-decked in the midst of a storm, and accompanied by music which comes somewhere between *Der fliegende Holländer*, Puccini and the Wolf's Glen, to the final deliberate waltz duet in which the ability of waltz rhythms to be potent as well as lilting is only too well demonstrated.

There is, in fact, a light comedy element in the show, but the Ariola disc omits it almost entirely in favour of giving us all the big singing and, if what contrasts there are largely lost as a result, I wouldn't have wanted to miss out on any of Lehár's heartfelt gipsy music. There are big showpiece songs, to be sure – the hero's macho 'Ich bin ein Zigeunerkind', the marvellous waltz 'Zorika, Zorika, kehre zurück', which returns powerfully as the finale, and the interpolated csárdás 'Hör' ich die Cymbalklänge' – but the level is held high throughout and the ensemble music is particularly potent.

The Ariola recording, with Robert Stolz at the head of the Berlin Symphony Orchestra, is a grand one. Margit Schramm is in superlative form as the landowner's daughter, Zorika, torn between her respectable fiancé and the romance represented by a sexy but self-centred gipsy who plays the violin. She tackles her difficult storm music with just the right amount of voice – this is not, after all, *Die Walküre* – and from then on, in solo or duet, she exhibits as many variants of passion as are required (and there are many) with accuracy, a driving style and a fine, vibrant voice. She even appropriates the popular csárdás from the second female rôle, which is taken by the excellent Dorothea Chryst, and does it so well that one can't complain.

Rudolf Schock chooses to play both the lovers. I don't know if this is supposed to be meaningful, but it works rather well. It also gives Schock the opportunity for a lot of macho singing, which he does to the manner born or at least acquired. The showy gipsy, Jozsi, suits him splendidly, even if he does just about come to grief on the biggest top note, and he gets a warmth into the more genuine Jonel which only bleeds into bravura when he sees some high notes coming.

Zigeunerliebe, especially without its little bit of comic relief (I should mention that the Ariola disc gives us one light number, the lovely 'Nur die Liebe macht uns jung'), is about as operatic as a show can go without being an opera, but it works best when it is sung by really good operetta voices, and this recording is the proof.

There are two double-disc versions of *Zigeunerliebe*, one from Urania in the original German, with Rosl Seegers and Herbert Ernst Groh, and the other in

Russian, on the Melodiya label. The German disc follows the outlines of the two-act version of the show (the original is in three), cramming the interpolated Act 3 csárdás into the second act and abandoning the rest of the old third act, which is mostly reprises, except for the final duo version of 'Zorika, Zorika'. It also omits Jolan and Kajetan, the light relief, and their two numbers. However, in spite of this rearrangement, the two Urania records contain the largest representation of the score available. Sadly, it is indifferently performed. Herbert Ernst Groh is a stolid, dark-voiced gipsy without much in the way of sex appeal or flair, but even he falls occasionally into the unpleasant vocal traps in which both Rosl Seegers (Zorika) and Ilse Mentzel (Ilona) spend most of the recording languishing: dreary, often unsure tone, a tendency both to wobble and stray from the note under the slightest stress, and a lack of any real vitality. Only Adi Appelt as a light-voiced Jonel sings agreeably. The first part of the recording is so limp it is surprising that the performers find the energy to pick themselves up a bit, as they do, for the second act.

The Russian version is infinitely better performed, but it is highly eccentric in its content. It retains the two Kajetan/Jolan duets, but omits several pieces of Acts 2 and 3, as well as both the long and large finales, which means that Jozsi's rôle is diminished not only by the loss of the merry 'Glück hat als Gast', but, more dramatically, his biggest number – 'Ich bin ein Zigeunerkind'. As a way of creeping at least a bit of this number in, it is briefly introduced as the show's finale, where it is strikingly less effective than 'Zorika, Zorika'. On the other hand, there are a couple of pieces included here which I don't recognize.

Much of the four full sides of this set are taken up by dialogue. At one stage, nearly half a side goes by without a note being sung. A lot of it sounds as if it might be great fun, for those who can understand it. There is some very heavy operetta acting going on, the chattering Jolan comes across hilariously even to the non-Russian speaker, and on the fourth side there is what sounds like a stand-up comedy act interpolated for what I presume is the actor playing Dragotin instead of his Act 3 song. The four stars of the recording are all first rate. D. Potapovskaya is an impressive, exciting Zorika who sets the show off on the wings of the wind with her sweeping performance of the storm scene, and her almost-operatic tones blend well with with those of V. Ivanovsky (Joszi), a rich but not heavy tenor of some style. A. Usmanov is contrastingly sweet and light as the put-upon Jonel, making a lovely job of his 'Zorika, Zorika', and A. Yakovenko sings Ilona's music with a vibrant warmth and self-possession, pairing delightfully with Y. Yakushev in 'Nur die Liebe' and waltzing happily through the duo which comes where 'Hör' ich Cymbalklänge' would normally be.

Eva

Apart from some original cast fragments reproduced on the Rococo label, *Eva* doesn't seem to have an original-language recording. There is a selection from this attractive score recorded in Spanish, which I haven't personally encountered, and one in Italian which shares a disc with a selection from the Italian musical comedy *Addio giovinezza*. This recording, part of the friendly and very old-fashioned sounding EDM 'Ritorno all'operetta' series, combines rather a lot of narrative with what is really an extended medley of ten pieces from the show performed by four fairly capable singers and otherwise limited resources. It is not for serious listening, but it gives at least an impression of Lehár's principal songs for the show, which are a much more standard set than those from *Zigeunerliebe*.

Oscar Straus

Ein Walzertraum

Oscar Straus – one 's' and no relation to those with two – was the first and the most immediately successful of the new set of composers to follow the way opened up by *Die lustige Witwe*. Although he was to have plenty of successes both at home and abroad over the following decades, it was his first winning piece, the bitter-sweet Ruritanian romance *Ein Walzertraum* (1907), that has remained his most popular in Europe, and its hit number, the glorious, graceful waltz duo 'Leise, ganz leise' one of the classic songs of Viennese operetta. The other lyrical pieces are in the best Viennese style, but one of the joys of the score is the cheerful balance maintained with some splendid ensembles and some particularly enjoyable light comedy numbers – the foolish violin and piccolo duet 'Piccolo, Piccolo, tsin, tsin, tsin', the delightful ladies' trio on temperament ('I weiss net') and the courtiers' worries over what will happen to the dynasty if the Prince doesn't get into his wife's bed ('Und die arme Dynastie').

The one complete recording of *Ein Walzertraum* is a 1970 set on the EMI Electrola label and features Nicolai Gedda as the Prince Consort whose marriage is threatened by courtly conventions, with Anneliese Rothenberger as his Princess and Edda Moser as the little violinist who sacrifices her own feelings to help the Princess win back her husband. All three are predictably excellent, but the highlight of the set is, of course, Gedda's expansive rendering of the tenor duet 'Leise, ganz leise' with the suitably self-effacing Willi Brokmeier. A touch more lightness and fun from the ladies – particularly Brigitte Fassbänder as the intermittently over-the-vocal-top mezzo-soprano royal confidante – wouldn't have hurt, but overall the set is a good record of what appears to be the show pretty much in its original state. The comedy rôle of Lothar has disappeared, and the music usually given to him (and to the comical King Joachim) is performed by the pleasant baritone Wolfgang Anheisser as Wendolin, but it doesn't really matter, for the songs are there. What are not there are the various interpolations that have accrued over the years, ranging from extra comic numbers written by the composer for the original London production, to the incongruous tipsy song taken from spare Straus to pad the part of the Princess in the current Volksoper version.

A selection from this set of two not very full records issued on a single disc has managed to take in all of the music except for the two little opening pieces and the last act Niki/Franzi duet. Unless you are keen on having the dialogue or every note of the score, this seems to be good value – certainly better value than the other principal selections on Telefunken and RCA (Peter Minich/Else Liebesberg/Eva Kasper), which cuts out four further pieces including two of the largest second-act numbers, or on Concert Hall and Primaphon (Rudolf Christ/Liebesberg/Renate Holm), which includes only eleven numbers and ultimately manages to squeeze most of them onto one side of a disc shared with *Hochzeitsnacht im Paradies*. Strangely, Ariola-Eurodisc seems to have bypassed *Ein Walzertraum* as a full disc, so fans of Rudolf Schock and Margit Schramm have to be content with a small selection on their 'Welterfolge Oscar Straus' record, where *Ein Walzertraum* shares space with numbers from *Der tapfere Soldat, Rund um Liebe* and *Der letzte Walzer*.

As *Rêve de valse*, the show had a particular success in France, and there have been no less than seven recordings made of the French version, including a truly splendid 1958 one on EMI-Pathé which stands head and shoulders above the rest. Baritone Michel Dens at his most tenorish is paired in the big waltz duo with the criminally wasted tenorino Claude Devos, who takes over the top line from his partner in time for the final B flat in most gentlemanly and agreeable style. There is a perfectly perfect Franzi in Liliane Berton, who is joined by Mado Robin (Princess Helene) and Solange Michel (Frederique) in a delicious if short version of the Temperament Trio, and by Pierre Germain (Lothar) for a properly comical Piccolo Duet.

Italy has turned out a double-disc *Sogno di valzer* as well as a selection in the EDM operetta series (backed with *Cin-ci-la*) and there is a sole selection of a dozen pieces recorded in English by EMI. *A Waltz Dream* was originally a failure in two George Edwardes productions in England (in spite of what the sleeve notes of this disc say). It didn't really take off in America either, and it has never become generally popular in the English language. June Bronhill, an ideal Franzi, is paired with popular tenor David Hughes (Niki), but she unfortunately takes that pairing too far by annexing the second tenor's half of the big waltz, thus disqualifying the record from any proper consideration.

Der tapfere Soldat

Der tapfere Soldat has never been regarded as a basic repertoire piece in its homeland and has not even been given a single excerpts recording there, the small selection on Ariola-Eurodisc's Straus compilation excepted. However, in its English-language guise as *The Chocolate Soldier* (a much better title) it has had a very much more prominent career, and its big waltz song 'My Hero' ('Held meiner Träume') has become a fixture of the soprano repertoire. 'My Hero' has been oft recorded, but larger selections from the show are surprisingly few and there is no representation of this most popular of operettas in the current catalogue. The sole British disc, a World Records recording with Stephanie Voss and Laurie Payne, has a meagre four songs (plus a non-Straus interpolation from the film version) on the back of a selection from Friml's *The Firefly*.

An American CBS selection with the stars of the film, Nelson Eddy and Risë Stevens, goes one song better, but Stevens joins Robert Merrill for the most substantial recording of *The Chocolate Soldier* – a two-disc version recorded on RCA in 1958. It is not a complete *Chocolate Soldier* any more than *The Chocolate Soldier* is a complete *Der tapfere Soldat*, but not too much is missing – Bumerli's last-act solo (perhaps because its title 'Why Is it Love Makes Us Feel Queer?' didn't quite fit in 1958), the march opening of Act 2, a little of the opening of Act 1. There have been some alterations, too – the duo 'The Chocolate Soldier' has been very oddly pushed from Act 1 to Act 2 and someone has tacked an extra section of 'My Hero' into the second-act finale – but the recording still, nevertheless, lets you mostly hear what this once so popular show is.

It is a shame it could not have done it with a little more spirit and gaiety. The performance is too often rather like old-time D'Oyly Carte, and much of the blame for this must go on the shoulders of Lehman Engel and his orchestra, who are square and unimaginative when they should be gay and comical. It must be shared by whoever did the casting. I know Risë Stevens starred in the film, but the film had a wholly different story, and her rich, mature mezzo-soprano sounds quite ridiculous singing the light, often soubrette, soprano music of the nubile teenage heroine of the show. When she joins in the two lovely all-female trios with Jo Sullivan (Masha) and Sadie McCollum (Aurelia) the balance is all upside down. The answer wasn't far away – the perky, bright-voiced Miss Sullivan would have been a splendid Nadina (and Stevens would have been a fine, swooning Masha) – but I suppose that would have upset the hierarchy.

The Metropolitan Opera's Robert Merrill as Bumerli lightens off his voice splendidly and with humour and, paired with a more suitable partner, would have been fine for the rôle, whilst Peter Palmer attacks Alexius's music strongly if occasionally approximately and Miss McCollum's mezzo-contralto mother is excellent.

However, although this *Chocolate Soldier* lies rather heavily on the stomach, it is the only real representation of the show on record and, until and if it is given another chance – preferably with Stanislaus Stange's awkward and unconsciously funny old translation replaced – it is all that is available (and not very) for anyone wishing to listen to a show which really is jollier and sweeter than it is allowed to be here.

Leo Fall

Leo Fall, a friend and contemporary of Straus, came to the fore round about the same time as the composer of *Ein Walzertraum* and, in the half dozen years before the war, he produced a series of outstanding and successful operettas that travelled the world. *Die Dollarprinzessin* (1907) is probably the best remembered, but *Die geschiedene Frau* (*The Girl in the Train*, *La Divorcée*) (1908) was a major international hit and *Der fidele Bauer* (*The Merry Peasant*) (1907) and *Der liebe Augustin* (1912) were other fine examples of the work of a composer who, in retrospect, has perhaps an extra sparkle of musical genius to spare over even his most famous and durable contemporaries.

I am at a loss to understand why Fall's marvellous operettas have been so neglected by recording companies. While the *Fledermice* fly out every few years, not one of these four memorable hits has been the subject of even one full record, much less a complete recording.

Die Dollarprinzessin

There have been a handful of selections from *Die Dollarprinzessin* issued on Philips, Polydor and Columbia, the Philips one paired (sometimes) with a selection from *Der fidele Bauer*, which has had an equivalently poor coverage. The Columbia disc backs *Die Dollarprinzessin* with a selection from *Zigeunerliebe*, starring Sári Bárabás and Heinz Hoppe, which takes in the song 'Lieber Onkel' not included on the recordings dealt with above.

Both shows on this record – and very different they are, with *Die Dollarprinzessin* tending clearly towards the light musical comedy genre – are sung by the same artists and are performed in the frustrating medley style. If this doesn't really allow you to get into the score it does, at least, give some idea of Fall's pretty, tuneful songs, beginning with the clickety-clacking of the little American typewriters, going on to introduce the star ('Das ist die Dollarprinzessin') in a choice waltz, and taking in an Automobile Trio and a comical display by 'Olga von der Wolga' in a show which treats America much in the same Ruritanian way that so many American shows treated central Europe. Bárabás, Hoppe, Christine Görner, Harry Friedauer and Hans-Maria Lins sing the music attractively without too much care for rôles.

The Philips recording does much better for amount of content – twelve separate numbers are given, if not in whole then at least in a substantial state. Unfortunately they are given in a nastily souped-up state, having been 'arranged' by someone called Bert Grund and rewritten by one Mischa Mleinek. Tatjana Iwanow spreads herself around lustily as the sexy cabaret star ('Ich stiege in der Finanzwelt') and most of the other performers skirt round the arrangements neatly, apparently in search of as much of the real *Dollarprinzessin* as they can find. *La principessa dei dollari* appears treated in the usual Italian style, sharing a disc with the Italian musical *La duchessa del bal tabarin* in the EDM series.

Der fidele Bauer

By the law of frequent repressings and rematchings, my copy of the Philips *Der fidele Bauer* is fortunately backed not with the phoney *Die Dollarprinzessin*, but with a Sári Bárabás/Rudolf Christ *Der Zigeunerbaron*. This is a joyfully lively recording of a colourful score. Erich Majkut sings the music of the old peasant of the title with clear, incisive tenor tones and with an attractive gentleness when necessary (as in the pretty 'Jeder tragt sein Pinkerl') but he attempts only limited characterization. Karl Terkal and Else Liebesberg, on the other hand, are a first-class singing pair in the principal tenor and soprano numbers. He rings all the bells with his vibrant waltz 'O frag mich nicht', she leads off the hugely happy 'Wir waren unser drei' and Bauernmarsch as the climax to the selection, and they come together very winningly in 'Morgen muss i fort von hier'.

There are other half-record *Die fidele Bauer* selections on Polydor and Columbia (EMI), and an EP on Amadeo, and I would suspect that any and all of them would give a representative selection of this happy score in the same way that Telefunken's little selection with Heinz Hoppe, Christoph Felsenstein, Benno Kusche and Sonja Schöner does in a jolly quarter-record medley.

Die geschiedene Frau

Die geschiedene Frau has been even less well done by, with an 45 EP Schock and Schramm recording on Ariola-Eurodisc, a treatment also given to *Der liebe Augustin* and to Fall's later, great and equally ill-treated *Madame Pompadour*, its largest recorded representation. Much of the content of these three discs (but unfortunately only two numbers and a chunk of the finale from *Die geschiedene Frau*) has been re-recorded on a compilation 30 cm record titled variously 'Welterfolge Leo Fall' and 'Und die Himmel hängt voller Geigen', the title of the best-known number from *Der liebe Augustin*. It is frustratingly little, but the record gives a tantalizing taste of the good things that are, for the moment, out of recorded reach.

EMI comes up with the nearest thing to a satisfying slice of early Fall with its lovely selection from *Der liebe Augustin*, which shares a disc with a splendid set of excerpts from his later *Die Rose von Stambul* and is discussed under the latter show.

Emmerich Kálmán

The attention refused to Fall has, in contrast, been poured lavishly onto his Hungarian contemporary Emmerich Kálmán, whose two greatest successes, the wartime *Die Csárdásfürstin* and the later *Gräfin Mariza* have both been frequently recorded. Kálmán's earliest works, dating from 1908 onwards, have received less attention, but *Ein Herbstmanöver* (*Tatárjárás* in its original Hungarian) (1908), *Der kleine König* (1912), *Zsuzsi Kisasszony* (1915) and, most notably *Der Zigeunerprimas* (*Sari* in America) (1912) are all represented in a lesser way on mainly Hungarian discs.

Der Zigeunerprimas, whose most celebrated song 'Mein alter Stradivari' gets some attention as a recital item, has one side of one of the less readily available

Qualiton records devoted to it (backed with *Zigeunerliebe*), but the other works are represented only by isolated numbers on the various collections of Kálmán's works. There have been several of these about over the years, but the only one I have is a selection on an American label, B. & F. Budapest Record Co. of Cleveland, Ohio (Selections from Beautiful Operettas by Emerich Kálmán (*sic*)), presumably transferred from a Hungarian original. One side is devoted to six pieces from *Csárdáskirálynö* (*Die Csárdásfürstin*), whilst the other is compiled of numbers from the four earlier works mentioned, plus one piece from *Marica grófnö* (*Gräfin Mariza*). The difference between the earlier, heavily Hungarian accented pieces and the definite Viennese swing of the later music is clearly noticeable.

Die Csárdásfürstin

It is *Die Csárdásfürstin*, however, that is the enduring element of Kálmán's earlier works. Its story is just another one about the lowly maiden and the high-born chap and their efforts to get together despite his parents and her pride. It displays, in the process of sorting out their affairs, one star romantic pair, one more light-hearted pair and, just for a change, one rueful older man, all with scenes and songs to deliver. But it is those songs, of course, which make *Die Csárdásfürstin* more than just another standard operetta. The score Kálmán composed for this show is indubitably one of his best: a happy mixture of Hungary and Austria, with a continuous series of melodious and rhythmic numbers. It begins with the Hungarian flavoured cabaret song ('Heia, heia in den Bergen ist mein Heimatland') delivered by Sylva, the heroine of the piece, in the course of her work, and takes in the lushly romantic duets 'Ja Mädchen gibt es wunderfeine', 'Heller Jubel' and 'Tausend kleine Engel singen' for the two lovers on the one hand, and, on the other, such delightfully jaunty numbers as 'Alle sind wir Sünder'/'Die Mädis vom Chantant', 'Ganz ohne Weiber geht die Chose nicht', 'Jaj Mamám' and the duet 'Mädel guck' for the less seriously romantic folk. In fact, the piece is sufficiently jolly in one of its many unserious, dancing moments to transform Mendelssohn's Wedding March into a saucy, rhythmic 'Hochzeitstanz' which at one stage becomes a csárdás.

Five full-length recordings have been made of *Die Csárdásfürstin*, three in German, one in Hungarian and most recently one in French, as *Princesse Czardas*. Ariola-Eurodisc put down a set with Dagmar Koller and René Kollo featured and in 1985 the Wiener Volksoper recorded their production, with Milena Rudiferia and Franz Wächter, amongst their live performance series, but easily the most significant of the German-language discs is, once again, an EMI recording, with Nicolai Gedda and Anneliese Rothenberger singing the rôles of the Austro-Hungarian lovers temporarily parted by social considerations.

This double-disc set takes in both a brisk text and the whole of the score plus one interpolated number – the hit song of *Das Veilchen vom Montmartre*, 'Heut' Nacht hab ich geträumt von dir' – added to make up for the fact that Gedda's rôle of Edwin doesn't actually have a genuine solo number. 'Last night I dreamt about you' is a sentiment that can slip fairly unnoticed into almost any romantic situation and, since this is a splendid number, there doesn't seem any reason why it shouldn't pop in to *Die Csárdásfürstin* instead of rotting on its crochets in the largely forgotten wilderness of *Das Veilchen*.

The casting on this recording is splendid from top to bottom. Anneliese Rothenberger is a glorious Sylva, using her warm, flowing voice in her cabaret song with a poised showiness which never becomes vulgarity, waltzing passionately through the expansive love duets, and swirling along with both the lushly romantic and the dramatic moments of the first-act finale in a way that simply could not be bettered, before bringing romance to its heights in the last dazzling waltz-duo 'Tausend kleine Engel singen'. Gedda takes hold of his extra song with ringing pleasure and joins Rothenberger in their handful of duets in a marvellous synthesis of two superb sounds. They have never been better together than they are here.

One of Gedda's great advantages as a performer of these works is his ability to switch from the richly lyrical to the light-hearted and even the comic with equal effect. Here, in three consecutive numbers, he bounces the rather deliberate but nice soprano Olivera Miljakovic (Stasi) through their little Schwalbenduett, wallops out the rhythmic Magyar melody of 'Jaj Mamám' with Willi Brokmeier (Boni) and pulls out all the sentimental stops with Rothenberger in 'Heller Jubel'. It is a very impressive display.

Willi Brokmeier is a model Boni, vigorous and bright of voice and full of personality, truly the life and soul of the cabaret club and the society ball, whilst Wolfgang Anheisser is equally enjoyable in the shorter rôle of Feri, and the two of them provide the most endearing moment of the whole set when they come together drooling politely over the cabaret chorus girls in the lilting 'Die Mädis vom Chantant'. Willy Mattes and the Symphonie-Orchester Graunke, which seems to have a special sympathy for this kind of music, play their part fully in making this an all-round first-class recording, one in which there doesn't seem to be a weak link anywhere.

The same cannot be said for the Volksoper recording. Putting in one strong, solid number for a songless hero is one thing (and they do, the same *Veilchen vom Montmartre* piece), fiddling around with the book bootlessly and shuffling about and snipping the score to no good effect is another. And when the resultant, messy *Csárdásfürstin* is performed at best quite attractively (Milena Rudiferia as Sylva), mostly just adequately, and at worst distinctly unpleasantly (Franz Wächter's Edwin), all the live-recording atmosphere and vitality in the world is not enough. With all its assets, surely the Volksoper can do better than this. It is the least good of the operetta-in-Japan sets.

The Hungarian recording is genuinely 'complete'. Stretching over three records, it includes both music and dialogue in full. This is fine if you can understand Hungarian, but otherwise it can become a little tiresome after the first hour or so. And, unfortunately, it is not in any case the libretto as written by Leo Stein and Bela Jenbach, but a heavily rewritten version concocted to feature the doyenne of Hungarian operetta, Hanna Honthy, in a major rôle fabricated for the occasion. Whatever you think of the speaking, however, the music gets splendid treatment. It is both sung and played with plenty of dash and vigour, with Erzsébet Házy a fine Sylva and György Korondi (Edwin), the very robust László Palócoz (Feri) and the characterful Róbert Rátonyi (Boni) all most enjoyable.

France's 1971 *Princesse Czardas* uses no dialogue and fits the entire score (but no overture, which is scorned as being unauthentic) on to one record. This one prides itself not only on sticking strictly to the music as Kálmán originally wrote it, without interpolation or cut and lacking only some *mélodrame* pieces, but also to the original orchestrations. It is, of course, in French, which detracts a little from all this authenticity, but the translation is a good one and the result is appreciable. It makes you wonder why those other productions had to try to 'improve' this excellent score, unless they were trying to edge in on the copyright.

The performance on this disc is generally good, although a little more Hungarian passion and dash here and there wouldn't have gone amiss. Michèle le Bris is a smooth and rich-voiced Sylva who produces some impressive moments, whilst the men are taken from that splendid pool of characterful tenors which France was able to call on at that time. Aimé Doniat (Boni) and Bernard Plantey (Feri) lilt delightfully through 'Les p'tit' demoiselles des variétés' (which sounds really good in French) and, if Henry Legay is not consistently at his best as Edwin, his best pieces are fine. If you want a *Princesse Czardas*, this one is much superior to the smaller selection issued by CBS – another 'family and friends' affair on which Merkès and Merval (Edwin/Sylva) and their son Alain (Boni) sing ten extracts with gusto and an over-the-footlights style, in keys that suit them, with lots of harp and fiddles. It is jolly, songs-from-the-shows stuff and not for those who like their *Princesse Czardas* straight.

Although the show has had its regulation amount of recordings in half-discs and medleys and EPs, often in tandem with *Gräfin Mariza*, there are just a few full-sized *Csárdásfürstin* selection records, beginning of course with a Eurodisc Schock-and-Schramm set of excerpts, and including others from CBS (Liselott Maikl/Hans Strohbauer), RCA (Erika Köth/Franz Fehringer), Saga (Friedl Loor/Mimi Coertse/Karl Terkal) and Summit. This last one is credited to the Operetta Ensemble of the City Theatre-Linz but, in fact, as I discovered when I began to listen to all these in sequence, what it really is is the Saga recording disguised under false names. There is no mistaking Karl Terkal's bright ringing tones, particularly when he helps himself to all of Boni and Feri's music as well as Edwin's, singing 'Die Mädis vom Chantant' as a solo, and soaring through the romantic duets with Friedl Loor and joining Mimi Coertse for 'Mädel guck' and the Schwalbenduett. When he arrives at the Sylva/Boni/Feri 'Jaj, Mamám' he solves the problem by cutting it to just a couple of lines and letting her sing one of them. Both the ladies, incidentally, have pretty voices, although Loor is a bit lacking in spirit in her opening number. The inclusion of two orchestral intermezzi means that several numbers including Boni's song and the second-act finale get left out, and there are some hectic slimmings, but even though this is a 'Karl Terkal and friends sing bits of *Die Csárdásfürstin*' disc, with no theatrical shape, it is perfectly enjoyable and Terkal himself is quite splendid. But I wonder how the Vienna State Opera Orchestra and Chorus and conductor Hans Hagen like being called the Operetta Ensemble of the Stadtstheater Linz and Franz Werfel?

The Eurodisc single finds Schock and Schramm both in their element, making this one of the best of that particular series. They are helped no little by Robert Stolz at the baton, who whisks the score along with a brilliance and swirling gaiety that is really irresistible. Thus encouraged – and this pair rarely need much encouragement – they fling themselves into their parts, and they and everyone else involved seem to have a splendid time. Schramm delivers a knife-bright version of her opening song, and swells to every bursting peak with Schock in their duets, whilst he (having appropriated 'Jaj, Mamám' and punched it to the wall to make up for the fact that Edwin hasn't a solo) sings quite splendidly throughout. Ferry Gruber gives a top-notch impersonation of Boni, teaming delightfully with Dorothea Chryst in a really cute 'Mädel guck', and if Julius Katona is a mite insecure as Feri it has to be remembered that he is playing an ageing rake.

Viktor Jacobi

Szibill

Although his operettas have not survived outside Hungary to the same extent that Kálmán's chief works have, Viktor Jacobi won international success in the years before the war with two exceptional works. *Leányvásár* (*The Marriage Market*) (1911) and *Szibill* (1914) were played throughout the world, encouraging Jacobi to move to America, where a budding Broadway career was cut short by a very premature death.

Jacobi's score to *Szibill* is one of the too little known joys of the operetta world, a marvellous mixture of lovely, light arioso and comic numbers. The delicate lyricism of the show's big waltz duet 'Illúzió a szerelem' and the gently tender sweep of Sybil's Letter Song are the antithesis of the big belt operetta where tenor and soprano steam through their emotional moments fortissimo, whilst the quaintly loping rhythms of the comedian's adorable duet with the heroine ('Félre csapom a kalapom') and the piquantly tripping measures of his teaming with the soubrette in 'Van Valami', 'Ha én vakahová megyek' and, above all, the delicious mazurka 'Gombhaz, hogyha leszakad', make their comic point wonderfully through their infectious rhythms and their dancing melodies.

The Hungarian record company Qualiton put down a selection from *Szibill* in 1964. The recording is not the last word in technical sophistication, but it is quite good enough to get across the beauty of Jacobi's music in some style. Marika Németh takes the title rôle of Sybil, an opera singer who masquerades as a Duchess to protect her soldier lover (Róbert Ilosfálvy) from disgrace and then finds herself face to face with 'her' Duke (Zsolt Bende), who seems determined to take the pretence into real life. If the fine voices of some of the principals are just occasionally a little insecure, their performances are nevertheless both individual and first rate. Németh and Bende achieve a splendid intimacy in their make-believe love scene, barely taking the tempting 'Illúzió a szerelem' above mezzo piano, and Ilosfalvy performs his part in Sybil's Letter Song with similar simplicity and taste. The comic couple, Róbert Rátonyi and Vali Koltai, are right on the mark in their numbers, singing with crisp and pointed ease, never vulgar or exaggerated, and they contribute enormously to the success of what is a truly heart-warming record.

The value of these performances is all the more obvious when they are compared with those on a short selection from *Szibill* included on another Qualiton record ('Illúzió a Szerelem – Jacobi Viktor operettjeiből'), made twenty years later, of a variety of Jacobi show numbers. Here the lovely *Szibill* music, grossly reorchestrated, is bumped along tastelessly, and two of the soubrette pieces, so appealing on the earlier version, are given a truly vulgar performance by a lady called Ildikó Hámori. Unfortunately the orchestrations throughout this record are deeply suspect (and if that's the Budapest Symphony Orchestra I'm very sorry for symphonies in Budapest), but some, though definitely not all, of the singing is rather better than the soubrette performance.

Leányvásár

Miss Hámori is also featured alongside some other fairly broad performers (including a romantic tenor who is almost comical in his posturings) in a selection of six pieces from *Leányvásár*, which make up almost one full side of this same sorry record.

There is almost as much to enjoy in *Leányvásár* as in *Szibill*. Being a thoroughly light romantic-comical piece (set, incidentally, in the goldfields of Ruritanian California), it does not have the lingering lyrical moments of the really romantic portions of the later show. It is the lively, rhythmic numbers of *Leányvásár*, such as the bouncy little 'Kettecskén' and the hilarious 'Gilolo', which are its special joy. Musical comedy meets operetta and the meeting is to the benefit of both. Even the waltzes swing. The over-the-top performances do less harm than they might to these jaunty numbers, but the singers on this 1984 recording are not in the same league as the players on an earlier version which, like the *Szibill* one, dates from the early 1960s and takes in a much larger piece of the score.

Like that *Szibill* record, it is not a masterpiece of fine technical recording, but the sound on this disc is respectable and the singing, if occasionally a bit wobbly, is also what I assume is idiosyncratically Hungarian. Marika Németh is again the leading lady, this time playing a saucy young American lass who goes out to imitate the plot of *Martha* and gets caught in the same marriage-market trap. She is at her most appealingly individual here, waltzing gently through 'Lucy belépoje' and giving her well-modulated all in the lovely, vaguely Pucciniesque 'Tele van szivem'. She is joined in several light romantic ensembles, notably the gloriously melodic first-act finale and the pretty, limpid 'Mondjad igazán', by Tibor Udvardy, generally more relaxed and thus generally more pleasant than in some of his other performances, as the backwoodsman who marries the unknowing heroine.

Anna Zentay is, as in most recordings of this period, the soubrette and she has the best of things in this show. She is occasionally harsh but attacks her numbers cutely, marching along her 'oompah-oompah' solo ('Tengerész-dal') and making a treat of her three duets with comic tenor Róbert Rátonyi – who is, as usual on these Qualiton discs, the most accomplished of all the performers. To hear the two of them hippity-hopping through 'Kettecskén' and 'No, de méltóságos' to Jacobi's gently bouncy dance strains and their very agreeable orchestral arrangements, and rattling off the rhythmic choruses of 'Gilolo', is pure musical comedy fun, as good as anything of its kind from any pre-war show from any country.

Pongrác Kacsóh

János vitéz

Pongrác Kacsóh's *János vitéz* (1904) is a special case amongst Hungarian operettas. There are no dashing ladies with sexy csárdás to sing, and waltz music and the other international operetta elements appear only when the wholly foreign French court impinges on the world of 'John the Hero'. *János vitéz* is built on a deeply romantic tale which has something of the Orpheus legend, Giselle or Peer Gynt to it, whilst remaining staunchly Hungarian in character to such an extent that it has become accepted more or less as the national operetta, before and above the internationally better known pieces. Kacsóh's music is in keeping with the nature of the show's tale, with much of the Hungarian national and folk-music styles in its score, and includes several extremely effective solos – the hero's 'Én a pásztorok királya', the touchingly plaintive soprano song 'Van egy szegény kis árva lány' and the French Princess's showpiece waltz, which strikes a pointedly artificial note amongst the warmth of the Hungarian music.

János vitéz has been twice recorded in full on three records by Qualiton/Hungaraton, which has also issued selections from these recordings. The first, made in 1963, starred Róbert Ilosfálvy in the title rôle of the piece, originally played *en travesti* by a soprano, and he is well supported by Anna Zentay as the hero's beloved Iluska and Mária Gyurkovics as the French Princess. The single recording has been for many years a pleasant way of making acquaintance with an important musical. The three-record set is strictly for Hungarian speakers.

When the second set was issued, in 1988, I felt slightly annoyed that even such a piece as this should be given a repeat recording when so much fine Hungarian operetta remains on paper. Then I listened to it. Firstly, it is probably the best-made record to have come out of Hungary that I have heard. The sound is clear and almost frighteningly immediate, the voices have been captured magnificently and the balance is impeccable. Then, on top of that, there is some superb orchestral playing and chorus singing from the forces of the Fövárosi Operettszinház, and the lead rôles are played by some of the most impressive new (to me) singers I have heard. Joszef Kovacs is the Janos – a clear, moving tenor who draws you to him – and the Iluska (Marika Oszvald) has the most beautiful, straight young soprano voice. To hear her sing her opening 'Van egy szegény kis árva lány' is quite ravishing. With voices like these available, I hope Qualiton will quickly record every Hungarian operetta in sight.

Andrea Zsadon tackles the coloratura of the French Princess's song with assurance, accuracy and fine tone and Sandor Suka plays the French King in the traditional way as a croaking ancient. It is only because all these folk are so very good that the Bagö (Gabor Garday) sounds a tiny bit stretched at the edges of his range.

Jenö Huszka

Bob Herceg and Lili Bárónö

Hungary produced other successful musical theatre composers whose careers spanned the pre- and post-war eras. Jeno Huszka turned out two pieces which had enduring hometown success, one on each side of the hostilities: *Bob herceg* (*Prince Bob*) (1902) and *Lili bárónö* (*Baroness Lili*) (1919), each with libretti all or partly by the same Ferenc Martos who had written Jacobi's two big hits. Huszka is no Jacobi, although his musicals are very pleasant. *Prince Bob* presents the joyous peculiarity of being set in Britain with a hero who is the son of the reigning monarch bent on marrying a commoner – a slight revenge for the many British musicals which used Hungary and its neighbours as the setting for more or less preposterous romances.

In the 1960s Qualiton issued an attractive recording devoted to Huszka's two hits using the same basic team that made such a success of Jacobi's two operettas. Like those discs it has been maintained in their catalogue since. An overture and four numbers from *Prince Bob* include an amusing Guards' March (it is hard to imagine the busbys of Britain marching to this very un-British piece) and some smoothly attractive songs for the hero neatly sung by Róbert Ilosfálvy, but the later *Lili bárónö* gets a more thorough treatment, with eight songs.

Gül Baba

Two further Huszka operettas, the Turkish-flavoured *Gül Baba* (1905) (based on another famous Hungarian semi-historical tale) and *Mária föhadnagy* (*Lieutenant Mary*), were given a similar treatment on another Qualiton disc of the same period, but in 1986 *Gül Baba*, apparently as the result of a television production, was given a full record of seventeen pieces to itself. As a recording, this is in another class from the tatty Jacobi collection of two years previously. Sound, orchestral playing and singing are all numerous notches up the scale, with a particularly attractive soprano, Katalin Farkas, and a splendidly vibrant and masculine tenor, Dénes Gulyás, leading the cast of what appears from this record to be a thoroughly romantic and picturesque piece rather than a comic operetta. It lacks the real genius of Jacobi, the fun and the passion, but, especially as performed on this recording, it is an enjoyable piece of distinctly Hungarian musical theatre.

More Enduring Operettas

Outside the works of the most important composers, there were several significant operetta successes on the pre-war and wartime stages of central Europe that have continued to hold the stage and which have had the honours of recording in various degrees. Czechoslovakia's Oskar Nedbal had his one lasting success with the colourful *Polenblut* in 1913, and Charles Cuvillier opened *Der lila Domino* (1912) in Berlin before taking it on to triumph in London, where the 1916 Schubert pasticcio *Das Dreimäderlhaus* proved even more successful under the title *Lilac Time*. Finally, Leon Jessel's *Schwarzwaldmädel* (1917) gave its composer his most enduring success.

Polenblut

In spite of its continued popularity, *Polenblut* has only twice been put on disc, by Ariola-Eurodisc and by Philips. The former is the one that is readily available. It displays a good, characterful operetta score which mixes a handful of nice waltz tunes – 'Ihr seid ein Kavalier', 'Mädel, dich hat mir die Glücksfee', 'Hören Sie, wie es singt und klingt' – and a lively march song for the hero with the occasional comic moment and some more specifically Polish styles and strains without pushing up any really memorable numbers.

Rudolf Schock is the footloose and financially frowsy Count Bolo and Margit Schramm is Helena, who puts his affairs and his heart into order by the end of the last act, and both clearly enjoy their rôles. Schock's bravura style suits the part of the cocksure Count well and Miss Schramm neatly combines sweetness and strength as she waltzes and polonaises him towards marriage through the dozen numbers that make up this selection. In a particularly good supporting cast, Fritz Ollendorf is especially enjoyable as Helena's father, plumbing the bottom of the bass range with some rumbling E flats in his buffo assertions that 'Ich bin ein Diplomate', and Ferry Gruber as the Count's best friend and Helena's ally gives some pleasantly unforced character tenor singing. The bulk of the action and the singing, however, belongs to the two stars who come to a peak in the second-act finale with its big waltz. My one real complaint about this recording is that, for no obvious reason, it jumbles up the order of the songs, thus taking away the dramatic context of the music.

For collectors of oddities, a selection from *Polenblut* has been recorded in Czech (backed with the work of another Czech composer – *Rose Marie*) on the Supraphon label.

Der lila Domino

Der lila Domino, in spite of its huge success, has survived only on one little English HMV 45 EP, whilst a couple of bits of Cuvillier's other principal success, *Afgar*, appear on World Records's Alice Delysia compilation, transferred from the 78s made of the original London production.

Das Dreimäderlhaus

Das Dreimäderlhaus, however, with its processed Schubert score (originally very attractively selected and arranged by Heinrich Berté) has been liberally recorded it its different versions – *Chanson d'amour* in France, *Lilac Time* in England, *Blossom Time* in America, *La casa della tre ragazze* in Italian and *Harom a kislány* in Hungarian. French Decca actually put out a two-record set of the French version of the show, but the bulk of the recordings are limited to a single disc.

The two most often found German-language recordings feature Schock and Margit Schramm – separately. He is paired on a full Ariola-Eurodisc disc with Renate Holm, she on another on EMI with Adolf Dallapozza. The 1972 EMI disc, made with a certain amount of doubling of rôles and no chorus, is nevertheless a pretty good one and includes all but a couple of the musical items in the score. The three little Tschöll daughters, so ghastly in Adrian Ross's English translation when they insist on opening the show as 'Tilli and Willi and Lilli Veit, trim and tight, brisk and bright', are much more acceptable in German as the harmonizing Haiderl und Hederl und Hannerl Tschöll, especially when cutely sung by the girlish Schramm (unrecognizable as the same artist who produced such dramatic moments in *Zigeunerliebe*), Monika Dahlberg, and Hildegard Hartwig (who sounds only less youthful because she's a mezzo). Dallapozza is a fine bright tenor Schubert who unfortunately replaces the climactic three-handed second-act finale, with its rendition of 'Ich schnitt es gern in alle Rinden ein', with a solo version, rather despoiling the rôle of Schober (Peter Karner). Dahlberg doubles delightfully as the flighty prima donna who upsets his romance, whilst Benno Kusche has his moment in father Tschöll's number and splits himself in half when two of the rôles he is playing turn up on two occasions in the same number.

The Eurodisc record is less satisfying. It is arranged mainly to show off the voice of the irrepressible Schock. Schubert's serenade 'Leise flehen meine Lieder' is added at the top of the disc, and 'Ich schnitt es gern in alle Rinden ein' is again filched from the rôle of Schober. Practically any number in which Schock or Renate Holm (Hannerl) is not involved is cut. The exercise falls well short because, in any case, Schock is on a decidedly off day, Holm sounds far too mature and the romantic efforts of the Berlin Symphoniker are wasted.

Schock had an earlier go at an even more souped-up version of the show on EMI-Electrola (DaCapo). This one mentions the 1958 film on its sleeve, even though only Schock from the film cast is included. It certainly isn't a soundtrack, but probably a spin-off record, as it is dated 1958 as well. Schock pops in 'Leise flehen meine Lieder' again, but he doesn't sing it particularly well, any more than he does most of the rest of a warm, modest rôle which, for all that he appears attached to it, seems to suit his forthright style ill. Erika Köth is ideally cast as a lovely, fresh Hannerl, Erich Kunz for some reason gets to sing 'Der Lindenbaum', which he does delightfully in spite of a contest with some angel voices, and someone who I presume is Walther Hauck (no one is credited) makes a particularly warm job of old Tschöll's song ('Geh, Alte, schau') amongst the oddities of arrangement and allocation of numbers.

The most comprehensive, unadulterated and best sung *Das Dreimäderlhaus* is, however, none of these but a recording which I wasn't aware existed until I stumbled on it, very recently, in a Viennese second-hand shop. It is on the Amadeo label and shows no date, but, as it gives information about playing mono records on stereo equipment, it would seem to be from the early 1960s. This one gives the whole score and nothing but the score as played in the original *Dreimäderlhaus*, very nearly in the right order, recorded with a lively clarity and played with loving musicianship by the orchestra of the Theater an der Wien under Rudolf Bibl.

Peter Minich is Schubert, playing the rôle with some feeling for the very vulnerable character of the composer, and, even if the voice occasionally goes a little red in its upper reaches, that is not unsuitable. Ernst Schütz's Schober, a fine self-confident tenor, strides ringingly through the serenade and understandably gets the girl. The girl is again Miss Holm, but here she is in very top form, singing with simplicity and lovely tone. She is still not precisely girlish, and neither are her sisters, with whom she turns out a delightful 'three little maids' trio, but the singing is grand. Fritz Muliar (Tscholl) and Monique Lobasa (Grisi) complete the solo team impeccably, but amongst the most impressive elements of this recording are the supporting artists who make up the beautifully balanced quartet, quintet and sextet which are so important to the score. The ensemble music on this disc is perhaps its most successful single element, but the whole record is extremely enjoyable and it is also a fine and faithful representation of the show.

If you can put up with Tilli and Willi and Lilli (and there are worse rhymes than this), there is an 1959 EMI recording of a smallish selection from the English version (with the music further rearranged by G. H. Clutsam into what we know as *Lilac Time*), which is neatly produced and well sung. June Bronhill is a very forceful Lilli (or is it Tilli?), Thomas Round sings Schubert agreeably but less forcefully (which isn't too good in their duet) and John Cameron as a baritone Schober gets his part of the finale, but is handicapped by the words ('Yours is my heart') and the musical rearrangement and can do little with it but sing strongly, which he does.

The French stick closer to the German original musically, but they have Annette, Nanette and Jeannette Mühl, and, on the EMI-Pathé recording at least, do the men the opposite way round – a tenor Schober and a baritone

Schubert. This fits the usual cliché – the baritone usually loses the girl to the tenor – but it is less effective musically, and even Michel Dens, backed by perhaps not the very best Pathé cast, cannot seem to make things terribly exciting.

The American version, again musically rearranged (this time by Romberg), has replaced Lilli, Tilli and Willi by Mitzi and Fritzi and Titzi (I think) Kranz in Dorothy Donnelly's version. It appears in a brief selection in the Reader's Digest set of show discs, where seven numbers are sung by pretty Mary Ellen Pracht and a bundle of stalwart-voiced gentlemen headed by William Lewis and Richard Fredrick, and also on an Al Goodman recording which does some very strange things not only to Schubert but to Romberg. *Blossom Time* is very, very far away from the *Das Dreimäderlhaus* that is presented on the German recordings and it is abundantly clear that the further away from that first arrangement the versions of Schubert's life and music go, the more uncomfortable they come. Haiderl, Hederl and Hannerl have a very big edge on their sisters, and Amadeo's long-lost disc has equally as large an edge on the other main recordings of them.

Schwarzwaldmädel

Leon Jessel's *Schwarzwaldmädel* has become popular as the favourite example from its period of a folksy type of operetta, and it is easy to hear why. Jessel's score, set to a simple story of town and country folk, is a happy, lively, fun-filled affair which echoes the unpretentiousness of its book. Jolly, rhythmic numbers with country-dancing melodies make up the largest, and the best, part of the score. The waltzes are strictly limited. When they do appear, they are happiest when, in the image of the show's most attractive number, the little soubrette's 'Erklingen zum Tanze die Geigen', they are jolly country waltzes and not lurchingly romantic town ones. There is one of the latter – the first-act finale steams into a big-time waltz ('Muss denn die Lieb' stets Tragödie sein') – but I like to think that it is really a tongue-in-cheek affair, laughing at the silly town folk and their overblown romances. *Schwarzwaldmädel* is pure dancing and singing fun and, if occasionally it threatens to get bogged down, courtesy of an overindulgent conductor or singer, Jessel's bouncing beat soon gets things going again.

The piece has been recorded on its ration of one-half and one-quarter discs, and Ariola-Eurodisc devotes a full Schock-and-Schramm record to it, but the fullest treatment given to the show is on a delightfully lively 1976 EMI-Electrola recording with Willy Mattes at the head of the Stuttgarter Philharmoniker and a really spunky cast. The two tenor town lads who come to the country to escape a young lady who has intentions on one of them are played by Adolf Dallapozza (Hans) and Martin Finke (Richard). They burst on the scene with a wallop in the lusty 'Wir sind auf der Walz' and keep up the energy and, in Finke's case, the fun right through the piece. When Malwine, the lady in question (Dagmar Koller), arrives, they each get pinned down for a duet in waltz time which conforms to their capacities. Finke has well-sung fun with 'Lockende Augen holder Sirenen' and the more lyrical Dallapozza gets to pull out the sob stops in the finale.

Whilst all this is going on, the major subplot dealing with the village church organist (Benno Kusche) and his little maid (Brigitte Lindner) produce some of the best bits of the show. Miss Lindner, who is actually young enough to be billed as a 'mädchensopran' (girl soprano), is quite something. She has the most charming voice, and it is quite delightful to listen to her tiptoeing through her little shadow song and dance to a whistling accompaniment, or pinging out the notes of her pretty waltz. I could not stop myself thinking 'I hope she didn't grow up with a wobble' (which she didn't, as later records show). Benno Kusche, Herr Reliability himself, is as grand as ever.

There is a second and fairly unnecessary subplot involving a young village couple which is useful only because it introduces a delicate little solo for the girl in the last act. It also introduces a duo in the first, which is the main one of those 'boggy' bits, and here, oversung desperately, it is the only moment when the recording looks as if it might get embedded up to its ankles. Still, this version actually manages to fit the entire score, excepting one little children's chorus, onto its two very substantial sides, so one can't complain if completeness means you get the less good with the very good. I rate *Schwarzwaldmädel* and this recording very good.

The Eurodisc version is an unusual one for that set, as it includes a few bits of narrative dialogue. As a result it leaves off several numbers, including both those relating to the 'spare' couple and the main version of 'Lockende Augen', which is replaced in the running order by 'Malwine, ach, Malwine' pushed back from Act 2. The selection is done in suitably energetic fashion under the direction of Werner Schmidt-Bölcke, with Schock, Schramm and Karl-Ernst Mecker leading the townsfolk with lively extravagance (there is no doubt about 'Muss den Liebe der Tragödie sein' being a burlesque here), and basso Fritz Ollendorf (Blasius) and the delightful Lotte Schädle (a maturer Bärbele) at the head of the country team. Acceptable enough in itself, it doesn't come up to its fellow recording in any department.

My Ten Essential Records

DIE FLEDERMAUS: complete, with Julius Patzak and Hilde Güden (2 records, Decca DPA 585–6)

DER ZIGEUNERBARON: complete, with Nicolai Gedda and Elisabeth Schwarzkopf (2 records, EMI SXDW 3046); CD (EMI CHS 7 69526 2)

BOCCACCIO: complete, with Hermann Prey and Anneliese Rothenberger (2 records, EMI-Electrola 1C 157–30216–7); CD (EMI CDM 7 69096 2, highlights)

DER BETTELSTUDENT: complete, with Hermann Prey, Rita Streich and Nicolai Gedda (2 records, EMI 1C 30162–3); CD (EMI CMS 7 69678 2)

DIE LUSTIGE WITWE: complete, with Elisabeth Schwarzkopf and Erich Kunz (2 records, EMI SXDW 3045); CD (EMI CDH7 69520 2)

DER VOGELHÄNDLER: selection, with Peter Minich and Lotte Schädle (Telefunken 6.21256)

ZIGEUNERLIEBE: selection, with Rudolf Schock and Margit Schramm (Ariola-Eurodisc 89 886 IE); CD (Ariola 258 360–218)

EIN WALZERTRAUM: complete, with Nicolai Gedda, Anneliese Rothenberger and Edda Moser (2 records, EMI 1C 157 29041–2)

SZIBILL: selection, with Marika Németh, Róbert Ilosfálvy Róbert Rátonyi and Vali Koltai (Qualiton SLPX 6543)

DIE CSÁRDÁSFÜRSTIN: complete, with Nicolai Gedda, Anneliese Rothenberger and Willi Brokmeier (2 records, EMI C191–29066–7); CD (EMI CMS 7 69672 2)

Other Recommended Records

Die schöne Galathee: complete, with Anna Moffo and René Kollo (RCA RL 25108; or Eurodisc 87 583 IE); CD (CD 258 376–218)

Fatinitza: selection, with Ruth Müller-Inden, Klaus Lange and Kurt Lewa (Amiga 540–145) (45 EP)

Der lustige Krieg: selection, with Elisabeth Roon and Waldemar Kmentt (Vox PL 206000; or Summit SUM5003)

Eine Nacht in Venedig: complete, with Cesare Curzi, Nicolai Gedda and Rita Streich (2 records, EMI TC 157.29 096–6); CD (CMS 7 69363 2)

Wiener Blut: complete, with Nicolai Gedda and Anneliese Rothenberger (2 records, EMI 157.30 668–70); CD (CDM 7 69095 2, highlights)

1001 Nacht: selection, with Herbert Ernst Groh (Classics Club X163)

Valses de Vienne: selection, with Janine Ervil, Gabriel Bacquier and Colette Riedinger (Decca 215.758)

Gasparone: complete, with Hermann Prey, Anneliese Rothenberger and Gunther Wewel (2 records, EMI 157 46571–2); CD (CDM 7 69092 2)

Die Dubarry: selection, with Karl Terkal and Else Liebesberg (b/w Gasparone) (Fontana 701 513 WPY)

Der Vogelhändler: complete, with Julius Patzak and Wilma Lipp (2 records, Philips SBL 5215)

Der Obersteiger: selection, with Walter Schmidt, Jola Koziel and Beatrix Kujau (Amiga 5 40 184) (45 EP)

Die schönste Melodien von Carl Michael Ziehrer: (b/w Die lustige Witwe) with Harald Serafin and Mirjana Irosch (Philips 9105 054)

Und die Himmel hängt voller geigen: excerpts from operettas by Leo Fall with Rudolf Schock and Margit Schramm (including Die geschiedene Frau, Der liebe Augustin, Die Rose von Stambul, Madame Pompadour) (Ariola-Eurodisc 86 929 EE)

Der liebe Augustin: selection, with Sári Bárábas and Heinz Hoppe (b/w Die Rose von Stambul) (EMI-Electrola SMC 83 454)

Die Dollarprinzessin: selection, with Sári Bárábas and Heinz Hoppe (b/w Zigeunerliebe) (Columbia 33 WSX 699)

Der fidele Bauer: selection, with Erich Majkut, Karl Terkal and Else Liebesberg (b/w Der Zigeunerbaron) (Philips P08179L; or Fontana 701 514 WPY)

Der Graf von Luxemburg: complete, with Nicolai Gedda and Lucia Popp (2 records, EMI 157–28 982/3); CD (EMI CDM 7 69216 2, highlights)

Das Dreimäderlhaus: complete, with Peter Minich, Renate Holm and Ernst Schütz (Amadeo AVRS 9242)

Leányvásár: selection, with Marika Németh and Anna Zentay (Qualiton LPX 6527)

Wie einst im Mai: revival cast recording, and selection with René Kollo (RCA VL 30413)

Schwarzwaldmädel: complete, with Martin Finke, Adolf Dallapozza, Brigitte Lindner and Dagmar Koller (EMI-Electrola 1C 061–30 691)

Polenblut: selection, with Rudolf Schock and Margit Schramm (Ariola-Eurodisc 89 888 1E)

Bob herceg/Lili Bárónö: selection, with Róbert Ilosfálvy, Marika Németh, Róbert Rátonyi and Anna Zentay (Qualiton SLPX 6536)

Janos Vitez: selection, with Joszef Kovacs and Marika Oszwald (Qualiton SLPM 16770) (also available in 3-disc set with dialogue on Qualiton SLPX 16618–20)

The Lilac Domino: selection, in English, with Aileen Cochran and Charles Young (HMV GES 5778) (45 EP)

CHAPTER 4

LPs of America's Pre-LP Days

Early Days

America has, in more recent years, paid a certain amount of attention to the past glories of its native light musical theatre. It has begun to treat its heritage – for want of a less pompous word – with a respect and a seriousness (just sometimes, perhaps, too much seriousness) which the British, the devotees of Gilbert and Sullivan apart, have largely failed to show. The German and French language theatres and their parallel recording industries have busied themselves with reviving and recording their classic repertoires largely because of the almost total lack of modern light theatre music being produced on the Continent; the British, busy with the excitement of today, have practically ignored yesterday, but America has shown some interest in restaging the outstanding musicals of the past and also some equal care for preserving those revivals on disc alongside re-recordings of archive material which re-present the scores and stars of the pre-LP era for modern listeners.

This is a very reversal of the situation of the early part of the century. When the gramophone was first popularized, it was the British who leaped into action, recording vast amounts of show music, much of it original cast material, on 78 rpm discs, whilst America paid only spotty attention to the field. In fact, odd as it may seem, some highly successful American shows which played London between the wars are represented on disc only or largely in contemporary recordings made by British casts and on British labels. The coming of the LP age, coinciding as it did with the most prosperous period of Broadway's musical history, undoubtedly had a good deal to do with the change in attitude evidenced in America – a change for which we must be extremely thankful.

The earliest days of the substantial light musical theatre in America subsisted very largely on imported musicals – the internationally successful products of London, Paris, Vienna and Berlin – and it was some time before a significant native musical theatre established itself. When the first major hits began to emerge they were, more often than not, of the type that presented knock-about low comedy stories illustrated with popular songs, new or, very often, second-hand. Many of these songs survived as great popular hits, but the composition of the shows was fluid, and material flowed in and out of them at a producer's or performer's whim. They were not the kind of shows which presented a coherent score.

A number of the outstanding popular show songs from the latter years of the nineteenth century found their way on to 78 rpm disc and some survive to today, even though most people are now mostly unaware that they gained their fame in a stage musical. 'After the Ball', 'Reuben and Cynthia' and 'The Bowery', for example, all featured in the hugely successful *A Trip to Chinatown* (1890). An enterprising recording made in 1978 with Cincinnati's University Singers and Orchestra, which takes its title from the *In Dahomey* song 'I Wants to Be an Actor Lady', brings together a number of such songs, combined on a full disc with pieces from slightly later and more sophisticated shows and writers. The performances are often a bit insecure, but, amongst the always interesting material, there is a splendidly lusty version of May Irwin's famous 'Bully Song' from *The Widow Jones*, which deserves to be particularly signalled, alongside the ringing 'Stein Song' from Gustav Luders's musical comedy *The Prince of Pilsen*, the extravagantly burlesque duo 'Buckets of Gore' (*The Corsair*) and such better-known pieces as 'The Yankee Doodle Boy' (*Little Johnny Jones*) and 'How'd You Like to Spoon with Me' (*The Earl and the Girl*). This last number is performed by Kim Criswell, then a member of the soprano section of the University Singers.

Reginald de Koven

Robin Hood

The 1890s brought the first really important American musical shows of a more substantial kind, shows modelled on the various styles of European comic opera, and the first of these to make a significant mark was Harry B. Smith and Reginald de Koven's *Robin Hood*, produced in Chicago in 1890. Its most enduring song, the wedding hardy annual 'O, Promise Me', has been often recorded and reused, but nothing resembling the show's full score was brought to LP until recently when a radio broadcast performance (undated and unidentified on the sleeve) was transferred to disc on the AEI label. It is an odd recording, with the songs linked by rhyming narration and dialogue and the quality badly obscured by the crackles of time, but through the noise one can recognize the charm of the score and some excellent singing.

De Koven subsequently achieved some success with several other pieces in a similar vein (*Rob Roy*, *The Highwayman*, *The Fencing Master*, *The Tzigane*), but *Robin Hood* remains his only enduring success. Another composer whose stage reputation rested on one work was John Philip Sousa, better known nowadays for his march music. His *El Capitan* has been regularly revived, but unfortunately none of these performances has made it onto record.

Victor Herbert

The one composer who has emerged from this period with a solid reputation, and who has become regarded as the founding father of the musical theatre in America in much the same way that Gilbert and Sullivan have in Britain, is the Irish-born, German-educated Victor Herbert. This is not the place to analyse this assumption nor the varying and often considerable merits of Herbert's writing, merely to register the fact that, between his first work, *Prince Ananias*, in 1894 and his last posthumous production in 1924, he became generally regarded as the most important of Broadway's composers. Herbert shifted from operatic burlesque through comic opera, children's musicals, farce musicals, and vehicles for a whole range of singing and comedy stars to veritable grand opera in a vigorously versatile display of composing art. He achieved some great success – not just in one narrow area – and many utter failures, and the best of his music survives today as the principal representative of the period.

Herbert comes to us on two types of recording. On the one hand there are the records of his enduring hits – *Naughty Marietta, Mlle Modiste, Babes in Toyland* and *The Red Mill* – made under modern conditions and on their merits; on the other there are the archive recordings compiled with historical considerations in mind. These last, like all of their kind, are not made for easy listening. They are scratchy, squeaky re-recordings of very old material, to which I personally find no pleasure in listening. They are interesting insofar as they show contemporary performance styles (though I do not believe that performance for stage and for recordings were necessarily related) and artists (the same comment applies), and they are worthy in that they sometimes allow us to hear music otherwise unrecorded, but they are not for an evening's enjoyable listening.

The chief of these archival compilations is a three-record set assembled by Allen G. Debus and issued by the Smithsonian Institution in 1979. It includes early recordings from *The Fortune Teller, Babes in Toyland, Mlle Modiste, The Red Mill, Naughty Marietta, Sweethearts* and the operas *Natoma* and *Madeleine* and a booklet full of some learned writing. It would, perhaps, have been preferable to have incorporated some of the lesser-known Herbert works here, as almost all these musicals have been recorded at least partially under modern conditions – and it really is more pleasant to listen to Mary Smith recorded in 1988 than no matter what distorted star of 1898. This is a set, really, for those interested in *Natoma* and Mr Debus's notes.

Naughty Marietta

The Smithsonian has, however, come up trumps in the alternative field. They have issued a two-disc recording of the most famous of Herbert's works, *Naughty Marietta* (1910), which is the most comprehensive recording of any American work of the pre-war period. This recording is apparently based on the Broadway opening-night version of the show, with Herbert's score and original orchestrations tactfully tailored by Frederick Roffman, who did some considerable rewriting of the piece for its 1978 New York City Opera production.

To those whose knowledge of Herbert and *Naughty Marietta* is limited to Jeanette MacDonald and Nelson Eddy on film, this set will be a revelation. Alongside the famous songs which were made international successes by the movie, you can now hear the remainder of the score – delicious chorus and ensemble writing and finales in direct line of descent from Sullivan rather than from the more recent and then currently idolized *Merry Widow* genre, lively comedy songs and some lovely orchestral music. *Naughty Marietta* was not just a little bundle of bon-bons, but a varied score of shapely proportions.

The recording, of course, does not have MacDonald and Eddy, but it gains from that. It is a very real sounding performance – you can almost see the action going on – and if the singers occasionally sound a little effortful at the edges of their range, that doesn't seem to matter. Judith Blazer in the title rôle gives a charmingly perky and Italianate interpretation of Marietta's dialogue and music and tosses off the show's title song and the bravura Italian Street Song splendidly, and Leslie Harrington, who restores the Eddy rôle to its original heroic tenor range, is at his best when most relaxed in 'I'm Falling in Love with Someone'. The comedians and the happily unpretentious chorus catch the flavour of the whole affair marvellously and the orchestra, under James R. Morris, turns out warm and well-tempered playing which is a pleasure to listen to. Once you have heard the glorious quartet 'Live for Today' and the first-act finale on this set, you can't really be happy again with a *Naughty Marietta* selection which omits them.

Prettily boxed (Miss Blazer, on the cover, looks as good as she sounds), the set is accompanied by an excellent booklet of notes, principally by Roffman, discussing the history of the piece and describing its textual and musical layout, which is marred only by the occasional factual slip (Louis Ganne's *Hans le joueur de flûte* described as 'a German operetta', for example). It would have been nice to have had a libretto, or even a lyric book, but given the ravages wrought on the piece over the years, this would perhaps have been difficult. In any case, the whole enterprise is a hugely successful one, and the recording highly enjoyable.

There are many other records featuring *Naughty Marietta* selections, several related to or influenced by the MGM film. The stars of that film can be heard on RCA, performing the principal songs that survived into the film version ('Ah, Sweet Mystery of Life', 'Tramp, Tramp, Tramp', 'I'm Falling in Love with Someone', The Italian Street Song, ''Neath a Southern Moon'), and Eddy pairs with the attractively straightforward soprano Nadine Conner (who sings rather better than he does) in a slightly larger 1950 selection on a ten-inch Columbia record ('It Never, Never Can Be Love', 'Naughty Marietta' and 'Live for Today' turned into a duet), but the official film soundtrack waters down the real stuff with half a dozen concocted songs which do not belong to the original show.

Two one-sided *Naughty Marietta* selections which have further Herbert interest are Capitol's disc top-billing Gordon MacRae, which also features a selection from

The Red Mill, and the RCA Doretta Morrow record, which backs up with a selection from *Mlle Modiste*. In spite of these and other starry names, however, both pleasure and historical interest point to the Smithsonian set as easily the most valuable recording.

The Red Mill

Of Herbert's other works, *The Red Mill* is the best represented on record. Although it was chiefly a comedy show, a couple of its songs, 'Every Day Is Ladies Day with Me' and 'Moonbeams', won considerable popularity and ensured its survival as a recording prospect. There are several recorded selections, including two which take up complete discs. One of these, on RCA, is based on the 1945 revival and includes, in what is a pretty meagre set of excerpts, one song that was added for the occasion; the other, by the Gregg Smith Singers on the Turnabout label, is much more comprehensive (thirteen songs instead of eight), splendidly played in tasteful arrangements which are as far away from the too prevalent Mantovani and Robert Wagner Chorale syndrome as can be, and mostly adequately if a bit characterlessly sung.

Unfortunately, the sleeve notes on this disc are embarrassingly incorrect. The Herbert Foundation, which supported the recording, can only be made to look silly by a claim that *The Red Mill* was the longest running musical up to its time when, in fact, it had something like half the run of pieces produced a decade and more earlier. A little more bravado on the disc and less on the notes would have been an improvement, but there is still plenty to enjoy in the music and in the livelier performances such as that from soubrette Samantha Genton.

More Victor Herbert

Although its favourite numbers, 'Kiss Me Again' (recorded on 78 by Galli-Curci) and 'I Want What I Want When I Want It', have been much used recital numbers, *Mlle Modiste* has not won a comprehensive recording. Someone called Starline Productions of Glendale, California, advertised a 'complete' cassette-only version of the show, presumably taken from the radio, with Gordon MacRae and Dorothy Kirsten starred, but failed to deliver the goods when I approached them. Thus, one side of a disc in the old Readers' Digest boxed set (backed with *Die Fledermaus*) is still the most representative if scarcely generally available selection. It incorporates eight of the very comic opera numbers from the show's score, including a particularly fine bass-baritone 'I Want What I Want' from Kenneth Smith. Jeanette Scovotti negotiates the lashings of coloratura encrusted on the heroine's songs for Fritzi Scheff with panache and accuracy, and two free-flowing American tenors tackle the charming 'The Time the Place and the Girl' (Arthur Rubin) and the fairly awful 'Love Me, Love my Dog' (Robert Nagy).

Babes in Toyland, on the other hand, has been paid more attention but almost always in rather heavily adapted versions. The most considerable of these is the Decca soundtrack from the 1961 Walt Disney film with Ray Bolger, Annette Funicello, Ed Wynn and Tommy Sands which, although it pops in several songs manufactured from other Herbert material and a couple of non-Herbert additions, nevertheless contains versions of ten numbers from the original show. Putting aside the revamped versions, we are left with an old Decca disc with Kenny Baker (backed with *The Red Mill*), and the selection included in the Reader's Digest boxed set. This has seven numbers performed by legitimate voices, as they were intended to be, and allows you to hear just why this piece has remained so popular for so long (it isn't always evident on the 'rearranged' versions). The famous March of the Toys, the delightful 'Toyland', beautifully sung here by Mallory Walker, Mary Quite Contrary's Irish waltz about her 'Barney O'Flynn', 'I Can't Do the Sum' as sung by the little soprano heroine (Mary Ellen Pracht), and such charming light operatic ensembles as 'Never Mind Bo Peep, We Will Find your Sheep' and 'Go to Sleep, Slumber Deep' are all very pretty pieces of what was evidently a most attractive score.

A few numbers from both these shows appear on the 1985 compilation from radio broadcasts, issued on AEI as a double-record set under the title 'A Treasury of Early Musical Comedy' along with songs from Herbert's *It Happened in Nordland*, *The Only Girl*, *The Princess Pat*, *The Fortune Teller*, *The Velvet Lady* and *The Girl in the Spotlight*. The quality on these recordings is necessarily patchy, but they are later in time and more enjoyable than most similar transfers.

A 'complete' cassette version of *The Princess Pat* with Gordon MacRae and Dorothy Kirsten was another amongst the list advertised by the mysterious Starline, but, in a more regular vein, both RCA and MMG (the Gregg Smith Singers) have issued acceptable selections from *Sweethearts* (1913), a piece which has retained some popularity in spite of a fairly impossible libretto and a score which is not in the same class as those for *Naughty Marietta* and *Mlle Modiste*. Unfortunately, the best of Herbert's early works – *The Serenade* and *The Fortune Teller* – in my opinion considerably superior to *Sweethearts*, have been largely allowed to escape. If the Smithsonian should ever be looking for a new Victor Herbert project, perhaps this is where it might start by looking.

Several Herbert recital records have been issued, including one by Eleanor Steber (Columbia) and another, more recently, by Beverley Sills (EMI), which instructs us cavalierly on its cover that it must be filed under 'classical'. Both contain largely the same repertoire. It would have been nice to hear these operatic ladies tackle Alice Nielsen's rôle from *The Fortune Teller* or some of the less remembered music Herbert created for Fritzi Scheff rather than yet another 'Ah, Sweet Mystery of Life' (which, no matter what happens, will always be associated with Jeanette MacDonald and the film), but I suppose it wouldn't have been commercial. Of this pair I prefer Sills (accompanied by André Kostelanez) to the hootier sound of Steber.

Kerker, Cohan, Luders and Caryll

Most of the other turn-of-the-century Broadway composers are generally and perhaps a little unfairly passed over today as hacks, but from their stable there did emerge one important hit show, Gustave Kerker's *The Belle of New York*. Always more appreciated outside America than at home, it has survived on disc only in a little selection by Mary Thomas and Barry Kent on the British EMI label. A film soundtrack featuring Fred Astaire filches the title but not the score of this 1897 musical comedy. As for Kerker's contemporaries, it seems that the works of Ludwig Englander, Julian Edwards and their brethren are gone beyond recall.

The new century brought several new writers who had something to offer, without any particularly new areas being explored. George M. Cohan, with his lively, song-strewn farcical musicals, was the natural successor to the *Trip to Chinatown* genre and Harrigan and Hart, whilst Luders and Pixley, with their musical comedies, and Ivan Caryll, exiling himself from England with the last works of a memorable career, followed the British 'Gaiety way' in musical comedy.

Cohan's work appears on several compilation discs and also on the original cast album of the 1968 musical *George M*, based on his life. But only the five songs which made up the score of his musical play *Forty-Five Minutes from Broadway* have been given a record to themselves, once again through the auspices of AEI, in a broadcast transfer featuring Tammy Grimes in the rôle of Mary ('It's a grand old name'), created for Fay Templeton. This recording, however, is not just music. It is a full-scale potted show, with more dialogue than music, splendidly performed by Miss Grimes, Larry Blyden and Russell Nype, and gives a good idea of just what the Cohan shows were like: bright and very low comedy, accents and just about everything else played for laughs, plus some breezy numbers including the rollicking title-song, Nype's insistence that 'I Want to Be a Popular Millionaire', and, of course, the enduring 'Mary', endearingly performed in duet by Blyden and Miss Grimes. One additional Cohan number, the pantomime injunction 'Always Leave 'Em Laughing', is squeezed into the story (as almost any number could be) as an enjoyable extra. This disc highlights the attractions of this most simple form of musical comedy and makes me wonder why Cohan's more famous *Little Johnny Jones*, revived in 1980, is still unrecorded.

Selections from the Luders/Pixley *The Prince of Pilsen* and Caryll's *The Pink Lady* have been issued on a radio transfer by AEI, who apparently have a lot more of these radio broadcasts they intend slowly to leak out to us. I am going to contradict myself on the subject of transfers as pleasant listening, and say straight out that, no matter what its technical drawbacks, this recording is a joy. The music of Luders and, particularly, of Caryll shows us that Herbert was no more head and shoulders above his musical contemporaries than Sullivan was in Britain. It is one of history's little distortions. This is light theatre music of the most agreeable and enjoyable kind and these are two charming selections, splendidly sung by the smooth and virile baritone Charles Kuhlman and the delightfully clear soprano Jessica Dragonette. If it has been impossible totally to level out the sound values and clean away all of the surface noise, this, in a perverse fashion, adds even a little period feel to the recording.

   The Pink Lady side comes out the better of the two, both as material (the highlight is the famous *Pink Lady* waltz, 'My Beautiful Lady') and in recording quality, but the whole record is great fun. It is equipped with some very readable sleeve notes which err only in insisting that *The Prince of Pilsen* was not produced in London. In fact, it ran for 160 performances at the Shaftesbury Theatre in 1904, proving itself one of the most successful US exports to date. *The Pink Lady* followed in 1912 with similar success (124 performances) and was also produced in Paris.

The Broadway Boom

The Great War coincided, more or less, with a turning point in fashions and fortunes in the musical theatre. A burst of splendid activity showered over Broadway as, under the impetus of a group of writers and composers whose talents ranged across the whole theatrical spectrum, from the lightest song-and-dance comedy to the richest of comic opera, America found its feet in the manufacture of light musical theatre. The now familiar names which mean Broadway started to build their careers, as Otto Harbach, Rudolf Friml, Jerome Kern, Guy Bolton, P. G. Wodehouse, Vincent Youmans, George Gershwin, Sigmund Romberg, Oscar Hammerstein II and many others forged the first great period of the Broadway musical in the decade following the war. By and large the librettists and lyricists have tended to become forgotten by the general public – the exception being Hammerstein, who is largely thought of only as one head of the creature 'Rodgers-'n'-Hammerstein' – whilst the composers and songwriters have become celebrated and, in the hands of some over-enthusiasts, practically canonized, as their music goes through performance after performance and recording after recording, often mashed into unrecognizable shape by vocalists and arrangers incapable of performing the pieces as they were written. Fortunately there are a reasonable number of more theatrically conceived recordings as well, even though much of this music falls into the category of being 'saved by the British 78 rpm cast recording'.

Rudolf Friml

Prague-born Rudolf Friml had got into his stride before the Great War, with the production of his charming musical *The Firefly* (1912), but it was another dozen years before he produced the two shows that ensured his fame – *Rose Marie* and *The Vagabond King*. Of the twenty musicals he composed they are the two which have lasted into the current repertoire and have had the honours of world-wide production and recording.

Rose Marie

Larger and, more often, smaller chunks of *Rose Marie* have been widely recorded but, surprisingly, mainly outside America. There are two film soundtracks that bear little resemblance musically to the stage score (four and three numbers respectively), the earlier of which presents Nelson Eddy and Jeanette MacDonald in the 'Indian Love Call'. Otherwise, I have been able to discover only one side of a Columbia ten-inch record, again featuring Eddy, a disc in the Readers Digest collection, and an orchestrally-orientated Al Goodman LP containing seven nicely sung but orchestrally souped-up pieces.

The rest of the recordings originate either in Britain or in France, in both of which countries the show has been enduringly successful. The original 1925 Drury Lane cast recordings, featuring Edith Day in the title rôle, are gathered together on a compilation disc of Friml material, under the title *Rudolf Friml in London*, put together by Michael Kennedy and Chris Ellis in the palmy days of the World Record Club. Unfortunately, the quality of these recordings is very poor and all one can tell is that Day and partner Derek Oldham had fine voices and that comic Billy Merson didn't.

Amongst a handful of half-records, there are two larger selections, one from the World Record Club dating from 1960 and the other from RCA put out two years earlier. The WRC disc presents a delightful leading lady in Barbara Leigh, erstwhile London star of *King's Rhapsody*, paired with a tenor Jim Kenyon in opera star David Hughes, and the romantic sections of the score are splendidly sung. The comedy songs, which are in any case the weak part of the *Rose Marie* score, are, however, not so happy, and the re-orchestrations, while unoffensive enough, are sometimes scrappy.

The RCA recording is an enterprise on a different scale. This is meant to be a definitive disc. If it isn't, it is perhaps due largely to lack of taste. It has its definite plusses, amongst which can be numbered a richly sung baritone Jim (Giorgio Tozzi), a bell-like Rose Marie (Julie Andrews), a smashing Mountie Malone (Frederick Harvey), and a selection which includes the three concerted finale sections as well as the large part of the solo and ensemble numbers. It has some enthusiastic but rather lushed-up orchestrations and a heavily Jewish Hard-Boiled Herman (Meier Tzelniker), who, unlike other English Hermans, at least attempts to sing his main number. Unfortunately it also has a croony chorus from the Mike Sammes Singers, who haven't got out of the 1950s, and, worst, a perfectly awful performance of 'Totem Tom-Tom' by a lady who thinks she's Rosemary Clooney on a languid afternoon and who nearly scuppers the whole disc single-handed – well, double-handed, for

I guess conductor Lehman Engel permitted or even encouraged this awful anachronism.

I don't suppose there's much more than a curious pleasure to be gained from listening to *Rose Marie* in French, but it is interesting to see how much more respectfully the French recordings treat the show's music. The only full-scale disc is a Merkès and Merval affair which is for devotees only, but André Dassary and Michèle Claverie pair a short selection with an equally brief group of songs from *Le Chant du Désert*, and Pathé-EMI pair an often-reissued half-record with a flipside of *No, No, Nanette*. This last disc brings together perhaps the most happily blended pair of 'Indian Love Call' lovers in Guy Fontagnère and Lina Dachary but, hamstrung by cross-casting with *No, No, Nanette*, it commits the unusual (for Pathé) bloomer of featuring the comic Duvaleix distinctly uncomfortably in the martial Mounties' Song.

The RCA disc comes out, in spite of its faults, as the best for both quality and quantity, but it would not rate a second look if the most recent *Rose Marie* recording had managed to find itself a vinyl home. Somewhere in a vault at the Smithsonian Institution are the ready recorded tapes of a complete *Rose Marie* whose issue on disc, in the same style as the *Naughty Marietta* project, was apparently aborted by the closure or serious diminution of the Institution's recording programme. It has been leaked on a pirate tape, as these things are, and I have thus been able to listen to a *Rose Marie* that is ideally played and immaculately sung (with a particularly glorious performance from the lady playing Rose Marie), and which is a credit to all concerned and to the American musical theatre and its recording industry. I suppose we can only wait and hope that the disc will one day appear.

The Vagabond King

The Vagabond King, with its period plot and dashing hero is, on the whole, a more dramatically and musically satisfying piece than *Rose Marie*. Its emphasis, most notably in its music, is on the vigorous and the romantic, and the comedy sections are not as obviously dragged in as in the earlier piece. Friml, at his best when at his most lyrical, produced much of his finest work in this score and, if 'The Song of the Vagabonds', 'The Huguette Waltz', 'Only a Rose' and 'Love Me Tonight' are marginally less well known than the *Rose Marie* hits, that is probably due to the fact that the picturesque Rocky Mountain musical has had a more extensive stage career.

The immensely singable music of this score has tempted many well-known vocalists to try it and there is a goodly line of recordings of the show, most of which, however, date from early LP days and are not readily found today. Several of these are almost wholly orientated towards the music of the hero and heroine – Earl Wrightson and Frances Greer (RCA), Gordon MacRae and Lucille Norman (Capitol) and Alfred Drake and Mimi Benzell (Decca) all include only the beautiful 'Huguette Waltz' from the rest of the score. But another short selection, in the Reader's Digest list, leaves this number out completely, including instead Huguette's second number, 'Love for Sale'.

A recording made by Oreste, the star of the 1955 film, is even more lopsided, as he not only pinches the mezzo-soprano waltz for himself, but interpolates three numbers credited (I think very dubiously) to Friml and to Johnny Burke. A flamboyantly vulgar tenor, he yields to the obvious temptation to belt and wallow his way through this most Hollywoodized of the generally over-lush versions of the score with the aid of operaticky soprano Jean Fenn, and the result is decidedly over the top. A British recording with popular tenor John Hanson and soprano Jane Fyffe (backed with *The Student Prince*) avoids some of these vulgarities and introduces Julie Bryan with fine versions of both the Huguette songs, but it inserts a laughable showpiece number, not by Friml, for its greedy star, which renders the selection ridiculous.

The two most substantial recordings of *The Vagabond King* are an RCA version with Mario Lanza and Judith Raskin, and a British World Record Club edition with Edwin Steffe and Lissa Gray. The former sadly omits the atmospheric 'Scotch Archers Song', the latter the second-act 'Nocturne', and both the comedy Serenade sequence, but the bulk of the score in the right kind of balance is there.

The Firefly and Further Friml

The favourite songs from *The Firefly* – the waltz 'Sympathy' and the Italianate serenade 'Giannina mia', not to mention 'The Donkey Serenade', which was fabricated for the film based on the show from a spare piece of Friml music, have had regular performances and, as a result, there have been several selections from this show put on record. The most substantial, and the only two-sided LP, is an old ten-inch RCA disc starring Allan Jones, who created 'The Donkey Serenade' in the film version of the show. This contains seven original songs plus, of course, 'The Donkey Serenade'. There is also a British recording with Laurie Payne and Stephanie Voss, which takes in just five songs one one side of a pairing with *The Chocolate Soldier*. The current catalogue has not had a *Firefly* available for a long time, and the rest of Friml's work, which included some other fine successes such as *High Jinks*, *Katinka* and *The Three Musketeers*, is only represented on the previously mentioned 'Rudolf Friml in London'.

This double-disc set consists of transfers from contemporary 78s made of the London performances of *Rose Marie*, *The Vagabond King*, *The Three Musketeers* and *The Blue Kitten* as well as an orchestral medley of tunes from *Katinka* but, sadly, omits *High Jinks*, which was liberally recorded by its original and very successful London cast. The transfers from the 1920s records are mostly as well made as is possible, and the recording has the great advantage of showing to those for whom Friml is only the romantic operetta composer of 'Indian Love Call', 'Only a Rose' and 'Rose Marie' that he had a wider span of abilities. On the one hand, there is the splendid martial music of *The Three Musketeers*, on the other the lilting popular strains of such delightful pieces as 'Cutie' and 'The Blue Kitten Blues'. There is also some material that is very routine, but this set is a must for anyone interested in looking further into the works of Friml than the two great hits.

Sigmund Romberg

Although he supplied music for all types of show over the first ten years of his musical life in America, from the lightest of revue to the botching of great foreign pieces like *Das Dreimäderlhaus* and *Die Rose von Stambul*, Sigmund Romberg, like Friml, found his fame in a series of picturesque and full-throated musical successors to the Continental operetta and the Daly's Theatre musical. In the space of less than four years he produced the three enormously popular musicals which made and have maintained his fame, *The Student Prince* (1924), *The Desert Song* (1926) and *The New Moon* (1928).

The Student Prince

The Student Prince, with its demanding star tenor rôle, has won world-wide popularity for its principal songs, even though it has earned an extended stage run only in America. Like *Naughty Marietta*, it owes its fame in the rest of the world very largely to its celebrated film version, which featured, behind the dashing face and form of Edmund Purdom as the Ruritanian prince who finds freedom and love in old Heidelberg, the voice of Mario Lanza at the peak of its powers. Unfortunately, the film version saw fit to gut and restuff the score of the show and, although two recordings feature the voice that is widely connected with the rôle of Prince Karl-Franz and the major songs of *The Student Prince*, neither is a full representation of the stage score.

HMV's 'Songs from the *Student Prince* and Other Melodies' is exactly what it says. Only the five numbers the star performed – 'Golden Days' (borrowed from another character), the Drinking Song, 'Deep in My Heart, Dear', the famous Serenade ('Overhead the moon is beeeeeeeming') and the part-sung 'Gaudeamus Igitur' – get an airing, alongside some extra material slipped into the movie to allow this almost one-man show to become even more monodramatic. One of these, Nicholas Brodszky's 'I'll Walk With God', has since become a throbbing tenor regular on Sunday broadcasts. The other side has Lanza singing such pieces as 'I'll See You Again', the *Carousel* soliloquy and 'Dein ist mein ganzes Herz'. It is all good showy stuff, sung with more emotion than you would believe possible or tasteful, but when the star soars upwards from his uneven middle register, demanding impressively on the leger lines that we 'hear my serenade..!', it also verges on the irresistible. The second selection, on RCA, repeats the same material – with a different soprano picking up the duetting crumbs but not being allowed her own solo – but has four further numbers, including 'Just We Two', which rightly belongs to two subsidiary characters.

For a more comprehensive look at the stage *Student Prince*, which actually does have other characters in its cast, it is necessary to look elsewhere. Fortunately, there are plenty of other options. Unfortunately most of them don't measure up too well. Putting aside those selections that offer little more than Lanza's discs – which means ignoring the efforts of Nelson Eddy (Columbia), Lauritz Melchior (Decca), Donald Dame (RCA) and William Lewis (Reader's Digest) and the unsatisfactory archive material assembled from early American and British performances on Monmouth and World Records – we are left with a half dozen discs which more or less provide the bulk of the score.

The most substantial of these is probably the Goddard Lieberson Columbia recording of 1952, which features operatic vocalists Robert Rounseville and Dorothy Kirsten and a rather splendid men's chorus who don't get credited for their individual bits. In some ways and at some times, this is a fine recording. It is not the fault of the performers or the producer if, when all the music of this show is put together without its intermittent dialogue, it sounds a bit like a rather hectic male-voice choir concert with a lonely soprano obbligato. I think the problem is that, having chosen to use a group of weighty voices, which add great éclat to the student songs and other ensembles, Lieberson has got himself into a problem with the soloists' tessitura. Both Rounseville and Kirsten (who sacrifices the lyrics mightily for the sake of getting up to the notes) get very tetchy at the top of their big voices and discomfort immediately sets in. All the fine singing elsewhere gets forgotten under the influence of just a few unpleasant sounds at the highpoints of effort.

There is almost as much material on Columbia's 1963 recording, another which boasts a fine operatic cast and some new and sometimes curious Hershy Kay orchestrations which swing merrily along under the baton of Franz Allers. Jan Peerce is the Prince here, devoting a richer and darker tenor to his panoply of songs without pinching anything belonging to anyone else. He may not have the easy showmanship of Lanza, but when you get down to sharps and flats this is actually the better voice and, since he has sufficient measure of the music to pull out just the right number of stops at just the right moment, it is an impressive performance. The duets come off particularly well and the reason is not far to find. Roberta Peters is easily the best recorded Kathie. She fires off a salvo of impeccable coloratura to announce her arrival, and launches into her 'Come Boys, Let's All Be Gay Boys' with shiny tone, clean diction and easy accuracy, before falling in with Peerce for 'Deep in my Heart, Dear' and the top line in everything else in the score. Georgio Tozzi is the very warmest of baritone Dr Engels and the students, particularly Robert Sands as Detlef, are a brighter, younger, less seriously choral team than on the previous disc, whilst Lawrence Avery and Anita Darian mix light tenor and not-so-light soprano cleverly in 'Just We Two'. Musically, then, this is a fine recording, and the intrusion of some reasonably awful snippets of speech (in which none of the artists manner to marshal a minimum of naturalness) and what to me is not the right ending cannot be allowed to affect its superiority.

Gordon MacRae (Capitol) is wise enough to take the music down a bit when he turns Prince Karl-Franz into a baritone but, although this means he can make a virile job of the solos, he is in his turn stretched in the duets, and, after Lanza, one can't really accept a baritone in the rôle. The British tenor John Hanson has made two recordings as the Prince, a rôle which he played in London in the late 1960s, but not only does he fail to measure up vocally, he interpolates two additional songs written by himself on a rather embarrassing disc which thinks so little of the show's real composer as to bill him on the sleeve as 'Sigmund Rombug'.

Fifty years after its first production, *The Student Prince* was staged in Heidelberg itself, where it has since become a regular attraction at the Summer Festival. In 1979 this production was put on record with the Hamburg State Opera Chorus and Orchestra supporting Erik Geisen, the American tenor who had taken the star rôle since the première, under the Kanon label. This is a recording which, from a purist point of view, is maddening. The script and score have been fiddled with, largely for the benefit of the leading man who, as if he didn't have enough taxing material to sing, is allowed to follow Lanza (who presumably was able to record his version in bits rather than playing it end to end) and annex both the Drinking Song and the top line of 'Gaudeamus', thus wiping the second tenor rôle of Detlef right off the stage. But this version goes even further and gives the same treatment to the actors playing Tarnitz and Princess Margaret. It snaffles their one duet, 'Just We Two' so that, apart from soprano Celia Jeffreys as Kathie (who is allowed to keep 'Come Boys, Lets All Be Gay Boys' and her lines in the duets presumably because even our hero can't sing duets with himself), only the bass-baritone Dieter Hönig gets a look in, with two halves of 'Golden Days'.

Although the piece might make a better star vehicle thus manipulated, it really doesn't make a better show. From time to time it is nice to hear someone else rather than Karl-Franz. And it is particularly maddening because this Karl-Franz is really rather splendid. It is one of those vibrant, rash and risky performances that goes for every high note with bravura and mostly gets them without sounding nearly as strained as some of the more famous exponents of the rôle. The serenade is particularly successful; 'Gaudeamus' the least so and thus the most annoying because one knows Geisen shouldn't be singing it. Hönig is a super Engel, Miss Jeffreys pleasingly at ease in the high parts of Kathie's rôle, and the orchestra and chorus first rate performing what the sleeve tells us are the original orchestrations. Maybe they are and maybe they aren't, but they are excellent, supporting and complementing the vocal performances without ever overwhelming them in a rush of lush Hollywood sound. Whilst on the subject of the sleeve, it has to be said that once again a foreign-language issue has fallen foul of the translation bug. Stephan B. Martin sounds very Anglophone, but he clearly isn't or he wouldn't have Karl-Franz and Kathie 'relieving' their bitter-sweet love affair!

The Desert Song

The Desert Song is arguably the best of the group of romantic comic operas that found such great success on Broadway at this time. It has a well-balanced book, neatly mixing the comic, the romantic and the colourful, and a memorable score. The deeply sentimental title song, the picaresque Riffs' Chorus, the sparkling soprano showpiece 'Romance' and its more dramatic fellow the Sabre Song, the saucy description of what it means to have 'It', and the remarkable juxtaposed trio of items on the nature of love ('Let Love Go', 'One Flower Grows Alone in Your Garden' and 'One Alone'), featuring respectively basso, counter-tenor and baritone voices, are all outstanding pieces in themselves and complementary components of a score which is typical of and an example to its period.

As in the case of *The Student Prince*, there are many recordings of *The Desert Song* – not only from America and from Britain but also from France, where the show takes second position only to *Rose Marie* in popularity amongst American comic operas. In looking at these discs, there is one notable point that comes immediately to view. With most shows, the selection made for a one-disc version is pretty regular, the same major songs being always included, the same lesser pieces being always omitted. With *The Desert Song* it is different. Of the twenty musical sections that make up the score, only one (the soubrette comedy number 'I'll Be a Buoyant Girl') is not included on at least one selection. The key numbers are, of course, always there – 'Romance', the Riff Song, the title song and 'One Alone' – but the various recordings pick and choose amongst the remaining numbers, some leaning to the comedy numbers 'It' and 'One Good Boy Gone Wrong', others preferring the incidental 'Song of the Brass Key' or the less well-known but equally attractive 'Margot' or 'Then You Will Know'. It is a fact that makes a point on the broad value of the score.

Many a famous performer has partaken of a *Desert Song* on disc, but the results are of varying quality. A Columbia recording featuring Nelson Eddy and Doretta Morrow is a disappointment – he sounds abstracted and she, although singing prettily, doesn't achieve take off either. Perhaps she is too busy wondering why she doesn't prefer David Atkinson's robustly sung Paul Fontaine to the unenthusiastic Pierre of Eddy. Gordon MacRae does rather better on Capitol, supported stoutly by Lucille Norman, but, as on their *Student Prince* recording, they are undermined by very suspect orchestrations and conducting.

There have been a whole host of British recordings made of *The Desert Song*, beginning with the original London cast, whose version has been transferred to LP by World Records and Monmouth-Evergreen. Edith Day was clearly a glorious Margot and Harry Welchman a fine-voiced Pierre, but the quality of these recordings, although appreciable given their age, simply does not allow them to be considered, for listening pleasure, in parallel with their more recent counterparts. Robert Colman, Peter Grant, John McNally and John Hanson have all had an LP-age go at the Red Shadow, but none of their recordings come anywhere near the splendid HMV selection made by Norman Newell in 1959.

This recording consists of a well-chosen cross-section of the score, including all the big romantic pieces as well as the two numbers allotted to the comedy rôle of Bennie, the splendid Riff Chorus and its feminine equivalent the French Military Marching Song, and both 'The Song of the Brass Key' and the second-act finale. The *coup d'éclat*, however, is in the casting. Edmund Hockridge is a splendidly heroic baritone Red Shadow and the heroine's music is given an incomparable rendition by the one and only June Bronhill, whose articulate, accurate, bright-voiced singing cuts out the silhouette of a simply perfect Margot. There is also a remarkable performance of the 'three faces of woman' sequence – Inia te Wiata using the basso end of his voice to effect in 'Let Love Go', a pure-voiced tenor who touches on the counter-tenor (Leonard Weir) giving an incisive 'One Flower Grows Alone in Your Garden', and Hockridge topping the set with a deeply-felt 'One Alone'. The 'Brass Key' number is given rather a 1950s sexy treatment by Julie Dawn, and Bruce Forsyth (a name to feature on the record cover at that time) is a rather limp and adenoidal Bennie. This is not my idea of Bennie, but Forsyth is altogether more with it than Gene Gerrard's London original was. The orchestrations by Brian Fahey are a bit flowery but mostly much more harmless than those used on the American recordings, and the sum total is a very pleasant *Desert Song* with more than a little touch of class.

The two recordings of *Le Chant du désert* offer a choice between quantity and quality. Unfortunately the quantity also has the authenticity and the quality anything but. It is the TLP 1985 disc which has the quantity – a dozen selections, all the principal pieces of the show including nearly eight minutes of the Eastern and Western Love sequence. It has a capable tenor Ombre Rouge (Jean-Marie Joye) and a jolly comic (Koen Crucke) cavorting through his description of 'Ca!', but Claudine Granger's Jenny (alias Margot) is too wobbly and shrill to be appreciated, the Clémentine is awful, and the orchestra is thin and tinny.

There is a much briefer and more intense pleasure in the half-record of excerpts issued by Decca in tandem with a similar slice of *Rose Marie*. The orchestra and chorus of Raymond Legrand are the real thing, even if their arrangements are very odd and chronically slow, and André Dassary and Mathé Altery are soloists of top quality. The selection begins with a long orchestral pot-pourri, continues with Dassary singing the title song and a very unmartial Riff Song, Altéry with half of 'Romance' ('Rêver'), him again with 'One Alone' and, very oddly, her finishing up doing a first rate imitation of a soubrette with the comic 'Ca!'.

The New Moon

The score of *The New Moon* is very much better known than the show itself for, like *The Student Prince*, it has been successful on the stage only in America. Its international fame is, again, not unconnected with the wide dissemination of two varying film versions made in 1930 and 1940 respectively, the latter of which featured Nelson Eddy and Jeanette MacDonald.

Its score is a superb one, featuring the beautiful 'Softly, as in a Morning Sunrise' (when you listen to this, stop and give Oscar Hammerstein credit for his moving lyric), the marching song to beat them all in 'Stout-hearted Men', the haunting 'Lover, Come Back to Me', the ultimate romantic duo 'Wanting You', and the delightful soprano waltz 'One Kiss', all of which have gone down as all-time favourites. With five enormous hit songs, *New Moon* is a recording natural, but, sadly, most producers have limited themselves to recording little more than the five hits, often ignoring the comedy songs and the ensembles, and the *New Moon* crop of discs is a disappointingly scrappy one.

The most shapely selection, a total of ten numbers, comes from a Capitol issue with Gordon MacRae and Dorothy Kirsten, issued in Britain on World Records. Inevitably the music has been homogenized by an arranger with a taste for violins and glue, and equipped with the Robert Wagner Chorale, but the fine cast overcome these handicaps bravely. MacRae's fine, round-edged baritone ranges from the macho 'Stout-hearted Men' to the lyricism of 'Wanting You' without any audible effort, and even steals 'Softly, as in a Morning Sunrise' from the tenor and does it well enough. Dorothy Kirsten is a lovely Marianne, sweeping through the underrated 'The Girl on the Prow' and putting real thought, as well as a succession of beautiful notes, into 'One Kiss'. The smiling little soubret piece 'Try Her Out at Dances' gets a delicious performance from an ideal pair of light comedy performers (Jeannine Wagner, Richard Robinson), and, having been rude about the Wagner Chorale, I owe it to truth to say they they provide on this occasion a particularly pretty girls' chorus and a very un-Wagnerian (Robert) group of men.

There is a second ten-number selection, drawn from the original London cast recordings, starring Evelyn Laye and Howett Worster, which takes more notice of the dramatic context and who sings what. It also includes the comedy song 'Gorgeous Alexander' and the song 'Paree' not played in New York, which isn't recorded elsewhere. Through the haze of the years, you can hear what a superb Marianne Evelyn Laye must have been, light and incisive of voice, and as clear as the proverbial bell, but in the end the haze, some boringly flat performances from the men and the somewhat erratic tempi and notation relegate this recording to the same drawer that contains all the other archive recordings.

Both film soundtracks have been transferred to LP on the Pelican label. The earlier one, which uses the five big numbers and makes up the rest with non-*New Moon* material, stars a rather effortful Lawrence Tibbett and the very fine Grace Moore, whose assurance and charm almost makes you forget the aged sound of the recording. The 1940 soundtrack has yielded up the same five pieces performed by MacDonald and Eddy, transferred very well indeed to modern record, topped off by MacDonald's performance of the interpolated number 'I Was a Stranger in Paris' (with terminal high note) and Eddy singing something called 'Shoe Shine', which doesn't seem to have anything to do with anything until it turns into 'Softly, as in a Morning Sunrise' – confusing. The second side of this disc has the stars singing five pieces of *I Married an Angel* taken from a 1942 radio broadcast.

Eddy and operatic soprano Eleanor Steber put down another, more correct, selection of eight numbers on Columbia. Eddy sings all the men's rôles, ranging from a rather unenthusiastic 'Stout-hearted Men', through the more lilting 'Marianne' as a duet, up to the two big sings ('Softly' and 'Lover'), and also tries (not very hard) to be funny in 'Gorgeous Alexander'. Steber is a strong-voiced Marianne, long on power and short on sweetness, who makes a really serious try at being a soubrette for 'Gorgeous Alexander'.

There are various other selections, ranging from one in the Reader's Digest set to a British HMV disc with Elizabeth Larner and Andy Cole, which takes in six numbers ('Marianne' is the extra one) nicely rather than impressively, but *New*

Moon has not made it onto record in French (*Robert le pirate*) or in any other foreign language.

Apart from these three big successes, little of Romberg's work has been systematically recorded. Original star Wilbur Evans and his material from the late work *Up in Central Park* (1945) have been preserved on another JJA archive recording and in a Decca pairing with *The Red Mill*; the odd number from *Nina Rosa* and from *Forbidden Melody*, played in France as *Le Chant du Tzigane*, were recorded there by their star, André Baugé; and Romberg's last show *The Girl in Pink Tights* (1954) was, in the LP age, given a cast recording; but from the mass of other shows of the Romberg opus only the odd piece has appeared.

Jerome Kern

Jerome Kern had been around in the world of the musical theatre even before Friml, contributing to shows in both Britain and America since soon after the beginning of the century, but his principal contribution and the series of stage works for which he is known today began in 1915 with the success of his little musical comedy *Very Good Eddie*. Amongst the shows that followed from Kern's versatile pen are the light comedies *Oh, Boy!* and *Leave it to Jane*; the charming song-and-dance show *Sally* and its successor *Sunny*; the very much more musically and dramatically substantial *Show Boat*, rightly regarded as the greatest product of its era; a pair of would-be operettas on Continental lines in *The Cat and the Fiddle* and *Music in the Air*; and the musically mature but textually confused *Roberta*. With Kern being regarded in America as the father-figure of the modern American musical theatre – and he deserves the accolade for *Show Boat* alone – to Herbert's role of grandfather, these works have been given plenty of attention as well as a variegated array of revivals, and Kern is pretty well represented on record, if not always in the form of coherent show recordings.

Show Boat

No record collection of any kind would be complete without a recording of *Show Boat*, and there are, not surprisingly, plenty of them to choose from – something for every kind of taste. Firstly there are the archive recordings. Helen Morgan, the original Julie, performing 'Bill' and 'Can't Help Lovin' Dat Man', and Paul Robeson, the Joe of the London production, singing 'Ol' Man River', have been re-recorded many times from original 78s, and both artists appear on a brief selection on Columbia Special Products. Robeson and the rest of the original London cast of 1928 can be heard in a selection taken from contemporary 78s on World Record Club (backed with *Sunny*). However, perhaps the most novel of these recordings is a compilation made on RCA Victrola, which uses the Robeson and Morgan tracks slotted into performances from more recent RCA recordings featuring Robert Merrill,

Howard Keel, Patrice Munsel and Risë Stevens to compile a selection from across the decades. It is a sort of 'best of RCA' combination, but the proximity of the finely sung and played modern recordings has the effect of making, in particular, Robeson's strangely off-hand 'Ol' Man River', in a peculiar version by Paul Whiteman's orchestra, seem unimpressive. This disc is an oddity rather than an enjoyment.

The score of *Show Boat* has been a mobile thing over the years, songs and ensembles being added and subtracted both during the composer's lifetime and after for various productions, but most selection recordings incline to the solid Kern heart of the bulky score – 'Make Believe', 'Ol' Man River', 'Bill', 'Can't Help Lovin' Dat Man', 'Why Do I Love You?', 'Life on the Wicked Stage' and 'You Are Love'.

Until 1988, only one double-record version existed, a Stanyan release recorded by the 1971 London revival cast and including all but a couple of the pieces used in stage productions over the years as well as two from the 1936 film version. This production, extremely effective on the stage, is also pretty satisfying on record. The score, which has been orchestrated and re-orchestrated over the years into some widely differing forms (indeed no two of the many discs seem to sound alike), gets a sometimes highly individual retreatment here, partly to fit the very idiosyncratic performance of Cleo Laine as Julie. Whether you will like this set or not will depend partly on whether you approve Miss Laine's interpretation, which turns this originally soprano rôle into a mixture of cabaret and torch singing. I find her 'Bill' magnificent, and her 'Can't Help Lovin' Dat Man' with its scat singing exciting if distinctly unusual, but neither can be said to suit the context of the show in any way. If you spare a moment to think of the plot, no one could have doubted for an instant that this Julie was no regular Aryan.

Elsewhere there is a fine, easy, almost-tenor Ravenal (André Jobin), a really splendid Queenie (Ena Cabayo), a strong young Magnolia (Lorna Dallas) and a lively soubrette pair (Kenneth Nelson and Jan Hunt) who give a real vaudeville feel to their numbers. Thomas Carey is an erratic Joe, quivering on the edge of flatness, but he rises to a fine climax with some ringing baritone singing (rather than the bass which has become popular since Robeson) at the end of 'Ol' Man River'.

A single-disc cast album from this production was also issued on EMI and, recently, with most of the earlier *Show Boat* discs having gone from the current catalogue, was reissued by That's Entertainment Records in a splendid pictorial sleeve equipped with what I think are pretty good sleeve notes (I should, I wrote them). However, no one need bother with *Show Boat* sleeve notes while they can have Miles Kreuger's *Show Boat* (OUP), the definitive book on the history of this milestone show.

The London recording was the third in a line of *Show Boat* original cast recordings. The 1946 Broadway revival of *Show Boat* was the occasion for what is arguably the first LP cast recording – a ten-inch disc including eight numbers from the original score plus one of Kern's last songs, 'Nobody Else but Me', which was interpolated into this revival. It is a fine recording with good performances all round, but only to be found today by diligent searching in second-hand shops. The same can be said of the RCA recording of the 1966 revival at Lincoln Center, where William Warfield (the best recorded Joe), Constance Towers (a properly soprano Julie) and a sprightly Allyn Ann McLeerie (Ellie Mae) have the edge on a fine singing juvenile pair (Barbara Cook and Stephen Douglass). Warfield and Miss Cook recorded another version (like the RCA one, conducted by Franz Allers) on Columbia four years earlier but, in spite of a splendid Ravenal from John Raitt and some excellent choral singing, it doesn't match the later disc as an all-round recording.

Of the countless other *Show Boat* selection discs, the two RCA issues from which portions were taken for the 'best of RCA' compilation are both pleasant, although Howard Keel and Robert Merrill each elect to tackle the songs belonging to Ravenal and to Joe, taking away any theatrical sense from the recording. The Merrill recording, which uses Patrice Munsel and Risë Stevens, is more operatic in tone, whilst Keel's version is rather more relaxed, with a Julie (Gogi Grant) who is straight out of the 1950s hit parade. Other releases include a radio transfer with Allan Jones and Irene Dunne, the 1951 film soundtrack with Howard Keel and Kathryn Grayson, a British version, recently reissued on First Night, with Inia te Wiata (Joe), Shirley Bassey (Julie) and Dora Bryan (Ellie Mae) and, for those who like the esoteric or who speak Swedish, a splendidly individual *Teaterboten* paired with a Swedish version of Paul Ábrahám's *Viktoria und ihr Husar*.

To pick and choose between these widely different versions of the show is a matter of individual taste, but there is no longer any need to look back in time for a *Show Boat*, for 1988 saw the issue of what is without doubt the *Show Boat* recording for our times. This is a three-disc set from EMI, comprising two records of what would normally be considered an *intégrale* recording, a full score accompanied by some of the show's dialogue, and a whole further record made up of all the other material either written and not used for the original production or subsequently written for inclusion in the show or its film versions. It takes advantage of the discovery of a mass of Kern papers since the Stanyan issue and includes amongst the extra material such novelties as the imitation music-hall number 'A Pack of Cards' for Magnolia and Julie's similarly unused 'Out There in the Orchard'. The splendid Joe/Queenie duo 'Ah Still Suits Me', sung in the 1936 film by Robeson and Hattie McDaniel, is amongst the other items taken in here, but the set does not incorporate other Kern numbers, such as 'How'd You Like to Spoon with Me', which were subsequently interpolated into the score but not written specifically for it.

This recording not only has the advantage of completeness, or indeed hyper-completeness, it has all the other advantages beginning with an atmosphere of what can only be called authenticity. I wasn't about in 1927, but this is exactly how I would have imagined that this show would have sounded in performance at that time. The overture sets up the feeling with its clear, characterful orchestrations (apparently those written by Robert Russell Bennett for the first production) and some no-nonsense playing under the brisk, unsentimental baton of John

McGlinn, and the unpretentiously hearty choir which opens the show compounds the impression. It is an impression that is never lost throughout the recording. The music is never overplayed or, in spite of being cast with some big voices, oversung; it is performed in a straight and lively fashion, not pulled about or overdramatized as the songs have so often been over the years, both in the show and outside it, but just sung as the author and composer wrote them.

This policy – and it clearly is a policy – is fortunately (or, rather, by good management) put into action by an exceptionally well-chosen group of principal performers. Jerry Hadley, who plays Gaylord Ravenal, is the possessor of a free, masculine tenor voice which he employs in the scene of his first meeting with Magnolia (Frederica von Stade) with an enjoyable naturalness, making their duet 'Make Believe' into an attractive little scena instead of a Nelson-and-Jeanette sing, whilst remaining ready with the really ringing tones for the splendid 'Till Good Luck Comes My Way' and the real romance of the later 'You Are Love'. Miss von Stade's warm soprano just occasionally gives the feeling of being a mite mature for the character of eighteen-year-old Magnolia but she, too, sings with a pleasing straightforwardness and beauty of tone. She makes the most of her opportunities to open up in 'You Are Love', for the rôle of Magnolia is otherwise made up of rather lighter stuff which, happily, she (sometimes narrowly) resists the opportunity to sing too robustly. Her 'After the Ball' is quite beautifully done.

The rôle of Julie is taken by another experienced operatic performer in Teresa Stratas, who performs a jaunty 'Can't Help Lovin' Dat Man' with splendid simplicity and warmth, avoiding all suggestion of warbling. There is none of the torch singing approach used by Cleo Laine here; the song is performed as the simple negro folk song the text says that it is. 'Bill', in its cabaret context, gets more of a single-number delivery, but Miss Stratas never lets it get away from her, giving a finely controlled soprano performance.

The two black rôles are played to perfection. As Joe, Bruce Hubbard cruises through 'Ol' Man River' in a fine, relaxed baritone, without an ounce of melodrama, tackling it as if he'd never heard anyone else sing (or oversing) it, making the song of a piece with the show and not an isolated showpiece. Karla Burns as Queenie hollers out her bouncy ballyhoo in a cheery chest voice, and makes it one of the most enjoyable numbers of the whole piece. Last, but very definitely not least, Paige O'Hara's pouting little sunbeam of an Ellie Mae makes a sparkly mouthful of 'Life on the Wicked Stage' and joins with Frank (David Garrison) in their happy duets in true (and now far too rare) soubrette style. The dialogue sections of the recording are rather less adept in some cases than the sung portions, but what remains of the non-singing rôles of Cap'n Andy (Robert Nichols) and Parthy Ann (the very odd-sounding Nancy Kulp) are performed in good old over-the-top comedy fashion, fitting in well with the style of the work.

Such lesser-known pieces as the jaunty 'Till Good Luck Comes my Way', the marvellously colourful 'In Dahomey' and the cheerful interpolated dance number 'Goodbye, my Lady Love', all included in the body of the work, will no doubt come as a pleasant surprise to those whose *Show Boat* experience has been limited to a selection disc. The contents of the third record of this set, however, which reproduces for the sake of minor differences several chunks available on the main discs as well as the additional songs, are, by and large, going to be of minority interest. Although EMI are to be congratulated on taking such a scholarly attitude to the classics of the musical stage, there is little doubt that the majority of listeners are going to be interested principally in the contents of the first two records, and it is hoped that eventually a two-disc set may appear – perhaps even without the pieces of dialogue which have, in any case, been included only to show off the underscoring.

Very Good Eddie

The rest of Kern's works are very much less well cared for than *Show Boat*. Two of his early musicals exist in revival cast recordings – *Very Good Eddie* in a version produced in 1975 and *Leave it to Jane* from a 1959 off-Broadway reprise. The *Very Good Eddie* recording contains little more than half of the original show's material, as the score for the revival was crammed full of Kern songs taken from other sources. Since, in its original form, the musical content was largely a hotch-potch of slightly used and almost new numbers, mostly on well-worn themes, this makes little difference, and the resultant show and disc were and are a jolly selection of Kern numbers from twenty years of quite successful and not so successful shows.

The most popular song from the original *Very Good Eddie*, the rather cutesy 'Babes in the Wood', comes over less effectively nowadays than some of the other pieces – the comic lament of the undersized hero 'When You Wear a Thirteen Collar', the attractive duet 'Some Sort of Somebody' or the pretty waltz 'Nodding Roses', which gives some respite from the driving rhythms of the large part of the score – but the most enjoyable moments come from the interpolated songs, the crazy 'Left All Alone Again Blues' from *The Night Boat*, the ragtime 'I've Got to Dance' cut from the *Very Good Eddie* score before Broadway, and the comedy routine 'Katy-Did' taken from the 1913 revue *Oh, I Say!*.

This last number benefits on this disc from a typhonic performance from Ms Travis Hudson, whose over-the-top rendering of the part of the expansive singing teacher, Madame Matroppo, also includes a burlesquey interpretation of 'Moon Love' (not 'Moon of Love' as given on the sleeve), taken from Kern's London show *The Beauty Prize*. The rest of the cast give lively performances over a rather relentless orchestra without ever hitting any heights.

Leave it to Jane

The *Leave it to Jane* revival and recording, unlike those of *Very Good Eddie*, remained largely faithful to the show's original version, although the disc omits several numbers from the original score, all but one of which ('A Peach of a Life') were not used in the revival. This pleasant, unpretentious, little show with its cheery, childish story and its rhythmic, mostly unexceptional musical numbers has, like its predecessor, been somewhat weighed down with its share of the portentous (and to me dubious) claims to historical significance made for this group of Kern shows ('the new form of rational musical comedy'), cautiously referred to in Miles Kreuger's knowledgeable cover notes. But this production fortunately takes no heed of such considerations, and the cast perform both the eminently detachable songs which form the heart of the score ('Cleopatterer', 'The Siren Song', 'Sir Galahad') and the bright supporting music in a fittingly naive fashion.

A fine group of enthusiastic choristers punch out the 'rah-rah' and 'rumty' rhythms of the college boys' numbers, the breathless, almost-accurate soprano of heroine Kathleen Murray gives a winsome Siren Song, comical Dorothy Greener goes historical over 'Cleopatterer' and pouts out the very music-hall number 'Poor Prune' effectively, whilst Jeanne Allen provides some earsplitting yowling in the hearty duets ('Just You Watch my Step' and 'The Sun Shines Brighter') she shares with Angelo Mango in the show's chief comedy rôle.

This may not be a state-of-the-art performance or recording, but it has the great advantage of being neither overplayed nor oversung – some of the cabaret croonings of the Siren Song I have heard over the years would be disastrous in this context – and it seems to me a fair representation of a Jerome Kern score of this period, played pretty much as it would have been in its own time. It may not be the greatest show score in the world, but it is pleasant and representative and, as Kreuger summarizes in his notes, 'a nostalgic collection of considerable historical value and listening pleasure'.

More Early Kern

Probably the best of this group of early Kern musical comedies was the really lively *Oh, Boy!* (1917), but this score has not made it to modern recording in spite of two revivals at the Goodspeed Opera House in recent years. *Oh, Boy!*'s music exists only on another World Record Club compilation, 'Jerome Kern in London – The Early Years', in a series of well-transferred cast recordings from the original London production (rechristened *Oh, Joy!*) starring Beatrice Lillie. This compilation, once again of notable historical interest, couples a dozen numbers from the show with nine pieces from the later *Sally* (1920), three from Kern's London collaboration with Ivor Novello, *Theodore & Co* (1916), orchestral selections from his other London musicals *The Cabaret Girl* (1922) and *The Beauty Prize* (1923) and some individual interpolated numbers from other shows. Like the companion Friml record, it is a splendid archive document rather than a feast of easy listening.

Sally was Kern's most successful musical of the some thirty he composed or contributed to before *Show Boat*. Written as a vehicle for dancing star Marilynn Miller, its score included one of his biggest hit songs, 'Look for the Silver Lining', which has been sung incessantly and recorded numerous times since. However, apart from the transfers of the recordings made by Dorothy Dickson and the Winter Garden Theatre cast of 1921, which are displayed both on the 'Jerome Kern in London' set and an American Monmouth- Evergreen recording, the music from this show's brief score is preserved only on another (and elusive) World Record Club disc in a six-song studio cast selection.

Sunny (1925) also had its popular tune in 'Who?', which duly did the rounds; its music, too, owes its survival on disc to World Records (sharing the disc referred to above with *Show Boat*) and the London cast recording with Binnie Hale and Jack Buchanan. But *The Cat and the Fiddle*, *Music in the Air* and *Roberta*, as well as having their early recordings reissued on LP, with all that means with regard to sound quality, have all been the subject of modern discs.

The Cat and the Fiddle

The Cat and the Fiddle gets fairly summary treatment on an early ten-inch RCA recording from a couple of weighty singers in Patricia Neway and Stephen Douglass, and a slightly more sizeable one on a British Fontana disc (backed with *Hit the Deck*) which, like the earlier version, naturally features the show's top song 'She Didn't Say Yes' alongside five other numbers from the score. In spite of some 'plinkety-swoopy' arrangements with a harp-complex and the Mike Sammes Singers doing their disembodied best to imitate 'boop-de-dooping' angels, the very expressive baritone of Denis Quilley and the easy, compact soprano of Doreen Hume combine attractively in 'The Night Was Made for Love' and 'I Watch the Love Parade'. She also makes a very nice contrast between the light-hearted 'She Didn't Say Yes' and the more lyrical 'Try to Forget'. These lighter voices suit the songs much better than the sub-operatic, and even the backing cannot wholly spoil an attractively presented selection.

Music in the Air

Where *The Cat and the Fiddle* had 'She Didn't Say Yes', *Music in the Air* had 'I've Told Every Little Star'. It also had a 1951 New York revival with Jane Pickens, who subsequently recorded much of the score on RCA with the assistance of Al Goodman and his orchestra and chorus. The recording is not at all pleasant. Miss Pickens sings in the what can only be called 1950s style, which involves a lot of crooning in places where crooning was never intended and, in 'I've Told Every Little Star', aided and abetted by what are presumably Goodman's arrangements, she goes off into a paroxysm of improper rhythms. She is altogether happier in a more straightforward performance of the lovely, simple 'In Egern on the Tegern See' but the damage is done and the recording devalued.

There is far less of the score on the World Records selection disc (backed with *Roberta*), but it is much more kindly treated by Marion Grimaldi, Maggie Fitzgibbon and Andy Cole, who performs the attractive 'And Love Was Born' (which Ms Pickens omits). The lively 'When Spring Is in the Air', which is also missing from the RCA disc, gets a spirited rendition from Miss Grimaldi and a ubiquitous chorus alongside the show's main numbers – 'I've Told Every Little Star', the soprano showpiece 'I'm Alone' and 'The Song Is You'.

The film soundtrack, which features Gloria Swanson and John Boles, has been re-recorded on JJA discs ('Jerome Kern 1934–8') but in an almost unlistenable state, whilst on 'Jerome Kern in London' Mary Ellis performs one song ('I'm Alone') which she sang in the London production and two others which were Eve Lister's in the theatre.

Roberta

Roberta, which had probably the best score of these three works, unfortunately also had the worst book (although it is almost a dead-heat with *Music in the Air*), but this hurt neither its recording prospects nor its life in the cinema. Songs such as 'Smoke Gets in Your Eyes', 'Yesterdays', 'I'll Be Hard to Handle' and the 1935 film additions 'Lovely to Look At' and 'I Won't Dance' ensured it half a dozen larger and smaller recordings; both film soundtracks, under the titles *Roberta* and *Lovely to Look At* (1952), were also transferred to record. Since it was the films rather than the stage show that encouraged this batch of recordings, all include the two successful film songs and most re-allot 'Yesterdays', orginally sung by the veteran Fay Templeton as old Aunt Minnie, to the ingénue rôle. Most also indulge in the fashion for souped-up orchestrations.

The interpretations of Gordon MacRae, Lucille Norman and the piercing Ann Triola are completely scuppered by some unfortunate up-to-date arrangements on a Capitol disc which runs together almost the entire score of the stage show plus the two film numbers. The other most substantial selection, on Columbia, with Joan Roberts, Kaye Ballard, Stephen Douglass and Jack Cassidy, suffers less in this all-important department but it is, quite simply, a strangely dreary disc. An 'Ed Sullivan presents' selection with an unnamed English cast goes in for good singing and the odd burst of those angel voices which seem to infest so many recordings of the 1950s.

The two film soundtracks each include only five songs from the original stage show. Given the rather unsatisfying state of affairs all round, there seems to be as good a value as any in the other half of the World Records *Music in the Air* disc already mentioned, in which Maggie Fitzgibbon expertly milks 'I'll Be Hard to Handle' dry, Marion Grimaldi turns her fine soprano on to a thankfully straight version of 'Smoke Gets in Your Eyes' and 'Yesterdays', and Andy Cole lends her convincing support in the charming 'The Touch of Your Hand' without, by way of a change, suffering from an over-prominent chorus.

Yet more Kern

Material from some other lesser-known and less successful Kern shows has also been transferred to LP record both by World Record Club, on a second 'Jerome Kern in London' disc (which includes songs from his two last London shows *Blue*

Eyes and *The Three Sisters*), and on the JJA Records compilation mentioned above, which reproduces numbers from *High, Wide and Handsome*, *Sweet Adeline* and *Joy of Living*. The indefatigable AEI is responsible for a tardy issue of what is almost an original cast recording of *Very Warm For May* (1939), presumably taken from the radio. A score which includes 'All the Things You Are' (sung twice, once by cast members Hollace Shaw and Ralph Stuart and once by Tony Martin, who had nothing to do with the show) and five other attractive Kern songs, plus a stirred and shaken version of the *Guglielmo Tell* overture and other familiar items, is sung by a cast including Jack Whiting, Frances Mercer and Grace McDonald; chunks of dialogue are spoken by Eve Arden and others. They were all obviously very good, but this recording doesn't really give anyone a chance. It sounds like the soundtrack of a very old movie which the mould has got at.

Unfortunately, the largest amount of Kern theatre music available today on record is in the form of such archival transfers and, *Show Boat* apart, the composer's show scores are not by and large well represented in coherent modern recordings. Even the centenary of his birth in 1985 brought us nothing new in the way of recorded performances, but hopefully the time will come. In the meanwhile, it is a case of choosing between the grand selection of transfers available and the few and not always very satisfactory custom-made LP recordings.

Vincent Youmans

Vincent Youmans is largely remembered today for the show which, more than any other, epitomized the 1920s musical theatre – *No, No, Nanette*. At least, he would be if people could only remember that he wrote it. Decades of one-eyed proselytizing both in print and on the air have bullied the layman into believing that between the wars only Kern, Gershwin and Porter in the entire world wrote any theatre songs worth remembering, and yet here is the most often and most widely enjoyed show of the era coming from the almost unfashionable pen of a writer who is – most unfairly – given comparatively little attention.

No, No, Nanette

Youmans's story and the fascinating tale of the creation of *No, No, Nanette* can be read in Gerald Bordman's biography of the composer (*Days to be Happy, Years to be Sad*, OUP), and the the joyful score that evolved during the incident-packed putting together of this evergreen show is to be heard on a whole range of discs, including several recordings from stage performances.

True to form, World Records have preserved the original London cast recordings from 1925 featuring Joe Coyne, George Grossmith and Binnie Hale (backed with *Hit the Deck*), whilst the American Stanyan label has paired the same transfers with a selection from *Sunny*. They have, of course, that old wind-up gramophone sound to them, some odd tempi and a reasonably careless attitude to accurate pitch, but some of the tracks, like Irene Browne's 'Too Many Rings Around Rosie' and Binnie Hale's stylish delivery of the title song, with their genuine 1920s flavour, come across with a delicious, uncomplicated brightness. This recording ought to be obligatory listening for any company planning to do *No, No, Nanette* . . . or *The Boy Friend*.

In 1971 a major Broadway revival was staged – its even more fascinating story can be read in Don Dunn's classic tale of backstage backstabbing *The Making of No, No, Nanette* – and remained surprisingly true to the score of the show as established by usage. Its recordings omitted two songs written for the comedy maid, the first-act and second-act openers 'Flappers Are We' and 'A Peach on the Beach'/'The Deep Blue Sea', as well as the light-hearted 'Fight Over Me' from the original score, but included the two well-known songs introduced for the initial London production, 'I've Confessed to the Breeze' and 'Take a Little One-Step'. The Broadway production and its disc feature Jack Gilford, Helen Gallagher, Bobby Van and Susan Watson, with Ruby Keeler star billed in the lesser rôle of Sue, whilst the London follow-up has Tony Britton, Anne Rogers, Teddy Green and Barbara Brown, with Anna Neagle getting the banner headlines.

This was a Big Revival. The music was reorchestrated for a large orchestra, which could have swamped the light structure and fabric of the piece had it not been done with such affection and taste. A two-piano sound, the introduction of ukeleles, a firing squad of tap-dancers and other such touches may seem too 1920s to be true, but they work, even when the songs are extended with long instrumental dance breaks fabricated to fit the needs of the show's dancing stars. The two recordings of the material are, however, very different. The American one is very up-front, bright and brash and played with an enormous enthusiasm (though never burlesquing the material), whilst the British is inclined to the dainty, the charming and occasionally the pale. Somewhere in there you can tell that the production succeeded in America and failed in Britain.

The Broadway recording is just plain more enjoyable, and even the biggest purist would find it difficult to remain aloof when Helen Gallagher attacks the 'Where Has my Hubby Gone?' blues or Bobby Van gets on to his 'Telephone Girlie'. Gallagher's performance as Lucille is great fun – her songs sliced out cheerfully in a chest voice which is as unlike Irene Browne's petulant soprano as could be as she goes camping and vamping her way through 'Too Many Rings Around Rosie', throwing off what is virtually a challenge to Van in a frantically energetic 'You Can Dance with Any Girl at All' and burning up everything in reach in her blues.

Van's Billy is energetic and stylish as he bouncily romances on 'The Call of the Sea' and jazzes along the telephone lines with the help of the three featured flappers in good vaudeville style, and Susan Watson, in the title rôle, expertly takes the sugar out of the word ingénue in the very bright version of the title song and a prettily understated vocal to 'Tea For Two' with the neatly sung, spoken and danced Tom (Roger Rathburn). Top-billed Ruby Keeler, playing the important but nearly songless rôle of Sue, has 'Take a Little One-Step' to dance (and sing) to, and Jack Gilford (Jimmy) croaks out a friendly 'I Want to Be Happy' to complete a star cast who are without exception good fun.

The inclusion of the little scenes which make up in particular the finale of the second act adds happily to the theatrical feel of the recording and, in the end, although you know that *Nanette* never sounded like this in the 1920s, you have to go with it. It's a 1920s show done 1970s style and, if you're going to have a modern recording that takes advantage of all modern recording has to offer, then this is done as well as you could wish. My priorities would have kept the missing songs and dispensed with the dance music for the recording, but someone else obviously had other priorities.

Most of those missing songs can be found elsewhere, if you want them, for there are a number of studio recordings about, although, somewhat surprisingly, almost all of those issued in the LP years before these revivals are not American. Britain is responsible for most, including two which devote both sides of a record to their selection. A truly awful Saga recording top-billing Margaret Burton includes 'Flappers Are We' and 'Fight Over Me' but, amazingly, omits one of the show's highlights, the bluesy 'Where Has My Hubby Gone?' blues. A Columbia issue of 1969 gives the most comprehensive selection of all, even though it practically ignores the third act ('Hello, Hello, Telephone Girlie', 'Where Has My Hubby Gone?' blues, 'Pay-Day Pauline'). This version goes wholeheartedly English – not a true sin as the original play was set in Brighton – but succeeds only in patches. Some of the performances are fine, but others verge on the over-the-top and insincere and sometimes you feel that you are listening to an overstated repertory theatre production from a group that has successfully murdered *The Boyfriend* and gone back to look for more such meat.

No, No, Nanette has been particularly popular in France since its original production there in 1926, running through repeated revivals and becoming as much part of the standard repertoire as the favourite French musicals of the *années folles*. It has found its way onto two French recordings, one by Merkès and Merval (CBS) and the other on the EMI-Pathé series with that set's usual splendid cast, including Liliane Berton (Nanette), Duvaleix (Jimmy), Lina Dachary (Lucille) and Guy Fontagnère as Tom. Although it pairs the show with the other American hit of the French stage, *Rose Marie*, the Pathé disc includes practically the same material as the CBS one, and its cast scamper through the songs at a breathless rate as if in a hurry to fit everything on to the record. This version was decidedly not meant to be danced to – it would be a festival of twisted ankles. It is a joy to hear Duvaleix croaking out 'Heureux tous les deux' (I Want to Be Happy) and Berton lending her crystalline soprano to 'Non, non, Nanette', but the recording, for all its delights, must remain a curiosity.

Hit the Deck

Youmans's other principal success, *Hit the Deck*, appears on record in a smaller variety of versions. Seven songs from the show's basic score of ten, plus the interpolated 'Fancy Me Just Meeting You', performed by the original London cast (featuring Ivy Tresmand and Stanley Holloway), are preserved in predictable state on the flip side of World Records' *No, No, Nanette* transfer, whilst a couple of modern selections, also with British casts, concentrate mainly on the show's biggest song successes, 'Hallelujah!', 'Join the Navy', 'Sometimes I'm Happy' and 'Nothing Could Be Sweeter'.

Better value comes from the MGM reissue of the 1955 film score. Although this discards three of the original numbers ('The Harbor of my Heart', 'Shore Leave' and 'If He'll Come Back to Me'), apparently resituates those that are left into a different story, and swaps the comedy of the stage show for the smooth singing of Tony Martin and Vic Damone and the song-and-dance talents of Debbie Reynolds, Ann Miller and Jane Powell, it has a bonus of sorts in the shape of four other interpolated Youmans numbers. These include the beautiful 'More Than You Know' from *Great Day*, sung by Tony Martin, not to mention a less showy than usual ensemble version of 'Ciribiribin' – not, need I say, a Youmans piece – which somehow worked its way in as well.

Some of the songs get great treatment – Damone and Powell lazing through 'Sometimes I'm Happy' and the jaunty 'I Know That You Know', Debbie Reynolds and the boys whistling and dancing all over a little bit of 'What's a Kiss Among Friends', and Damone, Martin and Russ Tamblyn belting into the revival song 'Hallelujah!' in soft-grained three-part harmony, which wasn't quite the way it was written. Ann Miller was clearly a hoot on screen, howling and wriggling her way through the interpolated 'Lady from the Bayou', but I find it off-putting to hear Tony Martin crooning emotionally to the 'girl of my heart' in 'More Than You Know' when the song cries out for its original 'man of my heart'.

The Fontana excerpts disc, which includes the enjoyable little selection from Kern's *The Cat and the Fiddle*, takes a similar line with *Hit the Deck*, giving five numbers from the show plus 'I Know That You Know' from the film. The songs are performed here in something more like the straightforward way they were intended to be sung by Denis Quilley and Doreen Hume, who are again in fine form – even if they haven't the supreme assurance of Damone and Powell – and the twiddly orchestra and croony chorus are less harmful than in the Kern selection. 'The Harbor of my Heart', which doesn't appear on the other discs, is a pretty bonus, even if the arrangement does its best to make it sound just like any and every other song, and 'Hallelujah!' is pelted through in a style which is as little like revivalist singing as the film trio.

The score of *Great Day*, which included along with 'More Than You Know' the magnificent 'Without a Song' and a lively title number, did not make it to disc, but World Records have issued a selection from the recordings made of the 1926 London production of the less obvious *Wildflower*. Otherwise, Youmans's work exists on record only in isolated numbers.

George Gershwin

For a composer who is as retrospectively idolized as George Gershwin, the representations of his show scores on record are disappointing. Admittedly, the man who made his first big mark with the blockbusting single 'Swannee' was, through the largest part of his career, more of a songwriter than a score-writer, and the many gems of his theatre and non-theatre writing have been widely recorded on recital records. But that does not alter the fact that recordings of the shows composed by the extremely famous and versatile writer of 'Rhapsody in Blue', *Porgy and Bess* and *Shall We Dance* are thin on the ground.

Primrose

The earliest Gershwin show score available as such is that for *Primrose* (1924), written for London and containing a bundle of songs, including the bouncy 'Wait a Bit Susie', the comical 'Boy Wanted' and the soubrette 'Naughty Baby', dug up from Gershwin's left-overs from his days composing for *George White's Scandals*. These are set alongside some rather stiff baritone numbers for the show's sub-operatic hero (Percy Heming) and some pattery bits for the star comic, Leslie Henson. It is unexceptional stuff of the period, catchy and pleasant, cobbled together to suit a predestined cast and delivered by them in an unexceptional way. Needless to say, it is the much regretted World Record Club and Messrs Kennedy and Ellis who are again responsible for making this interesting piece of musical theatre history available.

The next five years added *Lady, Be Good!, Tell Me More, Tip-Toes, Song of the Flame, Oh, Kay!, Funny Face, Rosalie, Treasure Girl, Show Girl, Strike Up the Band* and *Girl Crazy* to the total of the Gershwin stage *oeuvre*. Most of these titles will mean little to anyone, and many people will doubtless be surprised that such a sizeable number of forgotten or largely forgotten shows were credited (or, in some cases, debited) to Gershwin and also, mostly, to his lyricist brother Ira, in this the busiest period of their theatre life. *Lady, Be Good!* and *Funny Face* have come through Hollywood films to modern revivals of a greater or lesser kind. *Oh, Kay!,* equipped with a much superior libretto to either of these, skipped the filming but still turns up in the theatre, and, although *Girl Crazy* still wins, I am told, some attention in America, by and large the other shows have been left behind by time.

Not so their songs: from these more than half-forgotten shows came such numbers as 'That Certain Feeling', 'Kickin' the Clouds Away', 'How Long Has This Been Going On', 'I've Got a Crush on You', 'The Man I Love', 'Strike up the Band', 'Embraceable You', 'I Got Rhythm', 'But Not for Me' and the ballet 'An American in Paris'. If one added up the number of times that little list have been recorded, 'arranged' within inches of their lives for jazz singers, hooted by opera singers, or just good old plain sung as they were writ (hopefully on the principle that if Gershwin was a genius he knew best), it would probably come to something equivalent to the entire number of Broadway cast albums issued through history.

Lady, Be Good!

Lady, Be Good! (1924) owed much of its initial success to the performances of Adele and Fred Astaire, recently established as stars in *For Goodness' Sake* (also known as *Stop Flirting*). Although one cannot see their celebrated dancing on disc, it is interesting to listen to their vocal performances, recorded during the 1926 London production, as transferred onto World Records. The Smithsonian has gone even further in attempting to re-create the original cast performance of this show by interleaving the seven London tracks – including Fred's 'Fascinating Rhythm' and 'The Half of it, Dearie, Blues', William Kent's 'Lady, Be Good' and the delightful, added 'I'd Rather Charleston' as sung by Fred and Adele – with recordings of 'Fascinating Rhythm' and 'Insufficient Sweetie' by Ukelele Ike (Cliff Edwards), who performed them in the New York production.

Some of this little mixture is accompanied by piano only, played by Gershwin himself, some by orchestra, and Ike's, obviously, by ukelele. Gershwin's playing does give some tips on how 'Fascinating Rhythm', as an example, is supposed to go – no lingering round here, strict time from top to bottom – and Ike plink-plonks his way through his version authentically like a coon-singing George Formby. All these recordings, however, some more some less, are decidedly archival in their sound and the compilation is interesting only as such.

Unfortunately, these transferred discs are practically all there is, for the 1941 film entitled *Lady, Be Good!* junked all but two of Gershwin's melodies in favour of 'You'll Never Know' and 'The Last Time I Saw Paris', and the 1968 London revival disappeared without putting its revised revised version on record.

Funny Face

Funny Face, which paired the Astaires with top comic Leslie Henson at London's Prince's Theatre, has been the object of the same kind of attentions from World Records and the Smithsonian as *Lady, Be Good!*. Seven of the show's numbers, including 'The Babbit and the Bromide', 'Funny Face', ''S Wonderful' and 'He Loves and She Loves', are performed in various versions to make up a complete LP record which has the same kind of elderly sound quality and less than perfect performances as its companion disc.

The last three of the songs named above (along with 'Let's Kiss and Make Up') survived into the 1957 film, where they were joined by *Oh, Kay!*'s 'Clap Yo' Hands' and some studio material which makes it about as representative of the stage show as the 1983 Broadway show *My One and Only*. This latter borrows its title song and four others from the real *Funny Face* and supplements them with twice as many others, culled from here, there and everywhere amongst Gershwin's works.

On the cast recording of *My One and Only*, Tommy Tune's pleasant light baritone and Twiggy's flat, nasal and very individual vocal sound come together in 'He Loves and She Loves' (with a lot of tippy-tapping dancing feet, and a chunk of 'Funny Face' sung by the chorus grafted into its middle) and a bit of vocal 'S'Wonderful' at the end of a vast orchestral version; Charles 'Honi' Coles takes a run at the title song; and 'Funny Face' is played as a sort of comedy duo for two not very funny-sounding performers. The few bars of the chorus 'In the Swim' pounded out by the girls' chorus get the best service on a rather disagreeable disc of ground-up Gershwin.

The one custom-made modern *Funny Face* recording is a World Records half-disc (backed with Lerner and Loewe's *Gigi*) of five songs and an overture. It is terminally infested, however, with the New World Show Orchestra, the Mike Sammes Singers and a couple of fairly awful, sloppy soloists. Maggie Fitzgibbon's one lush and loud interruption with 'My One and Only' can't save the ship.

Oh, Kay!

Like most scores of the period, the musical part of *Oh, Kay!* is comparatively brief – eleven numbers in all – but amongst those eleven come more than an average selection of songs that have stuck: the cute 'Do, Do, Do', the appealing 'Someone to Watch Over Me', 'Maybe' and two numbers that are blatantly pasted into the script but built to bring down the house – 'Clap Yo' Hands' and 'Fidgety Feet'. Not bad for one show. Once again London is the saviour of the contemporary performance and this time we get the first four numbers named above performed by Gertrude Lawrence, Harold French and Claude Hulbert, both on World Records (sharing 'George Gershwin in London' with two numbers from *Lady, Be Good!* and eight from *Tip-Toes*) and on a number of other labels.

The show was revised by the original co-librettist P. G. Wodehouse for a 1960 revival, which cuts out two of the original numbers, remodels a couple of others and pops in four spare Gershwin pieces, two of which ('The Twenties Are Here to Stay' and 'The Pophams') were plucked from the antique *Primrose* and fitted out with Wodehousian words. It is an unpretentious revival, performed with just the two pianos which made up the backbone of the original orchestration plus percussion, a raucous girls' chorus of six, and a lively sense of fun. Baritone David Daniels and Marti Stevens, singing Gertrude Lawrence's rôle of Kay with rather more breadth and weight than the original star could ever have done, supply the good voices (but not too much comedy) as they duet through 'Maybe', 'Do, Do, Do' and 'You'll Still Be There'. He annexes 'Clap Yo' Hands' from Larry (Eddie Phillips), who has to be content with a few crackly bars of 'Fidgety Feet' and the interpolated 'Little Jazz Bird' from *Lady Be Good!*; she has her biggest solo moment in her nightclubby version of 'Someone to Watch Over Me'.

Oh, Kay! is, however, more fortunate than the others of this group of Gershwin shows, for it has been given a full-scale studio cast recording of its complete, original, unaltered and unadulterated score, by Goddard Lieberson for CBS. This is a recording with several strong points. The score is laid out in its show order, attractively made up with some bright, rhythmic, busy orchestrations that maintain the duo piano sound, and cast with a group of well-known and/or strong-voiced performers. There is just one very big 'but' about it, and I am not sure whether it is to be laid at the feet of conductor, Lehman Engel, or Jack Cassidy, who sings the rôle of Jimmy. It is a question of tempi.

If Cassidy were any more laid back he'd be flat on the floor. 'Dear Little Girl' is almost a dirge, and in 'Do, Do, Do' the most lively thing about is the orchestra, which finally gets going underneath the dragging singers and almost – but not quite – manages to give them some semblance of spirit. If it were a matter of just one song, this unsuitable speed could be regarded as an eccentricity, but when it afflicts a whole series it becomes simply boring. In 'Someone to Watch Over Me', Barbara Ruick, freed from Cassidy, seems to want to move things on a little, but Engel drags her inexorably back to funeral pace, leaving her practically to come to a halt at the end of each phrase or breath while she waits for the orchestra. The song takes six minutes.

The highlight of the recording is Allen Case's vigorous baritone singing of 'Clap Yo' Hands' and his duos with Roger White, 'Don't Ask' and 'Fidgety Feet', in which the music is actually allowed to get going. Otherwise it is a case of a marvellous opportunity to put down a definitive recording gone to waste.

Girl Crazy

Of the other mid-period Gershwin shows, *Tip-Toes* is represented only by the World Record tranfers listed above, but *Girl Crazy* gets a Lieberson/Engel recording, featuring Mary Martin, on Columbia. It also gets a couple of other modern selections, and bits and pieces on the soundtracks of the various films, which utilized what they fancied of its score either under its own title or, in MGM's 1965 version, as *Where the Boys Meet the Girls*.

The Columbia recording fortunately does not suffer too much from the pecularities of the *Oh, Kay!* disc. Opening with a vigorous cowboy chorus, it soon begins to hasten on merrily through almost the entirety of a score which includes such standards as 'Embraceable You' and 'But Not for Me', originally sung by Ginger Rogers, and 'I Got Rhythm', created by the young Ethel Merman. Mary Martin takes these three numbers pleasantly, regardless of characterization. She proves most at home in a smooth, puzzled performance of 'But Not For Me' and just a little short of the biggest guns we have come to expect in 'I Got Rhythm'. She also takes the vocal in a dragging version of 'Biding my Time', which seems to indicate that Engel is indeed responsible for all this murderous lack of movement, and draws the comedy tunefully from a first-rate 'Boy, What Has Love Done to Me'.

Louise Carlyle delivers Merman's other big number, 'Sam and Delilah', with gusto and style, and jollies along the clip-clopping 'When It's Cactus Time in Arizona', which sounds like a Gene Autry cut-out, whilst Eddie Chappell turns his masculine baritone on to 'Treat Me Rough' in an enjoyable battle with the brass section.

This is a much happier recording than that of *Oh, Kay!*. Even though it makes no effort to present the score as a coherent part of a show, it does at least supply all but one number in a well-played and sung disc on which things like arrangements and sound – if not always speed – are all in good order.

Of Thee I Sing and *Let 'em Eat Cake*

When Gershwin shifted from the Boltonized show books of the 1920s with their blatant song slots and their bias towards low comedy and simple sentiment, in the direction of a much more literary and dramatic kind of libretto – as in the pair of political burlesques *Of Thee I Sing* and its less successful sequel *Let 'em Eat Cake* – he did not produce the same kind of show score as he had for his earlier works. Little of the scores of these pieces consisted of take-out tunes like his biggest hits of earlier years; rather the music belonged to the script in which it was enshrined and, as such, it sits pretty ill on recital records. In coherent show and/or cast recordings, however, it is a different question altogether, and a full-scale version of *Of Thee I Sing* makes for particular fun, as, in a delightfully varied score, it ranges through genteel burlesque of everything from Gilbert and Sullivan and *Florodora* to the Viennese waltz.

The original production of *Of Thee I Sing* (1931) missed the LP age by some way, but a revival in 1952 was caught on Capitol, a 1972 TV broadcast was issued on Columbia, and a concert performance at the Brooklyn Academy of Music in 1987 resulted in a tandem recording with *Let 'em Eat Cake*. The three recordings present some broad contrasts. The newest recording is far and away the truest representation of the Gershwins' score. The original orchestrations have been exhumed, the show has been cast with artists who can actually sing the notes and, most importantly, where the other two discs include only part of the show's score, this version somehow manages to fit all of it onto its two sides. It sounds as if it ought to be hands down the best, but somehow it isn't. It is thoroughly and respectfully correct, but it just isn't much fun. Firstly it is recorded in such a way that you have to turn it up to blasting level to get rid of muddy sound that obscures the lyrics, secondly it is equipped with a vast and omnipresent choir which might very well be intended to burlesque the American patriotic choir tradition but merely sounds vast, correct and rather as if they are singing a laundry-list, and thirdly the principal singers, in spite of making some very pretty sounds, mostly don't seem to get into the special spirit of things.

This lack is all the more evident when you listen to the other recordings. The 1952 cast recording is lively at the expense of almost everything else, but the television cast version is both tremendous fun and good. It has an immediacy and a theatricality to it which may have something to do with its being a soundtrack recording, and a brightness and clarity in its recorded sound and its performances which the 1987 version lacks. Carroll O'Connor and Cloris Leachman dig into the rôles of Mr and Mrs President with glee, Michelle Lee vamps out a suitably over-the-top cabaret style Diana Devereaux (which contrasts vividly with Paige

O'Hara's more legitimate version of the extravagantly jilted Southern belle on the newer recording) and Jack Gilford, as the cellophane Vice-President, makes far more of what little is left of his part when the dialogue is omitted than he does in the same rôle fifteen years later. Unfortunately, this recording gives you only part of the score, plus the song 'Mine' from Let 'em Eat Cake, which was interpolated for the 1952 revival. It includes the stars' numbers at the expense of the hilarious French Ambassador's song and the Supreme Court Justices' music, thus unbalancing and taking the edge off this skilful burlesque. Also, although the performances are vigorously enjoyable, some of the effects are missed – as, for example, in the burlesque waltz scena 'I'm About to be a Mother', where Maureen McGovern's immaculate 1987 trilling points up the parody in a way that Leachman's warm but less vocally versatile performance cannot.

It's a matter of taste, I suppose. If you're listening for pleasure, you'll get more fun out of the 1972 recording, but if you're looking for a scrupulous, full-scale version of Gershwin's score, then you will be better off with the newer disc, especially since you get the sequel thrown in as well. Since this last has only recently been issued, I suppose it is unlikely that in the forseeable future there will be a recording of the whole of Of Thee I Sing, libretto and all. Given the honours it has won and the importance of the text in relation to the score, it would seem worth doing, but the fashion of the intégrale has not become current in America.

After the failure of Let 'em Eat Cake Gershwin moved on to his theatre masterpiece Porgy and Bess and, like Offenbach with his Contes d'Hoffmann, disappeared beyond the boundaries of this book. Gershwin show music, of course, turns up on all recorded collections of the composer's songs, and many such a recording has been dedicated to his music over the years. The most substantial is undoubtedly the five-record fifty-three song set by Ella Fitzgerald on the Verve label, on which Gershwin's music has, of course, been arranged. The most recent is that by Kiri te Kanawa. I wish she wouldn't: she is undoubtedly one of the world's finest operatic voices, but this music isn't meant to be sung by an operatic voice any more than 'Dove sono' is meant to be sung by Elaine Paige.

Tierney and McCarthy

Irene

The 1920s turned up several other shows that were popular in their time and well enough liked thereafter to earn revivals and recordings under modern conditions. The most widely popular of these was Irene, based (like the equally successful Going Up) on a piece by playwright James Montgomery, with a score by Harry Tierney and Joseph McCarthy. Ingénue Edith Day and her 'Alice Blue Gown' made a splendid hit on Broadway before crossing the seas to London's Empire Theatre, where another triumph was in store along with, in the manner of the time, a comprehensive recording session. As a result, an original London cast recording of the ten numbers from *Irene*'s score survive (the finales, incidental pieces and the composite Act 2 opening are not included), transferred onto LP by Monmouth-Evergreen.

Much of what appears on this disc will be unfamiliar to those who know *Irene* only from its 1973 revival. Harry Rigby followed his resuscitation of *No, No, Nanette* with a similar job on *Irene* but, whereas he had restored the first show to the modern stage in pretty much its original condition, *Irene* underwent drastic changes. The libretto was heavily rewritten, a small half of the 1919 score was used, and the piece was decorated with both contemporary and modern songs from other sources, including such well-known McCarthy lyrics – to music by other composers – as 'You Made Me Love You', 'What Do You Want to Make Those Eyes at Me For' and 'I'm Always Chasing Rainbows'. Needless to say, 'Alice Blue Gown' and the charming title song were amongst those retained.

The wholesale cannibalism practised on *Irene* turned out a surprisingly attractive result, and both the Broadway production of this version, starring Debbie Reynolds, and the subsequent (and further altered) version as played in London ended up as cast recordings.

The Broadway disc shows that Rigby's team did as good a job on *Irene* as they did on *No, No, Nanette*. As in the case of the earlier show, they have made it into something bigger for the 1970s, but this time the dance element is much smaller and only occasionally does the music cannon off sideways into chunks of dance arrangements. The songs just occasionally get a bit big for their own good, but mostly the vigorous orchestral arrangements and playing beef up the score nicely.

Debbie Reynolds appears in the large star rôle of Irene, and makes her into an endearingly spunky lass, intermittently Irish, and unfailingly and attractively sincere. She has plenty of chances vocally, and runs the gamut most successfully, whether hollering out her conviction that 'The World Must Be Bigger Than an Avenue', jubilating over being 'An Irish Girl', or taking the quieter, more reflective moments of 'I'm Always Chasing Rainbows' or the lovely 'Alice Blue Gown' with a rough charm. George S. Irving as the couturier Madame Lucy has the other principal rôle, but rather less to sing. What he has he does with a grand comic flair, flamboyantly claiming that 'They Go Wild, Simply Wild Over Me', gambolling around with the glutinously Irish Patsy Kelly in a fragment of 'You Made Me Love You' and joining in the delightful quartet 'We're Getting Away With It' with ease.

The lesser rôles are all well taken: Irene's two friends (Janie Sell, Carmen Alvarez) stridently tempt her admirer, Donald (Monte Markham, more spoken than sung), into action in the hilarious 'Great Lover Tango'; Patsy Kelly grumbles out her answers to her daughter over a glass of beer in 'Mother, Angel, Darling'; Ruth Warwick aristocratically hoots out her description of 'The Family Tree'; and a super men's chorus performs two close harmony numbers, all adding to what is an immensely likeable recording.

London's version of the show made several alterations to the score as played on Broadway. Unfortunately the very funny 'The Talk of the Town', which actually got back into the score this time, did not make it to the recording, and the much cut 'Family Tree' was also left out. The additions are a top-notch new comedy number, 'Up On Park Avenue', a lovely ballad, 'If Only He Knew', written for the production, and the Sammy Fain song 'I Can Dream Can't I?' added to bolster the rôle of Donald for a singing actor.

Julie Anthony's Irene is less brawny than Miss Reynolds's; the voice is younger and clearer, perfectly lovable in the gentle moments and girlishly buoyant or occasionally quite lusty in the more out-front pieces. She makes a charming job of 'Alice Blue Gown' and 'Mother, Angel, Darling', jigs gaily through the 'Irish Girl', turns on the more sophisticated tones for her new ballad and a particularly effective version of 'I'm Always Chasing Rainbows' (turned here into a first-act curtain number) and comes full circle to end with a delightfully relaxed 'You Made Me Love You'.

Jon Pertwee makes a plausible rogue of a multiple-accented Madame Lucy in contrast to the gay-dog sparkle of Irving's American dressmaker, and Jessie Evans's splendidly broad Irish Mrs O'Dare doesn't attempt to sing, but there are on the other hand fine vocal values from Eric Flynn (Donald), who makes a model juvenile hero's job of his rousing hymn to 'Irene' and his soupy Sammy Fain number. Janet Mahoney and Jenny Logan as Irene's two comical satellites show that they well and truly deserved their extra numbers by giving a storming version of 'Up There on Park Avenue' and a determined 'Great Lover Tango', which make one regret all the more that 'The Talk of the Town' was not included on the record. The men's chorus is fine, although perhaps a mite less coriaceous than its American equivalent, but all the other areas are equal and the result is a second fine recording.

Neither of these versions will, of course, give you much idea what the original *Irene* was like. If that is your aim, then it is back to the Monmouth-Evergreen issue and Edith Day for such songs as 'Sky Rocket', 'Castle of Dreams' and 'To Be Worthy of You', which were not deemed worthy of a 1970s reshowing, or the enjoyable 1936 Lux radio broadcast (with advertisements and Cecil B. DeMille), which featured Jeanette MacDonald (who understudied the rôle on Broadway) in a potted version of the show that is mostly dialogue. But either of these versions of the new *Irene* is good as a record of that production and/or as forty-five minutes of pleasurable listening.

Tierney and McCarthy were also responsible for the score of *Rio Rita*, a spectacularly staged Broadway success which flopped briskly in London but whose title and title song have remained in the public consciousness largely through the success gained by the piece's picturesque very early talking-film version. It is the London cast again, however, transferred to Monmouth-Evergreen, which gives us a handful of the songs from *Rio Rita* sung by Edith Day and leading man Geoffrey Gwyther. The latter, incidentally, takes care to put on disc the song he wrote for himself to sing in the London version. There are a couple of other brief selections which share records with other shows (RCA with *A Connecticut Yankee*, Australian World Records with *The Great Waltz*), but these are rarities.

De Sylva, Brown and Henderson

Good News

De Sylva, Brown and Henderson's college musical *Good News* threw up 'The Best Things in Life Are Free' and 'The Varsity Drag', and scored a fine home success and a rather lesser one in London. It also served as the basis for two films, songs from the second of which (with June Allyson and Peter Lawford) made it to LP in several different combinations.

Good News was chosen by Harry Rigby to follow his revival successes with *Nanette* and *Irene*, but the production, with Alice Faye top-billed, was a quick Broadway flop in 1974. The only recording of it is a two-disc private issue largely billed as a 'limited edition of 1000', which has been stuck together from a variety of live performance tapes. It contains most of the original score (three numbers were omitted) plus a bevy of its writers' pops, including 'Button up Your Overcoat', 'You're the Cream in my Coffee', 'Life Is Just a Bowl of Cherries' and 'Keep Your Sunny Side Up', very attractively arranged, but the quality of the recording is so poor that it sounds like a not very successful set of transfers, and it can only be of interest for those anxious to have any recording, no matter how audibly mediocre, of this particular score.

The first disc contains the actual score of the show, and the second is filled up with various out-cuts and special occasion recordings. Alice Faye comes over with a pleasantly easy if rather flat light baritone. The production, incidentally, provoked a cover version by vocalist Teresa Brewer, which is more like a De Sylva, Brown and Henderson pops album and is for Teresa Brewer fans only.

The film soundtrack of *Good News* includes only six songs from the show, plus two others written expecially for the film version. It, too, is rather a disappointment. The sound on the record I have is only just all right, and neither Peter Lawford nor Joan McCracken sings very well, which leaves the attractive June Allyson to hold up the piece. She has a not very convincing go at 'The Best Things in Life Are Free', grabbing breaths in the middle of lines and only just making some notes, and though she does much better with the less sustained 'Varsity Drag' it is not anything to lift this recording out of the not-very-good class. For the moment *Good News* discs are bad news.

Walter Donaldson

Whoopee

The 1928 Broadway success *Whoopee* and its score by Walter Donaldson and Gus Kahn has been given a certain amount of attention in recent years. The show and its early recordings have been the subject of a comprehensive archive assembly by the Smithsonian. Someone has clearly done something quite miraculous to these recordings, for, given their age, most of them come over with a clarity and validity which so many of their contemporaries lack.

Eddie Cantor gives a precise, rather deadpan performance of his famous comedy song 'Makin' Whoopee' and puts across a selection of interpolated numbers in an incisive light baritone without showing his comic talents over much. As might be expected, the experienced singer Ruth Etting, heard in both her own 'Love Me or Leave Me', 'My Blackbirds are Bluebirds Now' and the lovely 'I'm Bringing a Red, Red Rose' (originally allotted to the show's juveniles), if also rather characterless, is more vocally impressive. The George Olsen band and its singers, who were also part of the original show, donate several other tracks.

The 1930 film, which in any case used little of the show score beyond the title number, and a 1978 revival, originating at the Goodspeed Opera House and ending on Broadway, both failed to make it to disc.

Cole Porter

The boom of the early post-war years did not continue into the 1930s and, apart from the later works of the composers mentioned above, the only theatre writers who emerged were Cole Porter, the legitimate inheritor of the songwriter's musical tradition, and the Richard Rodgers–Lorenz Hart team, whose work, begun in the 1920s, produced its principal pieces in the decade leading up to Hart's death in 1943.

The careers of Cole Porter and Richard Rodgers both straddle the imaginary line which has been drawn by commentators at the year 1943 and the production of Rodgers's *Oklahoma!*. It is a line that, since it coincides fairly much with the introduction of the long-playing record and the coherent original cast recording, is one which is useful for the purpose of this book, but please note that I'm not endorsing it when I split the careers of these two writers between this chapter and that dealing with later days on Broadway.

Porter's pre-war work, blending smooth words and attractive tunes to excellent effect, established him as a favourite songwriter, who, in collaboration with Herbert Fields and various other writers, produced a series of song-studded, star-vehicle musical shows which became a feature of the Broadway scene in the years leading up to the Second World War. The best songs from those shows have remained with us in the half-century or so that has followed. They have been recorded, re-recorded, and re-re-recorded in more and less recognizable versions, and have become accepted as part of the classic American song heritage.

The shows in which they were originally heard, however, have lasted less well, in spite of the often highly respectable authors who crafted them. *Gay Divorce, Leave it to Me!, DuBarry Was a Lady, Panama Hattie, Let's Face It, Something for the Boys* and *Mexican Hayride* all enjoyed highly satisfactory Broadway runs and, by and large, respectable London showings, but their names are not widely remembered. Only one show, the 1934 *Anything Goes*, has remained a theatre hardy, with regular productions up to the last and hugely successful 1987 revival launched from Broadway.

Anything Goes

Anything Goes has been given a full range of recordings, beginning with the reproductions of the original 1935 London cast 78s, featuring Jeanne Aubert, Jack Whiting and Sydney Howard. These have been assembled both on World Record Club's 'Cole Porter in London', along with a selection of cast recordings from *Kiss Me, Kate* and *Nymph Errant* and other items, and on a Smithsonian compilation, where Cole Porter himself gives his own rendering of three numbers and original Broadway star Ethel Merman can be heard kicking hell out of 'I Get a Kick out of You', 'You're the Top' and 'Blow, Gabriel, Blow'.

Merman went through this famous trio of numbers on disc on a number of occasions, once with Bing Crosby on the 1936 film soundtrack version, and again with Frank Sinatra and Bert Lahr in an unlistenably corny and dreary NBC-TV broadcast (backed with *Panama Hattie*) full of toothpaste-bright chat and monotonous singing. Both these recordings are full of extraneous Porter material, as is the 1956 film version with Crosby, Donald O'Connor and Mitzi Gaynor.

There are five modern cast recordings of *Anything Goes*: the first taken from a 1962 Broadway revival, the second from a London version of that same revival, whilst the third comes from the Lincoln Center production which followed *Me and my Girl* in bringing the carefree glitter of the pre-war musical back to a Broadway which had come to take itself and its product so seriously that entertainment had seemed in danger of becoming lost. The last two (and there will probably be more) are from reproductions of this latest version in other countries.

On the sleeve of the recent Broadway cast recording, Thomas Cott begins his notes declaring, 'Cole Porter's score for *Anything Goes* is one of the most glorious in the history of the American Musical Theater'. I wouldn't quarrel with that. But then he goes on to describe a production, nay, a version, of the show which chops that 'glorious' score up into pieces, layering it with one or two cut-out numbers from the show's pre-Broadway days and with songs sliced from other Porter works.

Admittedly, Porter's songs were often fairly loosely attached to their context and, like other writers of the same school, he often ended up using in his scores a song composed for quite another show, but I find it rather snobbish to allow Porter (and others) kudos as a writer of single theatre songs but to assume that they and their associates were incapable of building those songs into a score. The original *Anything Goes* score is neatly proportioned, mixing the stars' big show numbers and topical or point songs with less significant ensemble and choral pieces and with material for lesser characters that complemented the star sections without detracting from them. To add a bundle of Porter pops to this, I submit, is truly over-egging the cake. Recordwise, it makes what should be a show disc into little more than a recital.

I have always tended to blame whoever is supposed to regulate these things – and believe me, they are regulated, as is borne out by the tight hold generally kept by the Rodgers and Hammerstein office on the material they control – for allowing the recent depredations on Porter's works (witness the preposterous London *High Society* of a few years back) in order to earn a quick buck from the material before copyright ceases, but if one looks back to 1962, two years before Porter's death, one finds a really amazing musical pot-pourri in the rewritten version that played at the Orpheum Theatre, presumably with his blessing.

Eight of the show's thirteen basic numbers appear on the cast recording of the Orpheum production, along with 'It's De-Lovely', filched from *Red, Hot and Blue* for the 1956 film and used in every subsequent version, 'Friendship', from *DuBarry Was a Lady*, which also seems to have stuck, and four other borrowed bits. The book was changed, too – admittedly by Guy Bolton, who almost wrote the original – but unless you read the sleeve notes that doesn't really matter.

It is an agreeable if rather unexciting Porter recital, give or take a louche lyric, especially when Hal Linden is happily crooning his way through 'You're the Top', 'It's De-Lovely' and 'All Through the Night' with pretty Barbara Lang, or when Mickey Deems brings in the comedy with 'Be Like the Bluebird'. Eileen Rodgers in the rôle of Reno Sweeney makes her way staunchly and unpretentiously through 'I Get a Kick Out of You' as a solo, 'Anything Goes' with chorus and the inevitable tappy feet, and the extraneous 'Take Me Back to Manhattan', which suits her better. She is much more pleasant than Margery Gray (Bonnie), who squeals out the interpolated and rather uninteresting 'The Heaven Hop'.

The same piecemeal score was used in the London 1969 revival (although Bolton's name had vanished utterly from the credits, so goodness knows what had become of the book), which is remarkable for just two things. It was the first London production by twenty-three-year-old impresario Cameron Mackintosh, and it was such a speedy flop that the recording that was made was never issued. When a copy crept into the daylight in the early 1980s at London's Dress Circle, the mecca of British show record collectors, it wore a price tag of £1,000. This most expensive musical theatre record of all time now has a good home in California. I hope its owner never plays it. Like ancient champagne, it is better to look at than to use. Nevertheless, its well-known rarity prompted TER to release it, obviously with an eye to the collectors' market.

That brings us back to the 1987 recording. Having railed against this production's reorganization of the show, I now have to admit that this version makes up a very pleasant piece of listening. Although the text has, from the evidence of the notes, been once again rearranged, it seems to have been done with rather more tact than previously, and some sort of balance has been maintained in spite of the trimming of the chorus contribution. Most of the original show is there somewhere, even if not in quite the right order or always sung by the right character. 'It's De-Lovely' (which fits rather well) and 'Friendship' (which I've never liked and which doesn't) are the principal additions, along with 'Goodbye, Little Dream, Goodbye', which is so charming as to silence any protests.

The recording itself is a largely enjoyable one. The orchestrations are happy and unpretentious, supporting the singers rather than being a band, the sound is bright and free, and there are some fine performances. Howard McGillin in the star rôle of Billy is truly splendid; he makes a marvellously clean and straightforward job of 'All Through the Night' and 'Easy to Love', performing them as if he had never heard any of the hundreds of singing stars who have arranged and cabareted them to death over the years. He is equally convincing sparring sparkily with Patti LuPone's Reno Sweeney or romancing with the sweet-voiced Kathleen Mahoney-Bennett (Hope), whose original song, 'The Gypsy in Me', is sadly burlesqued by the fop of the tale (Anthony Heald) but who makes you, instead, want more of her replacement number 'Goodbye, Little Dream'.

Miss LuPone gives an idiosyncratic performance which seems calculated to deny the iron-trumpet standard set by La Merman. She often sings quite conversationally, avoiding any kind of effects, but just when you are beginning to appreciate this rather tasteful approach she pops in something really vulgar or inapposite and you have to start getting to like her all over again. I never quite got there. She doesn't get to sing the splendid 'Buddie, Beware', which has been sidetracked to the rôle of Bonnie (now called Erma and played with gusto by Linda Hart), and instead shares 'Friendship' with Bill McCutcheon who, in the comedy rôle of Moonface created by Victor Moore, croaks his way through the foolish 'Be Like the Bluebird'. She loses in the exchange, but Hart gives a fine, traditional version of the piece so we, I think, gain by it.

You have to be thankful to this version for restoring 'Buddie, Beware' – even if to the wrong character – and including both the leading man's songs (they were originally alternates) and the counter-melody to the Sailors' Chantey (if not all the verses). In fact, when you come down to it, if you like 'Friendship' and Miss LuPone, there's precious little to complain about, and, even if you don't, it is still a fresh and most enjoyable version of this eternally fresh and enjoyable show.

London's cast album of this version is another fine and happy recording. The superb McGillin repeats his Broadway assignment with extra breadth and punch and the rôle of Reno Sweeney is taken with swingeing vigour by Elaine Paige. The peerless Paige voice rolls out like molten bronze, and tracks like her 'You're the Top' with McGillin are simply splendid, but just occasionally the style of the music and the humour of the songs seems to escape her a little. Nothing, however, escapes Kathryn Evans's Erma. Her rendition of 'Buddie, Beware' is a simply stunning mixture of singing, style and personality which just leaps off the record. Of the remainder of the cast Bernard Cribbins (Moonface) and Harry Towb (Elisha) show up with agreeably more singing voice than most comedians, but no less comedy, Martin Turner struggles less exaggeratedly with the burlesque of 'The Gypsy in Me', and only the rather un-ingénueish ingénue (Ashleigh Sendin), with an uninteresting version of 'Goodbye Little Dream', does not at least equal her Broadway counterpart.

If I have to pick and choose between the recordings of this production of the show, however, I would have to pick Australia's *Anything Goes*, for one reason and one reason only: it is one of those recordings with a star performance at its centre that just won't allow you to go elsewhere. Australia's Reno Sweeney is Geraldine Turner (heard some years earlier being highly impressive in Australia's *Chicago*), and the rôle might have been written for her. She has not only a strong, vibrant chest voice, even and pleasant to listen to throughout its whole considerable range, but she has evident ability as an actress and, above all, as a comedienne. Laughter twinkles through even her lustiest notes, lending the songs that light-hearted shimmer that needs to go along with the trumpeting tones. The almost ribald gaiety of her mature and confident performance is irresistible. To hear her commanding 'Blow, Gabriel Blow' or insisting with undertones that 'Anything Goes' is one big, sizzling joy.

Her supporting cast is young sounding and pleasant. Simon Burke is a youthful Billy with an attractive light voice (if without McGillin's style), Marina Prior stops just on the right side of oversinging Hope (who has for some incomprehensible reason been given 'All Through the Night', with 'Goodbye, Little Dream' being cut), Jacqui Rae is a fine Erma and Peter Whitford a not very humorous Moonface. All the orchestral and recording values are good, but in the end it all comes back to that beautifully bright and belting Reno Sweeney.

With all this patch of *Anything Goes*es mushrooming through the record shops it is a shame that this should have been the next show chosen by EMI-Angel and John McGlinn to be given the 'authentic' treatment so successfully practised on *Show Boat*. This 'first recording of the original 1934 version' (quibbles possible here) has been lovingly put together with much of the original orchestration and the lost portions carefully reconstructed by Hans Spialek (the original co-orchestrator) and others. It is on one disc, boxed with a 143-page booklet of splendidly learned notes in three languages and a fascinating detailing by McGlinn of the reconstruction process and an hilariously tongue-in-cheek glossary of the many topical names, places and expressions which litter the lyrics.

The record contains the twelve pieces and two finales that made up the 1934 opening night score of *Anything Goes*, played in order, but with a little solo for Hope ('What a Joy to Be Young'), which had been cut before opening, inserted in Act 2 – one can only assume to bolster that lady's rôle. Two further cut numbers ('Kate the Great' and 'Waltz Down the Aisle') and the original version of the pared-down 'Bon Voyage' ('There's No Cure Like Travel') are added as an appendix. Why the inconsistency? And, if there were to be an appendix of cut songs, why not include 'Easy to Love' – by far the best of the group? Still, apart from this last, all the portions of the original *Anything Goes*, free from interpolations and alterations, are there.

Unfortunately, this is almost the only recommendation the recording has in its favour. The other is the orchestra and orchestrations. The rich, easy musical sound lined up by Spialek and Co. and produced by the London Symphony Orchestra under McGlinn is a glorious reminder of the days before all became subordinate to the rhythm section. Between them they make the music quite as rhythmical as it needs to be, and this recording is wholly successful when the band is indulging itself in the overture, entr'acte and dance music. Once the singing starts, the pleasure stops. After the triumph of the *Show Boat* casting, something has gone horribly wrong.

Kim Criswell (Reno) has one of those syringe-like voices that goes straight through you – squeezed, harsh, nasal tones that slice up your eardrums the moment she puts her foot on the accelerator. She has not a whit of humour, warmth or personality and simply can't touch Turner or Paige on any count, or Evans or Hart in 'Buddie, Beware' (returned here to its rightful owner). Cris Gronendaal is a pleasant but characterless Billy; Frederica von Stade is miscast as Hope to the extent that her sung admission 'I'm twenty-one' raises mirth and 'The Gypsy in Me' (also back with its original owner) becomes an operatic burlesque; and Jack Gilford's nearly voiceless Moonface is the nearest anyone gets to showing personality. Many of the minor rôles are poorly taken and the semi-detached chorus is unconvincing. It is devoutly to be hoped that these 'authentic' EMI-Angel recordings will continue, but it is equally heartily to be wished that all the hard work and devotion put into re-creating classic scores will be supported by intelligent and accurate casting.

More Porter

The other Porter pre-LP shows get limited attention insofar as theatrical records are concerned. The world, or the part of the world which sings songs and makes records, seems determined when paying their lavish attention to Porter to take him as a songwriter, ignoring the theatre context of his songs. Time and again, the most popular and the most frequently repeated of his show songs find their way into more and more Porter anthologies on disc, or even, as in the case of the theatrical compilation *Cole*, on the stage, but rare are the recordings that gather together the contents of one particular show, as it was written.

Just two songs from *Gay Divorce* appear on World Record Club's 'Cole Porter in London' – one of which is the ubiquitous 'Night and Day', the only scrap of the original work to survive into the score of the movie entitled *Gay Divorce*. The same WRC disc gives much more space to Gertrude Lawrence and Elisabeth Welch's songs from the unsuccessful *Nymph Errant*, but *Jubilee*, which did not make it to London, is only really represented by a series of demo tracks recorded by Porter himself on a Columbia disc, with fragments of *Leave it to Me* and *Let's Face It*.

Dubarry Was a Lady's songs can be gathered up from various recital records, but five songs from *Red, Hot and Blue*, including four by Ethel Merman, and 'Goodbye Little Dream' deliciously crooned through the haze of the years by Yvonne Printemps, appear together on a beautifully put-together Smithsonian Institution compilation of archive material. The rest of this recording is composed of eight pieces from *Let's Face It*, performed by Mary Jane Walsh, Danny Kaye and Hildegarde, and by Mary Martin doing her original interpretations of 'Most Gentlemen Don't Like Love' and 'My Heart Belongs to Daddy' from *Leave it to Me*. These transfers come from a late enough era of the 78 rpm record to sound, by and large, no worse than the soundtrack of a contemporary movie sounds now on the television and sometimes better. They are a mixed bag, for some of the *Let's Face It* material is mediocre stuff, but the best tracks on this disc are a treat – Mary Jane Walsh's pretty 'Everything I Love', Merman pounding out her amorous distress 'Down in the Depths on the 90th Floor', Martin's two classic performances, Danny Kaye going bananas in 'Let's Not Talk About Love', and the wonderfully delicate Mlle Printemps (whose track is placed right after four punches between they eyes from Merman) giving a lesson in how to woo every ounce out of a song, even when you can't pronounce the lyrics.

Some of *Panama Hattie* gets a representation on the back of the unfortunate TV disc of *Anything Goes* and on the JJA label ('Cole Porter (Music and Lyrics)') in a collection with archive selections from *Around the World in 80 Days* (1946), the revue *Seven Lively Arts* (1944), *Mexican Hayride* (1944) and *DuBarry Was a Lady*. *Mexican Hayride* appeared as an original cast recording on 78s, with four discs in a solid folder (*Panama Hattie's* box held only two), and the results are included on the JJA disc.

Something for the Boys

The one show which has been served up again in the shape of contemporary recordings and issued as something like a well-after-the-event cast recording is *Something for the Boys* (1943). Sound Stage Recordings transferred nine pieces sung by original cast members Paula Laurence, Ethel Merman, Betty Garrett and Bill Johnson onto a disc which was topped up by four pieces from Porter's *Seven Lively Arts*, but AEI did even better and assembled a good dozen portions of this lively and agreeable if unexceptional show, plus some bits of dialogue, on a recording that has both an enjoyable period sound and a period flavour.

The disc is Ethel Merman orientated, AEI preferring to give us Merman's version of 'I'm in Love with a Soldier Boy' instead of that recorded by Betty Garrett (who sang it originally), and of the duo 'By the Mississinewa' performed by Merman and Betty Bruce rather than that of Garrett and Paula Laurence included on the other compilation. Merman gets plenty of big, bouncy songs, which she delivers in standard style (even when she starts on 'I can see he'd be happier without me . . .'), and also a chance for some enjoyable tit-for-tat dialogue. She also joins in duet happily with the smooth and extremely effective leading man, Bill Johnson, whose 'Could It Be You?' is the most enjoyable track of a disc which even the sleeve admits is not made up of particularly memorable music.

Leave it to Me

As far as the earlier Porter pieces are concerned, only Germany has seen fit to record a modern production as a cast album. The 1988 Stuttgart disc entitled *Wodka Cola* is, in fact, basically a German-language version of *Leave it to Me*. However, its score is yet another Porter jigsaw, with 'From This Moment On' (*Out of This World*), 'Every Time We Say Goodbye' (*Seven Lively Arts*) and 'Where

Are the Men' (*Anything Goes*) pasted in to eight of the original fifteen songs of the score. Amongst these are 'My Heart Belongs to Daddy' ('Mein Herz gehört nur Daddy'), 'Most Gentlemen Don't Like Love' and 'Get out of Town'.

Whatever its qualifications as an accurate record of *Leave it to Me*, *Wodka Cola* is a good record of *Wodka Cola* and a pleasant listen. The arrangements of Dieter Glawischnig and the playing of the band are both excellent – atmospheric and fun, if not always deeply 'authentic' – and the cast, although not the slick singers we have heard so often in Porter music, mostly sing attractively and/or well. Of the lead players, Barbara Grimm delivering a piquant but unexaggerated 'Mein Herz gehört nur Daddy' and a gently touching 'Jeder Abschied ist ein kleines Sterben' is more successful than Anke Hartwig, who tries to wallop out her numbers in the way she thinks 'Broadway-Musik' should be done without having the equipment.

Rodgers and Hart

The Rodgers and Hart combination have been given a slightly wider (better would not be an apt word) coverage insofar as their 1920s works are concerned, but almost solely through the English connection. On the one hand, WRC's 'Rodgers and Hart in London' preserves original cast recordings of four songs from their *Lido Lady* (1926), played only in Britain and France, along with odd songs from *Peggy-Ann*, two interpolations into the London musical *Lady Luck*, and other items, whilst, on the other, both *Dearest Enemy* (1925) and a version of *The Girl Friend* (1926) have been given British modern recordings of sorts. A selection from their short-lived *Chee-Chee* (1928) sung by Betty Comden has been issued on Eva records (backed with a similar treatment of the Gershwins' *Treasure Girl*).

Dearest Enemy and *The Girl Friend*

The *Dearest Enemy* recording is a private one, made with little more than a piano accompaniment, and cleanly and capably sung by a small group of vocalists headed by a pretty ingénue in Michelle Summers (Betsy) and the soft-grained and rather languorous baritone John Diedrich (John), who share the show's most important number 'Here in my Arms'. *The Girl Friend*, recorded professionally by TER, is the result of a small-scale production in an English stock theatre. It is also very distantly related to the original Broadway show and score as, in spite of the claims made on the sleeve, only three numbers, 'The Blue Room', 'Why Do I?' and the title song survive, along with one cut before Broadway ('Sleepyhead') and four others interpolated for the original London production. Only two of these, 'Mountain Greenery' and 'What's the Use of Talking', both from *The Garrick Gaieties*, are by Rogers and Hart. A palpable attempt by TER to follow up the small-scale hit of their *Mr Cinders* recording, it has not the same quality either in its hotch-potch score, organization, performance or, most particularly, its skinny musical arrangements.

Another *Girl Friend* selection, on Epic, sharing a record with *White Horse Inn* and *The New Moon*, has room for only four songs sung by Doreen Hume and Bruce Trent.

A Connecticut Yankee

A Connecticut Yankee (1927) is the one show of the dozen from this period that has lasted with any vigour, but it has been poorly treated with regard to recording. The vigour and the one recording which does exist really belong to the 1940s rather than the 1920s, for it was the much revised *Connecticut Yankee* reproduced in 1943 that was responsible for its continuing popularity. The four 78 rpm recordings from this production issued by Decca were reissued by JJA on a disc shared with a similar selection from the Arthur Schwartz/Howard Dietz *Inside USA*, and more recently by AEI, which manages to spread them over two sides of a disc by ingeniously fabricating reprises from the original tracks.

Dick Foran, in the rôle of the Yankee transported back to King Arthur's times, takes some fine songs with him, but sings them with more smooth vocalizing and concentrated accuracy than spirit. Julie Warren, who joins him in 'Thou Swell' and 'My Heart Stood Still', is even paler, and the secondary couple, Chester Stratton and Vera-Ellen, duetting about a year 'On a Desert Island with You', are rather more lively, even if her quaint soubrette voice shows why she was dubbed in her films. Vivienne Segal had top billing and the best of the new songs, the highly comical 'To Keep My Love Alive', but she, too, sings this lip-smacking piece of material deadpan and not very accurately, almost as if she were afraid of the recording machinery.

The 1930s Roger and Hart shows have fared better. Like *A Connecticut Yankee*, *The Boys from Syracuse*, *On Your Toes* and *Pal Joey* have undergone major revivals which have resulted in full-scale recordings, whilst *Jumbo*, *I Married an Angel* and *Too Many Girls* are also represented on selections discs. The 1941 *By Jupiter*, the last of the partnership's works before Hart's death, also made it to disc.

Pal Joey

The most memorable of these shows is undoubtedly *Pal Joey* and it can be quite unequivocally stated that here was a case – probably the first case – where, instead of a successful show being the making of an LP record, an LP record was the making of a successful show. Columbia's 1950 studio cast recording of the score of *Pal Joey*, which had been only a limited public success in its 1940 production, won sufficient praise and popularity to encourage a Broadway revival in 1952 and, with fashions having changed, John O'Hara's sad and seedy musical with its unfamiliar anti-hero established itself as both the most substantial work of the Rodgers/Hart pairing and as an international success. The revival, which starred Vivienne Segal (the star of the 1940 cast) and Harold Lang, was also put down on a cast album by Capitol. However, since Segal and Lang had headed the cast on the rival Columbia disc, they had to be substituted for this recording and so, whilst the remainder of the show cast appeared on the Capitol semi-cast album, the two lead rôles were taken by Dick Beavers and Jane Frohman.

The later disc includes all the vocal music, but omits the dance sequences, whilst the earlier one drops, instead, two of the show's bundle of tongue-in-cheek cabaret songs and includes, in preference, some of the dance breaks. It also utilizes what would seem to be the original orchestrations for the show, and these are much more lively and imaginative than those used for the 1952 revival and recording.

Castwise it is nip and tuck, with the two recordings each at an advantage in turn. I prefer Vivienne Segal's straightforwardly soprano 'Bewitched' (or as it is known to non-pedants, 'Bewitched, Bothered and Bewildered') and 'What Is a Man?' to those of the rather detached and fruitier Frohman, but Beavers makes a much more virile and believable Joey than the limp and lightweight Lang. On Capitol, Helen Gallagher is strongly and appreciably featured in the originally subsidiary rôle of Gladys, zinging through her cabaret numbers 'That Terrific Rainbow' and 'Plant You Now, Dig You Later' and joining Beavers effectively in 'You Mustn't Kick It Around', but Elaine Stritch's version of the topical 'Zip' is performed on the 'end-to-end-as-loud-as-possible' principal and much more fun comes from Lewis Bolyard's tenorish burlesque 'The Flower Garden of my Heart'. On Columbia 'Zip' does no better in the hands of Jo Hurt and Barbara Ashley just belts Gladys's songs. Both recordings have pleasant singers as the juvenile, Linda, and it is perhaps no fluke that, given this, the duet 'Take Him' (Linda/Vera) is in each case one of the best tracks. Listening to this pair of notable recordings today, they are both just a bit disappointing in their lack of attempt at characterization. However, the spate of small label cover discs that followed didn't throw up anything to challenge them.

The film soundtrack includes a larger chunk from the original score than is often the case, some pieces metamorphosed into other forms, but it also includes numbers from *On Your Toes*, *Babes in Arms* and *Too Many Girls*. Its biggest advantage is the presence of Frank Sinatra as Joey – rather an upmarket Joey, with his classy voice and stylish presence – giving 'I Didn't Know what Time it Was', 'There's a Small Hotel' and 'The Lady Is a Tramp' as well as 'I Could Write a Book', 'Pal Joey' and his own reprise of 'Bewitched' (which actually belong to *Pal Joey*'s score) his enormously effective voice and delivery.

Jo Ann Greer glides gently through Rita Hayworth's music, making more points with the borrowed 'Zip' than the louder ladies, and bestowing an introspective warmth on a particularly effective 'Bewitched' and 'My Funny Valentine'.

No one else gets much of a look in. Gladys and the tenor have vanished from the score – only Joey gets to sing in the cabaret of this version, and the show songs, though listed on the sleeve, are instrumentals – and the sad loss of 'Take Him' practically cuts Trudy Ewen/Kim Novak out as well. This isn't really a recording of the score of *Pal Joey*, but what there is of *Pal Joey* amongst its score gets top-notch performance.

The most recent *Pal Joey* is a cast recording of a small-scale 1980 London revival. This version cuts down the orchestra severely, provides new orchestrations, and re-allocates some of the music amongst the characters – Gladys and the tenor have to all intents and purposes disappeared – but it alone of all the recordings presents the whole score (dance music apart) of the show in its original shape and correct order. The reduction of the band works rather well, particularly in the cabaret scenes and in the ballads, since *Pal Joey* is an intimate story with no big effects. The orchestrations that have been used here (and which are credited to four people) are adept and characterful, and conductor Grant Hossack handles them with skill. The performers are not always equally as skilled. You will not find accomplished singing on this recording – the nearest thing to it comes from the very young and firm-voiced Danielle Carson as Linda – but you will find one or two interesting performances. The most important is from Denis Lawson as Joey. This Joey you can believe in as a suburban medallion man. He establishes the character in his first lines and is utterly believeable thereafter. Since he sings his songs, particularly 'Do it the Hard Way', with a cocksure, eager style and a light but sturdy baritone, the whole performance is most convincing.

Sîan Phillips as Vera manhandles her very individual baritone growl through 'Bewitched', mixing successful lines with some that are less so in a characterization which keeps on threatening to develop into something spot on, but then doesn't. Chicago is a long way away when her precise British accent meets the very East End vowels of Miss Carson in a 'Take Him' which isn't quite the highlight it is on the other recordings. With Gladys gone, her solos in the cabaret music are shared out among the chorus girls. At the start they sound grand, a real bunch of second-raters who would be just the kind to fill up the stage of a downmarket Chicago nightclub, but then someone tells them to be funny, and the resulting performance of 'The Flower Garden of my Heart' is a horribly amateurish affair. It is followed by 'Zip', which also gets a 'mummy-look-at-me-on-the-stage' treatment from Darlene Johnson – what is it about this song? Is it so very difficult to play without vulgarity? – and suddenly the disc is much less interesting. A pity, as it would have been nice to have a good, full *Pal Joey*.

The Boys from Syracuse

When compared with such superior examples of its kind as *Phi-Phi* and *A Funny Thing...*, *The Boys from Syracuse* (1938), based on Shakespeare's *Comedy of Errors*, shows up as just a fairish musical. However, its score houses several Rodgers and Hart standard songs and it was undoubtedly these that earned it an off-Broadway revival in 1963. When that revival turned out a success, London (which hadn't bothered about it first time round) followed suit without imitating that success. These two productions not only produced two cast albums, but also prompted a third recording, in the Columbia series produced by Goddard Lieberson, and, as a result, whilst others of the authors' scores are unavailable, we have three full discs of *The Boys from Syracuse*. They are not the world's most marvellous recordings, but they do show up best and worst Rodgers and particularly Hart existing side by side in one show. The famous soprano ballad 'Falling in Love with Love', the lovely baritone 'You Have Cast Your Shadow on the Sea', and two more lively pieces in 'This Can't Be Love' and the musically charming trio 'Sing for Your Supper' are all most enjoyable, but several of the other pieces are so banal, in their words above all, that it is hard to believe they are from the same pen(s).

The off-Broadway cast recording is a pretty rough affair. Stuart Damon sings smoothly as the Antipholus with the most music and Karen Morrow has a lusty, shrewish go at the female comedy numbers, but other cast members are less happy. Soprano Ellen Hanley doesn't sound comfy in 'Falling in Love With Love' and Clifford David, stuck with 'The Shortest Day of the Year', doesn't seem to know what to do with it. It is all lively and good-humoured enough, very off-Broadway rather than 'on', but for a recording some tighter and more musically sound performances are needed.

The London disc is certainly better all round. Bob Monkhouse doesn't have Damon's voice, but he is an agreeable light comedy juvenile, leaving the real singing to Denis Quilley as the Antipholus with not very much to sing. Lynn Kennington quivers a little less over the big soprano number than Miss Hanley, and there is a particularly true and sweet Luciana from Paula Hendrix, who duets very prettily with Monkhouse in 'This Can't Be Love'. Maggie Fitzgibbon goes rather over the top with the comedy, in an accent which is neither Australian nor British nor American but distracting, and shares 'He and She' with Ronnie Corbett, who must have been a caster's dream as the 4 ft 10 comic. The opening scena, played by minor players, gets served very much better here, both in singing and in acting.

The best sung version is, without question, the studio recording. It lacks something in vigour, perhaps because some of the folk involved haven't any idea what they are singing about, but only in some places. The most notable of these is the opening scena, in which all the lines are impeccably sung but which doesn't allow the comedy to breathe at all. You get the horrid feeling that this bunch of session choristers didn't know it was there or else don't know what 'comedy' means.

The outstanding performer here is Bibi Osterwald, who takes not only the comedy rôle of Luce but also appropriates the song 'Oh, Diogenes', sung in the play by 'a courtesan'. She is wholly at home with her material and, even though it is some of the show's weaker material, makes it work for her as she sings merrily through her three numbers and joins the other two girls in an excellent performance of 'Sing for Your Supper'. Portia Nelson, who is something between a legitimate soprano and a nightclubber, treats 'Falling in Love with Love' with less respect than the straighter ladies, pulling it about quite a lot inside the limits the orchestra allows. It is an effective style, and the song sounds a good deal happier not being sternly vocalized. Holly Harris, in the soubrette rôle, falls into something of the same category and is equally good.

Since they don't sing together, Jack Cassidy takes both of the Antipholus rôles and makes his usual leisurely but agreeable way through the two big ballads, lurching into a more lively mode when 'This Can't Be Love' comes along. Lehman

Engel's orchestra is more with it than his chorus, but they have more to do as, along with the twelve sung excerpts on this disc (as on the other two), the second-act dance music is also included.

On Your Toes

On Your Toes makes an unusual cast recording, as its score is made up of just nine numbers and two important ballets, the famous 'Slaughter on Tenth Avenue' and 'Princesse Zenobia'. The songs include more than an average ration of Rodgers and Hart favourites – 'There's a Small Hotel', 'Glad to Be Unhappy' and 'It's Got to Be Love' are the most obvious, but the charming 'Quiet Night' and the splendid title number are at least as good, and the ballets are two marvellous pieces of dance music, pieces of a scope and size rarely attempted for the musical stage.

On Your Toes has had two major revivals, the first in 1954 with ballerina Vera Zorina starred, the second in 1982 with Natalia Makarova playing and dancing the rôle of the tempestuous dancer. Each of these prompted a cast recording, and a third disc, made by Goddard Lieberson for Philips, prior to these revivals, completes the list.

The 1954 cast recording is a very enjoyable one. It takes in the nine songs, one additional number, an overture, a finale and a version of 'Slaughter on Tenth Avenue', omitting only the sizeable 'Princesse Zenobia', and deals with all the elements perfectly well. The orchestra and its new arrangements are bright and sharp, Salvatore dell'Isola keeps the show bubbling along in spite of all temptations to the contrary, and the performers all deal with their numbers attractively – not an easy thing in a score which consistently tempts the ballad singers to soup-up and the comedy actors to go over the top. Kay Coulter (Frankie) sings 'Glad to Be Unhappy' and her halves of the two duets with Junior (Bobby Van) in a pleasant, warm, middle voice, and Van gives her an equally pleasant straight musical comedy response. Elaine Stritch (Peggy), singing with a clear character chest voice which will surprise those who know her only in latter day incarnation as a death-rattle baritone, has a good time with the rather deliberate topical song 'Too Good for the Average Man' and turns the added 'You Took Advantage of Me' into something dangerously like an eleven o'clock number.

The Philips disc falls for some of the temptations, and the most obvious one is forseeable. With Lehman Engel at the helm and Jack Cassidy singing Junior, you can bet there are going to be indulgent tempi, and you'd be right. Portia Nelson, singing Frankie and 'On Your Toes' and 'Quiet Night', gets dragged down with them, and the most enjoyable moment comes from the two duets ('The Heart is Quicker Than the Eye' and 'Too Good for the Average Man') sung by an excellent Peggy (Laurel Shelby). Once again, 'Princesse Zenobia' gets omitted and the space left by not including the interpolated number is filled with an entr'acte.

The recording made of the 1982 revival is in a different class to these two in aspiration and in technical expertise. It is a two-record set that includes every bar of available music from the show – a whole side of 'Princesse Zenobia' and another whole side of 'Slaughter on Tenth Avenue', leaving the nine songs, the overture and a quick reprise to make up the other two, rather brief, sides. It is also made with a broad digital stereo in contrast to the mono of the two early recordings, with vast attention obviously paid to the orchestral sound, which is, consequently, quite splendid. It is so splendid that, when the orchestra has to come back down to accompanying the less caringly looked-after singers, it occasionally threatens to swamp them.

The decision to record in full and all this fine studio work make what might have been a regular, ordinary cast recording into something rather better, for the performances themselves, though ranging from the all right to the jolly good, are not outstanding. Christine Andreas (Frankie) is the most accomplished singer, showing a fine, attractive middle voice and an intelligent approach to her songs, but her partner, Lara Teeter (Junior), is a pleasant light voice and no more. Dina Merrill (Peggy) goes for broke in her numbers, without being as accurate or effective as Laurel Selby or Elaine Stritch, although she has a fine partner in George S. Irving for 'Too Good for the Average Man'. The star of the record is, as someone clearly intended it to be, the orchestra. It makes a really splendid job of the two ballets, played in what is apparently as near the original orchestrations as the elderly arranger could muster to memory nearly half a century on, and provides a memorable record of some rather special theatre music.

I Married an Angel

I Married an Angel (1938), which originally starred Dennis King, Vera Zorina and Vivienne Segal, is not one of Rodgers and Hart's more interesting scores. The pleasurably swinging title song and a ballad asserting that 'Spring Is Here' are the most attractive of its songs, and it descends as far as a rather nasty little piece which sniggers about 'A Twinkle in Your Eye' in the same way that Victorian songs used to nudge-nudge about ladies' 'dimples'. This was one of three retained, alongside numbers from the film version, on Pelican's transferred radio broadcast disc with Jeanette MacDonald and Nelson Eddy (backed with *The New Moon*), but a more recent compilation made by AEI from radio and 78 rpm record sources virtually reconstructs the whole score of the show. The compilation is technically very well done and the sound suffers surprisingly little, but in spite of that and in spite of the fact that Gordon MacRae, Lucille Norman, Wynn Murray, Eve Symington and original cast member Audrey Christie all sing in the most pleasant, unforced Broadway style, it is not record whose content allows you to be too excited.

Too Many Girls

The score of *Too Many Girls* (1939) came under the very particular hands of Ben Bagley, the purveyor of a long series of mildly eccentric recordings of less-known songs by well-known composers sung by unlikely people. Partly because it originally opened on his sixth birthday, he left his usual format to put on record a not particularly coherent version of the score of this cute but not very remembered show. The teenaged heroine, singing of 'My Prince', is crackled out characterfully by the long-past teenage Estelle Parsons, Anthony Perkins croons warmly through the show's prettiest number, 'I Didn't Know What Time it Was', and the exceedingly camp Nancy Andrews honks out jaunty versions of the comic numbers 'Spic and Spanish' and 'Give it Back to the Indians' in an outrageous accent. And there is more where they came from, all equally unsuitable and fetching. The pointed 'I'd Like to Recognize the Tune', complaining about arrangers and their passion for wrecking composers' music, deserves to be engraved over the portals of the Musicians' Union.

Oddly orchestrated, if that is the word, for a small group, the songs are delivered in such a gleefully unpretentious style, everyone concerned clearly having loads of fun, that they sound more attractive than they ever could have done on the stage. Everyone ought to have a Ben Bagley record, and this is a very happy one to start with.

Babes in Arms

Jumbo, issued only as a film soundtrack which uses just five of the songs from the show (notably 'The Most Beautiful Girl in the World'), also gets a brief showing on a rare ten-inch RCA disc, shared with *Babes in Arms*. To squeeze the score of *Babes in Arms* onto one side of a ten-inch disc is rather liking getting a baby elephant into a bath – there is too much of it, and it can't really be reduced.

There have been continuous efforts to put *Babes in Arms* back on the stage since its original run and its successful Mickey Rooney/Judy Garland film. They have been regularly unsuccessful, but you can see why people keep trying. You just have to run your eye down the song list – 'Where or When', 'My Funny Valentine', 'Babes in Arms', 'I Wish I Were in Love Again', 'Johnny One-Note', 'The Lady Is a Tramp' and the less-known but super 'Way Out West'. Talk about every one a coconut . . . there are only four other numbers in the show. It has to be a percentage record of some kind.

The items on that famous list have been recorded in more shapes, sizes and disguises than any other show score I can think of. They've been crooned, jazzed, hooted and yodelled, and also given some of the most outstanding performances of any show songs from this era on a pile of records that would top the leaning tower of Pisa. Yet the score of the show, as such, has only been recorded once, and that on a version which makes no attempt at all to re-create it as a score, but simply trots out the numbers in their show order, performed by three soloists and an undertasked chorus.

The recording is one of Goddard Lieberson's series for Columbia, and the artists he uses are Mary Martin (billed big) and Jack Cassidy and Mardi Bayne (billed small). They all perform well. Martin sings with a strong, relaxed tone and sufficient character and delivers one of the straightest and least mannered versions of 'The Lady Is a Tramp' about (in spite of some words I don't recognize). Cassidy doesn't get much of a chance to stage one of his go-slows but puts across the less starry numbers with smooth charm, and Mardi Bayne tops the disc with her cute 'Way Out West' and a fine contribution to 'I Wish I Were in Love'. It is a three-person recital disc masquerading as a show disc (even the orchestrations are shared – Miss Martin has her own done by Ted Royal), but at least it exists. Perhaps someone will take up the challenge and give us a proper theatrical-style *Babes in Arms* recording, but I guess they would fall into the same trap the revival productions have. We've all heard these songs done over and over by the top singers of five decades; can anyone ever again find a bunch of kids who can compete with those versions?

By Jupiter

After *The Boys from Syracuse*, *By Jupiter* (1942) was another and rather happier venture into the classical past for Rodgers and Hart. It did not house the take-away tunes which the earlier show had – there isn't a recognizable title in the schedule – but it had a strong initial US run, a British production (which didn't make it to town) and, like *The Boys from Syracuse*, an LP age revival which resulted in its being preserved on record.

This recording includes all of the original score, even if the songs have been re-allocated among the characters, and, whilst it is no more a *Phi-Phi* or *Funny Thing* than *The Boys from Syracuse* was, it must have been quite a lot of unsophisticated fun of the sex-on-the-brain kind in the theatre. The score gets a much better service on this recording than the *Boys From Syracuse* one does on its equivalent disc. Sheila Sullivan (Antiope) and Robert R. Kaye (Theseus) sing the romantic music alongside the main story – she with a sparky soprano, which is well expended on the pretty song 'Nobody's Heart', and he with a very impressive baritone, which joins her attractively in 'Here's a Hand' and the almost rhapsodic 'Careless Rhapsody' and turns 'Wait Till You See Her' into a particularly pleasant track. Bob Dishy, top-billed in the rôle of the foolish Sapiens originally taken by Ray Bolger, larks his way through 'Now That I've Got my Strength' and the rather tiresome 'Life with Father' with limited vocal tone and joins the incisive Jackie Alloway (Hippolyta) in the show's most successful comedy number 'Everything I've Got', a number that had to be cleaned up to make it to the hit parades.

A second recording of a selection from *By Jupiter* on the Roulette label (backed with *Girl Crazy*) is a rather limp jazz-cabaret performance by two artists of limited talents and a small band who provide a fair example of the awful things that can happen to a score when you can't do anything to stop it.

Kurt Weill

The works of Kurt Weill have, over the years, been the object of a passionate and vocal following by a well-organized group of devotees of this composer's works. Although none of Weill's Broadway scores achieved the success of his music for

Brecht's *Die Dreigroschenoper*, the special enthusiasm of his following has prompted a good representation of the American part of his career on record.

The 1936 flop *Johnny Johnson* was recorded in full in 1957 on MGM (and more recently reissued on cassette and CD) with a cast including Evelyn Lear, Thomas Stewart, Burgess Meredith and the composer's wife, Lotte Lenya. The record has one of those ridiculous sleeve notes which get over-enthusiasts into trouble ... 'an important milestone ... preceding *Oklahoma* by seven years it was the first to arrive at this kind of integration ... unique ...'. The rather more successful *Knickerbocker Holiday* (1938) survives in the form of a transfer of a radio broadcast which includes a good handful of the songs.

Johnny Johnson

Johnny Johnson's story is an anti-war satire. Its score is an interesting and characteristically orchestrated mixture of the aggressive, sometimes almost hurtful, tones of the *Dreigroschenoper* and *Mahagonny* and of more straightforward light opera. It includes many pieces which are little more than fragments or incidental music (mostly in the harsher style) and only a handful of what could be called songs (mostly lyrical), from which several 'numbers' emerge effectively: Aggie's Sewing Machine Song, a sort of depraved wartime equivalent of the operatic spinning song, the heroine's long-lined 'O, Heart of Love', the Song of the Goddess delivered by the Statue of Liberty, and a curious, Berlinish Cowboy Song which hasn't a touch of country and western about it.

As with the Brecht/Weill pieces, the production of this recording often denies singing. Although such performers as future opera stars Evelyn Lear and Thomas Stewart are in the cast, there are only isolated moments (fortunately, including her big solo) when they are permitted to sing out. Lear's ballad is, indeed, very affecting, which it would not have been if less well sung. In some of the disc's best moments, Jean Sanders endows the Statue of Liberty with a richly maternal contralto voice, Scott Merrill gives dash to Captain Valentine's brief tango, and Thomas Stewart lets his fine baritone loose thrillingly in counterpoint to William Malten's spoken German counterpart in 'In Times of Tumult and War'.

Burgess Meredith as Johnny doesn't sing until the show's final moment but his singing is not comfortable and the number doesn't make its effect. Similarly, Lotte Lenya doesn't seem very happy in the little French piece 'Mon Ami, my Friend', which sounds like a pale copy of *Happy End*'s songs, and Hiram Sherman's psychiatrist is so over the top as to be not in the slightest bit menacing.

The various bits in between, even if you follow the synopsis, are rather too confusing to make up a very listenable and comprehensive show record, but the power of the piece and of its splendidly played music comes over strongly, and the best bits remain worryingly in your head.

Knickerbocker Holiday

The score of *Knickerbocker Holiday*, attached to a zany but tetchily political libretto, dipped in old musical comedy sentimentality and nineteenth-century Dutch-accent low comedy, retains very little of the qualities that make *Johnny Johnson* so effective. But its subject matter scarcely fitted the dramatic style which had been used in the earlier show. There is, of course, the gliding 'September Song', sung rather differently in context to the interpretations on most modern recordings, but nothing much else to arouse enthusiasm unless it be the rather conventional duet 'It Never Was You'.

The radio transfer which is the show's surviving recording features Maxwell Anderson's text as much as the pieces of songs included in a broadcast of almost an hour in length. Apparently made in the year of the production, it starred Walter Huston, the original star of the show, as Pieter Stuyvesant, and Jeanne Maddern, his leading lassie, in her original rôle, alongside a cast of actors who do not seem to be from the show. It is a very jolly little potted show. The inclusion of plenty of the accented comedy keeps things lively, and Huston gets to plays his scenes and sing 'September Song' twice in a nice crackly voice.

The piece has been issued twice, to my knowledge, the more recent being on AEI where, as with most of their material, it has been made to come across suprisingly well. An interesting disc, giving as it does a whole 1938 show in microcosm, but by no means one to put on for a musical evening.

Lady in the Dark

The more significant *Lady in the Dark* (1941) is the most popular of this group of Weill's works, and it has received attention from both theatres and the recording industry over the years. Recordings of original star Gertrude Lawrence, including her performances of her two set-piece numbers 'My Ship' and 'The Saga of Jenny', have been issued on RCA's Victor Vintage Series, whilst Danny Kaye (who came to fame performing 'Tschaikowsky' in this show) displays his numbers on Columbia ('Danny Kaye Entertains'). Miss Lawrence can also be heard on an AEI radio transfer disc which, like others of this series, is a potted show rather than a recording of the score. This one sounds rather like an episode of a soap opera, with the 'My Ship' theme floating in menacingly behind the dialogue which is, in any case, heavily modified stuff. The music is even more stripped down and, although 'My Ship' and 'The Saga of Jenny' get their due place, the three large musicalized scenas which are the backbone of the score are filleted into skinny extracts.

Miss Lawrence, giving a performance in the style of the time, was clearly superb in the rôle of Liza Elliott. Her dialogue is real and convincing, if occasionally just a touch Bette Davis, and her voice – a surprisingly steady and sweet light soprano, much better controlled than in *The King and I* – is more effective than that of many a 'singing actress'. Amongst the other members of this cast are Hume Cronyn as the psychiatrist to whom Liza pours out the dreams which make up the three musical scenes of the show, Gene Crockett camping up Danny Kaye's rôle of Russell to draw laughs from the studio audience, and Macdonald Carey as the man behind Liza's problems. Unfortunately, this is not one of AEI's better transfers technically. The dialogue comes out well, but the songs are badly distorted. The distortion and the filleting means that, in spite of Miss Lawrence, this record really isn't a starter.

A television cast version featuring Ann Sothern, dating from 1954 and likewise clipping out large pieces of the score, which was released on RCA, and a comprehensive CBS studio cast disc with Risë Stevens in the star rôle make up the tally to date. This last, made by Lieberson's successor Thomas Z. Shepherd in 1963, is much more if not wholly satisfactory. To begin with, it eschews text and instead includes virtually all the music. There have been a number of cuts of just a few lines made here and there in the various scenas, small enough ones to make me wonder if my script and the performing script are slightly different. The sleeve insists that the piece is 'musically intact' and the cuts are, in any case, insignificant enough not to mar the recording.

Operatic mezzo-soprano and sometime film star Risë Stevens takes the rôle of Liza. She has a beautiful voice, at its most attractive when she relaxes into a richly unpretentious chest voice which is anything but operatic, at its least when she succumbs to the temptation – just a couple of times – to switch into warbling on a high note, and she sings the songs splendidly. The more beefy 'Saga of Jenny' suits her better than the *fil de voce* 'My Ship'. It is just as well, though, that too much text was not included, for, for a lady whom I don't remember as being embarrassing as a film actress, she is distinctly uncomfortable when it is a question of dialogue. The best support comes from John Reardon (Randy), who sings the rôle of the film dreamboat with a glorious baritone, whilst Adolph Green, as Russell, happily exchanges the usual camp for coochy comedy and, less happily, struggles with his singing. He negotiates the patter of 'Tschaikowsky' in agile fashion, but when it comes to anything a little more sustained you can feel his larynx hurting. Still, the rôle of Russell is scarcely written for a vocalist with a capital V and Green's personality wins out.

One Touch of Venus

Weill's other main Broadway success, the score to S. J. Perelman and Ogden Nash's *One Touch of Venus*, is less extensively but effectively represented. Original stars Kenny Baker and Mary Martin recorded an attractive selection on Decca, which has been reissued on AEI, but that is all. Otherwise the score exists largely in piecemeal song performances and on recitals devoted to Weill works, which means some of the less obvious pieces have escaped. It is easier to pick the 'plums' from *One Touch of Venus* than from the earlier Weill works, as this is much more a straightforward musical play, with a traditional book and a series of individual songs. The songs include several very fine ones – the lyrically nimble and natural 'I'm a Stranger Here Myself', with its effectively loping melody, and the smooth ballads 'Speak Low' and 'West Wind' – and these give a strong backbone to the Decca recording.

Unfortunately this record has space for only seven songs – those sung by the two stars – plus the two exuberantly lush dance sequences, 'Forty Minutes for Lunch' and 'Venus in Ozone Heights', which give Weill the chance to include a little more of his more adventurous tones. Both the soloists are excellent. Martin uses her warmest, most attractive timbres on her solos, of which 'I'm a Stranger Here Myself' comes out the best (perhaps because it's the best song), and Baker's relaxed high baritone-to-tenor is allowed to float sweetly through 'West Wind' before he devotes himself to the altogether less successful humorous songs – the sniggery 'The Trouble With Women' and the 'cutesy' 'Wooden Wedding'.

For the record, two songs from the show plus mangled versions of three others made for the film version are enshrined on an Ariel disc called 'Kurt Weill in Hollywood', along with three pieces from the *Knickerbocker Holiday* film and others from Weill's Hollywood ventures *Where Do We Go From Here* and *You and Me*. There are rehearsal recordings (what next?) of several songs on a disc called 'Tryout' from DRG records, but the search for the rest of the *One Touch of Venus* score ends with Painted Smiles's 'Kurt Weill Revisited'. There you can find Chita Rivera singing 'Dr Crippen', 'Way Out West in New Jersey' and a mixture of 'Very, Very, Very', 'Vive la différence', 'How Much I Love You' and the title song. Which means that in the end not so very much got away.

The final works of Weill's Broadway period fall into the LP age where, in spite of their lack of success in the theatre, they too are well represented.

The only other works from this period that have, to my knowledge, been significantly recorded are Oscar Hammerstein's updating of Bizet's opera *Carmen* as *Carmen Jones* (1943) and Marc Blitzstein's *The Cradle Will Rock* (1938).

Carmen Jones

Carmen Jones has a Carmen who works in a parachute factory. Escamillo became Husky Miller, a boxer, Micaëla lost her pretty name to be christened Cindy-Lou and, from Bizet's famous score, Hammerstein turned the Habañera into 'Dat's Love', the Chanson Bohemienne into 'Beat Out Dat Rhythm on a Drum', the Toreador's Song into 'Stand Up and Fight', and the Seguidilla into 'Dere's a Café on the Corner'.

A large part of the score was originally recorded by members of the double-cast Broadway cast on 78s, and when the LP arrived soon after, it was also put out on the new format. It doesn't sound, on this disc, to be far from being just a straight *Carmen* translation, except for the drum passages in the Chanson Bohemienne. Muriel Smith is a firm-voiced operatic Carmen Jones, Luther Saxon a Joe (i.e. Don José) in the same vein, and Glenn Bryant an awkward Husky Miller whose teeth seem to get in the road of his tongue and his voice.

The film soundtrack of 1954, which managed to get in a little more of the score than the original cast recording, notably the Card Song, is generally a much less stiff and operatic performance. Twenty-year-old Marilyn Horne is the sweetly inviting singing voice of Dorothy Dandridge as Carmen Jones; she is unforced and sexy, with her soprano tones wide open in her 'Dat's Love', fresh and bouncy in her revamped 'Seguidilla', and more dramatic and substantial, showing the first tones of the mezzo-soprano she was to become, in the Card Song. LaVern Hutcherson sings his Joe (on behalf of Harry Belafonte) fairly straight, a bit strenuous in his 'Dis Flower', which zips between soft and loud without spending much time in between. Marvin Hayes's 'Stand up and Fight' sounds strangely like bits of two different voices taped together; one of the voices is fine and incisive, the other a sort of bottled-up throat-ache. Olga James's gentle Cindy-Lou is an attractively dizzy squeak which avoids the top notes of her music in a curious fashion, but Pearl Bailey stands out with her wholly unoperatic 'Beat out That Rhythm on a Drum', and the quintet 'Whizzin' Away Along de Track', with its odd, seemingly ill-assorted collection of voices, also takes the starch out of the score beautifully.

Virtually the same ground is covered on a British studio recording of 1962 from World Records, which features no less an artist than the young Grace Bumbry as Carmen Jones. Bumbry is the fruitiest of the three recorded Carmens, and the lower notes of her music roll out with the same dark frisson as they do when they are well sung in the opera. She is more operatic in her tone and her approach than Horne, and pays very much less attention to the words of her songs, concentrating mainly on producing a very lovely tone, which is, indeed, very lovely. The last notes of the Card Song, black as the nine of spades, are quite stunning.

The supporting cast are mostly excellent. Here is a Joe (George Webb) with a lighter, easier voice than either of the two previous artists – not very American GI, it is true, but a lovely performer with a special talent for mixed voice who makes his Flower Song both comfortable and believeable. Ena Cabayo (Cindy Lou) gives an intelligent, passionate performance, taking all Bizet's top notes but making 'My Joe' much more than just a piece of showy vocalizing, Elisabeth Welch slides gently through 'Beat out That Rhythm on a Drum' whilst the chorus provides the 'oomph' to the number, and Thomas Baptiste, who is very definitely no opera singer, gives a rhythmic and thoughtful 'Stand up and Fight'. This also gains from some help from the energetic Mike Sammes Singers, proving here that they can sing without slurping all over the barlines when they want to.

The Cradle Will Rock

The Cradle Will Rock has been cherished and, occasionally, staged through the years rather for its political content than any integral merits. Politics are clearly sometimes more powerful than music for, whilst so many meritorious works remain unrecorded, *The Cradle Will Rock* has been the object of several recordings, including a double-disc version of a 1964 revival, a single-disc transfer featuring the original cast and, most recently, a cast album of a brief season played to empty houses by an American company at London's Old Vic. Which recording you prefer really depends on how much of it you want.

My Ten Essential Records

NAUGHTY MARIETTA: complete, with Judith Blazer and Leslie Harrington (2 records, Smithsonian Institution Smithsonian N-026)

45 MINUTES FROM BROADWAY: songs and potted text, with Tammy Grimes, Larry Blyden and Russel Nype (AEI 1159)

NO, NO, NANETTE: revival cast recording (revised version), with Bobby Van, Jack Gilford, Helen Gallagher, Susan Watson and Ruby Keeler (Columbia S-30563); CD (Columbia CK 30563)

ROSE MARIE: selection, with Julie Andrews, Giorgio Tozzi and Frederick Harvey (RCA LSO 1001)

SHOW BOAT: complete, with Frederica von Stade, Jerry Hadley and Teresa Stratas (3 records, EMI 49108); CD (CDS 7 49108 2)

OF THEE I SING: selection, TV cast, with Carroll O'Connor, Cloris Leachman and Michele Lee (Columbia S-31763)

THE DESERT SONG: selection, with Edmund Hockridge and June Bronhill (HMV CLP 1274)

ANYTHING GOES: Australian cast recording, with Geraldine Turner (EMI EMC 792103)

PAL JOEY: members of the Broadway revival cast, with Jane Froman and Dick Beavers (Capitol ST774)

ON YOUR TOES: Broadway revival cast recording, with Christine Andreas (2 records, Polydor 8813 667-1); CD (TER 1063)

Other Recommended Records:

I Wants to Be an Actor Lady, and other hits from early musical comedies, performed by the Cincinnati University Singers and Theatre Orchestra (New World NW 221/Recorded Anthology of American Music)

Robin Hood: archive radio cast selection (AEI 1179)

The Pink Lady/The Prince of Pilsen: archive radio cast selections, with Charles Kuhlman and Jessica Dragonette (AEI 1172)

The Red Mill: selection, by the Gregg Smith Singers (Turnabout 34766)

The Firefly: selection, with Allan Jones and Elaine Malbin (10-inch, RCA LM-121)

Leave it to Jane: off-Broadway revival cast recording (Strand Sl 1002)

The Cat and the Fiddle/Hit the Deck: selections, with Denis Quilley and Doreen Hume (Epic LN 3569)

Music in the Air/Roberta: selections, with Marion Grimaldi, Maggie Fitzgibbon and Andy Cole (WRC T121)

Jerome Kern in London – The Early Years, including archive recordings of the original London productions of Sally, Oh, Joy! and Theodore & Co and medleys from The Beauty Prize and The Cabaret Girl (World Records SHB 34)

The Student Prince: selection, with Jan Peerce, Roberta Peters and Giorgio Tozzi (Columbia OS 2380)

The New Moon: selection, with Gordon MacRae and Dorothy Kirsten (World Records ST 1101)

Of Thee I Sing/Let 'em Eat Cake: Brooklyn Academy of Music concert performances, 1987 (CBS F2M 42522); CD (CBS M2K 42522)

Girl Crazy: selection, with Mary Martin, Eddie Philips and Louise Carlyle (CBS OL-7060)

Irene: London revival cast recording, with Julie Anthony (EMI EMC 3139)

Let's Face It/Red, Hot and Blue/Leave it to Me: compilation of contemporary recordings (Smithsonian Collection RO16 P14944)

By Jupiter: off-Broadway revival cast recording, 1967, with Robert R. Kaye, Bob Dishy and Jackie Alloway (RCA LSO-1137)

Babes in Arms: selection, with Mary Martin and Jack Cassidy (Columbia Special Products AOS 2570)

The Boys from Syracuse: selection, with Portia Nelson, Jack Cassidy and Bibi Osterwald (Columbia COS 2580)

Too Many Girls: selection, with Estelle Parsons, Anthony Perkins and Nancy Andrews (Painted Smiles PS1368)

Lady in the Dark: studio cast recording, with Risë Stevens, Adolph Green and John Reardon (Columbia OS 2390)

One Touch of Venus: selection, with Mary Martin and Kenny Baker (Decca DL 79122)

Knickerbocker Holiday: archive radio cast recording, with Walter Huston and other members of the original cast (AEI 1148)

Carmen Jones: selection, with Grace Bumbry, George Webb, Ena Cabayo and Elisabeth Welch (Heliodor HS-25046)

CHAPTER 5

Britain between the Great War and the LP

The end of the Edwardes era in the British theatre coincided not only with the First World War but with the general discovery by the British public of ragtime and of the variety-style revue, followed in succession by the explosion of a new-found passion for social dancing and dance bands, the first significant coming of the American-bred musical, and the growing glorification of light comedy stars, as the mainstream light musical theatre reorientated itself towards a kind of dance-and-laughter show that was part play, part dance (and, less significantly, song) revue, part star vehicle, and part musical fodder for the omnivorous dance bands and newly electrified gramophones.

The old Gaiety shows had certainly been made up of what were intended to be take-away tunes, but now that the one-step, the two-step and the fox-trot had replaced the old quadrilles and polkas and lancers, and the record player had supplanted sheet music as the favourite purveyor of home music, the accent was ever more on catchy music and on rhythm rather than on real melody or lyrics.

Recordings of dance music poured into the shops and homes of the country, and much of this music came from the theatres of London's West End where the public could go to see, at various times, the romantic and occasionally comical dancing of Adele and Fred Astaire, Jack Buchanan and Elsie Randolph, Cyril Ritchard and Madge Elliott, Roy Royston and Louise Browne, or the wholly light-hearted efforts of Laddie Cliff, Stanley Lupino, Richard Hearne or Lupino Lane, performed to the same orchestras that could be transported, by record, to their own living rooms.

This craze, and the rush of shows which obligingly fed it over the next decades, did not mean that the comic opera line of descent in the musical theatre – the inheritance of Daly's Theatre – disappeared. America's Friml and Romberg and the Continental melodies of Fall, Gilbert, Jacobi, Cuvillier, Benatzky and Lehár bolstered up a fallow period in British writing in the early years after the war until the best local composers, such as Vivian Ellis, Noël Coward and Ivor Novello, switched from lighter forms to give their attention to the more substantial romantic musical. They created a body of work which has survived in performance, popularity and on record to this day, whilst the made-for-dancing melodies of Weston and Lee, Tunbridge and Waller, Phil Braham, Herman Darewski, Melville Gideon, Noel Gay and even Ellis himself, having been enjoyed, danced to and superseded by more of the same rhythm, have been left behind. A quick glance down Ian

Bevan's detailed discography in my own *The British Musical Theatre* gives an idea of the considerable output of recorded music from even the most unsuccessful London dance-and-laughter shows of the time, and these recordings are only the straightly sung versions. Beyond them were lists and lists of band arrangements and medleys. Yet, apart from the very few that managed to make themselves into radio and dance-hall standards, these songs (and there were only songs – a finale or concerted number was practically unknown) survive only on elderly 78s, even though, amongst them, there lurks some highly enjoyable material. Revivals of *Mr Cinders* and *Me and My Girl*, two of the most successful of these star vehicles, have revealed scores that have deservedly gained a second life and, with a little fossicking amongst 78s and sheet music, there are certainly others of equal value to be discovered.

Sadly, up till now, few have bothered to fossick. The World Record Club, in its missionary work of transferring and preserving on modern records the shows and performances of the 1920s, 1930s and 1940s, has taken comparatively little interest in this lightest breed of British show. Only through the bias of some of the era's favourite performers such as Buchanan, Bobby Howes or Cicely Courtneidge, whose names are still sufficiently well remembered to sell a record or two, do we get a glimpse of the material of this period on compilation discs. World Records did, however, pay rather more attention to Ellis, Coward and Novello, both in original cast transfers to LP and in studio cast recordings but, from an historical point of view, there is still a fairly substantial gap remaining.

The War Years

Chu Chin Chow

The two phenomena of the Great War in the British theatre were the musicals *Chu Chin Chow* (with a score by Frederic Norton) and *The Maid of the Mountains* (music by Harold Fraser-Simson), both of which have subsequently been given a number of revivals and both of which have been recorded under modern conditions.

Chu Chin Chow's score has been taken up twice, on World Records in 1961 and on HMV in 1959, and, looking at the two sleeves in a shop, I would have been in no doubt as to which to buy. The WRC disc has a larger selection than its rival, and also a full cast including the magnificent Hervey Alan in the not-too-vocal rôle Oscar Asche wrote for himself, the tenor brothers John Wakefield and Edward Darling, sopranos Ursula Connors and Marion Grimaldi, Ian Wallace for the famous basso Cobbler's Song and another fine bass, William McCue, heading the Robbers' Chorus. It also has the original orchestrations, and, in its 1980 reissue, a far better, if not error-free, sleeve note (much taken from Asche's almost reliable autobiography).

The HMV disc has Inia te Wiata singing the songs belonging to four bass and baritone rôles as well as the comic tenor part, divides the feminine numbers between Julie Bryan and Barbara Leigh irrespective of character, has heavily expanded orchestrations, leaves out such numbers as 'Mahbubah' and 'I Built a Fairy Palace in the Sky', and is packed in a garish and unhelpful cover.

When you listen to them, however, there is a surprise in store. The WRC cast all sing charmingly (even if some of them are incomprehensibly given each other's numbers), the orchestra sounds suitably unobtrusive and pretty in turn, and it is all really rather boring. No one except Alan sounds as if they've bothered to find out what it's all about. They could be singing in Sudanese, and the comedy moments which make up such an important part of the show are quite lost.

The HMV disc goes precisely the opposite way. Inia te Wiata sings superbly, sometimes a clear, firm baritone, sometimes a darker, more covered basso, sometimes both at once, and he characterizes his songs splendidly. He is, obviously, well and truly at home both as a rather glum shoemaker, in what sounds as if it ought to be a definitive version of the famous Cobbler's Song, and as the fearsome Abu Hassan, declaring himself to the clashing of cymbals to be 'Chu Chin Chow of China' or heading the Robbers' March. But then he takes on not only the choral number 'Here Be Oysters Stewed in Honey' and gives it a ringing baritone performance, but the songs belonging to the star comedy rôle of Ali Baba, originally written for character tenor Courtice Pounds. He doesn't quite achieve the tenor part, but throws himself with glee into the comical 'When a Pullet is Plump' and the lively 'I'll Sing and Dance' rather like a really light-hearted Osmin.

The two sopranos and Charles Young (tenor), who make up the rest of the solo team, tackle their numbers with conviction and splendid voices. Barbara Leigh sings Alcolom's lovely, desperate lament 'I Long for the Sun' with a firmly centred soprano and a real passion, and Julie Bryan takes over that rôle to share with te Wiata a richly sung version of the comedy duo 'Anytime's Kissing Time', which is given rather more staunch service here than it was perhaps intended to have when sung by the original comic tenor/comedy soprano pairing. She also performs two of the numbers from the ingénue rôle of Marjanah, the stylish 'Cleopatra's Nile' and the lyrical 'I Love You So', with assurance. Young gets only the serenade 'Corraline', which he shares with Miss Leigh, and his no-nonsense tenor blends most happily with her clean soprano. The booming orchestrations, far from being offensive, seem to suit the spectacular fairy-tale aspect of the show perfectly and, as a whole, this is a highly enjoyable recording, and quite worth giving up the extra songs for.

The Maid of the Mountains

The favourite songs from *The Maid of the Mountains* have been recorded on a number of occasions. 'A Bachelor Gay' was long a popular solo with baritones, 'A Paradise for Two' appeared on a number of duet recordings, and the soprano solos 'Love Will Find a Way' and 'My Life Is Love' were both several times recorded by specialized recording artists, even though the title rôle of the show had become extremely closely associated in Britain with its original star, José Collins.

Miss Collins and the other members of the 1917 cast put down a large part of the score on contemporary record, and ten of these 78s have been assembled on World Records as 'the original 1917 cast recording'. Given the age of the original discs, it is an impressive transfer, and it is clear that the voices of Miss Collins and her baritone partner, Thorpe Bates, were first rate, but the sound is still the usual archival one, with the orchestra sounding like a barrel organ. If you don't mind that, this record is worth investigating, particularly as the second side also includes a couple of numbers from composer Harold Fraser-Simson's follow-up show, *A Southern Maid*, as well as numbers from the Sidney Jones/Paul Rubens *The Happy Day*, Victor Jacobi's lovely *Szibill* and Oscar Straus's *Der letzte Walzer*, in all of which Miss Collins starred in London.

In her homeland, the Australian soprano Gladys Moncrieff was even more and even longer identified with the rôle of Teresa than Miss Collins was in Britain. 'Our Glad', as she was fondly known, appeared regularly on the Australian stage as the maid of the mountains over a period of more than thirty years, creating a legend in the process. She also recorded most of the soprano music at one time or another, and these famous performances have been preserved on several Australian records devoted to the star, including a small format LP newly issued on the Discovery label of the four principal pieces.

An unsuccessful Emile Littler London revival in 1972 prompted a newer cast recording on EMI. You only have to listen to two or three tracks of this record to know why the revival was unsuccessful. The piece has been 'improved' by its producer. The libretto has been shuffled about and songs reorganized to allow the originally non-singing hero to take the bulk of the male music and to allow top-billed Jimmy Edwards to be his much-loved self more frequently than the script initially allowed in the medium-sized rôle of the Governor. 'The Song of the Vagabonds' from Friml's *The Vagabond King* (with ghastly new lyrics) and Harry Parr Davies's 'Pedro, the Fisherman' from *The Lisbon Story* have been tacked in and all the music has been reorchestrated in a most vulgar way. The whole thing is awful, and the throaty soprano of Lyn Kennington and the solid baritone of Australian Gordon Clyde have little chance against such odds. This is a record to be avoided at all costs.

Tacky orchestrations strike again on a Saga studio cast recording. This is a shame, because the record presents the largest selection of any *Maid of the Mountains* disc, and features two singers in Michael Wakeham and Madge Stephens (another Australian) who can really sing the material. Unfortunately, some really eccentric orchestrations, erratic production and idiosyncratic conducting spoil their efforts. All these three functions are carried out by the same person, a certain Merrick Farran, who would seem to have inspired the disc. He's picked everyone else really well; he just shouldn't have picked himself.

Miss Moncrieff's success in establishing the show in Australia doubtless accounts for an Australian studio cast recording (backed with *Balalaika*) made by the then active Australian arm of the World Record Club. It is sad that only five numbers were recorded here for, after the disappointing discs listed above, this one has the potential to be a winner. It has two fine singers in soprano Valda Bagnall and a splendid baritone, Neil Williams, to perform the main Teresa/Beppo numbers, orchestrations of a refreshingly sensible kind and a bright, clean recording sound. It also has horribly confused and inaccurate sleeve notes, but only the WRC José Collins record has anything in the way of a proper note, and that is an endearingly gossipy piece by Sir Geoffrey Harmsworth (*sic*). For a taste of *The Maid* – as the show was popularly known in theatrical circles, where there is always a tendency familiarly to clip titles – this half-a-record is undoubtedly the best bet, but for a larger meal one could do worse than trust in 'the original 1917 cast recording'.

The 1920s

The only other legacies from the war years to be found on LP are a selection from the Ivor Novello/Jerome Kern *Theodore and Co*, which appears on the WRC 'Jerome Kern in London' compilation, and half a dozen songs from the flop show *Houp-La*, recorded by Gertie Millar and served up with her *Quaker Girl* selection, also on World Records. The 1920s, however, are even more poorly served. Odd songs from Jack Buchanan's vehicles *Toni*, *Boodle*, *Battling Butler* and *That's a Good Girl* turn up on World Records, Music For Pleasure and ASV Living Era compilations of Buchanan material, and a few fragments of Laddie Cliff, Leslie Henson and friends appear on similar discs. There is a whole selection of crackly-sounding bits from London shows by foreign composers, including Szirmai's *Lady Mary* and Arthur Schwartz's *Here Comes the Bride* (JJA 'British Musical Comedies by American Composers'), more London Jerome Kern – the rather embarrassing *Blue Eyes* featuring Evelyn Laye as the girl who saved Scotland – on 'Jerome Kern in London', and the WRC release of the distinctly enjoyable original cast recordings from Gershwin's *Primrose* (the song 'Wait a Bit, Susie' is of the particularly sticking kind), but only the two shows that have made it into the 1980s exist in any kind of comprehensive recording.

Mr Cinders

Vivian Ellis's *Mr Cinders* achieved its original success in 1929 with Bobby Howes and Binnie Hale in its starring rôles. Their songs from that production have been reissued on World Records and, more recently, in an excellent set of transfers on EMI's 1986 'Binnie and Bobby', where numbers from *Yes, Madam*, *Please Teacher*, *For the Love of Mike*, *Hide and Seek* and *Magyar Melody* also get an airing. A more substantial and satisfying recording, however, resulted from a charmingly unpretentious revival in 1983 at London's tiny King's Head Theatre Club. That's

Entertainment Records thought it worthwhile to record this piece even whilst it was playing at its 100-odd seater venue so, when it moved into the West End, changing leading lady on the way, they had to re-record and reissue with the new star. As a result, there are (or have been) two *Mr Cinders* discs on the TER label, with different tracks slipped in to cover the rôle in question. Christina Matthews on the West End version is much superior vocally to her predecessor, Julia Josephs, making the later record the better prospect of the two.

After listening to so many recordings where orchestrations and choral arrangements have been souped up into that glutinous style favoured in the 1960s, this one is a total joy. Michael Reed's tiny two-piano-based group produces a happy, atmospheric sound which never overwhelms the delightful, light-hearted songs of the show's score, and the delicate harmonies of his vocal arrangements add a further charm and humour to both solos and ensembles. Such touches as the coloratura obbligati entrusted to the comedy soubrette rôle of Minerva, and the part-writing for the trio of flappers who replace the female chorus – so pretty as to disallow any kind of parody playing – are quite splendid.

The show's score remains almost intact in this revival, although the principal number 'Spread a Little Happiness' has been (not altogether logically) handed over to top-billed Denis Lawson in Bobby Howes's rôle of Jim. 'She's my Lovely' from *Hide and Seek* has been inserted to surprisingly good effect, and a new number by Ellis and original lyricist Greatrex Newman was added to bolster the rôle of Jill when Miss Matthews took over. This piece is, unfortunately, lyrically banal and does not fit well into the show, but it is interesting to note that fifty-five years after the original event Ellis had lost none of his joyful skill for melody.

This is one of those records where, even without the aid of the colour pictures on the sleeve, you can feel a theatre performance coming across. Lawson, better known as a film and TV actor, turns out a comic performance of sincerity and charm which sets the tone for the evening. He croons movingly through 'Spread a Little Happiness', crisply and comically spits out the patter lyrics of the hilarious 'On the Amazon', and joins the clear, friendly soprano of Miss Matthews in the fondly ridiculous 'I've Got You' and 'A One Man Girl' with a wry sentimentality that is just right.

The rest of the excellent cast are right on the ball too. Graham Hoadly as Lumley, Mr Cinders's foppish 'ugly' brother, is the epitome of period comic style, as he turns his perfect vowels and machine-gun vibrato to describing his 'Blue Blood' or wickedly declares how he could be 'True to Two' in a superbly understated performance. Fortunately, he becomes true to one when he meets up with silver-voiced Minerva (Diana Martin), who supplies the coloratura to his vibrato, rippling with a giggle up to her effortless top C as she delivers her lyrics with a naturalness and clarity, contrasting vividly with the plummy tones and modified vowels of too many other singers on too many other recordings. Not this one, though, and that is one of its greatest charms. This is a performance by people, not by vocalists and, oh, what a breath of fresh air it is!

Bitter-Sweet

Mr Cinders was an exemplary 1920s musical, angled towards light comedy and perhaps rather less dance than was usual, full of tripping rhythms and joyful tunes made to fit the fact that, *pace* Miss Hale, there was barely a genuine singer in the original cast. It was quite the opposite end of the scale from the other hit musical of the decade and the year, Noël Coward's *Bitter-Sweet*, which returned the home-made romantic musical to the London stage with a vengeance.

Bitter-Sweet's most famous number, 'I'll See You Again', has been sung on disc by a register of recording royalty from Joan Sutherland to Richard Tauber, Mario Lanza, Nelson Eddy and Gracie Fields. Both the original London and Broadway stars, Peggy Wood and Evelyn Laye, have left their versions of 'I'll See You Again' and 'Zigeuner', which survive transferred to WRC/EMI and MFP respectively. The WRC/EMI disc (which also includes selections from *Cavalcade*, *Ace of Clubs*, *Operette* and *Conversation Piece*) also features Ivy St Helier's definitive performance of 'If Love Were All', but a larger selection of the score appears on a number of other recordings.

There are three principal studio recordings that devote two full sides to *Bitter-Sweet*'s score. One of these, a 1969 issue on Columbia, features June Bronhill, but it is a sad disappointment. Bronhill is under par, the happy shine now gone from the voice, and she is supported by an effete-sounding Carl Linden (Neville Jason) who puts on a silly accent for the occasion, an unimpressive Manon (Julia d'Alba) and a typically awful 1960s orchestra and chorus of the kind just referred to above.

A World Records release with Adele Leigh is better, but by no means perfect. Miss Leigh sings pleasingly, but her then husband, James Pearse, is a hefty Carl who insists on turning his 'a' vowels into 'e' vowels and is much happier when he gets to the lusty baritonic 'Tokay' than in the romantic music. The most pleasant part of the recording is Susan Hampshire's thoughtful Manon. She sounds like the 'humble diseuse' Coward's lyrics identify her as, as she spins her light soprano conversationally through 'If Love Were All' and bounces saucily into her French cabaret number. The third recording, starring Vanessa Lee, and thus clearly worth consideration, is a rarity I have not heard.

There is also in existence a pirated recording of the songs from the 1940 Nelson Eddy/Jeanette MacDonald film. It is a curious affair, erratic in its arrangements and reorganization of the music, and at its best when MacDonald lends her beautiful, clear tones to the romantic music (though she gives a strangely jaunty and heartless 'If Love Were All'). However, the sound is pretty poor and the recording can unfortunately only be recommended to MacDonald unconditionals.

It is understandable that all of these recordings should wish to feature *Bitter-Sweet*'s big solo showpieces – the soprano music, Manon's two songs, the romantic duets and 'Tokay' – but desperately sad that, as a result, two of the finest pieces, the first-act finale and the glorious third-act sextet 'Alas, the Time is Past', are in each case omitted. As a result, I have spent the last few years going for my *Bitter-Sweet* to a pirate tape of a British provincial performance at the Northcott Theatre, Exeter, where these missing ensembles are intact and where there is a particularly fine lead performance by the young Jan Hartley-Morris.

It was undoubtedly this more than intermittently brilliant revival that sparked a more substantial London season by the New Sadler's Wells company in 1988 and, as a result, That's Entertainment Records – never one to let a significant light opera or romantic musical production pass without leaping into action – has come up with the genuine full-scale, double-disc recording of Coward's most important musical which has been for so long lacking.

It is a fine recording. The plusses are many and major, the minuses few and comparatively unimportant. Firstly, it is very pleasant to have the whole of the show, in sequence, rather than just the familiar bon-bons. The favourite highlights gain by being set in their musical and dramatic context, and the less well-known pieces of the score throw up some happy surprises for those whose knowledge of *Bitter-Sweet* has hitherto been limited to the hit numbers. Secondly, the version used is quite splendid.

The score has been reorchestrated by the same Michael Reed who did so well by the score of the contemporary *Mr Cinders*. This time he has not a tiny group at his disposal but a vast orchestra, and he runs the gamut with them, unafraid to swoop from full orchestra to a solo instrument, even a piano or a harp, within bars, varying the colours and personality of the music with marvellous effect and unabashed sentimentality. Since the orchestra plays the music with a vigour and vivacity which speaks of enjoyment, the result is first class. The chorus, at their best, are fine too. Only occasionally, in the many numbers in which they are involved, do they indulge in oversinging and yodelled words, and several members – notably the chorister playing little Effie in the first-act finale – do particularly well in their spoken lines.

At the head of the principal cast, Valerie Masterson as Sari Linden is the axle of the affair. She is in glorious voice and, even if she makes no attempt at differentiation in character or vocal tone between the girl Sarah and the elderly Marchioness of Shayne, it is a pleasure simply to hear her sing her songs. Although she opens up impressively on 'Zigeuner', it is not that piece, nor indeed the main version of 'I'll See You Again' which is the highlight of this performance, but rather a rapturous version of 'The Call of Life', a shiveringly moving last-act finale and, above all, a thrilling, dash-away performance of the underrated waltz song 'Tell Me, What Is Love?', which bursts out with the kind of passion that could perhaps have been used to good effect elsewhere.

It seems a little odd to have cast a voice such as Masterson's – surely on the heavy end of what was intended for the rôle – against the very light baritone of Martin Smith as Carl. Again, it seems odd to have Carl played as an earnest, young English gentleman rather than a romantic Continental. There are no accents here. At first, as he almost croons his way through his early lines, it sounds as if he has strolled in from another show. But, as the work progresses, the combination becomes more acceptable. If their first 'I'll See You Again' is a little uncomfortable, by the time the lovers get to the end of the show they are blending very effectively.

Rosemary Ashe (Manon) both employs the accent Smith eschews (why this inconsistency?) and makes a bravura display of the versatility and characterization Miss Masterson ignores. Her cabaret act is grand – well sung, and tasteless enough to show why La Crevette is working in a second-rate café, amusing soldiers. She attacks 'Bonne nuit, merci' with a marvellous, chesty vulgarity and swoons into a campy 'Kiss Me' with the safety catch off her soprano register. This is, after all, the original Carlotta of *The Phantom of the Opéra*. 'If Love Were All', impeccably sung, only lacks some of the warmth of an Ivy St Helier.

Elsewhere there is a lusty if occasionally gargled 'Tokay' from David Rendall, a determinedly belting and unhistorically unladylike group of 'Ladies of the Town', some nicely understated 'Green Carnation' boys, a slightly hasty version of the beautiful 'Alas, the Time Is Past', in which half a dozen chorus girls get solos and, typically, a couple grab their big moment with sub-Wagnerian glee, and some enjoyable pieces of orchestral dance music. The best moments of this well-organized and well-recorded set – the finales, 'Tell Me What Is Love', 'The Call of Life' and so forth – are thrilling, and the rest is never less than acceptable. Sixty years after its first production *Bitter-Sweet* and Coward have been well served.

The 1930s and 1940s

The 1930s and 1940s are, on the whole, little better looked after than the 1920s. Various 78s have been re-recorded onto modern discs, again usually in personality collections or on such discs as the JJA compilations of British productions oriented towards American interests.

Half a dozen songs from Cole Porter's flop *Nymph Errant*, performed by Gertrude Lawrence and Elisabeth Welch, turn up on WRC and MFP; and JJA, WRC and MFP have all plundered the songs recorded by Jack Buchanan and Elsie Randolph from *Mr Whittington* and *Stand Up and Sing*. World Records have rescued a chunk of the charming score for *Yes, Madam*, the follow-up to *Mr Cinders*, some of which also appears on the EMI 'Binnie and Bobby' disc, but, in spite of virtually the whole score being available on 78, no one has seen fit to try to reconstruct this eminently revivable piece on record. These lighter shows are, however, largely neglected by modern recordings and the only really significant recordings of shows from the thirties are those of the Noël Coward and Ivor Novello musicals.

Ivor Novello

The series of spectacular, romantic musicals created by Ivor Novello over the last fifteen years of his life produced a body of music that won itself a special place in the affections of a large public and also of many performers. His scores were unashamedly lush and sentimental, out-Hollywooding the movies with their gloriously sweeping melodies devoted almost entirely to the female voice. The formula Novello happened upon for the first show of the series, *Glamorous Night* (1935), in which he himself starred as a non-singing hero opposite a full-blooded operetta soprano heroine, was retained throughout the series, along with such regular features as contralto Olive Gilbert and her obligatory song(s) and the device of the operetta-within-an-operetta, which allowed Novello to write musical scenas of a kind in which he himself could never have participated.

Original Cast Recordings

Substantial recordings of all eight of Novello's last shows exist with their original casts, transferred onto modern recordings. Between 1925, and the general introduction of electrical recording techniques, and the mid- and late 1930s, considerable advances had been made in sound reproduction for the gramophone and, although these recordings are composed of material taken from 78 discs, their quality is of a much superior standard to the recordings of a decade earlier. They can be listened to often, under modern conditions, with almost as much comfort as a contemporary recording, and since, in this case, this allows us to listen to the musicals performed as they were intended to be, under the supervision of Novello himself, the original series of discs repays consideration.

In the 1950s, selections from *Glamorous Night*, *Careless Rapture*, *The Dancing Years* and *King's Rhapsody* were transferred onto ten-inch LPs by HMV. The sound on these is fine, but the discs are now difficult to find in good condition. However, the World Record Club comes to the rescue once again, with a reissue on a double-record set entitled 'Ivor Novello, the Great Shows', of the contents of these four records, topped up with such pieces as Elisabeth Welch's *Glamorous Night* solos and the 'bit of opera' scena from *Careless Rapture* (in which Novello is actually heard singing a bit of cod opera), not used on the ten-inch discs.

The title of this disc is is a bit misleading, as *Careless Rapture* was not one of Novello's notable successes, and *Perchance to Dream*, which was, is not included. But there is a simple answer: the *Careless Rapture* recordings belong to the HMV-EMI combine, whilst *Perchance to Dream* was recorded by the rival Decca. Needless to say, these selections are only that: six pieces from each of *Glamorous Night* and *Careless Rapture*, eight from *The Dancing Years*, and a collection of medleys, songs and music from *King's Rhapsody*, but they are fairly representative of the score in each case.

Glamorous Night includes four Novello favourites in its list and they get excellent renditions from their original performers. Mary Ellis, the show's soprano star, lends a rich operetta voice to the title song, Trefor Jones displays a really virile, easy tenor in 'Shine Through my Dreams' and the two join together splendidly in the duet 'Fold Your Wings', all three pieces being portions of the operetta-within and sung with and in appropriate style. Alongside these ringing performances, it is a contrasting pleasure to listen to Elisabeth Welch's dark brown rendition of

'Shanty Town' and the less impressive 'The Girl I Knew', which was later cut from the show.

Alongside this selection, the *Careless Rapture* side highlights an often unsuspected variety in Novello's writing at this time. From the superb tones of Mary Ellis, he turns for heroine to the rather shriller, more modern-sounding Dorothy Dickson, who tootles her way through 'Music in May' and joins the fun in the opera parody with Novello and with Olive Gilbert, who booms out her rich contralto impressively in 'Why Is it Ever Goodbye' and the concerted piece 'Bridge of Lovers'. The pretty 'Love Made the Song' is performed with operatic gusto by two small-part players, but a large part of the selection is devoted to the ballet music for 'The Miracle of Niachow'.

For *The Dancing Years*, Miss Ellis puts in a reappearance with the most famous of her Novello rôles, the prima donna (Novello always cast her as a prima donna) Maria Ziegler. She performs 'Waltz of my Heart' and 'I Can Give You the Starlight' splendidly, and gets impeccable support from Miss Gilbert in 'The Wings of Sleep' and from Novello's tenor *de toujours* Dunstan Hart in 'My Life Belongs to You' – again both portions of an internal operetta. She also performs 'My Dearest Dear' with Novello. Roma Beaumont as the teenage Grete sings the British musical comedy parody 'Primrose' in a suitably childish way, and once again a great dollop of ballet music, admittedly including the lovely Leap Year Waltz, goes in to complete the selection in preference to the show's other songs.

The *King's Rhapsody* selection is the least satisfactory. It is not that it is poorly equipped with voices: Vanessa Lee shows a lovely, clear soprano in her solos, Miss Gilbert, if a little less trenchant than before, is still growling out the low notes, and Denis Martin's warm, light baritone is no small change for the more ringing tones of his predecessors. The problem is that the makers of the recording have caught the German disease of running groups of songs together in irritating little medleys and, in consequence, only Miss Lee's beautiful 'Someday my Heart Will Awake' and 'The Violin Began to Play' and the trio 'The Gates of Paradise' get untrammelled performances. Again, instead of full versions of the other songs we get a huge ballet piece (Muranian Rhapsody) and, unexpectedly, the show's finale.

World Records followed up this recording by giving similar service to the three other Novello musicals available to them, *Crest of the Wave* and *Arc de Triomphe*, both failures, and the composer's last piece *Gay's the Word*, written not with himself and his 'team' in mind, but as a commission from comedienne Cicely Courtneidge to a text by revue author Alan Melville. It does not belong in the catalogue of Novello's romantic musicals, but it shows up splendidly on this recording as a first-rate example of the work of the Novello who collaborated in his early days on revues, popular songs and the light-footed turn-of-the-war shows. It also manifests, against the two flops, an undeniable quality.

Crest of the Wave was Novello's second show with Dorothy Dickson, and this time he tried to equip her with the sort of material she had succeeded with in Kern's *Sally*. It didn't work. She sounds fine enough, but it's poor stuff. Of the four songs recorded here, Olive Gilbert gives vast breadth to the attractive (and long) 'Haven of my Heart' and Edgar Elmes stalks lugubriously through the patriotic ghost song 'Rose of England', which became the show's only real survivor.

Arc de Triomphe is just as bad. Mary Ellis, in a vast rôle, sings decidedly more carefully than in her earlier hits and to less effect, whilst Elisabeth Welch makes the most of 'Dark Music', but Ellis and her unlikely partner, light baritone Peter Graves, sound oddly matched in 'Easy to Live With'. One suspects that if Novello had played the Novelloish rôle into which he instead dumped the hapless Graves, the song might not have lived to opening night.

Gay's the Word, in contrast, is bags of fun. Courtneidge is suffering pretty much from vanished voice by this stage in her career, but listening to her delivering Melville's chortling lyrics to 'It's Bound to Be Right on the Night' and 'Gaiety Glad', and even the schoolboy-smutty 'Bees Are Buzzin''' and popular but mediocre 'Vitality', you can gather the effect she had on an audience – rather like a beloved auntie who sometimes says naughty things.

Novello's lively tunes carry these songs through nicely, but he comes into his own with the music for the juvenile soprano rôle, which is played by Lizbeth Webb with one of the purest and prettiest soprano voices I've ever heard. She performs 'Finder, Please Return', 'On Such a Night as This' and 'Sweet Thames' quite beautifully. Unfortunately this last song is glued up in another of those pernicious medleys, which prevents the selection being played in sequence, but it is still a jolly representation of a good, typical latter day pre-war musical comedy – produced in 1951.

The Decca *Perchance to Dream* recording, made in 1945, is disappointingly slight in its selection. Muriel Barron proves once again Novello's fine taste in sopranos with a vigorous version of 'Love Is my Reason for Living', 'A Woman's Heart' and the Victorian Wedding Song; Olive Gilbert is not quite as lusty as of yore in her best ever vehicle, 'Highwayman Love', and Roma Beaumont describes her 'Curtsy to the King' in suitably awestruck tones. The whole is topped off by a finely blended 'We'll Gather Lilacs' from Misses Barron and Gilbert. That is it: six numbers – but six numbers pretty definitively performed. Issued originally on ten-inch LP, it has subsquently been reissued, on one occasion sharing a record with a very unlikely bed-mate in the form of a studio cast performance of *Salad Days*.

Studio Cast Recordings

The two WRC records, supplemented by this Decca *Perchance to Dream*, cover Novello's later work pretty well, but it is strange that, perhaps because of the availability in the 1950s and 1960s of the ten-inch discs performed by the original stars, few other versions of the most popular of these shows have emerged. There is, however, one set, mostly taken from BBC broadcasts and issued in the late 1960s on the Columbia TWO label, which includes *Glamorous Night*, *Careless Rapture*, *The Dancing Years*, *Perchance to Dream* and *King's Rhapsody* in more substantial selections than those given on the original cast recordings. These discs are rarities nowadays and, apart from the fact that they do contain the largest coverage of the five shows in question, there is little reason to seek most of them out.

The Dancing Years disc in this series, not taken from the BBC but produced by Norman Newell specifically for record, is a curious affair with a messy orchestra that harbours a demented harpist in its ranks, a pure-voiced Anne Rogers miscast in the lead rôle, Andy Cole on the verge of crooning the tenor music, and only Ann Howard, in a dignified mezzo, coming out of it all satisfyingly. Her reward is an extra number, for this disc contains the only recording of the song 'Spring in Vienna', added to the score after the London production in order to bolster Olive Gilbert's rôle. The other discs, which are BBC transfers, are rather better done, although their sound is by no means as perfect as one would expect, given their provenance.

The *Glamorous Night* contains all of the show's sung music, although it does not bother with 'The Girl I Knew' or the non-vocal dance music. It is a more than competent recording but it is unfortunately not terribly exciting. Rae Woodland is a committed heroine, singing with a firm, strong soprano and plenty of gusto and vibrato through the title song and 'When the Gypsy Played', and Robert Thomas joins her to perform the tenor parts of the internal operetta, 'Fold Your Wings' and 'Shine Through my Dreams', with an almost frenetic Italianate dash and a passionate big-theatre voice. The always enjoyable Monica Sinclair shows, in her healthy contralto and twinkling delivery, what 'Shanty Town' must have sounded like when the show went on the road and Elisabeth Welch's big number was very curiously handed over to Olive Gilbert.

Careless Rapture doesn't have all the vocal goodies *Glamorous Night* offers, but, on the other hand, it does in this series get a generally better performance of the complete score. Elaine Blighton, a pleasant middle-weight soprano, encompasses both the lyricism of 'Music and May' and the petulance of the soubrettish 'Wait for Me' successfully (although it is a bit of a battle with the orchestra sometimes), and Ann Howard does Olive Gilbert to a turn, driving through the black treacle of 'Why is There Ever Goodbye' and the 'Temple Ballet' music with fulsome tone. The men have little to do, but Jon Lawrenson, the most prominent, bounces tunefully through 'The Manchuko' and joins Veronica Lucas very successfully in a huge rendering of the amateur operatic society's rehearsal.

I do not have the *King's Rhapsody* disc from this series, but going by the *Perchance to Dream* recording, I'm not particularly sorry for the lacuna. This recording, which also holds the whole of the vocal score and even the 'Triumphs of Spring' ballet, is the least satisfactory of the three I have heard. It is an utterly competent and soulless affair. Elisabeth Robinson, in the tripartite soprano rôle, sings slowly and deliberately with apparently nothing but 'the sound' in mind, producing a dreary plummy performance and simply drowning 'Love Is my Reason' and 'A Woman's Heart' in consonantless vowels ('a wooomanislavetoereart'). Patricia Lambert in the leading rôle of Melinda/Melanie has less to sing but sings it much more attractively, and Ann Howard brings things momentarily to life with her 'Highwayman Love', but this is simply not the way to play light opera. It is Novello with all the life squeezed out of it. The BBC can do better and, since they apparently have the orchestrations, maybe now would be the time to try.

World Records issued a selection from *Careless Rapture* and *Glamorous Night* which includes 'The Manchuko' in its selection from the first-named show, but otherwise offers nothing that isn't on the original cast discs. Patricia Johnson does well at being not-Olive Gilbert and surprisingly well at being not-Elisabeth Welch, but Patricia Bartlett gets much too *Il Trovatore* with the soprano music for my taste. It is an unobjectionable disc, but one with nothing special to offer.

Selections from *The Dancing Years* have been issued on MFP (backed with *King's Rhapsody*) and as part of a John Hanson disc on which the sleeve admits that 'the script has been slightly re-written'. It has been rewritten sufficiently to allow Hanson – in the non-singing Novello rôle – to help himself to 'Waltz of my Heart' (no less!), 'Uniform', 'My Life Belongs to You' and a share of 'I Can Give You the Starlight'; he also manages to sneak in 'If You Only Knew' from *Crest of the Wave*. No further comment is needed.

The only other full record devoted to a Novello show is a 1969 revival recording of *The Dancing Years* which featured June Bronhill. 1969 means it is not vintage Bronhill, but that is still better than just about anything else, even although the lady has to put up with second-rate orchestrations and a weak supporting cast, including an over-the-top tenor who sounds like a caricature of Mario Lanza in his declining days, a wobbly mezzo Cäcilie and a very limp hero. But it is Bronhill, and in spite of a certain heaviness and what I am sure is a proliferation of high notes that don't belong in the score, she rattles off her numbers with inimitable style. Strangely, she is most at home in the interpolated 'Rainbow in the Fountain' (from Novello's professionally unproduced *Valley of Song*), which she skips through with the lightness and brightness of earlier years. This disc includes the *Lorelei* operetta sequence, otherwise unrecorded, and the Tyrolese Dance which opens Act 2 (and which would have been better left unrecorded).

Elsewhere, there are plenty of recital recordings of Novello material. The most recent examples include a straightly sung set from radio favourites Vernon and Marietta Midgely and, in devastatingly awful arrangements, a murderous recordful from popular singer Vince Hill. The most widespread seems to be a 1959 recording which includes Vanessa Lee, Marion Grimaldi, Ivor Emmanuel and 'the voice of Ivor Novello' in its credits, but also far too much of the Williams Singers and a set of up-to-date orchestrations.

Since the original cast recordings, Novello's musicals have been rather poorly treated by the recording world. By and large, it still pays to go back to those original performances, awaiting the day when his still much-loved and frequently sung works are given the treatment so recently won by *Bitter-Sweet*.

Noël Coward

After the international success of *Bitter-Sweet*, Noël Coward continued to write romantic musicals but, although he turned out some magnificent material in the process, he never again succeeded in melding text and music to such effect as in that first splendid work. *Conversation Piece* (1934), *Operette* (1938), *Pacific 1860* (1946) and his 1950 attempt to be more up-to-date, *Ace of Clubs*, were followed in later and LP years by *After the Ball*, *Sail Away* and *The Girl Who Came to Supper*, and all are substantially represented on record.

Conversation Piece

Conversation Piece was written as a vehicle for Yvonne Printemps and, in consequence, its star music was pitched at the brilliant French actress and soprano's level. The result included the famous 'I'll Follow My Secret Heart' to which, subsequently, such *dive* as Maggie Teyte and Joan Sutherland have lent their voices on record. Coward himself starred opposite Mlle Printemps and, in a fashion which Novello would soon follow, largely refrained from singing. Practically the whole of the solo music of *Conversation Piece* was the province of its feminine star, although there was the opportunity for a gentlemen's quartet to sing of being 'Regency Rakes' and a pair of ladies of the town (again) to muse that 'There's Always Something Fishy About the French' as light relief.

The original cast recordings have been preserved, once again, by World Records on a Coward compilation entitled, like the Novello collection, 'The Greatest Shows', and including original recordings from *Bitter-Sweet*, *Operette* and *Ace of Clubs* alongside the *Conversation Piece* selection, making the title as misleading as in the case of the Novello discs.

Naturally, the 1934 sound of the *Conversation Piece* songs is far from perfect, but what emerges is the charisma and highly individual vocal talent of Mlle Printemps. The lady did not speak English – she learned her rôle parrot fashion, and it shows up in a parade of amazing vowel sounds – but, although she is clearly happiest when leaping into the considerable French-language sections of her music, she is passionate and radiant in voice throughout the recording, and her second-act outburst when she declares her love for her partner-in-deception ('C'est assez de mensonge') is dazzling. The other selections, too, are well done, with the ladies, led by Heather Thatcher and Moya Nugent, making a fine job of the ensembles of the ladies of the Steyne and the male soloists giving a crisp version of 'Regency Rakes'.

In 1951 Goddard Lieberson persuaded Coward to appear in his original rôle on a double-disc quasi-complete recording of *Conversation Piece* with the opera star Lily Pons as his partner. Since the entire dialogue could not be fitted onto two records, however, it was decided that a linking narration would be provided, and Coward himself took on the job of supplying this. A studio cast including

Cathleen Nesbitt (Julia) and the young Richard Burton (Sheere) was assembled, and Lehman Engel was put in charge of the music. One would have expected a fine result. What eventuated, rather, was a fascinating document.

Lily Pons was a good choice for Melanie. She displays a pert vivacity in her dialogue, succeeding (at forty-seven years of age) in creating the young woman surprisingly well, and she sings, if at times tentatively, with a pleasant simplicity and plenty of her famously pure high notes. The performance lacks the temperament of Printemps's display, but at least Pons has rather more idea of the English. Nesbitt and Burton (neither of whom sing) give easy and sometimes impressive performances of their scenes and some of Coward's lines emerge with a glowing incisiveness. But, and I'm afraid it is a considerable but, otherwise the recording is less impressive, and I regret to say that this is almost entirely to be laid to the account of Coward himself: not Coward the author of *Conversation Piece*, but Coward the performer, and above all Coward the adapter for this project.

As a performer, he adopts a 'Frainch' accent that is spine-crawling (although it apparently did splendidly on the stage) and delivers his lines in a style which, perhaps simply because he is so very well known, makes you think, 'Oh, listen to Noël Coward putting on a silly voice.' Worse, he has written the joining texts in self-consciously twee verse and delivers them in person and unblushingly, breaking up the dramatic effect of the spoken scenes with their archness. The sense of performance is further dissipated by the fact that he annexes 'Regency Rakes', 'There's Always Something Fishy About the French' and the ensemble 'There Was Once a Little Village' and performs them in a fashion that has little to do with the show. This may all have been good for sales, but it is rotten for the coherence of the recording.

This uneven set has other disadvantages in some hilariously poor sound effects and the fact that the sides are laid out for auto-coupling, but in spite of its failings it is still interesting. Here is Coward, alongside some fine artists, performing a rôle written by himself presumably much as he did on stage in 1934, and here are Pons, Burton and Nesbitt making early LP appearances in one of the few attempts at recording an English-language musical with much of its dialogue. Yes, it is indeed interesting. But I'm not sure that it does *Conversation Piece* justice.

Pacific 1860

Neither *Operette* nor *Ace of Clubs* were successful on the stage, and their recording on LP is limited to the WRC compilation, but Coward's other stage failure, *Pacific 1860*, has been twice assembled from the six 78 rpm recordings made of the original cast performances.

It is easy to see why this piece attracted the attention the other two did not for, although the unfortunate libretto and the miscasting of leading lady, Mary Martin, sank the show in the theatre, the score for *Pacific 1860* contains some of Coward's very best writing. Fortunately, a very considerable portion of this was recorded – not, as in other cases, just the solo showpieces, but also ensembles, choruses and some orchestral music – and, although several numbers are unfortunately twinned on one side of a 78 with artificial linking material, leading to some odd choices of cuts, it is splendid to have here the most substantial original cast recording of any of Coward's pre-LP shows. The breadth of the selection means that the record gives us a kaleidoscope of Coward's varying styles of writing, from the soaring comic opera air to the crispest of revusical point numbers. It points up his most outstanding skills as a composer and a lyricist and also his little weaknesses and self-indulgences.

Pacific 1860 is unusual in that the star-billed players, Mary Martin and Graham Payn, have virtually none of the best songs. Payn displays a charmingly cultivated light voice in a neat almost-letter-song ('Dear Madam Salvador') and joins Miss Martin's soubrette soprano smoothly in their principal duet 'Bright Was the Day', which is not quite as good a song as it needed to be, but he is sacrificed on the altar of the horribly twee legend of 'Fumfumbolo', a number which belongs on the yet-to-be-made disc of sniggers from the shows. Miss Martin copes deftly with the 'hoppity-skippity' melody of 'One, Two, Three' and less convincingly with her more heartfelt songs ('I Never Knew', 'I Saw no Shadow on the Sun').

She and they just cannot compare with the glorious soprano music allotted to the thrilling Sylvia Cecil. Cast in the rôle of the heroine's duenna, Miss Cecil reaps the show's two outstanding numbers, the moody waltz 'This Is a Changing World', in which she displays a range of tone from a rich chest voice to a peerlessly floated top, and the featured line of the beautiful female trio 'This Is a Night For Lovers' (with Maria Perilli and Winefride Ingham), which is my own personal favourite piece of Coward music.

Alongside this lyrical music come a splendid barrage of lyric-effective pieces: one of the best of all Coward patter songs, 'His Excellency Regrets', the dying-to-be-naughtier tale of 'Uncle Harry' who got into missionary troubles, Daphne Anderson's deliciously pouting desire 'I Wish I Wasn't quite Such a Big Girl', a twitteringly dissatisfied bridesmaids' chorus, 'Pretty Little Bridesmaids' and a stalwart trio of not very resigned ageing ladies (Mothers' Lament).

On the That's Entertainment recording (the better and more recent of the two) you can hear that the sound is definitely not of today, but neither is it objectionably old. The orchestra comes up cleanly and attractively and peaks and crackles are rare. The songs are unfortunately not placed on the record in show sequence, probably due to the inseparable 78 pairings referred to, which is a shame. A little surgery might perhaps have been worthwhile. Still, this is a disc of great interest and many pleasures and, until the day comes when someone gets round to making a modern recording of this score with someone as outstanding as Sylvia Cecil featured, it will more than do.

More Coward

There have been many other discs compiled from contemporary recordings of Coward as both a composer and a performer, ranging from his earliest revue days to his later career as a cabaret entertainer using both his own and other people's material. Amongst the most interesting is a Monmouth-Evergreen compilation of the songs from *Tonight at 8.30*, originally performed by Coward and Gertrude Lawrence on HMV 78s. Since these medleys and their supporting dialogue take up less than two sides of a disc, they are supplemented by the same pair singing 'Some Day I'll Find You', from Coward's *Private Lives*, and a handful of other non-Coward songs, including the celebrated George Robey/Violet Loraine revue duet 'If You Were the Only Girl in the World'.

Most of these tracks, but curiously not all, are included on a World Records double-disc set which also includes a selection from *Cavalcade* and, on its second disc, a variety of Coward performances of songs, ranging from Kern and Porter to his own 'Don't Let's Be Beastly to the Germans'. This set seems more appropriate for those looking for Coward the performer, whilst the Monmouth disc is for a fuller representation of *Tonight at 8.30*.

A fine selection of Coward's many brilliant revue songs, mostly performed by himself, are gathered on a companion World Records set ('Noel Coward – the Revues'), whilst the two recordings of his acts – the one of Las Vegas, the other of New York – issued by Columbia both singly and subsequently as a set ('The Noel Coward Album') show him in a wide selection of his most amusing material.

Posford and Grün

Balalaika

The triumph of Novello's and Coward's glamorous romantic musicals sparked off a certain emulation, and the most successful of the shows resulting from this reaction was George Posford and Bernard Grün's *The Gay Hussar*, which finally turned up in London under the title *Balalaika* in 1936. *Balalaika* had a splendid run, became the first British musical to be mutated into a Hollywood musical, and found considerable success outside its homeland. Given the power wielded by its librettist, Eric Maschwitz, who used his influential position at the BBC to boost his own work shamelessly, it is surprising that no recordings of the original production, starring Muriel Angelus and Roger Treville, seem to have been made. In fact, no British recording of the show exists beyond an orchestral selection on 78. There are *Balalaika*s from America, Australia and even France, but not Britain.

The American disc, a relic of the film, has little to do with the stage show. Nelson Eddy gives his well-known rendition of the principal number, 'At the Balalaika', before the score turns to Romberg and Sammy Fain and forgets about Posford and Grün. Australia serves the show much better. Even though the selection is a short one of five songs and a truncated overture, it includes a healthy title song from Neil Williams and an uninhibited version of the show's big Rombergesque duet 'If the World Were Mine' (Williams and Valda Bagnall) alongside a couple of the almost incidental atmospheric chorus pieces, which comprised much of the original score, and an unpretentious Drinking Song. This selection forms the other side of the enjoyable *Maid of the Mountains* excerpts discussed earlier, and the disc serves admirably for a dip into both shows.

The French recording, the result of a Nick Varlan production of the early 1980s, is from the TLP label and thus, automatically, features Claudine Granger in the lead rôle alongside Jean-Paul Caffi and Gérard Chapuis from the stage production. They bellow and wobble their way through a score of which about half (the better half) belongs to the original show and the remainder to the accretions of the years composed by Robert Stolz and Jack Ledru, which sound mostly like burlesques of the most hackneyed elements of the French *opérette à grand spectacle*. This version of the piece is given out as the property of the French branch of Chappell, who have quite a lot to answer for to the show's basic publishers, EMI. The only reason to listen to this disc is if you like really ghastly records, or if you desperately need to hear the otherwise unrecorded 'Red Rose' and 'Be a Casanova' – in French.

Vivian Ellis

Jill Darling

The most appreciable and durable of the British composers of lighter theatre music between the wars (and a little after) was undoubtedly Vivian Ellis. His 1920s works, typified by the delightful *Mr Cinders*, proved his mastery of the fashionable songwriting styles, and he had further successes in a similar vein in the 1930s, most notably with *Jill Darling* (1934). This musical threw up one particularly popular song in 'I'm on a See-Saw', featured in the London production by Louise Browne and the young John Mills, but its charming score included a number of other fine numbers, mostly for the benefit of leading lady Frances Day.

Half a dozen pieces by the original cast, including piquant performances of the lilting 'Pardon my English' and the very pretty 'Dancing with a Ghost' sung and acted with the required Hungarian accent by Miss Day, have been gathered on a World Record Club disc along with a large selection from Ellis's most famous revue, *Streamline*; this latter including the song 'Other People's Babies' and the splendid A. P. Herbert humorous monologue 'A British Mother's Big Flight' performed by Florence Desmond. Miss Day's breathless Minnie Mouse-like performance gives a glimpse of an idiosyncratic but attractive performer, even if the songs do not get a particularly musical treatment. The sound is regular enough for 1934, though a plonky bass gets in the way of some of the lady's breathier gurgles.

Follow a Star

Another 1930s work, the not-so-successful *Follow a Star*, created to feature American 'belter' Sophie Tucker in a legitimate musical, had a score shared by Ellis and the star's pet US songwriters Jack Yellen and Ted Shapiro. A selection from this show was released in 1987 by ASV as part of a disc that was somewhat misleadingly entitled 'Follow a Star', as only four of the fourteen numbers transferred plus an overture and a medley are taken from the score. It is a shame that the two other available tracks from the show, notably the pretty 'The First Weekend in June' recorded by juveniles Jack Hulbert and Betty Ann Davies, were not included, but this is a disc dedicated to Ms Tucker rather than to show music. It has a fine biographical sleeve note by Geoff Milne, but the actual performance, well transferred, shows that this reputed 'red-hot mamma' was in truth rather luke warm at this stage of her career. She talks her way through most of her songs, allowing the voice to sing on only about half a dozen notes, in a display which can only be described as dreary to the non-devoted. This is not one for those who care about the music.

Bless the Bride

Ellis's other major hit came when he switched styles and ventured into the world of the romantic comic opera. Unlike Novello and Coward, he did not head for the lusher pastures of Ruritania or Vienna, but set his *Bless the Bride* in Victorian England and beastly, foreign France. With Georges Guétary as its romantic French hero, Lizbeth Webb as its English rosebud heroine, and a score which simply glittered with good things, *Bless the Bride* became a huge hit, gathering to the Adelphi Theatre as much of the town as flocked to the two great hits of the early days of the American musical theatre revival, *Oklahoma!* and *Annie Get Your Gun*, which had opened within the same month.

The great hits from *Bless the Bride*, 'This is my Lovely Day', 'Ma belle Marguerite' and 'I Was Never Kissed Before', remain concert classics of the genre, but sadly these three and the tenor rhapsody 'A Table for Two' were the only items recorded by the show's oustanding original stars. They were issued on 78, and subsequently both on a 45 rpm disc and, along with a piano selection played by Ellis, on LP on World Records in tandem with a larger selection from Ellis's *The Water Gipsies*.

Both Guétary, with his light, smooth tenor, and Miss Webb, with her matchless ingénue soprano, are superb in the material. He turns 'A Table for Two' into a paean of scarcely suppressed excitement, she is as sweetly pure as a parson's vowels yet full of intensity as she declares 'I Was Never Kissed Before', and their duet 'This is My Lovely Day' is all happiness and foreboding. His 'Ma belle Marguerite' is, of course, definitive. But that is all there is. It is an infuriating taster. You can only console yourself with the angry supposition that maybe the rest of the original cast were awful.

For a deeper dip into *Bless the Bride* we can turn to a 1968 EMI Music for Pleasure recording which comprises a dozen numbers. It is a very good recording, arranged, played and sung with obvious enjoyment and good production values and with casting that almost makes up for the regrets of the original cast version.

Mary Millar is a splendid Lucy Willow, a little less girlish in tone than Miss Webb, but sweet voiced, accurate and well characterized. She is well supported by a family of fine voices, led by Leslie Fyson and Joanne Brown, who perform their tongue-in-cheek ensembles with nice, almost-straight faces. Miss Millar slips ruefully through her wish to marry 'Any Man but Thomas T.', melts into the sad ballad 'The Silent Heart', and gives all the gaiety needed to 'I Was Never Kissed Before' (thankfully here restored to being a lovely trio instead of the Webb/Guétary duet version) and 'This is my Lovely Day' in what is a thoroughly enjoyable performance.

As her hero, Roberto Cardinale gives an adequate interpretation in a cabaret light baritone style, avoiding or faking the high notes expertly. If I hadn't heard Guétary, I know I should have liked Cardinale better, so it is perhaps unfair to complain. Taken on its own terms, it's a perfectly valid performance. Peggy Mount gives a splendidly felt version of the nanny's number, 'Ducky', but Charles Young as Thomas and Mary Thomas as Suzanne are shorn of their best opportunities, as neither his 'My Big Moment' nor her 'Mon pauvre petit Pierre' are included in the selection. For the record, Lucy's song 'Summer', the comedy numbers 'The Fish' and 'The Englishman', the jolly chorus 'Bobbing' and a good deal of other chorus, concerted and incidental pieces are also missing. This is all the more disappointing in that the treatment of all that is there is so satisfying, but since a record has only two sides I suppose something had to go.

More Ellis

Ellis continued to work with his *Bless the Bride* collaborator, A. P. Herbert, on three further musicals, all of which survive on LP courtesy of World Records. *Tough at the Top* and *Big Ben* both suffered from feeble book and lyrics and, although Ellis has a special affection for the former work, neither approached *Bless the Bride* in tunefulness and substance or *Mr Cinders* in gaiety and art. The World Record Club recording is in any case an unsatisfying one: it contains three of those irritating medleys, reminiscent of club comics and cabaret singers, which chop little bits out of a half-dozen songs and tack them all together in an incoherent sequence. In this case even Lizbeth Webb and Trefor Jones in *Big Ben* and the fine soprano Maria d'Attili and a rather dull Giorgio Tozzi in *Tough at the Top* can do little but sing their snippets routinely.

This particular recording, as a contrast, also includes the songs written and composed by Ellis for the musical version of J. B. Fagan's Samuel Pepys comedy *And so to Bed*. These are of infinitely superior stuff and artistically done, from charming harmonized ensembles and a winsome love duet with a period flavour to rollicking comedy for the star of the show, the accredited comic Leslie Henson. The character of the work means that these songs are more the accoutrements of a play with music than the score for a full-blooded musical, but as such they are highly successful. Henson comes over well in the recording and there is further interest in the youthful appearance of Keith Michell as King Charles, singing the title duet with the rather unsure soprano of film actress Jessie Royce Landis.

The Water Gipsies

The Water Gipsies, the last of the Herbert/Ellis musicals, just crept into the LP era and was issued on an HMV ten-inch disc in 1955. Once again Herbert served his composer pretty poorly, and the result would be a bit dreary were it not for a handful of lively pieces performed by the young comedienne Dora Bryan, who became the hit of the show. Amazingly, her best number, 'Why Do They Call Me Lily?', an anarchic catalogue song of girls' names, is omitted from the LP, but it appears on the World Record Club pairing with the *Bless the Bride* cast tracks listed above. Miss Bryan's monologue describing in 'naice' tones a naughty night in an hotel room, her rejection of the fellow concerned ('It Would Cramp my Style') and her generalization on the subject when her sister looks like following the same path ('You Never Know With Men') are good pieces of material given superior performance, but there's some very slow sentimental and bucolic stuff to get through on the way to the good bits.

One final Vivian Ellis show which has had a recording devoted to it does not really belong in our listings as it is very much unavailable. *Listen to the Wind*, a superior children's musical from 1955, was recorded by World Records on an EP which has become one of the rarest and most sought after of all British show recordings. If ever you see this collectors' piece, buy it not just for pleasure but for a considerable profit!

Noel Gay

Me and My Girl

The most popular musical of the London war years was undoubtedly Arthur Rose and Noel Gay's *Me and My Girl*, which braved its extended twice-daily run at the Victoria Palace through a large part of the hostilities. This custom-built vehicle for comic Lupino Lane, constructed to allow him to repeat the character of Bill Snibson (which he had created in an earlier musical comedy, *Twenty to One*), was more comedy than musical, its score in London consisting of a couple of choruses, a finale, the title song as put over by Bill and his girl, the famous 'Lambeth Walk' song-and-dance routine led by Lane, a duo between the star and the second girl, and one number apiece for the two lead girls and the character actor playing the solicitor – just eight musical pieces. Most of them did not make it to record. There was just one of those medley discs and, of course, Lane and Teddie St Denis singing 'The Lambeth Walk', a track which has subsequently reappeared on a couple of period compilation LPs.

The hugely successful London revival of 1985 soon put that right. The score was topped up with a series of other songs written later by the authors in order to turn the piece into a suitably standard-sized musical for the amateur market (on the professional circuits, on the other hand, the play was sometimes done with little or no music), plus some additional favourites from the Noel Gay song repertoire. The result was a brand spanking new 1937 musical. A London cast recording was followed by a Broadway cast recording, a Mexican cast recording, a Hungarian cast recording and a Japanese cast recording, as Bill Snibson set off round the world half a century after his conception.

The cast recording of the London production is a grave disappointment. The colourful simplicity and attractive personalities of the stage performance vanish somewhere between the theatre and the vinyl. The unfortunately fashionable casting in British musicals of posh actors who sing a bit can occasionally come off through a splendid acting performance or, more often, a charismatic display of personality, but to make a gramophone recording featuring the weakest part of such performers' artillery – i.e. their singing – seems foolhardy. On this recording only Susannah Fellowes (a former Evita) as Lady Jacquie combines an acting talent with an enjoyable singing voice, making a voraciously seductive job of her duet 'I Would if I Could'. Robert Lindsay, whose acrobatic comedy was the life and soul of the stage show, meanders rather dully through his songs, Emma Thompson, whose gawkily attractive Sally paired so neatly with him, brings no personality at all to disc, and only Frank Thornton (Sir John) of the other actors kids his character to life in song in the cheery arrangement of 'Love Makes the World Go Round'. Why is it that actors who sing a bit so often forget to act when they start to sing? The chorus does better, though there is one of those edgy, cutting voices in there somewhere slicing up the ensemble sound.

My complaints about this unsatisfying disc could go on – the Lambeth Walk's endless choruses are jolly fun on a stage full of whirling dancers, but not so much on disc; the Duchess's splendid obligato to 'Noblesse Oblige' is not much use if you can't hear it; and I was taken aback to see, in the little sleeve note by the late Richard Armitage (Noel Gay's son and the producer of the new *Me and My Girl*), the claim that 'the show stormed its way into theatrical history with a run of 1,646 performances including a transfer to the Coliseum while bomb damage to the V.P. was repaired.' Theatrical history? Perhaps. The Coliseum? Certainly not. *Me and My Girl* played the whole of its 1,646 performances over two and a half years (1937–40) at the Victoria Palace, and its Coliseum performances (208 of them) did not occur until the show was revived in 1941.

Fortunately, the recording of the Broadway performance of *Me and My Girl* is infinitely better in almost every way than the London one. Lindsay, repeating his acclaimed performance for America, has learned in the between-time to bring his stage personality to the recording studio. His US Bill Snibson is a much livelier, more interesting and stylish fellow altogether and, in his image, the show's entire performance is crisper, happier and much better sung. Nick Ullett is a splendidly not-over-the-top Gerald, Timothy Jerome parodies Gilbert and Sullivan impeccably as 'The Family Solicitor' and Jane Connell (Duchess) manages several ounces more voice than her UK counterpart. Jane Summerhays

(Jacquie) doesn't ooze the sexual temptation of Miss Fellowes, but she sings well, and orchestra and chorus are in fine form.

That leaves Maryann Plunkett's Sally, and leave her is what I'd like to do. This is the sort of performance that, to me, is the unattractive side of Broadway. The lady has a big, loud voice. It is much better trained, much more competent than that of the English Sally, and I find it wholly repulsive. Unrelievedly pugnacious, unshaded and charmless, this performer demolishes the lovely 'Once You Lose Your Heart', sounds as if she can't stand her partner in 'Me and My Girl', and when she starts on a sullen 'Take it on the Chin', to which Miss Thompson with her limited vocal means gives a not unpleasant kind of stubborn determination, my fist just itched to follow the lyrics.

It is a shame about this for, otherwise, this is a fine recording. It still has the endless 'Lambeth Walk' repetitions, but the number is much better built here under Stanley Lebowsky's experienced baton, and the Duchess is a little more audible in her obbligato, which is just as well for her as her other number, 'If Only You Had Cared for Me', has been cut to leave place for a further Bill/Sally duet, 'Hold my Hand'. The British slip sleeve is superseded by a colourful gatefold with production photos, and the inner sleeve features a knowledgeable and enjoyable note and synopsis by American musical guru Stanley Green, who has tactfully managed to suppress the misinformation on the British sleeve.

When so much is good, I suppose it is foolish to be put off by one sour performance but, if it were not almost perverse to vote against such a hugely successful version, I would be very tempted to go for pure pleasure to the Mexican recording. This cast has clearly never heard of Lupino Lane or Lambeth or actors who sing a bit. They have taken the script and score as (re)written and, note by accurate note, with every marked squeak, giggle and interruption and no preconceptions, they sing their way through *Yo y mi chica* in a splendidly uninhibited style. It is a jolly, up-beat performance, with a Bill (Julio Aleman) who croons his way lovingly through the title song and puts a wealth of warmth into 'A la luz de este farol' ('Leaning on a Lamp-post'), and Olivia Bucio as a no-nonsense Sally (for some reason rechristened Linda) who is capable of covering all the emotions of the rôle and who also shows in 'Lo mejor es sonreir' ('Take it on the Chin') how an impressively powerful voice can be expressive and enjoyable at the same time. She should be promptly exported to New York.

The orchestra plays with a lively dance-band dash (and a maddeningly obtrusive snare drum), the minor parts are more than adequately taken – Evangelina Elizondo as the Duchess comes the nearest of all Duchesses to conquering the chorus with her obbligato – and the technical side is not bad at all. I suppose if you are going to listen to *Me and My Girl* it ought to be in English, but for anyone who fancies Spanish, *Yo y mi chica* is well and truly worth a listen.

I'm not even going to attempt the Japanese title and, unless you are Japanese, I wouldn't bother with the disc either. This has got to rate as one of the most unlikely recordings of all time. Not only is it in Japanese, it is a two-record affair with dialogue and, what is more, played by an all-female cast! If the language isn't confusing enough, the proliferation of ladies' voices is – especially as the Lady Jacquie sounds like a man. I am told it was a great success in Japan, but for us poor Westerners this recording must range amongst the curios of the industry.

Noel Gay supplied the songs for a goodly number of other musicals, but, apart from including a version of 'The Lambeth Walk' recorded during an actual performance at the Victoria Palace, the only recording devoted to his work – MFP's 'The Hits of Noel Gay' – disappointingly bypasses these in favour of a transferred selection of his film and revue songs. Versions of 'The Sun Has Got his Hat On' and 'Love Makes the World Go Round', both of which found their way into the remade *Me and My Girl*, are amongst them, alongside Cicely Courtneidge's performance of 'There's Something About a Soldier', Jack Hulbert's 'Who's Been Polishing the Sun' and Evelyn Laye's 'You've Done Something to my Heart'.

Odds and Ends

Old Chelsea

Only three other shows of the pre-LP era have made it to LP in any substantial shape. One is the light opera *Old Chelsea*, a 1943 attempt by Richard Tauber to compose a show in which to star himself. The resulting score included the successful 'My Heart and I' and a couple of other attractive pieces set in an impossible libretto. Several of the songs were recorded on 78, but the score survives thanks to a BBC broadcast of a potted version of the show made for the benefit of troops serving overseas and released on the American Sounds Rare label. Its sound quality is fair, the singing of Tauber and Nancy Brown fine but their dialogue embarrassing. The celebrated Irish actress Maire O'Neill makes equally heavy weather of her lines, Carol Lynn sings prettily and the young Charles Hawtrey also takes to singing – not so prettily – in the juvenile comic rôle.

Love from Judy

Love from Judy (1952), a musical remake of *Daddy Long-Legs* by Eric Maschwitz and American Hugh Martin with more than a touch of *Annie* about it, was transferred to an LP entitled 'Three by Martin' along with selections from the same composer's *Best Foot Forward* and *Look Ma, I'm Dancin'*. It's a pretty enough score, with Jeannie Carson in the rôle of the orphan girl, Adelaide Hall attempting to follow Elisabeth Welch's success in the Novello works with a couple of black numbers, and June Whitfield doing a little spot of scene stealing with a comedy song about being 'Dum-dum-dum', but it is not one to get excited about.

Bet Your Life

After years of salvage operations on bygone American shows by British companies, the compliment was returned in 1988 by the surprising issue on the enterprising Blue Pear label of the contents of the four 78 rpm Columbia records of songs from the 1952 musical *Bet Your Life*. Like *Gay's the Word*, *Bet Your Life* was a show which looked back to the star-vehicle comedy musicals of the pre-war period, and it was concocted largely around the latest and last of such stars, Arthur Askey. However, its reproduction on LP is rather due to the presence in the cast of American vocalist Julie Wilson and of Sally Ann Howes, both of whom have a large share in the singing.

It is a highly enjoyable set of numbers, and Alan Melville's lyrics in particular show up with a sprightliness and deftness at least the equal of some of the more fashionable writers of the period. Askey reeling off tipsy thanks for an unlikely list of wedding gifts in 'Ta, Ever So', or going through a long list of pre-bed ablutions when a pretty bride awaits him in bed ('Now Is the Moment'), is the epitome of the English dialect 'little man' comic, and Miss Wilson's cabaret zing and Miss Howes's unpretentious soprano join effectively in duet in 'All on Account of a Guy'. Brian Reece, who missed out when the recordings of *Bless the Bride* were being made, has his chance here with 'I Love Being in Love' and shows an agreeable voice in what is probably the least of the eight numbers. The producers of this 'Limited Collectors Edition' warn on the cover that the sound on the disc is imperfect, and it must be admitted that, for 1952, the quality is a little disappointing. It sounds more like 1932. That aside, it is a most enjoyable selection.

My Ten Essential Records

CHU CHIN CHOW: studio cast recording, with Inia te Wiata, Julie Bryan, Barbara Leigh and Charles Young (HMV CLP1269)

THE MAID OF THE MOUNTAINS/BALALAIKA: Australian studio cast recording, with Neil Williams and Valda Bagnall (WRC ST 794)

MR CINDERS: London revival cast recording, 1983, with Denis Lawson, Christina Matthews, Diana Martin and Graham Hoadly (TER 1069)

BITTER-SWEET: London revival cast recording, 1988, with Valerie Masterson, Rosemary Ashe and Martin Smith (2 records, TER 1160); CD (CDTER2 1160)

NOEL COWARD – THE GREAT SHOWS: including original archive cast recordings from *Bitter-Sweet*, *Conversation Piece*, *Ace of Clubs* and *Operette* (2 records, World Records SH 179–80)

IVOR NOVELLO – THE GREAT SHOWS: including original cast recordings from *Glamorous Night*, *The Dancing Years*, *King's Rhapsody* and *Careless Rapture* (2 records, World Records SHB 23)

ME AND MY GIRL: Broadway revival cast recording, with Robert Lindsay, Maryann Plunkett, Jane Connell and Jane Summerhays (MCA 6196); CD (MCAD 6196)

YO Y MI CHICA: Mexican cast recording of *Me and My Girl* (Marcial Davila recording/unnumbered)

PACIFIC 1860: original archive cast recording, 1946, with Sylvia Cecil, Graham Payn and Mary Martin (TER 1040)

BLESS THE BRIDE: studio cast recording, with Mary Millar and Roberto Cardinale (EMI MFP 1263)

Other Recommended Records

Binnie and Bobby: including numbers from *Mr Cinders*; *For the Love of Mike*; *Yes, Madam*; *Please Teacher*; *Hide and Seek*; *Magyar Melody*; *No, No, Nanette* etc sung by Bobby Howes and Binnie Hale (re-recorded from 78 discs dating 1929–41) (EMI GX 41 2542 1)

Glamorous Night: radio cast recording, with Rae Woodland (Columbia TWO 243)

Careless Rapture: radio cast recording, with Elaine Blighton (Columbia TWO 260)

The Dancing Years: revival cast recording, 1969, with June Bronhill (RCA INTS 1049)

Perchance to Dream: original cast recording, with Muriel Barron and Roma Beaumont (Decca LF1309)

Arc de Triomphe/Gay's The Word/Crest of the Wave: original archive cast recordings (World Records SH 216)

Bet Your Life (b/w *Beggar's Holiday*): original archive cast recordings, with Arthur Askey, Sally Ann Howes and Julie Wilson (Blue Pear BP1013)

Three by Vivian Ellis: original archive cast recordings from *And So to Bed*, *Big Ben* and *Tough at the Top* (World Records SH 339)

Jill Darling/Streamline: original archive cast recordings, with Frances Day and Arthur Riscoe (World Records SH 263)

We Were Dancing: including archive recordings of Noël Coward and Gertrude Lawrence in *Tonight at 8.30* and *Private Lives* (Monmouth Evergreen MES 7042)

CHAPTER 6

The Continental Musical from Supremacy to Oblivion

The musical theatre on the Continent, like that in Britain, took more 'modern' paths in the years after the Great War. In France, where Messager had bravely kept the drooping flag of classic comic opera flying, a whole new breed of musical comedy appeared in the vanguard of the popular theatre – snappy modern pieces flowing from the pens of the *chansonniers*, the French popular songwriters, as exemplified most outstandingly by Henri Christiné and Maurice Yvain, and such bright, light, up-to-date comedy writers as the free-flowing Albert Willemetz. The new French musical was light, trivial, saucy, snazzy and, above all, of the moment, and its style was as far away as it could be from the period charm of *Véronique* or *Les P'tites Michu*. This new jazz-age style of show produced some notable hits, but it failed to blossom into a long-lasting tradition and, before much more than a decade had passed, the theatre directors of France began to turn their eyes elsewhere. A flirtation with Broadway brought such pieces as *Rose Marie* and *No, No, Nanette* to the French stage with great success, but that source, too, proved quickly insufficient and much of the most successful material played in Paris in the 1920s was borrowed from the German-language stage.

Austria, Germany and Hungary had been less swift to follow the dance-and-laughter styles picked up in the other main centres. With composers such as Lehár, Straus, Fall and Kálmán, all deeply part of the more traditional operetta world, still at their peak, there was much in the way of high-standard romantic comic opera being produced on central European stages, and very successfully produced too. An occasional turn into a modern dance rhythm was allowed by these masters of the light musical theatre, but basically their works rested on the same combination of romantic and light comic scenes and music that been popular since the turn of the century and before. The effectiveness of the style, and of these practitioners of it, was proven by the high rate of export – the best musicals of post-war Vienna, Berlin and Budapest graced with enormous success the stages of New York, London and Paris (and were sometimes even written with them in mind), whilst most of the best native writers of those centres of musical theatre continued to favour the more up-to-date light comedy with songs.

By the mid-1930s, however, both Continental veins had run disappointingly dry. The big names of the mid-European operetta were, to all intents and purposes, finished, and the best of the sparkling musical comedies of France's *années folles* had been and gone. The best Vienna could muster in the decades that followed were the comparatively slight efforts of the Waltz King by default, Robert Stolz, whilst Christiné and Yvain had to wait until the second war for a successor and the discovery of a French writer capable of taking up where they had left off.

This man was Francis Lopez who, with his librettist Raymond Vincy, suddenly and unexpectedly revitalized the French musical theatre. Like Rodgers and Hammerstein in America, this pair produced a series of classic musicals that won wide popularity. Unlike the works of their American counterparts, however, their shows did not go beyond the borders of their own country. Most of Lopez's best work was done by the mid-1950s and, after Vincy's death, the quality of his output dwindled embarrassingly amongst a series of feeble imitations and outmoded shows which were just about all that Europe seemed to be able to produce. When the LP era arrived on the Continent, there was barely a worthwhile new show to record.

Partly, at least, because of this, the popular shows of the earlier years remained in the repertoire, and, along with the classic shows of the nineteenth and early twentieth century, found their way on to disc. The German-language shows, the most internationally successful, won the most attention, but the jazz-age shows of France were not neglected, and much of the best of Lopez – the last of the best of which just squeezed into the era of the ten-inch LP – is well represented on record.

Henri Christiné

Phi-Phi

The two men who hold the reputation for putting the new-style French musical into orbit are librettist and lyricist Albert Willemetz and his composing colleague Henri Christiné, previously best-known as the writer of such popular songs as 'La Petite Tonkinoise', 'Je connais une blonde' and 'Je sais que vous êtes jolie', and the show with which they set the town in an up-to-date whirl was an ancient Greek burlesque called *Phi-Phi*. Ancient Greek it may have been in setting, but its characters and its satire were transparently Parisian and contemporary, and its songs were arguably the most delicious shower of comic light music heard on the world's stage since the heyday of Offenbach.

Regularly revived in France, *Phi-Phi* has been recorded on several occasions. In some ways the one double-disc *intégrale* on the Decca label is worthy of recommendation. Firstly, it is the only *Phi-Phi* to give us the full score – and the full score is unquestionably worth listening to. Secondly, the piece's music gets a lively interpretation from Edouard Bervilly and his orchestra, and it features two highly enjoyable performances from tenor Bernard Alvi as the sculptural Prince Ardimédon, singing with a smooth, sweet sympathy for the thistledown-weight music, and from Mireille, who makes the saucy heroine, Aspasie, a bundle of personality, cheating splendidly through the extreme notes of the rôle without compromising either the music or the acting in a first-class musical comedy performance.

Colette Riedinger is cast as Mme Phidias, a rôle which is traditionally given in France to a rather clapped-out ex-star soprano, and this most stringently attacking singer gives it a much surer and stronger vocal performance than is usual, but she really doesn't show much interest in the character, and her big comedy number goes for little more than a brightly acid sing. The thing which drops this set out of consideration, however, is the off-hand performance of the marvellous and crucial title rôle by Max de Rieux. This artist never gets the character and his comedy off the ground, and *Phi-Phi* without an adorably roguish Phi-Phi is pretty much a lost cause. So, for pleasant listening and a proper, solid-centred performance of *Phi-Phi*, we have to forego the full score and look at the excerpt discs.

Whilst a selection disc with the fine comedian Henri Gènes and Parisian star Marina Hotine is now rare in Europe, a more recent TLP version is still freely available in the shops. This is, hopefully, because the public has too much taste to buy it. It is a travesty of the piece – TLP at its frightful worst. The inevitable Mlle Granger does her familiar wobbly hooting in the rôle of Mme Phidias and Aspasie is played by Marina Florence, a fine dancing soubrette whose stage performances I have loved, but who is hopelessly miscast here and unable to get anywhere near the notes of her songs. Jean Laffont puffs and blows his way horribly through the title rôle, the chorus quite simply can't sing, and only tenor Jean-Marie Joye (Ardimédon) can be acquitted from the charge of torturing Christiné's music to death.

Given the amount of goodies in the score of *Phi-Phi*, it is inevitable that a selection disc has to omit something of value, but the EMI-Pathé selection recording of 1952 omits more than usual to allow for a linking narrative constructed by Pierre Hiégel. It is a delightful narrative (if occasionally not wholly reflecting the libretto), but the loss of the extra songs is particularly great in that everything about the parts to be found on this recording is quite, quite superb. The great comedian Bourvil is cast in the rôle of the naughty sculptor and, with his inimitable chuckling, gulping, twinkling delivery, he creates in a matter of seconds an unforgettable character who leads us with a happy heart through the hilarities of the story and the highlights of the score of this impish show.

After Marcel Cariven's sparkling overture, a delicious-sounding but unidentified group of girls opens proceedings with a very *Boy Friend*ish ancient Greek chorus declaring 'Oui, nous sommes les petites modèles'. Then Bourvil relates in his comically chesty but true tones how he met in the street the perfect maiden to model for his statue of Virtue ('C'est une gamine charmante') in a magnificent example of sung story-telling. Aspasie, the maiden in question, as sung by the gaily sweet-voiced and utterly ingenuous Gise Mey ('Je connais toutes les historiettes', 'Ah, cher monsieur, excusez-moi', 'Bien chapeautée') is, of course, anything but virtuous. By the end of the show she is, as our history books tell us, the famous courtesan and the mistress of Périclès. The rôles in question could have been made for this pair of performers, and it is very sad that their duet, 'Maître, lorsqu'on a vingt ans' is missing. Gone, too, are Phidias' solo 'Vertu, verturon, verturonette' and Aspasie's topical song (in which Douglas Fairbanks and Mabel Normand are amongst the celebrities who get a mention) 'Non, s'il faut que je vous explique'.

The bulk of the show's score is shared amongst these two stars and the artists playing Mme Phidias (Germaine Roger) and Ardimédon (Gaston Rey), who are busy cuckolding Phidias while he is out chasing Aspasie. Mme Phidias' burlesque hymn to Minerva, in which she vows to strip off and pose as the model of Virtue for her husband's statue rather than have another woman do so, is given a suitably sub-operatic performance by Mlle Roger, and both she and the characterful Rey have a splendid time with the comedy waltz rhythms of their sex duet (it can't be called a love duet) 'Ah! Tais toi!', one of the loveliest melodies in the piece, during which she attempts to keep her clothes on while he tries to remove them. Alas, their post-coital Duet des souvenirs is missing, as is his hilarious solo 'Tout tombe', in which he tries to explain to her that surrender is inevitable, as everything drops in the end by nature, and her description ('Je sortais des Portes de Trézène') of his attempts to pick her up.

The three concerted finales, bubbling bits of foolery each one, are all included and perfectly performed on a recording with which is hard to find fault. My only complaint, as with so many of this series, is that it isn't extended to two records, which might have given us not only the missing numbers but also the performance of the comic Rogers in the incidental rôle of Le Pirée (a ridiculous name, but one day he will have a port named after him).

Dédé

Of the series of happy, tuneful Christiné musicals that followed *Phi-Phi*, the most successful was the 1921 piece *Dédé*, a farcical comedy in which the young Maurice Chevalier took a featured rôle. Thirty-two years later, Chevalier recorded his part (which was not, incidentally, the title rôle) as a raffish, penniless nobleman mixed up in sexual shenanigans in a Paris shoe shop, in a quasi-complete adaptation on the Decca double-disc series. To those who know Chevalier only from his calculated incarnation as the plastic Hollywood Frenchman, this recording may come as a bit of a surprise. Here, in his native language, re-creating a rôle he first played at the age of thirty-two, the ageing star gives an altogether more agreeable and natural performance, and it is possible to feel the remnants of the genuine charm which made him his early fame in revue. Admittedly he is aided by material altogether superior to most of what he was dealt up in Hollywood. Albert Willemetz's dialogue and lyrics are genuinely and gently witty – kindly laughter is always bubbling under the play's saucily smiling surface – whilst the songs include two that were hits for the star in 1921, the laid-back piece of unflappable philosophy 'Dans la vie faut pas s'en faire' and a flippant hymn to sexual generosity, 'Je m'donne'.

The show is by no means all Chevalier and his material, however. There is a whole scoreful of splendidly melodious, foot-tapping songs: the lilting and reasonably incidental duet 'Ah! Madame, je vous trouve exquise', the charming, rhythmic and extremely catching 'Si j'avais su', an hilarious chorus of inept, striking shoe-shop workers ('Au nom de la Fédération'), fine songs for the other principal members of the cast – shoe-shop owner Dédé, who is trying to seduce the mysterious Odette, Denise, who is in love with Dédé, and the lawyer Leroydet, who is in love with Denise . . . you get the picture – and, above all, magnificently singable finales, full of action and fun, which can yet produce melodies such as the lightsome 'Pour bien réussir dans la chaussure' (Act 1) and the waltzful of lies 'Une femme de monde trompait son mari' (Act 2).

The Decca recording gives plenty of emphasis to the play by casting the splendid singing actress Marina Hotine as Denise, with Andrée Grandjean (Odette), Raymond Girerd (Dédé) and Marcel Carpentier (Leroydet) all finely suited in the other rôles. The singing is in the style of the piece – light and bright and comedic with not too much emphasis on lyrical vocalizing – though Mlle Hotine brings the bonus of a fine, unpretentious singing voice to add to her comic talents. The piece runs along merrily and gently, the orchestra is unobtrusive, everything very relaxed and pleasant. It is all done impeccably, but maybe Chevalier's ageing laid-back style has been just a little too infectious – a touch more spirit here and there would have been in order. Incidentally, if this recording is reissued again (and I hope it is), it would be kinder to cut off the star's unnecessary and unpleasantly self-aggrandizing personal introduction.

If it's a spirited *Dédé* you're after, there is a very good alternative. A 1973 Paris revival with popular performer Antoine cast in Chevalier's rôle – and billed larger than the title – resulted in a cast album on RCA Victor which gives a good selection from the show performed in a completely different manner. The piece has been reorchestrated in a 1970s style, which – apart from one or two slightly meretricious cabarettish effects – suits its lively tunes very well, and it is played by Jean-Daniel Mercier's orchestra with a driving vigour and enthusiasm that make you sit up, purist or no, click your fingers and enjoy.

Antoine and the rest of the young cast headed by Englishman James Sparrow (Dédé) and Corinne Le Poulain (Denise) may not be the world's greatest singers, but they attack the songs with such relish, splendid diction and pure fun that the result is a highly listenable recording. The big Chevalier numbers lose something from being speeded along, and Antoine lacks the old star's *métier* (though he wins hands down on youthful credibility), but the rest of the songs emerge as I like to believe Christiné would have written them had he been around in 1973. 'Si j'avais su' and 'Ah! Madame' come out particularly well, and the two finales – included in full – work a treat, whilst little tricks of rearrangement, such as the doubling of the octaves in the strikers' chorus to include a grumbling basso, all add to the fun.

Needless to say, some numbers have had to be omitted and, given Antoine's billing, it is the other characters who suffer. Odette (Béatrice Belthoise) has had both her numbers and her Tango Duet with Dédé cut, Sparrow loses his one solo number and Leroydet suffers the same fate. Still, what is left is appreciable, and I feel that, when you come to the end of a cast disc wishing you had seen the production, it has to be good. The fact that I have seen photos of this production, and the cast is all stunningly good-looking, only adds to my regrets.

Maurice Yvain

The first and best musician to follow Christiné into the world of the new French musical comedy was Maurice Yvain, composer, amongst other famous songs, of the internationally known 'Mon homme'. Yvain began his theatre career with the light-footed, gently jazzy score to a delightful piece of sexual nonsense called *Ta bouche* (1922) and followed it up with a string of similar pieces, from which *Là-haut* (1923) and *Pas sur la bouche* (1925) were the most successful.

Yvain's early work was not included in the Pathé-Marconi output, and it was left to Decca to give his three favourite works a representation on long-playing record. *Là-haut*, a second stage vehicle for Maurice Chevalier after his success with *Dédé*, was given the full double-disc treatment, whilst *Ta bouche* and *Pas sur la bouche* were the object of single-disc selections. Although *Là-haut* won a reissue, none of the three recordings seems to have been issued in great numbers and all three have become collectors' items today.

Pas sur la bouche and *Ta bouche*

Under its jolly, colourful sleeve, the recording of that delightful sex comedy *Pas sur la bouche* is a disappointment. The singers seem ill at ease with the obtrusively jazzy piano-based orchestrations (which I have some difficulty in believing to be the real 1920s ones) and the band and vocalists seem on the verge of going their separate ways time and again. Mezzo-soprano Suzanne Lafaye, curiously cast in the rôle originated by the revue star Régine Flory, and tenor Réda Caire, an equally odd choice as her suave, over-confident husband, hold back their voices in an attempt to give the lightness the music demands, but mostly succeed only in sounding tentative, and Caire's performance of the show's popular topical song 'Je me suis laissé embouteiller' goes for nothing.

Janine Ervil's petite soprano makes a much better stab at her song of sexual awakening, 'Est-ce bien ça?', and veteran *opérette* star Fanély Revoil, in the plum rôle of the heroine's aunt who ends up marrying her (the niece's) American ex-husband (!), launches into her numbers with style and occasionally more gusto than the equipment can take; but both these performers would, like Lafaye and Caire, clearly be happier in something less determinedly jazz-age. Only Souris, who takes the low comedy rôle of the concièrge and gives a gutsy revusical rendition of the song made famous by Pauline Carton, 'Par le trou', describing what the voyeuristic lady sees through her customers' keyholes, really seems at home.

Perhaps the most unhappy bit of casting of all, which is probably to be laid at the door of record producer Max de Rieux, is that of himself in the rôle of the American who, trying to win back his former wife, ends up succumbing to a kiss from her maiden aunt. De Rieux burlesques the American accent clumsily, blathers his way over the chirpy melody of the show's pretty title song, and is generally fairly hard to take.

To add to its woes, this recording does not bother to follow the show sequence of the songs, placing them in any old order, and omits the delicious second-act finale 'Sur le Quai Malaquais' and, less seriously, the comedy hiccup song 'Le Hocquet'. Thankfulness for having this piece on disc has to be heavily tempered by regret that it is so unsatisfactorily done.

The same group's version of *Ta bouche* is much better. Part of the reason is simply that the score of *Ta bouche* is superior – Yvain's musicianly and sophisticated adaptation of the new American rhythms into something wholly French is seen at its best here, and it is easy to understand why songs like 'Dans mon temps', the shimmy 'Un petit amant' and 'Ça, c'est un' chose', with their dancing tunes and amusing and almost invariably sexy words, became the popular favourites of their time. That the Conservatoire-trained Yvain's ability as a popular songwriter was supplemented by a talent for composing an outstanding ensemble can also be seen in this score, notably in the tricky second-act quartet 'Puisqu'un heureux hasard'.

Mlle Lafaye is cast with the Opéra Comique baritone Jacques Jansen as the pair of ingénues who decide, to the repeated sound of the insistent title tune, that the time has come to stop kissing and get down to the real thing – it would, after all, be terrible if they got married and found out they were incompatible in bed. Both succeed amazingly well in lightening off their voices, and his *double entendre* version of how things get done 'Machinalement' and her sweeping version of 'Non, jamais les hommes' are truly and trippingly performed. Fanély Revoil as the heroine's mother is much more happily cast here, and in 'De mon temps' she comes across rather like a sophisticated, sung version of Hermione Gingold in *A Little Night Music*. She is paired with de Rieux as the hero's father and he puts aside the excesses of *Pas sur la bouche*, copes nicely with 'Un petit amant' and joins her in a splendidly catchy duet in which the two fortune-hunting phoney aristocrats explain their lack of ready cash by claiming to have their riches in land and bonds respectively ('Des terres et des coupons').

To add to these plusses, the small, piano-based orchestra is again used here and it sounds much less effortful and authentic. This is altogether a pleasant recording of a really enjoyable show and definitely worth bringing out from under the Decca dust-sheets for a re-release.

Là-haut

Là-haut is rather different in character from these two jazz-age musicals. It was a vehicle for two music-hall stars, Maurice Chevalier and Dranem, and, in consequence, the score is made up largely of what is little more than a series of modern music-hall numbers written for two light comedians. The most successful single song from the show was Chevalier's 'C'est Paris' – 'le seul, le vrai paradis, c'est Paris' – but this comes over today as just another of those (mostly subsequent) songs endlessly glorifying Paris under all aspects, at all times of the year or whatever. It is neither Yvain's best melody nor Willemetz's best lyric. There is more fun in the catchy and comical plea for (sexual) tolerance 'Si vous n'aimez pas ça, ne dégoutez pas les autres' or the incidental story of the little girl who couldn't make up her mind to do anything, which was really the excuse for the punning title 'Ose, Anna'. I find it a slightly disappointing score after the bubbling joys of *Ta bouche*, but the huge popularity of the two stars made certain that their songs were well spread about, and they thus became remembered and accounted 'standards'.

The only recording of the work, on Decca, preserves Chevalier's performance as Evariste, who, having been killed in a car crash, pleads to go back to earth to visit his widow. The comedy of the piece is drawn from the fact that he is only allowed to go in the company of a guardian angel (Dranem), whose unshakeable presence at his side duly gets them into situations funny, confusing and embarrassing in turn or all at once. The recording is one made, like *Dédé*, late in Chevalier's career, and I find it a little uncomfortable. Perhaps it is just that here he seems unable to shed the plastic Frenchman of Hollywood identity as well as he did on the other set. Perhaps it is just that *Là-haut* isn't as good as *Dédé*. Perhaps it's the fact that the two lead rôles both survive on crackly comedy singing of not vastly different styles and it becomes a bit relentless. And it doesn't help that Roméo Carlès, cast as the angel here, is no Dranem at all, but one of those performers who seem to think all you have to do to be funny is put on a silly voice. Marina Hotine, who appears as the lady in the piece, supplies the genuine style on a recording that is interesting as a document but only mildly enjoyable as entertainment.

Chanson gitane

As the vogue for jazzy comedy musicals passed on, Yvain turned his hand to the reborn fashion for more traditional fare, supplying the scores for such pieces as the spectacular *Au soleil du Mexique* (featuring Fanély Revoil) at the Châtelet and, most notably, the 1945 production of *Chanson gitane* at the Théâtre de la Gaîté-Lyrique. This romantic tale of bygone love and revenge amongst courtiers and gipsies followed the paths beloved of popular musical theatre from *The Bohemian Girl* to *The Desert Song* and the umpteen *Zigeuner* musicals of the German-language stage, and like all of these it won considerable success. Much of this success was clearly due to Yvain's charming if eclectic score, which ranges from echoes of Messager and Bizet in its lyrical work to the popular comic song in its lighter music, including along the way some fine ensemble writing on the one hand and a successful potboiler borrowed from one of his own film scores on the other.

This musical pot-pourri is given a very superior rendition on a Pathé-Marconi recording of 1954, featuring three original cast stars in the tenor hero André

Dassary, the baritone villain Armand Mestral and the comic Rogers. The tenor rôle is clearly the star one, and Dassary swings into the showy strains of its songs with a will. It is a rôle that seems a natural for the Lanza–Tauber–John Hanson brigade (although it is unlikely they would have done it more justice than the young Frenchman), but *Chanson gitane* never got out of France. Liliane Berton sings the two very attractive soprano set-pieces allotted to the rôle of the Duchesse de Berry quite beautifully, and Gise Mey is the perfect soubrette in a series of duets and trios which range from the jaunty 'Au pas du petit poney' to the two most interesting numbers of the score, the complex second-act quartet and the duo 'L'Aragonèsa', shared with Maria Murano, the gipsy of the title. Mlle Murano (a specialist in gipsyish ladies) gets the show's popular song, 'Sur la route qui va', but doesn't seem to know quite what to do with it.

Chanson gitane is an accomplished and enjoyable score, even if it is also one which gives an effect of being written to order. It receives a more than accomplished performance here, and it is interesting to consider it alongside Yvain's earlier and more spontaneous shows and also alongside the then freshly successful work of Lopez which it frankly tries to emulate.

Reynaldo Hahn

Ciboulette

Little else of French musical theatre between the wars proved of sufficient note to become enshrined on LP, but amongst that little else there is one very notable exception. Reynaldo Hahn's *Ciboulette* was a consciously old-fashioned *opérette*, a deliberately *soigné* score in the Messager vein attached to a pretty and sophisticatedly unsophisticated book by Robert de Flers and Francis de Croisset. The piece had and still has theatrical success, but it found its greatest favour with the cognoscenti and became prized in knowledgeable circles as a *petit chef d'oeuvre* of rare delicacy. Perhaps it is. If so, I'm missing something. There is undoubtedly much in *Ciboulette* to appreciate, much that is charming, refined and pretty, and one splendid scene of open sentiment which is almost daring in its ingenuous emotion, but the piece's very refinement and lack of vulgarity translates too often, particularly on disc, into a pastel piece, lacking in colour.

Apart from one 45 EP including three numbers sung by Colette Riedinger, who is about the most unlikely Ciboulette I can think of, I cannot trace a Decca recording of *Ciboulette*, but EMI-Pathé on the other hand have shown it sovereign favour. They have issued both a selections disc (1952) and a new full-length version (1983), giving it a marked preference over more generally popular or significant pieces. Both these recordings are perfectly adequate ones. The older version is rather short on music and omits the popular 'Dans ma charrette', amongst other pieces, in order to include a linking dialogue of sorts composed by Pierre Hiégel. Unfortunately, this narration does not come off as well as the same writer's *Phi-Phi* adaptation, giving incorrect ideas of the story and adding nothing to the presentation of the music. The songs are, however, as well done as is usual on this series. Géori Boué is a fine, straightforward Ciboulette, Raymond Amade sings exquisitely as the slightly foolish tenor hero, Antonin, and when they come together in the lovely duet 'Comme frère et soeur' the result is a model of the genre. Roger Bourdin takes the rôle of Duparquet, the prosaic-looking middle-aged market official who turns out to be none other than the Rodolphe of de Musset (and Puccini) in later life. His moving recounting of his youthful love and the death of Mimi is the *opérette*'s emotional highlight, and it is a scene which, spoken over an orchestral background before moving finally into the song 'C'est tout ce qui me reste d'elle', can set the shivers going up your spine. Bourdin gets about seven out of ten on the shiver rating.

The complete recording is comparable with the earlier one in most departments. Orchestra and choir are fine, Mady Mesplé is very well suited to the rôle of Ciboulette, producing a small sweet tone in her singing and brightly perky in her acted scenes, Nicolai Gedda is tasteful and pleasant as Antonin, and José van Dam, like Bourdin, rates a good seven for his big scene. There is, perhaps, nothing on this set to equal the Boué/Amade performance of 'Comme frère et soeur', but it is pleasant to have the enjoyable text, even if some of it is given a pretty broad performance and, since *Ciboulette* is not really an *opérette* of highlights, it works rather better listened to as a whole.

Incidentally, a couple of the songs from this piece have been included on a record of the show *Il était une fois l'opérette* where, accompanied by two pianos and an organ, they are given an energetically vulgar performance by Eliane Varon and Dominique Tirmont. It doesn't work at all and makes you appreciate all the more the more elegant style of performance on both the EMI discs.

Hahn wrote plenty more stage music but, in spite of his highly regarded position amongst French composers of the period, little of it has survived on record. One of his collaborations with Sacha Guitry, the play *Mozart* (which featured Yvonne Printemps as the boy musician), is represented on EMI's 'Les Triomphes d'Yvonne Printemps' by two songs – the Air de la lettre and the Air des adieux – which the actress sings with such grave tones as to make me wonder if they have been transferred at the right speed. They are attractive pieces, in the vein of the more solemn moments of *Ciboulette* or of Massenet's *Manon*, and Printemps, right speed or no, is as irresistible as ever.

Unexpected *Intégrales*

If Decca ignored *Ciboulette*, they gave surprisingly good coverage to two other works: Roger Dumas' *Ignace* and Goublier's *La Cocarde de Mimi-Pinson*. The case of the former is explicable, as both on stage and on film *Ignace* was a vehicle for the comic talents of the much-loved stage and screen star Fernandel, and the 1967 double-disc recording features this popular performer in the rôle he had created over thirty years earlier. On record, of course, something is missing. Fernandel's singing voice had, by this stage, utterly gone, but even more importantly, without the distracting visual aspect the very basic nature of the comedy of *Ignace*'s script and songs shows up rather clearly. Amongst a barrage of unsubtleties, there emerge on this recording several attractive singing voices which are largely wasted, and a vast caricature performance of a 'heavy lady' by Madeleine Clervanne which makes Bertha Belmore and Edna Mae Oliver sound like ingénues.

La Cocarde de Mimi-Pinson was a patriotic romance that found success during the Great War, and its excuse for survival is simply that it is a charming little piece, bright and simplistic in the fashion of the wartime film romances in its tiny story of the seamstress who saves her employer's son from the bullets of the Germans by sewing a little tricolore good-luck charm inside his coat. Decca's two-record set gives it the kind of production it calls for, played in primary colours, and with its music – a mixture of pretty waltz songs, comical moments and marches – performed in an equally straightforward style.

Liliane Berton is Marie-Louise, the *Mimi-Pinson* heroine of the piece, and she delivers the delightful, waltzing Légende des petits rubans and the lilting Rondo de la cocarde in her lovely, straight soprano, which contrasts well, both in song and in speech, with the merrily sparking soubrette voice of Simone Sylvia. Peter Gottlieb is a sometimes rather effortful baritone hero, but Pierjac is an adorable *petit comique*, and one of the joys of this set is to hear him joining the creaking-door voice of the marvellous Pauline Carton in dreaming of their future together serving their clients behind 'Un petit comptoir en étain'.

The show has been adapted for record by Max de Rieux (who again produces and appears) in such a fashion that much dialogue real and remade is included but, unfortunately, three good numbers – the comic's Chanson de la c'rise and Zoë's Marche des infirmières and Couplets d'amour – have been left out. There is also a confusing synopsis which doesn't tally with what is on the record.

Vincent Scotto: the Marseille Musicals

In the 1960s the Véga label was responsible for the issue of two discs featuring the songs of the famous series of marseillais musicals which, beginning their career in the city that was the home of their composer Vincent Scotto (best known outside France for his song 'La Petite Tonkinoise'), and eventually of librettists Henri Alibert and René Sarvil, succeeded in bringing a refreshing whiff of unpretentious gaiety to the Paris theatre of the 1930s and 1940s, parallelling the success of equally famous marseillais plays and movies of Marcel Pagnol. Excerpts from *Au pays de soleil, Un de la Canebière, Trois de la marine* and *Arènes joyeuses* performed by members of Sarvil's touring company are spread over these two recordings, originally issued separately but subsequently re-released by Decca as a set. Each musical is given one side of a record, which consists of a half-hour compressed show with snatches of dialogue and short versions of the cheerily uncomplicated Scotto songs, including such hits as 'Adieu, Venise provencale' and 'Sur le plancher des vaches'. It is not a wholly satisfactory formula, but the recordings have the great advantage of an indubitable air of authenticity and some characterful performances.

Alibert, the original star as well as the author of these pieces, recorded much of their music in 78 days. A selection from the shows already mentioned, as well as some from *Les Gangsters du Château d'If*, *Le Roi des galéjeurs*, *Les Gauchos de Marseille* and *Le Port du soleil*, has been transferred onto a double-disc set on the Pathé label under the title 'A petits pas dans le midi' along with a couple of Scotto film numbers and a few other songs, including three by Georges Sellers, the musical director of most of the original productions of the marseillais series. Alibert sounds rather like a marseillais George Formby, the ukelele replaced by a jazzy combo and an accordion, and his pleasant voice was clearly the adjunct to a comic personality, which doesn't wholly come across on record.

Another popular singing comedian, the genuinely marseillais Andrex, also filled up a Pathé disc with songs from the four best-known *opérettes marseillaises*. His warm personality comes over nicely in short versions of the well-known songs, interspersed with heavily accented patter, and, when taken in comparison with Alibert's, the recording benefits from the more modern techniques. However, both these recitals suffer from the usual defect of one-man or woman records: after a while it all begins to sound a bit samey and, ultimately, dull. And, as is evidenced by the Véga recordings, Scotto is certainly not dull.

Un de la Canebière, which has survived into revivals in the 1980s, has also received the attentions of the TLP label. I gritted my teeth at the sixty-one francs I had to pay for what I was sure would be another awful record, and was pleasantly surprised. This is much better than the usual TLP fare. The principal credit must go to Philippe Fargues, cast in the Alibert rôle, who sings the songs with ease and vigour alternately, not to mention a very pleasant light baritone. If the essential comedy of Alibert, Andrex and Pierre Denain from the Sarvil recordings is missing, it is at least partly compensated by thoroughly enjoyable singing. You have to hold your breath when the inevitable Mlle Granger comes on, but she doesn't warble too much and, like all the marseillais shows, this is principally a vehicle for the leading man and his mates, so there is a lot of Fargues and not too much of the lady. Unlike the other recordings, this is actually a full-scale representation of one of the marseillais shows and, as such, is interesting and, in spite of the fact that someone seems to have fiddled with the orchestrations and suppressed the joyous jazz-band cum accordion version in favour of rather too many fiddles, enjoyable.

Other folk obviously commented on the comparative success of this disc, for TLP followed it up with their versions of *Trois de la marine* and *Au pays de soleil*, slimmed down to fit each on one side of a record. There are plenty of jolly songs here, even though some have been clipped down and, to make up for the fact that the chaps get all the best bits in *Trois de la marine*, the selection from *Au pays de soleil* crams in as many of the feminine numbers as possible.

Unfortunately Fargues hasn't been brought back for this recording, but he is agreeably replaced by Francis Lorca, a pleasant warm tenor who sings with a great deal of ease but an almost total lack of temperament and character. He almost gets off the ground in the most energetic moments of the rattling hit songs of *Au pays de soleil*, the swinging valse marseillaise 'A petits pas', the title song and the rousing 'Zou!', but by and large he is just pleasant. The energy comes from Edmond Carbo, who takes the comic rôle in *Trois de la marine*. He helps light up a sadly short 'Sur le plancher des vaches' and makes his idiotic 'Viens dans ma casbah' into the most enjoyable track on the record.

Claudine Granger is happy enough in the easy-flowing middle-range music of the two heroines, producing some pleasant sounds when she is taking it easy, but the moment she approaches the edge of the stave the voice starts waving like windy washing again and it's time to skip tracks. I'm sorry to go on about this lady, but she does put herself up for it. The sleeve of this record, which principally bills *Trois de la marine*, carries an wonderfully tacky illustration by the ubiquitous Okley which is related to the show's original logo showing the three sailors of the title. Only this time the middle sailor has disappeared and who is there, airbrushed, hand on hip and looking all of twenty-five? Mlle Granger.

Vincent Scotto, with hundreds of songs and many a film score behind him, was already fifty-six when *Au pays de soleil* started his fame as a theatre composer but, even when the marseillais series ground to a halt over a decade later, he was still at the forefront of the musical theatre and screen. His most successful stage piece of all, *Violettes impériales*, was produced in the composer's seventy-second year. It was a piece that had nothing of the insouciant gaiety of *Un de la Canebière* about it, for things had changed since those pre-war days. As in America, the war had coincided with the coming of new talent – talent which had capitalized on changing taste and found its moment with a frankly romantic, thoroughly tuneful musical play. In America it was *Oklahoma!*, in France it was *La Belle de Cadix*. The writers of *La Belle de Cadix* were librettist Raymond Vincy, lyricist Maurice Vandair and composer Francis Lopez, and their show set in motion a series of picturesque musicals built on the old romantic-comic lines which were to prove the backbone of post-war entertainment and the most durable entertainments of their era. Before we turn to the works of Vincy and Lopez, however, a quick glance at Scotto's one highly successful attempt at the romantic stage musical is called for.

Violettes Impériales

Violettes impériales is not first class. Yvain's attempt to be Lopez in *Chanson gitane* is much better. There are some good light-hearted moments and some attractive romantic pieces, such as Violette's solo 'Mélancolie', but when the leading man's big song, 'Il n'y a pas de Pyrénées', is so very reminiscent of 'La Fête à Seville' from Lopez's *Andalousie* of the previous year, credibility starts to wobble. Nevertheless, the piece was and is popular, and it has been the object of two recordings by the Merkès/Merval partnership, both on the CBS label. The later recording drops two of the numbers (not sung by the stars) from the list included on the earlier one, but it is marginally less weak in its casting of the subordinate rôles.

Surprisingly Merkès, who created the rôle of Don Juan in the show and has played it regularly since, is less good than usual, whilst Merval, who was not cast opposite him in either of the big Paris productions, is better than in the more classic works of their repertoire. However, neither approaches the performances on a Véga recording under Marcel Cariven in which André Dassary turns Juan from a baritone into a tenor and Nicole Broissin skips through Violette's music at the head of a supporting cast including such fine artists as alto Freda Betti, soubrette Rosine Brédy and character actor Serge Clin. If *Violettes impériales* is necessary to you, this is the one to have.

Do not, by the way, be misled by the ten-inch HMV record which proclaims 'Luis Mariano chante les airs du film *Violettes impériales*'. This may be the same story, but it is not the same music. For the musical film of the musical, which was itself made from a film, Scotto's score was dropped (apparently at the behest of Mariano) and Lopez was brought in to compose some songs for the tenor he had made famous in *La Belle de Cadix*. This disc contains four of them, plus some other non-theatrical songs.

Francis Lopez

The musical theatre works of Francis Lopez span over forty years and many a record. They range from his earliest days with the splendid and important *La Belle de Cadix, Andalousie, Méditerranée, Quatre jours à Paris, La Route fleurie* and *Le Chanteur de Mexico* in the late 1940s and early 1950s through a patchy set of pieces in the late 1950s and the 1960s, which still brought forward some fine works, to some rather desperate attempts with lesser resources in the 1970s and utter embarrassment in the 1980s, when recordings of 'the latest Lopez' became a world-wide collectors' joke. I have thirty Francis Lopez musicals on record (and there are a couple I don't have) and I have no intention of detailing each and every one to you, particularly the bad ones, which are simply not worth listening to, and the awful ones, which are only for amateurs of the 'so awful that its funny' brigade. I shall stick to the fine works of the earlier part of this curious composer's career.

La Belle de Cadix

La Belle de Cadix (1945), with its classic combination of the romantic and comic in script and music, really crystallized a format for the post-war musical in France. By putting the young tenor Luis Mariano into its large lead rôle and making him into one of the biggest popular singing stars the country had known in years, it also set up a formula in which the lead tenor rôle was to become predominant. Such performers as Tino Rossi, Georges Guétary, André Dassary and Rudy Hirigoyen soon followed where Mariano led. There was plenty of place for a leading-lady soprano, a soubrette, a cheeky little comic and even a big, goofy comic, but the leading man was supreme and the songs that he sang had in each show to include the full gamut – from the romantic to the energetic and even to the religious. None of this schema was set up, however, when *La Belle de Cadix* came along to sweep all before it, and the piece is all the more meritorious in that its proportions came out so very right first time up.

The *La Belle de Cadix* original cast recordings with Luis Mariano, originally issued on 78s, were reissued on a ten-inch HMV disc, and later re-recorded on EMI-Pathé as part of an exhaustingly comprehensive boxed set of Mariano's recorded work from his stage successes ('Luis Mariano – toutes ses opérettes'). While it is a very fair representation of Mariano's talent – an attractive, well-used tenor, light at the bottom and cleanly ringing at the secure top – and of the songs his performance helped to turn into hits, this selection cannot be and is not a balanced recording of the show, as little more than the star's music is included. Nevertheless, his performance of the show's best numbers, the rollicking title song and the more romantic 'Maria-Luisa' and 'Une nuit à Grenade', gives some idea of his and their attraction for the public of the time.

Rudy Hirigoyen, another tenor who surfaced in the late 1940s (and who was still performing the same rôles in the early 1980s), is the centre-piece of a more comprehensive *Belle de Cadix* recording, issued originally on Odéon and later on CBS. Hirigoyen is the antithesis of Mariano. Where Mariano's voice and performance are smooth, modulated and accurate, Hirigoyen is lusty, vibrant and rash. He goes for every note and every song with all vocal and emotional stops out. It means he sometimes comes to grief, but it is risky and exciting. In his hands, 'La Belle de Cadix' gets a really virile treatment, relaxed yet vigorous, whilst 'Maria-Luisa' and 'Une nuit à Grenade' both throb with a pop-singer passion, the rubato matched only by the vibrancy of the voice. The nostalgic 'Le Clocher de mon village' is almost crooned, yet the lively 'Fiesta bohémienne', in which all Lopez's Hispanic background swells forth, is carolled out above the chorus with all the football-crowd-pleasing energy in the world. It is an archetypal popular tenor performance, and I can't think of another in any language to beat it.

Fortunately, the supporting cast on this recording are equally as good as the star. The uncredited Maria-Luisa displays an unpretentious, easy soprano in her two waltz songs, 'Les Sentiers de la montagne' and the Valse du mariage; her equally uncredited macho gipsy lover provides a fine contrast to the sweeping star music in the deliberately scornful baritone song 'Le Coeur des femmes', an interesting piece of effective, unshowy writing, and the soubrette pair jolly their way through two bouncy little duos ('Pour toi, Pépita' and 'Ma gitane') in the most typical style. It is a well-dosed and first-rate musical comedy score, and this recording does it proud.

Andalousie

The original cast recordings of *Andalousie* (1947), with Mariano starred opposite Marina Hotine and Gise Mey, were also first released on 78 and reissued both on HMV and (in 1978) on an EMI-Pathé LP. To the seven tracks recorded by Mariano in 1947 are added two numbers by Mlle Mey, both of which belonged to the lead soprano rôle played on stage by Mlle Hotine (who is only heard briefly in one duet) and not her own soubrette part. To help spread the nine numbers on to a full record, a narrative has been added, along with background music made up from some of the songs that are missing. The verdict here is pretty much the same as on the *Belle de Cadix*. Mariano is at his best in the love song 'Je veux t'aimer' and the famously throbbing bullfighter's prayer to the Virgin ('Santa Maria') and a little less convincing in the more virile numbers, particularly when compared with Hirigoyen's brave and bullocking performance on Odéon/CBS.

This latter recording has the edge all round. It has some thrilling singing from its hero in the swinging title song, the battling 'Olé, torero', and such showpieces as 'Le Marchand d'Alcarazas' and 'La Fête à Seville', and he also manages to put an infinity of passion into both the prayer and the big love song without sacrificing his heroic tone. In addition, this recording looks a little wider in its choice of songs. It includes the delightful soprano Janine Ribot performing both the two numbers – one of which is the delicious tipsy waltz for the heroine, 'Ça fait tourner la tête' – performed by Mlle Mey on the other version and also the tuneful arioso 'Valse viennoise', which falls in the show to the 'other woman', as well as opening and closing ensembles. The entire comic music is still missing so, once again, the recording is scarcely a proper representation of the show, but it is an improvement and what is there is splendidly done.

A third version of *Andalousie*, with Aldo Filistad and Liliane Berton starred, was recorded on Philips. To my disappointment, I have been unable to track this one down. It would be a great pleasure to listen to Mlle Berton's version of 'Ça fait tourner la tête', and perhaps some of the comic music is there as well. But can Filistad out-Hirigoyen Rudy Hirigoyen? Can anyone?

Méditerranée

Corsican singing star Tino Rossi, who came late in his professional life from recording and films to the stage and there turned a fine reputation into a remarkable one, was the tenor hero of *Méditerranée* (1955), where he loaned his much-loved voice to the rôle of none other than a Corsican singing star. He recorded a selection from the score of his most splendid vehicle on Pathé with his stage partner Dominique Rika (one number) and the soubrette Gisèle Robert (two numbers), who was presumably used because the original cast soubrette, Aglaë, was under contract to Philips (for whom she put down her four numbers on EP).

Even more than Mariano, Rossi belongs to the singing style of his age. His attractive tenor voice is used in a crooning, confidential style that was the joy of a million French housewives but, for my money, it does not serve Lopez nearly as well as the tearaway vigour of Hirigoyen on the CBS cover version. Where Rossi muses tunefully on the fact that 'Demain, c'est dimanche', Hirigoyen celebrates the fact with reckless *joie de vivre*; where Rossi confides his troubles to 'Vièrge

Marie', Hirigoyen pours out his heart and voice to her and, although he greets his native Corsica in more measured tones and even essays the odd pianissimo, he cannot forbear to end the number on a sweet, falsetto top note in a showy but wholly enjoyable way which Rossi eschews.

The Hirigoyen recording, like his *Andalousie* and *Belle de Cadix*, has the additional advantage of giving more place alongside the star material to other artists and to the rest of the score. Janine Ribot is again Hirigoyen's opposite number and she makes fine, sweet work of her numbers, whilst Lisette Jambel and Jacky Piervil are comically ideal as 'Les joyeux campeurs' mixed up all unawares in the romance and nefarious doings on a Mediterranean cruise. As a *bonne bouche* there is even the superb Duvaleix as the local priest with a droll little piece on 'Les paroissiens de mon village'. In contrast to the Rossi version, which is basically a selection of songs, this one not only gives a set of fine and suitable performances of its lively material but also a very good feel of the show – comics and all, for once – and of its ambiance.

Le Chanteur de Mexico

Le Chanteur de Mexico (1951) was another extremely popular Mariano vehicle with, by this time, some songs which were so 'typical' and true to the successful formula that they were inclined to sound a little distressingly like homogenized versions of the successes of the previous shows. Put down on 78 discs by Mariano with huge success, and duly re-recorded on the many compilations of his performances, most of the show was subsequently recorded on CBS by Hirigoyen, who also headed the cast of an *intégrale* recording for Festival Musidisc. Hirigoyen is well at home on his excerpts disc, which compares with the original cast recordings pretty much as did the songs from *La Belle de Cadix* and *Andalousie*.

The big number here is 'Mexico', a piece simply drenched in tequila, in which Hirigoyen doses his effects with a masterly hand. He soars up on the first line of the refrain to a falsetto 'Mexiko ... Mexiiiiiiko', before indulging in a bit of flowery coloratura in the same register on the repeat, and finally opening up for a full-voice note to end the number. Local flavour is also in evidence in 'C'est la fête à Saint-Jean de Luz' (try fitting that to music) and in 'Il est un coin de France', which the star milks for more yearning moments alongside the vigorous 'ay-ay-ay-ing' of the chorus than you could imagine – not to mention the slightly more musically sophisticated 'Acapulco' and 'La Téquila' (which speak for themselves). He even gets a chance to give the French capital a plug with the rather routine (but devilishly catchy) 'Quand on voit Paris d'en haut'. He goes to the other extreme with a pianissimo rendering of 'Maïtechu' and a gently pretty love song, 'Rossignol de mes amours', and saves the dramatic open-throated moment of 'Adieu la vie', a piece which sounds too *Pagliacci* to be true, for eleven o'clock and the approch of the final curtain. I suspect if there were a word such as 'gamutissimo', it would have been invented for the splendidly uninhibited Rudy.

There are four whole numbers on this selection in which the tenor does not appear – a catchy waltz for the soprano, two pieces – one of which is the show's most enjoyable number 'Ca me fait quelquechose' – for the soubrette (and the unnamed one here is a little beauty), and the regular staunch baritone song, but a fifth cast member (who sounds as if it might be Pierjac) gets one of the best moments, in a really jolly duet with our hero, 'Quand on est deux amis'.

The complete recording gives you, in addition, one song for each of the male comics, a reprise, a finale and an opening chorus, plus sufficient dialogue to join up all the songs (even when this is difficult). Its 1977 date means that Hirigoyen is no longer a juvenile – and the cover photo takes no steps to hide the fact – but he is undiminished vocally, although practised style has taken the place of the rashness. The ladies of the cast are not quite up to their equivalents on the selection disc, but there are two splendid bonuses in a grand bass-baritone, Lucien Lupi, as the Indian chief singing to 'Guarrimba', god of war, and the always delightful Andrex performing the rather feeble 'Pauvre Cartoni'. Christian Borel makes a lively *petit comique*. It is a recording – the only recording – which gives you some idea of what a Lopez *opérette*, plot, parti-coloured acting, cues for a song and all, is like and, although I find that it misses just a touch of the swirling gaiety so essential to these pieces, it fulfils that purpose pretty well.

Le Chanteur de Mexico was and is one of the most popular Lopez works on stage and screen and, if I find it just a little less pleasing than the first three works, it is probably because I saw and heard the first three first, and *plus c'est la même chose* . . . .

La Toison d'or

Amongst the other romantic operettas of Lopez's first decade, *Pour Don Carlos* (1950) appears in the shape of ten already predictable numbers (two boleros including the hit of the show 'Je suis un bohémien', two rumbas, and titles like 'Le fête en montagne') recorded fairly honourably on 78 by its stars Georges Guétary (six) and Maria Lopez (four) transferred to a Pathé-Marconi disc and backed with Guétary's numbers from his *Le Baron Tzigane* film; *A la Jamaïque* (1954) was apparently recorded on the same label, although whether from the stage show or the film I have not been able to establish. Both discs are rarities. *La Toison d'Or* (1954), however, was not only recorded but reissued on the Pathé-Marconi series, with its original star André Dassary, and also on a less common Decca disc.

Dassary, whose fine tenor is more in the Mariano mould than in the Hirigoyen, is a stylish and attractive performer, and he gives a fine sing to the variety of numbers alloted him – the 'tritty-trotty' song of the road with its rollicking tenor line sailing along above the chorus, the biggish romantic 'L'Etoile bleue' and 'Jamais je n'aurais d'autre amour' and so forth. Unlike one or two others, he is not afraid to put himself up against a really fine leading lady. It was Riedinger in the theatre and here it is Lina Dachary, with a larger rôle – five solos! – than some of Lopez's sopranos, but not some of his best songs. What she has, she sings superbly. The one spot of some originality comes with a ringing title song intoned by the bass Lucien Lupi as the villainous High Priest for, once again, the light comedy numbers are left off the recording.

Viva Napoli

After a less prolific period in the 1960s, Lopez returned in 1970 with his first original vehicle for Hirigoyen in the staunch and tuneful *Viva Napoli*. The tenor was cast as no less a personage than Napoléon Bonaparte in a tale something like *I Was Monty's Double*, and he was equipped with a set of songs fit to rival those of Lopez's earliest shows. From the opening 'Aqua fresca' (very reminiscent of 'Le Marchand d'Alcarazas'), through the jolly duo 'Les Routes d'Italie' with comic Luc Barney, to the catchy martial 'Soldats! Je suis content de vous' and a bouquet of romantic songs, the star was able to run two parallel gamuts at one and the same time, one as the battling emperor and the other as the little water-seller who is his double. It all made for a marvellous rôle and, on the Philips cast recording, Hirigoyen makes the most of all its aspects.

A little bit of the splendid rashness has gone from the voice after thirty years as a leading man, and the passing of time is also evident in the arrangements – the plonky bass line of so many modern recordings, the insistent rhythm section, the croony chorus, and a reduction in personnel all round are in evidence – but there are big tunes in plenty and fine voices to sing them and the overall result is a pleasant one.

Nicole Broissin sings the numbers from the leading lady's rôle, including the delightful waltz 'Les Fleurs d'Italie', and also 'La Valse de la reine', apparently written by Mme Lopez and allotted to the small rôle of Queen Caroline, whilst Barney makes a really jolly job of the cowardly 'Aïe, mamma mia' as well as joining a rather weighty soubrette (Eliane Varon) in some truly lively duets.

Viva Napoli was, alas, only a temporary reprieve. From there on, Lopez's work is all downhill. Casts and orchestras decrease at first slowly and then vastly, arrangements go from dubious to awful, singers are older (thirty and forty years on, Guétary and Hirigoyen still star), wobblier (particularly the sopranos) or, in the case of a remarkably continuous line of striving young tenors, simply less charismatic. Some of the pieces, lavishly produced, had runs of a year or even two, but as time goes on they become more and more banal and the music far too often sounds like either a sad caricature of the early works, or a desperate attempt to catch on to some colourful element and make a show without straw. In 1989, the year of the bicentenary of the French revolution, the latest Lopez is on the road – it is called *La Marseillaise*.

Amongst the earlier works, however, there is a second series that contains some really splendid shows. Away from the larger stages with their *opérette à grand spectacle*, their costume romance and ringing music, Vincy and Lopez collaborated on some delightful smaller-scale musical comedies.

Quatre jours à Paris

The first and best of these works was the hilarious *Quatre jours à Paris*, produced at the Bobino in 1948 with the comedian Andrex in its starring rôle. The score consists largely of character pieces and dance numbers (one of the show's features was a splendid and very popular 'Samba brésilienne') and the love songs are of a very different style to those written for Mariano and Rossi. This, incidentally, didn't stop Mariano putting some of them down on disc, but both his recordings and those made by Andrex seem to have been confined to 78. The only real representation of the score on LP is on a comparatively recent Festival recording featuring Georges Guétary. It says 'enregistrement intégrale' on its cover, but this clearly doesn't refer to the original show, only maybe to what looks from the cover pictures as if it may have been a television presentation of a scaled-down version.

It says 'version 1979' in little letters, and it is soon evident that someone has been at Vincy's skilful script and Lopez's jolly score. Many of the numbers are missing (not the star's, of course) and musical director Jo Moutet has had a go at the light, dance-band style orchestrations, replacing them with a modern combo with oddly electrical instruments, some nasty scratchy percussion and an obtrusive bass, and the simple lilt of the numbers is regimented away by an unsympathetic drummer. Guétary himself sings the songs pleasantly enough, but the humour of an Andrex, so vital to the piece, is absent. Eliane Varon sings prettily as his beloved but only she and Katia Tchenko, in the low comedy rôle of the extremely plain housemaid, have their solos included. Incidentally, mediocre though this production is on disc, it must have been even more peculiar on TV, as the French penchant for casting lead (and presumably juvenile-ish) rôles with ageing stars means that Guétary romances the middle-aged Mlle Varon, whilst the voluptuous Nadine Capri (Amparita, her rôle almost gone in this version) and lovely Jacqueline Guy (Simone) are shoved aside. Worst of all, the extremely plain housemaid is played in very short skirts by the adorable blonde Mlle Tchenko. It is distinctly confusing. Please go back to the original.

La Route fleurie

The other musical comedy triumph of this era was *La Route fleurie* (1952), a careless romp to the Côte d'Azur by a bunch of penniless youngsters who end up about to be wed, rich and famous by the time two hours of Vincy and Lopez's fun and popular songs have led to the final curtain. *La Route fleurie* had the advantage, at its creation, of an exceptional cast. Georges Guétary, who had already appeared in Lopez's 'legit' *opérette Pour Don Carlos*, was the romantic lead, whilst the comedy was in the hands of two relative newcomers, Bourvil and Annie Cordy. It was a bill that was to turn out to be something spectacular.

Their performances were recorded by Pathé, and they make up a fine disc. Guétary is smoothly romantic in his description of 'Une dinette' (not unlike his 'A Table for Two' in *Bless the Bride*), passionate in his praises of his 'Mimi' and a skilful *chansonnier* in the cautionary tale of the 'Jolie meunière' who kept refusing fellows and ended up without one. Cordy boogies through her dumb blonde description of her latest fad, 'Subitiste', fools about declaring 'Moi, j'aime les hommes', and borrows the best song from a subsidiary rôle, a topical piece for a crazy French actress trying to rehearse the rôle of a cowgirl, 'La Belle d'Ohio'. But it is Bourvil with his half-sad, half-comical delivery who comes out as the most appealing, and not just because he has the most imaginative songs. Whether he is composing a poem about 'Les Haricots' to please his beloved, rushing about in a pith-helmet, madly describing imaginary life in 'Madagascar', shrugging out his life of failure in 'Pas de chance' or joining with Guétary in a rose-coloured view of 'La Vie de bohème', he is a total joy.

The other artists and their numbers are, unfortunately, omitted from what is, in any case, quite a full record but, more curiously, one of the show's best numbers, Mlle Cordy and Bourvil's nonsense duet 'Tagada-tsoin-tsoin', is also left off, along with Guétary's big number from the last act 'Il a suffi'. In their place there are 'Ma chanson' and 'Copains', two numbers which don't appear in my libretto and which I can only assume were cut. Or added. Doubtless there is a story behind all this but I'm sure that somewhere there is a recording of 'Tagada-tsoin-tsoin'.

La Route fleurie was revived at the Théâtre de la Renaissance in 1980 with a presentable young tenor, José Villamor, and the experienced Jacky Piervil, but the recording that resulted is not comparable with the original. It does, however, include both 'Il a suffi' and the song 'Je l'aime et puis c'est tout' belonging to Mimi, the fourth of the merry band, whose rôle was rather squashed out by the star presences in the original. A third recording, made by TLP in 1984, casts Hirigoyen and Henri Gènes (who took over from Guétary and Bourvil respectively in the original production more than thirty years earlier) and, having apparently failed to find an equally elderly soubrette, simply omits all the music belonging to Annie Cordy's rôle of Lorette. Like both the other recordings, it does not have the elusive 'Tagada'.

Annie Cordy's success in *La Route fleurie* earned her a starring vehicle of her own in Lopez's *Tête de linotte* (1957), which gave birth to a jolly Cordy record, and she was later paired with Mariano in the same composer's *Visa pour l'amour* (1961), an agreeable piece, of which the Pathé-Marconi recording has now vanished into the realm of the dinosaurs. From this time on, however, Lopez concentrated on the romantic-tenor-first variety of musical and Cordy and Bourvil went their ways into other shows, occasionally together, leaving the composer on his downward slope.

In case there is anyone else in the world who is trying to put together a complete collection of Francis Lopez discs – no easy task – I should add that up to 1989 the following of his works, apart from those already quoted, have been put down on cast recordings: *Les Temps des guitares*, *La Cancion del amor mio*, *Le Secret de Marco Polo*, *Le Prince de Madrid*, *La Caravelle d'or*, *Gipsy*, *Les Trois mousquetaires*, *Fiesta*, *Volga* (twice), *La Perle des Antilles* (played and recorded in two significantly different versions), *Viva Mexico!*, *S.E. La Embajadora* (shades of *Call Me Madam*),

Aventure à Monte-Carlo, Soleil d'Espagne, La Fête en Camargue, Le Vagabond tzigane, L'Amour à Tahiti, Les Mille et une nuits, Carnaval aux Caraïbes, Le Roi du Pacifique, Fandango, Aventure à Tahiti and *Rêve de Vienne. La Belle Otéro* and *La Marseillaise* will doubtless follow.

Apart from the works of Lopez, there was little in the way of native musical theatre successfully produced in France in the decades after the second war, although a regular stream of musical comedies and recordings made from them continued to swell on to the market. Several are undemandingly enjoyable enough, others, like France's first attempt at a rock musical, *Les Plumes rouges*, are rather blush-making, and others again are simply awful. Amongst them one or two can be picked out.

La Petite Lily (1950), the unexceptional songs from which were issued on a ten-inch disc, had the distinction of starring Edith Piaf (who sings nearly all the numbers) and Eddie Constantine; *Pacifico* had Bourvil and Guétary, some enjoyable moments, and a good run; *La Polka des lampions* borrowed the story of *Some Like it Hot* with a certain success and a more agreeable score than that attached to the same story on Broadway; *Monsieur Carnaval* and *Douchka* both featured scores by Charles Aznavour; and *Ouah! Ouah!*, *Pic et Pioche*, *Nini la Chance* and *Indien* all had Annie Cordy as an unforgettable star. It was *peu, très peu*.

Marguerite Monnot

Irma la douce

However, from this rather unpromising atmosphere emerged the first French international hit for half a century: Alexandre Breffort and Marguerite Monnot's *Irma la douce* (1956). Starting at the little Théâtre Gramont, where it found sufficient success to be transferred to a larger venue, it finally ended up, thanks to a particularly outstanding English translation, going via London and Broadway to the stages of the world. Its career was marked along the way by regular recordings.

There is no original cast recording as such. The best that the original production can throw up is a selection of four numbers included by the original Irma, Colette Renard, on a ten-inch recital disc (along with, amongst others, two songs from Chaplin's *Un Roi à New York*). She sings them marvellously, with a straight, characterful French cabaret *chanteuse* voice that needs no specious effects to get across the cheerfully simple personality of the lovable Irma – but there are only four of them.

The rest of the score had to find its way to record elsewhere. Viviane Chantel, an attractive *chanteuse*, and two male singers put eight numbers on to a well-sung but oddly formatted 45 rpm sized 33 rpm disc, and Zizi Jeanmaire and Roland Petit, backed by the Quatre Barbus as the rest of the cast, came the nearest to recording the whole score on another ten-inch disc from which only a couple of pieces were omitted. It is quite enjoyable, although Jeanmaire is a slightly tougher Irma, without that youthful vulnerability that Renard achieves, and Petit is a fairly ordinary Nestor. The Quatre Barbus perform their three numbers superbly.

Renard finally recorded the score properly eleven years later when she starred in a Paris revival of *Irma* – in fact, not only the score but also the text, for this two-record set is a live recording made at the Théâtre de l'Athenée during the run. It is an extremely well-made recording technically, the sound being as good as a studio recording and sometimes better, and yet it has a theatrical atmosphere, emphasized of course by the applause and laughter coming from the audience.

Renard has necessarily matured. Her voice is just a little less fresh and innocent, just a little more, how shall I put it, professional – but just a little and in the most attractive way. And she acts the rôle with all the spirit and character that could be wished. It is still a splendid performance, endearing and warm, rather like a French Gwen Verdon with a stronger voice. She trips out her 'Dis-donc' delightfully, cruises gently through 'Avec les anges' and gives a strong sing to 'Irma la douce' in a manner that never shows for an instant that she has been singing these songs fairly non-stop for eleven years.

She is partnered most effectively by the equally warm and likeable Franck Fernandel (Nestor), whose gently smooth baritone blends comfortably under the star's chesty tones in their duets 'Me v'la, te v'la' and 'Avec les anges' and whose acting performance is right on the button. René Dupuy, the creator of the rôle of Bob le Hotu and the director of the original production, bundles the action along as the narrator. He is assisted by a comically expert supporting cast, who help wind the show up to its more and more topsy-turvy second act, and a splendidly atmospheric band, using Raymond Legrand's original orchestrations, which keeps up the illusion of the *milieu* in which the story takes place.

It was hard to imagine *Irma la douce*, with its very special French *argot*, translating into another language, but David Heneker, Monty Norman and Julian More did a remarkable job, and the success of the English-language version bears witness to their skill. The London and Broadway recordings of *Irma la douce* show up some small differences. They are few and mostly insignificant, although America souped up André Popp's London orchestrations and revised the vocal arrangements, which are, in any case, less enjoyable than the bouncy, tinny Legrand ones used in France.

The leading players, Elizabeth Seal (Irma), Keith Michell (Nestor) and Clive Revill (Bob), are the same in each case, and both the London cast of *mecs* (including Ronnie Barker, Gary Raymond and Frank Olegario) and the Broadway one (with George S. Irving, Stuart Damon and Zack Matalon amongst them) give fine support in a rather fuller-voiced manner than the rougher French group. Miss Seal and Michell give fine performances of the songs. She sounds very like a rather larger English version of Mlle Renard, firm and forceful and only occasionally resorting to a touch of yowling, and his gently warm and unforced baritone pairs attractively with her in 'Our Language of Love' (otherwise 'Avec les anges') and points his 'Wreck of a Mec' ('La Cave à Irma') and the various comedy passages with a first-class flair. But for all the expertise and energy that the performers put out, they do not achieve the flavour of the French recordings.

If *Irma la douce* puts on a rather different guise in English, I leave it to you to work out what it is like in Swedish, Dutch or Israeli. I have heard only the last of these and it is so far away from Pigalle and the Théâtre Gramont that I thought for the moment I had put on the wrong record. There are some very strange instruments in the band, including an electric piano, some other highly electrified string instrument and some bongo drums (or is it a drum-machine part of the electric piano?), which simply murder the music. 'Dis-donc' is unrecognizable squeezed into the relentless beating of the band on what is a generally nasty and fairly incompetent distant relation of *Irma*.

A final *Irma* cast disc, from South Africa, is a really small-scale affair, played with just piano, accordion and drums and with three *mecs* instead of the regulation five. It has a sparky Irma in Jo-Ann Pezzaro, later to be the South African Evita and Mrs Barnum, who is so un-French as to be billed, Mussolini-like, on the sleeve as *Irma la duce*, and, in spite of the fact it comes nowhere near the other recordings in professionalism, does help prove that an undersized *Irma* is better than an overdone one.

Claude-Michel Schönberg

La Révolution française

Amongst the rock operas that followed *Jesus Christ Superstar*, the one that attracted perhaps the most attention in France was another not afraid to take on an enormous subject. *La Révolution française* (1973), staged first at the Palais des Sports and the following season at the Théâtre Mogador, took the form of a series of scenes following the most important events in the course of France's history in the five years of revolution, mixed with an apparently historic and unresolved love story between a revolutionary and an aristocratic woman.

La Révolution française was recorded in a double-disc set and reissued in 1989 on the occasion of the bicentenary. It is equipped with the most effectively presented libretto I have ever seen, laid out like a cartoon strip in a series of devastating drawings that catch the spirit of the piece marvellously, with the lyrics of the musical sections – they are rarely written in the form of songs – as their spoken 'bubble' text. Triumphant green, blue and bilious yellow faces glare from every corner of every page, alongside the famous names of history reduced to vile, glaring skeletal masks like something from a science fiction comic. Only the two lovers and Madame Sans-Gêne, doing the washing for a naked Napoléon, escape this devilish treatment.

The music that illustrates the illustrations is a seductive if occasionally uneven mélange of modern writing and arranging styles and classical influences on much the same lines as *Jesus Christ Superstar*. It also has many premonitions of *Les Misérables*, which is scarcely surprising, as amongst the authors of the piece are to be found the names of Claude-Michel Schönberg and Alain Boublil, composer and co-librettist of the later show. The score contains a wide spectrum of musical pieces, ranging from violent, heavily rocked moments from Alain Baschiung as Robespierre, the effortful Martin Circus as Danton and other loud revolutionaries, and the guttural Jean Schultes as Fouquier-Tinville, to gently lovely melodies for the sweet-voiced heroine (Noëlle Cordier). There are moments of comedy for Madame Sans-Gêne (Elisabeth Vigna) and in the spoken murder of Marat, and sections of genuinely affecting power, such as the words of King Louis (played very effectively by Schönberg himself) before his murderers.

La Révolution française is a vast undertaking which does not succeed in finding itself a coherent style across its very varied and always vibrant surface. Maybe my French history is missing something, but it is incomprehensible to me, for example, that the score should break out into dance rhythms when Talleyrand comes on the scene, dissipating the atmosphere built up in the previous dramatic scenes. But if, as a whole piece, the enterprise seems neither *poisson* nor *poulet*, it includes some splendidly exciting and moving moments. And you can always look at Bernard Monié's pictures.

Unlike the other main kinds of light musical theatre entertainment, the German-language operetta did not come out of the war period significantly changed. The old and not so old masters of the Viennese stage – Fall, Lehár, Straus and Kálmán at their head – were still there, still producing superb works in much the same style as in the previous decade, and some of the masterpieces of the popular operetta stage were born in the years following the war. The only significant difference was that some of them saw the light of day in Berlin, to where several of the star writers of the operetta had moved their centre of operations.

Leo Fall

Fall, whom I persist in believing to be the greatest of them all, made the smallest contribution by way of quantity to the post-war musical, for his death intervened in 1925 when he was only fifty-two. The last decade of his life, however, brought two of his finest works, the wartime *Die Rose von Stambul* and *Madame Pompadour*, as well as his own particular favourite, *Die Kaiserin*. As noted earlier, Fall has fared poorly in the recording world. None of these three works has even been deemed worthy of a record to itself. The highly popular tenor music in *Die Rose von Stambul* has ensured it several half-records, one of which, on RCA, twins it with *Die Kaiserin*, whilst others pair it with Fall's earlier *Der liebe Augustin* and *Der fidele Bauer* respectively. *Madame Pompadour* has only been stretched to a meagre EP on Ariola-Eurodisc and to a half-disc, backed with that other fine French courtesan, Millöcker's *Die Dubarry*, on EMI-Electrola. However, although the examples of Fall's superb works are few, they are sufficient to give huge pleasure and to whet the appetite for more.

Die Rose von Stambul

The most readily available record of *Die Rose von Stambul* is that issued in the wide-ranging Ariola series (paired with *Die Dubarry*) and, thus, featuring the inevitable Rudolf Schock. In fact, Schock is so heavily featured that the selection is more of a 'Schock sings the tenor bits from the show' rather than a genuine selection. The two most exciting tenor numbers, 'O Rose von Stambul' and 'Ihr stillen, süßen Frau'n', hold pride of place alongside the glorious waltz duo 'Ein Walzer muss es sein' (in which you get to hear snatches of an under-recorded Erika Köth), the third tenor piece ('Zwei Augen, die wollen mir nicht aus dem Sinn') and the betrothal scene with its featured tenor section.

This is not one of Schock's better recordings. He sounds nastily effortful on the frequent high notes and uneven elsewhere and, as already mentioned, the balance in the wonderful duet is poor. Fortunately, although we still await a complete *Rose von Stambul*, there is a much more extensive, better balanced and more happily performed 1964 selection from the show issued in the EMI Operetten-Gala series. On this recording Fritz Wunderlich takes the star rôle of Achmed Bey, and he gives a thrilling performance of the two big numbers, alternately soaring passionately up to the heights and caressing the text with the sweetest of tones. He is paired with Melitta Muszely, who helps him to make very much the most of their two duets, but, space ruling, the lady does not get to show her skills in any of Kondja Gül's solo music. What this recording does have, however, instead of the remainder of the tenor music, is three of the show's delicious comedy pieces, here given a simply adorable performance by Harry Friedauer (Fridolin) and Christine Görner (Midili). Their sprightly sweethearting to the wonderfully tuneful strains of 'Fridolin' and the 'Schmucki-Duett' and, with Hans-Maria Lins as Müller, in the cute 'Grosspapa' is a joy.

Although it is sad not to have the soprano music, there is of course a limit to what can be fitted on to one side of a disc and, given the limitations involved, the contrasting selection, showing as it does the range and richness of Fall's talent, is a well-chosen, if tantalizing one. The performance is uniformly outstanding, and Carl Michalski's orchestra, vibrant and laughing in turn, adds more than its share to the success of a recording which has only the failing of the very best selection discs – there simply isn't enough of it.

Der liebe Augustin

Just to make this *Rose of Stambul* disc even more delectable, the other side contains an equally splendid selection from Fall's earlier *Der liebe Augustin* (1912). The riches to be found here are no fewer than in *Die Rose von Stambul*, although they are different in character. The leading man in this essentially comic piece is a rather less glamorous figure than Achmed Bey and his music, in consequence, is less soaringly romantic. This does not prevent the show's principal duet, the lovely waltz 'Und der Himmel hängt voller Geigen' being any the less appreciable, especially in the tenderly wistful performance it is given here from Sári Bárabás and Heinz Hoppe as the Princess and her beloved piano-teacher whose destinies, after many a comical interlude, can finally be joined when it turns out that she isn't really a princess at all. In the meanwhile they have turned out two other memorable duets ('Es war einmal ein Musikus' and the yearning 'Sei mein Kamerad') which, along with the other splendid ensembles – notably the insistently waltzing 'Anna, was ist denn mit dir?' – make up the heart of another unfairly neglected score.

Madame Pompadour

There is a brief selection from *Der liebe Augustin* recorded by Schock and Margit Schramm on Ariola, and Schock is also responsible for the most appreciable recording of *Madame Pompadour* on a ten-inch EMI-Electrola (backed with *Die Dubarry*). It is a selection that rather scrambles through some of the show's vocal highlights – the seductive 'Ein intimes Souper', the comical 'Josef, ach Josef' and the showy 'Madame Pompadour' – whilst omitting others, notably the famously bouncing 'Pom-Pom-Pompadour'. Schock is in better form here, and Muszely as the sexy heroine and Karl-Ernst Mecker as the hapless Josef Calicot are fine, but ultimately the recording is unsatisfying as a representation of the show: there is just too little of it to get any idea of the score or the operetta. However, until someone gets around to a full-scale recording (instead of the umpteenth *Wiener Blut* or *Eine Nacht in Venedig*) it is the best there is.

An intriguing insight into this work and the way music of this type was tackled in the 1920s can be found on a 45 EP issued by Electrola in 1957. It has Fritzi Massary, the original 1922 Pompadour, performing 'Josef, ach Josef' with her husband Max Pallenberg (Calicot in the 1926 revival), and a number called 'In Liebesfalle' which she interpolated into the show. Hers is far from the thoroughly sung performance of Muszely or Schramm, and distinctly nearer to the style of a Marlene Dietrich or a Zarah Leander, whilst he is all broad comedy and little singing. It is also quite, quite irresistible.

Die Kaiserin

The 1980 RCA pairing of *Die Kaiserin* and *Die Rose von Stambul* is a slightly lopsided one. It is actually a record of eleven separately listed songs and scenes (but not actually individual pieces) from *Die Kaiserin*, with the much shorter second side filled up with another, different recording of Wunderlich performing the three tenor numbers from *Die Rose von Stambul* and, with Gretel Hartung, the two big duets. The variously-sized pieces of *Kaiserin* material, as on others of this series, are crammed together with no breathing space between the tracks. It is a rather clumsy kind of layout, but nothing can obscure the charms of this superbly lilting grand operetta score. No matter how awkwardly displayed, the sparkling music – romantic, vigorous or soubret – soars through, making you wonder just why such splendid material has been so little heard-of outside its home land.

The five soloists on this disc are uniformly excellent. Anny Schlemm, in the rôle of empress-to-be Maria Theresia, written for Fritzi Massary, twinkles through her dancing 'Zwei Fusserl zum Tanzen' in true prima donna style and serenades 'Du mein Schönbrunn' in broad and beautiful waltz-time as her eleven o'clock number. She is joined in the show's big, gliding waltz duet 'Mir hat heute Nacht' by the clear-voiced tenor Franz Fehringer, who has his finest moment in the hero's lilting and lively 'Dir gehört mein Herz' – a gift of a song. Willy Hoffmann and Gretl Schörg have fine fun with the thoroughly sung light comedy music and bass-baritone Willy Schneider is a model operetta father-figure, whilst the Cologne radio choir, in particularly good form, get plenty of opportunity to show off their abilities. It all just leaves you saying, 'more, please'.

Wunderlich's *Rose von Stambul*, on the reverse, is just dazzling. Don't worry that you already have the other disc; this one incorporates the solo 'Heut' wär ich so in der gewissen' (in which he gets not only to sing but to whistle!) which isn't included on the larger selection. His partner is a bit wobbly, but she isn't too much in evidence and cannot spoil what is one of the outstanding operetta performances of recording history – a brilliant performer perfectly cast in a rôle with brilliant material. It is a truly superb disc. And that runs me out of adjectives.

In recent years it has been seen fit to issue double and even triple or quadruple record appreciations of the favourite pieces of a swatch of composers from Kálmán to Künnecke, Dostal and Eysler – but, maddeningly, not Fall. The best that can be exhumed is a pot-pourri of pieces under the title 'Und der Himmel hängt voller geigen' made up of items from the various Ariola releases of Fall material featuring Schock, and including both *Madame Pompadour* and *Die Rose von Stambul* of his later works. This recording is a bit unsatisfying as, given the presence of Schock, it concentrates almost entirely on the lead tenor and other lyrical music to the detriment of Fall's outstanding lighter numbers. However, it has the merit, at least, of making even a small part of the works of this under-appreciated master accessible to the record-buying public.

Franz Lehár

Franz Lehár who, on the strength of *Die lustige Witwe* and, to a lesser extent, *Der Graf von Luxemburg*, has become regarded in the contemporary English-speaking world as practically the inventor and certainly the greatest practitioner of later Viennese operetta, continued a steady output in the decade during and following the war. *Wo die Lerche singt* (1918), *Die blaue Mazur* (1920), *Frasquita* (1922) and *Clo-Clo* (1924) rendered some attractive portions without attaining full-scale success, but other shows from this period had to undergo severe rewrites before finding acceptance – *Endlich allein* as *Schön ist die Welt*, *Der Sterngucker* as both *Libellentanz* and *Gigolette* and, in the greatest success of Lehár's post-war career, *Der gelbe Jacke* as *Das Land des Lächelns*.

The only LP selections I have been able to trace of *Die blaue Mazur, Libellentanz* and *Clo-Clo* are, oddly enough, in Italian – part of that adventurous EDM series which has also preserved *Frasquita* (this one even better represented in French though unfindable in German), *Eva*, Sidney Jones's *The Geisha* and a whole group of Italian musicals. *Schön ist die Welt*, on the other hand, has won several recordings, all but one of which, however, are either on EP or on half a record. The only substantial recording is the now unfindable disc with Karl Terkal and Lotte Rysanek in the same infuriatingly out-of-print Philips series which also put out the most extensive selections of other such little-recorded pieces as *Die Dollarprinzessin*, *Der fidele Bauer* and *Die gold'ne Meisterin*. A very good reason, even if there were no other, to haunt second-hand record shops.

Das Land des Lächelns

Das Land des Lächelns – otherwise *The Land of Smiles* – is a wholly different proposition. This combination of the favourite old 'East fails to meet West' story, popularized in such shows as *The Geisha* and *San Toy*, and a Lehár score of some seriousness, with more echoes of Richard Strauss than of Johann, was an enormous success at its first production and has continued through many a revival as one of the most popular of its composer's works. In keeping with its music, and in the strain that Lehár adopted in his post-war works, this is a piece where the leading characters seem to spend more time being miserable than joyous. The score, in consequence, does not glitter with the frivolity of *Die lustige Witwe*, but it does contain a selection of very fine sentimental and romantic solos and some particularly splendid finales.

Over the years there have been five double-disc recordings of *Das Land des Lächelns*, four in the original German and one in French (*Le Pays de sourire*), and numerous selections in German, French, Italian, Hungarian and also in English, in spite of the fact that the show has never won the success on English-language stages that it has achieved in other countries. Because of its large and impressive made-for-Tauber lead tenor rôle, with its highlight of Lehár's most famous song, 'Dein ist mein ganzes Herz' ('You Are my Heart's Delight' in Harry Graham's familiar English translation), *Das Land des Lächelns* has attracted the attentions of most of the LP age's most prominent opera/operetta tenors, from Nicolai Gedda to Giuseppe di Stefano, Fritz Wunderlich, René Kollo and Covent Garden Rhadames Charles Craig; as a result, many of the recordings contain some particularly fine singing.

Three of the original-language sets are on the EMI label. The earliest features Gedda as Prince Sou-Chong and Elisabeth Schwarzkopf as Lisa, his Viennese wife who has to renounce love when she is unable to adapt to the customs of her husband's homeland. Gedda again starred in the 1967 remake with another out-standing operetta performer in Anneliese Rothenberger, whilst the 1982 version featured Siegfried Jerusalem – Bayreuth's 1988 Siegmund and the Sou-Chong of the Volksoper in 1985 – alongside Helen Donath. It is no coincidence, I am sure, that all three of the female stars here have been happily associated on the operatic stage and disc with *Der Rosenkavalier*.

All three sets are enjoyable. The most recent is the most complete, recorded digitally, and comes in an attractive boxed set curiously featuring a Chinese setting and the two principals in modern evening dress. It is equipped with a German text of the lyrics and the linking dialogue as well as notes in three languages. It also takes great care to translate the credits and, thus, we are treated to the knowledge that 'tenor' is also 'tenor' in German and 'ténor' in French, that bass varies to baß and basse, soprano loses its 'o' in German and by equals von equals de.

The recording itself is less eccentric. Jerusalem is a fine Sou-Chong who tries very hard to build his rôle through the various stages of the drama. It is not easy. In Act 1 the Prince is supposed to be an inscrutable Chinee, letting his love for Lisa show awkwardly and with difficulty, and it is only in the last minutes of the act and, more fully, in the second act, notably in 'Dein ist mein ganzes Herz', that he is strictly able to open up his personality and his voice. Unfortunately, this means that the two big songs of the first act, the pensive 'Immer nur lächeln' and the gently blossoming Chinese love song 'Von Apfelblüten einen Kranz', should really be held right back to a gentle, introverted mezzo piano.

I am sure Tauber didn't hold back at all, but Jerusalem laudably lets fly only in the very highest spots. In consequence, the later acts gain in dramatic strength and his singing in the Act 2 finale is especially impressive. Unfortunately the rest of the recording is less so. Donath's Lisa is uneven, whilst Brigitte Lindner, who has graduated from child soprano to the soubrette rôle of Mi, doesn't sparkle as she might and ought, and sounds as if she's trying to prove she ought to be singing Lisa. Martin Finke is a useful and not too comical tenor Gustl. The orchestra is sometimes rather hefty handed, which only increases the show's tendency to negative emotions, whilst the dialogue varies from the extremely naturalistic to the grossly operatic in its performance.

The two Gedda recordings are rather more enjoyable as all-round efforts. The earlier, made in London under the aegis of Walter Legge, is, in fact, quite splendid – the performances are well paced, beautifully sung and not too badly spoken in the potted dialogue scenes. Gedda is smooth, thoughtful and beautifully restrained where necessary, perhaps a little light in the lowest register and also in his speech, which, thus, lacks the ultimate in authority, but he rises to splendidly graduated heights in the show's biggest moments. Schwarzkopf is quite simply glorious in tone, in phrasing and in interpretation, and her singing of the very Richard-Straussian phrases of 'Ich möcht wieder einmal die Heimat seh'n' is quite magnificent. The future Marschallin is right there. When the pair join in the most powerful moments of conflict of the second-act finale, the result is very special.

The rôle of the little Chinese princess, Mi, is taken with a charming daintiness by Emmy Loose, and her appealing rendering of 'Im Salon zur blau'n Pagode' shows how the soubrette, with lesser opposition than here, can sometimes steal this show from the leading lady. Erich Kunz employs his delightful baritone with lightness and sensitivity as the supportive Gustl. This recording includes the lengthy opening investiture sequence of Act 2 and omits the opening chorus to the final act but, except for the sake of completeness, this is not a great loss and it does not diminish in any way the appeal of a lovely set of records.

The German 1967 Electrola set finds Gedda in maturer, more assured form than on the earlier discs, singing quite superbly, and speaking with much greater authority. With this assurance, however, on the debit side has also come a certain tendency to operettic mannerisms – the note held a little too long, the stagey effect used where previously there was none. These may make for extra applause in the theatre, but on disc they are less attractive and this classiest of tenors has no need of them. But this is a small quibble over a grand performance, one which is well matched by the Lisa of Anneliese Rothenberger. Like Schwarzkopf, Rothenberger rises in brilliance as the emotional tension rises and the best of the music arrives: her 'Heimat' is marvellous – quite different in its tone to that of her predecessor, rich green where Schwarzkopf's is brilliant blue – and the peaks of the second-act finale are superbly mastered.

This Lisa sounds absolutely at home with the music and the rôle, and the same can be said for the crisp, light tenor Gustl of Harry Friedauer. Renate Holm's Mi has little chance to be anything else but cute, however, as the rôle has been incomprehensibly truncated by the cutting of her last-act solo. Surely this brief but essential piece of music was more important to the recording than the heavily sound-effected scene of chatter that opens the recording? Like the earlier set, this one also omits the Act 3 opening.

Ariola's Schock and Schramm set is a rather more stagey one than any of these. It goes in for a brighter sound and a bigger performance without much regard to dramatic context. Both the stars give their usual accomplished operetta performances, but the recording is a rather obvious one musically, every effect being delivered to order over a sometimes rather thumpy orchestra. It's hard actually to fault it, but it simply lacks the class of the Gedda/Schwarzkopf discs. Incidentally, the excerpts record drawn from this set amazingly omits the Act 2 finale – the heart of the show – and cannot thus be recommended except for those who particularly (and only) wish to hear Schock's lusty 'Dein ist mein ganzes Herz'.

Le Pays de sourire, which has proved one of the most successful of all German-language musicals in France, was recorded by Pathé-Marconi in 1957, in its standard French version by André Mauprey and Jean Marietti, with a cast of the regular Pathé stars, headed by baritone Michel Dens and Liliane Berton. Although both give their usual splendid performances, neither is a hundred percent at home in this piece, he finding the uppermost notes of the big tenor rôle a little bit effortful and she lacking the operatic sweep of a Schwarzkopf in the grandest moments of the music. Nevertheless, his 'Je t'ai donné mon coeur' is magnificently rich and easy – the baritone tones and the French lyrics giving it a quite different feeling to the Tauberesque version we all know – and her singing of the score's less powerful moments is quite ideal. Claudine Collart is a perfectly charming Mi, Claude Devos a Gustl with the easiest of voices and the most delightful style and Louis Noguera sings Uncle Chang's one scene more accurately than most. All in all, it is an excellent set, but there seems little reason to invest in a French *Land des Lächelns* when there is such a fine German one to hand.

The highlights of *Das Land des Lächelns* can be tidily included on one record, but several of the many selection discs make odd choices. Some feature the singer playing Mi to the expense of the Lisa, which entails the inclusion of the soubrette's last-act lament. However, since all the well-known pieces – the three big tenor airs, the Tea Duet, the Blue Pagoda, the Mi/Gustl duets and the romantic duet known to the English as 'Love, I Surrender to Your Mystery' – must invariably be included, the finales, which contain such an important part of the dramatic action of the show, do not always get their due. The Ariola disc mentioned above is not the only one culpably to omit the second-act finale.

The 1967 Vienna Volksoper record with di Stefano is one such disc. Soubrette Dagmar Koller is a first-rate Mi who is given good coverage, whilst Valorie Goodall (Lisa) only gets a real chance in 'Ich möcht wieder einmal die Heimat seh'n'. Somewhat harsh and heavy elsewhere, she negotiates the high phrases with surprising success. Di Stefano makes a royally ringing sound, opening up dashingly in all directions in a performance that is a natural for those who love a big sing, but rather less for those who look for a measured acting performance. Since this is only a selection, perhaps there is less ground for complaint on such a score. There is more over the fact that the Act 2 finale is omitted in favour of an overture.

The only English-language disc is that made of the Sadler's Wells Opera production of 1959. It features two excellent performances from Charles Craig, in rich and ravishing voice as Sou-Chong, and from June Bronhill as the most piquant of Mis, but shorn of her last-act lament. Elizabeth Fretwell's Lisa just doesn't go the right way somehow in 'If Yearning Could Carry Me Home Again' (otherwise 'Heimat'), and blurts a bit in other places. I have difficulty in accepting the Christopher Hassall translation used here, particularly when it starts off the song we all know is called 'You Are My Heart's Delight' as 'Love, Let Me Dream Again'. 'You are my heart's delight' may be a pretty silly expression, but we're used to it. All in all, in spite of Craig and Bronhill, this isn't really the ideal record, and it is better to stick to the German-language discs.

By the time that *Das Land des Lächelns* appeared, in its new and successful form, in 1929, Lehár was well and truly back on line. Beginning in 1922 with *Frasquita*, followed by *Paganini* (1925), he had subsequently added *Der Zarewitsch* (1927) and *Friederike* (1928) to his credit, and the new *Schön ist die Welt* (1930) and his final work, *Guiditta* (1934), followed on. These pieces were not in the wonderfully gay, frivolous style of his pre-war works. All, with the semi-exception of the revised *Schön ist die Welt*, leaned sternly away from the happy tones of earlier days towards an atmosphere of an often dark romanticism. From *Paganini* on, they were also written to feature the star tenor Richard Tauber, almost invariably in a situation where his character found his love in Act 1, lost her in time for the second-act finale, and, in spite of things being sorted out between them, had to renounce life-long happiness for reasons of state or money or conscience at the final curtain.

This unhappy ending type of show was considered sophisticated in comparison with the old happy-ending fairy-story operettas of the past, but it became itself no less of a formula in the years between the wars than its jollier elder sister had been in happier days. There was an attempt to add substance to the libretti of these pieces by making the hero an historical character – the violinist Paganini, Goethe and Alexis of Russia all became grist to Lehár's librettists' mills – but the amorous events attached to their characters were nothing more than the standard amours of operetta, bearing little relation to fact, and little was gained from the exercise except a recognizable title.

This series of shows found varying fortunes in Austria and Germany but, with the exception of *Paganini*, which became popular in both France and Italy, failed almost entirely to travel effectively outside the boundaries of the German-speaking world. Inside those boundaries, however, they have become, with different degrees of popularity, part of the standard repertoire and, partly for that reason and partly because of the opportunities they offer for a star tenor to display his wares, they are also well treated on record.

Paganini

Paganini is a rather 'let me show off my voice' operetta. But I suppose if you have a Tauber to write for the temptation is pretty great, and, since one of the results of the exercise was the song 'Gern hab' ich die Frau'n geküsst', better known to the last couple of generations of English tenors as 'Girls Were Made to Love and Kiss', the recipe seems to have, at least in part, worked well. There are several other sizeable tunes – the first-act duo 'Was ich denke' (replugged in the act's finale), the soubret waltz duet 'Mit den Frau'n auf du und du' and the soprano 'Liebe, du Himmel auf Erden' (also replugged) – and a lot of other big music, only rarely broken by a bit of lighter material, so it can all get a bit relentless. But the tenor most certainly has a star rôle.

The show has been put regularly on disc in larger or smaller excerpts and twice in two-record sets, once in German on the EMI label, and once in French on Decca. The two recordings are very different not only in language but in style and in casting. Whereas the 1978 German version features Nicolai Gedda in the Tauber rôle, the 1955 French set allots that part to the baritone Robert Massard.

The German set, with the the the Bavarian Symphony Orchestra and State Opera Chorus conducted by Willi Boskovsky, keeps the dialogue to a minimum, gets in all of the music, and generally gives *Paganini* all possible production values, starting with a first-class star. Nicolai Gedda has the rôle completely under control, from the moment he makes his first entry opening up with all flags flying in the showy, Italianate 'Schönes Italien'. He launches almost immediately after into the huge sing of 'Was ich denke' with his voice ringing richly. After a second helping of the same hectic music in the first-act finale, it is straight into a relentlessly big ensemble ('Wenn keine Liebe wär') and 'Gern hab ich die Frau'n geküsst' at the top of Act 2. Gedda does not flinch, and finds the opportunity to introduce just a few gentler tones between the expansive moments of the pop number of the show. There are two more big duets – bigger for him than for her – before its time for another finale and another act. Most of the mega-music has gone by this time – the second half of the show is rather like a decrescendo, which is not the most satisfying shape dramatically – but since the big guns have been out since page one, it is perhaps as well. It just remains for him to go his way, topping what would have been an affecting finish by the soprano with a blazingly vulgar final flourish, but Gedda does it with such style that you cannot object.

The rôle of Anna Elisa, the Princess who falls in love with the singing violinist, takes up most of the score that is not occupied by him. This, too, is a big-singing part and one that Anneliese Rothenberger takes in her stride. She expends her most lovely tones on her impressive entrance music, 'So ein Mann ist eine Sünde wert', her big second-act waltz and her tacked-in third-act solo, as well as joining Gedda most effectively in their regular duets. Her mid-weight voice runs cleanly on top of all that all-stops-out music rather than sitting on it, and the effect is both ravishing and dramatically much more effective than a bigger and more effortful sound.

Olivera Miljakovic (Bella) and Heinz Zednik (Pimpinelli), as the lightish comedy relief, are good but not terribly light. Bella has, at least, the excuse that she is playing a prima donna rôle, but it takes the isolated jaunty rhythms of 'Einmal möcht' ich was Närrisches tun' to get them sounding sufficiently different to the lead players. If it were a stage performance you'd harbour the unworthy thought that these two were, perhaps, the understudies. He, nevertheless, makes a sharply energetic job of his waltz 'Mit den Frau'n'. The most enjoyably light-hearted bit of music comes, at last and à propos of nothing, at the opening of the third act when an incidental rustic leads off a sort of drinking song. Since that rustic is sung by Benno Kusche, good singing, gusto and all-round pleasure are assured, and, after an hour and a half, it is a relief to hear a male voice which isn't a tenor.

The French recording is not really a success. If *Paganini* is less than wholly satisfying in German, it is even less so in French, and the performance on this set never really takes off. Massard, sacrificed to the French mania for casting Tauber rôles with a baritone, gives his all, but an outstanding baritone can make a very ordinary tenor and his Paganini is just that – ordinary. What are thrilling top notes in his baritone rôles become here slightly nervy preparation for even higher notes, and the tessitura clearly makes the singer uneasy. The voice is very beautiful, and 'J'ai toujours cru qu'un baiser' (as 'Gern hab' ich die Frau'n geküsst' becomes here) is lyrically done, but it all lies wrong for him.

Colette Riedinger as Anna-Elisa is no happier. Often harsh, sometimes insecure, she too is at her best in her big number 'Amour, toi seul sur la terre' ('Liebe, du Himmel auf Erden'), but it is not a pleasant performance. Roméo Carlès overdoes the silly voice again as Pimpinelli, and only Huguette Boulangeot as Bella sounds really comfortable.

Although it also suffers from baritone problems, the French Pathé selection disc of *Paganini*, with Michel Dens and Andrine Forli, is preferable to the complete version, but there are several original-language selections with tenor leading men which make more sense – Peter Anders on RCA, Herbert Ernest Groh or Rudolf Schock on Eurodisc – none of which, however, are in the same class as the display provided by Gedda and Rothenberger.

Der Zarewitsch

Der Zarewitsch is, of all this group of operettas, probably the least vivacious and also the most lacking in dramatic action. Although the show is laced with some traditional bickering from the servant characters, whose three duets provide musically what there is of light relief, the principal story of an apparently homosexual prince who falls in love with a dancing girl dressed as a boy but is then required to give her up when it is time to take the throne, gives birth mainly to a series of alternately gloomy or seriously amorous solos and duets, but to little in the way of theatrical action or of brilliance in its music.

Where *Das Land des Lächelns* had its Chinese element and *Paganini* its violin playing, *Der Zarewitsch* makes a stab at a Russian atmosphere by interpolating some balalaika music and the aforementioned gloom, but otherwise there is little in the way of individual colour in a score that is, like *Paganini*, devoted principally and predictably to the tenor rôle of the tsarevitch and the soprano part of his beloved Sonja. The piece is, of course, much more than competent musically, but it is rather short on memorable tunes – the one that there is, Sonja's introductory wondering 'Einer wird kommen', doesn't belong to the star rôle – and on concerted music, as the rather disappointing finales are largely dialogues between the two lead players. Tauber apparently declared the part of the tsarevitch to be his favourite Lehár rôle and the operetta is continuously produced to this day, so maybe it is more grateful to the singer than it is to the listener.

There are two principal recordings of *Der Zarewitsch* and the earlier of the two, made in 1968 and issued on EMI, certainly gives the piece as splendid a showing as anyone could ask for. Nicolai Gedda again takes the title rôle and sings it with a magnificence that more than justifies the claims of pre-eminence ingenuously made for him in the set's notes. He simply soars through the music with the most beautiful tone, making a thrilling sound on the much solicited top of the voice, and almost succeeds in making a convincing character in both song and speech of this rather uninteresting hero. He is splendidly partnered by Rita Streich, who displays an ideal mixture of vocal warmth and lightness as his Sonja, whilst the little prince of the comic tenors, Harry Friedauer, makes much of the incidental comedy rôle and its duets. In an interesting piece of casting, Hans Söhnker, who had played the tsarevitch in a 1933 film version, appears in the non-singing rôle of the Grand Duke who is charged with arousing the heir to the throne's interest in women.

The musical score, finely played by the Symphonie Orchester Graunke under Willy Mattes, is linked with a fairish text (some rather odd progressions notwithstanding), mostly spoken with enthusiasm, and the boxed set comes with substantial notes but no text. Perhaps this is just as well, as the English translation of the German notes, as so frequently with EMI notes, is often unintentionally hilarious. Surely a firm of this importance, which takes such trouble with its packaging, can spare a few pennies for a proper translator!

Trimmings apart, this is a fine recording and indubitably superior to the more recent version on Ariola-Eurodisc. This latter set, accompanied by the Müncher Rundfunkorchester under Heinz Wallberg, was made in 1980 with René Kollo and Lucia Popp as its leading players. Kollo tries really hard to put some energy and passion into his grey rôle, sometimes at the expense of a wholly pleasant sound, and Popp makes a lovely, thoughtful job of her music in spite of a tendency to a wide wave in the upper register, but the result is ultimately not comparable with the earlier set. Incidentally, this recording has seen fit to interpolate two numbers from Lehár's *Wo die Lerche singt* for the benefit of Ivan Rebroff as the Grand Duke. This has probably been done in a not unreasonable attempt to get some liveliness into the piece, but sadly the songs just sound out of place and have the unhappy effect of turning the man who should, in this type of operetta, be the most distinguished and authoritarian character about, into a foolish buffo. The accompanying leaflet clearly identifies the interpolations, and also offers a long historical and analytical piece on Lehár and the show which insists on going on at length on the real-life Alexei and his alleged relevance to the piece.

There have been a fair number of *Zarewitsch* selection discs, including a Telefunken one with Guiseppe di Stefano and Dagmar Koller, an elderly Decca/London version with Helge Roswaenge and Lisa Della Casa, and others with Wieslaw Ochmann and Teresa Stratas (Philips), Josef Traxel and Sonja Schöner (Eurodisc), Werner Hollweg and Popp (Philips) and Schock and Renate Holm (Eurodisc), as well as a shorter one on EMI with Fritz Wunderlich and Melitta Muszely (backed with *Das Land des Lächelns*) and a smattering in Italian on EDM (backed with *Clo-Clo*), but nothing in English.

On the London version, Roswaenge's strong masculine voice and Della Casa's almost tentative, liquid tones make an odd pairing in an almost medleyed selection, complete with twanging balalaikas, which has in any case a rather awkward old sound to it. The later Eurodisc recording, the only other of these I have heard, has the benefit of a perfectly splendid Sonja in a top-form Renate Holm. Her 'Einer wird kommen' is quite glorious and, although she is deprived of her second solo, her duets and finales with Rudolf Schock (all three finales are included) are splendid. Schock is in good form as the Zarewitsch, secure at the top and with only a rare mannerism, and Karl-Ernst Mecker and Helga Wisniewska are a particularly strong-singing but still jaunty light comedy pair. This disc goes a good way to giving this less obviously attractive Lehár work that much more 'popular' feel.

Friederike

With *Friederike*, Lehár took a semi-pause in his series of dark-coloured, passionate operettas to compose a vehicle for Tauber that took him neither to the Orient nor to the steppes of Russia but to the unexotic Alsacian countryside in a piece he described as a *Singspiel*. The comparative simplicity of the work did not take it that far, but there was no doubt that the colourings of *Friederike* were less empurpled than those of its recent predecessors. But there was still Tauber, and Tauber meant ringing tenor songs, and there was still the fashion, and the fashion meant an unhappy ending, although at least in this work no one got thoroughly passionate until nearly the end of the first act, nor thoroughly miserable until well on in the second. They also, perhaps as a result, had fewer big melodies to sing, and 'O Mädchen, mein Mädchen', duly reprised, was the only real bon-bon to come out of the score.

For many years *Friederike* existed on disc only in excerpts covering one side of a record, as on Ariola-Eurodisc (backed with *Schön ist die Welt*) and Telefunken (backed with *Schwarzwaldmädel*) or in Italian on Fonit-Cetra (backed with *Die Bajadere*), in even briefer selectons on EP, or simply as one number on a recital disc (inevitably the show's Tauber hit song 'O Mädchen, mein Mädchen'). In 1981 EMI amended that situation by putting out a full two-record set. It is a fair set rather than a really good one.

Things start well, with the Munich Radio Orchestra under Heinz Wallberg playing sweetly through an overture that starts with some charming flute music and develops to its climax more in the manner of Respighi than of Verdi. Two delightful actors playing the heroine's parents begin the play, but when the principal singers join in things tie up somewhat, for they are clearly less than happy with the gentle musical strains of the opening scenes. Helen Donath, in the title rôle, acts with sincerity and speaks and sings with clarity, but the operatic tremors in her voice fit the material ill – a much simpler voice or production is needed. Gabriele Fuchs (Salomea) is rather inclined the same way, and Adolf Dallapozza (Goethe) is simply uncomfortable, even unsteady and verging on the out-of-tune. Only Martin Finke (Lenz), who makes a delightful job of the pretty song about his little lamb, is relaxed, sweet-toned and happy in his singing.

Matters improve later on, particularly where the ladies are concerned. Fuchs warms up nicely for her grand second-act duet ('Elsässer Kind') with Finke, and Donath gets better and better the more miserable Friederike becomes, making a lovely 'unwoofy' job of her 'Warum hast du mich wachgeküsst?'. Dallapozza, however, continues to blow hot and cold and, although he does some nice things, never really settles into the rôle or its music in the way that a Gedda could be counted on to do. Since he is the lynchpin of the whole affair and has almost all of the show's big moments, the set has to be less than top notch. It is, however, for now, and probably for a long time, the only full *Friederike* around, so if it is *Friederike* you want then this must be for you.

Giuditta

Giuditta is the biggest sing of all Lehár's big-sing operettas. The rôles of the wayward Giuditta and Ottavio (the officer with whom she runs away to a life of passion and, finally, disillusion), created by Jarmila Novotna and Tauber, verge on the operatic in their scope. Quite why it is listed as a 'Komödie musikalische' I cannot imagine, as its story is unabashedly tragic and the bulk of its music enormously powerful and dramatic. This time it is actually the soprano who has the bon-bons of the piece, bon-bons which have become favourites with operatic singers looking for 'lighter' work, or with operetta sopranos yearning towards grander things. The provocative waltz song 'Meine Lippen so heissen sie küsst' is the most generally popular number, but 'In einem Meer von Liebe', with its lush sensuality, and the dramatic 'In die Stirne fällt die Locke' are both plum pieces. The tenor's biggest opportunity comes right at the beginning with the jubilant (and high) 'Freunde, das Leben ist lebenswert'.

Giuditta has been given two full-scale recordings, one by Decca and the other by EMI, but although the favourite songs have been often picked out for recital recordings, only Ariola-Eurodisc, who pair Rudolf Schock with Sylvia Geszty, have turned out a one-disc Giuditta, alongside a small group of smaller selections which include one in Hungarian.

Casting Giuditta is a tough proposition. There are few Novotnas and few Taubers around in a generation, and the two leading rôles are real brutes, making demands on the voices and acting abilities of their interpreters more cruel than many of the most substantial operas. Somewhere, I suppose, there must be absolutely the right performers for these parts, but I haven't heard them yet. The Decca recording has Hilde Güden as the tempestuous Giuditta, a piece of casting which, given the lady's supreme skill as a beautifully creamy-voiced vocalist, seems unlikely, and Waldemar Kmentt as Ottavio. Quite how they cope I do not know as this recording seems to have vanished these days, leaving EMI's 1985 set as the only readily available one.

EMI cast Nicolai Gedda as Ottavio and this seems another odd idea. The demands of the rôle would seem to need a very fresh, young, free voice and there is no denying that Gedda is not, here, quite the Gedda of yesteryear. But although the smooth, clear quality of the voice and apparently its capacity for the easy degrees of light and shade seem to have suffered a bit, he still has more *métier* than any other half dozen tenors, and he makes his way through Ottavio without accident and with many fine moments.

The rôle of Ottavio doesn't actually give too many opportunities for light and shade. He comes steaming on to the scene with the bullocking opening of 'Freunde! Das Leben ist lebenswert!' and within minutes is powering into a long and trumpetingly dramatic duet with Giuditta which seems to owe something to Richard Strauss or even to Wagner. Even when something a little more reflective, like the soliloquy 'Du Bist meine Sonne', comes along, it spreads vocal difficulties everywhere (Gedda is obliged to go into falsetto in one high soft spot) and ends up with yet another upper-register blast with all stops out. He spends practically the entire operetta being really miserable and frustrated and has regular, large songs in which to express his misery and frustration with all the power in a tenor's lungs, and there is not much a tenor can do here other than open his lungs. Gedda, of course, has vast lungs and knows what to do with them.

Edda Moser is the Giuditta on this set. My record players just don't seem to be able to take Miss Moser's voice. She comes over here much more dramatically convincingly than she did as the Merry Widow and the vibrato does not seem to be nearly so much in evidence, but her extremely powerful voice goes through some excruciatingly ugly tone colours as she steams up, without ever blenching or faltering, to the repeated dramatic heights of the rôle. When she is in her middle register and not steaming, things get very much easier to listen to, but it is just not the voice for me.

Lehár took a little of the sting off the relentless driving passions and music of the lead couple and their romance by introducing a soubret couple alongside them. Even their story is a sad little one of failure, but they provide some gentle and even sweet moments of nice, lightly-sung counterpoint to the main story, before they are swept off the stage. They are called Antonio and Anita, and they are played to perfection here by Martin Finke and Brigitte Lindner, whose deft, charming singing and acting is a veritable oasis in the storms of voluminous lust.

A selection from *Giuditta*, without dialogue, can be a pretty relentless thing – all those chunks of vast singing, end to end. Yet somehow the Ariola disc doesn't come out like that. It is, in fact, a distinctly different *Giuditta* from the one you hear on the full set, and the reason for that can be summed up in one name: Rudolf Schock.

The way this selection is set out, this is a recording of *Ottavio*, and it lays its hands open in fifteen seconds flat – the time it takes the needle to reach the first track and for you to be knocked out of your chair by the first phrase of Schock's trumpeting 'Freunde! Das Leben ist lebenswert!'. Before long you know you are not in the dark-coloured tragic tale you expected; you are in Mario Lanza-land. It isn't serious; it is just all spotlights and popular musical theatre, right down to the last little breaks in the voice. And is it an unworthy suspicion that his partner has been recorded down a touch in their duets?

There is a lot of Ottavio on this record, but it is clearly a rôle Schock enjoys and he sings it with spirit and steady top notes. With the chances she is given, however (she is deprived of 'In die Stirne fällt die Locke'), his Giuditta (Sylvia Geszty) more than holds her own. In fact she takes the rôle quite superbly. She never sits heftily on the music, but sings it with a very attractive variety of tone and volume and wonderfully easy high notes, making her Giuditta a very womanly character and not a two-dimensional operatic vamp. From the picture on the sleeve she clearly had the physical appearance to fit the rôle as well – it would have been worth seeing.

Ferry Gruber and Dorothea Chryst complete the solo team. They make their usual impeccable job of the two lighter duets, with him sounding all of eighteen (which he was certainly not). Add to all this a fine, clean recorded sound, some unturgid orchestral playing and a competent chorus, and the result is a very pleasant record – one which I find, all in all, more enjoyable to listen to than the more seriously conceived full set.

The four-number Hungarian representation of *Giuditta* (backed with Kálmán's *Marica grófno*) has been recorded by Gyözo Leblanc and Katalin Pitti, two performers with an infinity of Hungarian passion and style and strong, young voices. She tackles 'In einem Meer von Liebe' and 'Meine Lippen sie küssen so heiss' with a warm-blooded zest, and he gives every ounce of voice and soul to both solo and duet, in a pair of performances which are very appealing in this material.

Frasquita

The only sizeable recordings of *Frasquita* of which I know are single-disc selections in French and almost impossible to find nowadays, so it's scarcely a case of making a choice. If you can get any of them, you're lucky. One is a Véga issue featuring Maria Murano, Nicole Broissin and André Dassary, the other, on Decca, with Kleuza de Pennafort and Bernard Alvi, and both help to give evidence that the music of *Frasquita* includes more attractive pieces than just the one well-known number 'Hab' ein blaues Himmelbett'.

It is more the fault of Lehár and his librettists than of Mlle de Pennafort that her Frasquita often sounds like a poor man's Carmen, but when she and her authors take her hand off her hip and she relaxes a bit into duet with Alvi, the result is very pleasant. Although the lady has the title rôle in this show, the gentleman (modelled on the Tauber voice) has the big sing. Alvi thankfully doesn't attempt to give his music that big sing, and his free French tenor voice curls very attractively around music written for a very different kind of singer. Probably none of this recording sounds much like what Lehár intended, but then again the French première was, for some reason, played by opera star Conchita Supervia at the Opéra-Comique, so *Frasquita* has been subjected to some widely disparate styles of performance. Supervia's performance has also survived (if survived is the world for an unfindable record) transferred to LP on the Pacific label.

The Véga recording, which assures us that it is a *version abrégée*, gets a remarkable number of the show's songs – perhaps *abrégée*!? – very well performed onto two very full sides. Maria Murano, in spite of the insistent castanets, does not do a stage gipsy display, but sings her songs with a strong warm soprano and not too much passion, and Dassary shows in a very pleasant performance how much easier it is to sing Lehár's tenor music with a middle-sized voice. As a result the first-act finale sounds less like the end of *Carmen* and more like operetta. Nicole Broissin, Aimé Doniat and Gaston Rey perform the lighter material brightly. The only problem with this recording is that is sounds rather older than it can possibly be. Given the presence of Mlle Broissin, who has only just graduated to playing *Hello, Dolly!*, it has to belong in the 1960s – yet it sounds a bit like a 1940s transfer. Maybe my copy just knows that it is a rarity and is behaving as such.

For the record, Romana Righetti and Carlo Pierangeli supply half a disc's worth of *Frasquita* in Italian on the EDM series.

Oscar Straus

Following the successes of *Ein Walzertraum* and *Der tapfere Soldat*, Oscar Straus became international: in the years preceding and following the war he lived in Berlin, Paris and Hollywood and wrote for the British and French stages as well as for German-speaking audiences. He did not again find the success of his two most famous pieces, but *Der letzte Walzer* (1920), *Teresina* (1925), Sacha Guitry's *Mariette* (1929), and *Eine Frau, die weiss was sie will* (1932) were notable pieces, and his musical collage of music by Josef and Johann Strauss, topped off by an actful of his own very best melodies, as the score for the glorious *Drei Walzer* (1935) was a triumphant exercise, today unaccountably overlooked everywhere except in France.

Der letzte Walzer

Der letzte Walzer is the only one of Straus's own late pieces to have been recorded, and it has been done only once, on a now rather rare 1952 Remington disc issued on Period and on Vogue. Why this is I can't imagine. As a piece of gloriously Viennese post-war musical theatre it is streets ahead of some of the contemporary and later works that have been given regular recordings. In spite of its threatening story, it mixes gaiety and the most un-gloomy of dramatic moments in a perfect whirl of waltzing melody, rising to splendid heights in the magnificently rhythmic 'Tanze, Vera Lisaweta' and the swaying, bursting waltz of 'Das ist die letzte Walzer', and glittering away into classic fun with its light comedy numbers, headed by the delicious little dimple song 'Du hast zwei Grübchen' and the dancing music for the heroine's trio of sisters and their admirer.

The recording itself is a splendid one. It is billed as being conducted by Straus himself, then eighty-two years old, but I am told that the composer 'conducted' sitting in an armchair with a cigar whilst Max Schönherr did the work on the rostrum. Whatever the facts, the result is first rate, with the Tonkunstlorchester and chorus giving impeccable support to a very fine set of soloists, headed by Margit Opawsky (Vera Lisaweta) and Rudolf Christ (Dmitri). Opawsky, in the vast rôle written for Fritzi Massary, performs with a superb dash and spirit – her attacking 'Tanze, Vera Lisaweta' is a triumph – and a warm, even soprano that soars through the most demanding moments of the very demanding waltz duets and finales without the slightest blench or slip. She gets power and personality into this dramatic rôle and into the music, whether she is waltzing along in the most Viennese way (occasionally with a touch of the Hollywood in the orchestra), jubilating over her condemned lover's escape to the rhythms of what sounds like a Polish csárdás, or flirting determinedly to gain his pardon with a Frenchified 'ooh-la-la'. It is an outstanding performance.

Christ, as her partner, has a less expansive rôle, but there is still a good deal of it, and he has plenty of opportunity to display his clear, strong tenor in the repeated above-the-stave sections in the duets and finales as well as in one big solo number. Kurt Preger takes the light comedy rôle of Ippolith and makes a simply charming job of his dimple song and of the giggling polka 'O kommt, o kommt', which he shares with the three girls and a piccolo obbligato, whilst the rest of the cast, with very little to do, all do it more than satisfactorily.

The record contains almost the whole of the show's score – just the odd chorus and one of the comedy numbers are missing – and even the entr'acte and the balalaika opening to the second-act finale are included. Unfortunately, someone has seen fit to arrange the numbers in an eccentric order, beginning with the first two numbers of Act 2 before going into a mixture of Act 1 and Act 2, which seems to have no rhyme nor reason. It is a taping job again to sort them out. This little oddity does no harm, however, to a record that is a real beauty. If you ever see it, grab it. Yes, it is very hard to find, but maybe some day someone will dig up those master tapes and re-release it – you never know your luck.

Neither *Teresina* nor *Eine Frau* has been systematically recorded – merely the odd piece here and there, including transferred recordings of both original star Fritzi Massary and London's Alice Delysia singing numbers from *Eine Frau*, notably the famous 'Jede Frau hat irgendeine Sehnsucht' ('Every Woman Thinks she Wants to Wander'). *Mariette*'s original star, Yvonne Printemps, also recorded just a little of the material Straus wrote for her, and a seven and a half minute seduction scene played with Sacha Guitry, including the charmingly amusing Valse Improvisée, has been reissued on Pathé Marconi's 'Les Triomphes d'Yvonne Printemps'. This is a splendid compilation of archive recordings on which the star performs show music not only by Straus but by Messager, Hahn, Yvain and even a really first-class and personal comedienne's version of Offenbach's 'Dites-lui' from *La Grande-Duchesse de Gérolstein*. What a shame she didn't record the whole rôle.

Drei Walzer

It was Yvonne Printemps whose performance in the star rôle of *Drei Walzer* was largely responsible for turning Straus's piece from just another fine show into an enduring French hit. The show was rewritten around her, the leading man's rôle altered to suit her non-singing partner, Pierre Fresnay, and the piece turned much more into something like the Sacha Guitry 'plays with songs for Yvonne', such as *Mariette*, in which she had been so very successful. Composers of the calibre of Messager and Hahn had written scores for Mlle Printemps, but nothing like the sparkling series of waltzes – half a dozen show-stoppers all to herself – which Straus concocted from the works of the Strauss family – 'C'est la saison d'amour' and 'Te souvient-il?' from father Josef, the beautiful 'Je t'aime' and the sparkling 'Je t'aime, O Paris' from Johann – and, in the last act, brewed freshly from his own resources, the valse lente 'C'est le destin, peut-être' and the bluesy 'Je ne suis pas ce que l'on pense'. Just to give someone else one good song to sing, the waltz 'Comme autrefois' was included for René Dary in the show's third rôle.

Mlle Printemps recorded all six of her songs (some with orchestra, some with only piano accompaniment) and they were reissued on LP by EMI-Pathé, taking up one side of a disc that was completed by her celebrated 'Pot-pourri d'Alain Gerbault', some pieces by Lully which she had sung on stage in *Jean de la Fontaine*, 'Dites-lui', and 'Plaisir d'amour'. It is an adorable recording of a piquant personality, a very pretty and individual light soprano and some beautiful music.

As the French *Les Trois Valses* prospered, was regularly revived and even filmed, it was also recorded three times: on Decca with Suzy Delair, on EMI-Pathé with Mathé Altéry and, more briefly, also on Decca, with Colette Riedinger. Whereas Mlle Printemps's records take in only her own numbers, the two first of these later recordings both cover the show more generally, although each includes slightly different portions. The Pathé disc uses the opening theatre scene (a fine melody by *père* Strauss), a couple of little ensemble pieces, the comical Quattuor polyglotte and the incidental Duo de la synchronisation, whilst the Decca record, which seems to be taken from a complete set I would dearly love to get my hands on, orients itself more towards the story of the piece and the leading man's contribution, and takes in several spoken scenes and the drama of the second-act finale.

Both these are fine recordings. The star music of the Pathé version, conducted with a generously indulgent hand by Frank Pourcel, is beautifully sung by the young Mathé Altéry with a pure, natural and unmannered soprano which floats through the waltzing melodies with a simple grace that is most attractive. The more incisive comedic glitter of Printemps is, perhaps, lacking from the point of view of performance, but the singing is lovely. The few incidental lines of the leading man's rôle, originally spoken by Fresnay, are tactfully sung here by Altéry's real-life father, formerly a well-known light opera tenor, whilst Jacques Pruvost, with the genial 'Comme autrefois', and Pierre Germain perform the crumbs of score left to them with warmth.

Richard Blaireau lingers less over the music than Pourcel on the Decca recording, which is a much more characterful one without, for all that, suffering in the singing department. Suzy Delair has a fine, fresh soprano and a bright, comic actress's delivery and, if in her hands the three ladies have a rather more poised and sophisticated sound to them than those of the piquant Printemps or the unaffected Altéry, there is no reason why that shouldn't be acceptable. She sings the songs rather than the music, Strauss, Strauss and Straus or no, and she is never intimidated by these famous names into sacrificing all to a vocal line. Jean Desailly acts convincingly as the three lovers and the supporting cast are particularly good – Claude Daltys full of character as the old dresser (Couplets de l'habilleuse), Robert Pisani performing 'Comme autrefois' touchingly as the eighty-year-old of the play and joining with Robert Piquet in the lilting Duo des deux Brunner, and a notable list of performers including René Lenoty, Dominique Tirmont, Pierjac and the imposing Mary Marquet making a meal of the comical family reunion of horror-struck aristocrats who have learnt that their youngest member wishes to marry a *danseuse*.

It is difficult to choose between these two. There is more of the music on the Pathé disc and Altéry is really very attractive, but the Decca version gives a much more dramatic idea of the piece, treating it almost like a *comédie aux ariettes*. Having enjoyed the film enormously, I find the speech-and-song construction of the Decca recording brings back to my eye the marvellous Parisian scenes of three epochs painted there by Ludwig Berger, but I suppose that is rather like using a cast recording as a souvenir. There is probably going to be more general enjoyment in the more straightforwardly musical composition of the Pathé version – unless, that is, you can find that elusive complete set.

Emmerich Kálmán

Gräfin Mariza

After the Great War, Emmerich Kálmán continued, on the *élan* of *Die Csárdásfürstin*, to turn out more fine operettas. *Gräfin Mariza* (1924) has been the most internationally successful of these, but *Das Hollandweibchen* (1920), *Die Bajadere* (1921), *Die Zirkusprinzessin* (1926) and *Das Veilchen vom Montmartre* (1930) all found acceptance and popularity in their homeland and/or abroad.

Gräfin Mariza is Kálmán at his most blatantly and beautifully Hungarian. After moving purposely away from his roots with pieces with Viennese, Dutch, French and even Indian flavours, he returned to his native country and its rhythms and melodies to produce what is perhaps his most fulsomely rich score. Its numbers range from the leading lady's celebrated csárdás 'Höre ich Zigeunergeigen' to the vast tenor *valse lente* 'Grüss mir die süssen, die reizende Frauen', the famous gipsy song 'Komm' Zigán!' and, in a completely different mood, the comical, loping 'Komm mit nach Varasdin' (reminiscent of the best of Jacobi's comedy songs), the sweet, tender 'Schwesterlein, Schwesterlein' and some lively, dancing ensembles.

Selections from the operetta have been much more freely recorded than in the case of *Die Csárdásfürstin*, and there have been at least nine full-disc recordings put out from Eurodisc (Grobe/Schöner and Schock/Schramm), RCA (Wunderlich/Görner), RCA/Telefunken (Minich/Németh), Philips (Kollo/Házy), Decca (Glawitsch/Hoffmann), Karussell (Alexander/Hallstein), Concert Hall (Rysanek/Christ) and CBS (Loor/Strohbauer), as well as others in English, Hungarian and Italian. The operetta has also been put down on two double-disc sets, one, impossible to find, taken from a Leipzig radio broadcast performance of the 1960s, featuring Martin Ritzmann and Rita Zorn, and the other, a companion to the *Csárdásfürstin* recording in the EMI series, with Nicolai Gedda and Anneliese Rothenberger.

This last is, clearly, the most substantial representation of the show available, and it matches its *Csárdásfürstin* companion in brilliance of performance and production. Willy Mattes and the Symphonie-Orchester Graunke have some marvellous, swinging melodies and orchestrations to get their batons and bows into and they take advantage of every csárdás and waltz to fling themselves into the lilt of a score which is played here almost in whole. Only the little gipsy girls' chorus from the first act, the opening chorus from Act 2 and the first little piece of Act 3 have been, for some reason, omitted.

Anneliese Rothenberger, in the title rôle, is quite magnificent. She bats not an eyelash as she soars with heartfelt passion and the warmest and most beautifully even-toned voice into her demanding entrance number, taking up the csárdás rhythms as if Budapest-born. From this magnificent start she soars on, making Countess Mariza into a charming, warm-hearted woman and a real singing sensation.

Gedda gives his everything to the rôle of Count Tassilo, the impoverished nobleman whose aspirations to the love of the woman for whom he now works is requited, after many a storm, by the final curtain. He takes in the whole gamut before the first act is over, as he swings superbly through his first big waltz song, dreaming of happier days amongst the girls of Vienna, turns sweet and softer tones on his duet with his young sister, and flings all the extravagance of a Schock into his tipsy 'graunch-and-grind' rendition of 'Komm, Zigán!' before bringing it back in *sotto voce*, and to great effect, for the finale.

The plot moves on, and in the second act the two stars launch into duet with the driving waltz 'Einmal möcht ich wieder tanzen' and again, in more intimately gentle tones, with their confession of love 'Sag ja, mein Lieb, sag ja', confirming every ounce of the vocal made-for-each-otherness (in Kálmán, at least) that was so evident in their *Csárdásfürstin*.

The secondary rôles are again beautifully cast, with Willi Brokmeier making a marvellous job of the provincial Baron Zsupán and his splendidly jaunty 'Komm mit nach Varasdin', Olivera Miljakovic attractively straightforward and much more lively this time round as the hero's sister, and Kurt Böhme the icing on a very tasty cake as the unfortunately very little heard Popolescu. Edda Moser takes the small rôle of the young gipsy girl and sings her introductory solo with such ravishing tone that I can scarcely believe it is the same artist who tackled *Giuditta* and *Die lustige Witwe*.

Of the *Gräfin Mariza* selections that have passed my way, the Telefunken one attracts interest as it includes one of the pieces (the sweetly sung children's chorus) omitted on the EMI set. Of course, it leaves off other things and, although the whole of Act 1 is there, with its seven minutes plus of finale, along with the four duets and the finale from Act 2, it completely omits Act 3; in its English RCA pressing it even gives an altered two-act synopsis of the story which rounds off the plot and score! Peter Minich is a very different Tassilo to Gedda, singing his first waltz with rueful reflection and his tipsy song with clean tone and unexaggerated style, and Marika Németh is a surpringly soubrette-like Mariza, who gets more dance than fire from her csárdás but who clips out a delicious 'Komm mit nach Varadim' with a super Zsupán (Herbert Prikopa). This is a light-weight *Mariza*, more fun than thrills.

Concert Hall gives a very small selection – just seven tracks from Act 1 and the two Mariza/Tassilo Act 2 duets – in a more than reasonable production in which Rudolf Christ's very relaxed, almost casual, Tassilo sounds no match for Lotte Rysanek as a spirited and strong-voiced Mariza. She makes more than a fair fistful of her csárdás, but she also borrows Manja's opening number and the synopsis tries to justify this ridiculous robbery. Else Liebesberg and Prikopa are such an attractive number-two pair that it is sad to have none of their numbers together in this mini-*Mariza*.

The elderly Decca recording, which runs all the numbers together in one long medley, has an apparently fine leading pair in Rupert Glawitsch and Lore Hoffmann, but suffers very much from its age – on the copy that I have, at least. It is more respectable, however, than Karusell's disc, which is an odd affair, with curious 1968 arrangements for what doesn't sound like a very 'grossen Operetten-Orchester' and a pleasant group of singers who seem to think they've wandered in from *Die Blume von Hawaii* or *Glückliche Reise*. It is a sort of swung *Gräfin Mariza* for a world which needs such a thing.

Gräfin Mariza seems to have suffered from some strange hands, and I am sure there is better to found amongst the Eurodisc, RCA, Philips or CBS examples of the show than in these mini or medley or swung versions.

Italy's *Contessa Mariza* is a little narrated medleyfied affair with a lusty Italianate Tassilo (Franco Artioli) and middleweight Mariza (Romana Righetti), whilst the one English *Countess Maritza* from the New Sadlers Wells company makes yet another variation to the plot and supplies a new translation (by Nigel Douglas), thirteen numbers and an overture. It also has some very nice voices but a disappointing absence of atmosphere or feeling until Marilyn Hill Smith's Maritza arrives, well after half the first side is over. Even then it is inclined to trudge dreadfully in a performance that is sometimes so slowly and passionlessly conducted as to be infuriating.

The very short 1986 Hungarian selection of four numbers and an overture (backed with *Giuditta*) with Katalin Pitti and Gyözo Leblanc, not unexpectedly, has all the Magyar passion which Britain lacks and some marvellous orchestral playing (ditto) from the Hungarian Radio and Television Symphony Orchestra. Both soloists dash into the music of *Marica grófno* with the sort of energy and style that makes it leap off the disc and, even if they are not Gedda and Rothenberger, I'd rather listen to them in this material than some of the other perhaps more technically impressive vocalists.

Amongst the Kálmán material issued, reissued and re-reissued over recent years, shorter selections and numbers from the successful (and less successful) operettas of his post-war years have appeared tied in with usually larger chunks of his two favourite pieces. There is a 'Das schönste von Emmerich Kálmán' two-disc set, which includes highlights from *Die Zirkusprinzessin* and isolated numbers from both *Bajadere* and *Das Veilchen vom Montmartre*, another, called 'Das goldene Emmerich Kálmán', which gets in a couple of pieces of *Hollandweibchen* and *Bajadere* plus a number from the posthumous *Arizona Lady*, whilst the four-record set issued to mark what would have been the composer's 100th birthday in 1982 does even better, gathering together a mixture of archive material – Fritzi Massary, Gitta Alpar, Tauber and Girardi himself included – and more recent recordings to such effect that a dozen Kálmán shows are represented – some, like *Das Veilchen vom Montmartre* and the late and not so great *Die Herzogin von Chicago* and *Kaiserin Josephine*, by several excerpts. An interesting item, but strictly for real (and rich) fans.

As far as recordings devoted particularly to one operetta are concerned, however, Kálmán's other works have done rather less well. Only *Die Zirkusprinzessin*, issued in a one-record selection on Ariola-Eurodisc, has been given a significant recording in the original language. For *Die Bajadere* it is necessary to seek out Hungarian or Italian versions for a selection, and the only full-sized recording that exists – on two discs – is, like the same scale version of *Das Veilchen*, in Russian on the Melodiya label.

Die Zirkusprinzessin

The *Zirkusprinzessin* recording has Rudolf Schock as the mysterious Mister X, a disinherited aristocrat performing in circus incognito, and Margit Schramm as the Princess who has inadvertantly caused his downfall. Schock, always happiest in the most flamboyant rôles, flings himself into this large part with his usual crowd-pleasing style, Miss Schramm is in fine voice, and the two of them join together very pleasingly in their duets – the waltzing 'Leise schwebt das Glück vorüber', the intermittently gentle 'Ich und du, du und ich', and the nicely light 'My Darling, My Darling'.

Miss Schramm is right on form in her fine entrance solo 'Was in der Welt geschieht', and Schock performs the attractive chin-up number 'Wer wird denn gleich weinen, mein Kind', the heroic Hussar March, the showy circus music of the first-act finale and the dramatic declarations of the second with energetic style. He does, however, make a bit of a major mouthful of the show's most popular number, 'Zwei Märchenaugen', graunching and grinding his way with all stops right out through what is really only a jolly hymn to women and wine.

The supporting cast are fine, with the light comedy pair (Ferry Gruber and Guggi Löwinger), as a contrast to the lashings of romantic singing going on elsewhere, giving first-rate performances of their two duets. The splendidly silly little 'Liese, Liese, komm mit mir auf die Wiese' is salutorily deflating to any pompousness in the big love story. Unfortunately, the soubrette misses her main opportunity, as the entire third act is ignored on this record.

Qualiton have also issued a full-disc selection of *Cirkushercegnö*, sung in Hungarian, which includes a number of differences in its content. It is a capable record, with Erzsébet Házy in fiery form as Fedora, Tibor Udvardy rather steadier and less chesty than is often his case as Mister X, and a rather surprisingly muted Róbert Rátonyi paired with a bright and typically Hungarian soubrette, Valéria Koltai, in the light comedy material, but the show is not as energetically and showily served here as it is on the Ariola disc. Udvardy takes all the notes but makes very little of 'Máma itt, holnap ott' ('Zwei Märchenaugen') compared with the multi-coloured performance of Schock; the comedy pair, for all their attractions, perhaps hampered by an unimaginative orchestra, don't really get their numbers (two of which are puzzlingly not those on the other record) bouncing along; and although Hazy gives a really vibrant, positive performance, and orchestra and chorus get going spiritedly in the second-act opening, the best bits don't add up to as good a total as that achieved by the best bits of the alternative disc.

Die Zirkusprinzessin is an attractive operetta, trying just a little too hard to give its tenor, in particular, opportunities for the Tauberesque effusions popularized in *Paganini*. But if it is not quite up to the best of Kálmán's scores, it still has enough enjoyable parts to make up a good selection record, and most of them are to be found on the Ariola disc.

Die Bajadere

There is altogether better stuff, however, to be found in *Die Bajadere*. The show has probably survived less vigorously in the theatre than *Die Zirkusprinzessin* because it does not have the opportunities for spectacle and circus acts that the later piece presents, but musically and, thus, as a recording prospect it is superior.

The romantic and comic elements are well balanced. The comedy characters are amusing and their songs lively, rhythmic and tuneful, and the romantic pair have some of Kálmán's most attractive music to sing. The tenor romance 'O Bajadere' is liltingly lovely and surprisingly low set – no big showy high notes here – and the soprano declaring herself modestly 'Sterne der Bühne' (star of the stage) does so with lightsome waltzing ease. That is not to say that there are no big sentimental musical moments, but when the climactic duet 'Lotusblume, ich liebe dich' does come, it is all the more effective for being a real climax. Amongst the half-dozen comic numbers appear a particularly jolly foxtrot ('Der kleine Tanzkavalier') and a shimmy ('Fräulein, bitte, woll'n sie Shimmy tanzen').

The principal Qualiton recording of this piece is, unfortunately, not one of their very best. All the important parts of the score are there, and they get a fair representation, but the singing is not quite good enough for you to sit back and go 'aaah' with pleasure, as you should with this score. The ladies, the usually reliable Qualiton regulars Marika Németh and Anna Zentay, are both afflicted intermittently with the wobbles, and the principal tenor, Tibor Udvardy, sounds too often as if he is fighting a not very successful battle with the remnants of a voice. His 'O, Bajadere' is pretty uncomfortable, and he must be crazy to interpolate an extra high note when he can barely make the ones a third lower. The best singing comes from the two comic men, which is not the best recommendation in a score which has such attractive lyric music.

The double-disc Russian recording is an altogether superior proposition. It is not officially 'complete': two and a half of the seven and a half comedy numbers (one of which is on the other recording) are missing, and there are slimmings and cuts in the lyric parts, some of which are standard, others puzzling. It contains the sizeable second-act finale (which is not on the Hungarian disc) and apparently uses the big second-act duet 'Du, du, du' as a first-act finale – but on the whole this is musically a fair and nearly full representation of *Die Bajadere*.

Its other advantage over the Hungarian disc is that it is far better played and sung. The orchestra rips into the lush bits of the music in the most lavishly fulsome but definitely classy way and also copes not at all badly with unfamiliar things like the shimmy and the Boston. The two leading singers don't know what a hoot or a wobble is. Ludmilla Belobragina has a beautiful, rich but never plummy soprano which she uses with style and commitment throughout the long and often arduous music of Odette's rôle, maintaining an even, warm tone that is a pleasure to hear. A. Moksyakov is a fine *ténor-barytonisant* – precisely the right kind of voice for this rôle, which stays low for long periods – who nevertheless produces an heroic sound at the top of his voice when things get, as they do quite regularly, passionate.

Tamara Skmigra is a dazzler of a Marietta, skipping through her text (even if you can't understand a word) and her songs with sparkle and dash, and making her 'Der kleine Tanzkavalier' foxtrot a highspot of the set. Her two gentlemen – who put in a fair amount of speaking through the music, but show themselves more than capable of sprightly, accurate singing when they want to – help keep up the fun.

Even though the comedy folk are given a long leash, this set fortunately has much less in the way of dialogue on it than its companion *Zigeunerliebe*. There is never too long to wait through the stretches of Russian for another number, and every one is worth waiting for. Without the dialogue, there is just about enough music on these four sides to fill up one CD, so let's hope that Melodiya might think of getting into that market.

Das Veilchen vom Montmartre

Das Veilchen vom Montmartre, which has received a similar treatment from the Russian company, is a lighter and less romantic piece than *Die Bajadere*. I know little about this work, but listening to the Melodiya set it is evident that it has a lively, attractive score and a lot of light-hearted scenes for the three young garret-based artists and their Parisian girlfriends who are the principal participants in the rather harum-scarum story. However, after the high standard of the singing on Melodiya's *Zigeunerliebe* and *Die Bajadere* sets, this one is a little disappointing on the performance side. The lady playing Violette has some pretty music, but she also has an acid, shrill voice which turns the odd top note into a shriek, and the men in the garret have occasionally unreliable light voices which are not unpleasant but which do nothing to lift their jolly tunes into anything memorable.

The strains of popular American dance music were catching on in all parts of Europe in the inter-wars years, and it was not only the newer brigade of Austrian and German composers who came to prominence at this time who leaned gradually further and further towards the New World for musical modernities such as the tango, the one-step and the foxtrot, to mix with the Austrian waltzes and Hungarian native rhythms that had been the bases of the pre-war operettas.

Even the most unlikely pieces bent to the fashion, and the biggest international success ever to come from Berlin's musical theatre world, a pure old-fashioned stage-Tyrol piece decorated with a bundle of simple, catchy numbers and vast amounts of scenery and speciality acts, borrowed tango and one-step rhythms for its score. Shorn of much of the scenery and all of the speciality acts, *Im weissen Rössl* alias *White Horse Inn* alias *L'Auberge du Cheval Blanc* alias *Al Cavallino Bianco* retains its popularity all round the world more than half a century after its 1931 production.

Ralph Benatzky

Im weissen Rössl

There are plenty of significantly differing recordings of various versions of *Im weissen Rössl* – for the original score, composed basically by Ralph Bentazky (who had previously himself arranged Strauss's music for the score of *Casanova*), has known a good few interpolations and rearrangements through the years and its world-wide travels. Quite what is the 'real' *Im weissen Rössl* is a point which really doesn't come into consideration, it is simply a matter of which you like the best. The most comprehensive coverage of the show in its original language comes on three double-disc recordings: one from Amadeo, one from Ariola-Eurodisc, and the third and most recent from HMV/EMI.

The 1979 EMI recording, the only one now generally available, has an advantage over the majority of versions of the show in two very fine lead players. Peter Minich (Leopold) adeptly mixes comedy and tenorizing, speech and song, and only a few imperfect sounds, as the waiter at the 'Im weissen Rössl' inn whose efforts to win the heart and/or hand of his employer make up the main plot-line of the show. Anneliese Rothenberger (Josefa) who, in her fifties, has gone beyond the long-running ingénue soprano years that produced so many performance gems, here gives a warmly attractive performance that makes you realize just how little this star rôle has to sing. Norbert Orth gives a clear-voiced, romantic performance as Siedler, the desirable bachelor on whom Josefa has designs, and Hans Putz (Emperor Franz Josef) almost steals the show with his set-piece, a richly spoken version of the philosophizing 'Es ist einmal in Leben so', which helps Josefa to see her way clear to putting her hand where there is a heart awaiting, but sadly the two unexceptional supporting sopranos are very lumpy and lusty (being an ingénue is obviously considered a bar to vaster ambitions these days) and both seem ill cast.

Amongst the cheerful potted dialogue the friendly, familiar numbers tumble out – the lively title song, the jaunty Tyrolean 'Im Salzkammergut', Robert Stolz's vivacious interpolated waltz 'Mein Liebeslied muss ein Walzer sein' and his lilting 'Die ganze Welt ist himmelblau', Bruno Granichstäten's 'Zuschau'm kann i net' and the vigorous Heurige song written by Hans Frankowski, all liberally and happily conducted by Willy Mattes. According to the sleeve, Matthes is also responsible for the enjoyable new arrangement of the piece played here.

The arrangement is fairly wide-reaching, for the score has, for some reason, been further jiggled around, beyond even what has become the accepted revised version of the revised version. Several songs have been sideswiped into different positions and a couple of pieces, including the duet 'Es ist wohl nicht das letzte Mal', have got lost on the way. For English listeners, used to the British version of *White Horse Inn*, there is another and more startling omission – the famous march song 'Goodbye'. It is not there for the very good reason that it was not part of the original score, but added by Stolz for the London production. You could be forgiven for getting tricked over all this, as the sleeve of the recording irritatingly gives no musical breakdown at all.

The other two full-sized *Im weissen Rössl*s, which feature Erwin Gross and Waltraut Haas (Amadeo) and Peter Alexander and Ingeborg Hallstein (Eurodisc), both gave birth to one-disc selections, and from them you can see that there is not any particular point in pining over the vanished 'completes'. Neither is as enjoyable as the EMI version. The 1964 Amadeo single, which has been reissued to mark twenty-five years of Amadeo, is certainly unobjectionable and it crams a lot onto one record, including more dialogue than I can ever remember having heard on a show single. It has an agreeable Leopold in Gross and a shrewish Josefa (Haas) with an iffy voice, but both are a bit short on charm. Peter Minich at this stage played Siedler and he does so nicely, although there are already snatches of an incipient Leopold to be heard. Hedi Klug (Ottilie) has some capable (and unfamiliar) high notes. No one is credited with arrangements, so maybe this is quite near to the original.

The Ariola one certainly is nowhere near. It is far enough away actually to make excuses on its sleeve, pleading the fact that there were interpolations in the original show to justify a bundle of unhelpful new ones here. But these are not the only excesses to which it stoops. There are unattractive musical rearrangements (credited singly, with apparent pride), Peter Alexander gives a soap-opera performance as Leopold, and when Ingeborg Hallstein (a very lightweight Josefa) started putting coloratura into the title song I felt it was time to leave the room.

There have been two single-disc recordings from Telefunken (starring Minich again, and Per Grunden), of which I have heard only the former. It is a respectable if not wonderful version, its chief pleasure coming from the way Carl Michalksi dances the score along. Minich's Leopold is a little less relaxed than in his later recording and his Josefa (Marion Briner) is rather shrill and hooty when compared with Rothenberger, but there is a splendid Siedler (Frederic Mayer) who is actually equipped with the duet missing on the other records. There is also, in the overture, the yodelling section which I always enjoy.

In addition to these studio recordings, there are also two cast recordings, one taken from the Hamburger Operettenhaus and the second from the Mörbisch Festival of 1985. Hamburg's recording uses just a little text to link together the musical numbers, but drops a few smaller pieces of music and clips others to leave place for interpolations of the Radetzky March and 'Oh, du mein Osterreich' and a handful of reprises in its 'Originalfassung des Hamburger Operettenhauses'. It is a bright, good-humoured recording on which nothing gets lingered over as it scuttles through its store of popular melodies, cheerfully performed and played. Erich Kuchar (Leopold) sounds a suitably nice fellow and has an agreeable almost-tenor voice, but Sonja Knittel (Josefa) is less steady and accurate than in earlier days. However, like other members of the cast, she makes up in pure *joie de vivre* what is lacking in the fine points of vocalizing.

Mörbisch has yet another *Neufassung* to offer. Oddly, instead of using 'Goodbye' they have chosen to insert another marching song for Leopold, with the rather less catchy title 'Lass uns Abschied nehmen mit lächelndem Gesicht'. They have also added a song for Giesecke (presumably because he is played by the venerable former boss of the Volksoper, Karl Dönch) and, on the other hand, dropped the yodeller, the Cow Chorus, the finales and the third-act opening. They have also done something funny to the nice big orchestra, which has gained a snare drum. I can't be the only person to find that interminable scratching unpleasant.

Rudolf Buczolich is another nice-sounding Leopold, who actually gets to sing 'Es muss was Wunderbares sein' alone whilst the indignant Josefa (Dagamar Koller) prepares to smack his impertinent face, and makes a capable rather than endearing job of 'Zu'schaun kann i net'. Miss Koller performs her brief spoken sections sparkily, but like Knittel she seems insecure in her singing (is this the rôle to which sopranos run when they start to wobble?); Joachim Kemmer is an enjoyably extravagant Sigismund with a cute Klärchen (Gaby Bischof) to woo, and Ottilie (Elisabeth Kalès), Siedler (Harald Serafin) and Franz Stoss (Franz Josef) all do their work more than simply well, but, although it is perfectly good, this *Im weissen Rössl* doesn't have any particular excitements that might earn it preference over the best of the others.

Lucien Besnard's enormously popular French version, first staged in 1932, made its own free-handed alterations to the show, one of them being the inclusion of the by then proven 'Goodbye' ('Adieu, je pars'), another the addition of Anton Profès's very pretty 'Je vous emménerai sur mon joli bateau', and the success of the show in France is evidenced by three complete recordings and a swatch of selections.

The Decca set features Luc Barney, the star of over 1,200 performances in two vast Châtelet Theatre *Auberge du Cheval Blanc* productions, opposite Colette Riedinger, his co-star of 1953, and both are quite simply excellent. Barney, the possessor of an easy unshowy tenor and a happy personality, is ideally cast as Leopold and Riedinger makes a bright and bossy Josefa, whilst tenor Bernard Plantey and Huguette Boulangeot make light work of the romantic duets and Jack Claret bounces through the comedy fluently in a splendid and smilingly light-hearted version of the show.

Eliane Varon, who appeared in the 1968 production, is featured opposite Christian Borel on Festival, but neither this nor even Decca's very fine set can compete with EMI-Pathé's 1962 recording. This one offers the supreme performance of the one-and-only Bourvil, who is in his element as the lovable head-waiter of the White Horse Inn, sabotaging the more glamorous opposition represented by city lawyer Siedler in order to win his *patronne*'s hand with the most adorable mock-innocence. To hear Bourvil, in his crinkly, laughter-filled voice, inviting the tourists to 'Regardez ce soleil', courting his Josefa with winning charm ('Pour être un jour aimé de toi'), heading off casually to join the army in 'Adieu, je pars', tipsily drowning his sorrows in a tyrolienne, and playing out the final, foolishly happy scene of the show, is to hear musical comedy at its most irresistible.

Andrine Forli fills the rôle of Josefa convincingly, Michel Dens (Florès/Siedler) is as impeccably and tenorisingly baritone as ever in the two familiar Stolz duos he shares with the ever piquant and pretty soprano of Janine Ervil (Sylvabelle/Ottilie), and Pierre Germain is quaintly comic as the ridiculously vain Célestin/Sigismund in Robert Gilbert's humorous one-step 'On a le béguin' and in the little duo 'Quand parut le mois de Mai' with perky Clara (Colette Hérent).

Among the extras this version offers is the whole of the yodelling act, and Hannerl Hopperger's performance, interpolated into both the overture and the first-act finale, is nothing short of sensational, topping off a thoroughly enjoyable set which proves that some musicals, no matter how successful, actually can gain from being 'adapted'. *L'Auberge du Cheval Blanc* seems to me well and truly to have the edge on each and every version of *Im weissen Rössl*. But then, when you have Bourvil . . .

The French selection discs include a delightful series of excerpts from this EMI-Pathé set, as well as a Merkès/Merval selection for their fans and three separate versions with Luc Barney on Decca and on Barclay. On the last of these Barney helps himself to as many numbers as lie within his range, relegating his three co-performers to filling in the gaps, on what is nevertheless, because of the singer's warmly attractive personality, a thoroughly enjoyable recording. Philips's issue goes firmly for vocal values and finds them with a bright baritone Florès (Lucien Huberty), a delightfully unshowy Sylvabelle (Marina Hotine) and a top-notch pair of singing funmakers in Rosine Brédy (Clara) and Jacques Loreau (Célestin). There is a strong-singing, rather acid Josefa (Georgette Bourdin), but this otherwise fine disc is spoiled for me by the miscasting of strong-voiced baritone Guy Fontagnère, who is more heroic than comic and stretched at the top of his range as Leopold.

In spite of the piece's popularity on English stages, only a small handful of unimpressive studio cast recordings exist of Harry Graham's English translation, the most substantial of which are two selections of a dozen items apiece on Music for Pleasure and HMV. The latter, with Andy Cole and Mary Thomas featured, is an earnestly capable recording which just shouts 'session singers' at you. The favourite songs plop slowly out like neat little sausages, wrapped in vast orchestral and choral sounds, and things turn unintentionally funny when a girls' chorus is turned into a 1950s number for crooner Rita Williams. MFP's effort is a tiny bit more like the show in its better portions, in spite of the 20th Century Symphony Orchestra (!) and the Mike Sammes Singers and their respective 1950s arrangements. It puts in the opening chorus with a fragment of inexpert yodelling, casts the lead comedy tenor rôle with an enjoyable light comedy player in David

Croft (but then lets him sing songs belonging to other rôles), adds several fine
singers in Marion Grimaldi (Josefa), Barbara Leigh (Ottilie) and Leonard Weir
(Siedler – some of the time), but in the end it is still a 'Music While You Work'
version of the show and, like its companion, is better avoided.

Amongst the other successful composers of this era appear the names of Eduard
Künneke, Edmund Eysler, Paul Ábrahám, Nico Dostal and Robert Stolz, whose
long career continued beyond the Second World War and made him the last
representative of the long-lived and brilliant mid-European operetta tradition.
This group are unevenly represented on record and, in any case, mostly only by
their one or two important hits.

Eduard Künneke

The German composer Eduard Künneke, whose most substantial claim to fame is
the highly successful and continuously revived *Das Vetter aus Dingsda* (1921), has
had surprisingly good record coverage. His pretty, compact little operetta has been
five or six times recorded on selection discs and, most recently, issued by RCA in a
complete version on a two-record set. *Glückliche Reise* (1932) has also appeared in
several short selections, two paired with excerpts from *Das Vetter aus Dingsda*, and
Künneke's late works, *Die Grosse Sünderin* (1935) and *Traumland* (1941), were both
included in substantial selections in the RCA series.

All these shows are represented on a double-album compilation of the
composer's work issued as 'Das goldene Eduard Künneke Album', where they
share space with such less-known pieces as *Die lockende Flamme* (1933), *Das Dorf
ohne Glock* (1919),(*Die Blonde) Liselott* (1927), *Zauberin Lola* (1937) and *Herz über
Bord* (1935). Four numbers from *Liselott* and three from *Lady Hamilton* (played in
Britain as *The Song of the Sea*) also appear on an enjoyable and interesting EMI
TV disc featuring operettas about famous ladies ('Geschichten über Frauen der
Geschichte'), where they keep company with such other *grandes femmes* as Lehár's
Friederike, Fall's *Kaiserin* and *Madame Pompadour*, Katnigg's *Kaiserin Katharina*,
Kálmán's *Kaiserin Josephine* and the pasticcio *Die Tänzerin Fanny Elssler*.

Das Vetter aus Dingsda

Das Vetter aus Dingsda (The Cousin from Thingummyjig) is a delightfully lively
and tuneful piece, and the RCA set, a cleanly and crisply recorded modern digital
recording full of atmosphere (proving it can be done) is a model one, packed with
gaiety, enthusiasm and good music, well played by Heinz Geese and the Cologne
Rundfunkorchester and – with one important reservation – aptly and well sung.
Unusually, the four short sides of this set – the last is only fourteen and a half
minutes – include no dialogue.

The long-unseen 'Cousin' of the show's title is the man pretty Dutch Julia has
dreamed of marrying ever since they were children, but when she mistakes a

stranger who turns up at her home for her Roderich, two acts of complications ensue before the predictable happy ending. The rôle of the Stranger, a splendidly grateful one with its delicately insinuating 'Ich bin nur ein armer Wandersell', the tempestuous storm song 'Vor dem Himmel und den Weibern' and several duets which run the gamut with energy but without vulgarity, is taken by René Kollo. Kollo's voice was made (and is mostly used) for larger things than operetta, but he has proved before and does so again here that he can adapt happily to this type of singing. His tactfully gentle treatment of 'Ich bin nur ein armer Wandersell' is beautiful and, when he opens up with full guns blazing in the larger lyrical moments, the result is never incongruous.

Unfortunately the same cannot be said for his Julia. Grit van Jüten has the kind of soprano voice which just never lilts. Lashings of blonde hair and a good figure (as seen on the sleeve) may be effective on stage, but they do not make up for an over-covered middle voice, screechy top notes and insensitive singing. She just cannot cope with the thin-spun lines of the lovely, musing waltz song to the moon ('Strahlender Mond') and when she starts off the duet 'Do you remember when we played together as children . . .' your immediate thought is, 'that person was never a child.' She is at her best when all the stops are out, but that is not enough.

Angelika Wolff is a fine antidote as a spikily pert soubrette. Every time she appears you can hear her smiling, and her 'boomps-a-daisy' duet with the likeable Bully Buhlan ('Mann, o Mann') is a jolly joy. Benno Kusche, surely the best operetta 'father' (or, in this case, 'uncle') around these days, is effectively paired with a warm, semi-singing Evelyn Künneke (any relation?) as the heroine's aunt in the highly enjoyable and rhythmic ensembles, including the lively opening table-talk and the swishy foxtrot 'Sieben Jahre lebt' ich in Batavia', which make you forget that this is an operetta with a cast of nine and no chorus. Freddy Breck is a bright-voiced late arrival on the scene as the real Roderich.

So much is so very right with this recording, both in its content and its performance, that the one blot is a shame. If only Julia weren't such a very omnipresent rôle. But it is, and so instead of a really top-class recording we have instead a near miss.

There is no other way of getting *Der Vetter aus Dingsda* whole, and Kollo and Kusche, in particular, are not equalled elsewhere, but there is an adequate EMI-Da Capo pairing of *Das Vetter* and *Glückliche Reise*, taken from two 1959 EPs, which gives some bits of each. The bitty eight-number *Vetter* selection misses out the Storm Song (and the rest of the third act), as well as the table-talk and the bulk of the ensemble material, but it has Erika Köth playing out the lines of the Moon Song very prettily and Rudolf Schock doing a finely restrained job with the Wanderer's Song and the Childhood Duet. It is a sampler only, but a pleasant one.

Glückliche Reise

The *Glückliche Reise* selection shows up Künneke's versatility. This is a pure musical comedy, with barely an old-world tune or rhythm in sight. Tango, blues, foxtrot and rumba all combine in an upbeat score of dance music that mirrors what was going on in Britain and France whilst at the same time retaining a Germanic flavour. Pieces of eleven songs are fused together for a close harmony group, which is so 1950s that you can hear the perms in their hair, and five accomplished soloists, without much regard as to who sings what. Several of the songs turn out to be great fun – the cute 'Jede Frau', the tango 'Drüben in der Heimat', the happy 'Komm mein kleines Farmerbräutchen' and the title march.

Another *Glückliche Reise* selection, on Fontana, also paired with a set of *Vetter aus Dingsda* excerpts, features Rudolf Christ and Ruthilde Boesch.

Die grosse Sünderin

It is hard to believe that *Die grosse Sünderin* came, three years later, from the same pen as *Glückliche Reise*. This is a rather fine Really Big Operetta in the old serious musical style with leading rôles for tenor and soprano that are long, hard, high and endlessly demanding in a way that few others of any era are. There doesn't seem, from this recording, to be any comic content to speak of and, apart from a lively march number for the number-two couple and one vaguely humorous scene, the focus is constantly on Countess Sybilla and the gallant Schrenk, the amorous protagonists of the piece, singing their hearts out. Her melodious 'Ich bin die grosse Sünderin' and his hugely big 'Das Leben des Schrenk' are the highlights of the rôles originally played by no less artists than Tiana Lemnitz and Helge Roswaenge.

Maud Cunitz and Rudolf Schock take the places of this pair on the 1951 recording made under the baton of Franz Marszalek, conductor of the original 1935 production. To say that she succeeds better than he is a bit unfair, for the rôle of Schrenk is an above-the-stave marathon requiring the strength of a Siegfried and the tone of a Postillon de Longjumeau. Schock makes a very brave attempt and brings some parts off with a distinct brio, but in others the noise at the top of the voice is not the most pleasant. Still, if you were to give 'Das Leben des Schrenk' and the devilish 'Ein altes indisches Märchen' to ninety-nine percent of tenors of all ranks and kinds, rare would be those to make it the end intact.

Traumland

With *Traumland*, a musical comedy set in 1940s filmland, Künneke goes back to the *Glückliche Reise* style. There is a filmstar called Ellinor Molander and a composer called Irvin Willin to provide the love songs and a couple of lesser players to provide the jaunty numbers. It's all rather like the French Francis Lopez musicals of five or six years later. Irvin (given every ounce of voice by René Kollo) rhapsodizes super-lyrically 'Ich sing' mein schönstes Lied', which sounds like something that might have been written for a Mario Lanza film, and repeats with a song about 'three little words', whilst Ellinor (Ingeborg Hallstein) gets very Rombergish in 'Still träumt die Lagune' until the chorus starts to swing the number, and she succeeds in mixing soprano tones (and even a final top note) with a hefty tango rhythm in 'Nach sehnt sich mein Herz in stillen Studen'. Dagmar Koller, in what was clearly a marvellously protean star rôle, as perky Peggy, masters every kind of singing from husky cabaret to pert soubrette to legitimate soprano as she sings languidly about 'Sex-Appeal' (*sic*), duos catchily with her very pleasant Jack (Peter Fröhlich) in 'Täglich tausend Liebesbriefe' and 'Mädel gesucht' (that tune sounds familiar), and even gets to do a sort of 1940s Rose's turn, imagining her name up in lights, as the first-act finale.

The recording makes the piece sound rather like an oversize film score, but it is an interesting one, as few German musicals of this kind – most of them pretty ephemeral – have been preserved on record. And Künneke's qualifications as a composer, confirmed by pieces like *Der Vetter aus Dingsda* and *Die grosse Sünderin*, are clearly above those of many of his contemporaries.

Edmund Eysler

The unpretentious old-style musicals of Edmund Eysler were another kind of show which, in spite of some initial successes and overseas productions, were unlikely to have a long life or inspire recording. His *Die gold'ne Meisterin* (1927) rated a long-lost selection on Philips in the 1960s, and the song 'Küssen ist keine Sünd' from the earlier *Bruder Straubinger* is a regular tenor bon-bon, but that is about all. A few years back it seemed that at last this neglected composer was to have some representation on disc when 'Die schönsten Melodien – Edmund Eysler', a record made with the Volksoper orchestra and soloists and containing not only six pieces from *Die gold'ne Meisterin* but numbers from half a dozen other Eysler works, was announced. If it ever came out, it vanished very quickly. I scoured Vienna for it twice. So, poor old Eysler goes back to being a record rarity.

Kurt Weill

The European works of Kurt Weill are a difficult group to classify, but, rightly or wrongly, I leave such pieces as the remarkable *Der Silbersee* and *Aufstieg und Fall der Stadt Mahagonny* to the operatic world, and deal here only with *Die Dreigroschenoper* (1928) and *Happy End* (1929).

Die Dreigroschenoper

Die Dreigroschenoper (*The Threepenny Opera*), a wilfully politicized (or socialized if you prefer it) retelling by Bert Brecht of Gay's *Beggar's Opera* story, has been widely and continuously produced on the stage during the last three decades, since its tuppence-coloured political content and the purposely coarse and *grand guignol* style of performance inflicted on it became fashionable, but it has remained steadily to the fore ever since its production through the medium of its score. Some of what Richard Traubner in his book *Operetta* calls Weill's 'tinny, bouncy tunes . . . have become virtual lieder' – the Moritat (better known by its English title, 'Mack the Knife'), the Barbara-Lied and Seeräuber-Jenny (Pirate Jenny) – but, as the same author points out, Weill's musical *métier* made of Brecht's 'preaching' play a very considerable musical piece with a score including some 'unequivocally very great operetta finales'.

The big songs of *Der Dreigroschenoper* have been endlessly recorded, with the feminine numbers (here isn't the place to partake of the continuing argument as to which rôle ought to sing which numbers) often ground tastelessly into the dust by rattling imitators of what they perceive as Lotte Lenya's 'Berlin style' (listen to her early recordings and you will hear a tart little soubrette), and 'Mack the Knife' subjected to every kind of bilious crooning. After that it is with some hope of relief that you turn to some of the numerous and various complete and cast recordings.

The French, with their taste for the *intégrale*, have actually been responsible for a four-record *Opéra de Quat' Sous* (I have never quite understood why the extra penny got into the French title), taken from a live performance of a 1969–70 production by the Théâtre de l'Est Parisien. It is a production which is acted big and sung and played simple and rough, giving perhaps the air of somehow being pretentiously unpretentious. But, for what it is worth, *Die Dreigroschenoper* exists *in toto* in French if you have sufficiently unbroken wind to tramp around Parisian flea-markets looking for it.

In the original German, there are a number of recordings of the full score, with or without its various extensions, and with or without dialogue. What I have always understood to be the first of these, on Columbia, dates from 1958. It has small bits of linking material and announcements and it includes the deleted Ballade vor der sexuellen Hörigkeit and Lucy's 'Kampf um das Eigentum', and for all that it is supposed to be a 'definitive' recording (and it may very well be insofar as its content is concerned), it is pretty patchy in performance. There seems to be a sort of inverted snobbery that encourages the casting of this show with people who can't sing. I don't mean glorious singers. I mean people who can't hold pitch, control tone or sing a phrase without gasping for an ill-placed breath, thus losing all dramatic effect. If they think they are being 'authentic' they have only to listen to the archive recordings of the first Mackie, Harald Paulsen, to hear the kind of taut, precise, devastatingly effective performance on which the work prospers. This recording tends unfortunately in this wrong-minded direction. Eric Schellow's uneven Mackie is better done than the performances of most of the other players, but Lotte Lenya (Frau Weill and the first Jenny thirty years earlier) shows them all a thing or two in her original rôle.

A Vanguard recording from Vienna, which is said to date from 1950, fits the show onto one disc, yet is to all intents and purposes complete. This one is a bit of a curious mixture. The singing is certainly more accomplished – Kurt Preger's oddly sneerish Mack is an incisive but not oversinging high baritone, Mrs Peachum

(Rosette Anday) a nicely raddled operatic soprano and Lucy (Anny Felbermayer) an effective light soprano; but the Jenny (who is apparently a member of the Vienna State Opera) chooses to speak most of the Salomon-Lied and her duet rather than sing, and Helge Roswaenge goes too far the other way and performs the Moritat with too much careful vocalizing. Top billing goes to Liane, 'the sultry-voiced *chanteuse* of continental night-life', who plays Polly. She performs both Seeräuber-Jenny and the Barbara-Lied and switches back and forth between chalky chest tones in her big solos and a useful and unpretentious little soprano in the ensembles. Odd, but at least in tune, and occasionally, as in the Jealousy Duet, right on the button.

If I had to pick a German-language *Dreigroschenoper*, I would opt for the two-record Philips issue, drawn from a production at the Stadtstheater, Frankfurt, in 1966. Covering four short sides (and omitting Lucy's usually omitted number), it is a clearly and cleanly recorded version, played without dialogue and with the songs simply announced. It lacks perhaps in atmosphere – the performers sound as if they are acting in a vacuum – but it does give a good, straightforward rendering of the score as played by a capable cast. Unfortunately, the men in particular perform with all the received mannerisms that have become attached to the piece, a habit which is as annoying here as it is in such cases as 'received D'Oyly Carte' acting. The Streetsinger puts on a silly voice (I cannot believe the poor man really speaks and sings like that) and there is a good deal of rather risible 'spit-'n'-snarl' acting and singing, which has the effect of making all the actors sound indistinguishable from one another. However, once you have (in my case reluctantly) accepted the fact that this is how it is going to be, there is a lot to enjoy on this set.

The principal enjoyment is the Polly Peachum. Karin Hübner can belt and howl with the best of them (and did, as Berlin's Eliza Doolittle), but she doesn't. She acts out her songs marvellously, picking her points wickedly and making Seeräuber-Jenny, mostly sung in a strong, girlish soprano, infinitely more menacing and interesting than it is when battered across. Her Liebeslied is just that, and her Jealousy Duet with Ursula Dirichs's hectic Lucy is quite hilarious in its playing, and hugely effective musically as the two girls bicker away at each other in hateful harmony. She quite takes the centre of the show away from Hans Korte's Macheath, a roughly unseductive fellow who can clearly sing better than he allows himself to.

Edith Teichmann is a strong-voiced Jenny who appropriates the Ballade von der sexuellen Hörigkeit and delivers it with gusto in a two-part voice – a searing 'shout' on the chest notes and an effective and accurate head register. Franz Kutschera makes a regular if unexceptional Peachum, and Anita Mey is his semi-sung wife. The two of them support Miss Hübner excellently in the first-act finale – one of the several tracks on this recording which is extremely effective. If all of this version were as good as the best bits, we should have a definitive *Dreigroschenoper*.

There is apparently also a three-disc set (presumably, thus, with dialogue) put out by Polydor which is conducted by James Last, but I have not heard this.

It is possible for a 'selection' disc, like the Vanguard single-disc recording, to manage to hold practically all of the score, and a cast recording from Germany's Skarabaus Theater Company on the Neue Welt label leaves out only three musical pieces, but others take in less. Amongst the selection discs can be found a series of tracks issued several times on Telefunken, a dozen numbers in all, recorded by some original cast members including Kurt Gerron (Brown/Streetsinger), who also narrates on one curious-sounding disc, Erich Ponto (Peachum), Lotte Lenya (Jenny) and original conductor Theo Mackeben. A recent reissue of early Weill recordings on the German Vintage label includes recordings of Paulsen's fine Moritat and solo Kanonensong and also two early Lenya recordings, which I gather probably aren't Lenya at all but Fritzi Massary. Whichever it is, she is notably better than her more modern counterparts.

The original-language recordings I have managed to hear being somewhat disappointing, it is a relief to find one rather better amongst the English – or, rather, American – language ones. The 1954–5 production at the off-Broadway Theatre de Lys in a dapper translation by Marc Blitzstein helped establish *The Threepenny Opera* in America, and the recording of this important production, a single disc taking in all the score including the Ballad of Sexual Dependency, shows how finely it was played. Here, at last, is a group of artists who balance effective singing and acting performance with a swaggering style suitable to their subject without sombering into any self-indulgences.

Scott Merrill is a poised Macheath with an agreeably unforced actor's baritone who is the centre-piece of the show without giving a showy performance, supported by a characterful but never caricatured Peachum (Martin Wolfson) and Brown (George Tyne). However, it is the ladies who are the most impressive. Charlotte Rae is a splendid Mrs Peachum, a quivering middle-aged soprano with a lusty turn, delivering her Ballad of Sexual Dependency with salacious opportunism, and magnificent when she joins Mackie for 'How to Survive', whilst Jo Sullivan is an ideal Polly, a harsh little ingénue with a vixenish voice. Lotte Lenya's singing has become worn by the years into what people now like to think is 'genuine Berlin'. She has lost her top register, has difficulty with pitch, and is often obliged to speak more than sing. However, style and personal magnetism more than see her through in what was by all reports a stunning performance in the theatre, and her Tango-Ballad with Merrill comes off splendidly.

Style and magnetism are equally present in Beatrice Arthur's performance of Lucy, but it is a performance that rather seems to have wandered in from another world, or perhaps some downtown drag show. Miss Arthur is a female basso profundo and a comedienne, as her TV triumph in *Golden Girls* has confirmed. The effect here is a bit too original. Or perhaps I'm now indulging preconceptions on this show myself. In any case, it is great fun to hear her join Miss Sullivan in a 'basso-soprano' battle in the Jealousy Duet.

There is, at the time of writing, no competitor for this record. A 1976 New York Shakespeare Festival revival, in a different and avowedly more devotedly faithful translation and with the usual modern snippets of scholarly musical director's additions to the score, makes an unexciting recording. The acting is uneven, with the *grand guignol* edging in from time to time, the voices are less secure, and, in comparison with its predecessor, it is a rather limp thing. Even less satisfactory is the souped-up soundtrack of the 1964 film, recorded in both English and German. However, I gather that, in the ridiculous way these things occur, we are shortly to have not one, nor two, nor even three, but four new recordings of the show. It smacks of the television soap-wars. Wouldn't three of the companies like to spend their money on some other worthy and less-recorded shows?

Happy End

The theatrically unfortunate *Happy End* survives only because of its popular group of wholly incidental songs. The atmospheric 'Tsurabaya Johnny' and the Bilbao Song, largely thanks to Lenya's interpretations, have become concert and cabaret favourites. Those interpretations, not only of songs belonging to her own rôle of Lilian the Salvation Army girl but of the whole score, have been recorded on CBS.

Paul Ábrahám

Yet another composer of Hungarian origin, Paul Ábrahám, wrote several internationally played inter-war operettas full of exotic colour and everything from big-sing lyric duets to contemporary pop and jazz. Two of these, *Viktoria und ihr Husar* (1930) and *Die Blume von Hawaii* (1931), have survived on regular if reduced recordings, but his third success, *Ball im Savoy* (1932), has been left unattended apart from an EP on Odeon of four songs by the original cast (Gitta Alpar, Oskar Dénes, Rosy Barsony, Herbert Ernst Groh) conducted by the composer.

Viktoria und ihr Husar and
Die Blume von Hawaii

The most substantial recording of the pretty mixture of Hungarian and Japanese tones, romantic, comic, ancient and modern, that make up the score of *Viktoria* – one entire disc to itself – comes, oddly, from France, where the show has never been all that popular. Part of the TLP series, it includes all the show's principal numbers, omitting choruses and finales, but unfortunately, like most of this series, it is rather indifferently cast and played. Claudine Granger (Viktoria) is much happier in this rôle than in the more classic pieces she has recorded for the same label, and she makes a pleasing job of the charming 'Rote Orchideen', the Hungarian 'Schöne Petrowna' and even the more demanding duos 'Pardon, Madame' and 'Reich mir zum Abscheid noch einmal die Hände', but Bernard

Sinclair as her long-lost lover has fallen unpleasantly victim to the woof and the wobble, and the two soubrettes are a fairly hefty pair who threaten to sink their music in spite of some lively singing from Jacques Tayles, doubling as both their partners. Tayles shares the show's jaunty hit song, 'Mausi, süss warst du heute nacht', with the indifferent Elya Weismann.

Die Blume von Hawaii has not been given as large a treatment, even though several of its songs continue to be popular – particularly the strong, romantic 'Ein Paradies am Meerestrand' – and productions still flourish. As with *Viktoria*, an EP or half a disc is its regular helping, and more than half a dozen pairings of selections or medley-selections from the two shows have been issued. There is a particularly well sung and flavourful one on EMI/Columbia, taken from a pair of early EPs, which unfortunately fillets the numbers in order to fit thirteen *Viktoria* bits on one side. The lovely, smooth Sári Bárabás and the very stalwart Heinz Hoppe share the big music of the *Viktoria* love story, and Harry Friedauer takes control of the fun, even though the vocalists don't stick firmly to one particular rôle. The delicious Jacqueline Boyer's jazzy assertion that 'Meine Mama war aus Yokohama', Rex Gildo and Conny Froboess's bubbling 'Mausi', and Willy Hagara's lovely relaxed baritone fragment of 'Pardon, Madame' – more a dark brown Bing Crosby than a Georgio Tozzi – are just some of the pieces that demonstrate all the stylishness that is missing on the rather relentlessly old-fashioned operetta style French recording.

The *Blume von Hawaii* side, which also presents the songs without much care as to who sings what, is equally enjoyable. The juxtaposition of Hoppe singing a ringing solo, 'Ein Paradies am Meerestrand', with the cigarette and whisky-stained Bill Ramsey and versatile Sonja Knittel walloping out 'Wir singen zur Jazzband' demonstrates exactly what Ábrahám is all about. It is a combination that horrifies some serious operetta fans, but I find this mixture of musical styles – American-Hungarian musical comedy with lyrics joyously and fashionably mixing German and English – great fun. Willy Hagara richly crooning his love for 'Du traumschöne Perle der Südsee' to twanging Hawaiian guitars and angel voices is heaven. What a shame that this sampler could not have been a full-scale recording. And where are the other records of Mr Hagara?

Amongst the dozen or so short and potted *Die Blume von Hawaii* selections, there is actually one full disc of excerpts on the Polydor label which needs to be mentioned in order to stop anyone being tricked into buying it in mistake for the real show. It is an 'up-to-date' version, a painfully ineffectual performance by some inept and echo-aided crooners of a dozen numbers from the show, which have been turned into musical pap by a gentleman from Cologne called Hans Bertram with the aim of 'appealing not only to operetta fans but also to the young generation'. Pfui. And a black mark for Polydor, who might have given us instead a proper half-hour plus of Ábrahám's merry score.

Ábrahám's popularity has extended far enough for *Viktoria* to have been recorded in Swedish and for both it and *Die Blume von Hawaii* (*Fior d'Haway*) to have been included in the Italian EDM series, but unsurprisingly no English-language recording has appeared.

Nico Dostal

Although Nico Dostal's reputation, like Ábrahám's, rests principally on two works, the hefty-handed musical comedy *Clivia* and the more operetta-like *Die ungarische Hochzeit*, a number of his other works have had some surprisingly generous representation on disc.

Clivia and *Die ungarische Hochzeit*

Clivia is a piece about a film star and South American politics, a bit like Francis Lopez not quite at his best or a B musical movie score, and simply not in the class of Ábrahám's best work from the point of view of either melody or fun. The show was, however, sufficiently well thought of for RCA and Franz Marszalek to devote a complete disc to its score and for artists such as Renate Holm (Clivia) and Peter Minich (Juan) to perform it. They do so well enough, but apart from the favourite bits – the very jolly comedy tarantella trio 'Am Manzanares' with its unbelievable castanets, and Clivia's rather obvious solo 'Ich bin verliebt' (surely the most used title in German musicals) – it is a fairly unrewarding listen.

Nevertheless, others have also devoted record space to *Clivia*'s music, albeit on a lesser scale, and Telefunken, Ariola-Eurodisc and EMI have all produced limited selections. Eurodisc has even brought *Clivia* together with other Dostal selections on both one- and two-disc compilations, the most recent being a double-disc set devoting one side to each of *Clivia*, *Die ungarische Hochzeit*, *Manina* and *Monika*, all conducted by the composer. They omitted, on this occasion, *Die Vielgeliebte* (healthily represented on another Dostal compilation), previously issued on a Rudolf Schock-Erika Köth EP, the contents of which was also included in their earlier 'Nico Dostal – Welterfolge' compilation.

The four-show set, to which the Berlin Symphony Orchestra and such fine singers as Schock, Schramm, Sylvia Geszty, Ferry Gruber and Monika Dahlberg lend their talents, pretty much confirms the impression left by *Clivia* and prompts the thought that Dostal owes his considerable coverage a good deal to his own active longevity and a distinct lack of competition in the LP age. The romantic music is slightly overdone 'I am writing operetta' music, sometimes 'I am writing big operetta' music, and the less prominent comic sections throw up most of what is enjoyable in his works.

Die ungarische Hochzeit shows up as the best of the four operettas, but it is ultimately undistiguished operetta-by-numbers material. The largest representation of this show can be found (with difficulty) on a Telefunken ten-inch disc featuring Traute Richter and Herold Kraus, which includes nine numbers and the overture, and a sampler of its highlights and those of *Clivia* are paired together on an EMI-Electrola disc.

Robert Stolz

Dostal, of course, was a decided also-ran in the LP age to an even longer-lived, extremely active and rather more appreciable composer in Robert Stolz. Stolz led a full and vigorous career in all areas of the musical world, both as a writer and a conductor, from his earliest productions in the first years of the century, when one of his musicals actually starred the great man of the golden age, Girardi himself, to 1969 when his last operetta, *Hochzeit am Bodensee*, was produced in his ninetieth year.

He was a prolific and successful composer of film operettas, but several of his stage works also found success, notably two with film origins – *Zwei Herzen in Dreivierteltakt* and *Frühjahrsparade*. *Wenn die kleinen Veilchen blühen* (1932) won considerable success on the London stage as *Wild Violets*. Each of these pieces has been given recorded coverage, as have *Venus in Seide* (1932) and the late works *Trauminsel* (1962) and *Himmelblaue Träume* (also known as *Hochzeit in Bodensee*) (1969), which have been given recording preference over Stolz's early success *Die Tanz ins Gluck* (1921). Ariola-Eurodisc, for whom Stolz conducted an uncountable number of discs of Viennese music and operettas, were the chief producers of recordings of his stage works and *Zwei Herzen* and *Veilchen* have been issued on one shared disc, whilst *Venus in Seide*, *Frühjahrsparade* and *Himmelblaue Traume* each have a record devoted to themselves alone. The original cast recording of *Trauminsel* was issued by Philips.

Venus in Seide

Perhaps surprisingly, it is the lesser-known *Venus in Seide* that makes up the best record. Stolz, the lightest of composers, here takes on a traditionally romantic and Ruritanian subject which, in most hands, would have been the meat of a big-sing operetta, and produces his personal version of that lushest of styles with just a dash of Hungarian and Polish flavours. He comes out at the end of it with an attractive and unexaggerated score whose very large tenor role includes a pleasing variety of numbers and several duets with the lead soprano who, in her turn, beginning with a very stylish entrance song, is well rewarded musically. The soubret songs are light and bright and, like the rest of the score, could easily have been written twenty years earlier.

Rudolf Schock in the hero's role gives one of the best of all his recorded performances, well-paced and unmannered, his voice ringing with heroic ease, and Margit Schramm as his Polish inamorata is equally pleasing, whilst Ferry

Gruber and Liselotte Schädle are first-rate in the lighter roles on a recording which, under the composer's baton, gives his piece a performance of enjoyable unpretentiousness.

Zwei Herzen in Dreivierteltakt

The same cannot be said of the *Zwei Herzen/Veilchen* disc. As its title would suggest, *Zwei Herzen* has a score full of waltzes, including the pretty teenage 'Heute besuch' ich mein Glück', convincingly sung here by Renate Holm, and the title number, as well as a nice Heurige song and some jolly duos for the light comic rôles (Ferry Gruber, Adolf Dallapozza), but its lyric numbers are unimpressively done by Schock and Melitta Muszely. These two are even more out of place in *Veilchen*, a feather-light musical comedietta with delicate little tunes. The ripe and gusty Schock and warbly, mature Muszely pretending to be collegians in the sweet 'Du, du, du, schleiss deine Augen zu' are horribly unconvincing. The tunes are drowned in professionalism. Yet this recording is also conducted by Stolz, who presumably knew what he wanted, and I can only assume that he succumbed to that famous composer's disease which makes even the greatest think that their music cannot be oversung.

Trauminsel

Trauminsel is another Peruritanian operetta, set in the Yucatan – a departure for Stolz who was inclined to stick nearer home where Wiener Lieder were natural fodder – and its score is dyed lightly in local colour. It is decidedly better stuff than *Clivia* and has a pretty if not remarkable score from which the soprano 'Weit her an Yucatan' and the bouncy 'Mañana' emerge as the most agreeable numbers. Among the capable original cast is Wagnerian tenor Jean Cox.

Himmelblaue Träume

Himmelblaue Träume, set in Bodensee, returns to more familiar territory and has odd reminiscences of *Im weissen Rössl*. For the score, pieces of Stolz's 1934 operetta *Grüezi* are supplemented by his song hits from other sources – 'Du sollst der Kaiser meiner Seele sein' from *Der Favorit*, one of Stolz's best numbers splendidly sung by Muszely, 'Ich möcht einmal wieder verliebt sein' from the film *Liebeskommando* and so forth – and the result is a pleasant recording which has rather the feel of being a songs from his shows compilation, but is none the worse for that. All the singers – Schock, Schramm, Muszely, Gruber, Monika Dahlberg, Harry Friedauer, Helga Wisniewska, Erika Köth and Rosi Rohr – get something swingy and showy to sing and, without exception, do it well. My particular favourites are Friedauer and Dahlberg with the skipping 'Jedes kleine Mädel hat eine kleine Lieblingsmelodie', Muszely's bravura solo and Schock's very gentle performance of 'Auf der Heide bluh'n die letzten Rosen' (from the film *Herbstmanöver*).

Frühjahrsparade

More successful than any of these last mentioned discs is Ariola-Eurodisc's recording of the pretty, lively *Frühjahrsparade*, featuring members of the cast of the original 1964 Volksoper production. The uncomplicatedly charming and very Viennese score of this operetta is partly the same as that of the Hollywood film of 1941, and what is known to the English-speaking world as Deanna Durbin's 'Waltzing' reappears as 'Singend, klingend ruft dich das Glück' amongst a barrage of dancing and marching melodies and some attractively unforced lyric solos and duos for the prima donna and her tenor.

Stolz is at the baton on the recording, which is headed vocally by two contrasting sopranos – bubbly soubrette Guggi Löwinger, diving rhythmically into her 'Jój, Mamám!' and the happy 'Ich freu' mich', and the tasteful and touching Mimi Coertse, who makes much of her fine set-piece Vienna solos 'Wien wird bei Nacht erst schön' and 'Im Frühling, im Mondschein, in Grinzing in Wien' – and tenors Peter Minich and Erich Kuchar. *Frühjahrsparade* is one of those works where simplicity is a virtue, and the cast and composer have combined here to bring it to disc in a simple and effective way.

Apart from the Ariola issues, Stolz's operettas have been little recorded, but an unexceptional French disc including selections from *Fruhjahrsparade*, *Trauminsel* and *Wenn die kleinen Veilchen blühen* exists on the TLP label with Claudine Granger and Bernard Sinclair featured.

Kattnigg, Raymond, Schröder and Burkhard

Amongst the other shows from the circa-war era that have been recorded in any significant way are Rudolf Kattnigg's *Balkanliebe* (1938), Fred Raymond's *Maske in Blau* (1937) and *Saison in Salzburg* (1938) and Friedrich Schröder's *Hochzeitsnacht im Paradies* (1942). The first of these has been Schock-and-Schrammed by Ariola-Eurodisc in a half-dozen song selection. When the selection opens with Schock pulling out his utmost, singing yet another swingeing song about his 'Heimat' (homeland), it is clear that *Balkanliebe* is nothing if not old-fashioned, and sure enough it turns out to be a big-sing operetta score, agreeable enough but a bit relentless, on a disc which, given its artists, concentrates only on the romantic music. The other side is devoted to *Der Försterchristel* (1907) by Georg Jarno.

Fred Raymond (*né* Friedrich Vesely) was, as can be seen by his choice of name, quite the opposite to Kattnigg. He was a thoroughly modern 1930s composer of popular songs ('I Left My Heart in Heidelberg') and musical comedy. There are still romantic melodies in his shows to pair with the up-to-date dance tunes, but he is no writer of the big-sing operetta.

Maske in Blau

I don't care for his biggest success, *Maske in Blau*. Not even its soubrette hit songs 'Ja, das Temperament' – so reminiscent of something . . . is it Charles Strouse's *Annie?* – and 'Die Juliska aus Budapest', nor its South American songs, which are definitely reminiscent of quite a lot of Hollywood movies, nor 'Frühling in San Remo', which is is no 'I Left my Heart in Heidelberg'. However, the show has been freely recorded on more than half a dozen half-discs and EPs and even more substantially by Schock, Schramm and Marika Rökk (who gets the hit songs) on a whole Ariola-Eurodisc, so someone must like it.

Saison in Salzburg

On the other hand, I find Raymond's much less exotic *Saison in Salzburg*, with its unembarrassed Austrian fooleries, quite delightful. Its main recording is a selection on Polydor, where can be heard the clear tenor of Franz Fehringer doing the romancing of a Renate Holm in her sweetest voice and Peter Alexander and Herta Talmar making hay with various-sized fragments of the jaunty, silly, lighter songs of the score. Another 'temperament' number, 'Der Grosspapa von Grossmama', is much more fun than the more famous 'Juliska' and, from the lilting waltz hymn to 'Salzburger Nockerln' (a sort of sweet waffle which is the basis of the plot!) to the tuneful *gaucherie* of the comic love song 'Der Toni mit dem Vroni', the happy, gliding melodies of the real romance ('Warum denn nur bin ich in dich verliebt', 'Weisst du denn, wie schwer es ist'), and the polyglot, poppy 'Und die Musik spielt dazu', *Saison in Salzburg* is a jolly comedy musical through and through.

Hochzeitsnacht im Paradies

The Polydor recording pairs *Saison in Salzburg* with a similar selection from Friedrich Schröder's *Hochzeitsnacht im Paradies*, recorded with the same fine team of singers. This is another enjoyable light musical, whose title refers to a honeymoon in the Paradise Hotel where things go nearly as comically wrong as in Feydeau's famous farce of nearly the same title. The numbers range from fairly straight romantic pieces for the off-and-on happy spouses, to such merry pieces as the hero's 'Es kommt auf die Sekunde an' and an oddly Latin song about Venice, all played in a happy, big-band manner and jauntily and unportentously sung.

There are several other agreeable half-disc recordings of this piece, one ten-number one on EMI-Electrola (with a cast including Anneliese Rothenberger) on similar lines is backed with *Maske in Blau*, another and shorter one on Concert Hall with *Ein Walzertraum*. But the package with *Saison in Salzburg* is the happiest.

Ariola-Eurodisc devoted one of their 'Welterfolge' compilations to the composer of *Hochzeitsnacht im Paradies* – although 'worldwide success' in the case of Schröder seems a little exaggerated. This over-titled treatment was also given to post-war composers Peter Kreuder (*Wedding-Mary* (1971), *Madame Scandaleuse* (1958)) and Gerhard Winckler (*Premiere in Mailand* (1950), *Die ideale Geliebte* (1957)) with equal dubiousness. All these recordings disappeared from the shops with a remarkable speed and have never been seen or heard since. But they must be out there somewhere.

Feuerwerk

One composer who genuinely did have a worldwide success, however, was Paul Burkhard, whose musical *Feuerwerk* (1950) won a series of foreign and foreign-language productions on the back of the international popularity of its hit song 'Oh, My Papa'. The song, of course, has been widely recorded, but a *Feuerwerk* selection, labelled as such, has appeared only on an Ariola-Eurodisc 45 EP recording, with Liselott Ebnet and Brigitte Mira featured. A cast disc, under the title *Der schwarze Hecht* (the one-act musical from which the show was developed), which seems to approximate what we know as *Feuerwerk*, was recorded live in Zurich in 1981. In spite of top-notch performances from Inigo Gallo as extravagant Uncle Alois with his crazy circus song 'Man hat's nicht leicht', and a seductive and individual sounding Ines Torelli as Iduna, it is a cheerfully dreadfully sung affair, but it gives some idea of the dialect 'comedy with songs and a couple of pianos' that the show was in its early incarnation. In recent years it has reached the Volksoper. Quite what it sounded like there I do not know, but I have a suspicion that I would prefer this Zurich recording.

My Ten Essential Records

PHI-PHI: selection, with Bourvil, Gise Mey and Germaine Roger (EMI-Pathé 057.10840)

MEDITERRANEE: selection, with Rudi Hirigoyen and Janine Ribot (Odéon XOC 186/CBS 88.254)

LA ROUTE FLEURIE: selection, with Bourvil, Georges Guétary and Annie Cordy (EMI-Pathé 057.10532)

LES TROIS VALSES: selection, with Mathé Altéry (EMI-Pathé 2C 051–10847)

DIE DREIGROSCHENOPER: in English as *The Threepenny Opera*, off-Broadway revival cast recording, with Scott Merrill, Jo Sullivan and Charlotte Rae (MGM S-31210C)

L'AUBERGE DU CHEVAL BLANC (*Im weissen Rössl*): complete, in French, with Bourvil, Andrine Forli, Michel Dens and Janine Ervil (2 records, EMI-Pathé EMI 1C 161 12087–8)

DAS LAND DES LÄCHELNS: complete, with Nicolai Gedda and Elisabeth Schwarzkopf (2 records, Columbia 33CX 1114/5)
DIE ROSE VON STAMBUL/DER LIEBE AUGUSTIN: with Fritz Wunderlich (EMI Columbia SMC 83454)
DIE KAISERIN/DIE ROSE VON STAMBUL: selections, with Anny Schlemm, Franz Fehringer and Fritz Wunderlich (RCA VL 30407)
GRÄFIN MARIZA: complete, with Anneliese Rothenberger and Nicolai Gedda (2 records, EMI 157 29068-9)

Other Recommended Records

Ciboulette: complete, with Mady Mesplé, Nicolai Gedda and José van Dam (2 records, EMI-Pathé 2C167-73105-6)
Chanson gitane: selection, with André Dassary, Liliane Berton, Maria Murano and Duvaleix (EMI-Pathé 057.10846)
Ta bouche: selection, with Suzanne Lafaye and Jacques Jansen (Decca 215.922)
Dédé: complete, with dialogue and narration by Maurice Chevalier (2 records, Decca 115.057-8); or revival cast recording, with Antoine (RCA Victor 440.760)
Là-haut: complete, with dialogue, with Maurice Chevalier (2 records, Decca 115.198-9)
Un de la Canebière: selection, with Philippe Fargues (TLP 91013)
La Belle de Cadix: selection, with Rudy Hirigoyen (CBS 88 254)
Andalousie: selection, with Rudy Hirigoyen and Janine Ribot (Odéon XOC 168)
Viva Napoli: selection, with Rudy Hirigoyen, Nicole Broissin and Luc Barney (Philips 6521.010)
Irma la douce: revival cast live performance, with Colette Renard and Franck Fernandel (2 records, Véga 16.089-90)
La Revolution française: complete recording (2 records, Vogue LDM 30166)
Les Triomphes d'Yvonne Printemps: including archive excerpts from Les Trois Valses, Véronique, Ta bouche, L'Amour masqué, Mozart, Mariette and La Grande-Duchesse de Gérolstein: (EMI-Pathé 2C 064-12869)
Paganini: complete, with Nicolai Gedda and Anneliese Rothenberger (2 records, EMI SLS 5184)
Der Zarewitsch: complete, with Nicolai Gedda and Rita Streich (2 records, EMI 1C 157-29020-1)
Giuditta: selection, with Sylvia Geszty and Rudolf Schock (Ariola-Eurodisc 89 879 IE)
Die Zirkusprinzessin: selection, with Rudolf Schock and Margit Schramm (Ariola-Eurodisc 75447 IE)
Die Bajadere: Russian studio cast recording, with Ludmilla Belobragina (2 records, Melodiya CM 04313-16)
Das Vetter aus Dingsda: complete, with René Kollo, Grit van Jüten, Benno Kusche and Angelika Wolff (2 records, RCA RL 30867)
Der letzte Walzer: selection, with Rudolf Christ and Margit Opawsky (Vogue MGM 120002/Period RL1904)
Glückliche Reise: selection (b/w Das Vetter aus Dingsda), with Christine Görner and Kurt Wehofschitz (DaCapo CO47-28 129); or selection (b/w Das Vetter aus Dingsda), with Ruthilde Boetsch and Rudolf Christ (Fontana 701 515 WPY)
Die grosse Sünderin: selection, with Maud Cunitz and Rudolf Schock (RCA VL 30317)

Viktoria und ihr Husar/Die Blume von Hawaii: selections, with Heinz Hoppe, Sári Bárabás, Sonja Knittel and Willi Hagara (Columbia SMC 83458)

Saison in Salzburg/Hochzeitsnacht im Paradies: selections, with Herta Talmar, Peter Alexander, Renate Holm and Franz Fehringer (Polydor 237 159)

Venus in Seide: selection, with Margit Schramm and Rudolf Schock (Ariola-Eurodisc 89 872 IE)

Frühjahrsparade: selection, with Guggi Löwinger, Mimi Coertse, Peter Minich and Erich Kuchar (Ariola-Eurodisc 71 569 IE)

CHAPTER 7

Bonanza on Broadway:
the first part

It has become curiously fashionable to mark *Oklahoma!* as a significant and seminal show in the formal development of the musical theatre in America. It is a fashion I've never fully been able to understand – the show is, after all, a splendid old-fashioned romantic operetta – just as I have problems with the other easy cut-up of Broadway history habitually made at the Princess Theatre musicals of Bolton and Kern and Co. However, significant or not in form, there is no doubt that *Oklahoma!* was the most popular musical to arrive on Broadway since the great days of Friml, Kern, Romberg and Youmans and that it deserves to be marked with a white stone as the beginning of the second coming of the Broadway musical both on the home and the international scene. Given its position as one of the earliest Broadway cast recordings issued on LP, it also provides a very handy starting point for this particular section of this particular work. In fact, the five great classic works of Richard Rodgers and Oscar Hammerstein II, ranging from *Oklahoma!* in 1943 through *Carousel*, *South Pacific* and *The King and I* to *The Sound of Music* in 1959 provide a regular backbone to the first part of the Broadway bonanza years which are the subject of this chapter.

All these five musicals have received outstanding stage, film and record success and, by rights, all five should have their place in any but the smallest collection of show records. Since, however, to include all five in my representative list of ten from the first part of this period would mean omitting too many other fine works and lead to a kind of historical imbalance, the invidious task of comparing these five shows and their recordings arises. If pressed, I think I would have to admit personally to preferring *The King and I* in the theatre and *The Sound of Music* on film, but on record? A careful listening to the mass of discs of the shows made over the past forty years was necessary to help me make up my mind. It was a pleasant task, by and large, as none of the five loses anything in having its score displayed without the libretto – in fact, a piece like *Carousel*, shorn of its textual mixture of homespun drama and whimsy, positively gains – and all have been the subject of fine recordings as well as the most appalling desecration.

Rodgers and Hammerstein

Oklahoma!

The record of *Oklahoma!* that went round the world, and which turns up even in some households where not another musical theatre record is found, is the 1955 film soundtrack with its familiar cover featuring Gordon MacRae and Shirley Jones driving off in the surrey with the fringe on top in front of a violent orange sky which I assume is the proverbial sunset, since the whole point of the story is that they *didn't* go off in the surrey until the finale. It is a fine record of a fine film, with both the stars in excellent vocal form, his attractive clean baritone and her straightforward combination of unforced chest and soprano tones fitting effortlessly into a pair of romantic-bucolic rôles which are not at all as easy to perform as they might seem. The lollipops of the romantic part of the score – 'Oh, What a Beautiful Mornin'', 'The Surrey With the Fringe on Top', 'Out of my Dreams', 'Many a New Day' and the duet 'People Will Say We're in Love' all come out splendidly.

The support performances, too, are grand. Gloria Grahame is outstanding as Ado Annie, the girl who 'cain't say no', avoiding what can be and is on nearly every other recording of this show a soubrette performance of half-squawk and half-tortured vowels, and providing instead a cute-voiced and slightly bewildered outback nymphet who genuinely doesn't understand why she can't stop herself enjoying herself with men. She is marvellously paired with a cloth-eared, comical Will Parker (Gene Nelson), who suffers not at all from the pitiful bowdlerization of the lyric to his best number relating his naughty adventures in 'Kansas City'.

The orchestra, conducted by the show's original stage musical director Jay Blackton (who has a string of *Oklahoma!* recordings to his baton and has clearly helped to stop the orchestral excesses which attack so many show records), uses what are said to be the original Robert Russell Bennett orchestrations, but I find that orchestrally this version lacks some of the vigour and vitality of, in particular, the original stage recording. The edges seem to have been smoothed off and the score 'violinned' into something politer.

The original cast recording was first issued on a 78 rpm set and only in 1949 transferred by Decca onto LP. It, too, is a splendid recording, driven along by Blackton from the very first beats of the overture with the spirit and vivacity that were among the show's most immediate and attractive features, carrying you through tune after tune until you arrive at 'Oh, What a Beautiful Mornin'' and the gloriously sung, warm and unaffected performance of Alfred Drake as Curly.

His Laurey, Joan Roberts, makes her character a pleasant, healthy ingénue with an attractive singing voice, whilst the comedians Lee Dixon (Will) and Celeste Holm (Annie) treat their set-piece numbers like set-piece numbers, in a manner which, if a tiny bit stagey for record, obviously would have worked well as knock-'em-in-the-aisles theatre material. The biggest plusses for this version are Drake's Curly, unequalled on record, and Blackton's orchestra, but the minus – in comparison with later LPs – has to be the sound quality. It is not bad – not on the original Decca release anyhow, though the 1969 MCA repressing is horrible – but it is just not up to the sophistication of later recordings.

A good example of the improvements made over the years in this department comes with the RCA cast recording of the 1979 Broadway revival. Fortunately Blackton is still around to conduct and fortunately he brings with him both the orchestrations of the first production and the energy and verve that characterized that production. Added to first-class technical values, an increase in disc space, which allows pieces of the score previously omitted to be included, and some fine casting, this makes up a recording which, in spite of the fine competition that has gone before, is pretty irresistible.

The Curly of this revival was Laurence Guittard. His baritone is a lighter instrument than the very masculine-sounding voice of Alfred Drake; where Drake sounded like a grown man, this Curly is a boy, full of youthful energy and high spirits, capable of both the silly tantrum of hurt pride which lets him deny the existence of the surrey in Act 1, and the heartfelt emotion with which he begs Laurey to marry him in Act 2. Whether it played like that on the stage I don't know, but that's what it sounds like on disc and it makes a lot of sense, particularly as his Laurey is played by Christine Andreas as a determined country girl with a strong personality and an excellent unfussy voice, in the same mould as Shirley Jones and Joan Roberts but with just that little extra bite. It is a fine young-sounding pairing which takes a lot of the cardboard out of what too often become a rather silly duo of operetta juveniles.

The soubret pair, Harry Groener (Will) and Christine Ebersole (Annie), are not quite as successful as their romantic counterparts, playing their rôles, as in the original stage version, with that old-fashioned emphasis on being the comedy of the show, but he turns out a punchy performance of 'Kansas City' and, although she makes some pretty odd and unsympathetic noises in her big number, they join appealingly together in 'All Er Nuthin''.

The fact that the scena 'It's a Scandal! It's an Outrage!' and the solo 'Lonely Room', cut from the film and not recorded on the original stage album, are given an unaccustomed airing here means that the artists playing the comic Ali Hakim (Bruce Adler) and villainous Jud Fry (Martin Vidnovic) are briefly featured. Adler, a very Jewish-Persian Ali, clips through his piece with convincing fun, but Vidnovic, a fine singer, does not quite have the power for his number. Although it is written for a short-range voice, 'Lonely Room' is a starkly dramatic little solo of sub-operatic style and power which looks forward to the strongest music of *Carousel* and, if it is to make its effect amongst the charm and fun of the rest of the score, it needs to be sung rather more blackly than here. To this small quibble may be added another over the slightly unexhilarating performance of the hoedown 'The Farmer and the Cowboy', but, even if Jule Styne's unnecessary claim on the sleeve note that this is '*the* definitive cast recording of this musical' is an exaggeration, it is probable that it is indeed a more useful recording than either the film track or the original stage disc.

The success of this revival prompted reproductions in both Britain and Australia, but the discs that resulted – a badly recorded live-in-the-theatre affair in London and a rather ordinary one from Australia – do not compare with the American one; nor do the recordings made of the original London version of 1947, re-recorded in tandem with *Annie Get Your Gun* on Stanyan, which have the particularity of featuring the young Howard Keel as Curly.

Alongside Drake, Keel and Macrae, two of the other most famous baritone leading men of the American stage have recorded studio versions of *Oklahoma!* amongst the many such discs. John Raitt, a take-over Curly on the first 1944 tour and the original star of *Carousel*, gives a strangely mannered and unimpressive performance on Columbia alongside a Florence Henderson (Laurey) who seems to have trouble with the break in her voice, and some unnecessary and heavily billed new orchestrations. Nelson Eddy, on the same label, sings much better but sounds, amongst a wholly ill-chosen cast, like a Curly in a collar and tie playing opposite a middle-aged secretary of a Laurey (Virginia Haskins), and what is, if nothing else, the loudest Ado Annie on record (Kaye Ballard).

Oddly, probably the most enjoyable studio cast recording of *Oklahoma!* is in German. Ariola-Eurodisc were responsible for a selection rendered in a German version by Eberhard Storch which scatters the numbers about in any old order but comes up with a superbly relaxed and warm-voiced Curly (Benno Kusche), a sweet and true Laurey (Christine Görner) and a couple of very buffo comics (Fifi Brix and Heinz Maria Lins) who bounce the score along over some decidedly merry arrangements to great effect. The opening 'Die Farmer und die Cowboys' is a real 'get up and dance', whilst 'Wundervoll ist dieser Morgen' is given a rich, off-hand treatment wholly suited to its words, and 'Nur alles oder gar nichts' is a right little German musical comedy tiff. It is a bit worrying to read on the sleeve that Will Parker is a 'Zirkusreiter' and that the synopsis manages to omit Jud Fry altogether, but the fun of the record makes it a novelty worth listening to . . . preferably after a safe dose of one of the three major US recordings.

Carousel

Carousel, which followed *Oklahoma!* to Broadway in 1945, is a less frivolous and light-hearted piece than its predecessor both textually and musically, as befits a musical based on an essentially tragic play, and its libretto and its score, while recognizably from the same hands as *Oklahoma!*, have a different feeling to them. The music written for *Carousel*'s hero is much more substantial than 'Oh, What a Beautiful Mornin'', its sentimental songs have a ring of drama about them which contrasts with the gentle flippancy of 'People Will Say We're in Love' and there are no traditional low comedy characters to deliver set-piece songs like 'Kansas City' or 'I Cain't Say No'. Instead, there is a score that mixes drama and powerful singing, in such pieces as the hero's famous Soliloquy and the equally celebrated paean to self-sufficiency 'You'll Never Walk Alone', with truly poignant moments such as the heroine's simple 'What's the Use of Wonderin'', vigorous chorus numbers and the warmly personal 'Mr Snow' and 'When the Children Are Asleep', allotted to the delightfully drawn second-billed couple, Carrie Pipperidge and Enoch Snow, who replace the stand-up comedy with a much less extravagant kind of enjoyment.

It is a score which, with its contrasts and substance, lends itself marvellously to recording, and it is not surprising that there have been, as in the case of *Oklahoma!*, several fine discs made. Most of them include most of the score. There was just a little too much for the earlier discs to cope with and, in consequence, the hero's final piece 'The Highest Judge of All' or Mr Snow's 'Geraniums in the Winder' are in turn omitted whilst some other numbers also lose their introductory verses. Although this is regrettable from the point of view of completeness, it certainly doesn't harm the records for pure listening pleasure.

Again as with *Oklahoma!*, the best-selling record of *Carousel* has undoubtedly been its excellent film soundtrack. If there is a complaint about this disc, and I'm not sure there is, it is the same as that turned on the *Oklahoma!* soundtrack – the piece sounds just a bit too neat. When the orchestra strikes up the first bars of the Carousel Waltz, which replaces the usual pot-pourri overture in this show, it has just a mite too much of that Hollywood synthesized sound to it – but only a mite. And there are many advantages which soon swamp any such misgiving.

Gordon MacRae is supreme as the jack-the-lad Billy Bigelow. Even better suited here than as *Oklahoma!*'s swaggering cowboy, he uses his impeccably clean, masculine baritone to splendid effect, making a great little self-conversation of the Soliloquy rather than the feet-apart aria others favour, and building a believeable relationship with the sweet and straightforward Julie of Shirley Jones which comes across effectively in spite of the fact that the bits of spoken dialogue between the portions of song are often omitted, providing a hiccup in the dramatic continuity. The other principal cast members are fine, too. Claramae Turner gives a gently expressive performance of 'You'll Never Walk Alone' with a lovely, sympathetic tone, which is right for the show if wrong for the English football crowds who have adopted this number as a supporters' song. Barbara Ruick makes Carrie a friendly, conversational character with an attractive singing voice and Robert Rounseville's Mr Snow verges on the operatic without falling over the edge.

The selection omits 'The Highest Judge of All' and Mr Snow's little piece, which were not included in the film. This version also made a number of minor cuts and changes to the score and the lyrics (excising, no doubt for propriety's sake, Billy's 'My God' in the Soliloquy) and even fiddled a bit with the story. A little more of Molnar's original dark colourings, which have always seemed to me to mix ill with the final fantasy portions of the show (where the dead Billy is taken to heaven and back again like the hero of *Là-haut*), were eased out and Billy allowed to die by accident rather than at his own hand.

A more strictly accurate account of the original show can be found on the Decca cast recording of the 1945 stage production. This is another fine version, which has subsequently been re-recorded by MCA much more successfully than their parallel attempt with the *Oklahoma!* discs. John Raitt is the Billy here and, although

I personally give the palm for this rôle to Macrae, it really is nip-and-tuck. Raitt is vocally superb, his lovely light brown baritone, even throughout the whole of the rôle's range, making mincemeat of his music; it is only because Macrae is so very convincing dramatically that this performance shows up marginally less effectively in that department. Raitt's partner, Jan Clayton, is another of those splendidly unaffected contemporary American show singers able to mix a clear, straight soprano top register seamlessly into a pleasant unforced chest 'show' tone (alas, where have they gone in this age of shouters?), and both she and Jean Darling as Carrie give their songs a beautifully natural interpretation. The cast is completed by Christine Johnson, a nice uncomplicated mezzo who treats 'You'll Never Walk Alone' with clear sincerity, and another remarkable high baritone, Eric Mattson, as a particularly effective Enoch Snow.

'The Highest Judge' gets onto this record, and is given a first-rate performance by Raitt. It is also interesting to notice the variation in the words of the Soliloquy – a rather tame section seems to have been supressed after the first production. There are no complaints about this record, as long as you can find a copy which has good clean sound, but much to my surprise I find that, in preference to either of these fairly impeccable versions, I plump for an RCA disc of a 1965 Lincoln Center revival. It has more faults, perhaps, but also a list of advantages which for me more than compensate.

This revival starred Raitt, returning to his original rôle twenty years later at the age of forty-eight, and it was not to be expected that he would still be able to give the performance of his youth. He doesn't, but there's not a lot in it. It is not so much that he is a little diminished in voice – it is clear and vigorous if a tiny bit less fresh than twenty years previously – but his style has become somewhat conventional and studded with the little swoops and tricks of the artist who has been inveigled into cabaret once too often. This does not intrude to an objectionable level, however, and the cocky, rather objectionable character of Billy comes over well in both dialogue and song.

The ability to put over dialogue is important, given the way the show has been laid out for this recording. Full-length versions of the songs and their introductions have been skilfully linked with just sufficient spoken text to situate the songs in their context and, unusually, the dialogue pieces inherent in the numbers are also included. The result is a recording that has a sense of story and an atmosphere lacking elsewhere, and the omission of the number 'There's Nothin' So Bad for a Woman' (although 'Highest Judge' gets in) is a small price to pay in return.

The rest of the cast are uniformly excellent. Eileen Christy – whom I have never heard of before or since – is a model Julie, simple and appealing in expression and with a strong, easy, well-modulated singing voice, and Katherine Hilgenberg is an operatic Nettie who nevertheless produces a smashing show sound in her lower register and turns 'You'll Never Walk Alone' into a Jessye Norman prayer. But the real treat lies in a truly endearing Carrie and Enoch in Susan Watson and Reid Shelton: their performance of 'When the Children Are Asleep' is an object lesson in musical theatre performance. She is bright-voiced and sparkling with youthful piquancy, he combines his fine straight tenor with a sense of character and of gentle comedy too often missing in Mr Snows, who spend most of the performance thinking about the coming top note. The result is a performance in which not just the refrain and the top note, but every line gets its musical and textual due.

Franz Allers's orchestra was given new orchestrations by Don Walker for this revival, but they turn out to be pretty much in line with the old ones. Where they differ, they are innocuous enough not to spoil the enjoyment of what is a thoroughly well-played and up-beat version of a show that can too easily become down in the mouth and/or overblown under unsympathetic production circumstances.

Such circumstances are in evidence on the only other American cast recording, a television soundtrack from 1967. Robert Goulet, drowned in echo, pours his rich voice all over the rôle of Billy and pulls about the music he has to sing tactlessly, whilst Patricia Neway (Nettie) and Marlyn Mason (Carrie) oversing unpleasantly in a version that is as far from the virile simplicity of the original *Carousel* as can be.

Most baritones who have ventured even on to the fringes of the musical theatre usually like to have a go at the Soliloquy and it is not surprising to see, amongst the goodly list of studio cast recordings, discs with Robert Merrill and Alfred Drake starred. I do not have the Merrill recording, but Drake's version is not a success. The star gives a pompous and vocally uncomfortable performance as the seaside lout on a recording in which the main interest is hearing Met diva Roberta Peters (whose lovely voice is almost wholly free of operatic mannerisms) managing to sing in one breath lines for which most girls take two or three. This disc (which we are informed in big letters is originally mastered on 35/MM magnetic film) also takes some sort of a prize for over-the-top sleeve text: 'you are hearing a whole new musical world opening up before your ears – a musical world never known to listeners anywhere before.' Boring, isn't it? You can almost bet the disc will be a dodo before you start listening.

A new *Carousel* has been issued as recently as 1987. It too goes in for claims in big letters on the cover ('Newly Orchestrated', 'First Digital Recording') and it, too, sadly is a dodo. The new orchestrations are harmless enough and the digital process is probably responsible for only a bit of the boring sound. The fault is elsewhere. It is called pretentiousness. This recording ranges from the polite to the pompous, through some often indulgent orchestral playing and scraggy chorusing, to a set of solo performances that can only be called inapposite.

Opera bass Samuel Ramey is Billy, a stuffy, throaty Billy whose wooffy singing never thrills and who gets nothing of the character into Hammerstein's larrikin. If he wishes to swap his Mephistopheles for musical theatre, he should be set to listen to Raitt and Macrae twenty-four hours a day to learn how to open up, relax and soar with Rodgers's melodies. Barbara Cook, a marvellous Julie thirty years ago, gives a warm, feeling performance in the rôle, but it is a rôle she should never have now been asked to play. Her voice has a maturity wholly at odds with the character. She could have been a splendid Nettie, which would have spared us Maureen Forrester's uncomfortable performance. The RCA disc proves that an opera singer can tackle Nettie, but not like this! David Rendall (Snow) falls into the same awful trap, and the sole moment of listening pleasure on the disc comes from the one clever piece of modern musical theatre casting, Sarah Brightman's delicious performance as Carrie.

The other pleasure comes from Stanley Green's informative and interesting insert note, but even it comes to grief in its last paragraph, a paragraph one can almost see being inserted under orders. Trying to justify the unjustifiable casting, he writes: 'It is undeniable that one of the great accomplishments of *Carousel* is that, with the exception of Gershwin's *Porgy and Bess*, it was the first major breakthrough in bridging the gap between the two forms of lyric theatre'. Come off it, Mr Green. You are at least one century too late!

If I have gone on at rather more length about this recording than it would merit, it is because I see in it a worrying trend. The great American musicals of the 1940s and 1950s now seem to have arrived at classic status and thus, it seems, are becoming worthy both of being tricked out with 'significance' and of being given what are intended to be definitive recordings. Sadly, some of those producing the recordings do not seem to have a liking of or a trust in the musical theatre and its performers. They seem to have the feeling that this little 'art form' needs to be given the weight and the help of souped-up 1980s orchestrations and performers from another area, the more respectable world of opera.

There is no reason why singers who are successful in opera cannot be equally so in lighter music. It has been happening in the theatre for centuries and on disc with such recent performers as Robert Merrill, Regina Resnik, Nicolai Gedda, Elisabeth Schwarzkopf, Roberta Peters, Gabriel Bacquier, June Bronhill, Robert Massard and Frederica von Stade. But you do not sing Rodgers the same way that you sing Puccini, and if you can't tell or can't produce the difference, stick to what you can do. If EMI's modern *Show Boat* can get it so very right, there is no excuse for a depressing record like this MCA *Carousel*.

South Pacific

South Pacific, based like its two predecessors on a piece of established romantic fiction, continued Rodgers and Hammerstein's series of 'human interest' musicals and brought to the stage in a memorable love story a couple – an ageing expatriate Frenchman and a US Army nurse flung together in the arena of the Pacific war – whose dramatic dimensions were a light year away from the flimsy hero and heroine of *Oklahoma!*. In spite of its subject matter, however, *South Pacific* never took on the rather sombre colours of *Carousel*, and much of the credit for this can be attributed to its score, a winning combination of the gently romantic and the surprisingly low comic which eschewed the more dramatic moments and more obvious showpieces of the earlier musical.

There were, perhaps, fewer take-out tunes than before, but any show that contains in a well-balanced score such numbers as 'Younger Than Springtime', the inescapable 'Some Enchanted Evening' and its less often heard but even more beautiful partner 'This Nearly Was Mine' as love songs, such sparky soubrette numbers as 'I'm Gonna Wash That Man Right Outa My Hair' and extras like the impossibly atmospheric 'Bali H'ai' is doing pretty well.

It was and is noticeable that this score requires less real singing than the two earlier ones. With the rôle of the Frenchman, Emile, being created for opera star Ezio Pinza, its music is necessarily written in a legitimate vein, but there is no soprano. The heroine of *South Pacific* is a soubrette and limited vocal demands are made of her. Amongst the rest of the cast only the light baritone juvenile man, Lieutenant Cable (whose romance with the native girl Liat is the main sub-plot), and the low comedy lady playing Liat's mother, Bloody Mary (whose 'Bali H'ai' is, like 'You'll Never Walk Alone' in *Carousel*, the chance for the big female sing of the evening), need to sing well.

Once again, the soundtrack from the film, which helped engrave this show, like its counterparts, into the popular consciousness of places far, far away from Broadway and from America, has always been the most prominent amongst the cast recordings. Mitzi Gaynor and Rossano Brazzi, gazing into each other's eyes on the Todd-Ao cover, decorated most people's gramophones in my youth, and such was the potency of the picture that even my parents, who almost never went inside a cinema, drove to town to take in *South Pacific*. I remember they weren't very keen on the special effects which turned the Pacific skies odd colours during 'Bali H'ai', but they bought the record.

Actually, this soundtrack is not up to the *Oklahoma!* and *Carousel* ones. It isn't just the excess of fiddles, it isn't just the fact that it lacks a truly magnetic performance anywhere; somehow the whole thing just doesn't have a real presence. Don't ask me to explain that in detail, I couldn't. I wonder, perhaps, if it is because of the fact that only Mitzi Gaynor of the four stars actually sings her own rôle. The rest are dubbed. I've always been violently against dubbing, just as I've hated the idea of splicing in odd (usually high) notes into insufficient recorded performances or the now electronic 'correcting' of badly pitched or timed singing. It seems unnatural somehow. And I've always felt sorry for the dubbing singers, who are mostly uncredited, and wondered why they shouldn't just have had the rôle. Was it because they lacked presence? Maybe that lack of presence is felt when you hear the songs of this film without hearing or seeing the more magnetic actors who played the spoken and seen parts of the rôles.

Giorgio Tozzi was the voice of Rossano Brazzi here and he sings his music thoughtfully, opening up with a rich baritone and a purposefully hefty accent in his big moments. Bloody Mary was played by the original stage performer, Juanita Hall, but her 'Bali H'ai' was junked and preference given to the London Bloody Mary, Muriel Smith, who sings that number (backed by a whole heavenful of disembodied voices) and 'Happy Talk' in a characterful negro style. This might seem unsuitable for the rôle of a character described as a little wizened yellow Tonkinese, but since Rodgers and Hammerstein seem to have cast large black women rather than little yellow ones in this show from the start I guess they changed their mind.

Bill Lee croons 'Younger Than Springtime' on behalf of John Kerr and also gets 'My Girl Back Home', a song cut from the stage show but reinstated for the film. Mitzi Gaynor holds her own with the dubbers with a charming soubrette performance, but one that lacks a little in bite and fun and, since neither she nor Tozzi/Brazzi set the score alight, you end up with a competent recording which just doesn't thrill.

You soon see why when you listen to the original cast recording. From the overture, it is a differently felt performance as Salvatore dell'Isola and his orchestra swing into Robert Russell Bennett's splendid orchestrations with real vigour. Then, when you arrive at the Twin Soliloquies, where Emile and Nellie, together, are each wondering, separately, what the other thinks of them, and when romance blossoms in the voice of Ezio Pinza's Emile with 'Some Enchanted Evening', you know that this just couldn't be done better. It must help, of course, to have a rôle specially written for you as this one was for Pinza, but many a specially written rôle has had a less than perfect performance. This one hasn't. Pinza employs his superb, rich but never obtrusively operatic bass with utter mastery in a beautifully judged singing and acting performance, highlighted by a rendition of 'This Nearly Was Mine' which is utterly memorable. In fact, here I'll stick my neck out, and say 'probably the most memorable basso piece in all recorded light musical theatre'. The whole score sounds so very and wonderfully right, nestled warmly in the corners of such a splendid voice, that it makes you wonder why subsequent productions have insisted on casting this rôle, one of the few bass rôles in modern musical theatre, with usually clapped-out baritones and tenors. This recording and Pinza prove their error.

Mary Martin gives a good soubrette performance as Nellie, happiest in the rôle's most lively portions, such as the burlesque 'Honey Bun', to which she gives a bright, edgy attack; William Tabbert makes a youthful, intense Cable without oversinging; and Juanita Hall is a cute Bloody Mary, long on personality but a touch short on voice if you like 'Bali H'ai' to be given the 'You'll Never Walk Alone' treatment. I'm not sure it really needs it, since Bloody Mary's basic function is comical; but if this number isn't sung up the show is very lopsided towards male legitimate singing. The men's chorus, who have plenty to do in this show, notably in the popular 'There Is Nothin' Like a Dame' and 'Bloody Mary', are suitably hearty and suitably unlike the Mormon Tabernacle Choir and, like the rest of the cast, they give a fine backing to the outstanding performance of Pinza.

Originally recorded on Columbia, this 1949 mono recording was reissued in a fresh sleeve (with a fine photograph of Pinza and Martin together replacing the original design) which reproduced the original notes of Morris Hastings. If there were to be a new sleeve, it would have been nice to have had up-to-date notes that took consideration of what had happened to *South Pacific* in the time since its so very successful first production and first recording.

Amongst what has happened are, of course, several revivals. The most important American one was in 1967, when Tozzi appeared at the Music Theatre of Lincoln Center in the rôle he had voiced for the film, playing opposite Florence Henderson.

Its recording is less attractive than its first-rate fellow *Oklahoma!* and *South Pacific* discs. Tozzi is good enough, but he gets a bit 'wooffy' from time to time and, well, he just isn't Pinza. You miss that lovely, flowing richness that the original star provided. As for Miss Henderson, she is bright, harsh and unsympathetic – the sort of nurse you wouldn't want to be nursed by. Irene Byatt is a curious Mary, emitting a series of barely connected sounds in the name of singing with no care at all for the lyrics, and the men's chorus is distressingly broad. There is a difference between low comedy and buffoonery and silly voices.

The first British production, with Wilbur Evans and Miss Martin, was never issued on LP, two EPs supplying all the songs except Miss Martin's solos, but the 1987 London revival has been given a full though not fully satisfying recording. It is thin orchestrally and vocally. Emile Belcourt, who has sung tenor rôles in opera, but whose voice is now more a light baritone and a rather wobbly one at that, has no chance with his big numbers, which are robbed of all their intensity and their particularity by being sung by such a light-coloured voice. Gemma Craven often sounds vocally worn in Nellie's numbers, and even the chocolate cream voice of Bertice Reading, an actress and vocalist to whom I looked for a dazzling big, black Bloody Mary, is disappointing.

Of the many studio cast recordings, the best known is the most recent, a digital effort made by CBS in the wake of their success with a new *West Side Story* starring Kiri te Kanawa and Jose Carreras. Mr Seymour Gartenberg is credited on the sleeve with having the idea to make a *South Pacific* with the same stars. For ideas like this, men have been jailed. However, Mr Gartenberg probably took a percentage and went away happy, for this disc undoubtedly sold a lot of copies. It is also, in fifteen years of record collecting, the disc which I have seen make the quickest appearance and in the greatest numbers in second-hand shops. Carreras is hopelessly miscast in the rôle of Emile and the fact that his music is transposed up means that he is compared with and comprehensively outperformed by Mandy Patinkin, who makes a very intense but comprehensible Cable. Kiri te Kanawa amazingly just about makes it as Nellie. I don't know why an opera star tempted into light music should tackle a soubrette rôle instead of the many lyric ones available, but Ms te Kanawa lightens off valiantly, puts a happy sibilant smile into her voice, and all but succeeds in getting rid of the technical smoothness so needful for opera but so at odds with this bouncing music and, even more, with a character she can never pin down. The result is far from objectionable, but hundreds of soubrettes could have been more apt without sacrificing three-quarters of their trump cards. Sarah Vaughan's hot-and-cold, pitch-imperfect and occasionally jazzy Bloody Mary is in a different show, but it doesn't matter as this project hasn't been thought through and the result is a novelty disc for those interested in stars rather than for those who care for *South Pacific*.

The same comment goes for a Reprise disc of 1963 which gives 'Some Enchanted Evening' to Frank Sinatra, 'Younger Than Springtime' to Bing Crosby, 'There Is Nothin' Like a Dame' to Sammy Davis jr, 'Happy Talk' to

Debbie Reynolds and 'Bloody Mary' to the Hi-Los in a series of individually credited arrangements.

The King and I

The King and I (1951) reverted to the favourite East-versus-West subject of the old British musicals and, treating it in a sincere rather than the usual comical way, gave it perhaps its finest incarnation in the story of the English governess who brings Western learning and values to an Asiatic nation which, in the image of its king, is warily willing to be taught. The central rôle of the piece was that of the governess, Anna Leonowens, conceived for the actress Gertrude Lawrence and thus relying on her greatest assets – a charm and warmth of performance and a delicate sense of comic timing – and making as little as was possible in the way of demands on her rather unsubstantial singing voice.

The ultimate casting of the charismatic young Yul Brynner (instead of the rather different Alfred Drake) as the King meant that the leading male rôle also lacked somewhat in vocal values, and that all the lyrical singing, as a result, had to be channelled into the secondary rôles of the King's slave, Tuptim (soprano), her forbidden lover, Lun Tha (tenor), and the chief royal wife, Thiang (mezzo-soprano). This could have made the show lopsided, but somehow the strong central acting rôles and the charm of the simpler songs Rodgers and Hammerstein gave to Miss Lawrence ('I Whistle a Happy Tune', 'Hello, Young Lovers', 'Getting to Know You') made up for the fact that all the showiest music was sung elsewhere, and the musical knitted together as a very effective stage whole.

But somehow or other it doesn't seem to work as well on disc as on stage. Anna and the King do not have their book scenes with which to establish their importance, he has little to sing, and on most recordings her numbers are either undersung by an actress or oversung by the type of vocalist for whom they were never meant. *The King and I* is a very difficult show to cast effectively and, of all the discs I have heard, there is none which manages to get every rôle satisfyingly covered.

The original cast recordings, of course, centre on actress Annas. On the Broadway version, Miss Lawrence sings awkwardly and tentatively and her personality doesn't come through the songs in the same manner that it did in the theatre. Brynner performs his main piece, 'Puzzlement', very light and straight, giving little hint of the driving character into which his performance would develop in later years, and none of the singers are wholly convincing in their rôles.

The London version is much better. Herbert Lom is a much more authoritative King with a pleasingly handled voice, and Muriel Smith, in her rich but unplummy mezzo, gives a passionate performance of Lady Thiang's superb 'Something Wonderful' which is the best on any record. But Valerie Hobson, like Miss Lawrence, lacks confidence in her singing and, as a result, the accomplished voices of Ms Smith and the juvenile pair and the strength of Lom wipe her recorded performance out.

In the 1956 film version, the makers found a perfect vehicle for the dubbing system. They were able to use the perfect, but non-singing, Deborah Kerr to play Anna whilst using the versatile and vocally skilled Marni Nixon as her voice. Nixon was a splendidly assured and tuneful voice-of-Anna, giving her songs just the kind of warmth they needed without oversinging. She was teamed with a Brynner who had gained much more assurance since the original cast recording, and a marvellously warm Lady Thiang (Terry Saunders) whose solo was flooded with feeling. Reuben Fuentes provided a confident baritone to dub Lun Tha but, for some reason, the makers of the film decided not to replace the breathy, cabaret-style voice of the lovely Rita Moreno in the soprano rôle of Tuptim and the result is curious, to say the least. It is also, certainly, the reason for omitting the duet 'I Have Dreamed' from what is, otherwise, just about the nearest thing to a successful *King and I* disc.

Two American revivals have been recorded, the first from Lincoln Center and the other a return to Broadway by Yul Brynner, twenty-five years after the original production. The Lincoln Center's version, supervised by Rodgers himself, is a rather operatic one. The mezzo-soprano Risë Stevens (Anna) has splendid warmth in her voice, which must have rung beautifully in the theatre, but, try as she might, is too often too weighty for this rôle on disc. Lee Venora, soaring through 'My Lord and Master', gives probably the best recorded version of Tuptim's music and she and Frank Poretta, a fine full-throated tenor, provide the opportunity to hear their duets thoroughly well, if largely, sung. Patricia Neway (Thiang), on the other hand, goes a little too far with a plummy, operatic 'Something Wonderful', which rings uncomfortably false after the more openly sung and acted versions of Muriel Smith and Terry Saunders. This disc, incidentally, includes the music and narration of the celebrated 'The Little House of Uncle Thomas' ballet scena.

The Brynner recording, which includes even more of the previously unrecorded lesser musical pieces (they cannot be called numbers), is not so successful. He has more character and less voice than before, but he is not well supported, as the ladies, led by the perilous June Angela (Tuptim), all seem to have developed a fit of the wobbles.

Alongside these cast recordings there is the usual ration of studio albums and, although none is a winner, two of these produce isolated performances among the best. Barbara Cook, on Columbia, gets the elusive blend of voice and performance needed for Anna and, if she lacks a little of the gentleness which I feel is needed for the rôle, she makes up for it with commitment. Unfortunately, most of the rest of the cast overcommit, and, although there is much attack and much rich singing from such impressive vocalists as Jeannette Scovotti and Anita Darian, there is little in the way of sympathy for the piece or its characters. There are also some pretty meretricious and unfamiliar sounds in the orchestra and a quite risibly awful Lun Tha.

The British Music for Pleasure label was on the verge of bringing off something quite special. Norman Newell's disc cast June Bronhill as a marvellous Anna who sings the part clearly and easily, with effortless diction and a genuine view of the character. Better yet, it paired her with Inia te Wiata as the King, and suddenly you hear what the show would have sounded like if Alfred Drake had been cast in the rôle. It is a whole new slant on the King, with all imitations of Brynner set aside. Here is a rich-voiced, rich-hearted despot who makes 'Puzzlement' into the most important number in the first act.

Alas, the success stops here. The supporting cast on this recording is very weak and, dispensing with a Lady Thiang, Bronhill annexes 'Something Wonderful', which destroys any dramatic integrity it might have had. Still, the result is better than the RCA version, on which Dinah Shore gently swings the rôle of Anna and Patrice Munsel (who also helps herself to Thiang's number) and Tony Martin pair awkwardly in the lyric music.

There have been several foreign-language recordings of *The King and I* and the two I have heard do surprisingly well with it – given the lack of a wholly satisfactory English-language disc. The German cast recording – *Der König und Ich* – with Liselotte Ebnet, Hans Putz and a fine Tuptim in Dorothea Chryst, is an acceptable disc, but the Hebrew version, featuring Rivka Raz as a very warmly felt Anna with a pretty, straight voice, Aric Lavie as a simply sung and un-declamatory King and Michal Peres as a very appealing, young-sounding Tuptim, does better and is let down only by a rather aged-sounding Thiang.

Oh, that it were possible to take Miss Bronhill and te Wiata from one recording, Muriel Smith from a second, and Lee Venora and Poretta from the third and mix them all together to make a *King and I* with not just a feast of fine singing but all the other necessary values as well. Maybe it will happen yet.

The Sound of Music

If *The Sound of Music* has become the widest-known of Rodgers and Hammerstein's musicals throughout the world, it is very largely because of the cinema version which, in real terms, still remains the most successful musical film ever made. The image of Julie Andrews running over the top of her alpine hill to the strains of the show's title song is engraved in the cultures of nations who have probably never heard of *Oklahoma!*, and to this day a comedian only has to have the band strike up those first phrases and toss his or her arms up as if to run forward and an audience immediately goes into the thrill of recognition. That's popular culture.

In this case it's also good stuff, for the film of *The Sound of Music* is a magnificent one. It is also, strangely enough, the only one of the five Rodgers and Hammerstein films in which any significant alteration was made to the stage show in reorganizing it for film. Hammerstein having died before the film version was made, Rodgers wrote and composed two additional songs ('I Have Confidence' and 'Something Good') to add to the already substantial star rôle of Maria (Julie Andrews), whilst cutting the pair of comedy songs performed in the theatre by the supporting actors appearing as Max Detweiler and Elsa von Schräder ('There's No Way to Stop it' and 'How Can Love Survive') and a duo for Maria and Captain von Trapp ('An Ordinary Couple').

The amendments proved to be wisely made, for it was Julie Andrews who, along with the mountains, was the undeniable hit of the movie, and both songs fitted her sweet, flexible voice and sincere acting style splendidly. It also meant that Eleanor Parker (brilliantly cast as Elsa) and Richard Haydn as Max didn't have to be dubbed. Christopher Plummer, who had still a little to sing, was – by the same Bill Lee who had 'done' Lieutenant Cable in *South Pacific* – but with great tact.

The record cannot give all the thrills of the film for, although we get Julie Andrews, we miss the mountains. However, Miss Andrews even without mountains is still a durable treat. From the moment she takes off on those first notes of 'The Sound of Music' to her very last note in the show she gives a landmark performance. It is a remarkable voice, unlike any other I have ever heard, with its sweet, youthful unforced tone through the whole of its range, rock steady up to the very top notes, and with diction of a clarity and naturalness that verges on the impossible. She hasn't even heard of the dreaded modified vowel. However, the lady is by no means just a voice. She puts a personality into her songs, the personality of Maria von Trapp, and you can follow her from the joy of the opening number, through the breathless 'oh, help!' of 'I Have Confidence' and the simple joy of her songs with the children to the wondering, half-unbelieving moments of falling in love in 'Something Good'. It is a performance to treasure.

The Sound of Music is Maria's show and, after the alterations, it became even more Maria's movie. Very few of the rest of the cast are required to sing, the notable exception being the Mother Abbess, the last in the line of Rodgers and Hammerstein's 'big ladies with a big number' in succession to Nettie Fowler, Bloody Mary and Lady Thiang. The Abbess is no less well served than her forebears, for the authors endowed her with one of their most enduring songs, 'Climb Every Mountain'. Enduring, but also horribly difficult: the Mother Abbess is a lady of a certain age, and she is given a number which, to be given its fullest worth, needs to start off at the bottom of the mezzo-soprano voice with a deep, rich sound, yet needs to rise from there right through the whole range of the voice to a perilously high and sustained ending. Few make it.

The film cast Peggy Wood, the original star of *Bitter-Sweet*, to play the rôle, but dubbed her with the soprano voice of Margery McKay, who gives an agreeable performance. She chooses to lighten off the early part of the number in order to keep an even tone throughout, losing a little of the song's impressiveness but avoiding its pitfalls and emphasizing the lyric. Her subordinate nuns (who are irritatingly not billed on the sleeve, although Parker and Haydn who don't perform on the recording are) follow the same way, giving lighter vocal performances than is usual on the stage without losing validity. Dan Truhitte and Charmian Carr are suitably youthful in 'Sixteen Going on Seventeen'.

If you are intent on having a recording of *The Sound of Music* as it was intended for the stage, then this one isn't for you, but that is the only excuse for not preferring this to any and all of the other recordings of the work, for none other equals Andrews's performance, and any *Sound of Music* recording stands or falls on its Maria. In the stage recordings, the Marias seem to fall into two camps, one of out-and-out soubrettes and one of legitimate sopranos, and no one succeeds in the way that Andrews does in encompassing both registers and both styles.

Mary Martin, the star of the original production, falls firmly into the first category, although the term soubrette is perhaps a little misleading as a description of the lady at that stage in her career. She was forty-five years old and the maturity shows in the voice, stronger and more incisive than ever in the middle and a bit dicky when the break has to be encompassed. I'm afraid she sounds like Andrews's mother. She is backed by a group of enthusiastic kids and another of thunderingly chesty nuns (some plummier than others), including a Mother Abbess (Patricia Neway) of the effortful operatic kind, and there are stagey performances from the other supporting performers in a recording that is mostly a bit relentlessly unsubtle.

It is, however, much superior to the London cast album, on which Jean Bayless is overparted as Maria and a rather ill-assorted group of nuns is headed by opera star Constance Shacklock, teetering on the edge of the effortful and the unsteady. Eunice Gayson's intelligent Elsa, however, emerges as rather more aristocratic than the usual cabarettish vamp incongruously put in the rôle.

Australia did better with its original version, which cast June Bronhill as Maria. It isn't quite right. Though the singing is, of course, splendid, she falls into the overly soprano group, even if she makes a good stab at being nice to the children. Rosina Raisbeck almost conquers 'Climb Every Mountain' and there are pleasant performances from the supporting men and rather less pleasant ones from the Elsa and Liesl.

A second Australian production in 1983 took the opposite turn and cast Julie Anthony, London star of *Irene*, as Maria. She sings the rôle very pleasantly, and New Zealand's Anthea Moller turns up what would have been a super Mother Abbess had she not been drowned out half the time by some really horrible orchestrations perpetrated by the show's musical director, who just happens to be the producer of the record. If the Rodgers and Hammerstein office had heard this vulgar mess, with its twiddly piano and crass percussion, I fear Australia would have been doomed to life henceforth without Rodgers and Hammerstein.

This revival was probably encouraged by a London restaging two years earlier, for both took the new songs from the film and interpolated them in the show alongside 'How Can Love Survive'. Australia also kept 'No Way to Stop It'. The London revival made it to disc, but what was a charming performance by Petula Clark on stage is turned into an agony of mannered recording. The remnants of June Bronhill's voice wobble very distressingly in the music of the Mother Abbess. However, the worst thing here is the record sleeve, which must just about take the prize for the most vulgar and amateurish ever. It looks and reads like an amateur seaside revue.

The Sound of Music has won a number of foreign-language productions, but the only discs I know of are a Dutch issue (which I haven't got) and Spanish and French versions of the soundtrack. Teresa Maria sounds really cute and suitable in the Spanish version of the heroine's rôle, although the sound is a bit poor, but Mathé Altéry in French gets the soprano/soubrette mixture almost entirely right and gives a delicious rendition of a mediocre French translation. Both these recordings, however, omit 'Climb Every Mountain'! I can't believe it was snipped from the film – perhaps Margery McKay's English was kept? But why? Is there no Spanish or French mezzo capable of singing the jolly thing?

Needless to say, there are lashings of studio recordings of *The Sound of Music*, mostly with undistinguished casts, although England's World Record Club came out quickly with an alternative to the London cast recording with a list of performers that looked very interesting. Adele Leigh is a pretty soprano Maria, and Patricia Johnson a very impressive Abbess who, like Ms Moller on the Australian disc, is sabotaged by some tactless new arrangements, but Maggie Fitzgibbon plays Elsa like a tart and the men are a bit boring. It is a disc which never catches the spirit of the show in spite of its good intentions. Another disc features the show score sung by the von Trapp singers themselves.

The most recent *Sound of Music* (including the stage score plus the two extra film songs) was made at the end of 1987 amongst the short-lived (I hope) wave of recordings of musicals with operatic casts. If it is often more successful than the others, that is because there is music in this show which requires thorough singing. Thorough singing is what it gets. This is a respectful, careful, every-note-in-its-place recording, which is at its best when the operatic nuns (headed by Eileen Farrell as a Mother Abbess who wins an impressive battle against the orchestra in her number) are on, but rarely bright elsewhere except through its children. Frederica von Stade is a Maria who would never have been made to leave the convent. It is quite clear that she will grow up to be just like the operatic ladies scolding 'Maria' and will one day sing a magnificent 'Climb Every Mountain'. She does her best to lighten off, makes the most glorious sounds in her singing and projects a personality of charm, but she cannot avoid sounding deliberate and unspontaneous in what is essentially a soubrette rôle.

It is odd to hear Elsa, Max and von Trapp operatically sung, but Barbara Daniels (Elsa) relaxes quite effectively when not tempted by legato lines. The gentleman playing the captain insists in his biography that he is 'one of the most accomplished and applauded performers in the world today' (who allows artists to put themselves up to be knocked down with such statements?), which, of course, he isn't, but he has a pleasant, stiffish baritone. Rolf (Neil Jones) and Liesl (the charming Jeanne Menke) give a welcome taste of lightness on this operatic menu, but on the whole this is a very, very serious *Sound of Music*.

Lerner and Loewe

My Fair Lady

The same period that holds the great work of Rodgers and Hammerstein also holds that of another musical theatre pairing, Frederick Loewe and Alan Jay Lerner, who produced four highly successful shows including one, *My Fair Lady*, whose success went beyond the simple meaning of the word to become one of the all time great works of the theatre.

Like the Rodgers and Hammerstein musicals, *My Fair Lady* has many of the ingredients of the classic operetta, the soprano and high baritone/tenor juveniles, the low comedian and the patter man, the romantic story and the comedy subplot; all are brought to play in a musical of the 1950s which, in the manner of the period, differs in several ways from the traditional pattern. The libretto of *My Fair Lady* is a substantial piece of work, adapted as it is from a classic of the English-language stage in G. B. Shaw's *Pygmalion*. It is illustrated by an outstanding series of lyrics by Alan Jay Lerner which help to point Fritz Loewe's score away from the traditional operetta musical line-up towards the shape taken by the song-and-dance shows of the years between the wars. There are no concerted finales, no opening chorus nor any genuine ensemble of solo voices and, in fact, so far is the old musical format now abandoned that *My Fair Lady* does not include in its score so much as a single duet; the nearest approach to ensemble work comes by allowing the chorus to back some of the solo work. The fusion of script and songs has taken the place of the more consciously 'score' preoccupations of earlier years. Such was the musical of the 1950s and *My Fair Lady* is its supreme example.

On its first production on Broadway in 1956 the show won enormous success and the original cast recording made of that production quickly became as much a classic as the show and the production themselves. Looking at it today, when dozens of other *My Fair Lady* productions have been staged in dozens of languages and when umpteen other recordings have followed it on to the market, it is easy to see and appreciate the outstanding qualities of Columbia's original recording and its performers and performances.

Rex Harrison as Professor Henry Higgins and Julie Andrews as Eliza Doolittle, the cockney flowergirl he passes off as an aristocrat by teaching her proper speech, both give highly distinctive performances that have become known and recognized world-wide. Subsequent Higginses and Elizas have had to choose between copying their style and delivery or consciously playing and singing the rôle with different emphases in an attempt at individuality. The result has been that those who have copied have failed to equal the brilliance of the original, whilst those who have pointedly aimed for independence have always been handicapped by not being able to come up with significant improvements. Harrison and Miss Andrews and the rest of the original cast had, of course, the great advantage of being unaware at the time that they were playing and singing one of the ultimate classic shows and a scoreful of what were to be standard songs and they were thus able to perform their numbers simply as part of their stage rôle rather than as the standard singles they later became.

Harrison's mostly spoken and barely-sung performance of Higgins's songs gave a new respectability to the old style of patter performance. So much so, that he found himself thereafter credited by some as having invented the parlando style of delivery and, to this day, when such a style is adopted in a musical rôle, the name of Harrison is sure to get a mention from one of the younger writers on one of the more unworldly newspapers. What made the performance outstanding was not the fact that Harrison spoke through the musical lines, but the way in which he did it – elegantly and in a relaxed manner, taking the character of the spoken dialogue seamlessly through into the musical portions of the piece with the sublime and unselfconscious sense of self-superiority that makes Henry Higgins the eternal character he is. When he demands 'Why Can't the English?' (learn to speak), it is in amazement that anyone should contemplate crushing a vowel when it is so easy not to; when he describes himself as 'An Ordinary Man', and wonders why woman cannot fit meekly and in an orderly fashion into the fringes of his life in 'A Hymn to Him', it is from a genuine knowledge of the fact that he is the centre of the universe.

Harrison conveys all of this and more in a classy, effortless performance which has been imitated countless times since but never equalled, rising to a peak in my favourite number of the score, 'I've Grown Accustomed to her Face', as he wonders at the seeming questioning of his own sureness in the face of Eliza's departure. Here is an eleven o'clock number of enormous skill which needs no brass-throated belter to fling it at the audience's ears but which gently, probingly dissects the essence of the show and its central character. Harrison, still sure but sensibly startled, puts it across in a masterly fashion.

Julie Andrews's Eliza is a very different performance. It ties a virtuoso yet wonderfully natural acting performance, encompassing the development of the girl from a yowling cockney flowergirl, endowed by Shaw with some of the most unlikely noises ever heard on the stage, to an articulate and gracious lady in about two hours, with a singing performance that takes in equivalent extremes of style. In 'Wouldn't it Be Loverly' she combines lyrical singing with mangled vowels and a vigorous character, in 'Just You Wait 'Enry 'Iggins' the soprano tones give way to a boisterous but never coarse chest voice, bouncing out her frustrations against her unkindly teacher, and in 'I Could Have Danced all Night' she turns her suddenly perfectly tuned voice to a rapturous love song which in any other show would have been a waltz. Very few Elizas manage to encompass both the cockney and the lady halves of the rôle – Miss Andrews not only encompasses them, she makes you believe the two-hour transition in a way none other I have heard or seen (*Pygmalion* or *My Fair Lady*) has ever done.

The rest of the recording is equally exciting. Stanley Holloway – masterly casting as Eliza's dustman father – gives an honest-to-goodness English end-of-the-pier rendering of the comedy songs 'With a Little Bit of Luck' and 'Get Me to the

Church on Time' in an endearingly warm performance that doesn't sink into the exaggerations of low comedy; John Michael King, an eager Freddy Eynsford-Hill with a clear, attractive light baritone gives 'On the Street Where You Live' without the air of performing a standard that afflicts most Freddies; and Robert Coote gives an enthusiastically slightly-sung Pickering; whilst the orchestra and chorus under Franz Allers are impeccable in their performance of Robert Russell Bennett and Phil Lang's arrangements.

The same four stars, plus Leonard Weir as Freddy, performed *My Fair Lady* in London and, as the advent of the stereo recording had intervened since the original version, it was decided to re-record the piece with the London cast. It is an interesting document. After three years of playing their respective rôles, Harrison, in particular, performs somewhat differently. He sounds less suave, less easy. He has started to fiddle with his performance and has made it more pointed, more obvious, perforated with odd growling noises and, notably, a little more sung where previously it had been spoken. It is not an improvement, but one cannot ask a man to maintain a performance frozen over three years, and there was little chance of bettering the original. Miss Andrews has filed down the extremes of her cockney for British consumption, but Stanley Holloway has kept an amazing regularity on a recording which simply cannot compare with their first effort.

Only one English-language revival has made it to disc, a twenty-fifth anniversary production staged on Broadway with Ian Richardson and Christine Andreas featured. It, too, cannot compare with the original, for although Richardson shows signs of being an excellent stage Higgins he adopts an unpleasantly ranting style in his songs, losing the character's self-contented ease; Miss Andreas, whose singing and acting are both admirable, makes a slightly heavy Eliza and George Rose, who should have known better, makes Doolittle into a Broadway theatre cockney which sits ill alongside Holloway's unstagey style.

Needless to say, *My Fair Lady* was the subject of a Hollywood film, but it was a film noticeably less successful than the Rodgers and Hammerstein ones, and the recording shows up some of its worst mistakes. Harrison is back as Higgins again, pitching his performance somewhere between his Broadway and London styles, but the voice of Eliza is done by the queen of the dubbers, Marni Nixon, to fit with the speaking voice of Audrey Hepburn, and the result is rather weak. Since the arrangements have been Hollywoodized and the supporting singing is largely pretty mediocre, the recording is not among the better ones.

My Fair Lady has been one of the most popular musicals of its period on foreign-language stages. I don't know precisely how many recordings there are of the show in how many languages, but I have stage versions from Hungary, Germany, Holland, Denmark, Mexico, Italy, Sweden, Israel and Austria as well as French-, German- and Spanish-language soundtracks. By and large, the foreign Higginses attempt to copy Harrison's delivery (in a variety of sometimes quite free translations) and the results range from the pretty ghastly and the very aged-sounding to the more or less sung, and only occasionally anything that sounds elegant and classy. The Elizas range from the sub-operatic to the caterwauling with some wonderfully horrible noises, from basso rumbles to high-pitched screams, to replace Shaw's 'aaoows'. Doolittle gets the widest variety of performances, depending on the low comedy traditions of the country involved: Holland goes in for a heavily Jewish Alf whilst the Austrian actor sounds like Wilfred Brambell, and only one or two can sing.

The Swedish recording takes the wooden spoon for really dreadful technical and performance values, whilst the most enjoyable are those from Denmark and Israel. Lars Schmidt's Danish production has a classy, masculine Higgins (Mogens Wieth), an appealing middle-weight soprano Eliza (Gerda Gilboe), an idiosyncratic Alfie (Osvald Helmuth), who gives a very individual, lachrymose 'Get Me to the Church', and a pleasant light-voiced Freddy (Preben Uglebjerg) in a version which is mostly well played and which simply has an air of enjoyment about it. The second of two Israeli recordings (on the Acum label) goes full out for entertainment value. The sleeve is written entirely in Hebrew, so I have no idea of who is who, but it is a production that doesn't fall into the slough of reverence. The Higgins is fine, the Alfie bright and uncaricatured and the Eliza a veritable spitfire with a fine middle voice, who makes a meal of her music and turns out the most splendid original 'Just You Wait 'Enry 'Iggins'.

Studio cast discs have been legion over the years, but the most recent Decca recording is undoubtedly the most important. It is another in the Kiri te Kanawa series and, once again, shows the prima donna making a very sincere stab at a musical rôle. Naturally, the lyrical pieces of the score suit her the best and she sings pleasantly and easily throughout, but the weight in the voice cannot wholly be disguised and, in spite of the glorious ease with which she accomplishes the notes of 'I Could Have Danced all Night', she cannot attain the youthful rapture Miss Andrews gave to the number.

Jeremy Irons, like Richardson, has all the means to make a fine Higgins but, again like Richardson, chooses to add to his crisp and committed delivery an extremely aggressive and irascible interpretation, which soon becomes tiresome. John Gielgud (Pickering) essays a few notes in the extended version of 'You Did it', Warren Mitchell is a fine natural Alfie and the Freddy shows off his nice voice in his number without getting into the show. In spite of good orchestral values (and the inclusion of some previously omitted dance music) and a chorus that has much more personality than the usual bunches of session singers put together for these occasions, the recording comes out without much character. But, compared with the old original cast version, most do.

Brigadoon

Brigadoon, Lerner and Loewe's first successful musical, dates from 1947 and sticks a little closer to the standard comic opera style than the later show, using its chorus in a more traditional fashion and employing the soprano-soubrette-light baritone-tenor vocal line-up. Rather less usually, undoubtedly because of Agnes de Mille's success with the substantial choreography for *Oklahoma!*, it also included sizeable sections of dance. The show produced a number of songs that became popular, the baritone/soprano 'Almost Like Being in Love' being perhaps the most well known, but the score was a well-balanced one, with charming light solos for the soprano ('Waitin' for my Dearie') and tenor ('Come to Me, Bend to Me' and 'I'll Go Home with Bonnie Jean'), some regular saucy fun for the soubrette ('The Love of my Life' and 'My Mother's Wedding Day') and some genuine sentiment in the baritone song 'There But for You Go I' and the lovely final duet 'From this Day on', all balanced with picturesque chorus scenes both lively and dramatic. *Brigadoon* was a delightful musical and its success was undisputed.

The original cast recording of 1947 was made by RCA, their first venture into the field, and is a pleasing one. Marion Bell in the soprano rôle of Fiona has a fluid, rich soprano and sings her music impressively, whilst David Brooks, as the American who stumbles on her magical village and falls in love, mixes moments of popular crooning with such stronger singing as the part seems to require. Pamela Britton is a lusty soubrette and Lee Sullivan sings the tenor songs quite beautifully but, unfortunately, the recording omits the better of the two soubrette songs, 'The Love of my Life', along with other less important pieces of the score in what is, apart from the opening choruses, largely a selection of the solo songs from the show.

The MGM movie made some significant alterations in *Brigadoon*, banishing practically all of the comedy, including Meg and her two solos, and its recording is, in consequence, even shorter. It is also less satifying, as although Carole Richards and John Gustafson sing attractively as the voices of Fiona and Charlie, Gene Kelly's very croony version of the baritone songs really isn't quite comfortable. A pretty film it may be, but it does the score (and thus the record) no favours.

A TV soundtrack from 1968 is even less acceptable. It, too, cuts the soubrette songs and displays the numbers in any old order (which I hope doesn't reflect the broadcast order) but, worse, soups the truncated piece up in a highly tasteless way. Robert Goulet, top-billed as Tommy, does everything except rock or swing the music as if he were performing in cabaret, wasting his impressive voice in a really superficial and vulgar performance that makes the recording a total no-no.

A Broadway revival of 1980 did not make it to disc, but a 1988 London one did. It is a recording that has its advantages. With the exception of the chorus 'Jeannie's Packing up', it incorporates all the show's main music, including both the soubrette songs, the Sword Dance, the chase scenes with their dance and accompanying music and vocals and the bagpipe funeral music, and it also maintains Ted Royal's fine original orchestrations. Another advantage is the use of several genuine Scots performers who, since they have no need to worry about putting on the accent, sing more freely than some of their predecessors. More superficially, it has a smashing sleeve of coloured photos from the production and clear listings of both cast and music as well as slightly unsubstantial notes.

Sadly, the performance itself is patchy, with the romantic leads erratic in their singing, the chorus thin on top and the orchestra unexciting, but there is some compensation in a pleasingly natural solo tenor (Morris Clark) and, above all, a marvellous Meg from another Scot, Leslie Mackie. This is no standard soubrette, but a joyous performance from an actress-singer mixing a warm, confident voice with an impish sense of humour and making 'The Love of my Life' the feature of the show. Alas, only when she is singing does this recording really come alive.

Life is in abundance, however, in a Columbia studio cast recording from the series produced by Goddard Lieberson and conducted by Lehman Engel. From the opening music the difference is evident. In place of the rather church-choir sound of the British disc, the chorus bursts with energy and vitality, producing both the mystery of the Scottish mists and the bustle of the village market in a manner that is, admittedly, about as Scottish as bourbon whiskey, but most enjoyable. The soloists follow the same pattern, with Shirley Jones using her sweet soprano to good effect and Jack Cassidy ranging from gentle singing to strong without the sloppy croons and glides favoured by other vocalists. Frank Poretta sings up strong as Charlie, less ingratiating in tone than others, but more enthusiastic, and Susan Johnson, a Broadway take-over as Meg, gives a personality-loaded performance of her two numbers in 'hog-calling' style. There may not be gallons of finesse on this recording, but it takes the show by the throat and never allows it to get soppy or self-indulgent. Since it also takes in all of the songs – including 'Jeannie's Packing up' – if not all the dance and scene music, it seems to me to have the advantage all round.

Camelot

The 1960 musical *Camelot*, based on T. H. White's delightfully humorous retelling of the Arthurian legend, emerged as a mixture of gentle burlesque, genuine sentiment and overwhelming spectacle. The spectacle, which helped to ensure the show's success, can do nothing for a record, but there is sufficient charm in the score and pretty wit in the lyrics to make its recordings highly enjoyable.

None of the songs from this score attained the popularity of the *My Fair Lady* music, but the straight baritone ballad 'If Ever I Would Leave You' lifted handily from the show into many a vocalist's act and the rueful 'How To Handle a Woman' also won a certain success. The more burlesque and humorous numbers, the most effective on the stage, were less so out of context, and it is pieces such as Guenevere's pouting, schoolgirlish longing for 'The Simple Joys of Maidenhood', or Lancelot's too-good-to-be-true self-portrait 'C'est moi', which give extra pleasure on a cast recording.

The original cast featured Richard Burton as Arthur and Julie Andrews as Guenevere and the pairing, recorded on Columbia, is a very effective one. He sounds like both a king and a man in the delivery of his songs, a delivery that mixes the sort of speech you would expect from a celebrated actor, and much more accurate and pleasant singing than you would dare to hope for. His whimsical description of the beauties of 'Camelot' has just enough humour and his 'How to Handle a Woman' makes its wondering point perfectly.

Miss Andrews is deliciously tongue-in-cheek as she details in her perfectly articulated and innocent-sounding soprano the sexual frolics encouraged by 'The

Lusty Month of May' or invents ghastly ways of disposing of the worrisome Lancelot in the splendid 'Take Me to the Fair', yet simply moving in the straight ballads 'I Loved You Once in Silence' and 'Before I Gaze on You Again'. Between them they set and maintain the half-humorous, half-serious tone of the show finely.

They are aided in this by a fine performance by Robert Goulet as Lancelot. It is he who gets the show's big ballad, and he sings it gloriously, using his beautiful baritone to its very best effect and showing just what he is capable of when he follows the conductor's and composer's beat. He sounds virile beyond the realms of the possible, and he puts that sound to magnificently humorous use when he sends himself up splendidly in 'C'est moi'.

The disc includes practically all of the show, encased in a fine pictorial gatefold sleeve with good plot and cast notes, but the listing of musical numbers follows the theatre programme rather than the recording, which means that there is a slight difference in the order of numbers and one minor artist (Nimuë) is wrongly credited.

London's version of Camelot featured Laurence Harvey and Elizabeth Larner with Barry Kent as Lancelot. As a recording, it does not come up to the Broadway version, as Harvey sings poorly and both he and Miss Larner, who makes a beautiful vocal sound, lose nearly all the humour of the piece. Kent is much more successful, a fine stout baritone voice and just enough fun, but the record is not very satisfying. Paul Daneman, who succeeded Harvey, gives his Arthur on World Records, but although he has a better singing voice he surprisingly fails to get hold of the character and isn't up to his Guenevere (Patricia Michael), who gives a lovely all-round performance. This version, however, has the Lancelot singing the soprano song 'Follow Me', omits 'C'est moi' and 'Before I Gaze at You Again' and is, in consequence, not of much interest as a record of the show.

The film version of Camelot was an impressive one, but it was made with performers whose least talent was their singing. Consequently, the soundtrack, with everyone doing only what they do least well, is not very satisfactory. Richard Harris succeeds marvellously in making Arthur as appealingly boyish as the original book did, and he sings more than acceptably in a rôle which does not require too much real singing, but Vanessa Redgrave barely copes with her numbers and Gene Merlino, as the voice of Franco Nero as Lancelot, sings so unattractively as to make you wonder why he was chosen. Some lyrics and musical passages have been altered and extended or reduced, others, including the villainous Mordred's 'Seven Deadly Virtues' and the humorous 'Fie on Goodness', cut and, in spite of Lerner's enthusiastic claims on the sleeve, it is clear that the score has taken second place here to the film.

Harris subsequently appeared all over the world in the rôle of Arthur, and during a London run recorded the altered version of show which he favoured for TER. This inefficient revival gave me one of the most unpleasant nights I have ever spent in the theatre and, if the recording is less utterly awful, it is still far behind the others. Harris is less good than on the film disc and the rest of the participants unexceptional and, on top of that, 'Take Me to the Fair' has been cut. Avoid this one.

Paint Your Wagon

Paint Your Wagon, produced in 1951, is a musical built on a story of gold rush days in early America. It was not the commercial success that *Brigadoon* had been, nor that the two later pieces would be, but it was a show that had plenty to recommend it, not the least a score including several numbers that won considerable popularity. The outback song 'They Call the Wind Maria', sung in the show by a miner far from home, strumming his guitar for his lonely companions, became a favourite baritone number, whilst the lovely tenor song 'I Talk to the Trees', the gentle 'I Still See Elisa' – an ageing man mourning his dead wife – and the brave 'Wanderin' Star', in which the same man, having seen the town he has built up fade away with the gold seam that supported it, prepares to move on, were other outstanding solos. There was also some fine choral music, notably the opening 'I'm On My Way', a magnificently picturesque and stirring march setting the show in motion as men, greedy for gold, set out from all parts and all walks of life to head for the newest strike. Unfortunately, the score also held a couple of real rotters, which diluted its effect, but there was plenty in *Paint Your Wagon* to make up a fine cast recording.

The only full-scale recording made of the show's score was of the original Broadway production, and it owes its good and bad features to the way in which the show was cast. Comedian James Barton, featured in musicals on Broadway thirty years earlier and now in his sixties, played the central rôle of Ben Rumson, and he performs 'I Still See Elisa' and 'Wanderin' Star' effectively, with the characterful smidgin of singing voice left to him. Rufus Smith gets 'Maria', and his rough baritone gives it a reality and pathos not heard in the usual more richly and smoothly sung versions, in the same way that the imperfect singing of the other miners gives life to 'I'm on my Way'. These are not pretty concert performances, they are performances made to fit in the play.

Tony Bavaar, as the young Mexican who finally gives up the search for easy wealth and returns at the end of the show to lead a simple life at the side of Ben's faithful daughter, displays a pleasant tenor voice in 'I Talk to the Trees' and the lovely (if less known) 'Another Autumn'. The disaster of this recording is the one woman involved. Olga San Juan is cast as the teenaged Jennifer Rumson, the only female in the mining town and too young to understand why she troubles the men ('What's Going On?') until she herself becomes aware of the attractions of young Julio ('How Can I Wait?'). Sent hastily to school by her father, she returns at last to find the boy gone for gold ('All for Him') and, whilst everyone else forsakes Rumson town, she sits there to wait until he returns to it and her. Miss San Juan treats these numbers of girlish awakening like a forty-year-old club singer, chopping them out awkwardly in what can only be described as an ugly and ill-controlled voice, without an iota of understanding. She must have been cast on her name, sight unseen. A shame, for she goes some way towards spoiling an otherwise enjoyable recording.

Paint Your Wagon had a second chance when a 1969 film version was issued and brought 'Wanderin' Star' unprecedented notice. Grunted out by Lee Marvin at a double-bass pitch, the song made it to the hit parades as a novelty item and undoubtedly swelled the sales of the soundtrack. Strangely, I don't seem to remember having been offended by the music in the film, but as a disc it is very different. The score has been put to the knife and the bad songs removed along with some of the good ones ('How Can I Wait', 'Another Autumn'), the gaps being filled by five new pieces composed by André Previn which probably fit the revamped plot of the film better. It has also been eviscerated in another way, as the songs are pulled about horribly – 'On my Way' mangled to fit visual considerations and 'Maria' dolled up in Hollywood sound with Harve Presnell's fine baritone drowned in a battery of tambourines and what sounds like the whole of the men's department of the Mormon Tabernacle Choir; the result is a very poor representation of Loewe's music.

There are several studio recordings of *Paint Your Wagon*, inspired by the film, but there is no LP of the original London production. A pity, for with Sally Ann Howes cast as Jennifer, the heroine's music would have won a very different treatment to that meted out by Miss San Juan. A two-record set including selections from *Brigadoon*, *My Fair Lady*, *Paint Your Wagon* and the film *Gigi*, and entitled 'An Evening with Lerner and Loewe', shows what might have been when Jane Powell tackles 'How Can I Wait' in soprano tones, but the great voices of Jan Peerce and Robert Merrill rather iron the interest out of the men's songs and, in any case, the selection is short. *Paint Your Wagon* has yet to be done full justice on disc.

More from the 1940s

Alongside these two famous pairings, a whole series of other writers and composers worked with considerable success and, through the 1940s and the 1950s, each year saw more outstanding new musicals produced on Broadway.

Amongst the earliest came *Song of Norway*, an Edvard Grieg pasticcio; Leonard Bernstein's carefree tale of a day and night in the big city, *On the Town*; Herbert and Dorthy Fields's lively and enduring Western *Annie Get Your Gun*, with its popular Irving Berlin score; and the Elmer Rice drama *Street Scene* musicalized by Kurt Weill. The whimsical *Finian's Rainbow*, Frank Loesser's version of the classic *Charley's Aunt* under the title *Where's Charley?*, Cole Porter's back-stage musical comedy *Kiss Me, Kate* and a musical version of Anita Loos's delicious novel *Gentlemen Prefer Blondes* joined them amongst the pick of what the 1940s had to offer.

Song of Norway

Song of Norway (1944) followed in the famous footsteps of *Das Dreimäderlhaus* (*Lilac Time/Blossom Time*) by presenting a fictionalized operetta biography of a composer illustrated by a score made up from his own music. Robert Wright and George Forrest's adaptation of Grieg's piano and orchestral music was lushly done and, because of the breadth of the original melodies, developed into songs that demanded large and wide-ranging lyrical singing from its principal players. It was this music and such singing that, alongside the splendid physical production, were the main attractions of the piece and, thus, the several recordings of *Song of Norway* present the show at its best.

The so-called original cast recording is not quite that. Irra Petina, who played the rôle of the prima donna Louisa Giovanni on Broadway, was prevented contractually from taking part in the recording and had to be replaced by Kitty Carlisle. Miss Petina recorded her numbers separately (with the assistance of Robert Weede) and they have been subsequently transferred from 78 onto the JJA label (backed with *Up in Central Park* and *Winged Victory*).

The cast recording shows off some superb voices – those ringing, open, un-pompous light opera voices that America seems to produce so well – with Lawrence Brooks (Grieg), Helena Bliss (Nina) and, in particular, Robert Shafer (Nordraak) all producing quite remarkably thrilling sounds. None of them, however, has much of a way with a lyric and the words are made to sound even more stilted than they sometimes are. The little bits of dialogue used to help continuity suffer even more. But the music is given full value and, especially when the three come together in 'The Hill of Dreams' or when Brooks and Bliss tackle the show's top number 'Strange Music', this recording is vocally a great pleasure.

What was evidently a very large-scale revival at the Jones Beach Marine Theatre in 1958, featuring a viking ship, a floating iceberg, a waterfall and other such aquatic extras, was also put on record. This version has the advantage over the earlier one of improved recording techniques – the so-called enhanced for stereo with its aggravating echo goes near to spoiling the original LP – and yields little or nothing to it in the quality of its singers. John Reardon (Grieg), Helena Scott (Nina) and William Olvis (Nordraak) all have really fine voices and all of them pay much more attention to the content of the songs than their predecessors. Brenda Lewis as the tempestuous Louisa turns on a much weightier, almost mezzo tone for her rôle, which allows her both to contrast well with Miss Scott's soprano singing and also to have a good deal of well-judged fun with her material. Her performance of the showpiece 'Now' gives some delightful variety to a score heavy in romantic solo and choral music. A couple of small sections included on the earlier disc are omitted here, but they are sections of no great significance and all of the principal pieces of the score are included.

A British recording of 1960 is generally more lightweight than these two, and has fiddled about unnecessarily here and there with the score. Its chief advantage is Sadler's Wells Opera soprano Victoria Elliott, who is in truly splendid voice as Louisa and lacks only the humour of Miss Lewis's performance. The film soundtrack has not only fiddled with the score, it has revamped the book (squeezing encounters with Liszt and Hans Andersen as well as the previous Ibsen into Edvard

Grieg's life), cut half of the stage score and replaced it with new Grieg, Wright and Forrest pieces. 'Now' is amongst the casualties. So was the film.

On the Town

On the Town (1944) brought composer Leonard Bernstein and writers Betty Comden and Adolph Green to Broadway for the first time with a happy, episodic musical, reminiscent in form of the favourite old run-around-the-town shows of the nineteenth century, which followed three sailor boys out for a good time with the girls of New York on their twenty-four hours of shore leave. Based on a ballet, the show retained a very large and narrative dance element and a short score of songs, half of which were comic revue style pieces ('I Get Carried Away', 'Come up to my Place', 'I Can Cook Too' and 'Ya Got Me'); two were ballads ('Lonely Town' and 'Lucky to Be Me') and the last pair formed an opening ('New York, New York') and closing ensemble ('Some Other Time'), bracketing the events of the show. It was an effective score, with its exciting and imaginative dance music (which contains many a foretaste of the more famous dances of *West Side Story*) and perky, jazzy songs, a combination that makes up an unusually proportioned score for recording.

There is no original cast recording as such, but two discs have been issued featuring several of the original cast members. The first is a combination of transfers from 78s on Decca/Ace of Hearts, which, under a misguiding heading 'original cast album', includes contributions from original artists Comden and Green (who featured in as well as writing the show) in a frantic version of 'I Get Carried Away' and Nancy Walker giving a raucous 'I Can Cook Too' and a solo version of the quartet 'Ya Got Me'. For some reason, Mary Martin croons her way uncomfortably through the two ballads that belong to the hero and the glorious opening scena, 'New York, New York', is given a not very professional performance by some choristers.

The second disc, made by Columbia, is very much better. Comden, Green, Walker and a fourth of the original six stars, Cris Alexander, came back together in 1960 to put down a virtually complete version of the score, including the full eleven and a half minutes of the opening song-and-dance scene and the other principal dances, the Times Square and two Coney Island ballets, as well as all the show's significant songs. All of the first three artists are in markedly better form than on their earlier recordings. Comden and Green are much less frenetic and much more comprehensible in their comedy and Miss Walker substitutes a niftily stylish clip through the complexities of her jazzier comicalities for the more hectic performance of fifteen years previously. She joins Alexander happily in a well-paced and amusing version of the revusical taxi cab song, in which he keeps asking to be driven to sights that no longer exist and she, the driver, keeps putting on the brakes and encouraging him to 'Come up to my Place'. John Reardon, imported for the principal singing rôle of Gabey, uses his unpretentious legitimate baritone to perform 'Lonely Town' and 'Lucky To Be Me' in a lovely warm, relaxed style, and with the orchestra, under Bernstein himself, in equally good form, this is a clear and enjoyable record of the piece.

A genuine original cast recording of the show was made when, following the success of *West Side Story* and a flop 1959 off-Broadway revival, *On the Town* was produced in London in 1963. It flopped there, too, but not before CBS had recorded with the London cast almost as much material as they had put on their US disc. Some of the sections come out very well, with the three boys sounding fresh and fine in their opening paean to the big city and Don McKay making a particularly youthful, eager Gabey in his numbers, but others are less successful and the decision to leave out the spoken lines which help describe the action of the dances was a mistake. So was the choice of the noisome, nasal Carol Arthur in the rôle created by Nancy Walker.

Annie Get Your Gun

Annie Get Your Gun (1946) was one of the most successful musicals of its period and it has also proved one of the most lasting. Beginning with long runs on Broadway and in London, the tuneful tale of the sharpshooting outback girl who finds that 'You Can't Get a Man with a Gun' gave songwriter Irving Berlin, after thirty-five years writing for the Broadway stage, librettists Herbert and Dorothy Fields, and original star Ethel Merman their biggest musical theatre triumphs. Both as a stage piece and as a scoreful of catchy songs for performance or recording, the show became a world-wide success.

'There's No Business Like Show Business' is perhaps the most widely known of the *Annie* tunes, but the easily extractable ballads 'My Defences Are Down', 'The Girl That I Marry' and 'They Say That Falling in Love Is Wonderful', and the comedy songs 'Anything You Can Do (I Can Do Better)' and 'Doin' What Comes Naturally' – a right pair of 'sock it to 'em' vaudeville pieces – have all become standards. And that list doesn't even include the delightfully tongue-in-cheek 'Moonshine Lullaby', the joyful 'I Got the Sun in the Morning' and the winning duo 'Who Do You Love, I Hope?', three of the show's best numbers.

A score made up of such favourite numbers – for there is little ensemble work in *Annie* – virtually all of which fall, in fact, to Annie and her partner, Frank, is a natural for recording and the show has been put on disc a goodly number of times, beginning of course with the original cast recording with Ethel Merman. Just how much you like this disc depends wholly on how much you like Miss Merman's handling of the rôle. I don't much. There must have been something in her wildly acclaimed stage performance that doesn't come across on record. There is no doubt that she possesses a remarkable voice, clear and clarion-like, but that is it. There is little variation of tone or even of volume from one end of the record to the other, whether she is singing a comic song, a love song or, indeed, a lullaby. In the aggressive 'Anything You Can Do' and the jubilant 'Sun in the Morning' she can be heard doing what she does best, but since she has treated the 'Moonshine

Lullaby' and the wide-eyed 'They Say it's Wonderful' in the same way the effect is lessened. There is no feeling, no characterization and, worse, no personality in the performance – just a remarkable stream of sound, which does nothing for Berlin's mixture of old-fashioned and inspirational lyrics.

The recording is compiled of all Merman's bits, one after the other, regardless of the dramatic run of the show, with the two numbers on which Ray Middleton (Frank) turns his fine baritone and the refreshingly light 'Who Do You Love, I Hope?' tacked on at the end, and a rousing 'Show Business' to finish off. It doesn't really make up a satisfactory cast recording.

Merman recorded the *Annie Get Your Gun* score on two further occasions. In 1966, at the age of fifty-seven, she appeared at the Music Theater of Lincoln Centre in a revival which was put down on a cast disc. Remarkably, she sounds about half her age here: the voice is as lusty as ever and there is also much more character in the performance. It still isn't the wide-eyed outback girl of the script, but paired with another rich-voiced baritone in the splendid Bruce Yarnell as Frank, she provides a more enjoyable listen than on the first disc.

There are further plusses here in the fine original Robert Russell Bennett orchestrations and the two full sides of songs laid out in show order, but there is one significant minus, a minus that is the fault of the production rather than the record. For some reason, it was decided to cut the soubret characters of Tommy and Winnie and, along with them, their songs 'I'll Share It All With You' (recorded only by Wendy Toye and Irving Davies of the London cast on 78) and 'Who Do You Love, I Hope?', the one bit of light relief from the incessant stream of numbers for the stars, and to replace them with an unimpressive and ill-fitting duet, 'An Old Fashioned Wedding', for – guess who – Annie and Frank. The effect is to make the disc a rather relentless little more than two-handed concert, particularly in view of Miss Merman's unvarying style.

This is, however, the best of the Merman discs, for the third effort, a real granny Annie made in Britain in 1973, is not very impressive. Merman is not to blame – she is much the same as before, belting out the score one more time – but she is paired with a stiff, warbly Frank and scuppered by some common, scratchy-sounding orchestrations. At the age of sixty-four it shouldn't happen to a lady.

Mary Martin, who took the star rôle in the first US national tour of *Annie* in 1947, recorded her version a decade later following a West Coast production in which she starred opposite John Raitt. This version concentrates wholly on the two stars, omitting the soubrette numbers and the vigorous opening 'Buffalo Bill' scene in what verges on being a recital record for two. Both sing pleasantly, she performing with a smooth, croony tone and the polite delivery of a radio band vocalist, he with a clean-cut baritone and the odd interpolated high note, but emotion is never aroused – there is no attack and little characterization. There is nothing wild about this west.

The recording of the most recent revival is the first to treat the score as part of a dramatic performance rather than a series of hit numbers for a pair of stars. Britain's Chichester Festival 1986 production featured a different species of American vocalist in former pop singer Suzy Quatro in the title rôle, and she duly provides a different species of Annie. Here, at last, is the awkward, youthful, lovable character of the libretto displayed on a lively, atmospheric recording which looks to the show first and the star second and, as a result, helps both. Miss Quatro makes her lullaby a lullaby, her comedy likeable instead of brash, and she saves her big vocal guns for the big moments in a thoughtful and well-paced performance. Her light baritone Frank (Eric Flynn) supports well and 'Buffalo Bill' gets its best performance anywhere from Maureen Scott (Dolly) and company.

Unfortunately, however, there are 'buts'. Not only is this production of the revised 'Old Fashioned Wedding' version – no Tommy and Winnie, no 'Who Do You Love?' – but it has been fiddled with further. For a show that had such a huge success on its initial run, this one has been fiddled with altogether too much since. Chichester's fiddling extends to the songs, where lines and layouts have been vulgarly and unnecessarily stretched over some 'rickety-tickety' orchestrations infested by the sound of the modern drum kit. A shame, when so much else is so good.

The most notable of the studio recordings of *Annie Get Your Gun*, a 1963 version with a highly enjoyable Doris Day and a suitably vain-sounding Robert Goulet, suffers from the same disorder. Phil Lang's specially billed new orchestrations are gimmicky and offensive and the two stars, both in fine voice, are irremediably sabotaged. This recording throws up some odd lyric changes that seem to have come about because of the 1950 film version, a version which has itself found its way to record. Howard Keel, in his usual virile form, and a rough, vocally approximate Betty Hutton, perform eight numbers on MGM. What might have been can be heard on a pirate disc which preserves the music tracks put down by Judy Garland before she was sacked from the rôle of film Annie. It isn't vintage Garland, but it serves at least the music of Berlin's show rather better than the finished article and includes some of the pieces omitted from the official film soundtrack.

It is unfortunate that a musical such as this should not have one really outstanding recording and a little hard to understand why. It can be done. The Germans have done it. The one foreign cast recording I have is from Berlin's Theater des Westens and, although it isn't perfect, it is thoroughly enjoyable. Annie is played by Heidi Brühl, who captures the mood of each song happily, varying her tone and her delivery so adeptly that you don't mind the fact that she cannot blaze out the top notes in chest voice like Merman, and Frank is Robert Trehy, a fine baritone who makes a first-rate job of 'Die Frau meiner Träume' (The Girl That I Marry). The soubrets are in, with their number 'Zufällig trifft man sich', and because I was so glad to hear their lilting delivery of this pretty song I didn't quite fall off my chair when Colette Warren (Winnie) burst into a coloratura obbligato half way through. There are few such decorations in Rudolf Kühn's lively and suitable orchestrations, however, and the elements of the record all come together to make up what is probably the happiest *Annie* of all.

Street Scene

Street Scene (1947) probably ought not to be included in this survey. It is one of those works, like Gershwin's *Porgy and Bess* (1935) before it and Menotti's *The Consul* (1950) after, that intentionally attempted to bridge what was seen as the gap between the light musical theatre and opera and to create what Weill himself referred to as 'a Broadway opera'. *Street Scene* was commercially produced on Broadway for a regular run which eventually totally 148 performances but, having thereafter lain largely neglected, nurtured mostly in the hearts of those cognoscenti to whom it has always been a musical masterpiece, only in the late 1980s is it again finding significant attention. It is notable that that attention is not from the commercial theatre but from the opera houses. This is understandable for, in spite of its composer's avowed intention, the music of the piece was approached, from the first, in an operatic fashion, and the evidence of this is clearly visible in the only available recording of the show, an excerpts disc on CBS.

The music of *Street Scene* is almost entirely in a contemporary operatic idiom, featuring harmonies and a style of vocal line not normally associated with Broadway, and requiring strong and wide-ranging legitimate voices for almost all of its rôles. This is emphasized by the casting, as the four principal parts are all taken by operatic artists who sing their music with operatic tone and style; even when the score is at its most jazzy, the music is still demanding enough to require singers of scope. Polyna Stoska, who appears as the adulterous wife murdered by her husband, has the most substantial song, 'Somehow I Never Could Believe', and she renders it with the same full-throated operatic delivery required of Magda's 'To This We've Come' in *The Consul*. It is exciting, sombre and demanding and a fitting centre-piece to the show's first act, even if a little ponderously done by Miss Stoska.

Elsewhere, the most successful pieces are the least serious ones – the gossipy people of the street passing their time in small-talk ('Ain't it Awful the Heat?') or avidly discussing the murder ('The Woman up There'), a pair of passing nursemaids revelling in the gory details ('Lullaby'), the music of schoolchildren and the deliciously wide-eyed solo of an expectant father, one of the many folk who people the tenement block and the show ('When a Woman Has a Baby'). When the predominant dark tones close in again, and when the young lovers of the piece (finely sung by Anne Jeffreys and Joseph Sullivan) launch into duet, the marvellous naturalness of these segments is largely replaced by a textual and musical style akin not only to opera but occasionally to old-fashioned opera. I find it less happy, just as I find the one example on this recording of a switch into a blatant Broadway style ('Wouldn't You Like to Be on Broadway') awkwardly out of place.

The recording, well if seriously performed throughout, is a fine one, and it is equipped with an interesting sleeve note by the composer himself (although any indication of the cast and who sings what is lacking). It excludes a number of significant pieces of the show's score and, naturally considering its spatial limitations, includes virtually none of the spoken dialogue. This is a shame as a work of this kind really needs to be heard in its entirety.

However, given the forceful enthusiasm of the very vocal (and well-placed) spearhead of the world's Weill supporters – a group which must surely equal the 'mad-for-Gilbert & Sullivan' group and the 'rah-rah-Sondheim' team in its determination to boost their man's claim for supremacy above all others – it is unlikely that we shall wait very long for a full-scale *Street Scene*. In the meanwhile, this disc is a very satisfactory taste of an interesting and occasionally outstanding venture into bringing contemporary opera to the commercial stage, and my excuse for including it here is as a parameter in this survey of Broadway.

Finian's Rainbow

I've always thought that the reason I didn't like *Finian's Rainbow* (1947) was that its libretto, mixing sentiment and leprechauns with social intent and earnest homilies, was so unreadable. Listening to the recordings of the score, however, I find more reasons. The lyrics of this whimsical-topical show, amazingly from the pen of the celebrated Yip Harburg, include far too many feeble variations on overknown themes, punctuated with some horribly inept rhyming, and the slim Burton Lane score is made up mainly of catchy melodies of a reminiscent kind. I still dislike *Finian's Rainbow*.

It is quite clear, however, that a lot of people feel otherwise. It had a successful first Broadway run (725 performances), a 1960 revival, a 1968 film version and, according to one record sleeve (none of which, by the way, is game to take a shot at providing a synopsis of the libretto) has been played in a lot of college productions as well. Its short score includes 'Old Devil Moon', 'How Are Things in Glocca Morra?', 'If This Isn't Love' and 'Look to the Rainbow', all of which have won a degree of enduring popularity – a pretty fair average. The songs have won some success and currency outside America, which the show itself has not – it was a quick flop in London whilst the Broadway run prospered – but both show and songs get goodish notices from the Boswell of the Broadway musical, Gerald Bordman, so I must concede that perhaps there is something specifically appealing to American tastes in the piece.

The three American *Finian's Rainbow*s have each given birth to a recording. The original cast disc was the first such recording to be issued by Columbia and, in fact, it uses only the show's soloists with a borrowed chorus. Whilst of interest as a document, it is not the best of recordings. It has a muddy sound, and Robert Russell Bennett's arrangements sound more Hollywoody than is his wonderful wont. As for the performances, Ella Logan in the leading soubrette rôle (I'm sorry, I just can't indicate her part in the plot; suffice it that she is the singing star who gets most of the songs) is a very individual taste. She sings the part of the Irish lassie with a series of vowels reminiscent of a Scots Eartha Kitt and a tone which was clearly useful for getting to the back of the 'gods'. Neither are so hot on record. Donald Richards as her love interest and David Wayne as the leprechaun who doesn't win her sing attractively but don't get across much of the show. This is probably not their fault, as the songs are so very detachable as to exist healthily out of context, as witnesses the Reprise disc, where Frank Sinatra gives his 'Old Devil Moon', Rosemary Clooney does her thing to 'Glocca Morra' and Sammy Davis jr takes the protest out of the social protest.

The revival recording, featuring Jeannie Carson (who sounds as English as Logan does Scots), is rather better and, for a straightforward version of the show score, this is probably the best bet. However, the film soundtrack, in spite of sounding like clipped-out bits from a film soundtrack and in spite of the fact that the songs have been rejigged to give Fred Astaire, in the virtually non-singing rôle of Finian MacLonergan, his chance to share in the singing, oddly enough gives the most life to the songs.

Petula Clark – another Englishwoman being Irish – mixes the temperament of Logan with the smooth singing of Carson and not too many mannerisms to give a pretty, unaffected 'Glocca Morra', and blends nicely with Astaire in other moments which were originally hers alone. Astaire is enjoyable, Don Francks shows a warm baritone, and Tommy Steele as a leprechaun with a deluge of personality even makes the grimly awful 'Something Sort of Grandish' sound acceptable.

Where's Charley?

Where's Charley? (1948) brought composer-lyricist Frank Loesser to Broadway for the first time with a musical version of the famous British farce *Charley's Aunt*. Broadway success was followed by a 1952 film and a belated 1958 London production, following the triumph of Loesser's *Guys and Dolls*. *Where's Charley?* shows little that might indicate its writer would, just two years later, produce a musical of the quality of *Guys and Dolls*. It is a light, farcical piece, constructed on a severely mangled version of the original play (it combines two principal characters in one and thus upsets the whole form of the thing), decorated with agreeable pastiche period songs and with such features as a parade and a ballet scena (a *sine qua non* in the post-*Oklahoma* Agnes de Millinery days) blatantly pasted in to provide some spectacle. But it clearly worked.

For some reason, this long-running show missed an original cast recording. It was left to the London production to put the score down on record, and it has to be said that they did not do much of it very well. Star Norman Wisdom (playing the combined rôle of Charley and Fancourt Babberly-cum-Aunt) has fun with the show's favourite song, 'Once in Love with Amy', soubrette Pip Hinton sends sparks flying in a splendidly vivacious fit of jealousy over 'The Woman in his Room', and the pair join together humorously in 'Make a Miracle', in which she is thinking of the future in social terms and he is thinking of marriage.

Felix Felton gives a mock serenade with gusto and there is a vigorous march to the very un-English 'The New Ashmolean Marching Society and Conservatory Band', but that is about it. The pretty 'My Darling, My Darling', a plain little love duet, gets warbled to death by the number-two couple, who also just about trample down the lively quartet 'Better Get Out of Here', and a clever recap of the story so far, 'The Gossips', sung by a group of University girls getting ready for a dance, sounds half the time like a rehearsal for *Die Walküre*. These last two pieces, even ill served, show just a few seeds of things to come from Loesser, whom it is perhaps unfair to judge on an English period pastiche piece which allowed him little freedom of expression.

The film soundtrack, featuring original star Ray Bolger and using ten of the thirteen musical pieces in the show, must be better than this, but I have never been inspired to chase it to find out.

Kiss Me, Kate

Cole Porter's *Kiss Me, Kate* (1948) was in a different class to *Finian's Rainbow* and *Where's Charley?*. Here was a piece with a slick, well-proportioned libretto, with lyrics that sounded effortlessly original and amusing (notwithstanding a rather relentless emphasis on things sexual in Act 2), and with music that switched from the languid to the jazzy, from the burlesque to the cabaret or to a soaring ballad with equal effect in a score in which nearly every song played a part in building up the whole. In *Kiss Me, Kate* Porter and his librettists, Sam and Bella Spewack, made a musical that would prove popular not only in the usual venues but, without it ever being performed as an opera, in the opera houses of Europe (where it was the first Broadway musical to find general acceptance in the repertoire in the same way as *The Merry Widow* or *Die Fledermaus*.)

Given this international popularity, it is surprising that there are, in fact, only two and a half original cast recordings of the show. The first of these was that made by the very original cast as played at Broadway's New Century Theatre, with Alfred Drake (Fred), Patricia Morison (Lilli), Lisa Kirk (Lois) and Harold Lang (Bill) featured. Then, more than a decade after this original recording, a remake took place when the cast were reassembled to put the whole piece down again on the newly invented stereophonic system. By and large, the stars had lasted well. Drake is still in splendid voice, although he succumbs not only to some lyric changes but also to the temptation to insert an unwanted high note in 'I've Come to Wive it Wealthily in Padua', as if to prove he can still do it. Perhaps by this time he had played his rôle once too often. His sense of humour is welcome though, and he makes 'Where Is the Life That Late I Led' dirtier than I had ever realized it could be.

Morison is equally fine, the voice straight and clear and the songs sung unfussily, but Lisa Kirk's torch singing sometimes burns the edges of the notes a bit. The gangsters are played by Aloysius Donovan and Alexis Dubroff (are these names real, or are all these AD's Mr Drake playing Donovans and Dubroffs?) in Flanagan and Allen style, one an octave below the other, and the effect is hilarious.

The original London cast, also featuring Miss Morison with Bill Johnson, Julie Wilson, and Sid James as one of the gangsters, recorded only a limited selection, and these ten numbers have been transferred to LP on World Record Club's 'Cole

Porter in London' along with selections from *Anything Goes, Nymph Errant* and other Porter material played and interpolated in London shows.

The only other cast recording is that of a London revival of 1986 under the banner of the Royal Shakespeare Company. It is embarrassingly undersung and quite unlistenable to. If the fashion amongst certain modern British directors to cast musicals with actors who sort of sing has to be endured in the theatre, surely there is no need to put the teeth-curling results of their efforts to hold pitch, breath and rhythm on to record.

The MGM film version of 1953 was, like the original stage version, beautifully cast and played. Howard Keel and Kathryn Grayson took the rôles originated by Drake and Miss Morison and played and sang them with equal panache. Both are in splendid voice on the soundtrack and, for once, alterations made to the score for the film both in orchestration and musical layout seem only to help them. They gambol through 'Wunderbar' with their tongues firmly in their cheeks and make the most of an additional flush of obbligato to end with. Ann Miller as Lois makes a crisper, more svelte job of her version of the numbers than Miss Kirk and gets the bonus of the added 'From This Moment On' from *Out of This World*. The sound of the soundtrack issue is, however, not the best and, all in all, it is safer to stick with the modified original cast disc.

One certainly not to stick with is the TV soundtrack issued by CBS. This one is nasty: brash, vulgar orchestrations with insensitive rhythms and a drummer with a nervous twitch, music and lyrics fiddled with, and some mediocre performances – except one. Robert Goulet is on his best behaviour. He sings what Porter wrote the way he wrote it and, in spite of the orchestra, he sings gloriously. What a pity he couldn't have been transported to another record.

Another absolutely terrific Fred is on view on the German-language Eurodisc recording, where Peter Alexander and Olive Moorefield sing a selection from the show. Sadly, this is not a cast recording – Miss Moorefield tackles both Lois and Lilli with consummate success – nor a record of the full show, but it shows once again how German performances of the classic Broadway repertoire, which respect the musical values of the shows both orchestrally and vocally, make fine recordings.

Holland is apparently the only other non-English-singing country to have issued a recording of this show, but there is a perfect pile of other *Kiss Me, Kate* studio recordings, many from Britain, containing various selections. Undoubtedly the most starry is one in the Reprise series, which has Frank Sinatra, Dean Martin and Sammy Davis jr performing 'We Open in Venice', Dinah Shore and Johnny Prophet giving a very curious 'Wunderbar' and Jo Stafford tackling 'Why Can't You Behave?'.

Gentlemen Prefer Blondes

Anita Loos's hilarious novella *Gentlemen Prefer Blondes* and its archetypal not-so-dumb blonde heroine, Lorelei Lee, were naturals for transformation into a

Broadway musical and, with Loos and Joseph Fields in charge of the transformation, the result was a predictably fine one. In 1949 the diamond-digging Lorelei Lee, personified by the dazzlingly bubbling and excessively blonde Carol Channing, took the town by storm. The score of the show, written by Leo Robin and Jule Styne, lacked the brilliance of the tale and its heroine, lingering too much in the old-fashioned areas of topical jokes and luke-warm 'nudge-nudge' lyrics on the textual side and unexceptional dance and point music on the other. Nor was the music helped by having its vaguely period tones (the piece was set in the 1920s) stridently orchestrated and weighed down by some croony Hollywoodian vocal arrangements; but it gained very much indeed from a fine set of original performers who are pleasantly in evidence on the cast recording.

The jewel of the recording is, of course, Miss Channing who, even without the aid of her acres of Barney Google eyes, transports Miss Lorelei Lee off the page and into your heart. She lifts her two principal songs, 'A Little Girl From Little Rock' and 'Diamonds Are a Girl's Best Friend', into a different class with the aid of a voice which resembles nothing more than an adorable frog. Yvonne Adair, as Lorelei's less practical pal Dorothy, spends her warm, unexaggerated chest voice on the undistinguished 'I Love What I'm Doing', George S. Irving gives voice and thought in an attempt to lift the tacky 'I'm a'Tingle' and Jack McCauley as our heroine's pet millionaire and Eric Brotherson as Dorothy's preferred beau both sing their songs attractively.

It took *Gentlemen Prefer Blondes* nearly thirteen years to reach London, but when it arrived it had been given a tactful and very effective facelift. The ill-fitting arrangements had been junked and replaced by some cheerful and effective 1920s-type orchestrations by musical director Alyn Ainsworth. Several of the lyrics, notably to 'Diamonds' and the topical 'Homesick Blues', had been sharpened up, 'I'm a'Tingle' had been dropped, a share in the vacuous 'Sunshine' was reallotted to Lorelei, in whose hands it sounded much less vacuous, and an extra song, the cod 'You Kill Me', was inserted into the Parisian cabaret scene that opened the second act. Each and every one of the alterations was an improvement.

In consequence, the London cast recording, which, like the Broadway one, is endowed with a particularly fine cast, has, in many ways, the edge over its predecessor. It is brighter, clearer and more lively in its musical part and, as a result, the whole piece is given a lift. Dora Bryan (Lorelei) renders nothing to Miss Channing with a performance of deliciously arranged squeaks, croaks and yodelling all her own, Anne Hart (Dorothy) wallops out Dorothy's music with gusto, and all the men give their numbers impeccably, both alone and, in a crisp and tidy performance, in their ensemble moments with the girls.

In 1974 the show was revamped, revised and represented on the road under the title *Lorelei*, with Carol Channing taking up her old rôle a quarter of a century on in a piece which had her 'Looking Back' with the odd new song and the odd one appropriated from someone else's part. The London improvements were ignored, the old orchestrations were reorganized, 'I'm a'Tingle' was reinstated (although

'Sunshine' completely disappeared), and the result was recorded on MGM. By the time the show reached Broadway, however, improvement had again set in. 'I'm a'Tingle' was out, as was the distasteful opening number 'It's High Time', a crass piece about getting drunk, and the two new numbers which had survived ('Looking Back' and 'I Won't Let You Get Away') were supplemented by an even newer piece for the star ('Men'). The alterations were recorded and a new MGM disc, comprising bits of the old plus the new, issued. The show had a fair run, but recordwise, if you want Miss Channing, it seems to me that you are better off with the young and original version. Otherwise, the British *Blondes* are better.

The 1950s

The 1950s on flourishing Broadway found the writers of the 1940s expanding on their successes, joined now and then by a new member for their happy clan. Alongside the regular hits from Rodgers and Hammerstein and Lerner and Loewe, Irving Berlin followed *Annie Get Your Gun* with a second winner in *Call Me Madam*, whilst Frank Loesser triumphed with the most New York of all New York shows, *Guys and Dolls*, and then showed the range of his versatility with *The Most Happy Fella*, a piece of considerable scope which verged on the light operatic in its style and its substance. Leonard Bernstein composed the score for the comparatively conventional *Wonderful Town* before producing two dazzling pieces of an equally varying kind – the dramatic *West Side Story* and the skilful operetta burlesque *Candide*. Cole Porter turned demi-semi-French with *Can-Can*, and Wright and Forrest, following on the lines they had successfully established in *Song of Norway*, produced a Borodin pasticcio, *Kismet*. Jule Styne composed the scores for the oversized female stars of *Bells Are Ringing* and *Gypsy*, George Abbott, Richard Adler and Jerry Ross proved a new team to be reckoned with with two enjoyable pieces, *The Pajama Game* and *Damn Yankees*, and Michael Stewart and Charles Strouse came up with the youthful *Bye Bye Birdie*. But probably the most outstanding of the newcomers' offerings was Meredith Willson's delightful *The Music Man*, a warm and optimistic winner from a writer who sadly never equalled this first wonderful effort. And whilst all this large-scale action was crowding happily on to the stages of Broadway, a small musical called *The Fantasticks* made its first appearance in a tiny theatre far from the bright lights – the first appearance of a show which is still running today.

Call Me Madam

Following *Annie Get Your Gun*, it was not unnatural that Berlin's 1950 show, *Call Me Madam*, should again be a vehicle for triumphant *Annie* star Ethel Merman. This time the character devised for her fitted Miss Merman perfectly. As the brash and rich Washington party-giver promoted to Ambassador of an insignificant country for services rendered, she had little or no need to be anything else than what she so splendidly was – Ethel Merman, the personality and the voice. Berlin fitted her out with songs that displayed the famous voice at its best, whether declaring herself trumpetingly as 'The Hostess with the Mostes' on the Ball', conducting her unorthodox love affair with the Prime Minister of little Lichtenburg by informing him that 'The Best Thing for You (Would Be Me)', or briskly consoling her lovesick protégé in 'You're Just in Love'. Light and shade was not required in the character of Sally Adams – she was forthright, brisk and big; she was Ethel Merman.

Unfortunately, one of those record company battles which seemed to pop up regularly at this time prevented the making of a genuine cast album of *Call Me Madam*, and we have, instead, two part-cast albums – one with just Miss Merman, and the other one with everyone else and with Dinah Shore taking the star's place. Like so many half-cocked affairs, neither is very satisfactory. Decca, who had refused to release Merman to join the rest of the cast on the opposition RCA label, put out a disc which had the leading lady singing not only all her own songs but also the leading man's number 'Marrying for Love' and the chorus 'Washington Square Dance'. She was, at least, joined by Dick Haymes for 'You're Just in Love', but several of the other numbers were simply dumped unsatisfactorily in the lap of musical director Gordon Jenkins (who manages to get his name on the sleeve nine times, although all he does is wave the stick) and his orchestra and chorus. There is no disputing that Merman's performance is definitive, but this isn't a show album, it's a recital disc.

The official 'original show album' just doesn't stand up at all. Dinah Shore was a very odd choice to replace the implacably stentorian Merman. Her silky, relaxed style of putting across a number is just not what these songs were composed for and she, naturally, turns them into something quite different. It doesn't work. Paul Lukas as Prime Minister Cosmo has a suitably Continental accent and not a lot of sense of pitch, but Galina Talva as the local Princess who provides the juvenile love interest has more of both qualities. Russell Nype as the other half of the love interest gives the most accomplished performance, but this show was about Ethel Merman and without her it seems decapitated.

The British production of the show had to do without Merman and it used another American performer in Billie Worth in her place. Miss Worth gets very much nearer to the mark than Miss Shore – she has some of the Merman 'oomph' as well as some charm and she also remembers to act her numbers. She is partnered with a Cosmo (Anton Walbrook) who talks his way very curiously through his songs and who seems, to hear his accent, convinced that Lichtenburg is somewhere in the Punjab. Shani Wallis, a sweet voiced Princess, has found her accent even further East and, whilst I suppose such things shouldn't really matter, I find myself distracted by these odd sounds. It is difficult to remember you are listening to very American Irving Berlin when someone is sounding as if they are doing *The King and I*. It isn't a bad recording, but it isn't what the show needs.

The film version is the only refuge. Here you have Merman and a top-class supporting cast all performing the right songs in the right way. Admittedly several of the show's lesser-known numbers have slipped out of the score and two extraneous pieces, one borrowed from Berlin's 1940 *Louisiana Purchase*, have slipped in, but the essentials are there and this disc gives the most pleasant listening of that part of the score which it displays. Merman is in first-class form, daintily pile-driving her way from the rousing 'Hostess with the Mostes'' through the ragbag 'International Rag' (which is not a patch on the eliminated 'Washington Square Dance') to some quite unforgettable duetting with Donald O'Connor in 'You're Just in Love' and with George Sanders in 'The Best Thing For You'. These two men do more than just support their star, they both give fine performances, O'Connor in his genially relaxed light baritone and Sanders (is that really him?) turning such a smooth, warm Continental singing voice on to 'Marrying For Love' that you regret the loss of his other number. Carole Richards is the voice of Vera-Ellen, dancing to the massed ocarinas of the MGM orchestra in a cute and croony soprano which blends well with O'Connor in 'It's a Lovely Day Today'.

It would have been nice to have had the full score from this cast, but it is still the best bargain, even without. But it does make you think that, given the status of Irving Berlin in the American popular music world, his stage shows have not been very well served by the recording industry.

Guys and Dolls

1950 also brought to the stage Frank Loesser's second attempt at a Broadway musical. This one was nothing like *Where's Charley?*. Old-fashioned English farce and the kind of music suitable to illustrate it had gone right out of the window and, instead, he and his librettists Abe Burrows and Jo Swerling, building on the very idiosyncratic stories of Damon Runyon, brought out a musical which could not have been more American, more New York, more Broadway, more brilliant. Story, dialogue, song-text and music all combine to make a picture and tell a story with a style and character that are quite unique. Forty years later, *Guys and Dolls* remains one of the most outstanding achievements in the musical theatre.

The score of the show is a well-proportioned one, yet virtually every musical piece, taken separately, is a gem. Every kind of number appears, ranging from slick Sky Masterson's brave baritone philosophy in 'My Time of Day' and his vigorous gambling song 'Luck Be a Lady', the tunefully tipsy 'If I Were a Bell' of the mission girl, Sarah Brown, for whom he falls, and their sweeping, unguarded duet 'I've Never Been in Love Before', to the very individual comical pieces: dumb, trusting Adelaide's lament over her inability to get her long-term fiancé, Nathan, to the altar, the brash cabaret numbers ('Take Back Your Mink', 'A Bushel and a Peck') she sings at her club, the satirical revivalist number 'Sit Down You're Rockin' the Boat' and – my own particular favourites – two remarkable duets in 'Sue Me', in which Nathan protests his love to Adelaide, and 'Marry the Man Today', where Sarah and Adelaide share their thoughts on how to handle men. As if all that were not enough, there are magnificent ensemble moments – beginning with the opening

'Fugue for Tinhorns', in which the lounging guys of the town discuss racing tips in three-part harmony, passing by the chorale description of 'The Oldest Established Permanent Floating Crap-Game in New York' to the lively title song. Here, truly, is a score with everything.

Surprisingly, it has been very little recorded. Well, perhaps not so surprisingly, since, besides being one of the great shows, *Guys and Dolls* also has one of the great original cast recordings, and the record of the 1950 Broadway production, issued first on the Brunswick label, has been kept steadily available over the years in most parts of the world where musicals are known and loved.

From the moment the record begins with the short 'Runyonland' introduction – magnificently orchestrated like the rest of the show by George Bassman and Ted Royal – and Sam Levene, Stubby Kaye and Johnny Silver leap into their horse-racing discussion in music, you know that something special is on the way. And so it proves. Number by number, the effect grows. Robert Alda (Sky) and Isabel Bigley (Sarah) face up to each other defensively in 'I'll Know (When my Love Comes Along)' and you are not just listening to two excellent, natural-sounding voices singing a sweeping melody, but to two characters whose personalities shine through their music and lyrics. Adelaide (Vivian Blaine) hammers out 'A Bushel and a Peck' in a voice to rival Merman's, but wholly convincing you that she is this seedy cabaret singer before lapsing into the sniffles and stentorian miseries of her Lament. By the time you get to the second part of the second side, where she and her Nathan (Levene) are battling it out in 'Sue Me', Stubby Kaye is employing his remarkable character tenor on 'Sit Down You're Rockin' the Boat', and the two girls are plotting in scalding harmony to 'Marry the Man Today', you are wallowing in just about the nearest thing to perfection I've found on a show disc. Even the little piece 'More I Cannot Wish You', which can slip away ineffectively in a less than well cast production, is given an exquisite performance here by veteran Pat Rooney sr, whose gentle, crackly Irish tones take the sugar off its sweet sentiments. What else can I say? This is a record to be treasured.

The first *Guys and Dolls* cast recording to come out after this appeared in 1976, when a whooped-up production with black performers was brought to Broadway. Loesser's score underwent the sort of treatment only a dead writer could suffer in silence as his music was twisted about into corny upbeat arrangements by Messrs Danny Holgate and Horace Ott and his lyrics 'improved' by someone who doesn't own up on the record sleeve. Abe Burrows has his name in large letters credited with 'Entire Production Under the Supervision of', which presumably stopped him complaining. If you last through the overture on this disc, there are just one or two pleasant surprises, including some fine male singing in the opening numbers and a Sky Masterson (James Randolph) with a beautiful voice, but the offensive arrangements win out very quickly and I must admit to never having made it to the second side.

The orchestrations on the only other cast recording, from Britain's National Theatre production of 1982, are a little less awful but only a little. When the copyright of works such as this is so closely guarded, why and how are these arranging atrocities so often perpetrated? However, even disregarding the orchestra, this recording is not a patch on the standard one. Several of the principal performers sound very uncomfortable in their singing and only the assured Julia McKenzie (Adelaide), galloping into her cabaret numbers with abandon and ending her cavalcade of woes with a sneeze at Yma Sumac level, and David Healy (Nicely-Nicely), with a lusty 'Sit Down You're Rockin' the Boat', make the grade.

The original London production was little recorded, and the 1953 film has left a limited soundtrack, but one of the stars of the film, Frank Sinatra, headed an amusing collection on the Reprise series in which he nabs the numbers which, as Sky Masterson, he didn't get to sing in the film, and joins with Dean Martin and Bing Crosby in the 'Fugue for Tinhorns' and 'The Oldest Established'; the Maguire Sisters make hay with 'A Bushel and a Peck', Sammy Davis jr tackles 'Sit Down You're Rockin' the Boat' and Debbie Reynolds and Alan Sherman go over the top with 'Sue Me'. It isn't the show, but it's fun – the sort of fun you can safely enjoy knowing that there is a brilliant 'real' record of the score in existence.

The Most Happy Fella

Loesser followed *Guys and Dolls* with another remarkable show, *The Most Happy Fella*, which has an altogether different kind of an appeal and tone to the idiosyncratic comedy and joyous songs of its predecessor. *The Most Happy Fella* is a heart-warming and simple love story, peopled by a group of thoroughly likeable and real characters, and set to music that ranges from the almost operatic to the Broadway comedy song in its styles, yet makes up a score that is a coherent and impressive whole, with only one or two *longueurs*. Only rarely is there an echo of the *Guys and Dolls* music to be found, and *Where's Charley?* is lost in the mists of time as Loesser demonstrates both his strength and versatility as a composer and a talent for effective and natural lyrics which is second to none.

The show's musical high point, the duet 'My Heart Is so Full of You', deserves to rate as one of the most outstanding love duets of the light musical theatre, whilst the simply expressed 'Warm All Over' gives the listener the very same feeling it describes. The joyous Italianate male-voice trio 'Abbondanza', the yearning baritone song of wanderlust 'Joey, Joey, Joey' and the impressive quartet 'How Beautiful the Days', with its classic harmonies, are contrasted with a set of light and comedy songs – 'Standing on the Corner', 'Big D', 'Ooh my Feet' and 'I Like Everybody' – which recall the fact that Loesser was a highly successful writer of hit singles before tackling the musical theatre.

That Columbia recognized the style and status of *The Most Happy Fella* was evidenced by the fact that they chose to take the unprecedented step of issuing, as the original cast recording, a three-record set which included the substantial score of the show in its entirety plus a large amount of dialogue. It was an enterprise both intelligently conceived and splendidly executed.

Robert Weede starred as Tony Esposito, the middle-aged Italian farmer who attracts his waitress pen-friend into marriage by sending her a photograph of his handsome young foreman. The rôle is one which requires not only a splendid legitimate baritone singing voice, but also an acting ability and, above all, an exceptionally sympathetic, masculine warmth. Weede's recorded performance scores on all these fronts – his singing is unaffected, vibrant and superb and his characterization remarkable. You cannot help but love this Tony, and you wholly understand when Rosabella, his bride, is weaned from her initial repulsion and anger to love by the genuineness and generosity of spirit of the man.

Jo Sullivan (Rosabella) is no vapid *Oklahoma!* ingénue. When we first hear her she is a hard little city chippie, with a steel butterfly voice, until, little by little, she warms under the sun of Tony's regard and finally rises with him to the heights of 'My Heart Is so Full of You' and the show's beautifully tender final scene. Susan Johnson (Cleo) and Shorty Long (Herman) give their all to the comedy material, she in a scalding chest voice, he rather more lightly; Art Lund, as the handsome foreman, makes a truly splendid job of his big number 'Joey, Joey, Joey', performing in a relaxed yet strong-centred baritone to great effect; and the three choristers featured in the Italian ensembles are quite splendid in their spirited harmonies.

What works so very well here, apart from the outstanding performances from the cast and the never intrusive band, is its layout. You have only to listen to the perfectly good selection disc taken from this recording to realize the difference. There, the beautiful songs come out as just that, beautiful songs. On the full set, with the dialogue and story in their place, the musical portions are more than just numbers, they become the part of a magnificently crafted whole which is both effective and often truly moving. Perhaps *The Most Happy Fella* is overlong and occasionally overwritten, but it is also a triumph of positive writing – warm, real, likeable characters and wonderful melodies in a score which has something for everyone – performed and recorded in its original cast version at a level that could scarcely be bettered.

The London production of the show was also put down on record and it, too, is performed extremely well. Inia te Wiata was the London Tony and, if he does not succeed in making him quite the character that Weede does, that is possibly because he is only given the opportunity to perform the main portions of the music on the HMV single-disc issue. His impressive bass-baritone is put to good use but, again, Weede edges him out in clarity and *joie de vivre*. Likewise, Helena Scott (Rosabella), who has more pure vocal quality and expertise than her American counterpart, doesn't make quite the same effect dramatically. Art Lund repeats as Joe, Libi Staiger is a desperately piercing Cleo and Jack DeLon a first-class Herman on a recording that is comparable with the single-disc version of the Broadway cast but, when compared with the set, has the same minor disadvantages.

Wonderful Town

The rise and rise of Leonard Bernstein, which had begun with *On The Town*, continued in the 1950s with three further musicals. The first of these was *Wonderful*

Town (1953), a musical based, like *Gentlemen Prefer Blondes*, on a very well-known and established work (on this occasion the hit play *My Sister Eileen*). As with the first musical, his collaborators on the score were lyricists Comden and Green. The piece was, by its nature, one that followed the lines of most other such play-based musicals, taking a slimmed version of the original text and popping songs and set-piece numbers into its fabric. This pre-drawn outline left the writers little chance to do anything but provide the same sort of revusical numbers with which they had been so successful in *On the Town* and the composer to stick largely to straightforward songs and to dance music, but the team's skill both in lyrics and music meant that several of those pieces were of superior standard.

Heroine Ruth and her mantrap sister Eileen, just arrived in Greenwich Village from Columbus, huddle together in their rented room wondering in burlesque country harmonies whether they wouldn't have been better off staying in 'Ohio'; a squad of Irish policeman serenade 'Darling Eileen' in mock-Irish tones; the 'Conga' and 'Swing' get parodied in major routines; and 'The Wrong Note Rag' gives a tongue-in-cheek example of another musical genre. Alongside the musical fun and the freely utilized dance rhythms, the lyricists took the chance to have lyrical fun of their own, as when an ex-college man remembers what he got away with in class because 'I could pass a football' and Ruth kicks herself for knowing 'One Hundred Easy Ways to Lose a Man', suffers attempts to discourage her ambitions in the witty 'What a Waste' or, desperate to be a reporter, runs through a topical set of questions to a pack of uncomprehending Brazilians in 'Conga'. The fun was everywhere in the score of *Wonderful Town*, and only a couple of ballads for the man Ruth eventually gets and the winsomely tuneful 'A Little Bit in Love', the show's catchiest tune, approached the romantic.

Rosalind Russell was the show's original star, yet another in what was becoming a rather exhausting Broadway series – the overwhelming featuring of large-scale and very loud-voiced female stars – and she received 100% above-the-title billing on the Decca original cast album. By and large it is a good cast album. It contains all of the songs, although not all of Bernstein's appreciable dance music, and it is immediately evident that the piece is well suited to record. There is something intimate about the style of writing, the importance of the lyrics perhaps, which compels you to listen closely to the songs, and since Miss Russell in her chesty tones and the delightful Edith Adams (Eileen) in her versatile Broadway soprano are pretty nifty on their lyrics, they both come across very well. George Gaynes as the love interest has a rather glutinous baritone which doesn't perhaps fully do justice to his songs.

There are some very enjoyable highlights here, from which I'd pick Miss Adams's delicate handling of 'A Little Bit in Love' and the gruesome Conversation Piece at an ill-matched and frugal dinner party. This latter ends in a gabbling ensemble, with Eileen's voice shrilling above everything like a demented flute – a scene which lets us hear a little of what is to come from the composer in his next work, *Candide*.

Miss Russell took up her rôle again, alongside several other original cast members, five years later for a television version of the show, which was recorded on

Columbia. The disc includes most of the same material as the cast recording, and it has one advantage over its predecessor in a fine, relaxed, vernacular performance from Sidney Chaplin as Ruth's Bob, but Miss Russell is rather huskier by this stage and, in spite of a good performance by Jacquelyn McKeever, I miss the devilish piquancy of Miss Adams as Eileen.

The original London production, which featured Pat Kirkwood and Shani Wallis, put down only an EP's worth of the show, but a 1986 revival with Maureen Lipman recorded the complete set of songs. It is a largely inoffensive recording of this scaled-down production, the reorchestrations having been tactfully done (and often sounding like more than fourteen players), Miss Lipman showing up with a pleasant small voice and a lively comic sense, and the football song getting a better performance from the very youthful-sounding Nick Colicos than on either American disc. But ultimately it is a lightweight version which lacks the usual cast recording atmosphere. It also commits (among other misdemeanours) the sad sin of dropping Eileen's vocal line in the Conversation Piece and, thus, ruining the show's most intricate number. If the lady can't sing the rôle, why cast her?

Candide

Bernstein's next score was a rather different affair. *Candide* (1956) was an operetta burlesque based on Voltaire's famous work, and the classic stature of the subject gave the composer the opportunity to allow his talent for full-hearted, adventurous orchestral music – as demonstrated in the dance music for the two earlier musicals – to blossom fully. *Porgy and Bess* and *Street Scene* had taken a path away from the old songsmiths' scores of pre-war days towards a more operatic style; *Candide* took a parallel course, adding to their elements that most important one of all – humour. *Candide* was not only a brilliant musical score, it was one that rose both musically and lyrically to heights of wit and humour not often attempted in the musical theatre.

The first production was not a box office success and, in spite of its obvious merits, the show was clearly not quite right. Although the score bristled with fun, someone had forgotten to tell librettist Lillian Hellman that the piece was a humorous one. Fortunately there were enough people around who believed in the show to prevent it from going the way of other unsuccessful musicals and, from that day to this, *Candide* has gone through a series of metamorphoses and productions, as Bernstein and an ever-changing list of collaborators have attempted to perfect it. Their efforts have been regularly recorded: apart from the original 1956 cast recording, there exist also a double-disc cast recording of the successfully revised 1973 revival, another of the New York City Opera production of the so-called operatic version, and a single selection disc taken from Scottish Opera's revised semi-operatic version. Each and every one of them is enjoyable – the material alone guarantees that – but all four are markedly different one from the other, both in the musical content used and in the style of production.

The original 1956 selection disc does excellent service to the music. The principal singing rôles of Candide (Robert Rounseville), Cunegonde (Barbara Cook) and the Old Lady (the stirring Irra Petina) are all given impeccable interpretations, the orchestra makes a rousing job of the outstanding overture (a piece that bleaches the usual unimaginative pots-pourris) and all the rest of Bernstein and Hershy Kay's superb orchestrations, and the supporting cast turn in equally fine performances. If there is anything lacking, it is perhaps simply something in the way of sparkle, personality, humour – the true burlesque sense. When you follow the score through with the detailed plot synopsis given on the sleeve, you don't have a lot of fun, and Richard Wilbur's marvellously quirky and occasionally outrageous lyrics come as somewhat of shock. Like the original version of the show itself, the recording suffers from a rather heavy hand on its heart.

The 1973 version takes an utterly different standpoint. The libretto was wholly rewritten by Hugh Wheeler, with additional lyrics taken in from Stephen Sondheim and John Latouche, and it can instantly be seen that they are all three in splendid sympathy with the score and with the burlesque concept. Wheeler altered some of the characters and many of the plotline details, juggled the numbers around, and managed to fit much of the original score – suitably changed – into his new piece. To number all the variations that occur in the successive productions of *Candide* would take several pages, but they included on this occasion the addition of the author Voltaire to the cast as a narrator capable of taking on several other characters during the course of the show, the omission of the songs 'Quiet' and 'Eldorado', the switching of the love song 'My Love' from a male–female affair to a male–male one, and the manufacture of a new opening number. The show was presented in a highly original staging, with a cast of twenty-three playing all the many rôles and an orchestra of just thirteen.

The recording happily reflects the new approach. Firstly, Voltaire's narration is included, which gives the whole piece both coherence and an additional source of comedy, and also accounts for the spreading of the show over four record sides. Secondly, the casting is done in a completely different spirit. Candide (Mark Baker) and Cunegonde (Maureen Brennan) sound like the fresh, foolish young people they are supposed to be and, if these artists lack an ounce or two of the vocal assurance of their predecessors, they more than make up for it with a spontaneity and youthfulness, which works wonders for the piece without harming the music. The music does rather less well, however, with the small orchestra. The splendour and the sheer size of the original excitingly orchestrated sound and the variations of tone colour and special effects it makes available are lost, and, even though all the wholly orchestral parts of the work except the overture are omitted, the loss is continuously felt. What is gained, in this recording, on the dramatic side is rather lost on the musical one.

John Mauceri, the musical director of this revival, was also at the helm when the 'operatic version' of *Candide* was prepared for the New York City Opera, and he was materially involved when, once again, in spite of the fact that the 1973 version had been very successful, it was decided to revamp the show. The one long act was more conventionally divided in two, a new finale pasted together for Act I from disused music, 'Quiet', the comedy waltz 'What's the Use' and some of the more difficult music for the rôle of the Governor (played by the Narrator), which had been omitted last time round, restored, and further disused pieces made into an entr'acte number. The lyrics, needless to say, were subjected to their periodic going over as well. Some of the alterations worked, others did not. One which definitely did was the restoration of the full-scale orchestra, even if things were taken perhaps a little far by using an orchestra of fifty-two players.

This recording has little to do with either of the earlier ones in the way of style. This time those involved know what they have. They have splendid music and they treat it, by and large, splendidly. The orchestra knows it has all its best bits back and it revels in playing its way through some of the most outstanding stage musical music of the century. The singers know they have some glorious lines to sing and they sing them thoroughly. They also know what they have to do is funny, and the record company even puts in some of the opening dialogue – which is usually very funny – to help matters along. One or two of the cast such as Maris Clement (Paquette) and the Old Lady (Joyce Castle) actually strive with some success to be funny, but they are, alas, rather isolated.

In this area, a large part of the fault lies with the casting of John Lankston in the Narrator/Pangloss/Governor rôle. I suppose there are very few performers in the world who could cope with the comedy of the Narrator's part and the tenor vocalizing of the Governor's songs – I've been casting musicals for years and I can think of only one – but Lankston isn't he. His dialogue is unconvincing, his manner rather too reminiscent of the pre-war D'Oyly Carte Company, and his singing impeccable but dull. David Eisler (Candide) and Erie Mills (Cunegonde), equally, sing unimpeachably, but neither succeeds in raising the characters off the disc. Scott Reeve in the underwritten rôle of the stainless Maximilian is by far the most convincing, but, in this version, he is little heard in comparison with the leading players.

It was surely Mauceri's presence at Scottish Opera that resulted in *Candide* getting a showing there in 1987 and a subsequent London season with a 'Best Musical' citation at the end of it, and it was certainly he who again took charge of reorganizing the show's score. Most of the alterations made for New York were now discarded, other portions were modified yet again, and John Wells was brought in to play about with the libretto once more. The less happy new items of the operatic version all vanished but, alas, with them vanished not only the reinstated 'Quiet' but also the lovely 'Sheep's Song' which had never done any harm to anyone.

The recording of this version was unfortunately limited to just one disc, although it must be said there is little more on the two discs of the New York set, the second of which contains a bare half-hour's listening. I say 'unfortunately', for, whilst I had reservations about the overly philosophical and under-funny rewrites of this version and also its production in the theatre, I think that it comes the nearest yet to getting us the perfect *Candide* on record. I won't quibble any further over the content except to say that there is now a bit too much of Candide himself being soulful in the show, and altogether too little of Maximilian (Cunegonde has been given back her half of 'My Love') and Paquette, who added both variety and fun to the entertainment. The orchestra sounds a little less titanic than the New York City Opera pack and it is, fortunately, given its opportunity to shine in both the Paris Waltz and the Eldorado music, but what has been got particularly right this time is the casting. Mauceri and director Jonathan Miller have found the combination that works – the full-scale opera orchestra and chorus combined with a cast selected from amongst the very best young operetta actors and singers in Britain.

The impossible Voltaire rôle has, wisely, been split in two. The occasionally singing actor Nickolas Grace assumes the Pangloss portion with spiky ease, while the insinuating tenorizing of 'My Love' and the vicious operatic bravado of 'Bon Voyage' are given a simply marvellous rendition by the flamboyant, ringing Bonaventura Bottone. Candide himself is played with unaffected voice and style by the American guest artist Mark Beudert, and Marilyn Hill Smith proves herself to be the ideal Cunegonde. She masters the fearsome coloratura of the show's lemon lollipop showpiece, the burlesque Jewel Song 'Glitter and Be Gay', with easy precision and a deliciously enunciated sense of comedy, and establishes the character of the innocent but oft-ravished heroine even without the aid of the dialogue. Ann Howard is a contralto Old Lady (which works well) who is prone to the odd shrill operatic blast, but Mark Tinkler (Maximilian) alone misses the tone of things and 'wooffles' away in the back of his throat in what is left of his rôle.

You get greedy for the ideal recording when you think as highly of a show as I do of *Candide*. It hasn't come yet, but we seem to be getting nearer all the time as the various ideas of the writers and producers drop one by one into the winning slots. Perhaps we could take the entire existing score and the stars of the Scottish version, add Scott Reeve from New York and resurrect Irra Petina, stir in Mauceri and the orchestra of his choice, and come out with something quite unique. But since any record of *Candide* is better than no record of *Candide*, and the newest and happiest one should be with us for a good while, there is little reason to complain.

West Side Story

West Side Story (1957), which remains Bernstein's most famous work for the Broadway stage and one of the most internationally popular of all musicals of the period, turned right away from the world of the crisp, cerebral *Candide* to a subject about as different as could be imagined – the street gangs of contemporary New York – and a musical style that was coherent with that subject. The clicking and crashing rhythms of youthful modern dance were given full rein in a well-proportioned score that mixes energetic ballet with genuinely ingenuous ballads, a couple of comedy numbers and some powerful ensemble music, and illustrates extrordinarily effectively the show's moving tale of a modern-day Romeo and Juliet in the American urban slums.

Everywhere in *West Side Story* the emphasis is on youth and on energy and, in the casting of the show's original production, pure vocal ability was given less consideration than usual. Only the three featured players, Larry Kert (Tony), Carol Lawrence (Maria) and Chita Rivera (Anita) were required to stretch their voices over an extended vocal line; elsewhere, the boys and girls who made up the rival gangs of the Jets and the Sharks were selected on dance and personality criteria. The result was stunning on the stage but, perhaps more surprisingly, it is also stunning on record. The boys who click and explode their way through the opening 'Jet Song' with a self-confident bragadoccio, which is all the more real for the pathetic childishness that lurks transparently near its surface, sound shakingly real.

The atmosphere of the show, already aroused by the vibrant, clashing tones of the prologue, is set, and it is maintained, powerful and raw, throughout the piece, even when the Jet boys swap self-serious swagger for a bit of comic cop-baiting in 'Gee, Officer Krupke' and the Puerto Rican Shark girls flaunt themselves in a sparky, satirical number about 'America'. Against this background, the doomed romance of Tony and Maria is born and proceeds through a series of sentimental numbers that have become standards – 'Something's Coming', 'Maria', 'One Hand, One Heart', 'Tonight', 'I Feel Pretty' and 'Somewhere'.

Kert and Lawrence are ideally cast. Both are utterly believable in their rôles, singing their songs with a youthful unpretentiousness which is a pleasure to listen to and which lends enormous power to their tragic end. He is earnest, excited, full of spirit, with a clear, thrusting voice, she quiet and delicate, just touching the notes with her sweet, accurate soprano, and both are well aware of what it is they are singing about, what is happening. When they move smoothly into 'Tonight' you get the feeling that they are continuing the preceding spoken scene rather than singing a duet. Rivera, too, is splendid in her rôle, striking sparks with Marilyn Cooper and Reri Grist in 'America' and pulling out deeply felt tones for the great duet with Maria, 'A Boy Like That', which climaxes the show musically and prepares the ground for the final dramatic (unsung) climax. This recording takes in all the seventeen musical pieces of the score, splendidly orchestrated and performed, and splendidly recorded. There would seem no need to look further for a thoroughly first-rate *West Side Story*.

There is, in any case, not very far to look, for, surprisingly in view of its popularity, the piece has not been nearly as widely recorded in cast recordings as, for example, *My Fair Lady*. The original London production left only a 45 disc of Don McKay and Marlys Watters performing the romantic rôles, although David Holliday and George Chakiris (who played in the London version) are both featured as members of two of the bundle of British studio recordings that followed, which entrust the Tony/Maria songs to performers of specific singing abilities. Operetta star Adele Leigh and two former Eliza Doolittles, Jill Martin and Diane Todd, are amongst them. There is a Japanese cast recording, which covers two discs and includes enthusiastically acted dialogue as well as some perfectly competent singing, a more recent and below par Australian version with some indifferent singers and a really limp-wristed sounding Riff, and a short selection in Swedish (backed with *Stop the World*), but that seems to be all.

There have also been comparatively few studio cast recordings of *West Side Story*, but the most substantial is one made in 1985 with Bernstein himself conducting. It is a two-disc set on Deutsche Grammophon, including the full score and dialogue, equipped with full lyrics in four languages and with notes that make it hard to understand why the recording was made. Bernstein's well-known contemporary remark about how right they were not to cast the show with specialist singers in 1957 gets quoted alongside what appears to be a justification for trying an operatic treatment. But an operatic *West Side Story* is an anomaly.

Everything is fine whilst the orchestra is playing, but the moment Kiri te Kanawa, José Carreras (who sounds much more Puerto Rican than she), Tatiana Troyanos (who tries hard in chest voice, but gurgles sadly above the break) and the rest of the company begin to sing, the result is ludicrous and sometimes downright tacky. Nina and Alexander Bernstein as the speaking voices of the lovers drag things momentarily back to reality, but the singing is so lacking in youth, in vigour, in all the things that made *West Side Story* great, as to be almost offensive. I suppose these things must be tried, but it would be better to try them in private rather than on a large and grandly publicized (and sold) recording.

Where the stage and studio have been reticent, the screen has come up with the goods. The enormously popular film of *West Side Story* has given birth to a truly fine soundtrack. As in all stage-to-film ventures, the piece has necessarily been revised for the screen, but in this case the revisions have been fairly tactful and virtually all of the show's numbers have been retained, if not always in their original form. The prologue has been lengthened to cover the opening credits sequence, 'America' has undergone a lyric-lift, 'Officer Krupke' has been taken from its uncomfortable place amid the height of the drama and repositioned earlier in the show, and so forth. The score has also been reorchestrated by Saul Chaplin for an orchestra three times bigger than the original pit band that appears on the cast recording. This aggrandization, which does not usually work, somehow comes off here. As was seen in the reorchestration of *Candide*, Bernstein's music is of a character and texture that seems grateful for such an expansion and the results, particularly in the orchestral solo portions, are stunning.

The singing performances are also appreciable. Marni Nixon dubs the voice of Natalie Wood in the heroine's rôle and does her usual amazing job – this Puerto Rican teenager's voice was, not long since, being the voice of the very English Deborah Kerr in *The King and I* and was soon to be the cockney Eliza of *My Fair Lady*. Here Miss Nixon (who is nothing like any of the three characters in question) gives a performance of lightness and sweetness which fits the rôle delightfully. Tony is sung by Jim Bryant, and he too does a good job, but he suffers slightly from the dubbers' disease and lacks the spirit and vigour Kert displays on the stage recording. Rita Moreno's singing of Anita was apparently a three-voiced effort, partly done by herself, partly by the chameleon Miss Nixon and partly by another dubber. Whatever the method and mixture, the result is amazingly strong and effective, both in the high jinks of 'America' and the drama of the duet.

This is a first-rate recording, with the advantage over the stage one of the more expansive orchestrations, and the disadvantage of the facts that the performers have just that little less presence and character and that the 'Somewhere' dance music and solo version are omitted. It's pick and choose according to your taste. Mine takes me, just marginally, towards the show disc.

Whilst Bernstein, Loesser and Weill and their associate book and lyric writers were attempting in their different ways to leave behind the faithful old comedy-with-songs formula in the musical theatre, the era's favourite songwriters continued happily to plough the furrow that had yielded gold before and was perfectly capable of doing so again.

Can-Can

Cole Porter's *Can-Can* allowed him to spill a handful of American-in-Paris ballads through a gently amusing Abe Burrows libretto to considerable effect and a two-year Broadway run. The handful included the durable 'I Love Paris' – so often sung out of context since its introduction here that it almost seems out of place in its rightful position – 'C'est magnifique' and 'It's all Right with Me', as well as the intermittently amusing 'Never Give Anything Away', 'Live and Let Live' and 'Come Along with Me', in a score that nevertheless cannot truthfully be rated amongst Porter's better works.

Listening to the original cast album, it is hard to imagine how anything from this show survived to success. There is a wholesale lack of style and sophistication in every department, beginning with some strident orchestrations, a whole lot of banal 'naughty Paree' words and a general lack of genuine humour, all compounded by some fairly awful performances. The French singer Lilo in the principal rôle doesn't make a very pleasant sound and sometimes makes it off-key, whilst Peter Cookson, playing opposite her, must have seen *Kiss Me, Kate* and decided that all Porter melodies need the voice heroic, for he oversings his numbers consistently, robbing them of any nuance. It is not pleasant.

The London production followed the style of Broadway, and it was left to the film version to treat the material with a little more of the tact it requires. The tact began by rewriting the libretto and cutting half the score. Naturally, the favourites remained, but along with some of the more tasteless bits the cutting sadly lost us the simplest and most effective little piece in the show, 'Allez-vous-en'. To make up for this, a group of Porter standards – 'You Do Something to Me', 'Just One of Those Things' and 'Let's Do It' – was pasted in. However, in the hands of Frank Sinatra, Louis Jourdan, Shirley MacLaine and Maurice Chevalier, supported by the orchestrations of Nelson Riddle, the surviving songs were given thoughtfully sung performances which made them sound very much better than before. If you require a full-scale

Can-Can you have no option but to brave the cast recording, but for once I feel that in this case it is better to take the stage show bastardized and Hollywoodized.

It is certainly better than another 'Porter Pops in Paris' show staged in London in 1988. This *Can-Can* includes a half-dozen songs that don't belong amongst the sixteen it uses and imposes surprisingly meretricious David Cullen arrangements and/or new lyrics on some of them – not to mention some weak performances.

Kismet

If Porter did not improve on his earlier work this time round, Robert Wright and George Forrest certainly did. They applied their *Song of Norway* method to Eddie Knoblock's classic comedy drama *Kismet* and, with the aid of the culled works of the Russian composer Aleksandr Borodin, produced a stunning 1953 musical version of the piece which remains one of the most successful operettas of the American stage. There must be very many people all round the world who are more familiar with the melodies and words of 'Baubles, Bangles and Beads', 'A Stranger in Paradise' or 'And This Is my Beloved' than they are with the original source material from which those songs were developed. From the strange cries of the muezzins and the poet's voice intoning a *memento mori* which set the show in motion, through rich, baritone numbers for the beggar, Hajj, whose wits and wiles are the spring of this Arabian Nights story; soaring melodies for pretty Marsinah, his daughter, and the young Caliph of Baghdad whom she finally weds; moments of grisly comedy for the wicked Wazir and of slinky seduction for his wayward wife, the lovely Lalume, the score of *Kismet* is one of those in which one outstanding number follows another without fail.

Like so many other shows with a very definite set of vocal demands, *Kismet* has been the object of several fine recordings, beginning with its original cast disc. Orchestra, orchestrations and chorus are all that could be asked for, whilst Alfred Drake, at the head of the cast, is a first-rate Hajj, mixing a comic lightness of touch with a ringing baritone voice and bringing out the roguish character of this rascally hero through his songs. Doretta Morrow and Richard Kiley as the young lovers both sing well, but if there is a disappointment it has to be the vocally lightweight and rather crude Lalume of Joan Diener.

Drake was also the star of a 1965 Music Theatre of Lincoln Center revival, recorded on RCA Victor, and, as is usual with this series of revivals, all the values are well cared for. In spite of the fact that the show has been fiddled with here and there (partly, it would seem, as the result of the film version), this recording has the edge on the original. Lee Venora is a very attractive Marsinah, singing with a clear assurance, which seems to impart even more of the same quality to Drake when he sings alongside her. More musically adept than her predecessor, Anne Jeffreys also makes Lalume more interesting, and the supporting cast, including Henry Calvin repeating his original impersonation of the Wazir, are fine throughout.

The 1955 film soundtrack, which employed a larger part of the original score than was often the case at that time (plus one new number, 'Bored'), is an unfortunate recording. The sound has not been well transferred, the Wazir's number is missing, and, in spite of some top-notch casting, the result is just not good enough. Howard Keel is a darker-voiced Hajj than Drake, which should give him an advantage in the rôle, but he doesn't ring through as clearly as he usually does. Ann Blyth is a charming Marsinah, Dolores Gray a chesty Lalume minus the top notes, and Vic Damone a very relaxed Caliph, but there seems no reason to take a mediocre recording which lacks some of the score when there is a choice of good ones which are complete.

There was no British cast recording – three of the four principal players were the same in London as they were on Broadway – but there is a full-scale British studio recording of 1964. Just looking at the sleeve, this disc would seem to have several things against it. Firstly, it is one of those that trumpets a new sound recording system across its front cover – 'new phase 4-stereo spectacular' is the name of this one. Then the name of Mantovani leaps out in black type from the credits in place of the original orchestrator, and it cuts corners on its principal singers: there are only five and they have to share the lines and numbers of the minor characters amongst them.

The disc is true to its cover. Whatever new phase 4-stereo spectacular is, it produces a big, wide sound, but it is a sound that suits this work very well. Mantovani's orchestrators have, indeed, been at the score, too. But, by and large, they have been discreet and there are only a few places where the shrieking strings get out of hand. And the casting? Well, it is so impeccable with regard to the principal rôles that it is hard to object when such singers as Kenneth McKellar and Regina Resnik have a little extra to sing. McKellar's version of the opening 'Sands of Time' is truly beautiful and Miss Resnik's attack on the Eastern yodelling of 'Zubbediya' is quite simply a collector's piece. So, it seems rather a case of errors and eccentricities turning into virtues.

Robert Merrill is the Hajj of this recording and his performance is about as ideal as can be imagined. Like Drake, he mixes a sense of comedy with a superb voice, and the extra bit of vocal richness he possesses helps to make pieces like the exceptional ballad 'The Olive Tree' (which is the other collector's item on this disc) just that bit more impressive. He has plenty of range to display his personality and sense of humour in the witty, wordy 'Gesticulate' and the 'Rahadlakum' duet with Resnik, but it is in 'The Olive Tree' that he really comes into his own, the glorious clear baritone tones, with never a touch of the opera house throttle, being used to full effect in a beautifully judged performance.

Adele Leigh and Kenneth McKellar give a very fine 'Stranger in Paradise' and bass-baritone Ian Wallace is suitably malicious and gleeful in the Wazir's song, but the other triumph of this record is undoubtedly Miss Resnik. She starts with the advantage over the other Lalumes in having a magnificently rich mezzo-soprano, which she can manipulate through black chest tones to a purple middle register and a violent magenta top, but, added to that, she has an evident sense of humour and a natural sexiness which ooze, both, through her performance like plum juice. When she hints at the equivocal joys of Baghdad in 'Not Since Nineveh' (restored to its original state, incidentally), Sally Bowles's Berlin looks pale. You wonder just what Nebuchadnezzar's hanging gardens got up to. And when she vaunts the properties of 'Rahadlakum' you have to know your Turkish to realize she's only singing about a sweetie. It's a masterly piece of casting, and a great performance, which puts the icing on a really grand recording.

Bells Are Ringing

Bells Are Ringing (1956) brought Comden and Green together for the second time with *Gentlemen Prefer Blondes* composer Jule Styne (the first had been the indifferent revue *Two on the Aisle*), on a vehicle for Judy Holliday, the acclaimed star of *Born Yesterday*. The authors came up with an amusing book, which cast Holliday as an answerphone girl who gets over-involved with her clients, and with some revusically humorous and gently sentimental lyrics, which Styne set in a standard songwriter style. A couple of the best – 'Just in Time' and 'The Party's Over' – caught the fancy of contemporary crooners and of the public sufficiently to get a wide distribution.

The show owed much of its success to Miss Holliday's performance in the rôle created for her, but unfortunately that performance comes across poorly on the original cast recording. The blonde appeal which she apparently had on the stage disappears here, and there is a sad lack of warmth in her ballads and some frantic mugging in the comic moments. Everything is very stagey and overplayed. She is not alone in this fault, for Sidney Chaplin opposite her falls part way into the same trap and Eddie Lawrence in the rôle of the spiv Sandor, who is the lynchpin of the principal sub-plot, splatters himself all over the back wall of the studio with his effortful funnies. It is not a subtle recording, and it is not helped by some obtrusive vocal arrangements. The classy, unbrassy Robert Russell Bennett has turned in orchestrations that lift the tunes splendidly, but Herbert Greene and Buster Davis have jammed the chorus into practically every number, even the most intimate, bringing the songs to a phoney climax with a dose of what sounds like thirty-two part Hollywood harmony. After the umpteenth time it becomes a bad joke.

Bells Are Ringing was transferred to film in 1960, reshaped by its original authors and with its music doctored by André Previn. Styne supplied two new numbers ('Do It Yourself' and 'Better Than a Dream') and the weaker parts of the original score ('On My Own', the revusical 'Is It a Crime', 'Hello, Hello There', 'Long Before I Knew You' and the lyrically comical 'Salzburg') were dropped, along with the 'Mu-Cha-Cha' dance routine. The doctoring was wisely and perspicaciously done, the orchestrations effective and the chorus limited somewhat in their interference and, as a result, the soundtrack recording of the piece is very much preferable to the stage version. Miss Holliday, again at the centre of things, gives a much more controlled and less vulgar performance and, in spite of the ubiquitous chorus, gets a good deal out of 'The Party's Over'. Dean Martin, in the leading male rôle, makes 'Just in Time' a wholly different song, delivering it with warm-voiced sincerity but never losing the amused, masculine crackle that is his trademark, and Eddie Foy jr, with just one song ('A Simple Little System') left to his comedy rôle, proves that it is more effective to let comic song words speak for themselves than to shout them in a silly voice. The new numbers – particularly the counterpointed 'Better Than a Dream' – are also an improvement, so here again, as with *Can-Can* is a rare case of Hollywood winning out over Broadway.

Gypsy

Like *Bells Are Ringing*, *Gypsy* (1959) was constructed to order for a major female star, Ethel Merman, and, once again, Styne was paired with some classy collaborators in Arthur Laurents (libretto) and Stephen Sondheim (lyrics). The result was an extremely well-made show, which gave its star every opportunity she required, with a score in which the words often dominated the music and which, like *Bells Are Ringing*, turned out a couple of take-away tunes ('Everything's Coming Up Roses' and 'All I Need Is the Girl').

The music, however, did everything it needed to do for the star. Tactfully situated as much as possible in the loudest part of her voice, it cleverly dipped below that area just when a change in tone was needed, thus producing an acting-singing performance of rather more light and shade than had been the case in earlier Merman shows. Backed by some of the biggest, brassiest orchestration about, the score and the star rose together to some memorable peaks of sound. They rose for the first time shortly after the beginning of the show with an eleven o'clock number which took place around 8.30 p.m. ('Some People') then with another ('Everything's Coming Up Roses') about an hour or so later, and finally with the grandmother of all eleven o'clock monologues in the extended final 'Rose's Turn'. It was an evening of brass trumpets all round.

The rest of the characters had little to do musically, but they inherited the most tuneful of the songs. The two young daughters of the stage-struck Rose (Merman), pushed unwillingly into the theatre to fulfil their mother's dreams, sing longingly about 'If Momma Was Married', and Tulsa, a member of their touring act who ultimately elopes with older daughter June, plots his new dance routine in the songs and dance number 'All I Need Is the Girl'.

The original cast recording is memorable as a display of Merman in what was probably her best-fitted rôle as the loud-voiced, single-minded Rose. A line from her last number just about says it all: 'Hold your hats and halleluia, Momma's going to show it to you'. And she does. The brass trumpet rings out undimmed by time and, by device or by understanding, something resembling interpretation seems to have crept in. A lot of it is very, very loud – particularly in the final scena, but the writers have made it so that it is right for it to be very, very loud, so all you can do is sit back and let it kick you in the ears. It ought to be unpleasant, but it works.

The rest of the score is performed more than adequately with Sandra Church (as the daughter who turns out to be Gypsy Rose Lee) and Lane Bradbury (as the daughter who turns out to be June Havoc) combining in a particularly good 'If Momma Was Married' and Paul Wallace dapper in Tulsa's number, whilst Jack

Klugman, who knows he can't sing, makes agreeably characterful noises in the rôle of Herbie, Rose's dogged admirer.

It was 1971 before *Gypsy* reached London and, when it did, it was in a lightly revised version with Angela Lansbury starred. Many people will prefer the London recording. Lansbury gives a performance of much more finesse and character than Merman. She acts Rose instead of just being her, pacing her characterization through the show and the score, and the result is both less ear-shattering and, paradoxically, less impressive. The fact is that the rôle of Rose was not constructed for finesse, it was constructed, and devilishly cleverly constructed, for Merman.

That searing power and mindless determination, that relentless voice pounding at you from half past eight till the final curtain is all Rose. She isn't a lady of finesse. Lansbury, who has a fine voice, doesn't have that extra diapason and, when she has built up her climax, you don't get the Merman knockout punch. I've always resisted the Merman knockout punch, but here there is no doubt that it is effective. The rest of the credits on the London disc are all good (note Bonnie Langford as the unbelievably ghastly Baby June), but a *Gypsy* rises or falls by its Rose and this one, magnificent as she is, just goes down on a split decision.

Kay Medford (billed on the cover as 'Mrs Brice from *Funny Girl*' as if she were a soap starlet) had earlier made a UK studio recording of the *Gypsy* score for Music for Pleasure, but her swoopy, mannered vocal style and lack of both personality and vocal range put the disc out of court. A much better effort is the South African cast recording on which Libby Morris makes a good stab at Rose, producing some of the Merman power and a successful attempt at a brassy characterization lightened by a bit of crooning in the more personal moments. After a good start (partly thanks to little Miss Langford, again playing June, and Joe Stewardson's strong Herbie), however, this recording starts to fizzle out, from a mimsy Tulsa through a medium 'Everything's Coming up Roses' and the extended made-for-London version of the rather unprepossessing 'Together'.

Merman was gypped out of the film of *Gypsy*, which was made instead with Rosalind Russell, who was first in with the cash when the rights were free. It was and is our loss. Russell has none of the power and pzazz that the creator of the Rose gave to 'her' rôle, and her songs on the soundtrack, even with some helpful pieces of Lisa Kirk's singing voice rather clumsily pasted in, are little more than marshmallow when they ought to be full-strength chili.

The Pajama Game

Richard Adler and Jerry Ross came to Broadway's notice with the successful production of *The Pajama Game* in 1954. *The Pajama Game* is a piece which suffers from a mildly tiresome libretto and some silly characters and which draws most of its interest from its tuneful and high-spirited set of songs. Unfortunately, since the show's characters are almost entirely motivated throughout by greed or lust, the lyrics of most of the numbers veer particularly towards the latter subject in its varying degrees, which makes listening through the score a bit like reading a deskful of schoolboy essays on the same topic. However, amongst the simplest of the numbers there are some sweet pieces – the unpleasant heroine's pouting denial 'I'm Not At All in Love', a piece with the bouncy melody of first-class Richard Rodgers, the banjo-backed 'Once a Year Day', which illustrates the firm's annual picnic and its sexual shenanigans, the burlesque 'Hernando's Hideaway' and, the most popular of all, 'Hey There', sung by the hero to his dictaphone at the first stirrings of attraction. The slick, trendy dance number 'Steam Heat' also won notice, partly for its performance but partly also for its insinuating style.

There are two full recordings of the show, one from each of the Broadway and London original casts, and there is little to choose between them, very largely because the London cast seem to have done little more than try (very successfully) to give clone performances of their American counterparts, even to the extent of the West End's Elizabeth Seal pretending not to be able to sing very well in order to sound like Broadway's Carol Haney. Miss Seal and Australian Joy Nichols as the sharp little heroine of the show have the edge on their predecessors, but otherwise the Broadway recording is marginally better.

Its biggest asset is John Raitt, lending his clear, unpretentious baritone to the hero's numbers with effortless style. This is surely one of the most perfect light musical theatre voices of the era, combining an absolutely sure technique with a warm and winning tone and a relaxed delivery, and devoting equal care to both notes and words; his 'Hey, There' is a classic. Edmund Hockridge, on the British disc, is a little richer or heavier vocally, a little more hearty in performance, but still very fine. Eddie Foy jr in the principal comedy rôle delivers his material to the manner born (which, of course, he was) and teams up with a particularly good comedy lady in Reta Shaw for the not quite sufficiently funny 'I'll Never Be Jealous Again', a piece with which London's Max Wall and Joan Emney are a little less successful. Janis Paige, in the co-starring rôle, sings with a clear, chesty country tone and not too much subtlety, and Carol Haney, who made a personal hit with her stage performance, comes over poorly on record owing to the fact, already chronicled, that she doesn't really sing – something that can be largely covered up by the boys in 'Steam Heat' but is a little more exposed in 'Hernando's Hideaway'.

The film version of 1957 snapped up Raitt, Foy and Misses Shaw and Haney from the Broadway show and, in an admirable piece of casting, replaced Miss Paige with that singing steel sweetheart, Doris Day. Miss Day just about succeeds in making the boring Babe into a believeable and – even more difficult – likeable character, and her incisive, down-the-line singing is just what is needed. Her 'I'm Not at all in Love' really waltzes along, cocky and crisp. Raitt is a joy, whether duetting with himself in 'Hey, There' or with Doris Day, Foy and Shaw are right on the ball and Miss Haney has either had some help or come along strongly with her singing since the stage production. There's a touch of the silly voices amongst the smaller rôles, but otherwise it is a grand cast.

Inevitably some of the score has been lost on the way to the screen – 'A New Town Is a Blue Town', 'Her Is' and, sadly, Foy's 'Think of the Time I Save' are the most substantial bits – but I'd willingly swap them all for Miss Day. Once again it is a case of going for the stage recording if you need the whole score, but taking the film soundtrack if you are just looking for a finely done selection. It is beginning to look as though Hollywood did a better service to the musical stage than is generally accepted!

Damn Yankees

Damn Yankees (1955), the successor to *The Pajama Game* and, because of Ross's death, the last work the briefly-constituted team produced, was much more fun. Its hilarious story of a middle-aged man who makes a pact with the devil, allowing him to be transformed into a young star ball player who can help the local team win the coveted pennant, was full of opportunities. The score had a number of enjoyable moments, including two hit songs, the seductive 'Whatever Lola Wants' and the homespun philosophizing of 'Heart', and dance music ranging from the hoedown to the mambo.

The original cast recording is, however, not up to that of *Pajama Game* insofar as performance is concerned. Stephen Douglass, who takes the central rôle, has a strong baritone and several modest chances to use it, but elsewhere the singing often ranges from the just all right to the decidedly rough. Gwen Verdon, a dance and comedy knockout on the stage, doesn't come over in Lola's celebrated declaration of intention ('Little Man, little Lola wants you . . .') as appealingly as she has been known to elsewhere, and Ray Walton's talents aren't very well served by the unimaginative comedy song 'Those Were the Good Old Days'. The most enjoyable moments are those where the baseball team get themselves organized into harmonies and carol out their convictions on the efficacity of 'Heart' over talent and hard work, or list the temptations of the flesh that they have to put behind them in order to keep mind and body concentrated on 'The Game'.

The film version, the soundtrack of which was issued as *What Lola Wants . . .* , reused the entire Broadway cast with the exception of Douglass, who was replaced by Hollywood 'Adonis' Tab Hunter. Hunter is less of a singer than Douglass, but he has a fresh boyish sound. The only alteration in the score is made to lighten his vocal contribution – the duet 'A Man Doesn't Know' being replaced by the soupy new 'There's Something About an Empty Chair' for Meg (Shannon Bolin) alone. 'Heart' is still the highlight of the affair and, naturally, there isn't a lot to pick and choose between the two discs.

The Music Man

The Music Man was the maiden work of Meredith Willson. He wrote book, lyrics and music for this show, which popped up out of nowhere like a shaft of sunshine in the 1957–8 season and scored a tremendous hit. It is a gem of a piece, mixing the comedy of real life, a marvellous array of characters and delightful music with an inestimable warmth and positivity. If *Guys and Dolls* is the most New York of

Broadway musicals, *The Music Man* is surely the most American. There is more heart-warming truth in the Iowa folk of this tale of a tricksy travelling salesman finally shamed out of his shenanigans for the love of a good but difficult woman than in all the Ruritanian farmers and cowboys of *Oklahoma!* put together.

The score of the show is both inventive and attractive, making much effective use of speech and song rhythms (without the aid of a persistent drum), whether it be in the unaccompanied train-imitation of the opening chorus, the clucking of the townswomen's chatter in 'Pick-a-little' or the marching swing of the show's favourite number 'Seventy Six Trombones'; there is also of a happy variation of musical styles, from the half-spoken, half-sung numbers of the leading man to the simple soprano lines of his heroine's music and the harmonies of a quartet of local luminaries set to singing barbershop by the charismatic 'music man' to keep them off his back. It is perhaps a mark of the individuality of the *Music Man* score that there is no love duet until the very final number of the show.

The original Broadway cast recording is as much a gem as the show itself. Robert Preston as Harold Hill, the music man of the title, who gave one of the outstanding performances of all time in this rôle on stage, succeeds in making that performance come across on disc. He displays a charming, double-tongued duplicity in 'Trouble', in which he persuades the local folk of the iniquity of the newly installed pool hall and convinces them of the uplifting effects of a boys' band, rippling out the salesman's patter with trustworthy ease, and dazzling them with the tale of the day he saw 'Seventy Six Trombones' come to town. He sings his way through the wry, opportunistic words of 'A Sadder but Wiser Girl', but all the time the warmth in his characterful, crumpled voice assures you that there is a nicer fellow beneath the cynicism. When he discovers love for 'Marian the Librarian', the charm and the warmth are allowed to come out more, peeping from behind a protective jokiness, but when it is finally time to hear him join her in 'Till There Was You' the process has been completed. Harold Hill has come out.

Barbara Cook gives a model Broadway soprano performance as Marian, making her a no-nonsense small town girl, lusty and clean vocally, particularly in her longingly reflective 'Goodnight my Someone'. The harmonizing town councillors are performed gloriously by the barbershop group the Buffalo Bills. Their singing of 'Lida Rose' and the tongue-in-cheek 'Sincere' ought to be framed for posterity. All the supporting characters are fine: Eddie Hodges's lisping Winthrop, the child brought out from his taciturn shyness by the spell cast by Harold's musical promises to sing burstingly of 'The Wells Fargo Wagon', which is bringing him his shiny trumpet; Pert Kelton's vigorously match-making mother; Iggie Wolfington glutinously chorusing the dance number 'Shipoopi'; and the vicious womenfolk of River City with their vulturish 'Pick-a-Little' chorus, who are charmed into a more generous frame of mind by Harold's manipulations.

London's cast recording cannot hope to equal this one. There is a plausible Harold Hill in Van Johnson and a particularly attractive light-voiced Marian in Patricia Lambert, but neither the musical nor textual language seems to fall naturally onto the tongues of most of the cast and, although the numbers get good enough service in a score where only Miss Lambert and the quartet have anything in the way of legitimate singing, it just cannot compare with the Broadway disc.

The film version brings back the inimitable Preston, pairing him with sweet-voiced Shirley Jones. It is a perfectly agreeable recording of a film score which has only a couple of variations from the original stage version, even if Preston is just a touch less fresh than before (not surprising after his long tenure of the part on the stage) and Miss Jones is not quite at her tidy best. The Buffalo Bills and Miss Kelton repeat their stage rôles accurately and Buddy Hackett is the other important newcomer, giving a lively oddball 'Shipoopi'.

Bye Bye Birdie

Bye Bye Birdie brought the rock-and-roll music craze to the American musical theatre for the first time, a couple of years after *Expresso Bongo* had done so in Britain. Like *Expresso Bongo* it was a musical about the rock-and-rollers rather than a show made up of genuine rock-and-roll songs; both took a satirical look not only at the new breed of singing superstar the craze was producing but also at the people who were to be found behind and around those stars. There, however, the similarity stopped for, whilst *Expresso Bongo* was a piece where the satire was sometimes savage, the colours sombre and the ending realistically downbeat, *Bye Bye Birdie* was an evening of skittish fun from beginning to end, its parody of a pop star a bulging burlesque compared with the bitter, sullen Bongo, and its score a series of light-hearted and lively numbers and dance tunes.

The cheerful 'Put on a Happy Face', sung by Albert, the manager of pop star Conrad Birdie, to a group of fans watching their idol head off for the army, Conrad's 'A Lot of Livin' to Do', as he sneaks out for a night on the town, and 'Kids', a parent's lament for the awfulness of modern youth, were the most successful numbers, but Albert's girlfriend's complaint that he has gone into pop music rather than becoming 'An English Teacher' and his and her efforts to convince the unbelieving Press that Conrad is a 'Normal American Boy' were more substantial and substantially funny pieces, and the burlesques of pop ('Honestly Sincere') and ingenuous youth ('One Boy') were finely made in a bright, youthful show in which the accent was always on comedy.

The original cast recording probably doesn't represent the show at its very best. Chita Rivera as the put-upon Rosie shows off a strong, attractive chest voice and a real sense of comedy in her numbers and Susan Watson is cute as the fifteen-year-old who is chosen to be the recipient of Conrad's last pre-army kiss, but the throaty Dick van Dyke (Albert) and the husky-voiced, frantic Dick Gautier (Conrad) show up a little less well.

The London cast version is more or less comparable as, once again, it seems to be a case of the performers trying to do little else than reproduce the sounds of the original American disc. This is easy enough for Rosie, as Chita Rivera repeats her rôle, and I fancy has it a bit crisper by this second recording. Sylvia Tysick probably isn't as good a vocalist as Miss Watson, but she sings her numbers attractively, and

Peter Marshall (Albert) gives a more confident and clear 'Put on a Happy Face' as well as supporting Miss Rivera stylishly. The biggest difference is in the rôle of Conrad himself. Whereas Gautier burlesques pop, Marty Wilde is the real thing. It doesn't lessen the fun any and, since Wilde has the better voice, it is a positive gain. This, along with the fact that the British recording seems to have that little more ping and point to it, gives it the edge.

A film version with van Dyke, Ann Margret and Janet Leigh resulted in a soundtrack with ten of the show's numbers increased by one new one ('Bye Bye Birdie'), and also sparked a disc by Bobby Rydell, who had appeared in it in the minor rôle of Hugo Peabody. On a disc announcing him rather misleadingly as direct 'from his starring rôle' in the film, he has a go at all the songs he'd had to stand round listening to the rest of the cast sing. In a parade of characterless pop-singing and altered lyrics, the recording shows why.

Another disc with curious billing was a British HMV studio recording which features comic Sid James, who sings 'Kids'. Its casting is uneven. Peter Gilmore makes the best job of anyone of 'Put on a Happy Face' and Joyce Blair gives a nifty imitation of a Broadway singer as Rosie, but the teenage Kim is played by an overaged operetta singer who belongs in some other show and on some other record.

The Fantasticks

The Fantasticks (1960) was a new feature for the American musical theatre: a deliberately small-scale musical, conceived and built for staging in an intimate auditorium, which became a major hit in the same way that the miniature *The Boy Friend* and *Salad Days* had recently done in Britain. Unlike its British fellows, however, *The Fantasticks* did not ever make the move uptown to a regular theatre. It remained in its own cradle, kept its own character, and is still running at the time of writing, nearly thirty years later. The piece is a whimsical little parable of life in which two friendly fathers put obstacles between their children, knowing they will then rebel and get together. But when they do, they still have the obstacles of the real world to overcome before they grow to maturity through experience and can come to a really fulfilling relationship.

Tom Jones and Harvey Schmidt's score for *The Fantasticks* is an eclectic but attractive one, moving from the gentle, folksy melody and sentiments of the introductory 'Try To Remember' to the modernistic tones of the scientific duet 'Metaphor', the light comicalties of the fathers and the Spanish burlesque of the bandit El Gallo. The accompanying small two-piano-based group is most effective in the heavily rhythmic or gently simple numbers and rather less to the purpose when the melodies need to soar, but at its best the score is a pleasant relief from the growing sameness in the sound of the Broadway musical. 'Try to Remember' proved the hit of the show, even making it to the hit parades, but most of the rest of the score was too allied to the text to make much sense in isolation.

The Fantasticks has been played all round the world, but few recordings seem to have resulted and only the original off-Broadway cast is readily findable. It is an enjoyable one, featuring two performers – Jerry Orbach (Narrator/El Gallo) and Kenneth Nelson (The Boy) – who progressed to larger things, and who both give positive and pleasant performances here. Orbach's crackly baritone, warm at the bottom and forgiveably cheating at the top, is as full of personality as his gentle slices of narration, and Nelson is more than an ingénu, singing with splendid vigour when given the chance. Their driving duet 'I Can See it' gets the best performance on the disc. Rita Gardener as the Girl covers the wide vocal range of the part skilfully, and the two fathers throw themselves energetically into their parts.

There is always something lacking, with a recording like this, for those who have not seen the show. You have the little band and the medium-sized performances to indicate the style, but you need to know that this is performed on a bare platform, with a cardboard moon and a box full of props and the actors almost within touching distance, in order to get the full flavour. Unlike many other shows, you need to visualize this one as you listen to it.

More Broadway Shows

Amongst the major hits of the late 1940s and the 1950s there were many other interesting, if not always so successful, and quite successful but less interesting, shows which were consigned to record more or less in their musical entirety. There were, on the one hand, the lesser shows of the larger writers, including Rodgers and Hammerstein's *Allegro, Me and Juliet, Pipe Dream* and *Flower Drum Song*, Frank Loesser's *Greenwillow*, Cole Porter's *Out of This World* and *Silk Stockings*, Irving Berlin's *Miss Liberty*, Romberg's *Up in Central Park* and *The Girl in Pink Tights*, Kurt Weill's *Love Life* and *Lost in the Stars*, Meredith Willson's *The Unsinkable Molly Brown* and Jule Styne's *High Button Shoes, Hazel Flagg, Peter Pan, Say Darling* and *Do Re Mi*. On the other, there were pieces by less prominent or rising Broadway writers such as Harold Arlen (*Bloomer Girl, St Louis Woman, House of Flowers, Jamaica*), Harold Rome (*Wish You Were Here, Fanny, Destry Rides Again*), Gene de Paul (*L'il Abner*), Jerry Bock (*Mr Wonderful, Fiorello!, Tenderloin*), Albert Hague (*Plain and Fancy, Redhead*), Mary Rodgers (*Once Upon a Mattress*), Rick Besoyan (*Little Mary Sunshine*), Arthur Schwartz (*A Tree Grows in Brooklyn, By the Beautiful Sea*), Jerome Moross (*The Golden Apple*) and many others.

The listener who has enjoyed the principal works of the most famous writers will undoubtedly find further pleasure in recordings of their other shows, but there is also much among the writings and recordings of the rest of Broadway that repays attention.

Bloomer Girl

The Arlen show discs are mainly disappointing, given the composer's songwriting record ('Stormy Weather', 'That Old Black Magic', 'One for my Baby') and the renown of his musical film scores (*The Wizard of Oz, Cabin in the Sky*). The music of *Bloomer Girl* (1944), a scrappily texted piece attempting to ape *Oklahoma!*, is its best feature. It has a polite American operetta score, hampered by sometimes clumsy lyrics (it rhymes 'Utopia' with 'ya dope, ya') and leavened with a helpful handful of the Negro songs in which Arlen specialized. Two of these, 'The Eagle and Me' and 'I Got a Song', along with the deftly deprecatory duet 'Evelina' for the heroine (*Oklahoma*'s Celeste Holm) and hero (pleasant-voiced David Brooks), are the best moments of the original cast recording on which another *Oklahoma!* veteran, Joan McCracken, squawks a tuneless 'T'morra" amongst some other rather banal pieces. From a purely historical point of view, it is interesting to compare the play-within-a-play sequence of *Uncle Tom's Cabin* with the equivalent portion of *The King and I*.

House of Flowers and Jamaica

The far less theatrically successful *House of Flowers* (1954) makes a better record. Truman Capote's comical story of a battle for supremacy between two Haitian brothel keepers gets a rather modest treatment, no doubt on account of the more reticent manners of the times, but there is still far more character and far more fun here than in *Bloomer Girl*. The score is able to take up Arlen's favourite black rhythms with impunity and, even if the music is sometimes more US hit parade black than Caribbean, the disc includes many enjoyable pieces enjoyably performed, particularly by Pearl Bailey as the madam of the sweetly named House of Flowers ('One Man Ain't Quite Enough', 'Has I Let You Down?'). Diahann Carroll in the principal juvenile rôle makes the most of the pretty 'A Sleeping Bee' and 'I Never Have Seen Snow' in a voice which was at this stage still warm and interesting, and the comic numbers 'Two Ladies in the Shade of a Banana Tree' (Enid Mosier/Ada Moore) and the imaginative Turtle Song (Rawn Spearman), uninhibitedly performed, give a necessary variety to a score that was well enough thought of to warrant a 1968 revival. Much altered, the piece failed for a second time.

This seems a little unfair, given the long run which had been the lot of *Jamaica* (1957), another Caribbean-flavoured show, constructed as a vehicle for Lena Horne. It clearly accomplished its task of featuring Miss Horne to the utmost for more than a year on Broadway, but the resultant recording shows it to have been a rather synthetic piece, deficient in words and warmth.

St Louis Woman

It is almost incomprehensible that the same man could be responsible for *Jamaica* as for *St Louis Woman*, a 1946 flop in which the composer was paired with lyricist

Johnny Mercer. Here, at last, is the triumphant Arlen of 'Stormy Weather', displayed in a score in which every number reeks of class and of character: the easytime beauty with her 'Any Place I Hang my Hat Is Home', the pretty barmaid who insists that her man 'Legalize my Name', the cheerful, charming jockey hero who is 'Ridin' on the Moon' and the rejected mistress with her dazzling blues song 'I Had Myself a True Love'.

This is music of a different class to the other Arlen stage musicals, supported by lyrics which are also of a different class, orchestrated with force, humour and character. Everything is right. And yet *St Louis Woman* ran only three months, apparently handicapped by a poor book. Fortunately there was time for the show's outstanding cast to get their contribution onto record, now reissued on LP on EMI Capitol. If the quality of the sound is a millimetre short of modern, that only seems to add to the atmosphere.

Ruby Hill in the lead rôle has a searing, sizzling voice which gives 'Any Place I Hang my Hat' real sexuality yet brings genuine passion to 'Come Rain, Come Shine', and the young Pearl Bailey bubbles through the barmaid's two songs. June Hawkins turns on a remarkable voice, which soars from black chest tones to soaring soprano in her blues and in the revengeful 'Sleep Peaceful', whilst Harold Nicholas, in the hero's rôle, has a lightweight charm perfect for the part. Even the chorus are first rate, and the performance of the glorious funeral sequence ('Leavin' Time') rates with the best of *Porgy and Bess* as some of the most thrilling negro music in the musical theatre.

The Wizard of Oz

After many years as half the world's favourite film, *The Wizard of Oz*, with Arlen's famous score, was adapted for the stage, where it was widely played. It ended up in, of all places, Britain's subsidized Royal Shakespeare Company, and the resulting production (which doesn't seem to have too many RSC members in the cast, but does have an orchestra of forty) was recorded on TER. Larry Wilcox's very Hollywood orchestrations (angel voices included) are well played, and both the more-than-teenaged Gillian Bevan, who makes a brave stab at being Judy Garland, and the rest of the cast, adult and child, give pleasant reproductions of their material. But since the original film version is available on disc there seems no reason to prefer this recording.

MGM's 'electronically enhanced for stereo' soundtrack recording, including much of the dialogue as well as the music, and preserving through a slightly misty sound the memorable performances of Judy Garland, Ray Bolger, Bert Lahr, Jack Haley and that perfect pair of witches, Edwardian musical comedy star Billie Burke and the vile, green Margaret Hamilton, is in a different class.

Wish You Were Here

Harold Rome turned from revue to the musical play in 1952 with *Wish You Were Here*, a musical set in a holiday camp, which concerned itself with the love affairs of the young folk who have come there in order to find love affairs. Its principal attraction was an on-stage swimming pool and rather less, from the evidence of its original cast recordings (Broadway and London), its bouncy, inoffensive score. Youthful casts propelled the gentle and fairly innocent comedy and occasionally reminiscent tunes harmlessly into orbit, and Jack Cassidy in America and Bruce Trent in London were gratified with the title number which surprisingly proved an extractable hit.

Fanny

Bright, insignificant music and perky, inane lyrics were less suitable as illustration for another film-into-musical project, a telescoping of the three Marcel Pagnol pieces *Marius*, *Fanny* and *César* into one show. Rome made some attempt to take a broader Rodgers and Hammerstein sweep with numbers for Ezio Pinza and William Tabbert of *South Pacific* and Florence Henderson of *Oklahoma!*, but the result, as heard on the cast recording, lacked any kind of feeling for the characters, any atmosphere of the superb original tales and any kind of appreciable material for the fine original cast.

Destry Rides Again

Rome was altogether more at home with a third ex-film, the comedy Western *Destry Rides Again* (1959). This time the lyrics had some amusing local colour and, paired with some not too reminiscent melodies, at their best when jauntiest and/or tongue-in-cheek, provided several good comedy numbers. The brisk 'Hoop-de-Dingle' of the town drunk, nominated sheriff by the town's chief baddie, led into some lively dance music, whilst 'Tomorrow Morning', in which the gentle deputy sheriff, Destry, thinks too late of the smart answers he should have given his tormentors, 'The Ballad of the Gun' in which he numbers the fates of famous gunmen, and the mock trial 'Are You Ready Gyp Watson?', with its choral verdict of 'Not Guilty', are all highly enjoyable. The songs for the star lady, gangster's moll Frenchy, range between the brassy and the sentimental.

The original cast recording is a lively one which prospers chiefly because of the splendid performance of Andy Griffiths as the Huckleberry Houndish Destry. He tumbles through the comical spoken parts of 'Tomorrow Morning' and the double-talking 'Only Time Will Tell' with an endearingly warm and wide-eyed facility, creating a splendidly vivid character which has more than just the primary colours of so many other musical comedy characters. Dolores Gray as Frenchy is both brassy and sentimental and delivers her large part of the score in a strong-centred voice, whilst Jack Prince, the only other artist to get much in the way of a number, as the drunken sheriff, leads a stout-lunged male chorus to good effect.

There is, perhaps, a slight feeling that the whole thing is a little overdone. The orchestrations are just that much too lush and loud, and the wholly incidental introduction of a local madame and her girls overjams the bread just that much (though they undoubtedly brought colour to the stage show) in an effort to make a large musical.

Someone else clearly felt that beneath all the Broadway extras there could be a fine small musical, for in 1982 in London a production was staged with a cast of seventeen actor-singer-musicians replacing the fifty or sixty personnel of the original version – no madame, no girls, and minus several incidental numbers. A joy on the stage, it works a little less well on disc, where the guitar-based country orchestrations sound just a touch too thin under the friendly voices of actors Alfred Molina (Destry) and Jill Gascoigne (Frenchy).

Mr Wonderful

The early successful musicals of Jerry Bock – all but the first, *Mr Wonderful*, written in tandem with lyricist Sheldon Harnick – have all been put on record and, although each has its share of grand moments, none is really wholly satisfying. *Mr Wonderful* (1956) is a happily corny 'showbiz' piece constructed to feature up-and-coming song-and-dance star Sammy Davis jr, and it has not aged well. The big rock sequence in which Davis and his partners displayed their talents ('Jacques d'Iraque') now sounds naive and there are times when it all seems a little like cruise ship entertainment. But then Davis sings 'Too Close for Comfort' and something starts to tingle. It would have tingled earlier had the leading lady, the odd-voiced Olga James, made rather more of the show's other big hit 'Mr Wonderful'. There are moderated tingles again when Chita Rivera arrives to mug her way through 'I'm Available', and prizes for energy go to Pat Marshall and Jack Carter, who are vaudeville through and through as the variety pair who push the star up the scree slope to stardom.

Fiorello!

Pulitzer Prize winning *Fiorello!* (1959) doesn't have the hit parade songs of its predecessor, but it is technically much more sophisticated stuff, particularly insofar as Harnick's words are concerned. It is a little difficult for non-Americans to become impassioned over this piece about one nice American politician's rise to power accompanied by predictable love affairs and, as the writers lollop through the mainly unexciting events of Fiorello La Guardia's life, they are hard put to come up with exciting songs. It turns out to be the politicians who get all the best material whilst the ladies make do with modest material, which they deliver modestly.

The glum Republican politicians of New York, sure of an election loss, play wittily worded 'Politics and Poker' in polka rhythm (a cute touch) before erupting in amazement and harmony at the fact that 'The Bum Won' – their unconsidered La Guardia has pulled off a personal triumph and now they have to court him. Best of all, however, is the lilting little ensemble 'Little Tin Box', a splendid encapsulation of municipal jiggery-pokery, which wouldn't disgrace an *Of Thee I Sing*. The rest is less attractive. It's a recording without notable performances, too, but 'Little Tin Box' makes it worth a listen.

Tenderloin

The less successful *Tenderloin* (1960) makes its hit in a different area. Set in 1890s New York and dealing with the efforts of a crusading clergyman to clean up the city's red-light district (as good a way as any to get a lot of lusty, semi-clothed chorus ladies on a stage yet again), it proved a vehicle for a particularly good set of almost-burlesque Victorian music-hall songs. The juvenile man (strong baritone Ron Husmann) has the particularly effective weepy ballad 'Artificial Flowers' and the raunchy 'The Picture of Happiness', whilst the area's top tart (enthusiastic Eileen Rodgers) leads the company in a vigorous exposé describing 'How the Money Changes Hands' and the girls of the Tenderloin belt out the praises of 'Little Old New York'. It is all good, jolly fun, sometimes sounding rather like the Players' Theatre gone West, and it gets a good, jolly performance, even though the show's star, ageing Shakespearian actor Maurice Evans, is not always wholly happy as a vocalist. As in *Fiorello!*, however, not all parts are as good as the best parts and it was not until the next decade that Bock and Harnick came up with their finest work.

Plain and Fancy

In an era that gobbled up musicals gratefully, Albert Hague's *Plain and Fancy* and *Redhead* both found some success on Broadway but, from the evidence of the cast recordings, it is clear that they were not first-rate pieces. Any originality which they had was in their subject matter: the former delved into the puritan Amish sect for its characters and setting rather in the way *The Quaker Girl* had done half a century earlier, whilst the latter took the form of a London-based musical murder mystery. As far as their scores were concerned, however, they leaned too often on what were becoming standard song styles, and subjects and melodies that sounded hackneyed before you'd listen to them once, and reproduced them at a level that was below the best.

Part of the blame for this sameness has to rest with several prominent members of the small band of arrangers who had followed (without ever approaching the talent of) Robert Russell Bennett, and whose sausage-machine orchestrations and vocal arrangements gave every show score the same uninspired sound, robbing them of any individuality they might have. *Plain and Fancy* (1955) suffers badly from the orchestration disease. Several of its numbers are written with some charm and in line with the show's simple and sincere subject, but all the simplicity is arranged out of them. One which survived this treatment, the highly successful 'Young and Foolish', sounds as if it had been rescued from any one of a hundred Hollywood movies.

At the other end of the scale, the number 'City Mouse, Country Mouse' takes ingenuousness and simplicity too far. When a little freshness of approach was needed to a show-song topic dealt with so many times before, the writers just litter it with clichés. The cast recording does little to save the situation. There is an appealing performance by Shirl Conway as the outsider who brings whisky and the comic relief to the puritan family drama, and Barbara Cook sounds like a soprano Ado Annie in the secondary female rôle, but otherwise there is little success in lifting material which continually knocks itself down with musical and textual cliché.

Redhead

Redhead (1959) has the air of rather more fun but, in spite of two marvellous performers in the central rôles – Gwen Verdon, setting the whole affair awash with her personality and her catchy, throaty singing, and Richard Kiley giving forth with one of the best Broadway baritones of the time – it doesn't add up to much at the end of the recording. Since the record company had to keep the identity of the murderer secret, there is no explanatory synopsis on the sleeve and, in consequence, those songs which are anything but obvious ballads make little sense. You're never sure whether you are in the show-within-a-show or just in the show. You constantly feel that there is something that you ought to be seeing which you can't. That aside, and in spite of the fact that the lyrics are by Dorothy Fields, even the obvious ballads are only average. This record is a souvenir for anyone who loved the show only.

Once Upon a Mattress

I laughed a lot at the recording of *Once Upon a Mattress* (1959) when I first heard it, aged fifteen. I laughed all over again when I finally saw the show in the theatre. Then I laughed a whole lot more when I listened to the record again. This first attempt since Victorian days at a full-scale fairytale burlesque, parodying *The Princess and the Pea*, is wittily and tunefully (by Mary – daughter of Richard – Rodgers) written and the original cast recording gets the show across in exemplary fashion.

The Minstrel introduces affairs, singing us the old tale ('Many Moons Ago'), and then confides in us what really happened, sending us off on the joyously comical tale of braw, lusty Princess Winnifred who, with a little bit of help from some self-interested courtiers, triumphs over the devious Queen Agravaine and wins herself the henpecked Prince Dauntless as a husband.

This is not broad burlesque, it is parody of a sweet and warm kind, with a cast of characters who are a delight. Principal of these is Princess Winnifred, who arrives in court, having swum the moat because the drawbridge was up, declaring in stentorian tones how 'Shy' she is. When she offers to let little Dauntless call her by her pet name, it turns out not to be Winnie but Fred. Carol Burnett was the original Fred, and her performance on the record is quite hilarious as she 'gluggle-uggles' her way through the description of 'The Swamps of Home' or longs for a 'Happily Ever After', bumping and grinding her way lip-smackingly through a demolition job on the tales of Cinderella, Snow White and Rapunzel. It is a comedy-on-disc performance of the first level.

The supporting cast are all fine, with Jane White at their head as the reigning battleaxe of a Queen, determined to prevent her son from marrying, and scheming to test the Princess for 'Sensitivity'. Joe Bova is an eager, foolish Dauntless, and Matt Mattox as the Jester describes in the show's most popular tune his father's fourteenth-century talents as a tap-dancer ('Very Soft Shoes'). Unfortunately, the show's most charming number, 'Man to Man Talk', in which the mute King mimes the story of the birds and the bees to his ready-to-be-saved son, lacks a little of its point on disc, but Bova delivers it with such well-timed ingenuousness that not too much is lost.

The British production was also recorded on what was, for a long time, one of the rarest cast albums on collectors' lists. It has recently been reissued by DRG records but, apart from any historical relevance it might have, it's not of much interest. Jane Connell is no Carol Burnett and, although some other cast members perform well enough, the original recording is unquestionably and by far superior.

Little Mary Sunshine

Little Mary Sunshine (1959) was another gentle burlesque, this time of the American operetta style, which succeeded in compiling a long run off-Broadway. It is less effective than *Once Upon a Mattress*, largely because it never seems to make up its mind what it is doing. One moment it is a parody, the next an affectionate pastiche in the *Boyfriend* style, and the next it sounds simply like a second-rate imitation of every variant of 1920s writing imaginable. When it presents its version of 'Tell Me, Pretty Maiden' or 'Naughty Marietta', the numbers sound less tongue-in-cheek than simply pilfered. Although there are some nice moments, particularly a double sextet section which has the girls 'Playing Croquet' and 'Swinging' until visited by half a dozen *Florodorean* forest rangers ('How Do You Do?'), it is generally a bit short on wit both musically and textually.

Like *Once Upon a Mattress*, *Little Mary Sunshine* was a success in America and a failure in London but, on this occasion, the London cast recording comes out superior to the original, which is too often a strangely spiritless and undersung affair. The London recording has Patricia Routledge giving an amusing interpretation in the title rôle of a warbly overaged juvenile, Joyce Blair going as far over the soubrette top as is possible in an imitation of *The Boyfriend*'s Dulcie, Terence Cooper blustering out a heroic baritone and, best of all, Gita Denise as an aged Austrian soprano, all woof and wobble, remembering her youth in 'Do You Ever Dream of Vienna'. Unfortunately the British disc cuts her other number, 'In Izzenschnooken on the Lovely Essenzook Zee', which was cut in London, as well as 'Playing Croquet' and the *Naughty Marietta* song ('Naughty, Naughty Nancy'), but, in return, it incorporates two pieces ('Say Uncle' and 'Me a Heap Big Injun') not included on the New York version.

The Golden Apple

There is a significant element of burlesque also in an earlier work, *The Golden Apple* (1954), a piece which used the Ulysses legend as the basis for a satirical musical set in early twentieth-century America. *The Golden Apple* is one of those pieces that, in spite of failing to run, is spoken of by devotees with reverence. It is the sort of piece which, in spite of its meagre 125 Broadway performances, an author like Stanley Green will include in his *Encyclopaedia of the Musical* in preference to such as the record-breaking *Erminie*, which ran ten times longer. It is the sort of piece people talk of reviving, even though a 1962 restaging also flopped.

Listening to the original cast recording, it is possible to see why the piece aroused such keen emotions. And it is also not difficult to see why it failed. It is adventurous in style and sometimes in content, being made up of a series of sung scenes and a few more standard songs set amongst a limited amount of dialogue, and it was composed by Jerome Moross for voices of some versatility and scope.

The lyric style of John Latouche is literate, clever, and unusually poetic in its few ballad parts but, equally, subject to stylistic and taste lapses and not always comfortable with the music. *The Golden Apple* is adventurous but flawed. When it is at its best, such as in the ballads 'Lazy Afternoon' and 'Windflowers', the sweeping duo 'It's the Going Home Together' or the comical scenes 'The Judgement of Paris' and 'Doomed, Doomed, Doomed', it is splendid. Elsewhere it is less so.

The recording is naturally unable to fit in the whole of the piece, and instead a significant selection is joined by a sketchy narration. The result is rather bitty for easy listening, but then *The Golden Apple* is not that easy listening. It demands attention, for there is almost always something going on in the words. The easiest moments are the ballads, the languid 'Lazy Afternoon' sung chestily and not too loudly by Kaye Ballard as Helen and the more rangy 'Windflowers', a classy soprano song with the difficulties of which Priscilla Gillette (Penelope) copes adeptly.

The most exciting moments are those when the three Washington matrons representing Aphrodite, Minerva and Hera (the authors get their Latin and Greek a little mixed up here, or was it just that Pallas Athene had too many syllables?) burst into song. Together or individually Bibi Osterwald, Geraldine Viti and Portia Nelson are quite superb. Stephen Douglass is the stolid baritone Ulysses and Jack Whiting, least well served with a clumsy Gallagher-and-Shean piece for Scylla and Charybdis, is Hector.

It is sad that Latouche, who died two years later, and Moross did not have the chance to work further together, for *The Golden Apple* presaged the possibility of interesting things to come. Itself, it is of interest largely for the possibilities it holds, and for some first-rate bits.

L'il Abner

Gene de Paul and Johnny Mercer were the composer and lyricist responsible for the rousing score of the film *Seven Brides for Seven Brothers*, a piece many years later ineptly adapted for the stage and recorded in Britain in a version that watered down the film score with some fifth-rate new material. Although it did not approach the durability of this famous film, their good-humoured stage musical *L'il Abner* (1956), based on the well-known cartoon, also won success, playing a 693-performance Broadway run at the theatre which had recently hosted such successes as *Oklahoma!* and *The King and I*.

L'il Abner followed the comic adventures of the very countrified folks of the town of Dogpatch through a jolly, comic-strip plot, illustrated with some jolly, suitable songs and a few slower, less suitable ones. The score and the cast recording are at their best when things are liveliest, and their undoubted highlight is the tale of that latter day Duke of Plaza Toro 'Jubilation T. Cornpone', the founding father of Dogpatch. The score has a strong ration of wordful, topical songs ('The Country's in the Very Best of Hands', 'Oh, Happy Day', 'Progress Is the Root of All Evil'), which are bright and, now, not so comprehensible, but it also attempts some ballads which sit less happily in the mouths of two-dimensional characters.

Alas, the characters do stay two dimensional for, although Peter Palmer (Abner) and Edith Adams (Daisy Mae) both sing well, he always sounds like a nice, well-spoken young gentleman in a suit and she like a secretary. Anyone who has seen *L'il Abner* on stage or in strip will know that is just what they aren't! These two have most of the score, but Stubby Kaye, hot on the heels of his success in *Guys and Dolls*, has the best – 'Jubilation T. Cornpone' and the lively 'Matrimonial Stomp', which sounds just a mite too close to 'Sit Down, You're Rockin' the Boat' for comfort.

A Tree Grows in Brooklyn and By the Beautiful Sea

Most successful as a writer of revue material, Arthur Schwartz also composed theatre scores both in Britain and in America. He worked with Dorothy Fields on *A Tree Grows in Brooklyn* (1951), a very light piece with a vague Brooklyn *Carousel* flavour, and *By the Beautiful Sea*, a sweet, turn-of-the-century seaside showbiz tale, both of which, with the starring assistance of Shirley Booth, had reasonable Broadway runs. Both scores contain some attractive songs in the lightest vein which bear witness to the composer's revue and songwriting origins, and both records make pleasant listening without being in any way remarkable.

My Ten Essential Records

SOUTH PACIFIC: original cast recording, with Ezio Pinza and Mary Martin (Columbia ML/OL 4180); CD (Columbia CK 4180)

THE SOUND OF MUSIC: film soundtrack, with Julie Andrews, Margery McKay and Bill Lee (RCA LOCD/LSOD 2005); CD (RCA ND 90368)

MY FAIR LADY: original cast recording, with Julie Andrews and Rex Harrison (Columbia OL 5090); CD (Columbia CK 5090)

KISS ME, KATE: original cast recording, with Alfred Drake and Patricia Morison (Columbia DL 4140 / OS 2300); CD (Columbia CK 4140)

GUYS AND DOLLS: original cast recording, with Robert Alda and Vivian Blaine (Decca DL 8036)

KISMET: studio cast recording, with Robert Merrill, Regina Resnik, Adele Leigh and Kenneth McKellar (Decca PFS 4035)

CANDIDE: Scottish Opera cast recording, 1988, with Marilyn Hill Smith, Mark Beudert and Bonaventura Bottone (TER 1156); CD (CDTER 1156)

WEST SIDE STORY: original cast recording, with Larry Kert and Carol Lawrence (CBS 70025)

THE MUSIC MAN: original cast recording, with Robert Preston (Capitol WAO 990); CD (Capitol CDP 7 46633 2)

ST LOUIS WOMAN: original cast recording, with June Hawkins, Ruby Hill, Harold Nicholas and Pearl Bailey (Capitol EMI DW2742)

Other Recommended Records

Oklahoma!: revival cast recording, with Laurence Guittard and Christine Andreas (RCA CBLI 3572); CD (RCA RCD1 3572)

Annie Get your Gun: (Annie schiess los!): German cast recording, (Theater des Westens) (Philips 838 900 PY); or Lincoln Center revival cast recording, with Ethel Merman (RCA LOC/LSO 1124); CD (RCA 1124-2 RC)

Carousel: Lincoln Center revival cast recording, with John Raitt and Eileen Christie (RCA LOC/LSO 1114)

The King and I: London cast recording, with Valerie Hobson (Philips BBL 7002 or Stet DS015014); or Lincoln Center revival cast recording, with Risë Stevens (RCA LOC/LSO 1092)

Brigadoon: studio cast recording, with Shirley Jones and Jack Cassidy (Columbia CL 1132)

Camelot: original cast recording, with Richard Burton, Julie Andrews and Robert Goulet (Columbia KOS 2031); CD (Columbia CK 32602)

Paint your Wagon: original cast recording, with James Barton (RCA LOC/LSO 1006); CD (RCA 60243-2-RG)

Song of Norway: Jones Beach cast recording, 1958 (Columbia CL 1328)

On the Town: studio recording, with members of the original cast and John Reardon (Columbia OL 5440 / OS 2028); also available on CD

Street Scene: original cast recording (selection), with Polyna Stoska, Joseph Sullivan and Anne Jeffreys (Columbia Special Products COL 4139)

Gentlemen Prefer Blondes: original London cast recording, with Dora Bryan and Anne Hart (HMV CLP 1602 / CSD 1464)

Call Me Madam: film soundtrack, with Ethel Merman, George Sanders and Carol Richards (Ace of Hearts AH-137)

Wonderful Town: original cast recording, with Rosalind Russell and Edith Adams (Decca DL 9010)

The Golden Apple: original cast recording, with Priscilla Gillette, Stephen Douglass, Jack Whiting, Portia Nelson, Bibi Osterwald and Geraldine Viti (RCA LOC-1014; re-recorded Elektra EKL-5000)

The Pajama Game: film soundtrack, with Doris Day and John Raitt (Columbia OL5210)

Damn Yankees: original cast recording, with Gwen Verdon and Stephen Douglass (RCA LOC 1021); CD (RCA 3948-2-RG)

The Most Happy Fella: original cast recording, with Robert Weede (3 records, Columbia O3L-240)

Bells Are Ringing: film soundtrack, with Judy Holliday (Capitol W/SW 1435); CD (Capitol CDP 792060-2)

Destry Rides Again: original cast recording, with Andy Griffiths (Decca DL 9075)

Once Upon a Mattress: original cast recording, with Carol Burnett and Joe Bova (MCA-2079)

Gypsy: original cast recording, with Ethel Merman (Columbia OL 5420 / OS 2017); CD (Columbia CK 32607)

Bye Bye Birdie: London cast recording, with Chita Rivera, Marty Wilde and Peter Marshall (Philips ABL/FBL 3383)

The Fantasticks: original cast recording, with Jerry Orbach, Rita Gardener and Kenneth Nelson (MGM E/SE 3872)

CHAPTER 8

Bonanza on Broadway:
the second part

By the latter part of the Broadway boom years, the star writers of the 1940s and 1950s had largely passed out of contention. Following the death of Hammerstein, Richard Rodgers wrote his own lyrics for *No Strings* and, more felicitously, paired with Stephen Sondheim on *Do I Hear a Waltz?*, before frittering away into *Two by Two* and *I Remember Mama*. Apart from an ill-fated attempt to turn their successful film *Gigi* into a stage musical, the Lerner/Loewe team was also finished, and Lerner's subsequent collaborations with other composers were a shadow of the great days. Frank Loesser had one more splendid piece to contribute in *How To Succeed in Business Without Really Trying* (1969) and Bernstein a very much less successful one in *1600 Pennsylvania Avenue* (1976), but the days of Irving Berlin and of Cole Porter were gone.

Several composers and writers who had prospered in the shade of the greats during the 1950s came into their own in the next decade, including Bock and Harnick (*She Loves Me*, *Fiddler on the Roof* and *The Apple Tree*), Jule Styne (*Funny Girl*), and Stephen Sondheim who, although considering himself primarily a composer, had hitherto been represented on Broadway only as a lyricist (*A Funny Thing Happened on the Way to the Forum*, *Company*). The 1960s also brought a handful of outstanding new writers to contribute to Broadway's continued well-being, led by the versatile and witty Cy Coleman (*Little Me*, *Sweet Charity*), Fred Ebb and John Kander (with the harshly dramatic *Cabaret* and *Zorba*) and Jerry Herman (*Hello, Dolly!*, *Mame*).

Behind these central figures, other writers provided support and successful shows, but, as Broadway moved through the 1970s, it was noticeable that this support was growing sparser. Sondheim (*Follies*, *A Little Night Music*, *Pacific Overtures*), Coleman (*I Love my Wife*, *On the Twentieth Century*, *Barnum*), Herman (*Mack and Mabel*, *La Cage aux Folles*) and Kander and Ebb (*Chicago*) still held centre stage, with only Marvin Hamlisch (*A Chorus Line*, *They're Playing our Song*) of the newer writers bringing a really substantial contribution to add to their efforts. The great era of American musical theatre came to its dusk with the principal writers of the 1960s still providing the rather less strongly beating heart of its activity.

Rodgers without Hammerstein

No Strings

The first Richard Rodgers musical of the post-Hammerstein period was *No Strings*, which had a comfortable run in the 1962–3 Broadway season and a short one in London. From the evidence of its cast recordings, that run must have been due largely to the name of Rodgers on the bills, for *No Strings* comes across as a routine, characterless piece. The splendidly rich-voiced Richard Kiley and the incisive tones of Diahann Carroll start the Broadway disc – the better of the two – promisingly enough, with a bouncy performance of the show's hit number 'The Sweetest Sounds', but thereafter it is mostly a case of very ordinary songs and pointless point numbers in a score where enthusiasm of any kind seems totally absent.

Do I Hear a Waltz?

The contrast with between *No Strings* and Rodgers's next work is total. The 1965 *Do I Hear a Waltz?* was a failure and it rendered up no reusable bits to the hit parades or the cabaret circuits, yet the score as heard on its original cast recording contains some of the loveliest of Rodgers's show music attached to what are probably the best lyrics with which he was ever served. Clear, natural, unclichéd lines and rhymes, little poems which create a scene in a verse or a sentiment in a chorus, and which bring laughs seemingly effortlessly – the words in which Stephen Sondheim tells his part of the Venetian story of a spinster American secretary and the middle-aged Italian who offers her holiday love are quite outstanding.

From the moment the scene is set, with the newly arrived Leona gazing in excited wonder at Venice ('Someone Woke Up'), the songs carry you into the story. There is crisp humour set to apt and lively tunes, as Fioria, the *pensione* owner, crackles out her thoughts on her customers ('This Week Americans'), the visitors discuss the perils of flying ('What Do We Do? We Fly!'), Fioria and a young American guest angle the maid out of the room under the guise of a language lesson ('No Understand'), or the amorous Di Rossi instructs Leona in the art of 'Bargaining'. There are wonderfully atmospheric pieces as the lonely Leona sits in the bustling piazza ('Here We Are Again') and, especially, the beautiful trio serenade, where three women who have spent very different evenings look at the moon and think of their man ('Moon at my Window').

But, best of all, there is the series of songs that take you through the love affair between the two lonely people at the centre of the story, beginning with the tentative approaches of 'Someone Like You' and 'Thinking', taking flight into full-blown lyricism as he encourages her to 'Take the Moment' which is all that people like them can hope for, until finally her doubts are put aside in the whirling waltz 'Do I Hear a Waltz?' and he, in the score's most thrilling musical moment, asks her to 'Stay' in Venice a little longer. It is too good to last. Things go wrong and, as she leaves, sadder and wiser, their final goodbye ('Thank You So Much') is a gently limping little acknowledgement of 'a little but lovely time'.

The cast recording is a good one, and the particular plus is the performance of Sergio Franchi as Di Rossi. The rôle is written for a strong, masculine, legitimate tenor voice and Franchi fills all the requirements, rolling out the flowing phrases of 'Stay', 'Someone Like You' and 'Take the Moment' with rich, clear tone and comprehensive musical style. He also manages the comic moments of 'Bargaining', including some tricky gear shifts into falsetto, impeccably. Elizabeth Allen (Leona) manages her large rôle with aplomb and an incisive middle voice and Carol Bruce (Fioria) takes the lower notes of her part in a rough-edged voice which serves well both in her comic solos and in the wearily sexy notes of the Moon Trio. The material is marvellous, the performances fine, the disc a permanent pleasure, and surely here, if anywhere, is material for the operatic cross-over merchants looking for lighter areas to invade. Domingo or Carreras would have a splendid time as Di Rossi.

Frank Loesser

How to Succeed in Business Without Really Trying

Frank Loesser also left one of his most enjoyable pieces to the end of his career. *How to Succeed in Business Without Really Trying* (1961) has a vastly different score to *Guys and Dolls* and *The Most Happy Fella*, a fact which is scarcely surprising, given the style of Abe Burrows's satirically comical libretto and its cast of cardboard big-business characters. There is no room here for the fulsome romanticism of *Most Happy Fella* or of Sky Masterson and his mission lass. Everything in this score is wryly and slyly humorous, from the frenetic despair of the office staff unable to take their 'Coffee Break' to a chorus of secretaries serenading the one of their number who has achieved their united dream, to wed her boss ('Cinderella, Darling'). Even romance comes in the same style – she sighs in song about how she will be 'Happy to Keep His Dinner Warm' whilst he heads onwards to executive status, and he comes to realization of his love for 'Rosemary' in the middle of being seduced by his superior's sexpot. Perhaps the most enjoyable number is also the gentlest – the two young people head for home, only able to mumble 'Been a Long Day', whilst an older secretary recounts what they are really thinking.

There is little to choose between the three cast recordings of *How to Succeed*, all of which are suitably brightly and brassily performed. The American original has the advantage of Robert Morse's innocently ambitious hero, the English version gains points on a heroine (Patricia Michael) who invests her songs with altogether more than the very strong voice of her US counterpart, and the French disc (*Comment réussir dans les affaires sans vraiment se fatiguer*) wins hands down on its character men. In a pinch, I think I would plump for this last one for, although it does not have Loesser's lyrics, it is given in a clear translation which, in one or two of the songs, sounds even better than the original, and it is played by some really enjoyable artists. André Luguet takes the rôle of big boss Biggley with more character and voice than Rudy Vallée on the original cast recording, Evelyne Dandry is a charming but incisive Rosemary and Jacqueline Mille equally good in the other main female singing part. Jacques Duby in Morse's character of J. Pierrepont Finch is a bit approximate in his singing, but his personality comes through splendidly, aided by the fact that this recording has included introductory dialogue for the songs, setting them helpfully *in situ*.

Unfortunately, *Comment réussir dans les affaires sans vraiment se fatiguer* is a disc which has long been difficult to find, even in France, so, being more practical, it probably comes down to a choice between the two original-language cast recordings. I would cast my vote on negative grounds and, simply because I find the stressed metal voice of Bonnie Scott (the original Rosemary) hard to take, go for the London version.

Bock and Harnick

She Loves Me

Bock and Harnick's 1963 musical *She Loves Me* abandoned the boisterous American-ness of *Fiorello* and *Tenderloin* for a gentle middle European flavour and a featherlight story of love in a perfumery. Perhaps as a result of this attractive lack of harshness in an era where that quality was becoming very prevalent, or perhaps because the piece's small size has made it easy amateur and provincial revival material, this pleasant but patchy show has had some success since its original 302-performance run and has found some fond adherents. Its score is actually a bit of an oddity, consisting of several very lovely songs for its heroine (attractively sung on the Broadway disc by Barbara Cook) – the wondering 'Will He Like Me?', the gentle 'Dear Friend', 'I Don't Know his Name' and the little letter scena 'Ice Cream' – a jaunty title song for its hero, some ensemble and lightly comic fragments ('Perspective', 'Tango Tragique'), and about the same amount of truly banal and too-standard-to-be-believed pieces headed by the gigolo's witless ballad to 'Ilona' and her response 'I Resolve'.

Perhaps some pieces of this score had a point on stage which is not evident on record but, as it is, to display the whole of this light and uneven score spread over two entire discs as the Broadway original cast recording does is to stretch the whole thing too thin and to drown the worthwhile bits in the less worthy material. The London disc, which prunes, unfortunately prunes in such an ill-advised fashion as to make the record useless. Although 'I Resolve' has been replaced by a piece called 'Heads I Win', 'Ilona' is still there, and 'Will He Like Me?' and 'I Don't Know his Name' are not!

Fiddler on the Roof

Bock and Harnick's enduring triumph was *Fiddler on the Roof.* The 1964 production of this warmly human Russo-Yiddish musical comedy at Broadway's Imperial Theatre ran for 3,242 performances, making it the longest-running Broadway musical up to that time, and it quickly spread around the world, translated and recorded in almost as many languages as *My Fair Lady.*

Tevye, the village milkman of the little Russian village of Anatevka, is the central figure of the piece. It is through his eyes that we see the erosion of traditional Jewish family values as the younger members of his family determine to live their own lives on their own terms, and it is because his eyes will not see the threats from outside that they are unprepared for the anti-Jewish actions which eventually drive them from their home. Old-fashioned or no, Tevye is a pragmatic man, a man with a sense of humour, and the character evolved in Joseph Stein's libretto is a superlatively likeable one who seems to be almost actor-proof.

The first Tevye was Zero Mostel, who was heavily solo-billed above the title on Broadway and who sets the tone for subsequent Tevyes on the original cast recording. He is warm, gently comical and affecting in what was clearly a superb stage performance, which comes over maybe a touch less well on disc owing to his limited singing voice. It is not that the rôle needs to be heavily sung, but a little more would be nice. Nevertheless, the half-spoken, half-sung 'Tradition', the classic 'If I Were a Rich Man', 'Sunrise, Sunset' and the lovely, simple duet with Golde, his wife (Maria Karnilova), 'Do You Love Me?', where after twenty-five years of an arranged marriage Tevye suddenly needs to know the answer, are all splendidly done, although Karnilova sounds unbelieveably shrewish and harsh in her reponses.

There are few opportunities for big singing in this score, except in the chorus parts. The songs are either mixed with speech or else, as in the young peoples' numbers ('Miracle of Miracles', 'Now I Have Everything', 'Far from the Home I Love'), vocally undemanding which, since, with the exception of Julia Migenes (Hodel), the cast are vocally limited, is as well. The other values are fine, with the orchestral and vocal arrangements (by Don Walker and Milton Greene respectively) first rate, and a general air of warm reality coming through.

The London cast was headed by Topol, who makes an exceptionally fine record Tevye. He has more singing voice than Mostel, a gruffly attractive and sincere personality, and a thick accent which adds character to the interpretation without ever being incomprehensible. Unfortunately, the rest of the cast don't have the same qualifications. The accents are an hilarious bunch, ranging from a trio of daughters who sound like English country maidens (listen to them saying 'I wouldn't holler' in the 'Matchmaker' number) to Miriam Karlin's London basso as Golde; the voices – apart from a fine chorus – unexceptional; and the sense of character limited, except in a particularly good version of Tevye's marvellous Dream Sequence, in which the ghosts of Golde's grandmother and the butcher's wife are sneakily summoned up by the milkman to help his eldest daughter avoid becoming the butcher's second wife. This disc includes the Bottle Dance music, which makes it a fuller recording than the American one and considerably fuller than that made by London takeover stars Alfie Bass and Avis Bunnage who, with a group of session singers in the supporting rôles, put down a version without the Dream, without 'Miracle of Miracles', and without anything to recommend it over the original cast discs.

Topol was given a second shot at a recording when he was selected to star in the United Artists film version of *Fiddler*, the soundtrack of which stretches over two records and includes not only the Bottle Dance but also an extended opening title sequence featuring Isaac Stern's fiddle and the song 'Chavaleh', which was cut from the stage show. It does not, however, have 'Now I Have Everything', which was omitted from the film.

This is a recording that will not appeal to purists. There has been a certain amount of fiddling (no pun intended) with the songs – a stretching here, a little snip there, a change of words every now and then – usually without any obvious reason and presumably to make the audio side fit the visual. But this is, in every way, a very filmic recording. There is an orchestra in the best Hollywood tradition, which doesn't sound as if it could fit into any pit on Broadway, and a chorus that would spill off any stage, and new arrangements have been made to fit them. They've actually been made very well, tactfully enlarging the original textures and very rarely slipping into the old-fashioned Hollywood sound, but they register 'film' as opposed to 'theatre' very clearly.

Topol, too, has gone filmic. His performance is often pitched at such an intimate level, in a voice that is so gruff and throaty as sometimes to vanish altogether before a word is ended, that you have to hang on to some of his quieter lines to catch them aright. But then he launches into his richly splendid 'If I Were a Rich Man', and shoots right up to the other end of the sound and song scale. It is an idiosyncratic performance, sometimes paced at a speed that makes you wonder if he alone was responsible for this having to be a two-disc set, but it works, and at its best it works superbly.

The rest of the cast also come out well but, since, in spite of plenty of space being available, the record sleeve doesn't give a cast list (which always makes me suspect a rash of dubbing), I'm not sure whom to credit. The biggest credit needs to go to the artist playing Fruma Sarah, the butcher's wife, whose vocally demonic hauntings in the slightly stretched Dream Sequence are quite wonderfully done. Here is a case of film and film soundtrack actually being able to improve on a stage original. The lively young people all have character and all sing just well enough for the tone of the material – there is no overvocalizing – whilst Norma Crane makes a more believeably bluff Golde than her stage counterparts.

I have eight foreign-language cast albums of *Fiddler* on my shelves and, surprisingly, when you remember the poor standard of the export versions of *My Fair Lady*, they all range from the reasonably acceptable to the good – if sometimes very curious. The most curious is undoubtedly the double-disc, live-recorded Japanese version, which includes all of the dialogue as well as the music. It is certainly not a disc for easy listening. There is a slick, 'showbizzy' Mexican version, a fair Hungarian one with rather better orchestrations than some of the curious combinations to which Hungary is prone, and there are two Israeli versions with largely the same cast, one in Hebrew and the other in Yiddish. The latter, with Shmuel Rudenski starred (and a translation of his chief song as what sounds like 'If I Were a Rothschild'), is the better and, indeed, preferable to the German version (renamed *Anatevka*) in which the same actor starred.

Another Israeli actor, Yossi Yadin, was featured in the Austrian *Anatevka*, and he turns out to be the most appreciable Tevye of all – warm, uninhibited, funny and with a fine voice. Backed by the original Israeli Golde (Lya Dulizkaya) and some fine young singers, he makes this one of the two best foreign *Fiddlers*. The other is the French *Un violon sur le toit*, which has the advantage of being the best-sung *Fiddler* all round. Basso Ivan Rebroff lets his hair down with a vengeance (and some fine animal noises in 'Rich Man') as Tevye, former operetta star Maria Murano has matured into a rich-voiced Golde, the girls are sprightly if very French, Philippe Ariotti gives a lovely, earnest 'Prodigieux, miraculeux' ('Wonder of Wonders') and another leading lady of the past, Eliane Thibault, throws herself energetically into Fruma Sarah's scene. The show sounds perhaps a little less natural in French than in German or Yiddish, but it is a good record.

Of the studio recordings on the stocks, the Decca disc featuring Robert Merrill and Molly Picon (the film Yente, here being Golde as well) attracts the most attention, but it is a tacky affair with a dreadful narrative and the usual stock of British session singers in support, and all Merrill's beautiful tone and impeccable singing cannot stop it being a bore.

The Apple Tree

The Apple Tree (1966) took a diametrically opposite tone to *Fiddler*. The warmth and sincerity of the partnership's great work was replaced by a brittle and sometimes campy humour in a trio of short pieces, allegedly linked by a theme, which made up a theatrical evening. The three range both in style and in successfulness with the first piece, *The Diary of Adam and Eve*, based on Mark Twain, being by far the most substantial. The second, *The Lady and the Tiger*, was from Frank Stockton's famous tale which exists for and consists of its cliff-hanger ending, and the third was an affected little Jules Feiffer Cinderella piece called *Passionella*. All three were staged with a trio of principal characters (Alan Alda, Lary Blyden and Barbara Harris) and a small supporting cast.

The recording is a disappointment because the show is a disappointment. There are moments of tenderness and sweet comedy in the first piece as Adam and Eve get used to their surroundings, as the snake tempts Eve to 'Forbidden Fruit', and as Adam looks puzzled at the child Eve has borne and declares 'It's a Fish', but the second piece is made up mainly of two loud songs for Miss Harris (and can she sing loudly), and the third is poor, campy burlesque in which Alda's crazy performance of the accusing 'You Are Not Real' floats above the general level.

There is too much of the undergraduate revue flavour about the whole affair and insufficient real wit.

Alda is the most pleasant to listen to, Blyden is suitably oily as the Snake and has not much else to do, and Miss Harris runs the gamut from Eve to Passionella in her heaviest boots, where a more measured performance would probably have been more effective.

The Rothschilds

The Rothschilds (1970) survived longer than *The Apple Tree* but it, too, is far from the worth of *Fiddler*. It is, in some ways, an upper-class version of the earlier piece, dealing again with the problems of being Jewish in Europe (and, presumably, by extension, anywhere else), as it follows the ultimately successful efforts of the Jewish Rothschild family to get very rich and to get the ghettoes of Frankfurt abolished. Altogether better made than *The Apple Tree*, it comes out, however, as a rather stolid piece, with lots of stout male singing. Even when it is at its most humorous, as with the revusical number 'He Tossed a Coin', in which Mayer Rothschild (Hal Linden) uses cooked-up tales of Cleopatra and Julius Caesar to sell some ancient coins, it doesn't really take off.

Jule Styne

Funny Girl

Amongst the ten shows with which he followed *Gypsy* in the 1960s and 1970s, Jule Styne composed only a few which had more than a token run (*Do Re Mi* (1960), *Hallelujah, Baby!* (1967), *Sugar* (1972)) but within that group there was one outstanding piece that was capable of being classed with the best of Styne's earlier works – *Gypsy* and *Gentlemen Prefer Blondes*.

Funny Girl (1964) was loosely based on the life of revue star Fanny Brice and, very largely, her love for and marriage to gambler Nicky Arnstein. Around Isobel Lennart's expressive book, Styne and Bob Merrill created a series of songs (mostly for the overwhelming leading lady's rôle) which helped lift the piece right to the forefront of that favourite type of Broadway musical, the vehicle for a larger-than-life female star, which Styne had already served so well in *Gypsy*.

What made *Funny Girl* all the more effective and makes the original cast recording a quite outstanding one was the star that it served. Barbra Streisand must have been born with vinyl vocal cords for, as this recording and her subsquent career show, records just love her and she, in her turn, knows just how to treat them. On this disc, she fashions a performance and a character from the show's material that is quite stunning. She is larger than life without ever being grotesque, she takes flight emotionally in her songs in a way which in other hands could be embarrassing, and succeeds in being quite simply enormously moving, and, in a performance of continuous light and shade, she maintains an infinity of feeling whilst singing full out in a way few others can – it is never one of those larger-and-louder-than-life performances.

Styne and Merrill give her all the chances she needs. One moment she is fooling about proclaiming 'I'm the Greatest Star', the next delivering a splendidly gutsy rag, 'Cornet Man', or pouring her heart uninhibitedly into her pleasure at being one of the 'People' who need people. One moment she is providing gloriously 'klutzy' comedy in what is surely the best seduction-over-dinner song in the catalogue, 'I Am Woman', and the next she is opening all her valves in the self-affirming blockbuster 'Don't Rain on my Parade'. To come back to Streisand singing this last number as it was written after years of listening to other mangled versions provides a timely reminder that it is not just a drag artists's anthem or a cabaret singer's opportunity to crack a microphone, but a splendidly crafted show song.

The supporting cast don't get too many chances in *Funny Girl*, but what they get is worth having. A creaky Kay Medford as Fanny's mother leads the deliciously casual putdown 'If a Girl Isn't Pretty' and joins Danny Meehan in another prime comic number, 'Who Taught Her Everything She Knows?', whilst Sidney Chaplin as Arnstein lends a warm, masculine presence to his rôle and the song 'I Want to be Seen With You Tonight'.

This is a model show album, bringing as it does all the essence of the stage production to the listener, equipped with an outstanding central performance which takes it into the exceptional class. Streisand repeats her performance on the film soundtrack, as does Kay Medford, but the score has been disembowelled for film and, although all the main hits have been retained and, indeed, supplemented by interpolated songs of the highest class ('My Man', 'I'd Rather Be Blue'), it is sad to have to do without such enjoyable pieces as 'Cornet Man' and 'Who Taught Her Everything She Knows?'.

Bob Merrill

Carnival

Bob Merrill, the lyricist of *Funny Girl*, had an earlier success in 1961 with a delightful little musical called *Carnival*, a stage version of the successful Leslie Caron film *Lili*. On stage Anna Maria Alberghetti played the orphan girl, taken up by a circus, whose heart is won by the show's puppets until she realizes that her sentiments really belong to the misanthropic, crippled puppeteer. Merrill was responsible for both the simple, effective lyrics and the tuneful music of *Carnival*, creating a score that held that rare quality of charm, a quality well captured on the original cast recording.

Miss Alberghetti describes in her first, delicately coloured song how she came to the circus from 'Mira', and again uses the sweetest part of her soprano voice on the naive 'A Very Nice Man' before launching into two of the show's most attractive numbers, 'Yes, my Heart' and the waltz theme 'Love Makes the World Go Round'. Occasionally she overblows in the higher passages, but it is a truly attractive characterization and her songs with the puppets are adorable without ever getting sticky. Jerry Orbach uses his actor's baritone to good effect in the disappointed 'I've Got to Find a Reason' and then takes on all the voices of the puppets with great skill.

The humour of the piece is provided largely by the philandering magician, Marco the Magnificent (James Mitchell), and his lady friend, The Incredible Rosalie (Kaye Ballard). Miss Ballard, as lusty as ever, makes a melodramatic meal of the hilariously tipsy jealousy song 'Humming' and, if 'It Was Always You' sounds like just another love song, a quick glimpse at the sleeve (which unfortunately gives no synopsis, this being the era when sleeves were used to plug the show rather than aid the listener) lets us see that it is sung as Marco plunges swords into the box in which Rosalie is imprisoned.

It is a well-balanced score, well presented, and the disc makes you wonder why such an attractive show has not become a seasonal regular. It is, of course, less attractive when less well done, as the London cast disc (a rarity worth seeking only for its rarity) proves.

Stephen Sondheim

The rise of Stephen Sondheim as a presence in the American musical theatre took a significant step forward with the presentation of his first show as a composer, *A Funny Thing Happened on the Way to the Forum*, in 1962, five years after his first appearance on Broadway with the lyrics of *West Side Story*. Thereafter, apart from his venture with Richard Rodgers in *Do I Hear a Waltz?*, he supplied both music and words for all the shows with which he was connected. Between 1962 and 1979 there were seven of these produced and recorded, seven shows wide ranging in subject matter and in style and displaying what seems like a purposeful variation of his extremely considerable skills, sometimes with more success and sometimes with less. However, the cult that has grown up around Sondheim's work has meant that even the less good and less successful of his works have received continued attention from devotees and has even sparked a couple of major revivals and recordings.

A Funny Thing Happened on the Way to the Forum

A Funny Thing Happened on the Way to the Forum was a gentle step into composerhood. The show is, quite simply, one of the funniest musical comedies in the Broadway canon and, whilst the score is in no way subordinated to the libretto, it is very much affected by it, notably insofar as the kind of players envisaged for its principal rôles are concerned. With a cast headed by a set of sort-of-singing comedy actors, there was little scope for wide-ranging music and, in consequence, most of the songs are in the light comic vein, reinforcing and enlarging upon the crazy classical situations of the book.

They include some particularly fine examples: the opening declaration that the audience can expect 'Comedy Tonight', the ingénue's ingenuous admission that she has no talent except being 'Lovely', and the slavering assertion of that upright citizen Senex that 'Everybody Ought to Have a Maid' for quite the wrong reasons. In contrast, there are two splendid burlesque pieces for the operatic captain, Miles Gloriosus, who plays a key part in a plot it would take a whole page to detail.

The original cast recording has a particularly fine bunch of comedians on display – Zero Mostel as the consumingly central Pseudolus, Jack Gilford shiveringly insisting 'I'm Calm' in inimitable fashion, and David Burns as a strong-voiced Senex – as well as a couple of fresh-voiced juveniles for the play's version of Ancient Roman romantic moments. Two 'legit' singers in Ron Holgate (Miles) and the vigorous Ruth Kobart, who makes a fine dragon of Senex's wife, Domina, in her song about 'That Dirty Old Man of Mine', complete the line-up. Surprisingly, Mostel comes across on disc with less personality than on stage, but the remainder give their all. The only problem is that *Funny Thing* definitely loses something on record. It is enjoyable as a record, but nowhere near as enjoyable as it is as a show.

The London cast recording, headed by Frankie Howerd, shows up that fault somewhat when it includes little pieces of the dialogue. Immediately things perk up – but not enough. It cannot equal the original disc in any other area. As for the film soundtrack, it reduces the score to a frustrating fraction of its original length – five numbers only – and fills up the record with incidental music.

Company

Anyone Can Whistle (1964) was a nine-performance failure, although its title song remained popular as a single and it duly had its not very inspiring cast recording, but *Company* (1970) received a fine Broadway run and, in spite of what seemed to be a libretto dealing with wholly American middle-class preoccupations, found regular productions abroad.

It was an unusually constructed piece, rather like a revue in some ways, lacking a linear development, as it showed the relationships of bachelor Bobby with a series of his married friends in a succession of short scenes and of songs. Many of the songs became Sondheim favourites – the out-of-towner's vision of New York 'Another Hundred People', the air hostess climbing out of a foreign bed to go to 'Barcelona', a spiky serenade to 'The Ladies Who Lunch', the hero's childishly self-preoccupied 'Being Alive' – but the less obvious moments included such gems as the marvellous complaint of three marriage-bent girls, pecking away like sparrows at the eyes of Bobby's independence ('You Could Drive a Person Crazy'), or the crazed patter of the bride who insists that she is not 'Getting

Married Today', whilst a cynical church soloist comments on her dilemma as she gets her breath back between verses.

In total contrast to *Funny Thing*, its construction and its almost entire lack of need of a visual side make *Company* ideal record fodder, but the original cast recording (and the London version, which slips in an alternative leading man) turns out to be a rather strange one. It is one of the few recordings where the material almost wholly wipes out the performers. When you listen to this disc you listen to the songs, their words and their music, and you mostly don't know or care about the foolish, faceless characters of the play or the apparently interchangeable artists playing them. Only Beth Howland as the panic-struck bride and Elaine Stritch with her easily identifiable basso drawl make any impression as individuals.

The fact is that, without distorting the show, the material probably does not allow too much in the way of individuality. The songs are in charge and it is they that command our attention. The lyrics are truly thoughtful, modern and free of cliché, always admirable and, in such pieces as 'Barcelona', 'You Could Drive a Person Crazy' and 'Getting Married Today', novel and unmissable. The music is well fitted to the style and subject of the songs, and if it rises to the odd rather unnecessarily melodramatic climax, as in 'Being Alive' (cried to the skies by Dean Jones on the recording, with all the forces of Jonathan Tunick's orchestrations powering behind him), I guess that is due to theatrical considerations.

The sum total is a recording that is unlike any before it, and, like or dislike *Company* as an entertainment, you must admire the exceptional writing skills on view in the individual pieces that make up the show.

Follies

Follies (1971) has similarities with *Company*, although in some ways it is very different. Once again it deals in a semi-revusical way with the relationships of a group of people brought together, for the purposes of the entertainment, for an occasion. This time they are a group of ageing Follies girls, and their reunion proves the opportunity for some reminiscing and for some tardy and tiddly truths brushed briskly under the stagecloth at the end of the evening so that real life can go on. The characters – particularly the women – are bigger than *Company*'s everyday city folk, their emotions are more colourful and exaggerated and their songs, some in Follies idioms, include some more favourite Sondheim numbers such as the torchy 'Losing My Mind', the socked-out career catalogue 'I'm Still Here', and the elderly reprise of the very youthful 'Broadway Baby'.

With its very slim structure (it can't be called a plot) and series of loosely related songs, *Follies* is fine record material, and all three of the existing recordings have their highspots. The original Broadway cast recording is perhaps the least wholly satisfying. It suffers from being made with artists who were able to play the rôles on stage and, since the leading players are all of a certain age, there are quite a few vocal problems on display. It also suffers from a very curious editing which cuts out two of the show's most charming pieces ('Rain on the Roof' and 'One More Kiss'), and also the 'Loveland' sequence which explains the tone of the songs that follow. Perhaps the singers concerned were just too creaky. However, there are impressive performances from Dorothy Collins (Sally), Gene Nelson (Buddy) and Ethel Shutta (Hattie), some fine youngsters and a definitive delivery of 'I'm Still Here' from Yvonne de Carlo, who avoids both the campy and the 'look how loudly I can still sing' syndrome.

By the time of the London production, seventeen years later, some revisions had been made to text and score, and most are improvements – notably a wonderful piece of word-work in the emotional striptease 'Ah, But Underneath', which replaces the original 'Story of Lucy and Jessie'. It was, however, sad to see the reflective 'The Road You Didn't Take' dropped in favour of the jagged stichomythia of 'Country House', a very 1988 Sondheim piece which fits a little uneasily into this score.

The recording of this production is a double-disc affair, clad in a splendidly showy sleeve trumpeting 'first complete recording' and equipped with a finely printed book of lyrics which oddly calls itself a libretto. It has technical advantages over the original recording, a lusher sound and a more assured and expansive feel, as well as some slightly younger leading cast members and a useful pitch-hitching machine in the studio to help those older folk whose vocal cords were sagging slightly. The result is a set which has much to enjoy – Julia McKenzie's torchy 'Losing my Mind', the fragile beauty of Adele Leigh's 'One More Kiss', Lynda Baron's gutsy 'Who's That Woman?', Paul Bentley's tongue-in-cheek tenor deliberately enunciating the new and amusing lyrics for 'Loveland', plus coolly stylish performances from Diana Rigg (Phyllis) and Daniel Massey (Ben) and an agreeably energetic one from David Healey (Buddy). If elsewhere things are less effective than in the older recording, the sum total is nevertheless far better.

Shortly before the London production, a gala concert version of *Follies* was staged in New York. Massing a starry cast, the New York Philharmonic Orchestra under Paul Gemignani and the ritziest resources of the television and recording worlds, it too produced a double-disc set of the show's score, albeit the score as it existed before the revisions made for London. Thus, we have 'Jessie and Lucy', 'The Road You Didn't Take' and 'Live, Love, Laugh' rather than their replacements.

It is a splendid set, prettily packed and equipped with a lyric book, artist's biographies and some hefty notes. As for the record itself, it is magnificently played and almost entirely magnificently sung by a group of artists which includes some brilliant and, to the unknowing, unlikely bits of casting. Many of the characters come out more clearly on this non-cast recording than they do on the full stage records, and moments such as Betty Comden and Adolf Green's delicious 'Rain on the Roof' and Arthur Rubin's roseate serenade to 'Beautiful Girls' (in which the canny gentleman alters the notation to avoid the larynx-busting 'oo' sound on the top note) are little treasures.

In the central rôles, George Hearn (Ben) and Barbara Cook (Sally) are quite outstanding (a tendency on his part to overdramatize notwithstanding), whilst the very youthful-sounding Mandy Patinkin gives endless voice and spirit to the part of Buddy. Alongside them, Lee Remick (Phyllis) is outclassed vocally, but her numbers are less musically demanding. Amongst the featured rôles Comden and Green and Liliane Montevecchi, singing 'Ah! Paree!', stand out as the real thing, whilst opera star Licia Albanese (equipped with a less tactfully blending junior partner than Miss Leigh) delivers a big 'One More Kiss'.

The artists given the two big bon-bons of the show are always going to be on a tough line. 'Broadway Baby' and 'I'm Still Here' have become standard party pieces, fodder for the camp older ladies of stage and supper club. What do you do with them? Elaine Stritch growls and hacks out 'Broadway Baby' to a blasting reaction from the live audience (faded determinedly in and out), which probably says more about the audience than it does about her, and the powerfullly-voiced, lightly amused Carol Burnett builds 'I'm Still Here' on a long and thoughtful crescendo to a similar response. First-rate artists both, it is in no way their fault that these songs have now become almost impossible and that you have to return to Ethel Shutta and Yvonne de Carlo on the original cast disc to hear them sung as songs and not as nightclub monuments.

Even though a few individual items from the other discs may be preferable, there is no doubt that this *Follies* is the most accomplished and enjoyable of the three. The star concert format is clearly one with possibilities, one that hopefully will, following this splendid example, render more recordings of fine, lesser-known shows available.

A Little Night Music

A Little Night Music (1973) proved, if proof were necessary, the versatility of Sondheim as both a lyricist and a composer. Around a bitter-sweet period film story of the Swedish bourgeoisie, Sondheim and his librettist Hugh Wheeler created a sweetly cynical Broadway operetta with a score built up from a mass of variable waltz tunes and some brilliant yet poignantly human lyrics. The waltz rhythms also brought out the very best in Sondheim as a composer and here, for the first, and perhaps the only, time to date, he equals the quality of his words with that of his music in a series of dazzling ensembles, unobviously structurally sophisticated, lyrically admirable and rich and sweeping in their music.

The original cast recording is a fine one. Len Cariou, in the principal male rôle of Frederik, uses his appealingly crinkly light baritone to good effect and, when he partners the sweet girlish soprano of Victoria Mallory (Anne) and the hectic pubescent tenor of Mark Lambert (Henrik) in the superbly constructed triad of songs 'Now'/'Later'/'Soon', the result is a magnificent modern operetta moment. Glynis Johns in the star rôle of Desirée has – unusually for the star of an operetta – only a small croaky voice but plenty of personality to lend to her limited music, and Hermione Gingold, cleverly cast as the aged plaything of kings, mooning over the lost status of 'Liaisons', follows the same effective style. Laurence Guittard, as the fly in the evening's romantic ointment, has a handsome voice which makes his song 'In Praise of Women' into a bravura piece of chauvinstic display, in contrast to the directly sung 'The Miller Son', uncomplicatedly performed with a fine, unforced tone by D. Jamin-Bartlett. As with all the best operettas, however, the best pieces of *A Little Night Music*, all of which get a thorough performance on this disc, are the ensembles, and Sondheim's intricate anticipation of 'A Weekend in the Country', the cynical 'Remember', which sums up the whole attitude to life of the play's characters, and the twittering 'Perpetual Anticipation' are all particularly finely done.

A Little Night Music is the first Sondheim score compiled as a score and not as a series of extractable songs and it is, therefore, all the more surprising that it should yield up a hit parade song in the shape of the rather obfuscated 'Send in the Clowns'. If you don't know the show and you have ever actually listened to the words of this song, can you honestly say you know what it's about? It falls to the lot of Glynis Johns here, and her croaky sincerity makes you at least think you know what it is about.

The London cast recording is also very well done. There is less croaking and crackling here – whilst Jean Simmons (Desirée) and Joss Ackland (Fredrik) are not first and foremost singers they can hold a note – but there is a mite less appeal as well. A lovely girlish Anne from Veronica Page, a feeling Charlotte (Maria Aitken) and a freshly boyish Henrik (Terry Mitchell) are amongst the assets, and a noticeably older Hermione Gingold repeats her Broadway assignment and the wordfully revusical 'Liaisons' as Mme Armfeld on a more than acceptable recording.

The film version, which unworthily revamps, transposes and thins out the score, is of minimal interest. Too little of the original score remains and what does is mostly dubiously dubbed with all the disappointments that inevitably entails. Cariou and Guittard repeat their original performances alongside some pieces of Elizabeth Taylor in what should have been a better recording.

Pacific Overtures

This successful venture into Swedish operetta was followed by a pseudo-Japanese recounting of the nineteenth-century American 'invasion' of Japan in the esoteric *Pacific Overtures* (1976). After Broadway failure with a cast of Japanese performers, the piece was staged by the English National Opera with operatic vocalists incongruously 'woofling' their way through the adventurous but too often uninteresting music and occasionally opaque lyrics. Both versions were recorded, the latter on a two-disc set.

Sweeney Todd

The musical melodrama *Sweeney Todd* (1979) was by and large a more accessible piece, but its failure to find a major metropolitan run anywhere except on Broadway means that only the original cast recording represents the score of a very substantial show which has, since, become widely popular in a much smaller-scale version. Broadway's production was a vast, black affair physically, which is reflected in the double-disc recording. This is in every way a dark show and a dark score, moody and threatening throughout. Even in its apparently lighter and brighter moments and its gentle and romantic songs for the young lovers it is never free of a foggy pall of foulness and gloom. It is also a big show: its orchestra (supplemented here) and its arrangements are big and exciting, and many of its performances need to be and are big.

Oddly enough, the central and title rôle, taken by Len Cariou, is not one that is played up large. Cariou plays Sweeney Todd in a brooding fashion, deliberately spoken and sung with a shapely middle-weight baritone that cruises through such pieces as his bitter praise of 'Pretty Women' or the tale of 'The Barber and his Wife' and only bursts out into a passionate roar, supported by the massed sound of the orchestra, at the most enormous moments of the melodrama. In scenes such as the howling 'Epiphany' the voice perhaps lacks the genuine power needed to lift the music and drama to its highest peaks – but the music and drama are strong enough to lift him instead, and all is well.

Angela Lansbury as his accomplice, the pie-shop owner Mrs Lovett, gives a performance unlike any of those she has previously put on record. She raucously hawks 'The Worst Pies in London' in a big, broad London-accented characterization, which she can yet calm down to the much more effective and grim gentler moments of 'Poor Thing' and the horrible, coy flirtation of 'By the Sea'. It is a genuine melodrama performance, large without being ridiculous, and insinuatingly nasty without being like a pantomime character.

There are some very fine supporting performances too, notably from Edmund Lyndeck as Judge Turpin, the villain of the story, whose self-flagellating 'Johanna' is superbly played with all the sustained power that Cariou does not employ, and from Joaquin Romaguera as the fake Italian barber Pirelli, with his showy tenor mountebank's song. Victor Garber sings the juvenile version of 'Johanna' with an unpretentious youthfulness, Merle Louise mixes rich soprano and ugly chest tones effectively in the schizophrenic scenes for the mad beggarwoman, Ken Jennings gets both freshness and pathos into his rôle as the simple Tobias, and Sarah Rice, as Sweeney's lost daughter, gives Johanna a rather wan simplicity.

All in all, the set faithfully records the show as played on Broadway, and in many parts it is an impressive recording of a work with many impressive parts. Since its first production the show has found itself a home in revised versions at both the New York City Opera and in some of the smallest of Britain's small theatres. One of these, at the Cheltenham Everyman, I found infinitely more affecting and dramatic than the production on this recording, bringing the drama and the music slicingly to the fore without the aid or hindrance of the large forces originally used. It would be interesting to hear what both that variant of *Sweeney Todd* (at the time of writing just opening off-Broadway) and an operatic treatment sound like on record. But there is little to complain about in the recording that does exist.

Sweeney Todd was also produced as a television film, which was issued as a commercial video, mainly with members of the original cast. Miss Lansbury and Lyndeck star again, with George Hearn (a much more substantial voice) as Sweeney and Cris Groenendaal and Betsy Joslyn from the Broadway chorus upped to the juvenile rôles.

Cy Coleman

The 1960s introduced to Broadway the jazz pianist and songwriter Cy Coleman who proved himself, during a period of more than a quarter of a century, to be one of the most versatile and enjoyable composers for the modern American light musical theatre. Over seven shows he stretched himself with equal success from the standard star-vehicle musical comedy, through jazz, country and popular song strains to operetta burlesque.

Wildcat

Coleman's first score, *Wildcat* (1960), with lyrics by Carolyn Leigh, was a pleasantly jaunty, positive one, which threw up one hit song in star Lucille Ball's opening number 'Hey, Look Me Over' and several other attractive pieces, such as the charmingly lopsided love duo 'One Day We Dance' and the happily energetic country 'What Takes my Fancy'. The cast recording has Ms Ball in swingeing and uninhibited mood paired with a warm-voiced leading man (Keith Andes) and a fine supporting cast, putting over a merry mixture of musical pieces set into a rather conventional Texas tale of love and oil.

Little Me

There was nothing at all conventional about Coleman and Leigh's next effort, nor about its libretto, supplied by the young Neil Simon, hot on the heels of his first Broadway success with the comedy *Come Blow Your Horn*. *Little Me* (1962), adapted from the hilarious book by the creator of *Auntie Mame*, Patrick Dennis, was equally hilarious as a stage piece. A marvellously extravagant burlesque of the celebrity biography, it was a genuinely funny piece in its story, in its dialogue and in its musical numbers. Leigh found a new comical gear, only momentarily used in *Wildcat*, and Coleman composed an infectiously enjoyable score that ranges from a mid-European funeral dirge to a toffee-nosed ragtime, from slimy soft-shoe and French cabaret strains to burlesque vaudeville and operetta, in a pastiche rich in the good-humoured satire the book inspired.

The original cast recording features Virginia Martin as poor little Belle Schlumpfert who sets out to conquer society armed with only a fabulous pair of bazooms, and Sid Caesar as all the men whom she abused *en route*. He manages the essential comedy of the rôle and the songs the more effectively, whether as a lecherous eighty-eight-year-old, a French *chanteur*, a Ruritanian Prince or the myopic GI surnamed Poitrine, whose function is to give Belle her predestined surname and to put over the wide-eyed hymn to a 'Real, Live Girl'. Miss Martin acts up super-cute for her cod vaudeville turn 'Dimples' and wallops out her determination to get to 'The Other Side of the Tracks', but just occasionally the comedy gets less attention than the singing.

The London edition of *Little Me* had a longer run than the original, but its recording, in spite of the inclusion of the 'Rich Kids Rag', missing from the earlier disc, and some helpful snippets of dialogue to place the numbers, is less appealing. Eileen Gourlay is a delightfully pert Belle, and Avril Angers shows how to play the comedy as her older incarnation, but Bruce Forsyth doesn't make much of the multiple male rôle and his highly individual vowels become very wearing.

A revised *Little Me* produced in America and London in the 1980s was not recorded and, although the original Broadway recording is a most enjoyable one, I feel that this piece (surely a candidate for an integral recording, given the quality of its libretto) has not had its record due.

Sweet Charity

Sweet Charity (1966), a more legitimate kind of musical comedy, gave Coleman his biggest success to date. Paired, this time, with lyricist Dorothy Fields, he turned out a quality score of modern songs to fit the character and the tale of the 'klutzy', loveable nightclub hostess, Charity Hope Valentine, and her umpteenth unfortunate tangle with romance. Amongst the take-away numbers are 'Big Spender', 'If My Friends Could See Me Now', the burlesque of crank religion 'The Rhythm of Life', the driving 'There's Gotta Be Something Better than This' and Charity's winsome 'Where Am I Going'.

The title rôle of *Sweet Charity* was devised to fit the talents of Gwen Verdon and, even though her dance talent goes unseen on record, the original cast recording shows just how well that devising did its job. In this rôle, Miss Verdon is quite a phenomenon. She gets more feeling and more oddly vulnerable personality onto one inch of gramophone record than there would seem to be room for. Here she quivers happily on the verge of being taken for a ride through the length of the show, until her final halleluia 'somebody loves me at last!' It is quite something, especially as you know that five minutes later she's gone and lost the man yet again.

Helen Gallagher and Thelma Oliver as Charity's dance hall pals ride 'Big Spender' with brassy, modern style as it bumps and grinds its way into the classics list, and have steel-throated fun with the rhythmic 'There's Gotta Be Something Better than This' and 'Baby, Dream your Dream', whilst each of the four male principals performs his number competently. But *Sweet Charity* is very much Charity's show. She and the girls have the best material, and this team serves that material marvellously.

The London cast recording features Juliet Prowse as Charity. She gives a first-rate performance, and all you can really reproach her with is for not being Gwen Verdon. Josephine Blake and Paula Kelly do equally well in the other female rôles. Unfortunately, however, this disc chooses to omit Charity's fine Act 1 Soliloquy and also her 'I'm the Bravest Individual'. The film version, featuring Shirley MacLaine as another top class Charity, has eight numbers taken from the show score and three that were not, and Chita Rivera and Paula Kelly in support. There are omissions and alterations, too, in the 1986 revival recording. The Soliloquy isn't there, 'Bravest Individual' has undergone a weird reorchestration that makes it sound like somthing out of a disco, 'Rhythm of Life' loses its way somewhere along the line, and the original 'Sweet Charity' is replaced by the new number of the same name written for the film version. Debbie Allen heads the cast on a dry-sounding digital disc, lacking much in the way of atmosphere and feeling, except in a fine performance of the plastic film star's 'Too Many Tomorrows' from Mark Jacoby.

Sweet Charity is one of the few Broadway musicals of this era which spread itself through Europe, and three foreign-language cast albums are the result, each of which presents Charity differently. The Dutch Jasperina de Jong is a jolly soubrette with a pretty voice, Germany's Dagmar Koller is central to a rather unsubtle production, which makes less equivocal the nature of the work of the girls in the Fan-Dango Ballroom, whilst France's Magali Noël is a very sweet Charity, bubbling with girlish joy alongside a pair of *consoeurs* who are less brassy and more softly sexy than usual. On the whole, the French record is probably the most enjoyable of the three, although it has a rather stately 'Rhythm of Life' from legitimate vocalist Dominique Tirmont and a sadly worn Sidney Chaplin not quite coping with 'Too Many Tomorrows'. But none of them has Gwen Verdon.

See-Saw

The next three Coleman musicals on Broadway were as eclectic a series as the first. *See-Saw* (1973) was nearest to *Sweet Charity* in its outline, pairing a kookie girl with a city gent lover amongst the determined 1960s Bohemianism of youthful New York. New York provided the production numbers, the love affair the ballads, and both areas came up with the usual crop of smiling Coleman songs – 'Nobody Does it Like Me', 'He's Good for Me' and 'Welcome to Holiday Inn', all for the heroine, and the company show-within-a-show tune 'It's Not Where You Start'. The score and the original cast recording are vital, brassy affairs, energetically played and sung, but Michelle Lee and her character of Gittel Mosca don't have the warmth and appeal of a Charity. She sings her fine selection of songs with a tough, confident tone, leaving the little light and shade of the show to Ken Howard as her lawyer lover and the speciality numbers to Tommy Tune and the chorus of colourful New Yorkers who make up the diversions from the love story. It's all lively, youthful stuff, very much of its time and place, spankingly delivered.

I Love my Wife

There were no production numbers in *I Love my Wife* (1977). Four actors and four musicians were all that was needed to tell Michael Stewart's little tale of attempted wife-swapping in suburban America, and the contrast with the big, brassy sound of *See-Saw* is total and very welcome. Coleman's light, bouncy melodies, orchestrated by the composer with maximum elegance and effect for keyboards, clarinet, bass, drums and the odd instrumental double, are delightful, and Stewart's endearingly clever modern lyrics manage to make more songs out of the one subject – minor variations on the sexual basics – than you'd think possible. Unfortunately, even he can't make this lack of variety interesting when the songs are piled one after another on to a record, and it is probably no coincidence that the most enjoyable song – a lolloping little celebration of 'A Mover's Life' – is an incidental piece with nothing to do with the plot.

The songs are not demanding vocally and the original cast recording shows up a set of performers who never oversing them, but make no big impressions either. A South African album and an Australian cast recording, which adds a couple of instrumentalists and omits a couple of minor pieces, are made on the same lines, performing the score in the intimately friendly way it demands. Perhaps this lack of big effects was the reason that, in a popular music world big on big effects, this was the first Coleman show not to produce a song hit.

On the Twentieth Century

Right at the other end of the musical spectrum was Coleman's score to Comden and Green's book and lyrics for *On the Twentieth Century* (1978). This experienced and outstanding team of Broadway collaborators boosted the famous old play *Twentieth Century* into another dimension with a burlesque operetta score of unequalled brilliance – Coleman's musical witticisms and unerring melody blending with songful after songful after intricately clever ensembleful of Comden and Green's most stylish lyrics.

On the Twentieth Century gave me fourteen of my happiest evenings in the theatre and I have replayed the original cast disc – alas, the only one in existence, as Julia McKenzie's performance of an epoch in the London production sadly went unrecorded – consistently over the years since. It doesn't always quite do the show and the score justice, but it has for me that other all-important function of a show recording: it brings back the memory of evenings enjoyed in the theatre. Perhaps it is unfair to be even a little dissatisfied with a recording that has so much. The two star rôles of *On the Twentieth Century* are monstrously demanding, requiring not only comedy talents of the highest degree but also wide, soaring operetta voices which can be twisted into the most unlikely, but all the more hilarious, effects.

John Cullum as the flowing, extravagant Oscar Jaffee is right on line: you can feel him licking his lips over the flamboyant baritone heroics of 'I Rise Again' and burning out his tongue-in-cheek 'The Legacy', the eleven o'clock number to cap all eleven o'clock numbers. Madeleine Kahn, in the much more technically difficult rôle of Lily Garland, sometimes sounds less assured. Her transformation from piano-playing Mildred Klotz into a star in 'Véronique' lacks a bit of zest. However, by the time she reaches her big second-act showpiece, 'Babette', in which authors, composer, orchestrator Hershy Kay and the artist combine in a dazzlingly funny depiction of a star with a dilemma, she is under full steam and both comedy and voice unite in a treat of a track.

There is so much more – Imogen Coca as an elderly religious nut croaking tunelessly over a dainty soubrette melody about 'dirty doings' behind locked bathroom doors, a pseudo-philosophical close-harmony number declaring 'Life is Like a Train', a splendidly effective sextet with plot ramifications too complex to go into, train music which sounds as if it might have come straight out of a Weber storm scene, and a burlesque death duet to challenge *La Bohème*. All are things it is so easy to do just adequately and all, here, are without exception done superbly.

Space restrictions have meant that one or two sections have had to be omitted. How I would have loved to have a record of the hilariously funny audition scene in which little Miss Plotka, at her piano, sabotages a star's unconfident yodelling of 'The Indian Maiden's Lament', not to mention . . . Well, suffice it to say that this is another musical where the consistent quality of text and music are such as to deserve an integral recording. In the meanwhile, I will continue very happily to listen to the original cast disc.

Barnum

Coleman's twenty years on Broadway were celebrated by a second world-wide hit with the circus musical *Barnum*. In spite of the fact that the visual side of this show was an integral part of its appeal, and that the production, text and score were tightly linked in the construction of the entertainment, the songs alone make up a lively and enjoyable record – seven records, to be precise, for there are American, French, British, Italian, Australian, Dutch and Spanish *Barnum*s on disc, a fact that speaks for itself.

Barnum himself dominates the show, and he has a fine and varied selection of numbers, ranging from the energetic patter of his 'Museum Song' or 'The Prince of Humbug' to the gentle 'The Colours of my Life' and the countryfied duet 'I Like your Style' with his wife, Chairy, but the highlights of this score are the vibrantly colourful company numbers 'Come Follow the Band', 'Join the Circus' and the stylish narrative 'Black and White', which whisk the events and the entertainment along with all Coleman's accustomed vigour and positivity.

Each of the recordings has its good points – some more than others. Jim Dale is the star of the original cast album, and he presents an appealing character at the head of an agreeable all-round cast, in which Glenn Close is a pleasant, warm Chairy, and Terri White gives the best recorded versions of the up-beat 'Thank God I'm Old' in the character of Joice Heth, 'the oldest woman in the world', and of the bluesy bits of 'Black and White'.

The London disc, which adds a carousel opening and a 'rinkity' two-piano introduction and makes some minor changes elsewhere, has the edge, however, mostly because of Michael Crawford's incisive and overwhelmingly enthusiastic performance in the title rôle. Vocally more assured than Dale, he also conveys the manic, almost childlike passions that make up the man, with a wild sincerity that is quite irresistible. His supporting cast are mostly fine, with Sarah Payne making much more of Jenny Lind's meaningful arietta 'Love Makes Such Fools of Us All' than her lighter-voiced American counterpart, and Deborah Grant as a thoughtful, pretty Chairy. They are backed by particularly good orchestral and recording values.

The Australian recording has a cocky, mischievous and rather insensitive Barnum (Reg Livermore) but also the most impressively and affectingly sung Chairy (Gaye Macfarlane). The French disc features a lively, well-sung Tom Thumb (Jorge Rafael) and a pleasing Chairy and Jenny, but a hectic Barnum (Jean-Luc Moreau) without much obvious singing talent, whilst the tinkered-with Italian version, effectively led by Massimo Ranieri, is elsewhere not so satisfying. It is the Spanish *Barnum*, headed by two fine, warm personality singers in Emilio Aragon (Barnum) and an uncredited Chairy, which is, in all, the most enjoyable of these foreign-language recordings, but in the end you have to come back to Crawford for pure performance value.

In fact, the whole of that performance is available, for *Barnum* is the only West End production to have been filmed in the theatre and issued as a commercial video. It is a splendid recording, taken not from the original Palladium production but from the subsequent revival at the Victoria Palace, and thus uses a different supporting cast. Almost everywhere this is a gain and, in spite of the one or two corny music-hall jokes that have crept in to the script, and the loss of the buzzing audience-stage rapport that was engendered in the theatre, the whole show gets a thoroughly grand acting, singing and flamboyantly circussy representation.

Jerry Herman

Jerry Herman was another new name to appear on Broadway at the beginning of the 1960s and, before the decade was out, his celebrity and success had spread worldwide along with his enormously successful musical *Hello, Dolly!*.

Milk and Honey

Herman's first Broadway venture was *Milk and Honey* (1961), a mid-life love story with an Israeli setting and a lushly written score, which was duly recorded at the top of a goodly New York run. Opera singers Robert Weede and Mimi Benzell and the no less large and lusty-voiced Tommy Rall, backed by an omnipresent umpteen-part chorus and orchestra, give full-throated renderings of an end-to-end series of lyrical Jewish-flavoured ariettas and duets that seem to climax more often than a

Tschaikowsky coda, in a style perhaps not wholly in keeping with the modest love stories of the text and lyrics. Molly Picon, as the comic relief, has a man-chasing number in each half, each with some funny lines; the second ('Hymn to Hymie') notably prefigures Dolly Levi's chats with her departed husband in *Hello, Dolly!*.

Hello, Dolly!

Hello, Dolly! (1964) is a happy combination of a favourite stage plot, a title rôle full of comical opportunities, and eleven enjoyable musical numbers. Gower Champion's production, Carol Channing's creation of the rôle of Dolly Levi and the metamorphosis of the title song into one of Broadway's all-time mega-hits helped ensure that the show broke the Broadway musical long-run record, ultimately going on to be one of the most internationally played of all Broadway musicals. Surprisingly, the result has been only a limited number of cast albums, and New York and London account for half of these between them. Equally surprisingly, these aren't terribly satisfying.

The original cast disc enshrines what was clearly a magnificent stage performance by Carol Channing, and it is the record that anyone who saw that performance is going to want to have. To someone who didn't see her, it is rather less satisfying. The ineffable Channing croak has gone from being endearing to being excessive and even mannered. Some of the noises she produces have nothing to do with music or, come to it, with anything else. The timing and the comedy are there, but the sounds are plain ugly.

The music gets a hard time altogether: David Burns (Horace) also works on the remnants of what was never a great voice, Eileen Brennan (Irene Molloy), although spunkier than was later the fashion in this rôle, and even, possibly, a touch Irish, gives an unsure 'Ribbons Down My Back' and only Charles Nelson Reilly, a fresh, boyish Cornelius, skipping his way eagerly through 'Put On Your Sunday Clothes' as he anticipates a day in the big city, really delivers a record performance.

The London version is no better. Mary Martin has all the vocal quality that Miss Channing lacks, but she provides none of the comedy values. She, too, has a non-singing Horace (Loring Smith) and a Cornelius who isn't a patch on Reilly, and the recording comes out as a scrappy affair all round. Miss Martin was replaced at Drury Lane by Dora Bryan and, although a new cast recording was not issued, HMV put out a studio cast version featuring Miss Bryan and her Horace, Bernard Spear, alongside a group of session singers. Unfortunately, it isn't a very good recording. I say 'unfortunately' because the two top-billed artists show up with all the qualifications for their rôles (in which they were extremely successful) without actually quite clicking. Miss Bryan has both the comedy of the character and the voice to sing the songs and, when she is on line, she is great, but every so often she seems to wander off on a cloud and delivers a line or a phrase as if she had no idea what it meant. Spear is a nice Jewish Horace with a good singing voice and the occasional lapse of taste. The session singers are just dire.

Broadway also put out a second recording from its original production when the show was recast in mid-run with a black cast headed by Pearl Bailey and Cab Calloway. There can be no complaint about the vocal values here. Miss Bailey's indigo tones are glorious, Calloway is as sparky as a newt, the Cornelius has a legitimate bass-baritone of quality instead of the usual light comedy man's voice, and the Irene sighs out a pretty, romantic 'Ribbons' tastefully. The only trouble is, apart from Calloway (who is supposed to be the straight man of the piece), they are all very short on fun.

The final English-language cast disc comes from the film adaptation but, although this contains most of the original stage score, plus a couple of pieces cut prior to town, it is an uncomfortable version. It is *Dolly* synthesized into a Barbra Streisand vehicle, souped up to sound like a remake of *Funny Girl*, with languorously legato lines and lazy, uncredited orchestrations that take the zest out of the piece.

Beyond this frustrating group, there is just a handful of foreign-language discs – an acceptable Israeli one, German and Austrian ones featuring Marika Rökk as an ageing soubrette of a Dolly and a truly warbly Irene, a dubious Russian effort, and one from France. And there, lurking inside a violent puce sleeve with one of those marvellously awful Pierre Okley portrait covers that always make the artists look twenty years younger, slimmer and prettier than the photos on the back, is the Dolly, and indeed the *Hello, Dolly!* you've been looking for.

She is called Annie Cordy and, if you turn back to the French section of this book, you'll see that she bubbled to fame in 1952 in the comedy rôle of the musical comedy *La Route fleurie*. Here, twenty years of every kind of theatre, film and cabaret later, she is still bubbling (indeed, almost another twenty years later the same remark still applies), giving the rôle of Dolly Levi every millimetre of the apparently elusive combination of adorable comicality and fine, cheerful, uncomplicated singing it demands. It is a dream performance, which doesn't want to be described – just listened to.

Fortunately, everything else about the recording is up to Mlle Cordy's measure. There is a lovely, dreamy 'Ribbons' ('Un chapeau avec des rubans' in André Hornez's version) from Pierrette Delange (Irene), whose clear, unpretentious soprano is a joy; a splendidly wide-eyed and eager Cornelius with a sparky light baritone (Jean Pomarez); a well-judged and -sung Horace (Jean Mareuil); and a conductor (Caravelli) who attacks the score with a rare and unselfconscious *joie de vivre*. The whole adds up to a delicious surprise, one of the best foreign-language recordings of any Broadway musical and, incontestably, the best Dolly and *Hello, Dolly!* about.

Mame

Dolly and *Hello, Dolly!* were followed by Mame and *Mame* (1966), another larger-than-fiction lady of a certain age blasting her way into Broadway's heart and on to the hit list. In translating Patrick Dennis's immortal Auntie Mame to the musical stage, Herman did not take the high comic route chosen by Simon, Leigh and Coleman in *Little Me* but instead provided the lady with a selection of variously jolly and sentimental numbers, plus the boost of a title song in the 'Hello, Dolly' vein which was built up by this master of the extremely massed chorus reprise to an end befitting the 'Halleluia Chorus'. If this was rather the mixture as before, it was a flavourful mixture which found many takers.

Angela Lansbury was the musical incarnation of Mame, and she gives her rôle a fine performance on the original cast recording. She has a friendlier voice than some of the more strident *grande dames* of Broadway, making her lively numbers likeable and her one final quieter moment in the reflective 'If He Walked into my Life' most effective. If Mame comes across as rather less madcap than between bookcovers, the excess comedy is channelled into the rôles of best friend Vera (Beatrice Arthur) and secretary Agnes Gooch (Jane Connell). Miss Arthur, as all who have watched television's *Golden Girls* series will know, has a very intriguing bass-baritone voice, but the musical comedy burlesque 'The Man in the Moon (is a lady)' doesn't really take off and her tit-for-tat cattiness with Miss Lansbury in 'Bosom Buddies' ought to be funnier. The same goes for Gooch's solo, describing in gleefully unrepentant terms a plain girl's fall from innocence, on which Jane Connell exercises one of the strangest singing voices I can recall.

Both these ladies repeated their rôles in the film version, alongside Lucille Ball's Mame. The soundtrack includes nearly all the score, dropping 'That's How Young I Feel' and replacing it with a song for Robert Preston in the previously songless rôle of Mame's husband. It is a surprisingly bland song and a bland record. Surely the story of Auntie Mame is a funny story?

There was no cast recording made in London, where Ginger Rogers starred, due to financial considerations; a Mexican version with Silvia Pinal is unexceptional, and elsewhere only single songs seem to have been recorded (it is unsettling to hear the French serenading 'Mah-may'). So, although it leaves you rather unsatisfied, the original cast recording is, for the sake of Miss Lansbury, the only contender.

Dear World

After the success of *Mame*, Herman was less fortunate with his next three shows, *Dear World* (1969), *Mack and Mabel* (1974) and *The Grand Tour* (1979). Although *Dear World*, based on Giraudoux's *The Madwoman of Chaillot*, had a short run, its score – the most adventurous and characterful of Herman's works to date – makes an enjoyable record. Lansbury stars again, and has something to get her comical teeth into, even though the composer insists on ballads as her main diet and isn't quite able to give up his 'everybody join in the last time round' formula. There is a splendid Tea Party sequence in which the Countess (Miss Lansbury) and her equally dotty friends (Jane Connell and Carmen Matthews) wander conversationally through vaguely connected subjects, several of the ballads – 'I Don't Want to Know', 'I Was Beautiful' and 'Kiss Her Now' – are charming, and the atmosphere of the story, delightfully and helpfully related on the sleeve, comes clearly through the score and the recording.

Of *The Grand Tour*, based on another famous play (*Jacobowsky and the Colonel*), the same can certainly not be said, and that leaves *Mack and Mabel*.

Mack and Mabel

After Broadway failure and a considerable period of the cast album appearing in cut-out bins, *Mack and Mabel* was given a second life. Assiduously plugged by one British disc jockey on one British radio station, the score of *Mack and Mabel* gradually gained currency and finally a cult status amongst a particular group of English musical theatre devotees. Suddenly West End auditions were flooded with girls demanding throatily 'Look What Happened to Mabel', insisting that 'Time Heals Everything' and wanting to be 'Wherever He Ain't', and of actors who sing attempting 'I Won't Send Roses'. The disc came out of the cut-out bins, librettist Stewart sat down to rewrite the book, which was being blamed for not supporting this now favourite score, and the show was spoken of in hushed tones usually reserved for Weill or Sondheim.

I'm not sure I can tell now whether *Mack and Mabel* is a good show, or a good score. When you've heard something so often, you can't remember whether you like it or not, you just know that you know it. I *think* it is a good score; it certainly has some fine numbers, and even more certainly it has a very fine cast album. Robert Preston (Mack) and Bernadette Peters (Mabel) have two of the most appealing, personality-full voices ever to grace a cast recording. They radiate enough warmth between them to set a whole show alight, and that is exactly what they do. Since they have three-quarters of the score to themselves, the record is a truly memorable one. Preston makes you believe in every word he sings in that crinkly, comfortable baritone. When he tells Mabel 'I Won't Send Roses' it sounds wholly reasonable. When he declares 'I Wanna Make the World Laugh' you know that he will.

Miss Peters goes from the girlish delight of 'Look What Happened to Mabel' through the youthful lovelornness of 'I Won't Send Roses' and the passionate fury of 'Wherever He Ain't' to the wistful torchiness of 'Time Heals Everything' and makes you feel for her – no, for Mabel's – every mood. But no performers, no matter how great, can achieve all this without first-class material, so I guess that answers the earlier question. When the stars aren't weaving their magic, Lisa Kirk intrudes with the chorus and two standard old-time Broadway pieces ('Big Time', 'Tap your Troubles Away') just to bring you back to reality.

The *Mack and Mabel* cult in England resulted in the staging of a live recorded concert version at the Theatre Royal, Drury Lane, on the lines of Broadway's *Follies* effort, but, since many of the cultists are the same people who believe implicitly in the superiority of Broadway performers, many of the artists on the disc were imported from America. It is an often enjoyable if slightly incoherent representation of the show, with Jerry Herman's narration decimated presumably to allow all the songs to be fitted on to the single disc. Frances Ruffelle produces shivers with her singing of 'I Won't Send Roses', Paige O'Hara (why is she billed as Pattie?) gives a fine 'Look What Happened to Mabel' and George Hearn and Denis Quilley's introduction of what actually sounds like a group of 'Hundreds of Girls' is impressive, whilst Tommy Tune tackles the tongue-in-cheek 'Tap your Troubles Away' to the delight of a tactfully edited audience which goes wild for anything in tap shoes.

The score is all there except for 'My Heart Leaps Up', which is replaced by the cut-out 'Hit 'em on the Head', happily played by a fine (uncredited) orchestra, and well recorded under what must have been difficult circumstances. It is a fine souvenir for the members of the audience, a gift for disc jockeys, but in the end a concert which cannot compare with the cast recording.

Kander and Ebb

Cabaret

Songwriters John Kander and Fred Ebb got together on Broadway with the recently re-released score for the 1965 musical *Flora the Red Menace*, but found real success with their second collaboration, *Cabaret* (1966), a remarkable musical adaptation of *I Am a Camera*, John van Druten's stage version of Christopher Isherwood's Berlin stories with their desperate little heroine, Sally Bowles. The show had a successful run on Broadway and a lesser one in London, but the international propagation of the score of *Cabaret* was principally achieved by the 1972 film adaptation, in which Liza Minnelli and Joel Grey helped 'Cabaret', 'Maybe This Time', 'Mein Herr', 'Willkommen', 'Money, Money' and 'Two Ladies' into general circulation.

The recordings of the original stage versions are not on the whole very satisfying. The Broadway disc has Joel Grey leering persuasively at its helm, still some way from the gleeful portrait of epicene debauchery familiar to filmgoers, Lotte Lenya singing staunchly as Fräulein Schneider – the respectable face of Berlin – and Jill Haworth charging her way fairly insensitively through the rôle of Sally. London comes off slightly better, with Barry Dennen's reproduction of what Grey's performance probably developed into during the run, a less lusty Schneider from Lila Kedrova, and Judi Dench an intermittently more vulnerable Sally, sometimes showing the cracks in the girl's facade of foolish bravado.

The film version goes some distance from the original stage piece. The story is partly different, the rôle of Fräulein Schneider practically disappears, along with her four numbers, her Jewish lover and his one number, and the musical burden is placed virtually wholly on Miss Minnelli (Sally) and Grey. There are only five numbers from the original show left, plus pieces of a couple more, and 'Mein Herr' (replacing what for another artist would have been the more suitable 'Don't Tell Mama'), 'Maybe This Time' and 'Money, Money' (in place of the original 'Money Song') come in to make up a reduced but highly satisfying score.

Much of the satisfaction comes from the performance that score gets from the two stars. Grey has honed his numbers till they are like little dentist's drills, and delivers them with a spiky, salacious style that many have tried since to imitate without getting anywhere near equalling. Miss Minelli simply transforms Sally Bowles. Forget Isherwood, forget the silly, self-deceiving lass from Chelsea, London: Liza Minelli's American Sally Bowles performs her on-stage numbers with a sophisticated vigour that would have got her out of the Kit-Kat Club into a job at the Folies-Bergère in a flash, empties herself into 'Cabaret' and 'Maybe This Time' with consummate art and vocal quality, and wipes all and any competition right off the floor. I don't suppose Sally Bowles has been played as she was written since, and I don't suppose she ever will be. This is what you call taking a rôle and making it your own.

It is sad to lose such pieces as 'What Would You Do?', the breathless 'Perfectly Marvelous' and 'Why Should I Wake Up?', but the exchange is a more than worthwhile one, as all the three new songs on the soundtrack are splendid. A London revival of 1986 attempted to meld the stage and film scores together, taking in 'Maybe This Time' and the newer 'Money' but retaining 'Don't Tell Mama', in what seemed like the ideal compromise. Unfortunately the recording that was made of this production shows up a set of embarrassingly inept performances.

There is much more mileage in the only foreign-language version I have tracked down, a 1970 Viennese disc of the stage score on which Joel Grey's rôle is taken, not unsuitably, by a woman (Blanche Aubry). The piece sounds good in German, and the cast mostly have its measure. Aubry sometimes overdoes the gusto (imagine 'Two Ladies' with three ladies), but Lya Dulizkaya is an impressive Fräulein Schneider and Violetta Ferrari an adequate Sally.

Zorba

Zorba (1968) is in a different world to Cabaret. Red-blooded and vital, poignant and dramatic in turn, it is illustrated by a score which contains few 'numbers' in the accepted Broadway sense, but builds itself out of the sung narration of a Greek chorus, pieces of sung and semi-sung scenes, choruses and a handful of solos to the great advantage of both the drama and the atmosphere of the piece. The leading rôles of Zorba and Hortense, the sweet, ageing cocotte who loves him, are dramatic ones on which the vocal demands are not broad, and the big singing falls to the narrator and to the juvenile pair, acting out their tragic love story in parallel to the gently sad one of their elders.

There are four cast recordings of Zorba, all a little different in layout and content, and all giving different vocal values to the principal rôles. On the original cast album Herschel Bernardi and Maria Karnilova combine their acting with more than sufficient vocal talent, making an effective star pair, whilst Lorraine Serabian displays a searing, ethnic-sounding voice as the narrator. A 1983 revival, on the other hand, paired at its head Anthony Quinn and Lila Kedrova, the stars of the non-musical film Zorba, the Greek, sacrificing singing for what were clearly exceptional acting performances. The sacrifice is, in effect, not one, for the two actors come through triumphantly on record, and Miss Kedrova's gentle little death scene ('Happy Birthday') is enormously moving. The narrator (Debbie Shapiro) is more Tin Pan Alley than ethnic, but the other values are good and there is even an extra (unnecessary) song ('Woman') for Quinn.

A well-made Viennese recording features erstwhile *Fiddler on the Roof* star Yossi Yadin with Luise Ullrich and Dagmar Koller in a more vocally orientated version, but the recent Hungarian version with Ferenc Bessenyei featured sacrifices too much of the show's feeling to be enjoyable.

Chicago

Kander and Ebb's third important musical, *Chicago*, was called 'a musical vaudeville' by its authors, an expression that describes it pretty well. It tells its black-and-tinsel comedy story of jazz-age crime in a series of pastiche musical turns, character songs and plot numbers intermingled with the sounds and stage business of the 1920s, as Roxie Hart and her fellow murderess Velma Kelly, with the help of twinkle-toothed defence lawyer Billy Flynn, attempt to capitalize on their notoriety to make careers in show business.

Chicago was Kander and Ebb expanding the area they had dipped into with the narrator's material for *Cabaret*, and the result was a flip and funny musical, stylish and satirical, and full of first-rate numbers ranging from the raunchy 'Cell Block Tango', in which half a dozen merry murderesses relate the circumstances of the crimes they insist they didn't commit, to the hot sounds of Velma's 'All That Jazz', the cool ones of Billy's slimy creed ('All I Care About'/'Razzle Dazzle') and the tinkly jazz of Roxie's 'Funny Honey'.

The original cast recording is a splendid record of the show and the performances that helped make it a hit. Gwen Verdon is Roxie, wide-eyed as a weasel and as winning as ever, Chita Rivera is Velma, burning up the boards with her snappy jazz style, and Jerry Orbach is a perfect, ivory-smooth, three-faced Flynn who knows just how to bamboozle the world with his 'Razzle Dazzle' and a fetching baritone. The smaller rôles, all drawn just that much more colourfully than their cliché – the dragon wardress (Mary McCarty) with her baritone voice, the deeply liberal newspaperwoman (M. O'Haughey) with his coloratura soprano, Roxie's unwanted nebbish husband (Barney Martin) admitting memorably to being 'Mr Cellophane' – are equally well taken in a piece where the concept is wholly successful and both the material and the performance are exceptional.

If it weren't for the outstanding quality of the original cast disc, I'd have no hesitation in recommending the other available cast recording made by Australia's Sydney Theatre Company. Once again, the piece is well cast throughout, some splendid voices being topped by Nancye Hayes's less girlish, stronger Roxie, Geraldine Turner's vibrant, belting Velma and a genuine cabaret turn from Judy Connelli as Mama Morton. If you miss Stanley Lebowsky, his blazing Broadway band, and the stylish announcements from the bandstand in the original, there is still plenty here to get your ears into.

Kander and Ebb followed up *Chicago* with two musicals for Liza Minnelli, with whom they had had a close association over some twenty years, but *The Act* (1977) and *The Rink* (1984) joined their first Minnelli musical, *Flora, the Red Menace*, on the less successful list, along with *The Happy Time* (1968) and *70, Girls, 70* (1971) all of which scores are preserved on cast recordings. *The Rink* won a very brief London run in 1988, attracting such vocal attention from those who regretted the long absence from London stages of that Broadway institution, the glamorous older lady with the big belt voice, that a limited issue cast disc was made after the show had folded.

Charles Strouse

Charles Strouse and the Schmidt/Jones team, both of whom had put their heads into the musical theatre with no little success round the turn of the decade, were others who had further contributions to make during the 1960s and 1970s. Strouse followed *Bye, Bye, Birdie* with *All American* (1962), *Golden Boy* (1964) and *It's a Bird, It's a Plane, It's Superman* (1966), all duly recorded, before striking comparable success with his first *grande dame* musical, *Applause* (1970). A musical adaptation of the backstage drama *All About Eve*, it starred Lauren Bacall, featured a title song that caught on, and was duly exported to London. Two further musicals, *I and Albert* (1972) and *The Nightingale* (1982), were produced in London with negative results and cast recordings (the former, curiously, with as much of the personnel as could be reassembled many years later), but Strouse finally hit the big one with his collaboration with Martin Charnin on the score for *Annie* (1977).

Annie

The story of little orphan Annie and her curly-headed climb from Miss Hannigan's orphanage to Daddy Warbucks's mansion was the perfect family show. It also turned out a winsomely catchy set of songs, headed by the child's optimistic wishes for 'Tomorrow', the villains' dreams of 'Easy Street', the cute 'You're Never Fully Dressed Without a Smile' and a real wicked-witch number about 'Little Girls' for the horrid Miss Hannigan.

Annie mark 1 is the Broadway cast album. It is a lively affair with a trenchant-voiced Annie (Andrea McArdle), who just makes the top notes of 'Tomorrow', a suitably invective Miss Hannigan (Dorothy Loudon), a Daddy Warbucks who can sing (Reid Shelton) and a vigorous supporting cast. It is in all aspects better than its London equivalent, and has the edge on the other English-language disc, from Australia, which boasts an attractively less effortful Annie on the credit side and some fiddling with the score and orchestra on the debit.

The film version is a misjudged affair. Half a dozen numbers from the stage score have been given the heave-ho, including the jolly hymn to 'NYC', and four new pieces and one resuscitated one have been tacked in. They are poor stuff, glutinously orchestrated, and in consequence the classic Miss Hannigan performance given by Carol Burnett, who gurgles and shrieks her way through 'Little Girls' like a banshee on a bender, is lost amongst the debris. The film soundtrack was also issued in French, and I deeply suspect that Amélie Morin who sings Annie is not a very little girl. An uncredited French lady (note to the actors' unions – why are these people almost never credited?) makes a fair stab at imitating the inimitable Miss Burnett.

If *Annie* sounds a little odd in French, it sounds even odder in Danish, where it is played with a reduced orchestra and the most ear-splitting of Annies, but things go very much better in Spanish. Carmen Pasucal is the most appealing Annie of all. She has a voice that is not all bawl, makes a charmingly varied and no less effective job of 'Mañana', and holds her own effortlessly against the adults, who sing rather less well than she. Serenella is a gruffly spooky Miss Hannigan, but Pastor Serrador's vocal insufficiencies mar what might otherwise have been incontestably the best of all *Annies*. As it is, it is best to play safe and go with the original Broadway disc. At least you know what you are getting.

Schmidt and Jones

110 in the Shade and *I Do! I Do!*

Schmidt and Jones had no *Annie* with which to follow *The Fantasticks*, although their subsequent musicals also exist on disc. *110 in the Shade* (1963), a musical version of *The Rainmaker*, has some enjoyable numbers, such as the lively showpiece 'Rain Song', the amusing 'Poker Polka', an effective quarrel scena ('You're Not Foolin' Me') and a particularly strong and dashing-voiced leading man in Robert Horton, but it was less successful than the two-handed *I Do! I Do!* (1966), which was recorded in both its Broadway and London productions. Robert Preston and Mary Martin are more at home with this ultimately intimate musical history of an American marriage than their British counterparts (Anne Rogers and Ian Carmichael), but although its sentimentality is well judged and there is sufficient humour in the material and the performances, this fifty-year song-cycle isn't very exciting listening. *Celebration* (1969) turned back to the *Fantasticks* style without the same effect.

Marvin Hamlisch

Although fine new musicals continued to appear on Broadway through the 1970s, the decade saw few fresh and successful writers arrive to supplement the stars of the 1960s. The most notable addition to the musical forces was Marvin

Hamlisch, who moved to the theatre from the film world to create the score for the most successful Broadway musical of the decade, *A Chorus Line* (1975), and confirmed that success in no uncertain way with a splendid set of songs for the virtual two-hander *They're Playing our Song* (1979).

A Chorus Line

A Chorus Line is a backstage musical for modern times, made up of a series of portraits of the group of dancers who are auditioning for places in a show, and following their fortunes through their tryout to the final selection. The score mixes exciting dance-based ensembles and set-piece songs, all of which are built on clear, truthful, colloquial lyrics by Edward Kleban and which are a mile away from the old songwriters' inconsequentialities. The nervous thoughts of the dancers percolate through the pounding of the test dance routine in 'I Hope I Get It', three girls blend their memories of youthful dance classes as an escape from unlovely homes in perhaps the loveliest musical portion of the score ('At the Ballet'), and images and preoccupations of puberty swirl energetically together in 'Hello Twelve, Hello Thirteen, Hello Love'. Then a single character steps forward with memories of an unsympathetic teacher ('Nothing'), or of more physical worries ('Dance Ten: Looks Three') or, indeed, vocal ones ('Sing'). And so it goes on, with each number adding something and yet being enjoyable and effective on its own.

The original cast album does every musical piece full justice. There is energy and tension in every line of the ensembles, a marvellous mass of intermingled voices in 'Hello Twelve' and three girls, with the dazzling Kay Cole soaring up to the top notes, interlace plaintively in 'At the Ballet.' The solo numbers get equally fine service, whether it be in the perky comedy of Pamela Blair (Val) describing how she got 'tits and ass', Priscilla Lopez's cautionary tale of 'Nothing' or Wayne Cilento's frenetic, nervy description of his introduction to dance ('I Can Do That'). The show's take-away number, its big final ballad 'What I Did for Love', is beautifully sung by Lopez, with 'One', the audition piece that becomes the motto of the whole affair, coming close on its heels to end this shapely score on a high point. *A Chorus Line*, the longest-running musical in Broadway history, is a remarkable piece, and it has been given here a remarkable recording.

The film version, made a decade later, has none of the same impact. The soundtrack shows that songs have been rearranged, reshaped. 'Hello, Twelve' and 'Sing' have gone in favour of a piece called 'Surprise, Surprise', and the big song-and-dance solo 'The Music and the Mirror', featured with such power by Donna McKechnie in the original show, has been replaced by a different number using only a little of the original material. It would seem that this has been done to make the show more contemporary, but none of the alterations are improvements, and the orchestrations, based on what sounds like a muppet gone mad in the rhythm section, obliterate the lyrics and sometimes even the music. Since none of the players' singing voices come up to those of the stage cast, the disc has nothing to recommend it.

There is more joy in a Norwegian recording which, although it lacks the polish of the American one, gives an eager, thoughtful presentation of the score, and even in an Austrian one where there is little passion but an interesting amalgam of American style and old world voices. To hear admittedly light legitimate voices combining in 'At the Ballet' only emphasizes the beauty of that number.

They're Playing our Song

Far from the concept style of *A Chorus Line*, *They're Playing our Song* is a lively, witty comedy with songs, telling the up-and-down love story of a popular composer and his lyricist to a text by Neil Simon and a score by Hamlisch and lyricist Carol Bayer Sager. The nine numbers that make up the score were all in various popular song idioms and three of them, 'Fallin', 'Workin' it Out', 'I Still Believe in Love', are actually represented as the hit parade work of the show's two characters. All are musically and lyrically warm, funny, likeable and/or affecting, as well as fitting those characters snugly, in a score which complements its libretto perfectly.

The songs make a fine disc, even apart from the book, and the original cast recording is hugely enjoyable. Robert Klein is He, full of husky energy and personality, bopping his way crazily through 'Workin' it Out' and ruefully reflective as he hopes She may return to 'Fill in the Words', the words to his music. Lucie Arnaz is She, warm and unshowy in her singing, making her effects none the less tellingly for neither crooning nor blasting, and bringing out both the comedy and sentiment of the rôle and the songs effortlessly. All the other values are unimpeachable – the scoring, the playing and the backing vocalists who represent the actors' alter egos – although I'm not sure why it was decided to leave the very brief overture off the recording.

They're Playing our Song went round the world (although surprisingly not into the film studio), and there are five other discs as evidence. The London one (Tom Conti/Gemma Craven) is capable enough, but lacks the character and finesse of the original, whilst Australia's outstandingly successful production resulted in a rather disappointing recorded version with both John Waters and Jackie Weaver giving very lightweight performances. The contrast between Miss Weaver and Spain's Macaria is vast – where Miss Weaver twitters, the Spanish lady almost growls. Both she and her partner (Mauricio Herrera) have very individual voices which make *Están tocando nuestra canción* a droll listen.

Austria's awkwardly live-recorded *Sie spielen unser Lied* is actually better than any of these. Peter Fröhlich has both voice and personality, but his partner, Michaela Rosen, sophisticated and silky in her delivery of both music and the bits of dialogue that are included, is strangely lacking in spark. In the end, it is the Italian *Stanno suonando la nostra canzone*, with Luigi Proetti and Loretta Goggi, which comes out clearly ahead of the other foreign-language discs. Two top-class performers in a lively, well-recorded performance that brings out both comic and musical values make it a valid alternative to the original.

Stephen Schwartz

Of the other writers who found more than an isolated success during this period, Stephen Schwartz did best, making a hit with his first offering, *Godspell* (1971), and following up with *Pippin* (1972) and *The Magic Show* (1974) as well as the well-regarded if unsuccessful *The Baker's Wife* (1976).

Godspell

Godspell is a small-scale, youth-orientated piece that tells Bible tales in a series of modern-speak conversations and bouncy songs. It proved to have a quite phenomenal appeal for the young and for anyone else who could understand it, and it spread around the world to such effect that I can number on my shelves cast recordings from America, Britain, Australia (two), France, West Germany (two), South Africa (two), Kenya, Sweden, the Netherlands and Spain. There is also a film soundtrack. Youths of the 1970s will probably enjoy the original cast disc best, youths of the 1980s and 1990s will prefer the British disc, where they can find the young Jeremy Irons singing 'Prepare Ye the Way of the Lord', the young Marti Webb giving 'Bless the Lord', the young Julie Covington singing 'Day by Day' and the young David Essex in 'Alas for You' and 'Save the People', and no credit for the caster who spotted all that blossoming talent.

Pippin

Pippin is a conventional book musical, but it has some of the same feeling about it that *Godspell* has, with its jaunty words full of 1960s sentiments, its gentle pop music and its neat, well-made numbers. Several of the songs, such as the introductory 'Magic to Do' and the hero's yearning for a 'Corner of the Sky', proved to have a life beyond the show, but the burlesque humour of 'War Is a Science' and the tunefulness of 'No Time at All' and 'Spread a Little Sunshine' were more appealing than the show's more wispy moments. The original cast recording is not very impressive for, in spite of an energetic Ben Vereen ('Magic to Do'), a jolly Irene Ryan ('No Time at All') and a gently pleasant vocal performance from Jill Clayburgh, the singing is weak, notably from John Rubenstein in the show's title rôle. If you are keen to hear *Pippin*, perhaps there is more to be found in the Australian or South African versions.

The Baker's Wife

For all its tempestuous history and its failure to reach Broadway, there is much more of quality and substance to be found in *The Baker's Wife* than in *Pippin*. Given a subject and characters of depth and warmth in the Pagnol/Giono *La Femme du boulanger*, Schwartz has written here with real sincerity. He has succeeded far better than the authors of the more successful *Fanny* in composing a series of songs which, at their best, capture both the atmosphere of the piece and also the unspectacular characters of the kindly middle-aged baker, his errant wife and her village Lothario.

In 'Merci, Madame', the baker's joy at bringing his beloved wife to a new home where they can live their undemanding life together is happily drawn, whilst she sadly reflects on her unwillingness to make even a gracious response to his 'Gifts of Love'. The lover tosses off his provincial pride in 'Proud Lady', the wife sees her troubled story in the lovely tale of the 'Meadowlark', and the abandoned baker simply blinks away his realization of the cruel facts of life in 'If I Have to Live Alone'.

If some of the other recorded material is a little uneven, this is perhaps the legacy of a score that was often changed during its run. Only some of the show's bundle of in-and-out numbers are recorded on the Take Away Tunes album which features the stars of the show, Paul Sorvino, Patti LuPone and Kurt Peterson. Sorvino's gentle light baritone is effectively used, well contrasted with Peterson's more lyric tones, and Ms LuPone is particularly good when she puts the harshness right out of her voice in 'Gifts of Love' but undeniably impressive when she opens up in 'Meadowlark'. It is a fascinating recording, full of might-have-been. Listen to this one, and wonder why *The Baker's Wife* died on the road when many other musicals of much lesser quality came to town, and died all over again in London in 1989.

Hits and more Hits

Alongside the works already mentioned in this chapter, Broadway hosted and toasted a significant number of works in the 1960s and 1970s from writers whose successful contribution to the musical theatre was limited to one or maybe two works. Mitch Leigh's *Man of La Mancha* was perhaps the most notable of these, *Grease* (Jim Jacobs/Warren Casey) the most enduring, but there were other enjoyable successes in Burt Bacharach's *Promises Promises*, Sherman Edwards's *1776*, the small-scale off-Broadway *Dames at Sea* (Jim Wise) and *You're a Good Man Charlie Brown* (Clarke Gesner), *The Wiz* (Charlie Smalls) and *The Best Little Whorehouse in Texas* (Carol Hall). The Geld/Udell partnership scored twice with *Purlie* and *Shenandoah*, whilst Galt MacDermott's follow-up to *Hair* (1967) included *Two Gentlemen of Verona* (1971). All of the titles quoted here were among the many shows recorded in an era when a cast recording had become the norm for all but the most obvious flops.

Man of La Mancha

Man of La Mancha (1965) is a largely dramatic musical based on the tale of Don Quixote and set with a score of songs and ensembles, of which the largest and best part, including the show's two most successful pieces ('The Impossible Dream' a lyrical crescendo of a number expressing man's need for illusions towards which to strive, and the driving title number), fall to Quixote himself.

The original cast recording features Richard Kiley in the star rôle, and his performance is a truly classy one. Virile and dignified, with his beautiful baritone voice lending a splendid ring to the knightly numbers and a genuine warmth to the sentimental ones, he gives a definitive interpretation of his part and his music. The three other principal rôles are not all as satisfyingly taken. Robert Rounseville as the padre is splendid in his singing of the attractive 'To Each His Dulcinea', but leading lady Joan Diener (Aldonza) is extravagantly earthy and dramatic and not always very pleasant to listen to, and Irving Jacobsen (Sancho Panza) has such a funny voice that it is difficult to understand what he's saying. In fact, the lyrics suffer quite a lot, but the recording is thoroughly worth its vinyl for nothing else than Kiley's remarkable singing.

The London disc undoubtedly has the edge as an all-round record. Keith Michell's fresh, unpretentious baritone gives a different flavour to the star rôle. The heroic glory of Kiley is replaced by a less sophisticated but highly appealing vocal quality. Michell introduces us to the innocent side of Quixote and, in the final moments, he rises magnificently to his death scene without falling into melodrama, a comment that certainly cannot be applied to Miss Diener, here repeating her big Broadway performance. Bernard Spear is a cheerfully comical and characterful Sancho with no diction problems, and Alan Crofoot, even if he doesn't equal Rounseville in pure vocal magnificence, is a fine padre. In fact, one of the most enjoyable numbers on this enjoyable record is 'I'm Only Thinking of Him', in which Crofoot joins with the pure-voiced Patricia Bredin and a galumphing, fruity Olive Gilbert in a nicely pointed performance of the hypocritical trio.

In 1972 Columbia put together a high-profile cast for a studio recording of Man of La Mancha. The enterprise seems from the list of its credits as if it should work fine, but it turns out to be disappointing on most counts. TV star Jim Nabors, chosen for the lead rôle, is out of his depth with the Quixote music, Marilyn Horne (Aldonza) sings simply gloriously but paradoxically makes you long for just an ounce or two of Diener's vulgarity instead of tidily measured oratorio diction, and Jack Gilford (Sancho) has all the character but far too little voice for his lines. The best value on the record comes from former Metropolitan Opera star Richard Tucker, in splendid voice as the padre.

The soundtrack of the not-very-successful film is just inadequate. It has Peter O'Toole speaking, but not singing, Quixote, and he has been given a 'suitable' singing voice rather than a thrilling one. I don't know whether it is Sophia Loren sort-of-singing Aldonza, but if it is, that is the only excuse for it. With the two star rôles bereft of any vocal values, there isn't a lot to listen to and, since the sleeve prefers to give some splendid colour stills from the movie rather than tell you who anyone is, the supporting cast who actually can sing the remaining tampered-with parts of the score are anonymous.

The foreign-language recordings of *Man of La Mancha* are a mixed bunch. There is a not very exciting Mexican one where the Aldonza gets star billing above the Quixote, and a fairish Austrian one, but the most interesting are those from France and Germany. The French production is hugely energetic. Jacques Brel is featured as a passionate and wayward Quixote, striking into 'L'Homme de la Mancha' with wild, dramatic vigour and milking 'La Quête' with every bit of rubato possible (and some that is not) in a performance that seems to inspire Miss Diener (again) to even greater extravagances than before. There is a fine supporting cast, ranging from a chirpy uncomplicated Sancho (Jean-Claude Calon) and a smooth padre (Louis Navarre) to some attractive female soloists. The disc omits the overture and the Barber's Song but includes Quixote's confrontation scene with 'the Enchanter', which is not recorded elsewhere.

The German recording is rather more conventional and rather more even. It has Gideon Singer, also the Quixote of the Israeli recording, as a vigorous, strong-voiced leading man, equally impressive in song and speech, and Dagmar Koller giving a fair impression of a German version of Miss Diener (blonde, by the evidence of the sleeve), without the wilder excesses and with a rather more attractive voice. The Sancho goes over the top in places, and the padre's lusty tenor is a bit frayed at the edges, but 'Ich denke nur noch an ihn' (I'm Only Thinking of Him') gets its best performance here, thanks to two high-class singers (Vera Clifford, Adrienne Horusitzky) in a cast where the vocal values have been well cared for. And that is always a good thing from a record point of view.

Grease

Grease, a lively musical that amiably parodied the teenage generation of the 1950s, was a Broadway long-run record-breaker, and the original cast recording shows up its attractions. The authors have put together a score that is full of the friendly foolishness and simple tunefulness of the 1950s hit songs – the dreamy 'Summer Nights', the teenage disaster songs 'It's Raining on Prom Night' and 'Alone at a Drive-In Movie', the motor car number 'Greased Lightnin'' and the energetic all-pals-together 'We Go Together'. Put across here with youthful glee and infectious high spirits, they make up a happy, enjoyable disc. Barry Bostwick (Danny) and Carole Demas (Sandy) lead the team, he hollering his way through his numbers with all the zeal of an aspiring rocker, she catching the parody element nicely and turning on the power when needed.

Adrienne Barbeau (Rizzo) has two of the best songs – the bitchy 'Look at Me, I'm Sandra Dee', ridiculing Sandy's chocolate-box image, and the show's one serious song, 'There Are Worse Things I Could Do', in which she effectively defends her less than pure lifestyle – and she delivers them with gusto and voice, whilst Alan Paul croons out with acute humour his angelic advice to Frenchy, the 'Beauty School Dropout', to swallow her pride and go back to high school. The sum total is a recording that is both fun, particularly for those with fond memories of the 1950s, and well done.

Grease did not repeat its hometown success overseas, and a Mexican disc (under the title *Vaselina*) is the only other cast recording I have encountered, but the show had a second coming when the 1978 film version had a huge and international success. The soundtrack, issued on a double-disc set, includes most of the stage score ('Alma Mater', 'All Choked Up' and most of 'Alone at a Drive-In Movie' have gone) but also interpolates a series of songs by other writers, including the two numbers that became the film's biggest hits, John Farrar's 'Hoplessly Devoted to You' and 'You're the One That I Want'. Both are in the tone of the film, which is altogether less parodic than the stage show, although another new song, 'Sandy' (written by Louis St Louis, the musical director and arranger of the original show to replace 'Alone at a Drive-In Movie') catches the burlesque tone more obviously. The one piece that simply does not fit is the unimpressive new title song by Barry Gibb, which is much more 1970s than 1950s. As if that weren't enough in the way of music, there is also a handful of old songs, ranging from 'Blue Moon' to 'Hound Dog', delivered by the group Sha-Na-Na, helping to fill the four sides available.

John Travolta (Danny) and Olivia Newton-John (Sandy) perform attractively, he with more cocky smoothness than Bostwick, she much more the gentle ingénue until her moment comes in the final reel; Stockard Channing is a tough and effective Rizzo; and the real thing, in the person of 1950s star Frankie Avalon, coos out 'Beauty School Dropout' quite beautifully. Elsewhere the dubbers move in. To many people, *Grease* is epitomized by Travolta and Miss Newton-John and by Farrar's two film songs, but to those coming to the show with a clear mind I would unhesitatingly recommend the stage disc, which has a vigour and a presence not so much in evidence on the soundtrack, a performance not diluted by a complete side of Sha-Na-Na, and less 1970s overemphasis on the thumping bass.

1776

Sherman Edwards's *1776* went back a good deal further than the 1950s for its action – to the signing of the American Declaration of Independence. This may seem an unlikely subject for a musical, but the result is a pleasant and clever show and score, with a lot of what could have been very faceless Congressmen deftly delineated as interesting and even amusing characters, and a neat balance maintained between the personal and historical elements involved. Little of the score is in the nature of extractable songs, although the pretty waltz 'He Plays the Violin', in which Martha Jefferson explains her taciturn husband's attractions, is the most obvious of the individual items, but there are effective set pieces for the rather buffoonish Richard Henry Lee ('The Lees of Old Virginia'), the vehement Edward Rutledge ('Molasses to Rum') and, showing the real effect of the war against England, away from the talking-shop of Congress, a moving little song for an unnamed courier telling of a friend's uncomplicated death on the field ('Momma, Look Sharp'). Elsewhere, Congress choruses and John Adams keeps up a longing and exasperated correspondence with his wife, Abigail, in conversational duet, both to good effect.

There are two original cast recordings of this show, from Broadway and London, and it is difficult to choose between them on merit. Both give the score good service and each has its high spots. The American disc has strong, splendid singers in Clifford David (Rutledge), Ron Holgate (Lee) and Betty Buckley (Martha), but the British one has an incomparably better Congress, a rich, crackly Benjamin Franklin (Ronald Radd), a delicious teenage-sounding Martha (Cheryl Kennedy) and more vocal values from Lewis Fiander in the important rôle of Adams. The vocal sum total comes out just in favour of the latter, but there is sometimes an indefinable something lacking dramatically. I thought, perhaps, it might be the fact of English accents on such a very American subject, but then remembered that in 1776 Americans didn't have American accents.

The 1972 Columbia film featured Daniels, DaSilva, Howard and Holgate from the Broadway show alongside Virginia Vestoff and Blythe Danner in the feminine rôles, and included most, but not all, of the score.

Promises, Promises

Promises, Promises (1968), a musical based on the film *The Apartment*, was another to have an impressive Broadway run as well as some overseas success. Like *How to Succeed in Business Without Really Trying*, it centres on a young man trying to make his way up in the business world, and this particular young man's method is based on lending his bachelor apartment to his superiors for their extra-marital affairs.

Unlike the Loesser musical, this one does not come over as well on record as on the stage. There is less character, less humour, and the songs, with their use of angel voices and fadeouts and orchestrations heavy on the cymbals and drums, sound as if they belong to another medium – film, television or the popular song market – rather than the musical theatre. Given the film, television and popular song background of writers Hal David and Burt Bacharach, this is understandable. The most enjoyable moment is the delightfully silly office Christmas party song-and-dance 'Turkey Lurkey Time', and the most successful number the significantly simple guitar-accompanied 'I'll Never Fall in Love Again', which became hit parade material in the hands of Bobbie Gentry.

There are cast recordings from New York, London and Italy (*Promesse, promesse*). Of the two English-language discs, the Broadway one is the better, with Jerry Orbach singing in his usual attractive style as an easy, convincing young hero on the make and Edward Winter energetically using his fine, strong baritone as the randy big boss. Jill O'Hara, as the heroine after whom both of them lust, is tempted by her material into doing things to her twenty-one-year-old voice which probably explain why she's not been heard of since. 'Turkey Lurkey Time' gets a great send off, and a quartet of itchy businessmen give plenty of vigour to the rather distasteful 'Where Can You Take a Girl?'.

The prize for charm, however, goes hands down to the Italian disc, a truncated recording featuring only the ten numbers in which Johnny Dorelli and Catherine Spaak were involved. He cruises very pleasantly through his numbers, and she, not having the vocal equipment of Miss O'Hara or Betty Buckley on the London recording, instead invests her part with a warm femininity which, over the less rowdy orchestrations used here, is most agreeable.

Dames at Sea

There was plenty of fun in both *Dames at Sea* and *You're a Good Man, Charlie Brown*, both of which had successful seasons off-Broadway and continued their careers overseas. *Dames at Sea* (1968) is to the 1930s what *Chrysanthemum* and *The Boyfriend* were to earlier decades and *Grease* to a later one, a loving and lovable re-creation of the musical and theatrical (and, in this case, movie) styles and foibles of a bygone era. There are multiple echoes of *42nd Street* (the show's hero and heroine are even called Dick and Ruby) and other such pieces, and of many a favourite, familiar song, including a marvellous parody of the torch song in 'That Mr Man of Mine', the heroine's infinitely ingenuous 'Raining in my Heart' and 'The Sailor of my Dreams', the ghastly tale of what befell 'Singapore Sue' and a gem of a do-you-remember 'Beguine' in a score that is full of lyrics and tunelets that are cute but never twee.

New York and London both issued cast albums of the score but, in spite of Sheila White's sublimely 'kewpie-doopie' heroine on the UK disc, the American recording is the better. Bernadette Peters is adorable as Ruby, gasping out her wide-eyed numbers and never going over the edge of loving parody, and David Christmas is equally attractive as her sailor-songwriter lover, whilst Tamara Long wallops out her torch song, taps herself to death in 'Wall Street' and hurtles the 'Beguine' back at Steve Elmore's comical Captain with raucous energy. The cast of six all give happy, pointed performances, the tiny orchestra supports with Jonathan Tunick's delightfully characterful arrangements, and a good time is had by all.

A 1989 British tour (reorchestrated and with a cast of eight) recorded by TER has a comical cover with notes by author Robin Miller which catches the eye, but the performance doesn't catch the fond flavour of the piece in the same way the earlier discs do.

You're a Good Man, Charlie Brown

Whereas *Dames at Sea* developed from an even smaller-scale show, *You're a Good Man, Charlie Brown* (1967) evolved from a 1966 concept album. By the time the piece reached the stage, the ten little numbers that comprised this original disc had been supplemented by a couple more, and the resulting cast recording topped up the light-music content of the show by including two spoken scenes. It is a fresh and wholly endearing record, cute in a totally different way from *Dames at Sea*, each spoken and sort-of-sung piece a little Peanuts picture-strip on its own. There is Charlie Brown trying hopelessly to fly his kite or relating the terrible tale of the lost baseball game, Snoopy the dog daydreaming of heroics against the world war flying ace the Red Baron, or, more prosaically, of 'Suppertime', loudmouth Lucy dispensing hideously inaccurate 'Little Known Facts' or declaring her intentions to be a Queen when she grows up, and little Linus making a brave attempt to abandon his inseparable blanket. It is sweetly hilarious to listen to the Peanuts gang trying to write a 'Book Report' for homework and heartwarming to hear them sing of 'Happiness' in words and music that perfectly capture the spirit of the famous comic strip.

The cast recording claims, on the sleeve of the British pressing, to be recorded live, but there doesn't seem to be any evidence of this. All the players bring their characters to life beautifully – which in this piece is altogether more important than being able to sing the few-note range of the music – making an enjoyable and unusual show recording. The 1972 TV soundtrack has basically the same content, though Lucy's Queen scene and the Peanuts pot-pourri are omitted and some other fragments included instead. The piece hasn't been souped up too much for television, but one or two of the performances are a little less appealing than on the stage disc.

The Best Little Whorehouse in Texas

The Best Little Whorehouse in Texas (1978) was another small-scale musical which grew sufficiently to end up in a Broadway house and, subsequently and excessively, in London's Theatre Royal, Drury Lane. A satirical, topical piece aiming its barbs mostly at media and political hypocrisy, it charted the attempts of a self-important television personality to get a small-town Texas brothel closed down on moral grounds, illustrating its very funny and sometimes moving book with a score of pleasantly natural country-styled numbers by Carol Hall. Far from the *grandes dames* and slickness of the biggest theatres, Hall's warm, smooth, colloquial and often funny lyrics and gently catchy melodies provide the basis for a really enjoyable cast recording.

From the moment the scene is set by the locally coloured leader of the six-piece band that accompanies the show, describing the history of the Chicken Ranch where Miss Mona and her girls operate ('Twenty Fans'), the songs introduce a character or set the story on its way with an attractive ease and, although sex is at the base of the whole tale, it never breaks in at snigger level. *The Best Little Whorehouse in Texas* is about business. At the head of the cast, Carlin Glynn is Miss Mona, singing her songs with a strong, no-nonsense personality and a warm country voice that never overwhelms the material, particularly affecting as she comforts a new recruit ('Girl, You're a Woman') or thinks back to her early days ('The Bus From Amarillo'). Elsewhere there are excellent numbers for the adenoidal, inhibited waitress who longs to have the courage to be more adventurous ('Doatsy Mae') and for the double-talking politician ('The Side-Step'), both of which get superb comic performances from Susan Mansur and Jay Garner respectively. There is also a youthfully aggressive 'Aggie Song' for a bunch of footballers looking forward to their first visit to the whorehouse, and a touching farewell ('Hard Candy Christmas') as the girls leave their banned home to go their separate ways. Perhaps the most impressive of all, however, is the warmly practical summing up of the town's sheriff (the superb Henderson Forsyth), regretting what has happened to the 'Good Old Girl' who was almost his lover.

The company nature of the piece is purposefully advertised by listing the cast on the sleeve without their rôles, but they have a point here. It doesn't really matter who they are. All the performers of the original *The Best Little Whorehouse in Texas* come across with a humanity and naturalness that light up the material they have to deliver.

Just how good they are is shown up by the film soundtrack. Burt Reynolds and Dolly Parton star, and the lady chucks out most of Ms Hall's songs in favour of a couple of dogs of her own. There are half a dozen of the original numbers left, and many fewer reasons to bother with this record.

The Wiz

The Wiz (1974) also suffered from being made into a film, but it did leave behind a sufficiently good original cast album to give it a fair and proper representation. This all-black version of *The Wizard of Oz* is a super-lively affair with a rocky, jazzy, gospelly score by Charlie Smalls, played and sung in a vibrant, edgy, electric-sounding manner by a rip-roaring cast of singers.

Stephanie Mills is Dorothy and, like that more familiar Dorothy – Judy Garland – the voice she turns on to her rôle is no child's voice. It is a strong, compact, clear, modern pop voice which copes with the wide demands of her final ballad, 'Home', effortlessly and picks up the energetic hustling of 'Ease on Down the Road' (this show's equivalent of 'Follow the Yellow Brick . . .') with crisp vigour. There isn't a lot of innocence to be heard, but there's plenty of singer.

There are other fine performances and songs: Ted Ross as the richly funny cowardly lion tops the list ('I'm a Mean Ol' Lion'), Tiger Haynes as the tin man oozes his way through 'Slide Some Oil to Me', André de Shields comes on as a slinky Wizard, Mabel King as the horrid Evillene has a merry, dark-voiced tantrum with 'Don't Nobody Bring Me No Bad News', and Dee Dee Bridgewater gives welcome warmth to the good Glinda's 'If You Believe'. There are one or two songs that show up a little as padding (Aunt Em's long-winded vocalizing in 'The Feeling We Once Had' and a rather 'rumpty' everybody-be-happy chorus), and the pop techniques in backing and fading sometimes sit a bit uncomfortably, but as a whole the recording is a vigorous, energetic and enjoyable one. No one sleeps while this is on.

Purlie

The Wiz had been preceded in 1970 by another largely black musical in *Purlie*, the work of composer Gary Geld and lyricist Peter Udell. The show had a good run but has not confirmed itself in the most popular repertoire. Having not seen the show on stage, I can only assume that what seems, from the synopsis on the cast recording sleeve, to be a rather straggly plot with incessant mentions of that overworked 1960s word 'freedom', must have been at fault, for the score and the original cast recording are both quite remarkable.

The first side opens with a magnificent crescendo of a gospel chorus, 'Walk Him up the Stairs', featuring a soloist (Linda Hopkins) with a voice that would skin rabbits and a thrilling choral sound, then moves on to introduce our hero, Purlie (Cleavon Little), a virile, punchy, characterful 'New Fangled Preacher Man', his deliciously weaselly sounding brother (Sherman Hemsley), who wriggles out of direct action by declaring 'There's More Than One Way of Skinnin' a Cat' and, best of all, little Lutiebelle, the girl who is the lynchpin in Purlie's plot to rip off the devilish white overlord of the area. Lutiebelle is played by Melba Moore, who is possessed of a voice that is nothing short of glorious – powerful yet not hard, rich and fresh, skittering through all its registers from ringing chest tones to zinging top notes. She has two marvellous songs in her admission of love for 'Purlie' and her jubilant, joyous showpiece 'I Got Love', and she flings herself into them with staggering ease.

The gems don't stop there, either. The villain of the piece explaining to his would-be songwriter son the laws of natural selection ('Big Fish, Little Fish'), the boy's clumsy efforts to write a folksong ending in the final scenes with success with the happy 'The World Is Coming to a Start', Purlie's staunch 'The Bigger They Are the Harder They Fall' and the cotton-pickers' procrastinatory chorus 'First Thing Monday Morning' are all hugely enjoyable. It is splendid stuff and helps to prove that all the best recordings don't necessarily come from the most famous and longest-running shows. This is one of the very best of Broadway records.

Shenandoah

Geld and Udell had a longer run with *Shenandoah* (1975) and it, too, is the subject of a fine recording. *Shenandoah* is an unfashionable musical with those who write about musicals. It is a deeply sentimental piece with a homely feel to it, a score that sings about 'Violets and Silverbells' and 'sugar and cinnamon', and introduces a little black boy and a little white boy singing a duet, and so forth: what the sophisticates would call 'corny'. Corny it may be, but it gave me a little weep in the theatre in one of the more than a thousand performances of its Broadway run, and even the recording alone can bring up a lump. It's a little more difficult for those who have not seen the show, as the sleeve gives no synopsis. The little boys' duet loses much of its point if you don't know who they are, and, as the dramatic Civil War events of the second act are not related in song, you lose the point of the final numbers.

The central performance is that of John Cullum as the humanitarian Virginia farmer who tries not to become involved in the wasteful foolishness of war. His thoughts and his principles are worked into a series of effective monologues, which form the ossature of the score, and Cullum's fine baritone helps give authority and sincerity to their delivery. There is drama and pathos, too, in the song of a young soldier (Gary Harger) heading his way home to the South through the ruined countryside, simply because it is 'The Only Home I Know', but there are plenty of more lively moments to contrast with these more serious elements.

Penelope Milford, mooning over a backward lover, turns a lusty charm on her lilting worry that she will soon be 'Over the Hill' and joins with another attractive singer in Donna Theodore in the catchy country strains of 'We Make a Beautiful Pair', whilst youngster Chip Ford shares two lively if lyrically obvious pieces – the winsome kids' duet 'Why Am I Me?' and a swinging hymn to the inevitable 'Freedom'. All the players sing well, catching the southern and period flavours effectively and without exaggeration, and representing the score in fine fashion.

Hair

Hair is a difficult piece to deal with. It is less a show, much less a recording and more a phenomenon then anything else. An eclectic collection of characters, chunks of dialogue, musical fragments and a group of songs strung together on a spider's web of a story, it is simply a hotch-potch declaration or celebration of the preoccupations of the 'make love not war' generation of the American 1960s. That it should have had the enormous success it did on its first showing in America (helped considerably by some unaccustomed nudity) is one thing; that it should have survived through repeated showings all round the world over the next twenty years, whether as a period piece or not, is another, and one which earns it a place alongside the other major Broadway shows of the 1960s.

Given the nature of the score, what I find even more surprising is the huge number of cast recordings that have been made world-wide. Many of the long list of pieces itemized on the sleeves of these records are little more than fragments, ranging from tiresome catalogues of 'naughty' words, whether on sex, drugs or race, to atmospheric bits which seem to me to mean little or nothing out of context. The principal songs – in the generally accepted meaning of the word – which come along at intervals include the winsome 'Aquarius' (which became the hymn of *Hair*'s people), but there are more substantial pieces such as the plaintive 'Easy to Be Hard', the jolly 'White Boys/Black Boys' sequence and, my own favourite, the unrhymed 'Frank Mills', a sympathetic tale of unfortunate love which is rather like a modern version of the Joyce Grenfell Hampton Court maze sketch.

Hair has always been a very mobile entertainment. Its original off-Broadway version, which was recorded, included all the principal numbers, but the show was heavily revamped before presentation on Broadway and a considerable list of musical bits and pieces was added, including the finale 'Let the Sun Shine In', and the resultant new version, with its up-town cast, re-recorded.

This second disc, which includes almost all the material which was used in the Broadway production, can fairly be considered to be the standard *Hair*, if such a thing exists. Its cast, including authors Gerome Ragni and James Rado (and rather less of Melba Moore and Diane Keaton), enter into the spirit of the piece with alternate vigour and fashionable languorousness, and Lynn Kellogg and Sally Plimpton take their chances in the biggest numbers with power and delicacy respectively.

Later in the run, members of the cast took part in a further recording, under the title 'DisinHAIRited', which included most of the other material written for the two versions of the show and either cut or not recorded on the Broadway disc. This process was also followed in London, where the principal cast album (with Paul Nicholas, Oliver Tobias, Peter Straker and Annabel Leventon) was supplemented by 'Fresh Hair' (where Elaine Paige joins the company), both discs containing a little less material than their American equivalents.

The film soundtrack, which stretches its material over two records, contains basically the same selection as the Broadway cast album. John Savage, Beverley D'Angelo and Treat Williams star in a recording which, coming more than ten years after the original stage production, manages to maintain much of the feeling of the piece, even if the technical skills in evidence make it all sound a bit sanitized.

On the other discs, the selection varies, with various pieces of the score floating in and out of what was an equally unstable book. Australia contributes one more English-language *Hair*, but otherwise there is a choice between versions from Finland, Brazil (in Portuguese), France, Israel, Denmark, Norway, Sweden, Japan, the Netherlands, Italy and Mexico. There are also no less than three different German versions, including one in which the cast includes Donna Summer (née Gaines) and one double-disc set with dialogue (*Das ganze Hair*).

Two Gentlemen of Verona

Two Gentlemen of Verona (1971) is a more conventional book musical. A modern-language version of Shakespeare's play, it is illustrated with a lengthy score of light and enjoyable pop music of considerably more scope than *Hair*. The lyrics, relaxed and very much of the period and mileu, are effectively combined with the melodies and their arrangements in a score that becomes a little incoherent when listened to without the aid of a synopsis. Quite why there is neither a synopsis nor a cast list on the original cast double disc is a puzzle, since the sleeve is a triptych affair full of photos and excess art-work. Perhaps the producers assume a working knowledge of Shakespeare.

Whereas the American cast recording includes the whole score, the London version (which takes in one new number) is limited to one disc and thus covers only a selection.

My Ten Essential Records

HELLO, DOLLY!: original French cast recording, with Annie Cordy (CBS 65115)
FUNNY GIRL: original cast recording, with Barbra Streisand (CBS BOS3220)
FIDDLER ON THE ROOF: film soundtrack, with Topol (United Artists UAD 60011)
DO I HEAR A WALTZ?: original cast recording, with Sergio Franchi and Elizabeth Allen (Columbia KOL 6370)
SWEET CHARITY: original cast recording, with Gwen Verdon (Columbia KOL 6500); CD (Columbia CK 2900)
CABARET: film soundtrack, with Liza Minnelli and Joel Grey (ABC ABCD752); CD (MCA 250 428–2)
A LITTLE NIGHT MUSIC: original cast recording, with Len Cariou and Glynis Johns (Columbia KS 32265); CD (Columbia CK 32265)
A CHORUS LINE: original cast recording, with Priscilla Lopez (Columbia PS 33581); CD (Columbia CK 33581)
ON THE TWENTIETH CENTURY: original cast recording, with John Cullum and Madeleine Kahn (Columbia 35330)
PURLIE: original cast recording, with Cleavon Little and Melba Moore (Ampex A-40101)

Other Recommended Records

Carnival: original cast recording, with Anna Maria Aberghetti and Jerry Orbach (MGM E/SE3946 OC)
How to Succeed in Business Without Really Trying: French cast recording (*Comment réussir dans les affaires sans vraiment se fatiguer*), with Jacques Duby and Evelyne Dandry (Philips 77.988 L); or London cast recording, with Warren Berlinger and Patricia Michael (RCA Victor RD-7564)
A Funny Thing Happened on the Way to the Forum: original cast recording, with Zero Mostel (Capitol WAS/SWAO 1717)
Little Me: original cast recording, with Sid Caesar and Virginia Martin (RCA LOC/LSO 1078)
Man of La Mancha: original cast recording, with Richard Kiley (Kapp KL4505/KS5505); CD (MCAD 31065); or original London cast recording, with Keith Michell (MUPS-334 or MUCS-123)
You're a Good Man, Charlie Brown: original off-Broadway cast recording (MGM 1E/S1E-9 OC); CD (Polydor 820 262–2 Y-1)
Hair: original Broadway cast recording (RCA LOC/LSO 1150)
Zorba: revival cast recording, 1983, with Anthony Quinn and Lila Kedrova (RCA ABL1–4732); CD (RCA RCD1 4732)
Dames at Sea: original off-Broadway cast recording, with Bernadette Peters and David Christmas (Columbia OS 3330)

1776: London cast recording, with Lewis Fiander (Columbia SCX6424)

Company: original cast recording, with Dean Jones (Columbia OS 3550); CD (Columbia CK 3550)

Follies: live concert recording, 1985, with Barbara Cook, Lee Remick, Mandy Patinkin and George Hearn (RCA HBC2–7128); CD (RCA RCD2–7128)

Godspell: London cast recording, with David Essex, Marti Webb and Jeremy Irons (Bells 203)

Grease: original cast recording, with Barry Bostwick, Carol Demas and Adrienne Barbeau (MGM 1SE-34 OC); CD (Polydor 827 548–2)

See-saw: original cast recording, with Michelle Lee and Ken Howard (Buddah BDS 95006); CD (CDRG 6108)

Dear World: original cast recording, with Angela Lansbury (Columbia BOS 3260)

Mack and Mabel: original cast recording, with Robert Preston and Bernadette Peters (ABC H830)

The Wiz: original cast recording, with Stephanie Mills and Ted Ross (Atlantic SD 18137)

Shenandoah: original cast recording, with John Cullum (RCA ARL1–1019); CD (RCA 3763-2-RG)

Chicago: original cast recording, with Gwen Verdon, Chita Rivera and Jerry Orbach (Arista AL9005)

I Love my Wife: original cast recording, with Lenny Baker (Atlantic SD 19107); CD (DRG CDRG 6109)

Annie: original cast recording, with Dorothy Loudon, Reid Shelton and Andrea McArdle (Columbia PS 34712); CD (Columbia CK 34712)

The Best Little Whorehouse in Texas: original cast recording, with Carlin Glynn and Henderson Forsythe (MCA 3049)

They're Playing our Song: original cast recording, with Robert Klein and Lucie Arnaz (Casablanca NBLP7141); CD (826240-2-M)

Sweeney Todd: original cast recording, with Len Cariou and Angela Lansbury (RCA CBL2–3379); CD (RCA 3379-2-RC)

Barnum: London cast recording, with Michael Crawford (Air CDL 1348)

The Baker's Wife: studio cast recording, with Paul Sorvino, Kurt Peterson and Patti LuPone (THT 772)

CHAPTER 9

Thirty Years of British Musicals, 1950–1980

In spite of its vigorous track record in the world of show music under the régime of the 78 rpm disc, Britain was much slower than America to move forward into the era of the long-playing record. Whereas Columbia had issued both the 1946 Broadway revival of *Show Boat* and the original cast recording of *Finian's Rainbow* on LPs in June 1948, it was 1954 before the first long-playing recordings of new London shows appeared – *The Boyfriend* (HMV) and *Wedding in Paris* (Parlophone) on ten-inch discs, Coward's *After the Ball* (Philips) and *Salad Days* (Oriole) on twelve-inch. The presence of two such enormous hits as *The Boyfriend* and *Salad Days* amongst the earliest show LPs can only have helped the new type of record establish itself, and in the same way that the original cast recording had caught on in America, long-playing records of the newest shows quickly became an effective and popular part of the theatrical and recording business. The ten-inch format was soon abandoned – the HMV issue of the flop musical *Wild Grows the Heather* in 1956 was the last of such records – and although the occasional lesser show contented itself with the issue of 45 rpm singles or extended-play records, the twelve-inch LP became the standard cast album.

Musicals from the Old Masters

The pre-war style in musical theatre had by now had its day, and even the most important of the writers who had supplied its scores had given their best work. Vivian Ellis had just one final venture with *The Water Gipsies* (1955), but Coward, among his many other activities, submitted *After the Ball* (1954) to London, *The Girl Who Came to Supper* (1963) to New York and *Sail Away* (1962) to both. All three of these differently styled works were confided to record.

After the Ball

After the Ball, a romantic operetta version of Wilde's *Lady Windermere's Fan*, is, on record, a mixture of enjoyable highlights and what can only be called less enjoyable parts. Most of the happiest pieces of this score are the incidentals, and almost all are the satirical portions: Graham Payn, as the Australian Mr Hopper, shocking a London society gathering with his tongue-in-cheek tale of his wild and woolly origins; Irene Browne (Duchess of Berwick) growling out her ageing longings for 'Something on a Tray' at the end of each tiring day; or three classy soprano ladies (Pam Marmont, Lois Green, Marion Grimaldi) singing their way with twittering matter-of-factness through Coward's witty and bitter lyrics on a man's right to adultery in 'Why Is it Always the Woman Who Pays?'.

The lyrical musical is attractive, with Lady Windermere's lovely 'Clear, Bright Morning', beautifully sung by the precise and pure soprano of Vanessa Lee, registering as the outstanding solo, and a charming duet 'I Knew That You Would Be My Love' with Peter Graves (Lord Windermere) the most enjoyable of the rest.

The big disappointment of the stage show was Mary Ellis's Mrs Erlynne, and the record shows why. The fine voice of *Glamorous Night* is, to put it bluntly, shot, and what remains here of her rôle are two unimpressive numbers distressingly shakily performed. The other casting disaster of *After the Ball* was Irish tenor Shamus Locke as Darlington. His only remaining solo, 'Stay on the Side of the Angels', although referred to on the sleeve, was ultimately not included on the record. There are, nevertheless, one or two fairly awful numbers amongst the remainder, but the best bits and the assured performances of Miss Lee, Graves and Payn make up for them.

Sail Away

Sail Away, a generally more successful piece, lost its soprano star in a rewrite on the road and thus, almost by accident, Coward finally came somewhere near writing the revusical musical comedy for which his talents so clearly fitted him. The show has a modern setting, a brash, tart heroine and a lot of the satirically drawn middle-class folk whom Coward always sketched so acutely. All the opportunities were there and they were gleefully taken: *Sail Away*'s score includes four outstanding comedy numbers, as well as a couple of pleasing ballads for the leading man.

Coward himself put most of the *Sail Away* score on record for Capitol, but the two principal recordings are those made by the Broadway and London casts. Both these star Elaine Stritch, both include Grover Dale in the juvenile rôle, but there are several small differences in the lyrics and one alteration to the score: where the Broadway disc includes the number 'The Little One's ABC', the London version uses 'Bronxville Darby and Joan'. All else being equal, this means the London recording has to be preferred, as this last, perceptive song is one of the gems of the show, particularly as performed by Sydney Arnold and sixty-six-year-old Edith Day, hissing comfortably at each other 'We're a dear old couple, and we hate one another . . .'

Elaine Stritch gives a big, gutsy comedy performance as ship's hostess Mimi Paragon. She is particularly successful in her encounter with one of those ghastly booklets that teach you 'Useful Phrases' in your preferred foreign language, and in flinging herself extravagantly both into a woeful plaint of job dissatisfaction in 'Why Do the Wrong People Travel (and the right people stay back home)' and a baleful warning to a shipload of Americans ready to swarm over the inconveniences of Europe, 'You're a Long, Long Way from America'.

David Holliday sings rather a lot of ballads of which the gentle 'Don't Turn Away From Love' and the title song, 'Sail Away', lifted from *Ace of Clubs*, are the most agreeable. But the male honours are pilfered by John Hewer in a dual rôle as the ship's purser and an Arab Fagin singing two very funny versions of 'The Passenger's Always Right', the first instructing his coven of stewards in the obligations of their job, the second organizing a motley band of thieves, beggars and pimps to supply the arriving tourists with whatever their heart (or any other part of their body) may desire.

As in *After the Ball*, not all parts are as good as the best parts, but once again there is more than enough fine, funny material here to make the record more than a little worthwhile.

The Girl Who Came to Supper

The same, alas, cannot be said for *The Girl Who Came to Supper*. This musical version of Rattigan's *The Prince and the Showgirl* comes across as a feeble imitation of *My Fair Lady*. José Ferrer is the princely gentleman, Florence Henderson the common girl whom he doesn't in the end get, whilst Tessie O'Shea supplies the cockney knees up. The score is a pale shadow of real Coward, and the recording never really comes to life unless you are enthused by the hatchet-voiced Miss O'Shea doing what amounts to a quarter of an hour's cabaret act, including several goes at 'London Is a Little Bit of All Right', 'What Ho! Mrs Brisket', 'Don't Take Our Charlie For the Army' and 'Saturday Night at the Rose and Crown'. Miss Henderson, a tough little lady with a firm Broadway soprano, gets her chance to do her turn in the second act with an insufficiently funny potted burlesque of an Edwardian musical comedy, but Ferrer wanders unhappily through his songs as if aware that it is all a bit misbegotten.

A Wedding in Paris

Amongst the other shows whose inspiration came largely from pre-war sources, the small-scale *Romance by Candlelight*, with a score by American songwriter Sam Coslow, disappeared quickly, leaving for trace only a now rare but still undistinguished EP of four songs, but the lively *A Wedding in Paris*, with a score by the Viennese expatriate Hans May, proved an attractive piece which also made an attractive record. It is a ten-inch disc, and not that easy nowadays to find, containing eight numbers which it is still old-fashioned enough to call 'vocal gems'.

This is not technically the very best recording of its time, but the songs – a fetching blend of Vienna, the London Hippodrome and Hollywood – are an enjoyable little group. The star pair, Anton Walbrook and Evelyn Laye, have two songs apiece. She sings hers with elegance and a well-preserved voice, and he speaks his in suave, accented tones which make a particular success of the *roué*'s creed 'Strike Another Match'. The juvenile pair, soprano Susan Swinford and Jeff Warren – the possessor of a very attractive light baritone – perform the other numbers, including a particularly happy duet, 'I Have Nothing to Declare', and a charming waltz-time title song. *Wedding in Paris* may not have been a blockbuster, but its score and this recording are a pleasant way to pass a half-hour if you are lucky enough to dig up a copy.

Wild Grows the Heather

There are also pleasant things to be found in the much less successful and equally scarce *Wild Grows the Heather*, a musical adaptation of J. M. Barrie's *The Little Minister*, with a score by pre-war showman and composer Joe Waller and his musical amanuensis Joe Tunbridge. There is a touch of *Brigadoon* in its determined Scottishness and a slice of culture shock when the little minister bursts into 'He's Got the Whole World in his Hands' as a finale, but there is first-rate singing from a cast and massed chorus headed by Bill O'Connor, Valerie Miller and soubrette Eira Heath. The atmospheric and melodious title song, in particular, shows that Waller and Tunbridge – composers of many successful shows – were better than the hack writers they are too often rated.

With the pre-war musical on its way out and the big new products of Broadway occupying most of London's major theatres, the next era of British musicals took root in the small club and repertory theatres. Small-scale shows, where the lack of production values necessarily threw more attention on to the writing, these pieces brought forth a new generation of musical theatre writers. From the Bristol Old Vic came Julian Slade, from the Players' and Watergate club theatres Sandy Wilson, from the Unity and the Mermaid Lionel Bart, and from Windsor Julian More, who soon paired with Monty Norman and David Heneker; from all of these men came the shows that were the London successes of the following decades.

Julian Slade

Salad Days

Slade's early promises with his revue *Christmas in King Street* and the music for Sheridan's *The Duenna* quickly led to his most successful and enduring show, the light-hearted and revusical *Salad Days*, which broke all London long-run records with its transfer from Bristol to the Vaudeville Theatre in 1954. The show's success encouraged a number of cheap label studio cast recordings, but apart from a 45 EP made from the original Australian production, only two cast recordings of *Salad Days* exist – the original 1954 LP and a version made by That's Entertainment Records in 1982, which brought back together most of the members of a 1976 West End revival. The two recordings are somewhat different in approach, and which of the two you prefer is rather conditioned by the way you like your *Salad Days* served up.

The original cast recording, featuring a group of actors mostly with limited singing talents, plays a dozen numbers from the show as they were written to be performed, with the simplicity and unpretentious charm that were a good part of the reason for the show's great success. There are no big performances, no expansive characterizations, no musical effects, just an end-of-term romp played for good, straightforward, light fun. The one member of the cast who is called on to sing significantly is Eleanor Drew (Jane), who is given the heroine's two charming lyric solos, 'I Sit in the Sun', in which she ponders her mother's efforts to get her married, and the lovely waltz 'The Time of My Life'. It is hard to imagine either these or any of the rest of Jane's music being better or more aptly sung, for Miss Drew has a sweet, true soprano and an actress's care for words which combine in a lovely performance. James Cairncross has the most to do otherwise, switching deftly from lofty in the governmental 'Hush-Hush' to louche in the naughty tale of 'Cleopatra', and John Warner gets a little more music than masculinity (but not a lot of either) into his duets with Miss Drew.

The revival recording is a rather souped-up *Salad Days*. The two-piano accompaniment has apparently been rearranged, filled up with extraneous flourishes and thumping, and is played for all the world as if it were trying to pretend that it wasn't a two-piano accompaniment. The vocal lines, too, have been heavily rearranged, resulting, in one or two cases, in amusing and effective moments, but too often in a muddy, overwritten sound which is the antithesis of what *Salad Days* is at its best.

If these are the drawbacks, however, there are more than sufficient gains to palliate them. Nearly thirty years on, the show is given a much more accomplished recording and performed, in line with modern tastes, in a much more characterful way. There is also more material on this record for, by cutting out the linking dialogue and the final medley of reprises of the original cast recording, room has been made for the inclusion of the burlesque cabaret song 'Sand in my Eyes' and the mothers' lament 'We Don't Understand our Children', as well as for a fuller version of the hectoring parental 'Find Yourself Something To Do'; all three get first-rate performances from a very accomplished cast.

This production put its star values in Sheila Steafel and Elizabeth Seal in the rôles of the two mothers, and it is sad, given the very revusical nature of the piece and the fact that neither lady has much to sing, that it was not therefore judged useful to include some of their spoken material – the beauty parlour monologue, for instance. We are left to our hunger a little after hearing Miss Steafel tearing 'Sand in my Eyes' to shreds like a marinated Marlene Dietrich, cooing back and forth to Miss Seal about the unfairness of children, or joining with the characterful Barry Martin to persuade their son to go to work, whilst quelling the interruptions of the embarrassing Aunt Prue (Tricia George). Martin makes a fine job of 'Hush-Hush', but hands over 'Cleopatra' to the energetic Malcolm Rennie (the doubles in *Salad Days* seem to be of movable parts), who plays it with what I think is a Jewish cockney accent. Christina Matthews is a charming Jane, and Adam Bareham and Osmund Bullock complete a well-chosen cast which suffers only by sometimes being made to make the show more complicated than necessary.

Slade and his collaborator Dorothy Reynolds followed *Salad Days* with a series of West End musical shows in a largely more constructed but equally unpretentious style: *Free As Air* (1957), *Follow That Girl* – an adaptation of *Christmas in King Street* (1960) – *Hooray for Daisy* (1959–60) and *Wildest Dreams* (1961), and Slade followed up with two pieces with other partners in the more substantial book musicals *Vanity Fair* (1962) and *Trelawny* (1972). All but *Vanity Fair* were treated to a full-scale cast recording.

Hooray for Daisy *and* Wildest Dreams

Of the Slade/Reynolds shows, *Hooray for Daisy* and *Wildest Dreams* both originated in repertory theatres, and their light, easy-going scores were written with the same two-piano accompaniment that had proved so effective in *Salad Days*, although both required a little more in the way of singing abilities from their cast than the earlier show had done. *Hooray for Daisy* (a very rare recording nowadays), set in the action of an amateur pantomime, mixed numbers from the show-within-a-show with songs concerning the various romances going on amongst the cast. There is, thus, some comedy in the fact that no one but Eleanor Drew, again the leading lady and again a pleasure to listen to, can really sing.

On the one hand, a local worthy playing the front half of the cow has an amusing 'Soft Hoof Shuffle' and the principal boy and girl enjoy a bouncy harmonized duet; on the other the real-life boy and girl have a lilting 'Madame, Will You Dine'; but it is all very light and very whimsical and, partly because the sleeve gives no indication of what the songs are, it doesn't really take off.

In *Wildest Dreams* Slade allowed himself to get a little more ambitious musically and there are several interesting and enjoyable numbers, but, since Anna Dawson, a more than worthy replacement for Miss Drew, is the only competent singer around, the listening does become less than satisfying. It is also a little shocking to find a boogie woogie number in the middle of this politest of English scores.

Free As Air

Free As Air, written for metropolitan production, has an orchestra, a larger cast, and a soubrette (Patricia Bredin) who opens the recording with a voice certainly not made for a repertory theatre. The gently decorative numbers that make up the score rarely come across with either the simple charm of *Salad Days* or the substance of a comic opera, and the result is a recording of a show that seems neither chalk nor cheese. Lovers of curiosities can hear *Free As Air* in Dutch on the Philips label, the only recording I know of of a Slade work in a foreign language.

Follow That Girl

The qualifications that hang over *Free As Air* cannot, however, be applied to *Follow That Girl*. As a recording, at least, this is the easily the best of the Slade/Reynolds pieces. It has the catchiest Slade melody ('Follow That Girl'), the funniest of all the collaborators' numbers ('Life Must Go On'), and the most consistently tuneful and humorous score, and it is also far and away the best-performed recording of the shows of the Slade canon.

The happy median is reached with the use of a small piano-based band as an accompaniment, supportive and never intrusive, and here at last a group of effective singers are satisfyingly mixed with the semi-singing actors. Susan Ham sh re is the heroine, and if she has not the skilful voice of Misses Drew and Dawson, she has a very charming youthful presence and more than enough soprano tones to make her performance wholly enjoyable. She is paired with a fine singing hero (an amorous policeman!) in Peter Gilmore, whilst the bigger singing and a goodly dose of burlesque comedy go to Marion Grimaldi and to Patricia Routledge. Newton Blick and James Cairncross from *Salad Days*, playing and singing opposite them, seem to have profited vocally by the experience of the earlier show.

Follow That Girl has an advantage over its fellows, perhaps, in that it is more overtly humorous. Adapted from a revue, its numbers each justify their presence and the genuine laughs come one after another. Philip Guard and Robert McBain, giving each other excuses for not restricting their social and sex lives after the apparent disappearance of the girl they professed to love, are hilarious; Patricia Routledge and Cairncross 'Waiting for our Daughter' in Victorian parlour duet form no less so; and the 'Three Victorian Mermaids' who are squeezed into the action give a galumphing touch of the merry music hall to this happy parody of the late Gaiety Theatre musicals.

Miss Grimaldi and Blick ride through their several numbers with great *élan* – describing the theft of their baby son whilst 'Shopping in Kensington' or halting the fleeing heroine on the brink of a bridge so that the artist can capture the plight of the 'Solitary Stranger' in oils. It is all such fun that it makes you want to see the show on the stage, which must be a fine recommendation for a cast recording.

Trelawny

By the time *Trelawny*, a musical version of Pinero's *Trelawny of the Wells*, arrived on the London stage under the management of the young Cameron Mackintosh, much had changed or was changing in the musical theatre. In 1972 both *Jesus Christ Superstar* and *Joseph and the Amazing Technicolor Dreamcoat* appeared. But there was still a place for the well-crafted classic-based musicals that had been popular over the past decade, and *Trelawny*, from the evidence of its recording, deserves to be classed amongst the most enjoyable of these.

Slade's score – his most substantial musically – illustrates Pinero's play in a very attractive way, mixing lively characterizations and numbers for the theatre folk with some particularly fine, simple sentimental numbers. Avonia Bunn (Elizabeth Power), looking forward to her big opportunity as principal boy, launches merrily into 'The Turn of Avonia Bunn', and the comics Gadd (David Morton) and Colpoys (Teddy Green) declare eagerly 'We Can't Keep 'em Waiting', but it is in the simple avowal of Arthur Gower ('Arthur's Letter'), in the yearning 'The One Who Isn't There' and in the clear, moving duet between Rose (Gemma Craven) and Sir William (Max Adrian), that the score is at its most effective.

The cast play the material well, the actors portraying actors rarely lapsing into the clichéd imitation music-hall performances liable to infest any musical with a Victorian setting, and although there is no notable solo singing – indeed, the music neither demands nor wants showy vocalizing – the characters, with Ian Richardson's Tom Wrench at their head, emerge splendidly.

Slade, who can be heard at the piano in the recordings of his earlier shows, has recorded a number of discs of his own material, the most comprehensive of which, on the Overtures label, is 'Julian Slade Looking for a Piano'. Here he performs, amongst other items, three songs from his university musicals *Lady May* and *Bang Goes the Meringue*, two numbers from the 1967 *In Pursuit of Love*, and two from his stage adaptation of Fraser-Simson's *Winnie the Pooh* cycle of songs, as well as the original *Christmas in King Street* versions of four pre-*Follow That Girl* pieces. An earlier recording, on Oriole, with Eleanor Drew, Jane Wenham and John Neville amongst the performers backed by a seven-piece group, also includes material from his musicals *The Merry Gentleman*, *Lady May* and *The Comedy of Errors*, as well as songs written for the plays *Two Gentlemen of Verona*, *The Duenna* and *The Shoemaker's Holiday*.

Sandy Wilson

The Boy Friend

Sandy Wilson's 'new 1920s musical' *The Boy Friend* (1953) has survived through thousands of metropolitan performances and hundreds of smaller theatre productions world wide as one of the favourite British musicals of all times, and the winning charm and loveable humour of such songs as 'A Room in Bloomsbury', 'I Could Be Happy with You', 'It's Never Too Late to Fall in Love' and 'Won't You Charleston with Me' have gone round the world several times and on to record as many times again.

The original Players' Theatre production was recorded on an HMV ten-inch disc (in a particularly attractive photographic sleeve) and subsequently re-released on a twelve-inch record by Music for Pleasure. This is the real *Boy Friend*, accompanied just by piano and not-too-intrusive drums, with only four 'Perfect Young Ladies' with four boyfriends to people Mme Dubonnet's finishing school. It is a delightful recording, with Anne Rogers and Anthony Hayes giving definitively sincere renditions of 'I Could Be Happy with You' and 'A Room in Bloomsbury', John Rutland and Maria Charles doing the same for 'It's Never Too Late to Fall in Love' and Violetta bouncing Frenchly through 'It's Nicer in Nice'. It is interesting to listen to the tune of 'The Riviera', which obviously underwent changes after this disc was made. The record does, however, have some sad drawbacks. A ten-inch disc is not big enough to hold all of *The Boy Friend*, and in consequence 'The You-Don't-Want-to-Play-With-Me Blues' and 'Safety in Numbers' are missing, and other pieces, including the title song which is cut to one chorus, painfully truncated.

The original Broadway cast album, the next to arrive chronologically, was a twelve-inch disc, and both the missing numbers were restored, along with the various pruned away verses, choruses and the obbligato to 'Poor Little Pierrette'. This time it was 'Nicer in Nice' that was squeezed out. The pianos have been replaced by an orchestra, playing the Ted Royal/Charles Cooke arrangements which are lively and affectionate, the population of the school has swelled and, all in all, this is *The Boy Friend* inflated to uptown size. Julie Andrews (Polly), Ann Wakefield (Maisie) and John Hewer (Tony) head the cast attractively, but affairs are vocally sabotaged by an embarrassingly awful Mme Dubonnet.

The 1968 London and Australian revival recordings are the first to include all the songs (the Carnival Tango dance music goes instead), and the 1970 American revival and the British thirtieth anniversary production go a little further and include the Act 2 finale, the former disc managing even to retain the Tango. There is also a film soundtrack to the film which was not *The Boyfriend* and which, although it includes all of the show's numbers (plus a couple of others), is best ignored.

The first London revival disc has some fine performances – Cheryl Kennedy and Tony Adams are an appealing leading pair, Marion Grimaldi gives Mme Dubonnet both voice and comedy and Frances Barlow is a spirited Maisie – but some insensitive and aggressive orchestral playing and a bit of unbalanced recording spoil what should have been a good record. The later British revival gussies up the show irritatingly, stretching the songs with superfluous dance breaks and complicating them with harmonies, false finishes and unnecessary alterations to familiar lines. It is also not very well performed, only Jane Wellman as a sweetly uncomplicated Polly and Derek Waring, briefly heard as Percival Browne, coming up to the mark.

As well as being the most complete, the second American disc also comes out top orchestrally, with some bright, tight playing of the Royal/Cooke arrangements which compares favourably with the excesses on the other records. There are also first-class performances from a splendidly on-the-bouton Jeanne Beauvais, warbling her way sentimentally through Mme Dubonnet's songs ('your 'eart is 'igh . . .'), and from Ronald Young as an eager Tony paired with a sometimes surprisingly uningenuous Polly (Judy Carne), whose TV exposure earns her 100% above-the-title billing.

Sadly, there are some less apposite interpretations. Hortense (Barbara Andres) and Maisie (Sandy Duncan) barely get around to singing, preferring to speak and/or squawk their songs. So, a perfect *Boy Friend* this is certainly not, but given its extended content and its tidy, unfussy playing it probably comes out as the best all-round bet if you are looking for extended content and unfussy playing, even though it does rather leave you longing for an Anne Rogers, a Maria Charles or a John Rutland.

Valmouth

Wilson followed *The Boy Friend* with a variety of pieces – some, such as *The Buccaneer* (1953), *Divorce Me, Darling* (1964) and *His Monkey Wife* (1971), constructed for the Players' and for other club theatres, and one, *Valmouth* (1958), written for a slightly larger stage and for a larger lady, the American actress and singer Bertice Reading. It was a violent change of gear. Whereas one of *The Boy Friend*'s most popular aspects was its genial and utter apparent lack of sophistication, *Valmouth* was sophisticated beyond anything previously attempted in the light musical theatre. To make a musical from the material contained in the extravagantly esoteric comic novellas of Ronald Firbank was like trying to contain a river of quicksilver. But Wilson did it, and did it with exceptional artistic – if not commercial – success.

There are two recordings of *Valmouth*, one made with the cast with which the original production transferred to the West End, the other of a memorable Chichester Festival Theatre revival of 1982, where several important actors repeat the rôles they had created a quarter of a century before. Both have much to recommend them.

The original production is accompanied by a small orchestra featuring an electric organ sound, eccentric and amusing and in keeping with the show's originality, which always allows the all-important words of Wilson's witty songs to come clearly through. It includes virtually all of the score. Cleo Laine had by this time taken over Miss Reading's rôle of the mysterious masseuse Mrs Yajnavalkya, and she performs it with a warm, musky tone and only a hint of the vocal mannerisms that were to become her trademark. There is, perhaps, little in the way of *sous-entendre* and *sous-sous-entendre* in her description of her 'Magic Fingers' and the accomplishments of her late husband 'Mustapha', but she makes a splendidly moving moment of her last farewell to the centenarian Grannie Tooke (Doris Hare) in 'I Will Miss You' and bounces happily through the description of dressing up in her 'Big Best Shoes'.

The two showiest numbers fall to the elderly and sexually infatuated Lady Parvula de Panzoust, and Fenella Fielding gets her teeth and nails into them with a devastating husky innocence. Her justification of her intent to fling a nubile shepherd into the hay 'Just Once More' is a connoisseur's joy. She flickers brilliantly through Wilson's hilarious lyric, and to hear her get her tongue around what must be one of the most esoteric rhymes in musical theatre, the cheeky pairing of 'put my *déshabille* on' and '*désorientée* papillon', is a delight. And when Lady Parvula speaks to her husband in heaven, with a *mea culpa* of her many misdemeanours since his death ('It Was Only a Passing Phase'), it really demolishes the convention for future use.

There are more such brittle, revusical numbers as well as a selection of more lyrical and even truly feeling songs, and they are all well performed – Patsy Rowland turning a crystalline plaintiveness on her suicidal lament 'I Loved a Man', Peter Gilmore as the tasty Arcadian wondering robustly 'What Do I Want with Love?', Geoffrey Dunn, frantically and camply Spanish, describing his Cardinal's seat at 'The Cathedral of Clemenza', Marcia Ashton with the cataclysmic chatter of one released from a vow of silence ('My Talking Day'), three old ladies twittering nostalgically over their young days when 'All the Girls Were Pretty', and the deceptively simple 'Niri-Esther', in which the hero (Alan Edwards) rhapsodizes jauntily over his bride-to-be . . . in duet with his catamite.

It is splendid, stylish, special stuff, well performed and recorded, with only a rather silly reprise of the favourite songs as part of the finale coming to break the atmosphere so well built up through the recording. My only other worry is that the sleeve carries no breakdown of the plot. To those who know *Valmouth* and its recondite characters, the full implications of the songs are clear, but 'Niri-Esther', for example, does lose something of its point unless you know that it is sung by a bridegroom to his boyfriend.

The later recording does away with the jolly reprises, includes the previously omitted 'What Then Can Make Him Come So Slow', and carries a brief synopsis written by Wilson himself. It also has Bertice Reading back in the rôle that was written for her, and suddenly a whole new dimension appears. Miss Reading's rich, chuckling, insinuating voice, masterfully used through its range of sound and volume, gives acres of extra meanings to the text of her songs, and the personality of Mrs Yaj takes on unplumbable, unspeakable depths. When she utters her 'Good Evening' at the top of her first song, the two words hold promises of goodness-knows-what to come, and come it does. The manic, multi-layered description of her 'Magic Fingers', the raging love-song (or is it a sex-song?) to her 'Mustapha', which brings a tingle to the loins and a lump to the throat, the arching, mystical 'Cry of the Peacock', the cackling jollity of 'Big Best Shoes', which leaves you wondering what on earth she is going to get up to when she's got them on, and the gentle moments of 'Little Girl Baby' and 'I Will Miss You' all combine in a performance which is quite extraordinary.

Most of the rest of the recording comes up to her example. Fenella Fielding repeats her Lady Parvula with added zest and point, Marcia Ashton has an extra eccentricity as the chattering nun, Robert Meadmore personifies purity in his beautifully sung 'What Do I Want with Love?', and the three old ladies – Judy Campbell droning an octave below, Jane Wenham twittering frantically on top, and Miss Fielding desperately holding on in the middle – make 'When All the Girls Were Pretty' a quivering hymn to faded glory. Mark Wynter gives every ounce of unequivocal romance to his love song to 'Niri-Esther' as played by Femi

Taylor, who glows with innocence as she longs for home 'Where the Trees Are Green with Parrots', Cheryl Kennedy teeters on the verge of tears and the note as the troubled Thetis, and Sir Robert Helpmann completes the principal cast as an archly fey Cardinal.

The artists are helped by some fine fresh arrangements by Richard Holmes, which replace the electric organ with a more versatile combination of instruments, and the *coup de maître* to a fine record is given by a splendid pictorial sleeve decorated with a design for the show by Andrew and Margaret Brownfoot, which captures the spirit of the piece marvellously – the three old beldames chattering over their table under the hooded eye of the resident priest.

The Buccaneer and *His Monkey Wife*

The recording of *The Buccaneer*, made on the occasion of the show's 1955 transformation from club show into West End musical, provides some light, bright entertainment and the opportunity to hear the comedian Kenneth Williams, in the rôle of the pubescent Montgomery Winterton out to save the traditional comic paper of the title, singing about 'The Facts of Life'. The 1986 President reissue of the previously rare cast recording of *His Monkey Wife* allows a wider audience a glimpse of another humorous and satirical Wilson score, topped by a classy revusical number on 'Marriage' as put across by Myvanwy Jenn and Bridget Armstrong as a pair of cynical denizens of Hampstead.

Divorce Me, Darling!

The underrated *Divorce Me, Darling!* once again finds Wilson at his affectionate and witty best, with a show that joyously does for the 1930s what *The Boyfriend* did for the 1920s. It is a much larger-scale work than its little predecessor, massing a big cast, a proper orchestra with some delightful pastiche 'so and so and his band' arrangements, and songs that cover the gamut of period styles, whilst sometimes making wide demands on a cast including some necessarily accomplished vocalists.

Its original cast recording struck a little trouble when the voice of leading lady Patricia Michael gave out in mid-session and understudy Jenny Wren had to step in for the last two numbers of Polly's part, but Miss Michael's lovely clear soprano only occasionally shows signs of being in trouble as she sighs sweetly through the delightful 'Whatever Happened to Love', even though she has to put up with a rather ham-voiced Tony in the duet 'Back Where We Started'. Maria Charles is back to join Geoffrey Hibbert in the comic highlight of the score, 'On the Loose', where Dulcie and Lord Brockhurst take 'It's Never Too Late to Fall in Love' to its next stage accompanied by a highly amusing series of imitations of orchestral instruments; Joan Heal grinds her way throatily through a Marlene Dietrich impersonation in 'Blondes for Danger' and stagily bemoans an actress's life in 'Lights! Music!'; Anna Sharkey flings a gutsy three-octave voice into the rhythms of

'Swing Time Is Here to Stay'; Irlin Hall, as the manhunting American Hannah van Husen, belts her way through 'Here Am I (But Where's the Guy?)' with aplomb; and everyone joins in the catchy title song with infectious enjoyment.

It is a happy recording, displaying a score whose charming ensemble music helps give it more substance than the collections of moveable songs that comprised many genuine 1930s musicals, and which is performed for the most part with style and humour.

Like Slade, Wilson has recorded his own material both as a pianist and as a self-accompanied vocalist – his most substantial selection, taken from his solo show at the Players' Theatre, being recorded on the Overtures label in 'Sandy Wilson Thanks the Ladies'. It includes numbers from each of the shows already mentioned, but also several revue songs from the 1950s and three from unproduced shows.

David Heneker

David Heneker, military man turned songwriter, began his second career, in the musical theatre, at the age of fifty-two with one of the outstanding musicals of the 1950s, when he combined with Julian More and Monty Norman on the score for the hard-hitting Wolf Mankowitz piece *Expresso Bongo* (1958). The team followed up with *Make Me an Offer* (1959) before Heneker went solo to turn out his biggest successes in *Half a Sixpence* (1963) and *Charlie Girl* (1965), and continued with a startling longevity with *Jorrocks* (1966), *Phil the Fluter* (1969), *Popkiss* (1972), *The Biograph Girl* (1980) and *Peg* (1984). All but the enjoyable but unsuccessful *Popkiss* won original cast recordings, and Heneker's unobtrusively skilful lyrics and unexaggerated melodies have, by and large, been well served on disc.

Expresso Bongo

Expresso Bongo is an aggressively original piece, the seedy, often down-beat story of a young rock singer's rise to fame via the gutters of Soho. It pulls no punches in its script or in its songs, which are a mixture of tart parodies of modern rock and some fine thoughtful solos and characterfully comical songs. The recording of the original production top-bills Paul Scofield, Hy Hazell, James Kenney and Millicent Martin, all of whom are splendidly cast.

Kenney is the youthful anti-hero of the piece, belting out 'Don't You Sell Me Down the River' and 'Expresso Party' in energetic imitation of Tommy Steele, Britain's top pop singer of the time, and milking the sickening mother-loving appeal to a more general public in 'The Shrine on the Second Floor'. Scofield, as Bongo's small-time cockney agent, shows up an easy, attractive singing voice in two first-rate pieces, cocky on the way up ('I Never Had It So Good'), rueful on the way down ('The Gravy Train'), and Miss Martin gives a feeling performance of two good pop ballads ('Seriously' and 'I Am') and an Alma Cogan imitation of a pop singer to close out the show on a semi-optimistic note. Hy Hazell, cast in a rôle not dissimilar to the Vera Simpson of *Pal Joey*, as the predatory, ageing actress who takes Bongo under her wing and her bedspread, is particularly well supplied. She joins in a brittle, revusical catalogue of rich purchases with a society friend ('We Bought it') which is both humorous and bitter at the same time, before turning on cabaret tones for the painful recognition of the inexorable advance of 'Time' in a moving ballad whose lyrics ring uncomfortably true.

There are one or two numbers in which the writers rather lose their modern attitude – a set-piece comedy patter song contrasting operatic and pop matters in a series of purposefully anguished rhymes ('Nausea') and a cynical, sub-*Dreigroschenoper* piece with atom bomb preoccupations ('Nothing Is for Nothing') – but it is a well-balanced, effective score put over in good style.

A film version of *Expresso Bongo* was responsible for a 45 EP disc of four songs sung by its young star Cliff Richard, which was the first British show record to make its way on to the hit parade. However, only one of the four songs contained on the disc belongs to the show, the other three, including the single 'A Voice in the Wilderness', being written for the film version which largely ignored the show score.

Make Me an Offer

Heneker and Norman's *Make Me an Offer*, based on a Mankowitz novel, was another successful contemporary musical, set amongst the vendors of the London street markets, and the score's lightly orchestrated mixture of conversational musical pieces and unobvious ballads is extremely effective. The corny stage-cockney excesses seen in too many other musicals are avoided in a show that takes a naturalistic style, and even in its comic songs maintains an unforced lyrical line that moves away from traditional songwriting.

The original cast recording features Daniel Massey as honest Charlie, the young antique dealer who, through an everyday market swindle, gets the chance he needs to straighten out his personal and professional life. Massey, like Scofield, is an actor who can sing this type of material splendidly. His performance of the opening 'Pram Song', frustrated thoughts set in motion by tripping over the pram in the overcrowded flat that he, his wife and their baby son occupy, sets the tone of the show, and his lilting longing for for a little shop of his own ('I Want a Lock-Up') is the most tuneful moment of the piece.

The ladies of the show don't quite manage the same happy mixture of acting and singing – Diana Coupland as the wife sings her numbers warmly but rather carefully, Dilys Laye as the disturbing influence is pointed but sometimes vocally uncomfortable, and Sheila Hancock does silly voices in the ironic 'It's Sort of Romantic' – but the comedy is well served elsewhere.

Meier Tzelniker, as a colourful street trader, disserts on the nature of business ('All Big Fleas') and joins battle with a rival (Wally Patch) in the Needle Recitative scene with spiky Jewish humour; and there is a clever series of scenes – 'Break

Up', 'The Auction', and the rapped 'Knock-Out' – which follow the process of the auction that is the heart of the second-act action. On a capable recording, only the massed chorus going on about being in the 'Portobello Road' leans towards the obvious, and this unpretentious and effective score gets a good performance, from Massey and Tzelniker in particular.

Half a Sixpence

With *Half a Sixpence*, a version of H. G. Wells's *Kipps* written as a vehicle for rock star Tommy Steele, Heneker went it alone, supplying lyrics and music for a score which, as Steele took the show from London to Broadway to Hollywood, was to become his best-known work. In each venue a recording was made, followed by a whole swatch of cover versions as original cast understudy Roy Sone, pop singer Marty Wilde, budding personality Des O'Connor, and jazzmen Count Basie and Gordon Beck all had a go at 'Flash, Bang, Wallop', 'If the Rain's Got to Fall', 'Half a Sixpence' and the rest of Heneker's lively, characterful score.

The three recordings of the show on which Steele appears contain a number of variations amongst them. The London disc covers the complete score as it was played in the original production, with the exception of the chorus number 'A Proper Gentleman' and the second-act opening, but the Broadway disc omits – as the Broadway version of the show did – 'The Oak and the Ash', 'I'm Not Talking to You', 'The One That's Run Away' and the dual number 'I'll Build a Palace for my Girl' and 'I Only Want a Little House', as well as 'The Old Military Canal', adding in replacement 'A Proper Gentleman' and 'The Party's on the House'. The film version tinkers again with the contents of the piece and reinstates 'I'm Not Talking to You' and adds 'I Don't Believe a Word of It', 'The Race is On' and 'This Is My World', whilst dropping 'Long Ago' and 'The Party's on the House'. It also generally goes in for all sorts of filleting, rearranging and choreographing.

Steele's Kipps is a memorable creation – simple, masculine, warm, loveable and, above all, youthful, with all the extremes of vigour and vulnerability that involves. Unable to split a sovereign like the rich folk do, he presents his girl tentatively, sincerely, with a 'Half a Sixpence', then not long after, with equal sincerity and a dash of desperation, he is all eyes for a different girl, wretched that 'She's Too Far Above Me'. But, lurking under the teenage heartaches, high spirits are never far from the surface and they burst forth with joyous vitality when Kipps looks eagerly forward to a date ('If the Rain's Got to Fall') or celebrates his wedding in music-hall style ('Flash, Bang, Wallop'). There are other fine moments too, as when Kipps and his Ann share childhood memories with affecting simplicity ('Long Ago') or imagine in parallel songs the houses that represent what they want out of life ('I'll Build a Palace'/'I Only Want a Little House') in a score, a character, a performance of real delight.

Unlike the score, that character and Steele's performance remain remarkably constant through the three recordings made over some four years. The Broadway version and the film soundtrack give evidence of perhaps a little more assurance and even a touch more maturity which, whilst making things go more slickly, does mean that you lose a little of that bright wonderment that is so effective in the first record, particularly in pieces like the lovely 'She's Too Far Above Me'.

As it happens, that first recording has the edge, in any case, in practically every other area. Heneker's undecimated list of light-fingered tunes are light-handedly orchestrated and brightly and sensitively played, the recording is straightforward, clear and uncomplicated, and the rest of the cast all play their parts to perfection. Marti Webb is a very young, very sparky Ann, vixenish when on the defence ('I'm Not Talking to You'), unsentimentally tender when she wants to be ('Long Ago'), but always firm and determined. Her voice is not yet the super-confident, soaring instrument of the creator of 'Tell Me on a Sunday', but it is fresh and strong and suitable, so suitable in fact that it was she who was chosen to dub the vocal lines for Julia Foster's film performance, a job which again she fulfilled effectively. James Grout (Chitterlow) gives the few lines he has to sing with unexaggerated style, Anna Barry (Helen) lends 'The Oak and the Ash' the cool kind of soprano it requires, and the chorus, who have much more to do than either of them, are endlessly on the ball.

The Broadway disc has too much of the music missing to make it valid – the loss of 'I'm Not Talking to You' and 'The One That's Run Away' is particularly regrettable – and the replacement numbers are not an improvement on the lost material. Although Polly James is a strong Ann, she is hamstrung without both her biggest number and the final double song, and neither Chitterlow nor Helen has anything left to sing in this thinned down version. The film soundtrack has similar limitations, and there is no reason to prefer either to the healthily reprinted original cast recording.

Charlie Girl

Whilst Heneker's next work, *Charlie Girl*, ran in the West End for seven years, his last shows played out their lives in few more weeks. However, taken as recordings, the merits of the five pieces concerned are not necessarily commensurate with these figures and Heneker's unshowy skills are on display in a series of appealing records.

The popular attraction of *Charlie Girl* (a collaboration with John Taylor) is evident in a group of recordings of its lively, accessible score, beginning with the original cast recording with Joe Brown and Anna Neagle, continuing with an Australian cast disc (Johnny Farnham/Anna Neagle), a Music for Pleasure studio recording featuring Jessie Matthews, and a cast recording of the show's 1986 revival with Paul Nicholas and Cyd Charisse.

The energetic cockney performance of Joe Brown, the sweet and quavery voice of Miss Neagle declaring 'I Was Young (When This Last Happened to Me)' and strong singing from Christine Holmes in the title rôle, smooth Stuart Damon as the Prince Charming of the affair, and a croaky, enthusiastic Hy Hazell as his American mother all go to make up an enjoyable original cast recording, which has the edge on its Australian equivalent. This latter has equally energetic performances from a very young and very lively pop-singing Farnham (Joe), a smooth Peter Regan (Jack Connor) and a broadly punch-packing Mamma (Margo Lee), but it leaves out several songs including my own favourite, the counterposed 'Bells Will Ring' and 'I Love Him' sequence, and 'Like Love', which reduces the rôle of the rather careful Charlie (Geraldene Morrow) to just one song and the appeal of the score by several notches. It does, however, include the interpolated number 'Liverpool', which doesn't appear on any of the other recordings.

The MFP recording gathers an experienced cast together, with Regan, repeating his slick Jack, Anne Hart and Cheryl Kennedy as Charlie alongside Miss Matthews, who shows an appreciably well-preserved voice in 'I Was Young'. However, a young 'discovery' called Bobby Lynton is a feeble Joe and once again the score is shorn of some of its most enjoyable moments.

For the whole score, well recorded, invigoratingly played and splendidly sung, it is best to turn to the most recent recording. *Charlie Girl* underwent some revamping for its revival, the two most obvious alterations being some happy new orchestrations and the replacement of 'I Was Young' with a new number, 'When I Hear Music, I Dance', to suit the talents and reputation of the top-billed Cyd Charisse. Miss Charisse has perhaps even less voice than Miss Neagle, but there is a whole choir of Hollywood angel voices to help her through her big number and a lot of charm and fun in her pairing with the bubbling Dora Bryan, who puts much less belting and much more humour than her predecessors into the rôle of Mrs Connor.

The voices of the piece are elsewhere. Paul Nicholas, the original Jesus of *Jesus Christ, Superstar*, doesn't bother with the hefty cockney accent of the original, but turns on a lazy charm and a warm, light pop voice for Joe's numbers; Mark Wynter's classy, vigorous baritone serenades his own reflection with his tongue firmly in his cheek; and Lisa Hull is a delightful, young Charlie, equipped with a really fine, even voice which she never feels the need to push into a pseudo-pop sound. Her outstanding performance of the rocky 'Like Love', skittering effortlessly from chest regions up to stratospheric skat, is the highlight of the record.

Jorrocks

Jorrocks, a thoroughly enjoyable score devised for a classic period script, has a little of the feel of *Half a Sixpence* without, owing to its subject and characters, having that piece's light-hearted energy or outstanding numbers. Its cast recording is an impeccable rendition of the music, with Joss Ackland a Dickensian, rich-voiced hero standing head and shoulders over the show; a grand collection of English eccentrics headed by Paul Eddington, Willougby Goddard, Michael Malnick and Thelma Ruby; and Cheryl Kennedy as an ingénue who declares tunefully and energetically, 'I Don't Want to Behave Like a Lady'.

Phil the Fluter

If *Jorrocks* followed in the footsteps of *Half a Sixpence*, *Phil the Fluter* had more of the make-up of *Charlie Girl*, with its mixture of pop star (Mark Wynter), comedian (Stanley Baxter) and beloved star lady (Evelyn Laye). Its score is a combination of well-known songs by Percy French, who was the subject of the libretto, and original Heneker numbers. 'Abdul Abulbul Ameer', 'Are You Right There, Michael' and 'Phil the Fluter' get rousing performances, but the most enjoyable moments come in the new material as Miss Laye, without attempting to sing, declares 'They Don't Make Them Like That Any More', or joins with Wynter in happy duet ('I Like It') in which she ventures a few husky notes and he rips away in a lively baritone. Sarah Atkinson and Caryl Little sigh that they can't compete with 'Mama', and the latter dissects her apparent lack of charms in 'How Would He Like Me'. Unfortunately, Baxter, the nominal star of the affair, comes over rather ineffectually, resulting in a show and a recording which are rather lopsided.

The Biograph Girl

There is, all round, more enjoyment in the recording of *The Biograph Girl*, a small-scale show about early Hollywood. A cast of a dozen, impersonating such film luminaries as D. W. Griffith, Mary Pickford, Lillian Gish and Adolph Zukor, and a tiny band skip happily through a mixture of alternately lively and reflective numbers with a touch of wryness here and there and occasional moments of satire. Griffith (Bruce Barry), supported by the whole company, sings richly of a world of films 'Beyond Babel', ponders on the way life, like a film, goes into 'A Gentle Fade', and sourly looks from an unpromising present to a future where he will be hailed as 'One of the Pioneers'. Mary Pickford (Sheila White) pouts for the benefit of the press of how 'I Like to Be the Way I Am in my Own Front Parlour', and, in the most effective moment of the score, reflects with her co-workers on what might be the future of their work ('Put it in the Tissue-Paper').

Peg

Peg, a musical version of *Peg o' My Heart*, was another small-scale work but, instead of being allowed to remain small like *The Biograph Girl*, its recording shows it to have been souped-up with excessive orchestration and given some uncomfortable performances, starting with a fairly charmless and often loud Peg. Under it all, some typically charming Heneker tunes and lyrics can be heard trying to get out, and Patricia Michael's moving song 'When a Woman Has to Choose' shows the composer and lyricist at nearly eighty years of age still producing his best work.

Lionel Bart

In the half a dozen years during which Lionel Bart was active in the musical theatre he was responsible for all or some part of half a dozen shows, notably the words and music of one of the most popular of all English musicals, *Oliver!*, and the magnificently gritty *Maggie May*, as well as the lyrics of the splendidly roistering period piece *Lock Up Your Daughters*. *Blitz!*, which produced a song or two amongst its scenery, *Fings Ain't Wot They Used t'Be*, and the disastrous Robin Hood burlesque *Twang!!* completed the UK work-list, and all were preserved on LP record, with results varying from the memorable to, in the case of *Twang!!*, the utterly dismal.

Oliver!

Oliver! is both the most widely successful and the most widely recorded Bart piece. London and Broadway both put down their original cast versions, which share a shelf with the 1968 film soundtrack and several foreign-language versions – Israeli, Dutch, Hungarian – as well as the predictable clutch of studio recordings. The two principal cast recordings are both good, but, in spite of the fact that they share several lead players, the director and the orchestral arrangements, there are some noticeable differences between them. In the time between the London and Broadway productions the show has been allowed to 'develop'. That is to say, various bits of business and ad libs have become enshrined in the score. The same goes for the cast. Three years after London, their Broadway performances have an assurance, even a cavalier slickness that was not there before. This may be preferable, it may not be – it's a judgement best left to the individual.

The London disc gives a good representation of the show and the score. Georgia Brown's Nancy is definitive – a genuine, unclichéd East End girl played with a superb mixture of off-hand toughness and vulnerability, throatily whacking out the sexy lines of the pub song 'Ooom-Pah-Pah' or pouring her soul and voice into the beautiful 'As Long As He Needs Me', as she hopelessly recognizes that her love for the brutish Bill Sikes will always get in the road of finer feelings. The performance of this ballad here is perfect, an unshowy, matter-of-fact admission of the woman's feelings expressed for no one but herself to hear. It would never again be the same, for soon the Shirley Basseys of this world were to leap on 'As Long As He Needs Me' and turn it into the biggest torch since the Statue of Liberty.

Ron Moody's Fagin is a fellow with such a wide range of funny voices that it is sometimes hard to tell which is the character, but he makes a crisp job of 'You've Got to Pick a Pocket or Two' and 'Reviewing the Situation' as he turns Dickens's villain into a cute rogue. Something of the same kind of transformation comes over most of the other baddies of the *Oliver Twist* story, as Mr Bumble, Mrs Corney and the undertaking Sowerberrys all become splendid figures of fun. Hope Jackman (Corney), making up to the beadle (Paul Whitsun-Jones) with the fake bashful threat 'I Shall Scream', is hilarious and Barry Humphries, in pre-Edna Everage days, is gratingly obsequious as the undertaker accompanying his tuneless wife in 'That's your Funeral'.

The children of the piece are very appealing. You mustn't stop to think that it is odd for a workhouse to accomodate only the sweetest little sopranos with middle-class accents. There is not a basher in earshot, and Oliver himself (Keith Hamshere) is the whitest and most youthful of them all. But he's no accomplished choirboy, the voice is frail and barely supported, and to hear those little-boy-lost tones singing Bart's lovely 'Where Is Love?' is truly effective. Martin Horsey (Dodger) supplies the more energetic singing in 'Consider Yourself' but, once again, the childish element remains. This Dodger is a kid, not a thoroughly slick teenage Street Arab.

The American cast recording, which was actually made whilst *Oliver!* was on its pre-Broadway run in, contains the same material as the London one with the exception of 'That's your Funeral', which at that time had been temporarily cut from the show. It also features London take-over Dodger Michael Goodman, who was succeeded by David Jones, later of Monkees fame, for the Broadway opening. Georgia Brown, Hope Jackman and Danny Sewell (Sikes) from the original London cast all repeat their rôles here (as did Humphries) and it is noticeable that Brown's Nancy has ripened into much more of a star performance. 'As Long As He Needs Me' still has that soft-centred toughness, but the voice opens up much sooner and much more vibrantly than before as she delivers the number with a considerable breadth and surety. There is more performance too in Bruce Prochnik's Oliver, a surer, less childish Oliver than Hamshere, and one with the at least slightly less perfect vowels more suitable to a workhouse boy.

The funny voices (and a good few dropped-in lines) seem to have become by this time a built-in part of the rôle of Fagin, but Clive Revill handles them with aplomb and more of a singing voice than Moody does, giving a fine performance of a rôle pitted with received mannerisms, and Willoughby Goddard makes Mr Bumble into a foolishly comical buffoon alongside Miss Jackman's delightfully ghastly Widow. This is perhaps a more accomplished *Oliver!* recording, but in being so it loses some of the personality of the original disc.

The soundtrack of the highly successful film retains most of the show score, stretching it here and there to choreographic needs, but it drops the comedy songs 'I Shall Scream' and 'That's your Funeral' as well as Sikes's 'My Name'. It also submits most of the music to a syrupy filmic rearrangement, which is a shame since, floating on the syrup, the singers give by and large a good rendition of their songs. Shani Wallis is a more conventional Nancy than Miss Brown, and she expends her strong chest voice on a version of 'As Long As He Needs Me' which is stretched out to climax as often as Casanova. Moody repeats his original performance, Mark Lester is a softly tentative Oliver and Jack Wild a copybook cockney sparrow Dodger. There is a vocal bonus with the casting of the very individual tenor of Harry Secombe as Mr Bumble.

Of the foreign versions, the Israeli *Oliver!* is a rather disappointing effort, although Shraga Friedman's Hebrew Fagin is naturally able to do without the funny voices and Rivka Raz makes a well-judged job of Nancy. The Dutch version comes out like one of those faithful reproductions now in vogue, all-round capably done but not very exciting. But the Hungarian? This 1985 recording is a collector's piece for its genuine tastelessness. It opens up with a jollified orchestral arrangement of 'Oliver', with little boys voices singing the one word over and over, which is pure horror. Its Bumble-cum-Sowerberry is an overacting basso, its Mrs Corney-Mrs Sowerberry a crooner who gets violins behind her each time she sings and who borrows 'Umpapa' to expand her rôles, the Oliver (who seems to be related to one of the perpetrators of the recording) has the echo turned up full for safety, Bill Sikes whispers 'Minden alvilági gengszter' with more humour than menace, Fagin swings along merrily with a full range of voices and other noises, 'That's your Funeral' gets treated like Zorba's Dance, and 'Consider Yourself' is entrusted to a chesty dame who sounds as if she's saying 'Come Up and See Me Some Time' and who turns up on side two with a breathy 'Neki így kellek még' (As Long As He Needs Me). Quite what has happened to 'Who Will Buy?' I can't quite decipher. Hungarian Radio should have both their arrangement department and casting director confiscated.

Maggie May

Maggie May, a colourful and tragic tale of the Liverpool docklands and its people, was as modern and realistic a musical as *Expresso Bongo* and as effective on the stage. As a recording it is less obviously attractive. The reason for this is that the score of *Maggie May* isn't made up of straightforward show songs, but often of sung and spoken scenes and fragments with music. There is a handful of traditional-sounding folksy pieces – 'Dey Don't Do Dat T'day', 'Leave Her, Johnny, Leave Her', 'Right of Way', 'Stroll On', 'We Don't All Wear the Same Size Boots' and the explanatory opening 'Ballad of the Liver Bird'- complemented by only half a dozen pieces that can be regarded as a 'number'.

'It's Yourself I Want' and 'The Land of Promises', the nearest thing to a big ballad for the show's rough and tough prostitute heroine, were, however, both effective enough to get themselves recorded by Judy Garland, along with the brisk title song and 'There's Only One Union', a jaunty little piece in which Maggie and her mate Maureen put the local men's pigeon-chested preoccupation with petty politics in its place.

The original cast recording features Rachel Roberts as Maggie May and Kenneth Haigh as Casey, the man she loves and sees killed by the graft of the tinpot Caesars of the dockyards. Miss Roberts has a strong, harsh voice, which is heard to its best in the lively duet 'I Told You So' with Maureen (Diana Quiseekay), and which she brings down to a strangely ugly croon for the moving 'It's Yourself' and 'The Land of Promises'. Haigh's actorish light baritone does service for his lively praise of 'Maggie, Maggie May' and his drunken insistence that 'I'm Me', and Barry Humphries as the Balladeer and the dockers who make up most of the rest of the cast follow on the same lines.

The cast album originally consisted of two records, the bulk of the score on the official album, and the remaining four numbers on a 45 EP. These were combined on a That's Entertainment repressing of 1983, finally bringing the full score of *Maggie May* together on one record.

Blitz and *Fings Ain't Wot They Used T'Be*

Blitz and *Fings Ain't Wot They Used T'Be*, a couple of noisily cheerful theatrical cockney pieces, are at the opposite end of the sophistication scale to *Maggie May*. *Blitz* is the more substantial of the two. It throws up a couple of obvious music hall numbers in 'Who's That Geezer Hitler' and 'Down the Lane', a song so very standard East End-y that it is hard to believe it comes from the pen of a genuine East Ender, and a photofit Vera Lynn number (actually sung by Miss Lynn), but also a group of less out-front and much more attractive numbers. From these the often broad-playing, brass-lunged cast, headed by the bellowing bass-baritone Amelia Bayntun and the pleasingly gentle juveniles Graham James and Grazina Frame, mine the most enjoyable moments of the recording.

The original cast album of *Fings Ain't Wot They Used T'Be* – recorded live in the theatre – sounds a bit like amateur night at the Dock and Duck. The sound is rough, the singing even rougher, the accents so exaggerated I suppose they can only be real. Anyone who is attached to the score (which I am not) will get better value from the HMV studio recording, in which Joan Heal, Alfred Marks, Adam Faith, Sid James, Tony Tanner, Alfie Bass and even, briefly, Bart himself appear.

Lock up your Daughters

Before his triumphs as a one-man musical writer, Bart had his earliest theatre success as a lyricist in tandem with composer Laurie Johnson in the hugely enjoyable musicalization of Henry Fielding's *Rape upon Rape* as the comical, unselfconsciously bawdy *Lock up your Daughters*. *Lock up your Daughters* is a true musical comedy – that is to say, every single number (and scene) has a comic content, even when things are at their most dramatic or sentimental – and, as a result, its score makes splendidly chuckleworthy listening. Whether it is the libidinous Mrs Squeezum pondering itchily 'When Does the Ravishing Begin', the blue-eyed heroine relating an attempted seduction 'On a Sunny Sunday Morning' or the massed company warning each other to 'Lock up your Daughters' in lascivious London town, the piece and its cast recording (made by the original Mermaid Theatre cast, and not that of the West End transfer) are tuneful and funny through every track.

Stephanie Voss and Terence Cooper are the young lovers who have to avoid the perils of London on their way to each other's arms, and they make delightfully ingenuous duettists in the longing 'Lovely Lover' and the rapturous 'Kind Fate', although Miss Voss's easy soprano and accurate comic timing get their best chance in the cheeky 'On a Sunny Sunday Morning'. Richard Wordsworth, a first-rate singing comedian in the best Gilbertian tradition, as a wriggling, sniggering villain, Hy Hazell as his wife expending her bosomy tones longingly on 'When Does the Ravishing Begin' and lashing into the revengeful 'I'll Be There', and Frederick Jaeger prowling after feminine flesh in a sexy light baritone ('Red Wine and a Wench', "Tis Plain to See') are the rather attractive sounding perils they have to negotiate. Jauntily accompanied by a lightweight band under the direction of the composer, with lively orchestrations that hoist the ex-Elizabethan story firmly into the present day, they give the show a neatly unexaggerated performance which makes a fine show into a very agreeable record.

More Shows that Started Small

Whilst Wilson, Slade, Heneker and Bart were producing their successful series of works through the 1950s and 1960s, other writers came up with shows which either followed their fashions or, occasionally, successfully took a line of their own. At the beginning, many of these musicals came from the club and repertory theatres and, most notably, from the Players' Theatre, newly rich and ambitious after the West End success of *The Boy Friend*. *Twenty Minutes South*, *The Crooked Mile* and *Johnny the Priest* all won cast recordings, but, in spite of Elisabeth Welch's contribution to the second of these, they were unremarkable shows on disc, and the tiny New Lindsay Theatre's *Chrysantheumum* and Windsor Theatre Royal's *Grab Me a Gondola*, both of which transferred to London from their original homes, have left much happier recordings.

Chrysanthemum

When I first heard the original cast recording of Robb Stewart and Neville Phillips's *Chrysanthemum*, I was at a loss to understand why such an effervescently funny and joyfully tuneful musical wasn't being played the world over, particularly by theatre companies with limited resources. I immediately sought out and read the libretto and wondered a whole lot more. It is a little gem, a wickedly accurate parody of Great War-time theatre and music made into a show which in any case stands up as a connoisseur's hoot and a layman's belly laugh, and which, with its combination of witty, tongue-in-cheek lyrics and tunes, makes the most delicious of recordings.

Pat Kirkwood and Hubert Gregg are star billed, she as Chrysanthemum Brown – the prototype of Hollywood's Thoroughly Modern Millie – and he as the true blue Englishman to whom she gives her heart. She turns her rich band-singer's voice to a variety of numbers, lively as in 'Saturday Night', soulful as in 'No More Love Songs', and comic as in her impersonation of the one and only 'Shanghai Lil', and joins in love duets cutely rhythmical ('Is This Love?') or swooningly waltzy ('Love Is a Game'), playing her rôle with poise and with sufficient humour. The bulk of the cleverest and funniest material goes to Gregg, performing with an upper lip so stiff it must have been double starched and a fine mastery of crisp delivery and effective timing. He speaks as much as he sings, particularly in his marvellous telephone song, hysterically British as he battles with a series of wrong numbers when trying to get through to Scotland Yard; or bossily warning his teenage sister to 'Watch your Step' amongst the perils of London town in a paroxysm of hilarious rhyming which pairs 'read a' with 'Ouida', 'scorned' with 'demi-monde', 'marries' with 'Buenos Aires', 'London' with 'un-done' and 'double entendre' with 'Poule de Londres'. If this sort of thing is your cup of tea (and it is certainly mine), *Chrysanthemum* is a gold mine.

Pretty soprano Patricia Moore and elegant light baritone Roger Gage are perfect as the juvenile lovers of the piece, equipped with a charming variant on the popular Weather Song of the parodied period, and veteran baritone Raymond Newell as the heroine's father shows that the deep brown voice which set the ladies quivering in the 1920s and 1930s is still in excellent form in the 1950s.

Unfortunately, the limitations of the single record has meant that several numbers from the score ('Sinner Me', 'Ships at Sea') have been omitted. But, even more sadly, there is no recording of the American production of *Chrysanthemum*, which starred Patrice Munsel, for the rewrites that were made to bolster the lady's rôle put more humour into her part, and the two fresh songs that were added for her are as hilarious as the best of the rest of the score. Nevertheless, the London cast record (reissued in 1979 on the American AEI label) is more than sufficient until the inevitable revival of *Chrysanthemum* spawns a more comprehensive one.

Grab Me a Gondola

Grab Me a Gondola is a light-hearted comedy piece written by Julian More and James Gilbert, whose experience in revue is evident in its bright, topical score. As in the case of *Chrysanthemum*, the songs are too numerous to fit on the cast recording, but fifteen numbers make it on to a lively disc in which Joan Heal, Denis Quilley and Jane Wenham play the largest part.

Miss Heal has the showiest songs in her rôle as a very up-front Diana Dors film star, out chasing publicity and Mr Quilley in the setting of the Venice Film Festival, and loudly detailing her Shakespearian ambitions in 'Cravin' for the Avon' and her sexual ones in 'Man, Not a Mouse', but the rest of the cast get the best of the numbers. Jane Wenham uses her attractive English soprano on the very pretty ballad 'Bid Him a Fond Goodbye', Quilley lilts attractively through his 'When I Find That Girl', and there is a very funny quintet in mock-operatic style about a broken-down motor car. In good revue style, everyone in the small cast gets a go: *Glamorous Night* tenor Trefor Jones uses his ringing tones on a song about 'Chianti', Guido Lorraine as an Italian prince has a wry 'my-wife-doesn't-understand-me' piece, Donald Hewlett and Johnny Ladd have a name-dropping number, there's a nice piece for the boys about the unreliability of newspapers, a jaunty one for the girls about 'Star Quality', and finally – a West End first – a rock number headed by Joyce Blair and Jay Denyer to wind things up with a nod to the very latest craze. It's a bit of a grab bag, but the best pieces are fine, and the less good ones have the merit of being gay and unpretentious.

Belle

More's erstwhile colleagues Wolf Mankowitz and Monty Norman were responsible for a less successful but enjoyable piece in the Doctor Crippen musical, *Belle*. The concept had the tale of the piece told in 1910 music-hall style, as a show-within-a-show, and equipped with numbers written by Norman, some more, some less in the music-hall idiom. Many of them are scarcely developed songs, rather a verse and chorus or two, illustrating the story or helping it along, but there are several pieces that stand out – a gently tongue-in-cheek soprano number for Ethel le Neve ('I Can't Stop Singin') and the hit of the show, 'The Dit-Dit Song', based on the celebrated telegraph arrest of Crippen at sea.

The recording is a jolly, if rather fragmentary, affair, which would have gained no little in coherence had the record company thought to put a decently detailed synopsis on the sleeve. It doesn't contain any particularly accomplished singing, but apart from the material for Ethel (Virginia Vernon) there is little opportunity for it. Perhaps the cleverest performance is by former Sadler's Wells soprano Rose Hill as the vile and quickly murdered Belle, who performs 'Bird of Paradise' in a shuddering series of deliberately off-key notes. The rest of the cast bundle along in a variety vein, with Nicolette Roeg and Davy Kaye proving that it isn't necessary (or correct) to bellow or belt music-hall material, and if it is sometimes a little difficult to tell if and when the show has its tongue in its cheek, the result is a friendly show and recording.

Songbook and Poppy

Norman's shows over the next couple of decades didn't win the honours of a run or a recording, until in 1979, in collaboration with More, he produced the small-scale *Songbook*, a spot-on burlesque of the endless compilation shows which, in the wake of *Cole* and *Cowardy Custard* had swamped the lazier stages of the country. *Songbook* followed the fortunes of the fictional songsmith Mooney Shapiro through a career which found him in the right place at the right time all of the time, illustrating this abysmally eclectic biography with the enjoyably awful fruits of Mooney's plagiaristic pen. A cast of five skip merrily through Hollywood, the depression, Americans in Paris, the 1936 Olympics, the war, Broadway cute and Broadway pretentious, and the pop world in a series of wickedly orchestrated songs, pulling out several plums on the way. Gemma Craven and Diane Langton guy the musical-with-a-message in the splendid 'I Accuse', Miss Langton does a top-hole Cicely Courtneidge in 'Bumpity Bump', Anton Rodgers gushes out 'Je vous aime Milady' and knocks some favourite American blind spots in 'Messages'.

Norman later supplied songs for another burlesque, *Poppy* (1982), this time telling a cruel tale of the opium wars between the nasty Brits and the noble Chinese in the style of British pantomime. Its score is less clever and, as performed by the Royal Shakespeare Company, less well played and sung on its unimpressive cast recording.

Successes of the Sixties

Stop the World, I Want to Get Off

Anthony Newley and Leslie Bricusse struck success with their first effort at a musical together when *Stop the World, I Want to Get Off* (1961), a vehicle for Newley, turned into an international hit. It also found great success in the recording world, with both 'What Kind of Fool Am I?' (three times, with Newley, Shirley Bassey and Sammy Davis jr) and 'Gonna Build a Mountain' making it to the hit parades as singles, and the issue of a series of cast recordings.

There is not a lot of difference between the London and Broadway recordings, but difference there is in spite of the fact that Newley starred in both productions, supported in each case by Anna Quayle and the Baker twins, the only other characters who get to sing anything alone. There is little variant in the contents – the American version includes the 'Family Fugue', which the original cast disc omits – but there is a difference in Newley's performance. What begins in the British recording as a rather gauche, engaging interpretation, simply sung, has been replaced by the time of Broadway consecration with a much slicker and more starry style. 'What Kind of Fool Am I?', instead of being a quaintly puzzled enquiry, has turned into the full eleven o'clock number. It is almost as if Newley takes himself for Shirley Bassey. It is, of course, a perfectly legitimate way of performing the song and the rest of the rôle, but, hit songs or no hit songs, *Stop the World* was always a little show (Newley takes the trouble to vaunt its simplicity on both record sleeves), and the later recording is starting to sound just a bit like a cabaret act instead of a musical. Miss Quayle throws herself into her various incarnations as the 'Typically English' wife of our hero (and her Russian, German and American equivalents) with some extravagantly revusical characterizations, and chorus and orchestra do what they have to do (pretty much the same in each version), but *Stop the World* and its recordings exist principally for their star, and stand or fall by his performance.

Sammy Davis jr brought the show back to Broadway in 1978 in a revamped, modernized, relocated version. There is a larger supporting cast, new and flashy orchestrations, an extra song ('Life is a Woman') to add to the star's already impressive list of solos (Family Fugue/'Nag, Nag, Nag' goes to make room for it), and some rewriting elsewhere, none of which is an improvement. Davis himself, partnered by Marian Mercer, sounds remarkably like Newley.

There is also a film soundtrack (Tonny Tanner/Millicent Martin), a German cast recording, a Swedish studio cast recording and a 45 of Beatrice Lillie – an interesting casting thought – singing 'Typically English', but *Stop the World* is by

Newley for Newley and comes across best done by him, first time round, with the simplicity he himself advocated.

The successor to *Stop the World*, *The Roar of the Greasepaint*, *the Smell of the Crowd* was unable to repeat the stage success of the former piece and folded before reaching London, but once again it proved to be a fertile field for the cabaret vocalist, and 'Who Can I Turn To?' and 'On a Wonderful Day Like Today' became torch-singing and holiday camp favourites respectively. Norman Wisdom, star of the British version, recorded the big ballad and 'The Joker' on a 45, but only when Newley joined the show for Broadway did the full score get released. The recording includes a couple of other fine songs ('Nothing Can Stop Me Now', 'The Joker') and it also shows the first signs of Newley's metamophosis from a lively popular singer into a braying caricature of himself. This becomes more evident in a third dip into the same well in *The Good Old, Bad Old Days* (1972), where the good songs are less notable and Newley decidedly unattractive.

A selection of Newley and Bricusse numbers, including some from sources other than their collaborations, were made into the score for the short-lived *The Travelling Music Show* (1978), which featured television personality Bruce Forsyth, then at the peak of his celebrity.

Although Bricusse's other success came mainly in the film world, he continued to supply material for the stage. From the recordings of *Pickwick* (1963), *Kings and Clowns* (1978), a translation of the Italian musical *Aggiungi una posta alla tavola* called *Beyond the Rainbow* (1978), *Goodbye, Mr Chips* (1982) and *Sherlock Holmes* (1989), which used his words and/or music, *Pickwick* shows up as easily the most successful. Its jolly Cyril Ornadel score features the well-known 'If I Ruled the World' as sung on the original cast recording in the very individual character tenor of Harry Secombe. Teddy Green, a lively Sam Weller with a jolly explanation of how to 'Talk' yourself out of trouble, who details in duet 'The Trouble With Women', and Anton Rodgers playing 'A Bit of a Character' as a smooth Jingle, share the best moments of this bit of 'comic-strip Dickens'.

Robert and Elizabeth

Australian composer Ron Grainer's best-known and mostly widely recognizable piece of music is undoubtedly the television theme tune to the *Doctor Who* series. It is a long way from that atmospheric little piece to classic operetta, but Grainer, in his first attempt at a stage musical, succeeded in turning out what is probably the most substantial light operatic score to have graced the British musical stage since the days of Messager's *Monsieur Beaucaire*.

The rôle of Elizabeth Barrett Browning in *Robert and Elizabeth* (1964) was evolved around a June Bronhill at the peak of her powers, and the composer took full advantage of his star's vocal brilliance and stamina in writing a dazzling series of solos and duets for her character. Not too many musicals demand the sustained power of her tempestuous defence of love in the song 'Woman and Man' nor, indeed, the lengthy top D in alt which comes at the end of it. But this score is not just fireworks. The combination of Ronald Millar's intelligent, natural lyrics and Grainer's exceptional music covers the whole breadth of operetta styles, from Elizabeth's longing soliloquies 'The World Outside' and 'Tied to a Bed' and her lovely duet with Browning 'I Know Now', to the most warmly comical moments provided by the younger members of the family wistfully pondering on 'The Girls That Boys Dream About' or galloping jocularly about in 'Pass the Eau de Cologne', and to father Barrett's powerful denunciation of 'What the World Calls Love' and Browning's impetuous declaration 'I Said Love'.

Miss Bronhill shares the limelight on the original cast recording with Keith Michell as Browning, and the two produce some of the most vibrant and exciting singing on musical theatre record. This is possibly Miss Bronhill's finest recording, certainly one of her best. The voice is clear, silver-shiny, even, and as solid as the Pyrenees throughout its range, rising to magnificent peaks of sound time and time again. 'Woman and Man' is a thrillling moment, and she scales the devilishly written and demanding heights of Elizabeth's second-act soliloquy without batting an eyelash or noticeably changing a gear. Michell's Browning is wonderfully complementary to this virtuoso performance whilst being played in a wholly different way. His light, vigorous baritone, which has no whiff of the operatic world anywhere near it, bursts with youth and clarity and excitement as he jubilates ('The Moon in my Pocket'), frets ('Frustration') or badgers his beloved to follow him out of her father's house with single-minded passion ('In a Simple Way'). There is no doubt that she must follow him – this man is irresistible.

Angela Richards sings with charming freshness as Elizabeth's younger sister, but few of the remainder of the show's cast have much to do. John Clements, top-billed as the elder Barrett, rather lacks the vocal power and passion that characterize this famous rôle, Jeremy Lloyd is a fine foppish Surtees Cook, and a pleasant but rather faceless group of brothers sing their music acceptably, but they pale into insignificance alongside the two star performers.

The difficulty of finding a new June Bronhill always made a major repeat of *Robert and Elizabeth* unlikely, and the high reputation of the original cast recording forestalled the making of any new disc, so the 1987 Chichester Festival production and its recording on the First Night label were both interesting and a little daring. The results, however, were extremely positive.

The new Elizabeth Barrett Browning is the young soprano Gaynor Miles and her performance, which obviously has to be compared with Bronhill's, stands up very well. It is a lighter voice, more silvery, with a firm vibrato, and one which is not in the least afraid of the rôle's vocal extremes, all of which are accomplished with a certain bravura. However, Miss Miles doesn't depend just on beauty and brilliance of voice. This Elizabeth is thoughtful, dramatic, impassioned to the point of producing shivers in the second-act soliloquy, rhapsodic in 'The Real Thing' and even fun in her part of 'A Simple Way'. If there is not quite the perfection of technique and tone that Bronhill achieves, it is more than compensated by the intelligence and passion of the interpretation.

Mark Wynter, as Browning, makes less of a tearaway youth of the poet, playing in a more poised style than Michell, singing in a warm baritone which is at its best in the gently pensive 'Escape Me Never', yet full of energy in 'Frustration' and 'A Simple Way'. He relaxes handsomely into an attractively smooth number, 'Long Ago I Loved You', which, cut from the original production, found its way back into the score at Chichester.

There are, in fact, a number of other differences between the score on this recording, which in any case uses a smaller cast and orchestra than before, and on the original. The opening number, 'Wimpole Street', has been shorn of its ballet and reduced to a lesser length, 'Escape Me Never' has been remodelled, and Mr Barrett's important 'What the World Calls Love' and Dr Chambers's reprise of 'The World Outside', which were not recorded in 1964, are both included this time, alongside 'Long Ago I Loved You'. Each of these inclusions or alterations is a gain.

There are other gains, too, further down the cast list. John Savident gives Mr Barrett's two pieces all the black passion they call for, the brothers and sisters are a splendidly youthful and lively lot, who, with the help of contralto Jill Pert's rich-voiced Wilson, make 'The Girls That Boys Dream About' into one of the highlights of the disc; baritone Gareth Jones's reprise of 'The World Outside' is ringingly sung; and the chorus and orchestra sound fresh and vital throughout.

To choose between these two recordings is impossible for me. The second has many advantages, yet I cannot easily bypass the original version which has been one of my favourites for a quarter of a century. Either is a treat.

Grainer wrote little subsequently for the theatre, but two of his other pieces have been preserved on record. *On the Level* (1966), a bouncy, contemporary piece about schoolchildren and examinations, was in a completely different musical style from *Robert and Elizabeth* and, in spite of some enjoyable moments, *not* on the same level. Sheila White squeaking out her teenage urges in 'Bleep-Bleep', Gary Bond muddling romance and exams in a busy nightmare scene, and a lyrically pointed finale were the highlights of a patchy piece. There was yet another style in *Sing a Rude Song*, a little musical on the life of Marie Lloyd as seen by Ned Sherrin and Caryl Brahms, where Grainer's jaunty original songs were mixed with relevant music-hall songs. Marie, in the person of an oddly subdued Barbara Windsor, does most of the singing, but Maurice Gibb of Bee-Gees fame turns up to claim his share as husband number two.

Canterbury Tales

One of the most successful musicals of the 1960s was the musical version of the *Canterbury Tales*, with music by Richard Hill and John Hawkins. This was partly due to the cunning way in which, under the protection of being based on a classic, it allowed on to the stage a certain amount of what would in those months prior to the abolition of the censor still otherwise have been called 'sex-'n'-violence' and just called it 'bawdy'. The show's score (whose bawdy subject matter and lyrics now seem quite gentle) is a lively collection of musical fragments and short twentieth-century medieval songs. On the original cast recording, these are helpfully linked by lines from the tales, which situate the various musical bits in context and help keep the comic tone up.

Nicky Henson, Billy Boyle and Gay Soper sing the music attached to the various sexy, young characters they play in the course of the evening with a pleasant ease; Wilfred Brambell, of *Steptoe and Son* fame, is the various grubby old men and Jessie Evans a rough-edged Wife of Bath, both with more character than voice; whilst Pamela Charles lends a legitimate voice to the evening's theme song 'Love Will Conquer All'. The tactful combination of text and music makes a highly enjoyable recording, and it is unfortunate that the same kind of layout was not used on the Broadway version which, instead, although including some dialogue, concentrates largely on the songs. As a result some pieces don't mean very much. This is unfortunate because, by and large, the performances on the Broadway disc are, if not necessarily more suitable, on the whole more vocally accomplished.

Ed Evanko, Sandy Duncan and Bruce Hyde are fine as the young people, George Rose is splendidly pointed in the older rôles and Edwin Steffe who, as the host, has appropriated 'Where Are the Girls of Yesterday' from the Clerk of Oxenford, is a proper singer who makes the 'Song of Welcome' a song instead of the original jolly howl. Hermione Baddeley (Wife of Bath) also has an extra song, but is very much not a proper singer, and she speaks her way energetically through 'Come on and Marry Me, Honey'. Martyn Green, the D'Oyly Carte comedian, reads Chaucer's lines in clear, English tones, though without the warm ease of author Martin Starkie (who replaced original cast member James Ottoway for the London disc).

The content of the Broadway show had a number of variations from the London production and, in consequence, five pieces from the original do not appear on the later disc, being replaced by three others. In this way, the whole of the amusing music for The Priest's Tale is omitted, making one final reason for preferring the original record.

Amongst the numerous other 1960s musicals that found their way on to record, mostly as cast recordings, there were a wide range of subjects and styles – crass, louche low comedy in *Instant Marriage*, teenage comedy with some light-handed John Barry songs in *Passion Flower Hotel*, lashings of routine stage cockneyisms in *The Match Girls*, made-to-measure operetta in star tenor John Hanson's own *When You're Young*, ill-musicalized Noel Coward in *Mr and Mrs*, and some very dubious classical adaptations in *Our Man Crichton*, *The Young Visiters*, *Two Cities* and *Ann Veronica*. Laurie Johnson of *Lock up your Daughters* fame provided a vehicle for Harry Secombe in *The Four Musketeers* and classical composer Wilfred Josephs dipped into the musical theatre with the score for Houdini biomusical *Man of Magic*. However, the two most enjoyable of this crop of not-so-successful (and sometimes truly awful) shows were *Virtue in Danger*, the best of the attempts in the wake of *Lock up your Daughters* to turn a Restoration play into a musical, and a loose-limbed revusical vehicle for female impersonator Danny la Rue, prowling about in disguise on behalf of British intelligence declaring *Come Spy with Me*.

Virtue in Danger

Virtue in Danger is a politely salacious musical version of *The Relapse*. It doesn't contain any big, obvious numbers but it has a pleasant, well-made period-modern score by Bernard and Dehn which gives the feeling that it would fit well into the play. The original cast recording has the benefit of some particularly fine actors, headed by John Moffat (Foppington), Barrie Ingham (Fashion), Jane Wenham (Amanda), Patricia Routledge (Berinthia), Richard Wordsworth (Coupler), Hamlyn Benson (Tunbelly Clumsy), Patsy Byrne (Hoyden) and Alan Howard (a non-singing Loveless), who partake of some amusing moments in mostly more than adequate singing voices. The barely wounded Foppington's panicky howls for succour ('Hurry Surgeon'), the meeting of Hoyden and Fashion under the gooseberry eye of the girl's nurse ('Nurse, Nurse, Nurse'), Miss Routledge's sultry Spanish duo 'Wait a Little Longer, Lover' with Basil Hoskins (Worthy), and Miss Wenham's sweet singing of the pretty 'I'm in Love with my Husband' are amongst the best moments of a recording that represents its kind better than other attempts in the same area.

Come Spy with Me

Come Spy with Me comes from the opposite end of the musical spectrum. It is a jolly burlesque of such glamorous spy stories of the time as the James Bond tales and the television series *The Man From Uncle*, which also takes revusical swipes at anything else that comes within coo-ee. Hero Danny (La Rue), lift girl Mavis Apple (Barbara Windsor) and the dashing Agent VO3 (Gary Miller) chase the baddies and their all-important virility drug through two acts and fourteen numbers with titles like 'Assassinating Rhythm', the lift girl's 'Life Has its Funny Little Ups and Downs', and Danny's 'rumpty' 'A Far, Far, Better Thing' as he goes off disguised in his high heels to stalk the foe. It has the feeling of the British film comedies of the 1950s (the presence of ubiquitous civil-servant actor Richard Wattis in the cast only increases that feeling) plus some brightly British, fun-filled songs by Bryan Blackburn.

La Rue appears in both masculine and feminine garb, and has his main number ('More to Me Than Meets the Eye') performing strip-cabaret in the dreaded Rice Room, but the bulk and the best of the songs fall to his two co-stars. Miss Windsor makes a cute job of her lift number, revels comically in a desperate-danger telephone monologue, and yodels lovingly over the swish VO3 ('Mister What's-His-Name'). On account of Miller's fatal illness during the show's run, his rôle of VO3 was taken on the recording by popular vocalist Dennis Lotis, who croons so silkily through his invitation to 'Come Spy with Me' that you can practically see his teeth glint. Needless to say, at the other end of the scale, the baddies are as bad as can be – they even have a song about the 'Great, Great Welfare State'. *Come Spy with Me* is all good, silly fun, and not for those who take their musicals desperately seriously.

Andrew Lloyd Webber and Tim Rice

The first years of the 1970s saw the arrival on the scene of a pair of writers who were to dominate the musical stages of the world for the next two decades. Lyricist Tim Rice and composer Andrew Lloyd Webber started small with a fifteen to twenty-minute long school production of their cantata *Joseph and the Amazing Technicolor Dreamcoat* in 1968. But the international success of *Jesus Christ Superstar* (1972), which prompted a reassessment of an enlarged *Joseph*, and their subsequent triumph with *Evita* (1978) established them and their new style combination of modern-speech lyrics and effective blend of pop and classical musical elements as the most popular contemporary musical-theatrical idiom.

Jesus Christ Superstar

Jesus Christ Superstar began its life as a gramophone recording. Having initially failed to find a producer for the theatre, it instead found one in the recording industry, and it was to due to the success of that original recording of the full score by MCA Records that the piece subsequently made its way to the stage. Its success on its first production on Broadway resulted in world-wide exposure and a flood of records, including cast recordings from a dozen countries. After New York, Denmark was first off the mark, and Sweden (twice), Germany, France, Australia, Britain, Spain (twice), Japan, Brazil and Mexico all followed suit. There was a film adaptation and numerous studio cast versions, as *Jesus Christ Superstar* added to its record as the longest-running West End musical the qualification of being also its most widely recorded.

The effect made by that early double-disc recording is easy to comprehend. *Jesus Christ Superstar* is a sizzling piece of work, ringing with youthful energy, performed by a group of mostly established singers whose deliberate rock vocal excesses are always held in check by the solid and real musical bases of the score. It is played with exuberance and even sometimes excess volume by varied combinations of instruments, in which the electric guitar sound is always prominent. The piece is not done theatrically. There are fade outs and poppy repetitions which disappeared when *Jesus Christ Superstar* was transformed into a stage piece. It is, as it claims, a rock opera for record, but one that had originally been conceived for the stage and could easily be changed back.

The performances on this set of recordings, in retrospect, seem young and even unsophisticated. Over the following years, *Superstar*'s score has been smoothed into a less flamboyantly aggressive article by a series of vastly professional and accomplished vocalists. In 1990 you would not hear this music sung in the untied rock style which Murray Head (Judas) and Ian Gillan (Jesus) of the group Deep Purple let loose on their material in 1970. It depends on your taste which style you prefer. Both these men, working in Lloyd Webber's favourite rock tenor register, have exciting wide-ranging voices, but Head possesses by far the more power of the two and makes a much stronger presence. His 'Heaven on their Mind' and 'Damned for All Time' are greatly impressive. Gillan comes to a peak in the show's most remarkable sequence with Jesus's Gethsemane soliloquy, a true test for any aspiring rock (or non-rock) tenor.

Just to give the devil a full hand, the other most impressive performances here come from the Priests, headed by basso Caiaphas (Victor Brox) and tenor Annas (Brian Keith), singing their plotting in menacing octaves. The rôle of Mary Magdalene is taken by Yvonne Elliman, who turns gentle folky tones onto her calming 'Try Not to Get Worried' and opens up into something rather more powerful at the climax of a version of 'I Don't Know How to Love Him', which is sung to a regular guitar rhythm and never allowed to wallow in the way that is now customary. The orchestra and chorus are highly effective and seemingly vast in personnel, and the sum total is an impressive *Superstar*, which was not soon to be superseded.

In fact, only four further complete versions of the show followed this original one. Telefunken put the West German cast recording down in full, the entire Spanish production was recorded on Pronto, and the Japanese, who have a penchant for going the whole hog in these matters, did the same, leaving the film soundtrack as the only other English-language representative of a double-disc *Superstar*.

This last set incorporates two pieces not found on the original recording – one included in the stage production ('Could We Start Again, Please?') and another, a piece introducing the Priests ('Then We Are Decided') composed specifically for the film. It is a fine recording, with a strong, clean-voiced Jesus (Ted Neely) who rises to heights of human misery in his Gethsemane scene, and a vibrant, passionate Judas (Carl Andersen) who paces his performance through to a savagely bitter death scene. From the Broadway cast, Miss Elliman repeats her Mary, Barry Dennen his highly emotional Pilate, and Bob Bingham rolls out a remarkable Caiaphas. If this version lacks a bit of the rawer attack that was employed on the pre-production disc, it has, on the other hand, more clarity and dramatic shape, and, ignoring the fact that the film itself was not a success, it can be considered a perfectly viable alternative.

The German recording, irritatingly packaged in a box with no descriptive details bar a cast list, is another good recording. It has a part-German, part-British cast, with Oliver Tobias, a manically powerful Judas, well and truly eclipsing the less impressive Jesus (Rainer Schöne). The remainder of the principals perform the material in more or less the manner established on the original recording. The Japanese, on the other hand, on a disc made seven years later, take sometimes slightly different lines. Mary Magdalene is, for example, a gentle soprano, a deviation which is quite effective as a calming contrast from the violent rock music of the two principal men. Here, for the first time, the Jesus very definitely is the Superstar. Takeshi Kaga sings his music stylishly, alternately with power and with gentleness, and makes a much more successful character than his Judas (Minoru Terada), who is reduced to impotent shrieking in a rôle which seems beyond him. This set, incidentally, is beautifully packaged, with all the necessary information given in both Japanese and English and a text in Japanese. The Spanish double-disc set is a perfectly competent one, on which the Judas (Teddy Bautista) also somehow acts as musical director and arranger and plays keyboards and harmonica (ah! modern technology!), and on which the show's producer (Camillo Sesto) plays Jesus. Both men perform their rôles capably, but you get the feeling that they're calculatedly putting all the rock crackles into their voices. There is more spontaneity elsewhere, but somehow there is a phoney feeling hanging around this performance.

Of the selection discs, the original Broadway and London cast recordings are the most widespread. The Broadway recording has Elliman (Mary), Bingham (Caiaphas) and Dennen (Pilate) in common with the film soundtrack, plus a fine clear-voiced Jesus (Jeff Fenholt) and a vigorous Judas (Ben Vereen), and is generally superior to the British disc. This omits Judas's death in favour of Simon Zealotes's song (more widely included in selections generally), and is both a much less extravagant performance stylistically and mostly less excitingly sung. Paul Nicholas, however, in spite of not really having the vocal range for the rôle of Jesus, imbues his Gethsemane scene with moving understanding.

Australia's cast recording – the only other in English – has advantages over both of these. An enthusiastic, well-sung version, it includes 'Poor Jerusalem' and the Last Supper sequence and omits Herod's Song and the Priests' Trio in return. The leading players are well matched, with an explosive Judas (Jon English), who revels passionately in every beat of the high notes that others barely reach, and a contrastingly clear and firm Jesus (Trevor White), who has a little difficulty at the bottom end of his range, but who goes from the gentlest moments of the rôle to the searing climax of Gethsemane impressively and accurately. The Mary (Michelle Fawdon) is affectingly sweet-voiced, and the representatives of Peter, Simon and a rough and unaristocratic Caiaphas all perform well alongside a highly emotional Pilate (Robin Ramsay), who, as a billable name artist, gets good exposure on the recording.

I haven't been able to lay hands on the Danish, Brazilian, Mexican or earlier Swedish recordings, but the four foreign-language selection discs I do have – French (1972), Spanish revival (1984), Swedish revival (1985) and Hungarian studio cast (1986) – show the variations that have come into the playing of *Superstar* over the years. The orchestration on the later recordings has shrunk and/or softened, the singers have adopted more 'modern' styles, and technical quality has also moved onwards. Taken on their own terms, all four are perfectly fine records. The French version – not perhaps the most interesting of adaptations – has the most beautifully plangent Mary (Anne-Marie David) and a good all-round cast, in spite of a Jesus who, though he sings well, seems to feel obliged to put in some unnecessary scalded cat noises just to prove how 1972 he is. America's Bob Bingham (Caiaphas) takes grateful advantage of the open 'a' sounds of the French lyric 'cela m'agace, cette populace' to pound out some even blacker bottom notes than ever, and Michel Mella makes an interestingly insinuating fellow out of the often not terribly exciting Simon Zealotes. Just an ounce more of everything from the Judas and a touch less mannerism from the Jesus and this would be a first-rate disc.

The three recent recordings have all had a good fiddle with the orchestrations and, although they make up for some of the ensuing loss of musical breadth with good sound recording, good singing and lashings of echo, something of the piece's original style is lost. The Swedish record comes up with fine singers for Jesus and Mary, but a Judas who skives the higher notes of his rôle, and it makes do without the Priests, which is always a shame. The Spanish disc, which seems dominated by a drum kit and a bank of electric keyboards (it's the same Teddy Bautista of the original Spanish recording twenty-five years later), may be thin on instruments but certainly not on commitment, volume or style. Its singers, too, are extremely good. All the characters come across much more stoutly than on the earlier Spanish version and Pablo Abraira (Jesus) makes a very respectable job of Gethsemane. Whatever this record may lack, it is very enjoyable to sit back and listen to.

There is another fine, mostly unmannered Jesus (Sándor Sasvári) on the Hungarian disc and, indeed, the excellent artists on this record all perform the show very much by the book. There is an operatic basso Caiaphas, who produces a splendidly easy dark sound but lacks some of the quirky vileness of the early, less well-equipped players and, indeed, of his fellow Priests, who perform in the accepted 'wicked-witch' style.

When you come to the end of it all, with *Jesus Christ Superstar*s for all ages and countries, and none of them what you would call a bad recording, it is still – in spite of perhaps better vocal performances and more effective characterizations elsewhere – difficult not to give best to that first, irrepressibly sparkling studio cast recording. For a single-disc treatment, I'd be tempted to the Australian recording, but the film soundtrack, the full-scale German set, the French cast album and the recent Spanish disc all give their own enjoyment, and doubtless some of the other *Superstar*s which I haven't yet been able to lay hands on do as well.

Joseph and the Amazing Technicolor Dreamcoat

Such alteration, or evolution, as occurred in *Jesus Christ Superstar* was as nothing beside that which the authors' perennially popular *Joseph and the Amazing Technicolor Dreamcoat* went through in its development from fifteen- or twenty-minute children's cantata to hit Broadway musical. Most of the stages in between have been documented on record, and as a result there are a number of different *Joseph* discs to be found.

The first recording, made in 1968, is the original twenty-minute's worth, expanded by half as much time again to fill two sides of a long-playing record.

In comparison with the *Joseph* of the 1980s, this recording clearly shows its origins, not so much by the sweetly careful singing of the school choir but by the folksily gentle and occasionally limp and mumbly singing of the principal lines by the group Mixed Bag and David Daltrey. It is a very polite recording, but then again it is a sort of family affair – Rice performs Pharaoh's Song, Lloyd Webber's organist father produces string sounds from the Hammond organ, and the conductor and choir are those from Colet Court for whom the piece was originally commissioned – and the tentative parts of the presentation are almost endearing. The sleeve of this disc, incidentally, is a beauty. You get the most angelic photograph of the two now famous youngsters, a good laugh or a slight twinge (depending on your age) at the pictures of the performers dressed up in their zippered leather jerkins and long hair, and a piece of prophetic writing from the *Sunday Times*'s Derek Jewell, the piece's and the writers' earliest critical champion – 'The names on this disc aren't yet well known, but . . . that situation will change swiftly. *Joseph* is splendid enough in itself. It could be the start of something even bigger.'

The next stage of *Joseph*'s development was its production, after the success of *Superstar*, at the Young Vic. Now increased to some forty minutes in length (and the authors already looking less angelic), it was again put down on record, this time with a rather more professional cast, by the Robert Stigwood Organization. The energy level is higher here: some of the humour of the lyrics starts to be brought out by the articulate Narrator (Peter Reeves), easy-voiced Gary Bond as Joseph puts more into and gets more out of his rôle, and Gordon Waller, from the pop duo Peter and Gordon, gurgles happily through a first-rate Elvis Presley impersonation as Pharaoh, complete with screaming fans.

No sooner had that record been made, with the writers asserting that these were 'the final-ever lyrics', than *Joseph* transferred to the West End and promptly proceeded to grow not once but twice more. Several lively tongue-in-cheek pieces were added, such as the burlesque Western carol 'One More Angel in Heaven', the parody *chanson* 'Those Canaan Days' and the rhythmic Benjamin Calypso. And so another record was made, this time by MCA, of a show which, with the inclusion of so much friendly burlesque material, had rather changed its character. It had also gained in performance for, although many of the London cast, notably Bond, Reeves and Waller, were the same as those who had appeared on the previous recording, they and the piece had gained considerably in crispness, clarity and confidence. The recording of *Joseph* Mark 3 was again several notches up in energy and style. The new numbers added fun and colour both to the show and to the disc, which was in every way a cut above the previous efforts.

A selection from the South African production and a larger one from Ireland – a very rare recording – followed, and Music for Pleasure issued a lively but 'sessiony' disc in 1979 featuring Paul Jones, the Joseph of a recent West End Christmas season, with Rice this time singing the Narrator and Waller repeating his definitive Pharaoh. Yet again there has been some reallocation of lines among the characters, but this time *Joseph* remained fairly static as to content.

In 1982 *Joseph* was given a Broadway production and a cast album on Chrysalis. Once again there were minor rewrites (including a limp little prologue) and wholesale reallocation of lines. The rôle of the Narrator, as had first been the case on the umpteenth year of the British tour, was cast with a female voice. Highly successful in the theatre, this production comes over unattractively on disc. The happy simplicity of the show is overlaid with some mannered and even campy performances and the gentle burlesque is trampled to bits. Bill Hutton is a pleasantly sweet-voiced Joseph, but Laurie Beecham as the narrator is both uncomfortably squashed-sounding and not very intelligible, whilst Tom Carder (Pharoah) drowns his lyrics in gruff Presleyesque noises.

Israel and Mexico seem to have been the only countries to issue non-English-language *Joseph*s. Mexico's I have not heard, but Israel's 1980 disc, which also uses a female voice as Narrator, is a rather unenthusiastic one.

Evita

With *Evita*, the dramatic story of Argentine dictator's wife Eva Peron, Rice and Lloyd Webber necessarily broadened into a more sophisticated musical and lyrical style. They produced a powerful and beautiful score in their own modern operatic idiom which, first heard on a double-disc recording, proved to be the basis for one of the most successful musicals of the decade and, statistically at very least, of all time. When it reached the stage in 1978, *Evita* began a career in which it would overtake the records established by all but *Jesus Christ Superstar*, both for the longest-running West End musical and also for the most widely recorded British show.

The original concept album was followed by several studio cast recordings, hastily recorded to cash in on the rise of 'Don't Cry for Me, Argentina' and 'Another Suitcase in Another Hall' to the top of the hit parade, before the London stage production's cast album arrived. Broadway followed, then Australia, and the floodgates opened as Spain, Austria, Mexico, South Africa, Japan, New Zealand, Brazil and Hungary all turned out single- or double-record cast albums from their productions. Even in Argentina, where the show was banned, half a dozen extracts were put out on a twelve-inch EP.

The original recording, looked at in hindsight, demonstrates that very much of *Evita* has remained quite unchanged since the very beginning. One section, Che's 'The Lady's Got Potential', disappeared on the show's way to the stage, and the cast albums didn't have the benefit of the London Philharmonic Orchestra, but otherwise the differences, both in content and in style and performance, are small. Julie Covington's Evita and C. T. (Colm) Wilkinson's Che make a fine scrapping, street-fighting pair. There is no forgetting that this powerfully acted Eva comes from a small-town, cheap-living background. She is no lady. Covington is also very individual vocally, singing through the rôle's wide range with a strong, dramatic, dry voice which carries neither warmth nor vibrato. It is almost anti-singing, but it makes a very definite character. As for Wilkinson, he is a marvellous Che, stylish and biting and with a thrilling voice, and there are other fine performances in Barbara Dickson's little Mistress with her reflective, folksy 'Another Suitcase in Another Hall' and Tony Christie's medallion-man Magaldi singing 'On This Night of a Thousand Stars'. The recording has, incidentally, no bands between the sections of the show, an operatic parallel Lloyd Webber was to use again in *The Phantom of the Opera* to insist on the integrity of the piece as a whole, rather than as a series of 'numbers'. The point is well made, but since the 'numbers' are individually listed on both the sleeve and the centre of the record, perhaps less than fully effective.

The London cast album is a single-disc recording which, nevertheless, takes in the heart of the show. It has Elaine Paige as Eva. The sharp and dirty fingernails of Covington's Eva are less in evidence here, but the single-minded character is clearly and effectively drawn and the singing is both searing and superb. This is a much more accomplished voice. Harsh and dramatic, insinuating and demanding, she soars chillingly to the vicious high chest notes of 'Rainbow High' and turns callous and mocking tones against David Essex's Che with devastating effect. The balance of the conflict is different here from that on the earlier record. This Che, finely and coolly sung and played, is never going to be a real threat to this Eva; an irritation, dripping sardonically away, nipping at her heels, but never getting at her throat. Also, unlike the first recording, this one poses a contrast between Che and Peron, and Joss Ackland's less extravagant singing and playing makes the President into a plausible and solid character, highlighting the effusive bickering of Essex's narrative. Mark Ryan as the vain tango-singer, sitting precariously on the edge of his high notes, and sweet-voiced Siobhan McCarthy's vacant little Mistress complete the cast, alongside a theatre chorus and orchestra which prove quite sufficient in strength for such ravenous climaxes as 'A New Argentina'.

MCA chose to return to the double-disc format for the Broadway cast album, producing the first (and only listenable) full English-language version of the stage *Evita*. This recording moves even further away from the gutsy invective of the concept disc. Patti LuPone has no trouble encompassing the vocal range of the rôle of Eva, but she does it with a different kind of voice, more lyrical and easier of delivery, neither hacking out the music like Covington nor burning her way through it like Paige, but saving her biggest cartridges for one or two occasions like the demanding high portions of the first-act finale. This means that the character comes across more self-possessed and less aggressive and makes the tit-for-tat with Che a less obviously dangerous one. It also means that you don't get the black thrills of such moments as Paige's 'Rainbow High'.

Mandy Patinkin's smoothly mocking Che, sung in an impressive lyrical modern tenor, sounds as if he would have the edge on this Eva in a showdown. Jane Ohringer (Mistress), Mark Syers (Magaldi) and Bob Gunton (a Peron who, alone of the principals, adopts an accent) fulfil their rôles in the established way, and there is a first-rate singing chorus on a recording which ultimately lacks a little passion.

Of the other English-language *Evita*s, both the Australian and South African recordings have accomplished Evas, but the full-length live-performance New

Zealand version is best passed by in embarrassed silence. Australia's warm-voiced Jennifer Murphy has impressive moments in a stylish performance which, however, only just makes the top notes, and South African Jo-Ann Pezzaro (who unfortunately leaves two numbers to her second string in a foolish piece of democracy) gives an intelligent and well-paced performance in a fine, strong voice just lacking the searing quality of an Elaine Paige. Neither, unfortunately, gets much of a battle going with their Che, as both John O'May and Eric Flynn sing the notes of their rôle with smooth precision, but scarcely get up steam as a protagonist.

The two full-length Spanish-language recordings (Spain and Mexico) use different translations, and the Spanish recording – it seems to be a habit in Spain – also takes its own way in the area of orchestration. This is a shame as, otherwise, it has many advantages, including good singing and plenty of attack throughout, and a well-paired, energetic Eva (Paloma San Basilio) and Che (Patxi Andion). Mexico's Eva (Rocio Banquells) also gives a shapely and well-sung performance, but neither she nor Sra San Basilio can come up to the Brazilian star, Claudia, who is undoubtedly the best of all the foreign-language Evas. She has a magnificent, easy voice which she uses with both strength and dramatic impact, pinging out the exciting high notes of 'Rainbow High' and 'Buenos Aires', building her 'Nâo chores por mim Argentina' impressively, and taking liberties with the music in an extremely sexy 'Ponho o mundo teus peu' ('I'd Be Surprisingly Good for You'). She is opposed by a vigorous, lip-licking Che (Carlos Augusto Strazzer), and a Magaldi (Hilton Prado) who takes himself much less seriously than some of the other occupants of his rôle. A little-heard but rich-voiced Peron (Mauro Mendonca), a plaintive Mistress (Silvia Massari) and a particularly strong group of male choristers contribute to make this a very satisfyingly performed Evita. Once again, the orchestrations have been fiddled with – 'Orquestracões adicionas' are credited, but in some places it seems to be a bit more than that – but this on its own is not sufficient to damage a fine recording.

Of the remaining recordings, the Hungarian version comes out the best. Equipped with a stallion-voiced, bile-spitting Eva (Kriszta Kováts), a slicingly characterful and rocky Che (Sándor Szakácsi), a heart-throbbing Magaldi (Attila Bardóczy) and a pretty but desperately over-echoed Mistress (Anikó Nagy), it attacks the score with a great energy which only occasionally produces excesses. Sadly, it chooses to omit 'Rainbow High', but what is there gets a committed performance. Austria's Eva (Isabel Wiecken) and Che (Alexander Goebel) expend useful voices and some curiously uneven interpretation on a selection which includes a vicious-sounding 'Rainbow High' and an equally bilious 'The Money Kept Rolling In'. This recording contains a bit too much 'wicked-witch' acting and it does not gel as it might.

The Japanese changed the famous white dress (Dior would have died rather than be credited with the crimplene monstrosity pictured on the sleeve), but produce a reasonably standard version of the show, apart from some draggy tempi (notably in a gentle 'Don't Cry for Me, Argentina') and the fact that they boast the world's only legitimate soprano Eva, oddly paired with a quasi-pop Che. Perhaps this combination of voices could work, but it is not what the show's history has accustomed us to and, in any case, not well enough done here.

So many *Evita*s, and more, doubtless, to come, but Elaine Paige's definitive vocal portrait has installed itself as the Evita of all time and is unlikely ever to be bested. For my taste, I should have preferred her paired with a more aggressive opponent, one on the lines of Colm Wilkinson, whose original Che is still head and shoulders above the rest. So, I compromise: for a selection, the London cast album with Miss Paige, for a complete *Evita*, the original concept album – and for something a bit more exotic, a swift visit to Brazil and the amazing Claudia.

More Shows of the 1970s

Behind the successful front of the three Rice/Lloyd Webber shows, the usual collection of successful and not so successful 1970s musicals made their way to record. One of those failures, *Jeeves*, actually had a score by Lloyd Webber, venturing into period pastiche in collaboration with playwright Alan Ayckbourn. The unexceptional *Jeeves* cast album (which hides one or two unexpectedly pretty numbers under indifferent performances) is, however, a gem alongside the recordings of such fellow flops of the period as the dreadful *Pull Both Ends*, *Tom Brown's Schooldays*, *What a Way to Run a Revolution*, *Bordello*, *I and Albert*, *Mardi Gras*, *Ride, Ride!*, *Drake's Dream*, *Liza of Lambeth*, *Big Sin City*, *Bar Mitzvah Boy* and *Colette*.

Fortunately the 1970s held a few pieces of better and more successful material than these, mostly in the old style, but just occasionally attempting something different. *The Card* (1973) and *Billy* (1974) were both in strict line of descent from the *Half a Sixpence* style of musical, *Hans Andersen* (1974) was fashioned for *Half a Sixpence* star Tommy Steele from Frank Loesser's famous film score of 1952, and *A Day in Hollywood – A Night in the Ukraine* (1979) was pure old-fashioned burlesque, but *The Rocky Horror Show* (1973) and, more expansively, *Tommy* (1975) took their musical inspiration from more modern sources.

The Card

Tony Hatch and Jackie Trent's jaunty score for *The Card* was no *Half a Sixpence*, but on record it was given as good a service as could have been hoped for from a cast featuring the earlier show's leading lady Marti Webb, Millicent Martin and, in the part intended for Tommy Steele, Jim Dale. In his first musical star rôle Dale gives an affectionately cheeky performance as Arnold Bennett's cutely ambitious Denry Machin.

Billy

Where *The Card* had Dale, *Billy* had another rising young star, Michael Crawford. It also had a fine, imaginative score from John Barry and Don Black which carried the daydreaming 'Billy Liar' musically through a series of dream o' day fantasies and a less comfortable set of encounters with real life. Crawford, in his stage musical début, was equipped with some fine songs and he performs them on the cast album with an irresistible mixture of cocky charm and febrile intensity. The twin soliloquies, the happily self-deluding 'Some of Us Belong to the Stars' and its echoing 'I Missed the Last Rainbow', the nearest Billy gets to facing the truth, are a touching pair of numbers, to which Crawford gives a fine mixture of bravado and pathos, alongside such more comical moments as his throttling condemnation of the affectedly trilling Gay Soper (Barbara) as 'The Witch' or his tactical admission of some of his worse 'Lies'.

The rest of the fine cast have good moments, too. Elaine Paige as rough-as-guts Rita pairs threateningly with Miss Soper in parallel thoughts of their mutual 'fiancé' in 'Any Minute Now', Bryan Pringle and Avis Bunnage as Billy's long-suffering parents harangue their incomprehensible offspring in 'And', and Billy Boyle joins Crawford in a rhythmic look at Yorkshire folk in 'Happy to Be Themelves'.

Hans Andersen

Hans Andersen (1974) brought Steele back to the musical theatre a decade after *Half a Sixpence* to give his inimitable treatment to the songs made famous by Danny Kaye: 'Thumbelina', 'Inchworm', 'Wonderful Copenhagen', 'I'm Hans Christian Andersen', 'The King's New Clothes' and 'No Two People (Have Ever Been So in Love)', plus a few more taken from the Loesser leftovers or composed for the occasion by Marvin Laird. The success of the stage show prompted a handful of cover albums, with Bernard Cribbins and Jon Pertwee both having a go at being Tommy Steele. Pertwee also included one song, the leading lady's 'Have I Been Away Too Long', cut in rehearsals and another, 'In your Eyes', which was never in the show. The former number was reprieved when Steele played a second West End run in a slightly revised version of the show three years later. The original cast recording was doctored for the occasion and re-released without the now cut opening chorus, but including the song in question, the lively 'Happy Days' (unrecorded first time round), and the replacement 'Dare to Take a Chance'.

Steele's vigour and charm are splendidly suited to the material, and both the Loesser standards and the lesser-known and new songs are invigoratingly performed. That is about it. There is little else for anyone else to do. The rôle of Jenny Lind is decorated with a lovely ballad, 'Truly Loved', but otherwise it's pretty much all Hans. Colette Gleeson is the Jenny of the original disc, giving a sweetly sung, natural-sounding performance. She is replaced in the revival by Sally Ann Howes who, equipped with the reinstated number, is more operatic but rather less appealing. Maybe I am biased in preferring the original recording. If you look down in the tiniest print amongst the chorus you will find, alongside the name of TV astrologer Russell Grant, that of the author of these lines.

A Day in Hollywood – A Night in the Ukraine

A Day in Hollywood – A Night in the Ukraine (1979) was a tiny one-act musical paired with a tiny revusical concert, which grew from its extremely tiny off-off-West End home to end up, with the concert substantially revamped but the musical more or less intact, as a Broadway hit. The musical (*A Night in the Ukraine*) was a very loose musical version of Chekhov's *The Bear*, as performed in the style of the Marx Brothers' *A Night at the Opera*, and equipped with half-a-dozen comical musical pieces in the best revue tradition.

The little British production did not make its way to record, but the Broadway version did. The six-cast, three-piano, one-bass recording includes the Richard Whiting medley and three new songs by Jerry Herman, as well as three songs by the original authors and a tap-danced recital of the Hollywood Production Code, all of which made up the *A Day in Hollywood* portion of the show. It is a little record of a little show, but none the less enjoyable for it. The score of *A Night in the Ukraine* comes across with plenty of humour, with David Garrison, impersonating Groucho Marx declaring himself in excruciating rhymes as 'Samovar the Lawyer' or courting the rich and rich 'Natasha', getting the best moments. Richard Whiting takes up a fair chunk of the rest of the record, but there is fun, especially for the film fan, in 'I Love a Film Cliché', in Peggy Hewett's burlesque of Jeanette MacDonald ('Nelson'), in Priscilla Lopez's sweetly sad tale of an usherette turned actress turned usherette ('The Best in the World') or in the catchy how-to-compose song 'It All Comes out of a Piano'.

The Rocky Horror Show

The Rocky Horror Show is another little show, but one which has grown in fame and fortune until it has become a world-wide cult both on stage and screen. On the way it has spawned a half-dozen recordings, beginning with one by the very original cast from the minuscule Theatre Upstairs at the Royal Court.

This recording, taking in thirteen numbers along with some snatches of narrative reminiscent of a children's record, is a loud and energetic nine-handed, five-musician affair, recorded with more enthusiasm than technical perfection. Tim Curry is a knockout as the crisply English 'Sweet Transvestite from Transexual, Transylvania', mixing leather jacket and Mae West in disturbing style, with Christopher Malcolm (Brad), deftly blending wide-eyed comedy and fetching 1950s singing, and Belinda Sinclair (Janet) doing good work as his 'victims'. The rest of the cast are unfailingly lively and fun, and the result is a disc that successfully reproduces the special atmosphere of the show.

The recording of the first American production in Hollywood is a more substantial one. There are three extra numbers ('Eddie's Teddy', 'Planet Shmanet

Janet' and the Charles Atlas Song), double the number of musicians, and slicker recording and singing, but apart from Curry, who repeats his London performance with variations, and Meat Loaf, in the Eddie/Dr Scott double rôle, there is also a sad lack of the humour that is the show's mainstay.

The other English-language recordings both come from Australia. The original cast album has more humour and a frenetic, strong-voiced, rather over-feminine Frank 'n' Furter (Reg Livermore) whilst a second Australian selection disc (served up in a plastic bag, as the maufacturers made the sleeves too small) gives only six numbers on a suitably ghastly piece of soft pink plastic.

The film soundtrack (*The Rocky Horror Picture Show*) reverts to the smaller band of the original show and to many of the original performers, but it makes other alterations. 'The Sword of Damocles', 'Once in a While' and 'Planet Shmanet Janet' have disappeared, and some of the other numbers have been reorganized, expanded or reallocated. There are fine, spunky repeat performances from Curry, maintaining his spoofily sexy but definitely male performance third time round; from the splendidly sinuous Richard O'Brien (also the author of the piece) as a definitive Riff Raff, here annexing the opening 'Science Fiction' and giving it a chillingly faceless performance; and from Little Nell (Columbia), Patricia Quinn (Magenta) and Meat Loaf (Eddie). They are teamed with an impeccable tongue-in-cheek All-American pair of 'goodies' in Brad (Barry Bostwick) and Janet (Susan Saradon). A bit of the raw energy of the original performance may have gone, but this soundtrack leaves little wanting, especially for the many millions to whom this movie is midnight madness.

For lovers of extreme curiosities there is a disastrous in-theatre German-language recording from Essen issued by Ariola, with a bald, black Frank in a leopardskin midi-skirt whose numbers are largely excluded from the record, a male usherette, a wobbly soprano Janet, an indiscriminately whistling audience, and chunks of Deutsche Texte. This is actually such a bad record, it isn't even a curiosity.

The Mexican disc (*El show de terror de Rocky*) is more proficient but ordinary. Its curiosities are the solo above-title billing of the unexceptional artist playing Chelo (as Janet has been renamed, presumably to rhyme with 'cielo!', which does duty as 'dammit' in the translation), an equally unexciting Carlos (ex-Brad), who is also musical director, producer and keyboard-player, and an uncharismatic Frank who, like everyone else, has to battle against an over-loud band.

Tommy

Tommy, devised as a recording by the group The Who, was ultimately adapted for both a film and a stage performance. The latter was of such insignificance as to put this piece squarely back into its own area, where pop music fans will know whether they prefer the original recording or the film track, with its Elton John 'Pinball Wizard'.

My Ten Essential Records

VALMOUTH: Chichester Festival cast recording, 1982, with Bertice Reading, Fenella Fielding, Mark Wynter and Femi Taylor (TER 1019)

THE BOY FRIEND: original cast recording, with Anne Rogers, Maria Charles and Anthony Hayes (10-inch, HMV DLP 1078; re-recorded MFP 1206 and Stanyan SR10008); or Broadway revival cast recording, with Judy Carne, Jeanne Beauvais and Cy Young (Decca DL 79177; re-recorded MCA 2074)

EXPRESSO BONGO: original cast recording, with Paul Scofield, James Kenney, Hy Hazell and Millicent Martin (Nixa NPL 18016; re-recorded AEI 1110)

HALF A SIXPENCE: original cast recording, with Tommy Steele and Marti Webb (Decca LK/SKL 4521; re-recorded TER 1041)

CHRYSANTHEMUM: original cast recording, with Pat Kirkwood and Herbert Gregg (Nixa NPL 18026; re-recorded AEI 1108)

OLIVER!: original cast recording, with Ron Moody and Georgia Brown (Decca LK/SKL 4105; re-recorded TER 1042)

ROBERT AND ELIZABETH: Chichester Festival cast recording, 1987, with Gaynor Miles and Mark Wynter (First Night Cast 8); or original cast recording, with June Bronhill and Keith Michell (HMV CLP1820/CSD1575; re-recorded EMI ON532; DRG/Stet DS15021; AEI 1111)

JOSEPH AND THE AMAZING TECHNICOLOR DREAMCOAT: studio cast recording, with Peter Reeves, Gary Bond and Gordon Waller (MCA MCF2544)

JESUS CHRIST SUPERSTAR: original studio cast recording, with Murray Head, Ian Gillan and Yvonne Elliman (MCA MKPS2011-2; Decca DXSA7206; re-recorded MCA 10000)

EVITA: original cast recording, with Elaine Paige and David Essex (MCA MCG3527); CD (DMCG 3527)

Other Recommended Records

A Wedding in Paris: original cast recording, with Evelyn Laye, Anton Walbrook, Susan Swinford and Jeff Warren (10-inch, Parlophone PMD 1011)

Sail Away: original London cast recording, with Elaine Stritch and David Holliday (HMV CLP 1572; Stanyan SR 10027)

Salad Days: London revival cast recording, with Elizabeth Seal, Sheila Steafel, Christina Matthews and Adam Bareham (TER 1018)

Follow That Girl: original cast recording, with Susan Hampshire, Peter Gilmore, Marion Grimaldi and Newton Blick (Oriole CSD 1307)

Trelawny: original cast recording, with Gemma Craven, John Watts and Ian Richardson (Decca SKL 5144)

Divorce Me, Darling!: original cast recording, with Patricia Michael, Joan Heal, Maria Charles and Geoffrey Hibbert (Decca LK/SKL 4675; re-recorded TER 1077; DRG DS15009)

His Monkey Wife: original cast recording, with Bridget Armstrong and Robert Swann (President PTLS 1051)

Make Me an Offer: original cast recording, with Daniel Massey, Meier Tzelniker and Diana Coupland (HMV CLP1333/CSD 1295; re-recorded AEI 1112)

Charlie Girl: revival cast recording, 1986, with Paul Nicholas, Lisa Hull, Mark Wynter, Cyd Charisse and Dora Bryan (First Night Cast 3)

Jorrocks: original cast recording, with Joss Ackland, Thelma Ruby, Cheryl Kennedy and Paul Eddington (HMV CLP/CSD 3591)

The Biograph Girl: original cast recording, with Bruce Barry, Sheila White and Kate Revill (TER 1003)

Lock up your Daughters: original cast recording, with Richard Wordsworth, Hy Hazell, Frederick Jaeger, Stephanie Voss and Terence Cooper (Decca LK 4320 / SKL 4070; re-recorded AEI 1120)

Maggie May: original cast recording, with Rachel Roberts and Kenneth Haigh (Decca LK/SKL 4643; re-recorded with extra material on TER 1046)

Grab Me a Gondola: original cast recording, with Joan Heal, Jane Wenham and Denis Quilley (HMV CLP1103; re-recorded AEI 1119)

Belle: original cast recording, with George Benson, Virginia Vernon and Rose Hill (Decca LK 3497/SKL 4136; re-recorded TER 1048)

Stop the World, I Want to Get Off: original cast recording, with Anthony Newley and Anna Quayle (Decca LK 4408/SKL 4142; re-recorded TER 1082)

Virtue in Danger: original cast recording, with Barrie Ingham, Patricia Routledge, Jane Wenham and John Moffat (Decca LK/SKL 4536; re-recorded TER 1079)

Come Spy with Me: original cast recording, with Danny LaRue, Dennis Lotis and Barbara Windsor (Decca LK/SKL 4810)

Canterbury Tales: original cast recording, with Nicky Henson, Billy Boyle, Jessie Evans, Wilfred Brambell and Pamela Charles (Decca LK/SKL 4956; re-recorded TER 1076)

The Rocky Horror Show: film soundtrack (*The Rocky Horror Picture Show*), with Tim Curry, Barry Bostwick and Susan Saradon (ODE 78332); CD (ODE CD 1032; OSVCD 25653)

Billy: original cast recording, with Michael Crawford, Elaine Paige, Gay Soper, Brian Pringle and Avis Bunnage (CBS 70133)

Songbook: original cast recording, with David Healey, Gemma Craven, Diane Langton, Anton Rogers and Andrew Wadsworth (Pye NSPL 18609)

A Day in Hollywood – A Night in the Ukraine: original Broadway cast recording, with David Garrison, Priscilla Lopez, Frank Lazarus, Peggy Hewett, Kate Draper and Stephen James (DRG SBL 12580); CD (DRG SBL 12580)

Hans Andersen: original cast recording, with Tommy Steele and Colette Gleeson (Pye NSPL 18451)

Evita: complete original concept album, with Julie Covington and Colm Wilkinson (MCA MCX503); or Brazilian cast recording, with Claudia and Carlos Augusto Strazzer (Som Livre 403.6273)

CHAPTER 10

The 1980s

The 1980s have, during their course, brought forth fewer and fewer new musical shows to add to the repertoire of the world's stages. The costs of production and of running a modern stage musical have dissuaded many producers from attempting to launch new pieces and, with the Continent having all but dried up as an initiating source and the once fertile stages of America in decline, only Britain has turned out much in the way of successful new musical shows. Even there, however, the handful of big international hits, often reproduced breath for breath around the world, as if they were enshrined on film, mask a general hollowness behind. There are fewer successes. What there are are bigger successes, and successes which are getting to a public that might not have previously gone to a musical or bought its record, but the percentage of failures is great.

In contrast, however, to the 1960s and 1970s, when many a new and sometimes worthy show escaped unrecorded, the 1980s have seen a passion to put even the most utter theatrical failures on record. It is an unquestionably useful way of keeping a score alive in an age when the printed vocal score has become virtually an anachronism, and music that is still alive can always hope that someone will take a fancy to it and give it another chance on the stage. But although this passion for posterity is all very fine for posterity, it is not quite as fine for an unalerted record-buying public. There are not a few of these discs that ought to have a health warning on them. But, again, there are the good ones and the outstanding ones. By and large, as usual, these are the successes, but, as always, there are some pleasant, often small-sized, surprises.

Andrew Lloyd Webber

The outstanding personality of the musical theatre of the 1980s has undoubtedly been composer Andrew Lloyd Webber who, with his scores for *Cats* (1981), *Song and Dance* (1982), *Starlight Express* (1984), *The Phantom of the Opera* (1987) and *Aspects of Love* (1989), has been responsible for filling musical theatres around the world for unprecedentedly extended runs as well as filling many a record with music.

Cats

Cats is, to date, the phenomenon amongst this list. Both its London and Broadway productions are still continuing at the time of writing, moving steadily towards the first decade of their runs, and other productions – or, rather, reproductions – of the piece, from Hungary, Japan and Austria to Australia and France, have confirmed the appeal of the show with their sometimes record-breaking successes. There is no doubt that *Cats* is set to become one of the most notable events in the history of the musical theatre, if, in fact, it has not already.

Largely a setting of the poems from T. S. Eliot's *Old Possum's Book of Practical Cats*, the show is necessarily episodic, relying more on its concept, its style, its remarkable dance staging and the personalities of its cat characters than on any narrative line to see it through the evening. On disc, of course, you have none of that, with the exception of the characters. A record of *Cats* consists very largely of a series of little portraits in words and music of Eliot's (and, you must now say Lloyd Webber's – if not also Trevor Nunn and Gillian Lynne's) family of felines: Mr Mistoffolees the magical cat, Skimbleshanks the railway cat, Gus the theatre cat, Macavity the mystery cat, the Rum Tum Tugger, great lumbering Old Deuteronomy and poor, bedraggled Grizabella, the glamour cat.

They are a delightful set of songs, but a set is indeed what they are. I remember when the first, now rarely seen, 45 rpm recording of Paul Nicholas singing 'Mr Mistoffolees' and 'Old Deuteronomy' came out, in November 1980, before the production of the show, being vaguely disappointed. The songs seemed repetitious and not particularly tuneful and Nicholas a mite unenthusiastic. In fact, they were an odd pair to choose, for the former in particular is constructed very much as an accompaniment to action and, on the stage, is illustrated by more visual elements than almost any other number. What was to be the hit song, however, was not even written at that stage. When it was, Grizabella's tortured 'Memory' became one of the most popular show songs of the decade.

The numbers of *Cats* work best when they are heard as a set, either in the theatre or on a cast recording where, the fascinating and atmospheric overture passed and the 'Jellicle Cats' introduced, the contrasts between the bouncing foolishness of 'Mungojerrie and Rumpleteazer', the sleazy bump-and-grind of the female cats on the lookout for 'Macavity', the pop caterwauling of the 'Rum Tum Tugger' or the heroic burlesque of 'Growltiger's Last Stand' make for a lively, varied record. To date, there have been seven double-disc recordings of the complete *Cats* score, beginning with the British and American cast recordings and continuing with their equivalents from Japan, Australia, Holland, France and the German production in Hamburg. Austria and Hungary limited their recordings to one disc, which meant omitting a significant amount of the show, but there is no single-disc *Cats* recording issued in the original English.

The London cast recording presents almost the entire show in its original state, being thus the only one of the seven to use the delightful if difficult 'Billy McCaw' ballad, subsequently and rather sadly replaced by the showier burlesque aria 'In quella tepida notte' in the second-act Growltiger sequence. There are many happy items – Sharon Lee-Hill and Geraldine Gardner turning searingly confident voices (not always the case in this cast) onto the swinging tale of 'Macavity', Brian Blessed's audibly bloated and bespatted 'Bustopher Jones', Bonnie Langford and John Thornton's ineffably 'cutesy' pair of innocent cat-burglars, Paul Nicholas's tongue-in-cheek rocker, and Stephen Tate and Susan Jane Tanner's theatrical-piratical pair making much of the show's funniest section as Growltiger and Griddlebone are all enjoyably painted characters. The 'Macavity' section is particularly successful, but the highlight of any *Cats* recording has to be 'Memory', and this definitive performance, building up inexorably from Sarah Brightman's petite, pure introduction to Elaine Paige's rich and powerful top notes, excitingly taken in full chest voice, is indeed the feature of this recording.

The Broadway cast album offers a few variations to the score, such as an unattractive rewrite of 'Mungojerrie and Rumpleteazer' which sounds momentarily as if it is going to be that old song called 'Love and Marriage', the rearrangement of the sections of 'Grizabella, the Glamour Cat' and, of course, the suppression of 'Billy McCaw'. Many (but certainly not all) of the performers have the edge on their British counterparts insofar as slickness and vocal sureness are concerned, but, as so often in reproductions, the piece has been broadened in performance, the shades and shadows of the original repainted in primary colours. The Rum Tum Tugger (Terrence V. Mann) and Bustopher (Ken Page) are broadly burlesqued, Gus (Stephen Hanan) is no longer a lovably grouchy old cat but just a singer getting ready for his aria, and Grizabella (Betty Buckley) tears her oddly altered song to a tatter. The disc produces some fine moments, notably in such parody parts as Growltiger's new aria, which is superbly sung by Hanan, but the warmth of Blessed, Tate and Tanner, the shining innocence of Brightman, the zaniness of Langford, the off-handed ease of Nicholas are missed, and the alterations are not improvements.

Australia's cast recording falls between the two earlier sets. Textually, it retains the American 'Mungojerrie and Rumpleteazer' and prefers the Italian aria from the revised score, but in performance it avoids the larger exaggerations of the American version, giving mostly a crisply sung and enjoyably played interpretation. John Woods is a clear-voiced operatic baritone Bustopher/Deuteronomy with clipped accents but without exaggeration, Jeff Phillips a characterful Tugger who stays well on the right side of pure parody, and Gary Ginivan and Laura Bishop get some of the cuteness back into the cat-burglar song. Marina Prior is a pleasantly girlish Jellylorum pairing with a really first-class Gus/Growltiger (Grant Smith), who gets both the elderly pathos and the cod-operatic bravura into the part, and Robyn Forsythe and Kerry Woods mix accents amusingly in their splendidly zingy double-act as Demeter and Bombalurina. Grizabella here is Debbie Byrne, who gives an affecting performance. Husky and ragged sounding, with none of the incisive harshness of Buckley and little of the soaring sureness of Paige, she makes a characterful, actress's job of 'Memory', which makes one think just what this song, now regularly shredded Shirley Bassey-style in cabaret, would have been like had it been created, as intended, by Judi Dench. Would it, indeed, have become the world-wide hit that it is? All round, this is a fine recording of the show as played in Australia, and a more satisfying choice than the Broadway set for those who want to own a record that includes the post-London alterations. Me, I prefer the show as played in London and as performed by Paige, Blessed and Co., even if there are vocal weaknesses elsewhere.

By and large, it is difficult to get enthusiastic about most of the *Cats* recordings that followed the original one for, although they are all well enough done, there is little or no originality in any of them. Each will be fine in its own country, for those who want to hear what T. S. Eliot sounds like in German, Dutch, Japanese or French, but there is rarely anything in them that can earn them preference over the original recordings.

The German disc, a surprisingly good-sounding one in spite of being made live in the theatre, gives the impression of being a photofit *Cats* (American version), except of course that it is sung in German. The performers are all good, all have attractive voices and all pitch the level of their performance neatly between the natural and the out-front. There is absolutely nothing wrong with it, and it would probably sound less uninspired to me if I hadn't heard half a dozen other performances and productions of the show all sausaged-out in the same mould. Such are the perils of the modern rage for reproductions rather than productions. The most interesting performance is Andrea Bogel's Grizabella, which blends what sound like legitimate mezzo-soprano tones with more modern ones; she gets down with rich ease to the low notes which are a problem to many other singers.

This record has one advantage over the English-language ones. Like them it is wrapped in inner sleeves that include the lyrics, but unlike them it actually tells you which character is singing what, which makes sense of putting a cast list on the cover.

The Dutch record, another very capable live recording, has little Dutch clones instead of little German clones (in language, anyhow, as there are some very un-Dutch names in the cast list, amongst them the German production's Rum Tum Tugger – who sounds altogether more flamboyant in Dutch). Otherwise it differs very little from the other except in that it has rechristened Eliot's cats with names ranging from Antimakassa to Ghiselbert Smit (ex-Bustopher Jones). Ruth Jacott, another agreeably low voiced Grizabella, partnered with a sweetly childish Nancy Nijenhuis, handles 'Herrinerung' (Memory) impressively in spite of having to reach for the top notes, and there are a very gutsy Demeter and Bombalurina to wallop out 'Van Zonderen' ('Macavity'). Once again, there is really nothing to criticize except for a lack of individuality.

There is infinitely more fun and even a little variety in the Japanese set. Some of the voices sound so very cat-like. The cockroaches, who sound like the Carlyle Cousins with pegs on their noses, could very well be cockroaches, and the Siamese cats are, naturally, quite impeccable. There is a particularly spunky Rum Tum Tugger, assisted by kittens who dare to squeal *before* they are supposed to, according to the *Cats* production bible; a delightful 'Mungojellie and

Lumpletezer', who are lucky enough to have the original English version of their song back; a Silabub who sounds just like a Japanese Sarah Brightman; and a nicely incisive Jellylorum, who spits out her English names gleefully, supporting a fine Gus/Growltiger who masters the pathos better than the higher passages of Italian opera.

The Grizabella sings 'Memory' with a mixture of sweetness and smoothness which is unlike any of the other Grizabellas. No raddled she-cat, this one, but when she takes the top notes (which I would have expected her to take in head voice) in a rough and effortful chesty rush, the effect is rather spoiled. I can't tell you who any of these artists are as the sleeve gives credits in Japanese only, but they are on the whole a fine team, and it is a thoroughly enjoyable record, even without poor old 'Billy McCaw'.

The French have never been too quick at picking up on English-language musicals, but *Cats* finally arrived in Paris eight years after its first production with a part-French, part-international cast, played in French. Listening to the record, with its 'translations' which are fairly distant from Eliot, I would guess that this reproduction (American version) was cast for dance talents, for as a recording it is disappointing. The men, in particular, are weak, being almost without exception distractingly affected and/or effeminate sounding and/or undervoiced.

There is an accomplished soprano Griddlebone (Marie Illes), who is sunk by a frantic, posturing Growltiger, and a useful Bombalurina (Cristina Grimandi) and Demeter (Laure Balon), but the Grizabella has a young-sounding, unwieldy voice which isn't managed to best effect. All in all, the good pieces here are well outweighed by the poor ones. It is not a patch on its Japanese equivalent, nor even on the other foreign-language double-disc *Cats* recordings and, for isolated items, certainly not the equal of the vibrant, energetic selection from the Austrian production.

This single disc isn't much use as a record of *Cats* – it omits, for example, the whole of the Growltiger sequence – but there are some very fine items. Rich-voiced Joachim Kemmer gives a splendid version of 'Gus, the Theatre Cat', the usually undersung 'Mister Mistoffolees' and the Rum Tum Tugger get simply electrified by the British actor Michael Howe (in tidy German) in a manner that utterly eclipses all other tenants of the rôle, Angelika Milster gives a poised solo version of 'Erinnerung' with splendidly easy top notes, Steve Barton and Valda Aviks lead a lively 'Gumbie Cat', 'Macavity' is quite simply flayed alive by the red-hot Jutta Bryde and Ute Lemper, and Bueneventura Braunstein and his splendid uncredited partner almost make 'Mungojerrie and Rumpleteazer' Mark 2 sound as good as Mark 1. It's the old cast recording story: you find an exceptionally well-cast production and the recording is not complete. A shame.

All round, the original disc remains the best as a complete record of *Cats*, and for high highlights a dip into the Theater an der Wien selection is warmly recommended. Whichever record of *Cats* you choose to listen to, there is absolutely no doubt that it is more enjoyable if you have seen the show. But, then, is there anyone still left in the listening world who hasn't seen it?

Song and Dance

The entertainment called *Song and Dance* was compiled from two short Lloyd Webber works – his song-cycle *Tell Me on a Sunday*, and the Variations on a Theme of Paganini for cello and orchestra, which were staged as a one-act dance piece. Both halves of the entertainment had been recorded before the production of the stage show, but the staging of *Song and Dance* resulted in a new, two-disc recording made live on the first night in London. Further recordings of the song-cycle were made by America's Bernadette Peters and, again live, Germany's Angelika Milster. A made-for-video and television recording, featuring Sarah Brightman in the song-cycle, was also issued on record.

The London recording, starring Marti Webb, shows the Song section of this skilfully constructed and intimate show in its most satisfying form. Several new songs – 'The Last Man in my Life', 'I Love New York' and 'Married Man' – have been added since Miss Webb's original 'Tell Me on a Sunday' recording, warmly filling out the bitter-sweet story of the roller-coaster love life of a middle-aged English woman in America, and the piece has been reorchestrated for the sixteen-piece combination used in the theatre (as opposed to the London Philharmonic Orchestra which played for the first recording).

On the debit side, this set suffers from the problems of most 'live' recordings and is a little rough in its sound here and there. The orchestra sounds a bit fuzzy and turgid in the overture and Miss Webb takes a little while to achieve lift off. When she does, however, she is superb. The rôle fits her magnificently and she gives a splendidly normal performance, making the woman of the piece into a real and likeable person in spite of her hapless but never hopeless failure to get her life into order, and sings with clarity and vigour and no specious effects. The piece and Miss Webb carry the story through crisply, with the aid of the repeated 'Let Me Finish', 'It's Not the End of the World' and Letters Home, and peak regularly in the set-piece songs such as 'Tell Me on a Sunday', the soaring 'The Last Man in my Life', the gentle 'Come Back With the Same Look in your Eyes' and the final 'Nothing Like You've Ever Known'. There is time off, as well, for the light comedy of 'Capped Teeth and Caesar Salad' and the black humour of the vicious 'Let's Talk About You'.

Song and Dance went through a series of mostly minor alterations and reorganizations during its London run. These are included in the second English recording along with 'Unexpected Song', a vocal version of the theme of the Dance section, which replaced 'The Last Man in my Life' and some mostly unfortunate lyric alterations. 'I Love New York' and 'I'm Very You, You're Very Me' were both cut. Sarah Brightman sings splendidly, proving once more how well her voice is suited to record, but she sounds extremely young and never succeeds in creating the battered but optimistic woman of the piece in the way Miss Webb does. She is delightful in 'Capped Teeth and Caesar Salad' and dramatically incisive in the powerful parts of the music, but 'Unexpected Song' is not as effective or enjoyable as a climax to the first part of the show as 'The

Last Man in my Life' and, although she performs it most attractively, it is always an 'item'.

Further and considerable alterations, including vast lyric rewrites, intervened for the American stage production, from which the Song section only was recorded by Bernadette Peters. 'Unexpected Song' held its place instead of its predecessor, and was featured in a new overture, and the two cut numbers stayed out, with two new ones – 'English Girls' and 'So Much to Do in New York' (a rewritten 'It's Not the End of the World') going in instead. 'Nothing Like You've Ever Known', not used in the stage show, was included in the record. The rewrites are disastrous. The whole thoroughly believeable character so successfully created by Black, Lloyd Webber and Miss Webb in the original cycle has gone out the window, being replaced by an adolescent, adenoidal kook with an IQ of ten, which Miss Peters plays in a lazy, strung-out manner, chewing up her words until they are often incomprehensible. It is all 'oh so very theatrical, darling', and quite the opposite of the original piece: a very disagreeable transformation and an unpleasant record.

The German-language version, more excusably, also makes alterations in the lyrics – for some reason 'capped teeth and Caesar salad' become 'blue Jeans und weisser Smoking' – and resituates its opening in Munich, but it largely retains the original musical layout ('Der Mann, bei dem ich bleib' ends the first part) and also captures the feeling of the show much more successfully. Angelika Milster has a strong wide-ranging voice which she employs stylishly and effectively, and if she lacks a bit of the wry vulnerability Miss Webb achieves, she makes the anti-heroine of the piece into a believeable character of her own, both gutsy and accident-prone, which is perfectly valid and extremely enjoyable.

Starlight Express

With his score for *Starlight Express* Lloyd Webber took a deliberate turn towards the youth-pop market. Since the concept of the show – a spectacle on roller-skates – was angled the same way, this was not illogical. However, for those who had watched with appreciation the growth of his influential style of theatre music, with its hybrid of classical and popular elements, it was not the kind of score expected or, really, wanted from the composer.

The long run achieved by *Starlight Express* in Britain confirmed that the show's creators had been commercially correct in putting together their wheelie-opera but, from a musical point of view, it was a case of the score and what story there was accompanying the spectacle rather than the other way round. The most important songs were aimed at the hit parade: Lon Satton and Ray Shell singing 'I Am the Starlight' backed with 'Starlight Express' and Michael Staniforth's 'CB'; Jeffrey Daniel's 'AC/DC' in two versions – straight and twelve-inch extended; and Stephanie Lawrence's version of the show's big ballad 'Only He Has the Power to Move Me' were all issued singly.

The original cast album, a two-record set including all of the songs and some of the substantial incidental music written to accompany the skating races which are the backbone of the show, was largely recorded live in the theatre. The schoolboy smuttiness of the lyrics wears thin very quickly, and the driving drumming rhythms, electric orchestrations and fake American accents also get tiresome – though doubtless there are folk who like some or all of these things – making two whole records of *Starlight Express* without visuals rather a long affair.

The values on the recording, however, are all fine. Sound is representative, the orchestra booms and bangs along energetically, and the singers all do what they have to do. Michael Staniforth as the two-faced little caboose, Lon Satton as the soul-singing paterfamilias of steam, and a brochette of bopping carriages headed by Frances Ruffelle (Dinah) get the most characterization into their performances. Daniels is just audible over the rhythm section in his 'AC/DC'. The most enjoyable moments of the recording come in the straight parodies, such as Ruffelle's hilarious countrified 'U.N.C.O.U.P.L.E.D' and Jeff Shankley and Staniforth's 'One Rock 'n' Roll Too Many' (which seems to have strayed in from another show), and in pieces like the jolly, energetic ensemble 'Freight'.

There was no Broadway cast album issued, but a studio recording of a dozen numbers performed by the sort of people who come 'courtesy of' various record labels was made in America. It includes 'Make Up My Heart', added for the Broadway production, and two versions of 'Engine of Love' (metamorphosed into and from 'CB'). Lloyd Webber describes the record on the sleeve as being a concept album after the event, and it is an apt description. The songs are sung, regardless of character, by the type of modern pop voices that best suit their idiom and are tricked out with doubling, backing, pop-style arrangements and so forth to sound like very superior examples of hit-parade fodder.

A couple of the singers are of that wallpapery breed who blend in with the band, but there are some first-rate moments when the really strong pop tenor of Peter Hewlett gets into his stride with 'Engine of Love' and 'There's Me' and duets through 'Only He' and 'I Am the Starlight', the latter in a really zingy pairing with Richie Havens. Havens puts a match to 'Light at the End of the Tunnel' and Marc Cohn does everything a pop singer can do with 'One Rock 'n' Roll Too Many' and 'Pumping Iron'. The feminine side of things, alas, is clearly less strong and 'U.N.C.O.U.P.L.E.D' isn't included. However, even given that misjudgement, this is far and away the best recording of the music from *Starlight Express*, as opposed to a recording of *Starlight Express*. Hewlett's 'There's Me' is an anthology piece. But then again neither he nor the other performers on this disc had to be able to do pirouettes on roller-skates. Just one complaint here – I wish MCA would make flat records; the one I bought was dome-shaped enough to want to leap off the turntable.

The unfortunate Japan/Australia touring company sent out from Britain apparently recorded the show as well, but the only foreign-language *Starlight Express* recording to date is one from Germany. It, too, has a half-British cast, but is sung in German and pastes a plug for Ute Lemper and Johnny Logan's version of 'Du Allein' across the front of the sleeve. They weren't in the show, but their track is slipped in to the detriment of Maria Jane Hyde and Steven Michael

Skeels. The recording has an introductory scene, explaining the whole action of the piece as happening on a child's railway set, which is welcome, and Sabine Grohmann's translation seems to have got rid of most of the sniggers ('ya gotta keep it going all night' probably doesn't have the same nudge-nudge connotations behind it in German anyhow), which is equally welcome, even if the cast persist in singing 'nobody can do it like a steam train' in English! It is played with plenty of energy, sounds good in German, and gets some lively performances. Logan and Lemper are fine, but Skeels and Trevor Michael Georges do rather more with 'Only He/You' in the previous track and Natalie Howard (Dinah) and Miss Hyde (Pearl) also come over attractively in what is an enjoyable selection.

The Phantom of the Opéra

With *The Phantom of the Opéra* Lloyd Webber returned to the idiom that displays him at his best. This piece, built on a melodramatic period story, mines the richest veins of lyricism, waxing alternately extravagantly sentimental and flamboyantly dramatic, in the best tradition of the romantic theatre. The score follows the story at every turn, building through the first act, via the mysterious duet which introduces the spellbound Christine to 'The Phantom of the Opéra' and the Phantom's weirdly spun 'Music of the Night', to the comical and musically marvellous 'Prima Donna' septet and the final love duet 'All I Ask of You' (Christine/Raoul), which culminates in the Phantom's curse and, to a tidal wave of orchestral sound, the sabotage of the great chandelier. Again, in the second act, after the wild musical pageantry of the opening 'Masquerade', the melody and the moments of musical humour mix together until the climactic production on stage of the Phantom's *Don Juan Triumphant*, with its soaring duet 'Past the Point of no Return' which stretches on into the final dramatic scenes.

It is a remarkable, multi-colourful score and one that is a natural for a full-scale, full-blooded recording. At the time of writing there have been three *Phantom* sets recorded, the first from the original London production, the other two from Japan and Austria, Broadway having passed owing to the fact that the two star players from the London production repeated their assignment in America. All three have been made with care and taste, if with slightly different content and casting.

London's *Phantom of the Opéra* is on two records, but the amount of music involved has meant that the piece has had to be slimmed here and there. This makes for a few lumpy transitions, but all the important pieces are there, and the libretto provided with the set, marking out the various cut pieces, means that a quick read replaces the usually brief clipped sections. The recording keeps the voices well forward over the large orchestra, and, although there are some odd choices of levels and balances from time to time, on the whole it is a most successful enterprise which allows the show to grow through its two acts of mighty moments and melody up to its dramatic finale.

The well-known performances of Michael Crawford and Sarah Brightman as the Phantom and Christine are faithfully recorded. She, with her pure, perfectly-measured tones in a rôle made-to-measure for her, not unnaturally records the better, succeeding in giving not only a lovely clear rendering of her music but also a fey, almost unstable portrait of a heroine fresh out of *The Mysteries of Udolpho*. He, in contrast, has rough edges to his voice and a range which necessitates modified vowels in the upper reaches, but the febrile, haunting personality of the Phantom comes powering through his sung lines as through his spoken ones, and the character so effectively created in the theatre can be heard equally on the record.

Rosemary Ashe, as the deposed prima donna, Carlotta, gives a dazzling soprano performance, her stratospheric roucoulings hitting each note dead between the eyes as she rides along on top of the sextet like a computer gone haywire. The septet itself, which I persist in finding the highspot of the show, doesn't quite come out right. The difference between the impeccable operatics of Miss Ashe and the much less accomplished vocalizing of a couple of the other participants hasn't been homogenized down into a happyish middle area, and it is a case of water and oil. They don't mix.

Steve Barton is a pleasant hero, John Savident and David Firth are briskly amusing as the beleaguered managers of the opera house, the chorus make a very fine sound in their infrequent appearances, and only a couple of the players – the Meg and the Buquet – come over as really insufficient vocally. It is a set which may not be the perfect *Phantom* but it does have a good number of elements in it which are very nearly perfect.

The Japanese, once again, have turned out a splendid recording with their *Phantom of the Opéra*. In some ways it is even superior to the British original. The first advantage is one of layout. The Japanese (no names except those of the technicians are given in English, so I have to generalize) have chosen to include the music of the piece rather than to make the discs tell a story, and this means we get all of *Hannibal* and *Il Muto* and the ballet music instead of the bits of linking dialogue and musical fragments. For me, this is an undoubted improvement, and the chorus and the singer playing Piangi (both badly cut in Britain) must think so too. The second advantage is one of balance. The technical folk seem to have worked out a happier sound balance. You don't have to turn the volume up to a murderous level to get quality from the orchestra – which incidentally plays quite rapturously under its anonymous conductor – and the singers have all been given the same sort of level treatment instead of being trickily turned up or loaded with echo.

Balance, too, describes the casting. The show is played here more operatically than in Britain. Everyone can sing 'legit'. This means that the ensemble work is much more satisfying, and that 'Prima Donna' comes over as an exciting, homogenous piece of vocal crochet work, rather than suffering from a vanished line and/or some effortful blasting through the texture of the music. It also means that on a number of occasions you feel you could almost be listening to a 1990s *Turandot*, particularly as the man playing the Phantom has a strong and stylish legitimate voice. It is very exciting, this kind of performance, and it set me, as I

listened, to daydreaming of a *Phantom* recording with the old Austrian forces –
Gedda (Phantom), Schwarzkopf (Christine), Streich (Carlotta) – or a French one
with Robert Massard, Liliane Berton and Mado Robin. I think there is little doubt
that a cast of this kind will one day come to record this piece, for the power of the
music becomes very evident when it is given such a style of performance.

Having said this, the singers on the Japanese disc, unfailingly competent, do not
all live up to the originals. The Phantom does the best, mixing a fine voice with
obvious temperament and drama, but the Christine, in spite of a pure, accurate
voice, does not achieve the wonderment, the fragility of the character that Sarah
Brightman creates. As for the Carlotta, she is not in the same class as Ashe as a
vocalist, and I haven't yet made up my mind whether it is funny to have a Carlotta
who hoots and wobbles and doesn't quite make it up to her notes in *Il Muto*. I think
perhaps not. But if it really is her making the frog croaks, she deserves a career
as an impersonator. Raoul sings attractively, as Raouls all seem to do, the Firmin
and André are a smooth light opera buffo pair and the Meg is almost as effective
vocally as the Christine, which is a great relief, but although this set has the more
even casting, it lacks the outstanding star performances of the British recording.

The Austrian cast recording, like both its predecessors, is a fine, well-made set
over which one can only nit pick and make comparisons. It manages to include
both the opera sections unclipped and some dialogue and, like the British disc,
is wrapped in the most amazing sleeve and inner sleeves and supplied with a full
German libretto. Like the Japanese version, it goes in for strong all-round vocal
casting, but it does not achieve quite the same richly romantic playing from its
conductor and orchestra that the Eastern set does.

The Phantom is played by Alexander Goebel, Vienna's Che in *Evita*, and, as
you might expect, it is a different performance from those of both Crawford and
the Japanese. The former's withering acting performance and the latter's fine
combination of legitimate singing and acting are replaced by a big, broad, almost
over-the-top Phantom with a modern rock tenor voice. For my taste, he does too
much and thus misses the effects, which are best made with less obvious effort,
but he can sing the notes and he is certainly a contrast to the rest of the cast.

Luzia Nistler is a charming Christine, clear voiced and young sounding, and
paired with a particularly warm Raoul (Alfred Pfeifer), whilst Wolfgang Pampel
and the Volksoper's Jack Poppell are a splendidly sibilant pair of producers. The
best performances on this recording, however, undoubtedly come from the grand
opera end. Sergio Lombana is the best Ubaldo Piangi to date, and Priti Coles,
equipped with a bigger voice than Ashe but with all her style and security in
the stratosphere and also a mean hand with the dialogue, has a field day with
Carlotta's rôle. When these last five get together with the appreciable Meg
(Alexandra Young-Schmidt) and Giry (Diana Bennett) in the septet the result
is very fine, except that someone is in there fiddling with the buttons, bringing
voices up and down, instead of just leaving them to sing. The operatic excerpts
get done particularly well in this version, but you can't help, again, thinking of
Crawford and Brightman.

Aspects of Love

After the romping romanticism and musical adventures of *The Phantom of the Opéra*, Lloyd Webber's 1989 *Aspects of Love* is a comparatively intimate and delicately put-together piece. The heightened tones of the previous show and the witty, contemporary style of the Tim Rice musicals are both wholly abandoned in a musical love story which, textually, is told in words that are nearer to natural, everyday speech than those of any other musical of recent times. The musical part, too, is written with a different palette of colours, with the show's themes being skilfully crafted in and out of one another in musical dialogue and also featured in several full-sized set-piece songs. Those songs render nothing to their predecessors in effectiveness – the hit-parade success 'Love Changes Everything', the blazing, fearful 'Anything but Lonely', the rapturous love duet 'Seeing Is Believing', the wild, stamping funeral oration 'Give Me the Wine and the Dice', the comical 'She'd Be far Better off with You' – and in some of its quieter moments the work attains an unusual beauty – not a word that often springs to mind when listening to show music.

The original cast recording of *Aspects of Love* is a really splendid one. It is technically impeccable, with a clear, full sound and the performers' voices very rarely swamped by an orchestra which is both light and rich at the same time. It also, on the CD issue, manages to get the end of Act 1 at the end of the disc, which allows you a touch of theatrical illusion. That illusion is, however, rather threatened by the very nature of the show, for *Aspects of Love* is laid out in a series of often swift-changing, almost cinematic scenes, and those who do not know the piece will find its recording very difficult to follow. It is like listening to the soundtrack of a film without being able to see the pictures: you aren't always aware when the scene has changed, or what the progression between scenes is. A good knowledge of the show's action or a libretto is almost indispensible for listening through this recording comprehendingly.

The performers on the recording are each and all great, achieving that blend of acting and singing that so few other recorded casts do. The bulk of the action falls on Michael Ball (Alex) and Anne Crumb (Rose). Ball sings with a radiant, unmannered modern tenor which reaches the highest notes without the suggestion of head-flung-back vocalizing, and he conveys the character of a very young man who grows up to be a very young man most effectively. Miss Crumb plays with a nice mixture of warmth and semi-sophistication which suits her rôle perfectly, and a blooming singing voice that can swell from an intimate, tuneful whisper to the powerful anguish of 'Anything but Lonely' or the sexuality of 'Seeing Is Believing' without becoming harsh. And she, like Ball, succeeds in making a character who is ultimately rather foolish extremely likeable.

At the heart of affairs is George (Kevin Colson). George enters after half an act is gone and dies before the big singing starts in Act 2, but whilst he is on, and in spite of the fact that he has none of the showiest bits of singing, he is, no small thanks to Colson, indubitably the centre of the piece. Colson makes him a warm, superior, relaxed and sexy man, blithely self-assured in the first act, gently, ruefully ageing ('Other Pleasures') in the second, before twisting himself into jealousy and death – and at every moment compelling. Kathleen Rowe McAllen (Giulietta) hammers out the funeral scene chirpily, Paul Bentley makes an endearingly gentle moment of 'My Shining Leading Lady' and Diana Morrison is delightful as the eventually teenaged Jenny, whilst the company support the soloists with vigour and some splendidly natural singing.

Aspects of Love could really not have asked for a better cast recording.

Tim Rice

Chess

Lloyd Webber's erstwhile collaborator, Tim Rice, combined with Björn Ulvaeus and Benny Anderssen of the group Abba to produce the other significant large-scale musical of the 1980s in Britain, *Chess*, a love story set against the background of the international chess world and its politics. Rice's unmatchable combination of tongue-in-cheek humour and imaginative expressiveness, full of hidden joys (who else would write a line like 'I see my present partner in the imperfect tense'?), made a remarkable musical play from the words of *Chess*, words which were splendidly supported by an effective and sometimes outstanding musical score in the pop/classic mould.

The sung-through score of *Chess* leans towards the pop side of this combination, but more on account of its highly electrical orchestrations and by the voices chosen rather than the actual writing of the music, which is firmly based on the soundest of classical principles.

The leading feminine rôles of Florence and Svetlana are written in the chest range (only the chorus get to sing above the stave), and the two leading male rôles of the Russian and American chess players are composed in the pop tenor mould as crystallized in the Jesus/Judas combination of *Jesus Christ Superstar*. The character parts of Molokov and Walter, the behind-the-scenes manipulators of the Russian and American sides, are placed in the usually neglected bass register, and add considerable weight both to the solo humour and to the breadth of the ensembles.

Chess threw up several individual numbers which made the hit parades in more than one country. The heartfelt duet 'I Know Him So Well' was the biggest success, followed by the less likely 'One Night in Bangkok', a thumping 'poppy' hymn on avoiding the horrors of the town, but they were just the tip of iceberg in a vibrant and varied score. Florence's beautiful ballad 'Heaven Help my Heart', the angry, battling 'Nobody's on Nobody's Side', the raging tenor showpiece 'Pity the Child' for the American and the winged Anthem for the Russian are all remarkable theatre songs. They are supported by some fine ensembles – the Mountain Duet and 'You and I' (Florence/Russian), the quartet

'A Model of Decorum' and the exciting concerted Endgame – as well as richly classical incidental music.

Chess was issued as a concept recording before the production of the show but, since the three stars of the recording subsequently played their rôles in the theatre, there was, unfortunately, no cast recording. *Chess* on stage differed somewhat from the layout on the original recording, with various portions of the play being switched around and new scenes being inserted for the sake of the continuity of the reorganized show. The record, however, contains all the principal songs and ensembles as played in the show (the 'Soviet Machine' being the largest loss), and Elaine Paige (Florence), Tommy Korberg (Russian) and Murray Head (American) give quite superb performances in the three dramatic star rôles.

Korberg's rendering of the Anthem that closes the first act is one of those performances that makes the hair stand up not only on your neck but (even if you don't have any) all down your back. With his open, straight-as-a-swallow tenor voice, both expressive and attractive, he contrasts excellently with the manic, howling upper-register tantrums of Head's American and his spiralling 'Pity the Child' and dry 'One Night in Bangkok'.

Paige runs the gamut with a magnificent ease, pelting into 'Nobody's on Nobody's Side' with cutting fury, cruising through the wondering 'Heaven Help my Heart' and rising rapturously and romantically (not an adjective one normally thinks of in connection with the Paige voice) to the heights of the Mountain Duet in tandem with Korberg, whose voice blends marvellously with hers. The celebrated duet for the two women, performed with Barbara Dickson, is quite stunning.

There is little if nothing that one can say against this top-notch recording. It is a thrilling exposition of an exciting piece of modern musical theatre before the event. The chorus, perhaps, lack a little in the way of bite and enunciation, the Embassy Lament came out better in the theatre sung by only two men, and it is sad not have the comical 'Soviet Machine', but I can't really think of anything else. When you have seen the show as many times as I have it is, of course, a little unnerving to have so many pieces in the 'wrong' places, but it is amazing what can be done with a tape machine if it bothers you.

The American production of *Chess* recorded a one-disc selection which shows that the piece underwent the same sort of revamping on the other side of the Atlantic that *Song and Dance* suffered. The insert notes put in evidence a tacky rewrite of the story (what was wrong with the enormously effective original one?) into which some of the songs now fit ill. Others, including 'Someone Else's Story' (Florence), 'No Contest' (Freddie/Walter to the music of 'Florence Quits') and a lullaby (Florence and a new character, her father Gregor), are new pieces, whilst elsewhere lyrics are altered freely and 'The Story of Chess' becomes a solo instead of a chorus. This last is, alone, in one way an advantage for, although the musical texture suffers, the lyrics can now be heard. However there is nothing in any way remarkable about the additional pieces of music, which seem to have been half-heartedly inserted for all the wrong reasons.

The principal performances, although undeniably accurate and competent, are not in the same league as those on the original recording. David James Carroll (Russian) has a clear and efficient tenor which simply lacks the star-quality warmth and personality of Korberg, just as Philip Caznoff, who makes Freddie unreservedly unpleasant and gives his music some splendidly assured, attacking top notes, lacks the husky magic Head achieved. Judy Kuhn has a fine, trenchant modern voice which she uses with versatility, but this recording never takes off in the way the other does.

Blondel

Rice's only other stage venture in the 1980s was *Blondel*, a burlesque of the Richard the Lionheart legend written in the vein of *Joseph and the Amazing Technicolor Dreamcoat*. Played as a big musical, it failed, but somewhere inside it there was a small-scale musical allowing itself to be swamped, and Rice's witty and amusing lyrics (when was there last an acrostic in a musical?) were the backbone of some enjoyable if musically unadventurous numbers which are enshrined on an original cast recording.

The harmony group Cantabile, acting as narrators, have many of the happiest moments as they swing a Benedictus, muttering 'on with the plot'. King John (David Burt) tries to persuade the minstrel that it is easier to write encomiums on him because there's 'No Rhyme for Richard' and Blondel (Paul Nicholas) wanders through the various countries of Europe seeking Richard to the accompaniment of some jolly national parodies, but there is also unfortunately a heroine called Fiona (Sharon Lee-Hill) with a big number called 'Running Back for More', which has precisely the opposite effect on the listener.

The two-disc recording is not a very exciting one. The principal players sing their material regularly, with Cantabile providing the most fun and the best singing. David Burt and Stephen Tate make energetic jobs of the rival Kings, but Nicholas's Blondel is a fairly faceless fellow and Miss Hill's Fiona has a strong-voiced but uphill battle against a misconceived character. Some fun bits only.

More London Successes

Behind this handful of large-scale successes, several other musicals of varying kinds made a mark and a record. Willy Russell's musical play *Blood Brothers* had two West End productions within the decade, plus several stagings outside Britain; a stage version of the old movie *Singin' in the Rain* also came twice to town; and the much-touted *The Hired Man* had a shorter but very loudly publicized life.

Otherwise, things were less fortunate, and pieces such as *Colette* (1980), *Windy City* (1982), *Andy Capp* (1982), *Goodbye Mr Chips* (1982), *Poppy* (1982), *Bashville* (1983), *Dear Anyone* (1983), *Hell Can Be Heaven* (1983), *Swan Esther* (1983), *The*

Secret Diary of Adrian Mole Aged 13¾ (1984), *Mutiny* (1985), *Time* (1986), *Budgie* (1988) and *Metropolis* (1989), all of which were recorded, added little to the wealth of the musical theatre.

Blood Brothers

Blood Brothers is a modern Liverpudlian tragedy, told in a good-humoured folk style and decorated with some pleasant, unpretentious songs and sung links accompanied by a nine-piece group. The musical content of the show is not large, so there is room on the recording for all of the several solos plus sung and spoken narrative sections and a little dialogue that sets the numbers in context. Oddly, for a show where the musical pieces are very much an adjunct to the play, there is no synopsis on the sleeve.

The songs, written in straightforward speech with pleasant, appealing melodies, are sometimes repetitive, but they include some fetching items: Mrs Johnstone regretting that life does not come on 'Easy Terms', or showing a touching optimism in 'Bright New Day'; two little boys, one a scruffy urchin and the other a tidy lad, both wanting to be like 'My Friend' as they kick cans along the Liverpool streets on a 'Sunday Afternoon'; Eddie refusing to speak his love to his friend's girl (I'm Not Saying a Word'); and the final numb wail of despair, 'Tell Me it's Not True'.

Barbara Dickson, in the leading rôle of the abandoned mother who gives away one of her twins and sets the fateful *Corsican Brothers* drama in action, has the largest share of the music, and she sings her material with an easy, folksy style to which it is ideally suited. She projects a strong, soft-edged and unemotional character who takes all life's blows as natural, and her 'Tell Me it's Not True' is quite devoid of anguish. Andrew Schofield is a hard-voiced, accented Narrator who urges things on between Miss Dickson's relaxed numbers, and George Costigan and Andrew C. Wadsworth make convincing children, each producing the uncomplicated acting-singing performances that Russell's songs ask for.

The London revival recording is a much more satisfying one as a show disc. Wrapped in an attractive sleeve which is more like a very colourful publicity leaflet and which, again, in spite of containing a lot of copy, doesn't give a synopsis, the record is one of a show that has been worked into shape over a long series of performances, and it is played in a more theatrical style than the original. And somehow the score, which has undergone only minor alterations (the reprise of 'My Child' as 'That Guy' is included instead of some of the narration), sounds much more substantial than before.

Kiki Dee is Mrs Johnstone, and she gives her songs a decidedly more characterful interpretation than Dickson did without losing anything in vocal quality. Hers is a warm, positively characterized performance, sung with a strong and bright folk-pop voice, and Mrs Johnstone comes out of this record as a very real person. Warwick Evans, as the Narrator, adds a good deal to the piece with his easy vernacular introduction and linking, and his splendidly sung warning of doom in 'Shoes on the Table' and 'A Man Gone Mad in the Town Tonight'.

Con O'Neill and Robert Locke are pleasantly natural as the two fated brothers, and the rest of company are displayed prominently throughout, giving a splendid atmosphere to the recording.

This is a first-rate show record from all angles. It has a strong feeling of the show itself, building up to a magnificently goose-pimply climax thanks to the excellent choice of cuts, notably the inclusion of the dramatic dialogue leading up to the final shooting, which adds oceans to Kiki Dee's really heartfelt performance of 'Tell Me it's Not True'. It is also sung, all round, by excellent unpretentious voices, acted, in both its spoken and sung portions, with a spirit and realness which are extremely effective, and played by its nine-piece band with enthusiasm and colour. It is a recording that quite simply does its show proud.

Rebecca Storm, who starred in the national tour and the Irish production of *Blood Brothers*, recorded six numbers, mostly from Mrs Johnstone's music, with a four-piece synthesizer-based band on the Portrait label. The songs have been turned around a little here and there to make them into singles, and stretched so that the six of them make up a very short LP. Without pretending to be a cast recording, it helpfully gives a plot synopsis on its sleeve, although without placing the numbers.

Miss Storm (a sometime *Evita*) has a strong and attractive voice, and she invests the songs with a little more passion and vivacity musically than Miss Dickson does, but without really making the words tell as they would seem to demand. This is more a recital record than a show disc and it naturally lacks the variety given by the men's numbers on the cast recordings, but Miss Storm's 'Sunday Afternoon' and 'Easy Terms' in particular are enjoyable tracks.

Singin' in the Rain

The recording of the stage show of *Singin' in the Rain* doesn't hold many surprises. It is a bright, happy and all-round fine performance of the score that was assembled for this production from those numbers used in the original film released to the producers at the time, plus one or two replacements. Subsequent revivals have, with the release of the remainder of the score, replaced 'Be a Clown', 'I Can't Give You Anything but Love' and 'Too Marvellous for Words', included here, with the original film songs 'Make 'em Laugh', 'All I Do Is Dream of You' and 'You Stepped Out of a Dream' as and when copyright allowed.

Assisted by some luxuriously Hollywoodian Larry Wilcox arrangements, and what sounds like a thousand-piece choir, Tommy Steele and Roy Castle ping through 'Fit as a Fiddle' and 'Moses Supposes' in impeccable style. Danielle Carson is an ideal soubrette with an adorable accent that gets no closer to Hollywood than Wapping ('Wood yew?'), and Sarah Payne (the Jenny Lind of London's *Barnum*) gleefully murders 'Temptation' in the rôle of the vile-vowelled Lina Lamont.

Steele, although recognizably Steele and thankfully not attempting any American accent, makes a fine job of being neither aggressively himself nor a demi-semi-Gene

Kelly, but simply performs the material in a warm, relaxed and unmannered style which is very pleasant to listen to. His flip-happy version of the title song is immaculate, and he joins Castle and Miss Carson in a lively, tap-filled 'Good Morning' which altogether makes you forget the original. The recording quite simply succeeds from all angles: it is a first-class record of the show as played and a highly enjoyable piece of general light listening.

The Hired Man

The Hired Man suffered, on its production, from having some excessive claims bruited about as to the significance of its score and composer Howard Goodall. Listening to the recording, a few years after the tumult and the shouting has faded away, what comes across is an agreeably simple, tough score with a strong rural flavour and some naïve songwords, sung over a little five-piece group by an enthusiastic group of mostly untutored voices, which sound good when they combine in the lusty rendering of the title song but less agreeable when attempting solo work with any kind of a range.

One of those irritating sleeves which doesn't tell you who sings what or where the songs fit in what story makes this disc fairly unmeaningful to anyone who hasn't seen the show, but there are a couple of strong and dramatic pieces in the first act – the duet for Emily (Julia Hills) and Jackson (Richard Walsh) and the final solos for John (Paul Clarkson), Jackson and Emily (the second of which is omitted), leading back to an ensemble and the booming title chorus, whose significance is fairly obvious. These pieces and the rest get an unfortunately ragged treatment on this recording which, amazingly (given that its two sides are far from full) omits, amongst others, my two favourite pieces from the score, the pretty duo 'Who Will You Marry Then?' and 'You Never See the Sun' which was given the most accomplished performance in the show by Clare Burt. All very curious and, in direct contrast with the *Singin' in the Rain*, not at all satisfying either as a record of the show or as general listening.

The French Connection

Les Misérables

After a long period in which the French musical theatre had stagnated sadly, with only the isolated *Irma la douce* finding its way to the stages of the world from amongst the reasonably tawdry and limited succession of original French pieces, low-lighted, most years, by 'the latest Lopez', the 1980s saw the sudden emergence of one of the internationally most successful musicals for decades in the shape of Claude-Michel Schönberg's *Les Misérables*. Like *Jesus Christ Superstar* and *Evita*, *Les Misérables* began its life on record. Schönberg and Jean-Marc Natel and Alain Boublil (the authors of the text) intended to follow the recording, made over a period of more than two years between 1978 and 1980, with a production on the lines of that given to their *La Révolution française* (1973), but in the end it was Robert Hossein, the Parisian king of spectacular stage productions, who produced the piece in Paris in 1980 for a season of 105 performances. Cameron Mackintosh's 'discovery' of the show led to its London production five years later in a translation by Herbert Kretzmer and, from there the world-wide travels of *Les Misérables* began.

At the date of writing, the show has been played in thirteen countries and is scheduled for more than a dozen others; and the result in recording terms has been double-disc sets from Britain, America and Austria, single discs from Hungary (*A Nyomorultak*) and Israel, and, for some devious reason, only a measly not-even-extended play 45 both from the Japanese, who are usually so expansive with their recordings, and from the Australians, where the cast themselves sabotaged the making of a full set by demanding extravagant payments.

The original French recording is a superb one, played and sung with passionate energy. It is cast with a thrilling selection of mostly young performers and guest artists of the quality of Adamo, Delpech, Sardou and the celebrated Mireille (the Manon of Broadway's original *Bitter-Sweet*), here in the tiny rôle of the Acheteuse de Cheveux. There are considerable differences between this recording and the show that has become such an international hit. The original recording and the original French production gave a fuller panorama of Hugo's novel, with Valjean, Javert and Thénardier just parts of the colourful whole which emphasized much more the students and their abortive revolution and the famous character of the child Gavroche. There are fewer solo numbers in this version, for the story has no time to stop for soliloquies. There is no 'Who Am I?' nor 'Bring Him Home' for Valjean, no 'Empty Chairs and Empty Tables' for Marius, no 'Dog Eats Dog' for Thénardier and no 'Stars' for Javert, whilst Eponine's song is a different number to the well-known 'On my Own'.

Undoubtedly the now familiar, rewritten version is showier and more theatrical, with its big solo opportunities for the leading players and its sharper focus on the Valjean/Javert combat and the Marius/Cosette/Eponine triangle at the expense of Gavroche and the host of secondary characters, but this original recording (made partly at the Studio Music Centre in Wembley, London!) is nevertheless a magnificent one.

A large number of the artists featured on the recording also subsequently appeared in the stage show, notably the actor Maurice Barrier (Valjean), who shows evidence of a fine, expressive and unpretentious singing voice, the young and ungrotesque Thénardier (Yves Dautin) and his attacking wife (Marie-France Roussel). There are especially fine performances from the spectacular, movingly dramatic Fantine (Rose Laurens) and the delightful, girlish Cosette (Fabienne Guyon, the Anna Held of London's *Ziegfeld*), who is in no way a legitimate soprano, but an appealing actress-singer with an effortless and versatile singing voice.

It is hard to imagine how those who did not make the move from disc to stage could have been bettered. The very young sounding Eponine (Marie) sends shivers down your back with her delicately played death scene, Jacques Mercier – a popular vocalist with a youthful rock voice – makes Javert's Soliloquy an anguished highspot, Richard Dewitte is a sweetly boyish Marius and the certified star, Michel Sardou, is a radiant Enjolras who is also able to produce shivers. Young Fabrice Bernard, a child artist who takes the considerable rôle of Gavroche, is simply great and never allows his material to sound like something out of *Oliver!*.

The original London cast recording takes us a good way along the road to the final version of the show. Made during the interregnum between the original performances at the Barbican Theatre and the West End opening, it covers two records, and, given the even more considerable length of the show at that stage, necessarily omits a certain amount of the material. The opening, with Valjean's soliloquy, the Thénardier waltz, and the 'Turning' sequence are amongst the portions left out, but Gavroche's song 'Little People', soon to go almost entirely under the knife, is included.

There are several outstanding performances on the record. Colm Wilkinson as Valjean has a mature and dramatic modern tenor voice which he uses to splendidly exciting effect in his confrontation with Javert (played by the straighter actor's baritone of Roger Allam – the same combination of voices as in France, but reversed), and with considerable beauty in the mixed-voice performance of 'Bring Him Home'. Allam, who has a very fine voice, sings his two big pieces superbly and gives strength and warmth to Javert in an interpretation of many shades, which keeps the piece from developing into a simplistic good versus evil contest. The most shining performance, however, comes from Frances Ruffelle as Eponine. Her plangent teenaged tones are used with an intelligence and feeling which turns the listener's stomach to jelly as she pours out her love for Marius in 'On my Own', and are quite capable of producing tears in her beautifully played death scene.

Michael Ball is a strong, masculine Marius – much more grown-up sounding than Dewitte – paired with a very sweet and extremely straight soprano Cosette (Rebecca Caine), whilst Alun Armstrong and Susan Jane Tanner as the Thénardiers have been turned here into the lowish comic relief. They both have incisive actors' voices and splendid diction, and roust 'Master of the House' along vigorously. Patti LuPone is a demonstrative but somehow rather calculated Fantine who cannot erase the memory of the scorching Mlle Laurens, and the supporting company are not always up to the standard of principals, but in general the piece is played in the best epic style. Such moments as the first-act finale, remoulded here on proven crowd-pleasing principles into a much more theatrically effective piece, the Javert/Valjean confrontation and anything in which Miss Ruffelle opens her throat are quite magnificent.

The Broadway recording goes one step further towards the show-as-it-is-played as, with Gavroche now almost gone, it has space to include several items not on the London disc ('Turning', the Thénardier waltz, the scene of Thénardier's attack on Valjean's house), although given the gaps on the records I wonder why they didn't include, at least, the show's opening sequence.

Wilkinson, who repeats his original rôle, has by this stage worked his way into it in an extremely effective way, playing with more weight and calculated effect than on the earlier version, whilst Terrence V. Mann sings Javert's numbers in an easy baritone, rising powerfully in sound when required, but without achieving quite the same dramatic quality that Allam does or the same conflict with Valjean. There are fine legitimate performances from a ringing Enjolras (Michael Maguire) and a well-matched pair of soaringly-singing lovers (David Bryant and Judy Kuhn), all impeccably in the mould of the smoothed-down piece of musical theatre that *Les Misérables* has now become. It is quite a way from the manic dash of Michel Sardou and his fellow performers on the much rougher, pop-vibrant concept disc.

Miss Ruffelle repeats her unmatchable Eponine, but too many of the other performances, which seem mostly to be overcooked imitations of their London equivalents, don't come off so effectively. The Thénardiers go thoroughly over the top, giving really grotesque unactorish performances, and a number of the ensemble catch the same disease – the lowlife equivalent of the ghastly pseudo-cockney performances once seen in too many London shows – and many of the piece's common folk verge on the embarrassing in spite of good, strong singing voices.

The complete show is recorded on a four-record set, compiled in four different studios around the world, using the pre-recorded backing of the Philharmonia Orchestra under Martin Koch and a cast taken from current and past London performers, a large group from the Los Angeles production, and soloists from New York, Sydney and Tokyo, combined by the wizardry of modern technology. It is quite something for a musical to be accorded such a comprehensive treatment and the recording is an appreciable achievement, with a number of notable highlights.

Sydney's Debbie Byrne is a deeply moving Fantine, giving easily the best English-language performance of the rôle in a tortured, vulnerable and vocally unexaggerated 'I Dreamed a Dream', and a beautifully underplayed series of scenes, finally fading away in a very believeable death. Another member of the Australian cast, Philip Quast, gives a splendid interpretation of Javert's rôle, mixing a poised acting performance and a warm, accurate voice, and a third, Anthony Warlowe, gives a first-rate straight-sung Enjolras. Michael Ball (Marius) repeats his original London performance with a stronger voice and less simplicity than first time round, paired with a pretty light soprano Cosette (Tracy Shayne) and a truly delicious Japanese Eponine (Kaho Shimada), childish and plaintive in voice and really affecting in her two big moments.

Not all the casting is as well done. New York's Gary Morris seems an odd choice for the rôle of Jean Valjean. He comes over as a very lightweight Valjean, vocally assured (except for the end of 'Who Am I?'), but lacking the powerful presence displayed by Maurice Barrier or the vigorous, driving vocal force of Wilkinson. He also sounds very young for the part, and a lot of the tension between the two main protagonists of the story is lost.

The Thénardiers seem to get broader (and less amusing) with each recording, and Barry James and Gay Soper (London replacement casting) graunch and grind through their rôles here in a disappointingly exaggerated display of 'wicked-witch' acting which seems to have found imitators in a few of the Los Angeles support cast.

The choral portions, with all the orchestra and large cast in full flight, are glued together in an enormously impressive fashion but, although the Philharmonia plays the accompaniment with sweeping vigour and breadth, I find that the music sounded more dramatic and effective in its original orchestrations than in this 'symphonic version'. Splendidly packaged with a full libretto including photographs from the various *Les Misérables* productions around the world, this is, however, a fine record of the show as finally played, even if it is not ideal in all its parts.

Austria's enjoyable double-disc recording gets in the opening of the show with Valjean's first soliloquy, the Thénardier waltz and 'Turning' in a vigorously conducted and played and generally well sung version which is the most legitimately performed of all. Reinhard Brussmann (Valjean) is a real operatic tenor, and even though he doesn't often permit himself to launch into full-throated singing, the security and vibrancy of his upper register allows him to tackle the music with great fluency. Since he also achieves a robust and dramatic characterization, he provides a fine centre for the recording, on which he is paired with a capable if rather shallow middle-weight baritone Javert (Norbert Lamla) and otherwise well supported. The young men make a vibrant group of singing rebels, the Cosette (Martina Dorak) sings especially prettily, and the Eponine does well at the fairly standard Frances Ruffelle imitation. Although silly voices, shrieks and howls are clearly *de rigeur* for the Thénardiers in the international *Les Misérables* production book, this Madame has a good go at actually singing some of the music, while Monsieur's funny voice is intermittent, for which relief much thanks.

Hungary's *Les Misérables* recording has gathered together most of the usual group of performers who play such pieces in Hungary, to good effect. Kriszta Kováts (formerly Evita) is Fantine, Sándor Sasvári (ex-Che and *Jesus Christ Superstar*) is Marius, Anikó Nagy (Mary Magdalene and Peron's Mistress) is Eponine, Pál Makrai (once Judas) plays Javert and Gyula Vikidál (ex-Pilate) is Valjean. Ildikó Hámori, who offended my sensibilities so deeply with her murder of Jacobi's operettas, has a jolly time making crow-screeches as Mme Thénardier. The result of this casting is, in direct contrast to the Austrian recording, the most pop-orientated of all the *Les Misérables* since the original French one. There are a few wild extravagances and a few duff notes, but this is certainly a spunky, lively version of the piece.

Israel, too, has produced an attractive *Les Misérables* recording. The scene 'At the End of the Day', which suffers in most recordings from second-rate playing by the small-part players who have the solos, gets an excellent performance as an opener to the selection, Dudu Fisher as a truly tenor Valjean sings 'Who Am I?' with a light but incisive voice and makes a triumphant job of the final top note which is so often a shriek, and Elior Yeini as a well-matched Javert gives a smooth 'Stars'. 'Master of the House' gets a jolly, characterful performance from Albert Cohen and Tiki Dayan and the young people all play their numbers in the established style with more than useful voices. The passionate tones of Avi Toledano (Marius) blend very beautifully with those of two sweet sopranos in Tal Amir (Cosette) and Shlomit Aharon (Eponine) in 'A Heart Full of Love'.

Les Misérables has become one of the internationally most successful shows for many a decade in its 'smoothed-down' version, and this series of generally appreciable recordings present the 'definitive' version of the show liberally. Enjoy them, but then go back to the French recording and remind yourself of the raw, dramatic panorama of Victor Hugo's tale as Schönberg, Natel and Boublil originally conceived it. Maybe Mlles Laurens, Marie and Guyon, and Messrs Sardou, Barrier and friends could now be let loose on the new *Les Misérables*: that would be quite a record. Maybe we will get it in 1991 when the new *Les Misérables* returns to Paris.

Starmania

The other singular success of the modern French musical stage is a piece called *Starmania* (by Michel Berger and Luc Plamondon). Half-French, half-Québecois, *Starmania* was originally issued as a concept album from which Claude Dubois' performance of 'The Blues du Businessman' (so much for the purity of the French language) made it to the hit parades. The show posted up its aims when it was first tried out on the stage in the middle of 1979 for just twenty-five Parisian performances, directed by original *Hair* and *Jesus Christ Superstar* director Tom O'Horgan, and it has maintained a presence, particularly in French record shops, ever since. It did not, however, follow the director's earlier works on to the world circuit.

A 1988 revival brought it back to the Parisian stage, making up, along with productions of *Cats* and *Cabaret*, a couple of 'the latest Lopezes' and a season of Offenbach's *Le Pont des soupirs*, one of the more lively twelve-month periods of musical theatre in recent times in the French capital. It also brought Dubois' single back onto the French supermarket shelves for a second coming.

Starmania is a very curious piece. A sort of science fiction melodrama with characters ranging from a black-leather clad villainess called Sadia (what else?) and a heroine who is a TV presenter, to a big businessman out to become President of the Western World, and a plot and action somewhere between *Batman*, *The Rocky Horror Show*, *Hair*, *Time* and the less inventive American comic strips, it is also the vehicle for a good deal of stage spectacle and a mass of relentlessly pounding youth-orientated rock music, occasionally blended with the strains of the French chanson. Its song titles give some idea of the level of its aims – 'Sex shops, cinémas pornos', 'Le Monde est stone', 'Ego Trip', 'Les Adieux d'un sex symbol', 'Paranoia', 'Un enfant de la pollution', 'Ce soir on danse au Naziland'. It is all very much for the pre-puberty crowd. Or am I missing a sort of double-bluff joke?

The original concept album on two discs, which I have, perhaps unfortunately, not heard, has been succeeded by two cast recordings. The first is a live-in-performance set of the original production made on four records and packaged up in a box with a booklet giving the titles of the songs, and lots of coloured photos of the extravagant costumes, but no libretto. This is a shame, as the singing style of a number of the performers makes it quite impossible to tell what they are saying. You have to trust the synopsis, and that isn't at all easy to do, particularly when (as in the set I bought) the labels are stuck on the wrong records.

Four records which include so much unvarying non-stop rhythm section is a bit much for anyone who isn't utterly immersed in 1970s (or is it 1960s?) rock-'n'-roll music. The less frenetic moments, when melody intervenes and the drummers take a break, include most of the best pieces of the show, particularly when they are served by voices such as the very attractive Françoise Thibeault as the comparatively sane waitress Marie-Jeanne ('La Complainte de la serveuse automate'), the fey France Gall as the sugar-sweet heroine Cristal and a splendidly stout-voiced Diane Dufresne as the filmstar Stella Spotlight or Etienne Chicot, who performs the 'Blues du Businessman' tidily. The other energetically rocking men all sound much like each other.

The highlights of the very successful 1988 revival have been live-recorded on two discs. Synthesizers have arrived by this time and so have higher wages, so there has been a considerable reduction of forces all round, and some new orchestrations are keyboard (and, of course, rhythm) based. This time some of the lyrics have been included on the inner sleeves.

The show is done rather less flamboyantly than on the earlier set and there are no performers of the standard of Mlle Thibeault amongst the efficient but largely unexciting cast, but this record displays the set-piece songs only, lifting them from the mass of music on the larger set, which seems like a good idea.

Everybody claps and squeals a lot on both of these recordings, so I guess there are a quite a lot of people who enjoy *Starmania* more than I do.

Latter-Day Broadway

Whilst *Cats*, *The Phantom of the Opéra*, *Les Misérables* and the produce of yesteryear from *The Pirates of Penzance* to *On Your Toes*, *Me and My Girl*, *Anything Goes* and the eternal *A Chorus Line* held the virtual monopoly on Broadway success in the 1980s, there was a continuous if reduced stream of home-made shows that continued to make a play for popularity, some with more but most with less success.

Of the established composers, Stephen Sondheim was represented by three pieces, *Merrily We Roll Along* (1981), *Sunday in the Park With George* (1984) and *Into the Woods* (1988), Jerry Herman found significant and exportable success with his musical version of *La Cage aux Folles* (1983), which was outrun as a world property only by a stage version of the favourite film musical *42nd Street* (1980), Kander and Ebb turned up two further mega-woman shows in *Woman of the Year* (1981) and *The Rink* (1984), Peter Udell and Garry Sherman gave *Amen Corner* (1984) and Alan Jay Lerner bowed out with the text for Charles Strouse's *Dance a Little Closer* (1983).

Names less well known and/or less usual in musical theatre circles were attached to *Dreamgirls* (1981; Henry Krieger/Tom Eyen), *Nine* (1982; Maury Yeston/Arthur Kopit) and *Big River* (1985; Roger Miller/William Hauptmann), which won runs considerably more than the few weeks or months that were the fate of so many musicals, and pieces like *The Tap Dance Kid* (1983; Krieger), *Baby* (1983; David Shire/Richard Maltby jr/Sybille Pearson) and *The Mystery of Edwin Drood* (1986; Rupert Holmes) also stood up for reasonable runs, but as often happens when large-scale musical theatre is suffering a drought, several enjoyable pieces poked their heads out from amongst the swell of compilation shows and revivals in smaller theatres.

The most remarkable of these was *Little Shop of Horrors* (1982), which won a world-wide success and even a movie, but there were interested audiences for varying periods and full-scale recordings for such pieces as *The March of the Falsettos* (1981), *Pump Boys and Dinettes* (1982), *Charlotte Sweet* (1982), *The Gospel at Colonus* (1985), *Three Guys Naked from the Waist Down* (1985), *Goblin Market* (1986), *Olympus on my Mind* (1986), *Nunsense* (1987) and *Romance, Romance* (1988).

Merrily We Roll Along

Merrily We Roll Along sees yet another three-quarters face of the ever-versatile Sondheim, with a short and unshowy score written as an adjunct to a version of George Kaufman and Moss Hart's successful play. It is a rather down-beat play with its sorry theme of the disabuse of youthful dreams and ambitions, but its gimmick, the telling of its little tale in reverse, has the effect of letting the evening get more positive and likeable as it progresses, rather than dissolving away into sad cynicism.

Sondheim's score follows this same progression and, on the original cast recording of the show, things get steadily more agreeable. There is little in the largely straightforward, conversational words of this show to excite the sort of admiration produced by the writer's most worldly witticisms, and the musical portion of the work is also a generally and pleasantly simple one. At least, I thought it was until I read the incredibly pompous note written by the composer and attached to the enclosed lyric book, explaining to all us poor ordinary folk how the score's thematic material is developed (backwards, of course) through the show. My immediate reaction was 'Tut, so much complexity to so little effect'. Anyway, these things are meant to be discovered by the listener, not rammed down his throat.

The two most enjoyable portions of the piece are a television interview ('Franklin Shepperd Inc'), where too much honesty proves disastrous, and a scene depicting two years of work by the three principals of the show in their struggle to make good as show-business writers ('Opening Doors'). But there are less enjoyable parts too, notably a rather under-par revue song about the Kennedys and some not very tuneful ensemble music. The piece is given an adequate performance by its young cast, but the record leaves you feeling that, in spite of the excellent synopsis provided, this score is rather too linked to its book to be wholly satisfying alone.

Merrily We Roll Along was a quick Broadway failure and subsequently underwent some rewrites, so this disc does not represent the show as it is now played by the schools and groups who have found its juvenile casting interesting.

Sunday in the Park with George

If *Merrily We Roll Along* is more 'difficult' than it seems, *Sunday in the Park with George* makes no concessions. It is just plain difficult. The first half follows the painter, George, who is 'sort of Seurat', as he composes his masterpiece 'A Sunday Afternoon on the Island of La Grande Jatte', introducing each of the characters who appears in the picture until they all come together in the artist's canvas at the end of the act. With this happy conceit is mixed the various stages of the failing relationship of the artist and his mistress. The second act, which centres on another artist called George, the illegitimate descendant of the first-act artist, wanders away into discourses on art patronage and criticism and the destruction of nature, before modern time comes together with the earlier age in its final scene, a meeting between George II and his great-grandmother, the mistress featured in the painting. Fortunately, a lengthy synopsis and explanation of what is going on is included with the original cast recording, along with the text to the recorded part of the show, but even then sticking the two halves together and making full sense (and/or relevance) of Act 2 requires effort and imagination.

The score is not much easier. Sondheim largely eschews both the lyricism and sharp wit of his most inviting works in his words, preferring to go for what I can only assume is intended to be an impressionistic (to say pointilliste would doubtless be going too far, but who knows) kind of writing, in line with the kind of painting the show deals with. There is considerable repetition, slow building up of lines through minor lyric changes and one line: 'That's the puddle where the poodle did the piddle', which sounds like a British seaside show at its worst. This from the author of *A Little Night Music?* Of course, there are crisp and amusing moments in the text, such as Dot's soliloquy as she swelters in the heat whilst modelling for George, and the introduction of the various characters in the painting, but George himself is a fairly waffly and pretentious fellow, and some of the passages of the second act go on puzzlingly.

The music is scarcely more inviting. I'm sure it is cerebral and probably complex, but it is not noticeably melodious. There are no long-lined tunes, no pretty songs, no jaunty or graceful or rhythmical dance melodies but, as with the lyrics, sections of music which seem to be painstakingly constructed, built up from smaller pieces, like the dots of Seurat's paintings. I feel it is rather like those modern painters who can draw from life beautifully, but prefer to give you three blobs and a triangle for a woman's body. Some will love it and some will hate it.

There is little opportunity, given the style of writing, for the cast to demonstrate their talents on disc. Mandy Patinkin (both Georges) has one or two moments when he can open up his voice, and he does it impeccably; Bernadette Peters is poutingly raucous as Dot and suitably aged as the grandmother, to the extent she sometimes sounds as if she and her voice are going to give up the ghost altogether; and the remainder of the cast sing staunchly through their stichomythia and ensemble work without getting the gratification of being allowed more than a few consecutive lines at the most. Maybe the same people who understand the backwards music in *Merrily* understand all this too. I don't, and I suspect that *Sunday in the Park With George* is for the Sondheim unconditionals and the amazingly intelligent.

Into the Woods

Into the Woods is a much more accessible piece. Like the old British burlesques and pantomime introductions, and like later works such as Caryl Brahms's *Titania Has a Mother*, it takes up the familiar characters of fairytale and plunges them into variants and combinations of their ancient stories, both before and beyond the traditional 'happily ever after'. It does, inevitably, have moral undertones and overtones and everywhere-elsetones, which are laid on thick in both story and song in the best fable fashion, but by and large they don't harm the story, for in a musical play we have become used to everything stopping for an illustrative number. The notes insist there are 'dark implications' in the piece, but that is making rather more of this simple mixture of story and take-it-or-leave-it symbolism and saws than it calls for. *Into the Woods* can be perfectly well enjoyed at face value, which almost certainly accounts for its success and makes its original cast recording an entertaining listen.

Two and a half pages of fine synopsis and a booklet of all the lyrics on the very full disc are included to help you make your way through the briars and thickets of the plot and to help set the numbers in their context. Although even with these aids I'm not quite sure why Rapunzel screams at the end of the second-act opening (except that she screams rather a lot).

The musical pieces of *Into the Woods*, mostly written in a sophisticated version of the jolly-song style beloved of children's shows, range from a jauntily silly title song to an X-rated attack by a dirty-raincoated wolf ('Hello, Little Girl') on Little Red Riding Hood, who comes out admitting ingenuously 'I Know Things Now', and a very funny duet for Cinderella's and Rapunzel's pining suitors ('Agony'), which later serves for their adulterous chase after Snow White and the Sleeping Beauty. The more serious numbers are the province of the Witch, the character who ironically has the most literal moral compunctions, as not too opaquely expressed in the waltz (hurrah!) 'The Last Midnight'. There are also some enjoyable ensembles, including a nifty quick-fire piece where all the protagonists try to escape responsibility for the fateful Giant's attack ('Your Fault').

The cast on the original recording fill their rôles effectively, with Robert Westenberg and Chuck Wagner particularly funny and full-voiced as the lecherous Princes (Westenberg also plays the Wolf splendidly), Joanna Gleason a smoothly sung and warmly acted Baker's Wife, Danielle Ferland a 'cutesy-pie' Little Red Riding Hood and Kim Crosby a pretty Cinderella. The all-important Witch is played by Bernadette Peters with a range of styles it is a little hard to comprehend – is she the same person before and after her transformation or is her character altered? – as she cackles horribly over the Baker's childlessness and the theft of her beans, and contrastingly pours out motherly hurt over Rapunzel or spouts morals in rich tones in 'The Last Midnight'.

La Cage aux Folles

One of the few Broadway musicals from this period to find itself productions outside America is *La Cage aux Folles*, a jolly adaptation of Jean Poiret's immensely successful romantic-comic play about a Tropézian gay couple and their son. It has a score, in Jerry Herman's best and most catching style, which has, in whole or in part, spawned a flush of recordings.

The show threw up a number of song hits, most notably the melodramatic 'I Am Who I Am', originally sung in the show by Albin, the female impersonator, as a defence of his right to live and be as he wishes, but subsequently jumped on by performers such as Shirley Bassey, Gloria Gaynor and Eddie Fisher and torn to many a tatter under all kinds of circumstances. The lively sing-along song 'The Best of Times' is another piece to have become popular outside the show, but the Frenchified 'Song on the Sand', the love song of the two men, which is more Trenet than Trenet, and the pretty, lilting 'Anne on my Arm', in which the son celebrates falling in love, are both also delightful songs.

The original cast recording gives a performance of the show's short order of music which it is hard to imagine bettered. Albin – otherwise Zaza, the queen of the drag show of the Cage aux Folles nightclub – is played by George Hearn, who lends his rich, operatic baritone to 'A Little More Mascara' and 'I Am Who I Am' with such masculine femininity as to avoid any feeling of tweeness or campery. Georges, the other half of the partnership, is played by Gene Barry with a crusty warmth and an endearingly creaky singing voice, which makes the 'Song on the Sand' into a most moving love song and gives a wealth of restrained emotion to the dramatic 'Look Over There'. When the two join together in a version of 'You on my Arm', it has just the same wondering joy in it as the version sung by the young boy about his girl.

John Wiener as the boy does his song attractively, the chorus of 'girls' sings lustily, and the Cocktail Counterpoint number, elsewhere grossly overplayed, gets a well-controlled performance. The orchestra under Donald Pippin gives really splendid support, rolling the music along and bursting forth with proprietorial breadth in its solo sections. *La Cage aux Folles* is splendidly served by this recording.

The British production, which also starred Hearn, was not recorded, but Australia's version was and it, too, is a fine record. Jon Ewing has a less dark baritone than Hearn, but it is a strong legitimate voice free of mannerisms, and he sings his numbers well. Keith Michell seems a little chary of committing himself to the emotion of Georges' rôle but he, too, sings with accuracy and charm, Gerry Sont gives the boy's song a fresh vigour, and all the other values are as near as could be wished to the original without quite coming up to it.

Berlin's Theater des Westens recording features an Albin (Helmut Baumann) with a considerably lesser voice than the two English-language versions. Rather than employing the rich legitimate tones of Hearn and Ewing, Baumann makes use of a limited light baritone, which is correspondingly less effective. Gunther König (Georges) comes out rather better, but the recording, whilst not in any way a bad one, just does not equal the other two. It is, certainly, by far preferable to the five songs recorded by Sweden's Jan Malmsjö who, by the cover photo, is in any case the most unfetching Zaza of the group.

42nd Street

42nd Street (1980), like the London *Singin' in the Rain*, brought one of the classic Hollywood musical films to the stage in a thoroughly delightful fashion. The original Warren/Dubin film score was, again, hotted up with additional material from other film musicals (*Go into your Dance*, *Gold Diggers of 1933*, *Dames*, *The Singing Marine* and *Hard to Get*) and the result was a show where familiar favourites like 'Lullaby of Broadway', 'Shuffle off to Buffalo', 'You're Getting to be a Habit with Me', 'Young and Healthy' and '42nd Street' were mixed with slightly less well-known pieces in effective proportions.

The original cast recording from Broadway is the only one I have at the time of writing, for the London production was not put on record and that from the recent Australian version has not yet reached me. Since it is as regular a recording as could be wished for, this is no problem.

Jerry Orbach as Julian Marsh, the producer who utters the immortal line about coming back a star, has little to sing in the show and thus does not appear on the recording until side 2, where he leads the performance of 'Lullaby of Broadway' and takes a chunk of '42nd Street', but when he does appear he proves to have been worth waiting for. The well-known, characterful baritone voice soars up to the notes of his verses, and you can just see the magnetic character gathering everyone around him as he weaves the spell of Broadway.

Orbach is well matched by Tammy Grimes as Dorothy Brock, the slightly ageing star who breaks her ankle and gives the little chorus girl her opportunity. Miss Grimes sings with a wry warmth and the kind of charisma that makes you understand why she is a star, and resists the temptation (succumbed to by some of her successors) to burlesque the rôle in 'About a Quarter to Nine', 'You're Getting to Be a Habit with Me' and the Shadow Waltz. Lee Roy Reams serenades 'Dames' in a fresh uncluttered tenor and Wanda Richert, as the little heroine, pipes her part agreeably, leaving us to hear in the volleys of tapping sections what it was that allowed little Peggy Sawyer to become a star.

Like that of *Singin' in the Rain*, this is a fine recording of a wholly enjoyable show, even if it is not a pure product of the 1980s. But if two such shows can be such block-busters in this day and age, perhaps it says something about what the public wants to see?

Woman of the Year

Woman of the Year is a slickly written musical play about the amorous problems of a 'strong woman'. Its score, by Kander and Ebb, is made up of a mixture of a lot of crisp light comedy songs and a few gentle ballads of the 'what's gone wrong' variety. Several of these are clearly marked out to be extractable singles, notably the heroine's tough assertion that she is 'One of the Boys' and her denigration of her high-flying talents in duet with an admiring, home-making woman in the very extended 'The Grass Is Always Greener'.

The original cast recording does not perhaps give the songs the best service that it might. The cast sound as if they are tired, as if the disc has been hurriedly put together the day after opening night, and since Harry Guardino's agreeable, crumpled baritone and Lauren Bacall's very similar tones dominate the disc, there is not much variety around. Still, the best of the comic pieces are enjoyable – Miss Bacall's performance of the quick-fire 'When You're Right, You're Right' and her put-down of her effete secretary ('Shut Up, Gerald'), and the vulturish 'It Isn't Working' and 'I Told You So' of the heroine's colleagues willing her marriage to fail. 'One of the Boys' swings along happily enough but, although 'The Grass Is Always Greener' apparently stopped the show on stage, it comes across less than hilariously on disc.

The performers are all adequate to their tasks, but the show as written is not an exciting one: it is a slightly down-beat romantic comedy with music and words to suit, and no one is ever required to open his or her mouth and grab you with a piece of singing. Given this, it would have been helpful to know the story, but the sleeve includes no synopsis, preferring a large list of credits down to the Choreographic Assistant, the Promotional Consultant and the Hair Stylist, who would seem to matter less on a recording than information about the recording.

The Rink

The Rink is an emotional piece about the mendable relationship between an ageing mother and the wayward daughter she brought up alone. It has none of the brittle comedy content of *Woman of the Year*, and its score, also by Kander and Ebb, is written in a different idiom, largely tailored to the talents of its two very vocal leading ladies – Chita Rivera and Liza Minnelli.

Rivera is vivacious, characterful and incisive, belting out her resentment at a life spent being 'Chief Cook and Bottle Washer' and asserting herself against the daughter who expects to wander back after fifteen years into a ready-made home ('Don't Ah Ma Me'). She makes more than most performers would of yet another number on the 'We Can Make It' theme. Minnelli isn't at her very best. The voice is a bit thick and she is inclined to chew up her words and notes, but Minnelli even at less than top notch is still better than most other performers of this kind of material at full value, and when the pair join together in 'The Apple Doesn't Fall Very Far from the Tree' things come to a fine peak. An ensemble of half a dozen versatile men supply a fine backing, lightening the dramatic story with some jolly moments like the happy, carnivalesque 'The Rink' and 'After All These Years', all of which make sense thanks to a comprehensive plot synopsis.

TER, which recorded this production, also put on disc a very brief London staging of the show, featuring Josephine Blake and Diane Langton, which seems a strange thing to do when you already have Rivera and Minnelli in the catalogue.

Amen Corner

Whilst other much weaker shows have won commercial recordings, it is odd to find the gutsy, effective score of *Amen Corner* issued only on a private disc made by the authors. A record-full of gospelly music with strong, healthy teeth, sung by a really stout-voiced cast headed by the searing Rhetta Hughes, it makes many other scores and singers of the period sound limp-wristed. I hope that someone will pick this record up for a full release one day, but for the moment it can only be bought from Udell himself.

Dance a Little Closer

Dance a Little Closer ran for one performance, but it was issued as a cast recording five years later. It is difficult to get enthusiastic about this recording. The material is far, certainly, from Lerner's best work, and although Strouse produces some sweet, lingering melodies the score doesn't start to invite you to listen to it until a long way into the first side. Part of the problem is in the performances. Len Cariou and Liz Robertson in the two large leading rôles sing accurately and with attractive tone, but without ever arousing emotion or interest in their very flat characters. They could both do with a little of the commitment displayed by Brent Barrett and Jeff Keller in their gay love song 'Why Can't the World Go and Leave It Alone'. You can't say it's bad, but it's very far from compulsive listening.

Dreamgirls

Dreamgirls was an exciting show in the theatre: exciting with its hectic 1960s Motown-type music by Henry Krieger and its infallible and vigorous 'gotta make it good in showbiz' story which led to the usual Cinderella ending by marginally different pathways; exciting, too, in Michael Bennett's staging. Its recording is exciting as well, but not in the same way. The score of *Dreamgirls* has been recorded, purposely no doubt, as a series of pop numbers rather than as a theatre score: no synopsis, no linking, none of the recitative or the lead-in material, just the songs baldly and barely presented as pop numbers begging for a play. I'm sure they won them, but although the individual songs don't suffer at all from this treatment, it doesn't do anything for them as a score.

The lollipop of the show and the recording is the dramatic 'And I Am Telling You I'm Not Going', sung by Jennifer Holliday in the rôle of Effie, the talented lead singer of an all-girl group who is given the heave-ho because her hefty bulk doesn't fit with the new svelte image planned for the girlie team. Effie objects with all her heart and soul, and Holliday tears down the ceiling in this bitter, resentful aria, peaking like a mandrake that has been ripped from its roots.

Many of the other numbers in the score are actually presented as pop songs in the show but, unfortunately, because of the presentation we have to guess which. One that stands out is the final 'One Night Only', Effie's big solo come-back number, which the now famous girl group covers in an attempt to destroy her. Thus, on the record, Holliday starts the number and it is taken over by the girls and the chorus.

Holliday's big, crazy voice, which sounds as if it is being torn out of her throat, gets the best chances in the show, but Loretta Devine, Sheryl Lee Ralph (the other two members of the group) Cleavant Derricks and Ben Harney have their moments as well, and all perform on equally high octane on a disc which never gives you a second to sit back. It is big, big, big all the way. Still, in spite of the lengthy apologia on the inner sleeve, written by the drama critic of the *Boston Globe* (why?) which tries to justify practically everything in sight without being asked, I'm not at all convinced that the record shows you *Dreamgirls* as a stage show. But maybe no one cares. And the songs, naked or not, still sound terrific.

Nine

Nine, a stage musical version of the Fellini film 8½, surrounds an immature Italian film director in prey to the mid-life crisis, that malaise beloved of American writers (and Italians?), with the crises and the women in his past and present life. Nothing much happens as the twenty-one women of the cast parade past us in review until this rather wimpish man, who isn't making the film he is supposed to have written, gets his (sex) life in order and the curtain can come down. The lack of significant action and the central man's bland lack of character don't matter too much on a recording; what matters is the score, and that is definitely not lacking in character. Maury Yeston's musical contribution to *Nine* is a multi-coloured affair – ranging from some clever, attractive ensemble music (well, if you have twenty-one female voices you might as well do things with them), including a splendid sung overture, to a wide variety of solos, of which the women get all the best items. In spite of the five solo spots given to him, there isn't much that can be done with the tiresome Contini (Raul Julia).

Karen Akers as Contini's wife delivers a gently explanatory 'My Husband Makes Movies'; Anita Morris as his mistress sings sex down the phone in a voice that goes from cutting chest tones to upper leger lines in what is supposed to be 'A Call From the Vatican'; Liliane Montevecchi as his producer goes into a number about the 'Folies-Bergère' in reasonably Gallic and sometimes off-key tones; Shelly Burch (the star of the non-existent film) needs him in an 'Unusual Way' in the most lovely but shakily sung single item of the score; Kathi Moss (the whore who taught him how) advises the use of the phrase 'Ti voglio bene' in a bosomy belt; and Taina Elg (his mother, oh yes) supplies a sweetly gentle moment reminding the boy of when he was 'Nine'. It is a score which is more demanding on its artists than many others, and not all the artists of the original cast are able to stretch their voices to all of its requirements, but when the girls are on, at least, the score and record of *Nine* are an interesting adventure.

The single-disc original cast recording was obliged to omit some of the show's music (although the cassette included additional material), but a 1988 Australian production spreads the piece over two very short records instead of one very full one. It doesn't include the extra material, but it is a decidedly superior recording which has many advantages over its Broadway counterpart.

John Diedrich (who is credited as director and apparently produced as well) plays Guido and, in spite of an accent that intermittently sounds like Nino Culotta out of *They're a Weird Mob*, he makes him a much less feeble fellow, acting energetically and singing with a strong, rich Robert Goulet baritone – particularly effective in the ballad 'Only with You', which sounds much less pale than before. However, singly or *en masse*, it is still the women's show and the women here are a perfectly marvellous bunch. From the moment they enthusiastically give out with the overture, or swell all over the harmonies and rhythms of the marvellous ensemble 'The Germans at the Spa' under the leadership of the splendid Sharon Jessop, it is clear that we are in for a first-rate performance. Maria Mercedes (wife) has warmth and poise and a richly cruising chest voice, Jackie Rees vamps a devastating 'A Call to the Vatican', Nancye Hayes zooms crisply and accurately through a 'Folies-Bergère' which sounds more authentic than the real thing, Caroline Gillmer (whore) radiates rough, rude sexuality and rich chest tones, and Peta Toppano shows that 'Unusual Way' really is the most beautiful part of the show when it is feelingly and beautifully sung. None of them, by the way, have accents . . . so why does he?

The only real faults with this fine set are peripheral. The cover is a mess: two discs slipped in one sleeve, no cast list, no indication of who sings what (that is on the discs and then it's erroneous), misspellings ranging from two of the stars' names and the musical director to the 'Follies Bergeres'. When Polydor reissues this set, hopefully a new cover will be in order. But in the meanwhile, it's worth having the bad sleeve for the fine recording.

Big River

The sleeve for MCA's recording of the score of the successful Huckleberry Finn musical, *Big River*, is an excellent one, informative and attractive, with a synopsis, pictures, lyrics on the inner sleeve, a proper cast list . . . all a show buff could ask for. The record itself is dome-shaped, of course, as is MCA's habit, but mine hasn't jumped off the turntable yet.

Roger Miller's lively country-style score is an ideal accompaniment for this picture-book tale, comfy and comical in turn, always tuneful and always thick-accented. The effective duos 'River in the Rain' and 'Muddy Water', as sung by Daniel Jenkins (Huck) and Ron Richardson (Jim), are highlights; Tom Sawyer's 'Hand for the Hog' sung by John Short, the vaudeville turn 'When the Sun Goes Down in the South' and John Goodman's 'Guv'ment' are nice comical moments; and there are plaintive slave strains in Carol Dennis's fine performance of 'The Crossing' and gentle sentimentality in the lovely singing of Patti Cohenour in 'You Oughta Be Here with Me' and 'Leavin's Not the Only Way to Go'. All the performers play their rôles with adept country style and character, and the sum total is a thoroughly enjoyable disc of a thoroughly enjoyable, unpretentious family musical. The successful Australian production has also put out a cast recording.

The Tap Dance Kid

Henry Krieger's *The Tap Dance Kid* is, like *Dreamgirls*, another black 'gotta make it in showbiz' show. This one, however, changes the wild world of pop music for that of dance, and centres on the ambitions of a ten-year-old boy to become a dancer against his father's commands. Krieger changes hats with ease, leaving the scalding sounds of Motown and Co. for an easy, bright, modern light music style in this second score.

The show's songs are mostly in a bright or sweetly sentimental vein: Hinton Battle as the kid's dancing uncle has fun with his 'Fabulous Feet', grandad taps his stuff in a dream sequence, the whole cast pounds out 'Dance if it Makes You Happy' and little Willie's fat, brainy sister counts her problems affectingly in 'Four Strikes Against Me'; whilst on the other hand, there are soliloquies for mother and for uncle's girlfriend and a comforting piece for uncle Dipsey ('Man in the Moon'), as well as a rather surprisingly serious eleven o'clock number for unyielding dad, which seems to have come from another show. The cast perform their material strongly, with Martine Allard as the young sister and Hinton Battle as Uncle Dipsey particularly enjoyable, in a show that is as cute as a button when it isn't taking itself too seriously. And that is most of the time.

Baby

Baby could only have been written in America. The baby in question is not the 'I can't give you anything but love' variety; it is the real kind, and the show deals with three couples and their reactions to having or not having a child. It begins with a little dissertation on the meeting of ovum and sperm, told like the introduction to *Journey into Space*, and the very first song manages to get 'spermatozoa' into its lyric (which must be some kind of a record), and goes on with a coy description of genetic getting-together. If this all sounds a bit pretentious and grim, it oddly enough isn't. The show keeps its sense of humour throughout, and it soon becomes more involved with the feelings and actions of the six straightforwardly attractive people who are its principals than with the mechanics of sex and giving birth.

Songs like the delightfully positive 'Fatherhood Blues', in which two of the men jubilate over impending fatherhood and the third determines not to give up trying, the funny 'The Ladies Singing their Song', in which every woman in sight pours advice and their grim but glorious experiences of childbirth over the young pregnant woman, or the older father's discovery that children are 'Easier to Love' than an adult wife, are both perspicacious and original as well as enjoyable.

The six lead performers are all as attractive as their characters, with the radiant Liz Callaway as the youngest mother coming over particularly well and even making the 'spermatozoa' lyric work, whilst Martin Vidnovic and Catherine Cox team warmly in the most difficult rôles of the couple trying all sorts of trying methods to conceive.

The Mystery of Edwin Drood

Another piece with a taste of originality – for these days, at least – is *The Mystery of Edwin Drood*, which presents a version of Dickens's unfinished story as a burlesque musical melodrama. The show is presented in the frame of a British Victorian music-hall performance and includes all the favourite elements of the genre – the dastardly villain, the pale persecuted heroine, the travesty hero – as well as a less expected element in that it has alternative endings, amongst which the audience is asked choose. Burlesque is, of course, only funny when it is written, composed and performed with total seriousness and talent, and *The Mystery of Edwin Drood* passes with flying colours on all these fronts. Rupert Holmes, responsible for both text and music, has come up with a score which is a marvellous mixture of the mock music hall and the parody light operatic, with lyrics both funny and fetching and melodies bouncy and beautiful.

The dramatic/romantic element of the story throws up the best numbers. The villainous Jasper's suspiciously frenetic 'A Man Could Go Quite Mad', the lovely spun-soprano 'Moonfall' for the wan heroine, and the pretty love duet of Rosa and Drood, 'Perfect Strangers', get performances of the top rank from Howard McGillin (a lip-smackingly horrid Jasper), perfectly pure, pallid Patti Cohenour (Rosa) and Betty Buckley (Drood). All partake of the marvellously melodramatic ensemble 'No Good Can Come from Bad', and Jasper and Rosa join together in a cracking and crucial duo to end the first act, which is a (if not the) highlight of show and disc.

The low comedy of the piece falls to George Rose as the Chairman, Cleo Laine as the enigmatic opium vendor called Princess Puffer, and a curious creature called Bazzard (Joe Grifasi), a small-part player in the company with ambitions to progress. This last has one hilarious song (which gets perhaps a slightly under-par performance on disc, certainly compared with the stage performance seen in London), but the music-hall goodies fall to the other two. Laine gives an over-the-top under-the-arches performance of the splendid 'The Wages of Sin' and 'The Garden Path to Hell', and Rose is as lively as a larrikin in his jaunty 'Both Sides of the Coin' and 'Off to the Races'. It is all super stuff.

The record includes the ending as played on the Broadway first night, which gives extra opportunities to Bazzard and to the Princess Puffer. The CD version of the show, however, manages to include all the variant endings, which is perhaps over-egging the pudding for the casual listener, but a joy for *Drood* fans, of which you will have guessed that I am one.

Little Shop of Horrors

From its small beginnings, way off-Broadway, *Little Shop of Horrors* has gone round the world. It must surely be the first off-Broadway musical to have been made into a major if not very marvellous film. It deserved better, for it is a very funny piece, spoofing the old horror movie genre deliciously in its tale of a frightful plant out to achieve world domination.

The original cast recording, in spite of irritatingly playing around with the order of the songs, is a splendid record of Alan Menken and Howard Ashman's story in songs, beginning with the bouncy introduction to the 'Little Shop of Horrors' sung in three-part harmony by a girl-group too girl-group to be true, before heading off 'Downtown'. There we meet gormless Seymour and his plant ('Grow for Me') and dumb blonde Audrey, who longs for sweet suburban life ('Somewhere That's Green') but is currently being womanhandled by a sadistic bikie 'Dentist'. Their troubles get giant-sized when the plant finds its voice and starts to demand 'Feed Me!' and shows a taste for blood.

Lee Wilkof is a first-rate wimp of a Seymour turning semi-hero for the love of Audrey in the lilting 'Suddenly Seymour' and even meditating murder ('Now'), Ellen Greene is a limply lovely little Betty Boop of a heroine, gushing vacuously over her longings for 'a matchbox of our own', and Franc Luz revels lusciously in pain as the ill-fated dentist with rock-and-roll tendencies, but it is the big, black voice of Ron Taylor, throatily howling out the plant's demands to 'Feed Me' or gloating over his 'Suppertime', that provides the very best moments of this happy disc.

For the film soundtrack, the score has been souped up into something larger, with a big orchestra and some all-round smoothing and sandpapering. The friendly and funny impression given in the stage recording of a devotedly B-rendering of a B-story of a B-movie has gone and we are in the slick and shiny world of A-movieland. Some reorganization and rearrangement has been done: 'Closed for Renovation', 'Mushnik and Son', 'Ya Never Know', 'Now' and 'Sominex' have all gone, and they have been replaced by the rhythmic 'Some Fun Now' for the three girls and 'Mean Green Mother from Outerspace' for the plant.

Rick Moranis gives a good performance in the mould established by Wilkof, Greene repeats her stage creation and Steve Martin is a less colourful dentist whose number has been unfortunately re- and overarranged. The three-part girls are very efficient but not very amusing, and utterly incomprehensible in their uninteresting new number. Levi Stubbs of the Four Tops is a magnificently lively, gravelly voice for the plant and he gets to do his thing wildly in the big, hectic new number.

There is altogether more fun in an Icelandic cast recording (*Litla hryllingsbúdin*), a disc which is not just a curiosity but a fine record of the show. A lively all-white group of performers is headed by an excellent wide-eyed, true-voiced Seymour (Leifur Hauksson) and a sweetly silly Audrey (Edda Heidrún Backman) with a strong, clear singing voice; if the plant has a little less rock-basso extravagance than the original, Ariel Pridan still makes a grand job of the rôle. This *Little Shop* cast is having fun.

The same can be said, with the bells of Notre Dame on it, for the French version. This starts off with the advantage of Alain Marcel's marvellously sparky and hilarious translation – just listen to the three girls clipping out the 'boopsy' rhyming of 'P'tit' boutique' for a start, then to Seymour's recipes for plant life in 'Pousse pour moi'. On it goes, with one bon-bon and bon mot following the last. It is a long time since I can remember a French show translation so imaginative and effective.

The performance, too, is fine. Fabienne Guyon is a superb Audrey, sweetly vacuous as she breathes out her longing for a home 'Au coeur du vert' and pulling out the pop-stops in 'Tout à coup, Seymour', and Vincent Vittoz is a cutely cornball Seymour who sings his numbers in a bright, energetic modern voice. The three girls are a lively, pointed trio and if Gérard Manzetti (Orin) suffers a little from over-echo, he is nevertheless a stylish sadist. Jacques Martial makes a splendid meal of the rôle of Audrey II in what is a very effective *Petite boutique des horreurs*.

March of the Falsettos

March of the Falsettos is a short five-handed small-stage piece about a bisexual middle-aged middle-class Jewish American (I'm afraid so), his wife, lover, son and psychiatrist. It won some fervent fans in the theatre, but, although the patterns of William Finn's words and music tie together neatly with each other in a swiftly and smoothly-running sung-through play style, the original cast recording is a slightly bewildering affair. A printed text of what you hear is provided and apparently most of the show is on the record, but I would have been grateful for a synopsis. I know everybody in the play felt angry with just about everyone else and that the wife went off with the psychiatrist, but, apart from that, I couldn't really say. And certain of the lyrics are what I could only call opaque, at least when divorced from the stage action.

Michael Rupert as the hero and Chip Zien as the psychiatrist flick through their rôles with style and pleasing voices, the support is fine, the band is fine, the recording is fine and I would guess the record is a very agreeable souvenir for those who liked the show.

Pump Boys and Dinettes

To call *Pump Boys and Dinettes* a musical is pushing things a bit. It has minimum action, and the half dozen performers, characterized as motorway service station attendants and waitresses, do little more than perform what they rightly call a 'musical tribute to life by the roadside' in nineteen loosely unconnected musical numbers in a jolly country idiom, composed by themselves. Musical or not, it's a 'damn cute l'il show' and it makes up a record of a refreshing simplicity and tunefulness. Whether it is the two girls touting the biscuits and smiling service at their Double Cupp Diner, getting tuneful over 'Tips' or wistful about a fouled-up relationship with a 'Sister', the boys gliding into unaccompanied four-part folk in 'Fisherman's Prayer', Jim Wann singing with touching sentiment over his 'Mamaw' or the unprepossessing piano-player fooling himself lugubriously over 'The Night Dolly Parton Was Nearly Mine', it is an endearing and unpretentious disc.

Three Guys Naked from the Waist Down

A small-scale musical on that subject beloved of large-scale musicals, how to be a star in showbusiness, *Three Guys* chose to deal with three boys who want to be comedians. Being off-Broadway, however, when these boys make it huge in commercial television they're aren't happy. Amongst a certain amount of heart-rending, one kills himself, one quits and the other sticks it. Michael Rupert and Jerry Colker's score is a bright one, but the piece as played by Colker, John Kassir and Scott Bakula seems a little effortfully comedic in its comedy parts and rather vastly emotional in such pieces as its big ballad 'I Don't Believe in Heroes Any More'.

A Danish cast recording seems, from its back cover photo, to want to emphasize the carefully provocative title.

Goblin Market

To base a musical on the poetic work of Christina Rosetti seems an unlikely idea, but the two-handed piece written by Polly Pen and Peggy Harmon, using the outline of the poem 'Goblin Market' and some of Rosetti's writings as lyrics, must have been a charming evening in a small theatre if the enchanting recording of its music, sung by original cast members Terri Ann Klausner and Ann Morrison, is anything to go by. Rosetti has had all sorts of subtexts inflicted on her work by scholars, but, as the record sleeve happily reminds us, *Goblin Market* is on its own an emotionally intricate piece about the two sisters who are its characters.

The delicate melodiousness of Miss Pen's atmospheric, period-flavoured music, strongly aided by some truly understanding arrangements for keyboards, violin and cello, is the basis for some exquisitely lovely songs which are well sung by the two performers. Several interpolated songs – excepting one by Brahms – are a little less effective than the original material, but the whole piece is a tiny, wondering delight.

Olympus on my Mind

As its title indicates, *Olympus on my Mind* (Barry Harman/Grant Sturial) is the unfailing classical burlesque returned to town. This one is a light-hearted version of the *Amphitryon*, with five principals and a chorus of three useful men, plus the backer's showgirl wife who carries through the show as a running joke. It is rather a similar line-up to that for *Phi-Phi*, but this show is not in the same class either in its comedy or in its music, both of which are occasionally agreeable without being in any way notable.

The trump card of the recording is the splendidly baritonic Martin Vidnovic in the double rôle of Jupiter and Amphitryon, sounding rather like the Miles Gloriosus of *Funny Things* in his series of musical numbers. He is well supported by the comical Frank Kopyc, horribly baffled by all the impersonations going on, and soprano Susan Powell as the legally virtuous Alcmene, but the running-joke Delores is a recording no-no. Inability to sing or act might be funny on stage and in one number, but on record and continually through the show it is a bore.

Two incidental queries: why are Jupiter and Mercury named in Latin and Alcmene and Amphitryon in Greek? And how come two of the sleeve photos are credited to Anita and Steve Shevett? I can just picture the pair of them with their fingers on the same button, waiting to click.

Nunsense

Dan Goggin's *Nunsense* is an entertainment in the form of a fund-raising concert (details in and on the record) by a bunch of crackpot nuns. Made up of a series of unlikely comic pieces, it obviously gains in the theatre from being ludicrously presented by a group of ladies in habits, but it still makes a happy, loopy entertainment on record. The nuns perform 'Tackle That Temptation with a Timestep', Sister Mary Amnesia does her vent act in 'So You Want to Be a Nun' and yodels out the show's highlight 'I Could Have Gone to Nashville', and the Reverend Mother gets an unsuitable attachment to a spotlight and waxes modest about her position in 'Just a Coupl'a Sisters' in a mass of showbiz allusions from *Gypsy* to *Die Zauberflöte*, from 'Swannee' to the Andrews Sisters.

The original off-Broadway cast perform their material with infectious gaiety, Semina de Laurentiis scoring the top points as she tosses off the showiest and most characterful parts of Mary Amnesia's rôle – switching from Queen of the

Night to Dolly Parton, hilariously – and the other wimpled ladies having various degrees of fun with various degrees of material.

Nunsense has spread like the good word, but the only other recording I know of is from the London production. It includes two pieces (the orchestral 'The Dying Nun Ballet' and 'Gloria in Excelsis') not on the American disc. It is also well performed, vocally stronger and more pointed comically in many places than the original recording, even if it occasionally seems that one nun might have been happier with another nun's numbers. Louise Gold is a versatile Sister Mary Amnesia who punches a mean country number, Anna Sharkey a zany Robert Ann with vast zest and a zingy upper register, Pip Hinton a graunchy-grindy Hubert of unlimited power, and Honor Blackman, as the Mother Superior, gives a fine and funny performance which is in another class from her other musical comedy recordings.

Romance, Romance

Romance, Romance, in accord with its title, is a combination of two one-act musical pieces about romantic love. Both are based on *fin de siècle* originals – one Viennese, one French – although in this manifestation the second piece is brought up to the present day. The first is easily the stronger of the two. The Schnitzler original, in which two rich people masquerade as poor folk in search of love and find each other, is prettily adapted and decorated with some charming, light new-period and frankly-new music by Keith Herrmann, including an attractive polka, a sparkly waltz and a torchy half-past-nine number ('The Night it Had to End'), and accompanied by crisp, characterful words which are very much happier than author Barry Harman's work for *Olympus on my Mind*.

Although its score is bright and jolly, Part Two has not the same character. Its Jules Renard story of a couple of old friends (m and f) who decide to have an affair, only to realize, before the fact, that their friendship isn't like that, translates reasonably well to modern times, but some of the modern numbers attached to it sound rather like sausage-songs, lacking the individuality of the best pieces of Part One.

Both halves are effectively performed by the relaxed light baritone Scott Bakula and the very individually voiced and piquant Alison Fraser (a sort of Carol Channing with top notes), assisted competently in Part Two by their spouses (Robert Hoshour, Deborah Graham). The result is an agreeable small piece, uneven but played with conviction.

The Gospel at Colonus

The Gospel at Colonus, a musical which retells the Oedipus legend in gospel terms, may have started off-Broadway, but it was by no means a small musical, presenting a cast of over sixty performers. It has been the subject of two recordings of almost the same material by the same cast which played it off- and briefly on-Broadway – Clarence Fountain and the Five Blind Boys of Alabama, the Institutional Radio

Choir, the J. D. Steele Singers and J. J. Farley and the Original Soul Stirrers. The later disc, on Nonesuch, includes two additional brief sections, although this is still far from the show's whole score.

Goodness knows how what all these people are singing on this record fits into the legend but, more importantly, the Bob Telson gospel music seems to be of a rather distilled, esoteric kind, lacking in those big, obvious heart-lifting numbers which mean 'gospel' to the uninitiated. Not until the last track on the first side ('Never Drive You Away') does this score supply a truly up-beat piece, and by then twenty minutes of what is clearly for specialists only has rather dulled the senses.

Charlotte Sweet

Like *Edwin Drood, Charlotte Sweet* is set in the British music hall where it, too, tells a burlesque melodrama tale of a sweet, pale and hard-done-by heroine finally rescued from villains of the deepest dye and restored to her own true love. This one has shades of *Les Saltimbanques* in its story, for the villains run a circus of extraordinary voices, and it is Charlotte's exceptionally high soprano (artificially aided by doses of helium) that they are after. There is plenty of enjoyable parody humour (things have come a good way from the obvious days of the *Little Mary Sunshine* kind of burlesque) from a group of comical characters who are given some lively music-hall tunes, both set-piece solos and narrative, in what is a highly enjoyable little piece of small-theatre entertainment.

The show gets a very broad performance on its two-disc original cast set, played to the accompaniment of a pretty and effective four-piece band (piano, two wind and percussion), with Mara Beckerman giving a particularly convincing performance as the stratospheric heroine.

My Ten Essential Records

CATS: original London cast recording, with Elaine Paige, Paul Nicholas and Stephen Tate (2 records, Polydor CATX0001); CD (Polydor 817–810–2)

CHESS: original concept album, with Elaine Paige, Murray Head and Tommy Korberg (2 records, RCA PL70500); CD (RCA VD 70500–2)

THE PHANTOM OF THE OPERA: original London cast recording, with Michael Crawford and Sarah Brightman (2 records, Polydor PODV9); CD (Polydor 831–273–2)

LES MISERABLES: original London cast recording, with Colm Wilkinson and Roger Allam (2 records, First Night Encore 1): CD (First Night Encore CD1)

BLOOD BROTHERS: London revival cast recording, with Kiki Dee (First Night Cast 17); CD (First Night CD17)

LITTLE SHOP OF HORRORS: original cast recording, with Ellen Greene and Lee Wilkof (Geffen GHSP 2020)

42ND STREET: original cast recording, with Jerry Orbach and Tammy Grimes (RCA CBL:1–3891); CD (RCA RCD1–3891)

THE MYSTERY OF EDWIN DROOD: original cast recording, with Howard McGillin, Patti Cohenour, Betty Buckley and Cleo Laine (Polydor 827 969–1 Y-1); CD (Polydor G 827 969–2-Y-1)

ASPECTS OF LOVE: original cast recording, with Kevin Colson, Anne Crumb and Michael Ball (Really Useful 841 126–1) CD (Really Useful 841 126–2)

GOBLIN MARKET: original cast recording, with Terri Klausner and Ann Morrison (TER 1144)

Other Recommended Records

Cats: Japanese cast recording (2 records, Canyon C40H0032)

The Phantom of the Opéra: Japanese cast recording (2 records, Canyon C40H0041)

Song and Dance: original London cast recording, with Marti Webb (2 records, Polydor PODV4)

Starlight Express: American studio cast recording (selection), with Peter Hewlett and others (MCA S5972)

Singin' in the Rain: London stage cast recording, with Tommy Steele (Safari Rain 1)

Les Misérables: original French concept album, with Maurice Barrier and Rose Laurens (2 records, Trema 310086–7); or excerpts (First Night Scene 2); CD (Trema 710 217/ First Night CD2)

Starmania: original cast recording, with France Gall, Fabienne Thibeault, Daniel Balavoine and Diane Dufresne (4 records, Warner Brothers WE324); CD (WEA 240 503–2)

La Cage aux Folles: original cast recording, with George Hearn and Gene Barry (RCA HBCI-4824); CD (RCA BD 84824)

Into the Woods: original cast recording, with Chip Zien, Joanna Gleeson and Bernadette Peters (RCA Victor 6796–1 RC); CD (RCA 6796–2-RC)

Merrily We Roll Along: original cast recording, with Jim Walton, Lonny Price and Ann Morrison (RCA CBL1–4197); also available on CD

Sunday in the Park with George: with Mandy Patinkin and Bernadette Peters (RCA HBC1–5042); CD (RCA RCD1 5042)

Dreamgirls: original cast recording, with Jennifer Holliday (Geffen GHSP 2007) CD (Geffen 2007–2)

Nine: Australian cast recording, with John Diedrich, Peta Toppano and Maria Mercedes (2 records, Polydor 835 217–1)

Big River: original cast recording, with Daniel Jenkins (MCA 6147); CD (MCAD 6147 010X 425)

Pump Boys and Dinettes: original cast recording (CBS FM 37790); CD (CBS MK 37790)

Baby: original cast recording, with Martin Vidnovic, Todd Graff, Liz Calloway and Catherine Cox (TER 1089); CD (CDTER 1089)

Nunsense: London cast recording, with Louise Gold, Anna Sharkey, Pip Hinton and Honor Blackman (TER 1132)

Charlotte Sweet: original off-Broadway cast recording, with Mara Beckerman (John Hammond Records W2X 38680)

La Petite boutique des horreurs: French cast recording, with Fabienne Guyon and Vincent Vittoz (HI 1740 121)

INDEX

Ábrahám, Paul, 301–3
Abraira, Pablo, 465
Ace of Clubs, 220, 228, 229, 239
Ackermann, Otto, 95, 104, 123
Ackland, Joss, 398, 447, 468
Act, The, 413
Adair, Yvonne, 347
Adamo, 494
Adams, Donald, 54, 57, 58, 63, 64, 68
Adams, Edith, 354, 381
Adler, Bruce, 313
Adler, Richard, 366
Adrian, Max, 438
Afgar, 147
After the Ball, 431
Aggiungi una posta alla tavola, 457
Aglaë, 256
Aharon, Shlomit, 498
Ainsworth, Alyn, 347
Aitken, Maria, 398
Akers, Karen, 508
A la Jamaïque, 258
Alan, Hervey, 215
Albanese, Licia, 397
Alberghetti, Anna-Maria, 392
Alda, Alan, 390
Alda, Robert, 351
Aleman, Julio, 237
Aler, John, 9
Alexander, Cris, 338
Alexander, Peter, 21, 284, 291, 307, 346
Alibert, Henri, 251, 252
Allam, Roger, 495
All American, 413
Allard, Martine, 509
Allegro, 372
Allen, Elizabeth, 386
Allen, Jeanne, 175
Allers, Franz, 100, 110, 128, 165, 317, 330
Alliot-Lugaz, Colette, 9, 45
Allister, Jean, 69, 73

Alloway, Jackie, 206
Allyson, June, 206
Alpar, Gitta, 287, 301
Altéry, Mathé, 168, 283–4, 327
Alvarez, Carmen, 188
Alvi, Bernard, 35, 41, 129, 242, 280
Amade, Raymond, 9, 12, 22, 27, 50, 129, 250
Amen Corner, 506
Amir, Tal, 498
Amour, Marthe, 129
Amour à Tahiti, L', 262
Amour Masqué, L', 309
Andalousie, 253, 255–6, 309
Anday, Rosette, 110, 293
Anders, Peter, 102, 175
Andersen, Carl, 463
Anderson, Daphne, 230
Anderson, Maxwell, 208
Anderssen, Benny, 488
Andersson, Gert-Ove, 130
Andes, Keith, 400
Andion, Paxti, 469
Andreas, Christine, 204, 313, 330
Andres, Barbara, 440
Andrews, Julie, 161, 324, 325, 328, 329, 330, 333, 439
Andrews, Nancy, 205
Andrex, 252, 258, 260
And so to Bed, 234
Andy Capp, 490
Angas, Richard, 72
Angela, June, 323
Angelici, Martha, 38, 47, 49
Angers, Avril, 401
Anheisser, Wolfgang, 134, 140
Annie, 413–4, 430
Annie Get Your Gun, 339–41, 382
Annie schiess los!, see *Annie Get Your Gun*
Ann Veronica, 460
Anthony, Julie, 189, 326
Antoine, 245

Antoine, Bernadette, 9
Anyone Can Whistle, 394
Anything Goes, 192–6, 212
Apartment, The, 422
Appelt, Adi, 103, 133
Applause, 413
Apple Tree, The, 390
Aragon, Emilio, 405
Arcadians, The, 84–5, 86
Arc de Triomphe, 224–5, 240
Arden, Eve, 178
Arènes joyeuses, 251
Ariotti, Philippe, 390
Arizona Lady, 286
Arlen, Harold, 372–4
arme Jonathan, Der, 114
Armitage, Richard, 236
Armstrong, Alun, 495
Armstrong, Bridget, 442
Arnaz, Lucie, 416
Arnold, Sydney, 431
Aronson, Margaret, 79
Around the World in Eighty Days, 197
Arthur, Beatrice, 300, 408
Arthur, Carol, 339
Arthur, Maurice, 34
Artioli, Franco, 286
Arundell, Dennis, 80
Ashe, Rosemary, 222, 485
Ashley, Barbara, 200
Ashman, Howard, 511
Ashton, Marcia, 441
Askey, Arthur, 239
Aspects of Love, 29, 487, 517
Asse, Christian, 11, 22, 44
Astaire, Adele, 183
Astaire, Fred, 183, 344
Atkinson, David, 167
Atkinson, Sarah, 448
Auberge du Cheval Blanc, see *Im weissen Rössl*
Aubert, Jean, 192
Aubert, Jeanne, 192
Aubry, Blanche, 411
Audran, Edmond, 3, 18, 40–1
Au pays du soleil, 251, 252, 253
Avalon, Frankie, 421
Aventure à Monte-Carlo, 262
Aventure à Tahiti, 262
Avery, Lawrence, 165
Aviks, Valda, 480
Ayldon, John, 77
Aznavour, Charles, 262

Babes in Arms, 205–6, 213
Babes in Toyland, 155, 158, 205
Baby, 509–10, 517
Bacall, Lauren, 413, 505
Bacharach, Burt, 422

Backman, Edda-Heidrún, 512
Bacquier, Gabriel, 23, 35, 42, 45, 105, 131, 318
Baddeley, Hermione, 460
Badorek, Wilfried, 112, 113
Bagley, Ben, 204
Bagnall, Valda, 218, 231
Bailey, Pearl, 211, 373, 374, 407
Bajadere, Die, 286, 288–9, 309
Baker, George, 54, 56, 60, 61, 62, 63, 64, 65, 66, 69, 76
Baker, Kenny, 209
Baker, Mark, 356
Baker's Wife, The, 418, 430
Bakula, Scott, 513, 515
Balalaika, 1, 193, 240
Ball, Lucille, 400, 408
Ball, Michael, 487, 495, 496
Ball bei Hof, 118
Ballard, Kay, 177, 314, 380, 393
Ball im Savoy, 301
Balon, Laure, 480
Baltsa, Agnes, 92
Bang Goes the Meringue, 438
Banquells, Rocio, 469
Baptiste, Thomas, 211
Bárabás, Sári, 112, 137, 267, 302
Barbeau, Adrienne, 421
Barbe-Bleue, 14, 52
Bardóczy, Attila, 469
Bareham, Adam, 436
Barker, Ronnie, 263
Barlow, Frances, 439
Bar Mitzvah Boy, 470
Barney, Luc, 259, 292, 293
Barnum, 404, 430
Baron, Lynda, 396
Baroux, Lucien, 40
Barrault, Jean-Louis, 19
Barrett, Brent, 506
Barrier, Maurice, 494, 498
Barron, Muriel, 225
Barry, Anna, 446
Barry, Bruce, 448
Barry, Gene, 503
Barry, John, 460, 471
Barsony, Rosy, 301
Bart, Lionel, 449–53
Bartel, Reinhard, 107
Barthelemy, Vivienne, 105
Bartlett, Patricia, 227
Barton, James, 335
Barton, Steve, 480, 485
Bartos, Rita, 112
Baschiung, Alain, 265
Bashville, 490
Basie, Count, 445
Basoche, La, 46
Bass, Alfie, 389, 452

Bassey, Shirley, 172, 456, 503
Bastianini, Ettore, 90
Bastin, Jules, 42
Ba-ta-Clan, 26, 51
Bates, Thorpe, 217
Battedou, André, 10
Battle, Hinton, 509
Battling Butler, 218
Baugé, André, 170
Baumann, Helmut, 504
Bautista, Teddy, 464, 465
Bavaar, Tony, 335
Bavards, Les, 27, 51
Baxter, Stanley, 448
Bayless, Jean, 326
Bayne, Mardi, 205
Beaumont, Roma, 224, 225
Beauty Prize, 175, 212
Beauty Stone, The, 79
Beauvais, Jeanne, 439
Beavers, Dick, 200
Beck, Gordon, 445
Beckerman, Mara, 516
Bédex, Henri, 11
Beecham, Laurie, 467
Begg, Heather, 67
Beggar's Holiday, The, 240
Belcourt, Emile, 321
Bell, Marion, 332
Belle, 455, 475
Belle de Cadix, La, 253, 254, 255, 309
Belle Hélène, La, 7–10, 12, 51, 52
Belle Lurette, 33
Belle of New York, The, 159
Belle Otéro, La, 262
Bells Are Ringing, 364, 383
Belobragina, Ludmilla, 289
Belthoise, Béatrice, 245
Benatzky, Ralph, 298
Bende, Zsoltan, 142
Bennett, Diana, 486
Bennett, Robert Russell, 172, 312, 320, 330, 340, 343, 364, 377
Benoît, Jean-Christophe, 9, 18, 25, 38, 40, 44
Benson, Hamlyn, 461
Bentley, Paul, 396, 488
Benzell, Mimi, 405
Berbié, Jane, 7, 44
Berganza, Teresa, 21, 22
Berger, Ludwig, 284
Berger, Michel, 498
Berlin, Irving, 339, 348–50
Bernard, Fabrice, 495
Bernardi, Herschel, 411
Bernstein, Alexander, 338
Bernstein, Leonard, 338, 353–61
Bernstein, Nina, 338
Berry, Walter, 94, 97, 108, 109, 116

Berté, Heinrich, 147
Berton, Liliane, 2, 5, 6, 8, 9, 17, 20, 37, 40, 41, 43, 44, 47, 49, 50, 51, 135, 180, 248, 251, 256, 271
Bertram, Hans, 302
Besnard, Lucien, 292
Besoyan, Rick, 372
Bessenyei, Ferenc, 412
Best Foot Forward, 238
Best Little Whorehouse in Texas, The, 424
Bettelstudent, Der, 109–11, 150
Betti, Freda, 40, 47, 50, 254
Bet Your Life, 239, 240
Beudert, Mark, 358
Bevan, Gillian, 374
Bevan, Ian, 215
Bevan, Stanley, 67
Beyond the Rainbow, 457
Bibl, Rudolf, 148
Bidault, Françoise, 30
Big Ben, 234, 240
Bigley, Isobel, 351
Big River, 509, 517
Billy, 471, 475
Bingham, Bob, 463, 464, 465
Biograph Girl, The, 448
Bischof, Gaby, 292
Bishop, Laura, 478
Bitter-Sweet, 220, 228, 239
Black, Don, 471
Blackburn, Bryan, 461
Blackham, Joyce, 10
Blackman, Honor, 515
Blackton, Jay, 312, 313
Blaine, Vivien, 351
Blair, Joyce, 371, 379, 454
Blair, Pamela, 415
Blaireau, Richard, 283
Blake, Josephine, 402, 506
Blanc, Ernest, 37
Blanc, Jonny, 128
Blanc, Pierre, 42
Blanzat, Anne-Marie, 44, 45
blaue Mazur, Die, 268, 269
Blazer, Judith, 156
Blessed, Brian, 478
Bless the Bride, 233–4, 240
Blighton, Elaine, 226
Bliss, Helena, 337
Blitz, 452
Blitzstein, Marc, 300
Blondel, 490
Blood Brothers, 491, 516
Bloomer Girl, 373
Blossom Time, see *Dreimäderlhaus, Das*
Blue Eyes, 178, 218
Blue Kitten, The, 163
Blume von Hawaii, Die, 301, 310

Blyden, Larry, 159, 390
Blyth, Ann, 363
Bob Herceg, 145, 154
Boccaccio, 107–9, 150
Bock, Jerry, 372, 376, 387–91
Boesch, Ruthilde, 296
Bogel, Andrea, 479
Böhme, Kurt, 94, 108, 131, 285
Boles, John, 177
Bolger, Ray, 158, 345, 374
Bolton, Guy, 193
Bolyar, Lewis, 200
Bond, Gary, 459, 466
Bonney, Barbara, 93
Boodle, 218
Booth, Shirley, 381
Bordello, 470
Bordman, Gerald, 178, 343
Borel, Christian, 258, 292
Borodin, Alexsandr, 362
Borst, Danielle, 33
Boskovsky, Willi, 91, 96, 104, 108, 116, 273
Bostwick, Barry, 420, 473
Bottone, Bonaventura, 72, 358
Boublil, Alain, 265, 493
Boué, Géori, 46, 250
Boulangeot, Huguette, 26, 27, 37, 105, 274, 292
Boulangère a des écus, La, 4, 34
Bourdin, Georgette, 293
Bourdin, Roger, 6, 250
Bourvil, 243, 260, 262, 292, 293
Bova, Joseph, 379
Bowden, Pamela, 69
Boyer, Jacqueline, 302
Boy Friend, The, 438–40, 474
Boyle, Billy, 460, 471
Boys from Syracuse, The, 201, 213
Bradbury, Lane, 365
Brahms, Caryl, 459, 502
Brambell, Wilfred, 460
Brannigan, Owen, 54, 56, 71
Braun, Horst Heinrich, 114
Braunstein, Buenaventura, 480
Breck, Freddy, 295
Bredin, Patricia, 419, 436
Brédy, Rosine, 43, 254, 293
Breffort, Alexandre, 262
Brel, Jacques, 420
Brendel, Wolfgang, 93
Brennan, Eileen, 406
Brennan, Maureen, 356
Brett, Jeremy, 127
Bricusse, Leslie, 456, 457
Bridgewater, Dee Dee, 425
Briercliffe, Nellie, 65, 68
Brigadoon, 331–3, 382
Brigands, Les, 15–17, 52

Brightman, Sarah, 318, 331, 332, 333, 478, 481, 484
Briner, Marion, 291
Britton, Pamela, 332
Brix, Fifi, 314
Broadbent, Elsie, 79
Brodszky, Nicholas, 164
Broissin, Nicole, 38, 93, 254, 259, 280
Brokmeier, Willi, 119, 130, 134, 140, 285
Bronhill, June, 6, 9, 20, 80, 84, 97, 127, 131, 135, 148, 167, 220, 227, 272, 318, 323, 326, 457
Brooks, David, 332, 373
Brooks, Lawrence, 337
Brooks, Nigel, 82
Brotherson, Eric, 347
Brown, Barbara, 179
Brown, Georgia, 449, 450
Brown, Joanne, 234
Brown, Joe, 446
Brown, Lew, 190
Brown, Nancy, 238
Browne, Irene, 179, 432
Browne, Louise, 232
Brox, Victor, 463
Bruce, Betty, 197
Bruce, Carol, 386
Brüder Straubinger, 297
Bruère, Louis-Vincent, 30
Brussmann, Reinhard, 497
Bryan, Dora, 172, 235, 347, 406, 447, 496
Bryan, Julie, 163, 216, 360
Bryant, Glenn, 210
Bryde, Jutta, 480
Brynner, Yul, 322
Buccaneer, The, 442
Buchanan, Jack, 215, 222
Bucio, Olivia, 237
Buckley, Betty, 422, 423, 478, 510
Buczolich, Rudolf, 292
Budgie, 491
Buhlan, Bully, 295
Bullock, Osmund, 436
Bumbry, Grace, 94, 96, 211
Bunnage, Avis, 389, 471
Burch, Shelly, 508
Burgthaler-Schuster, Gertrud, 95
Burke, Billie, 374
Burke, Johnny, 163
Burke, Simon, 195
Burkhard, Paul, 114, 306, 308
Burles, Charles, 6, 9, 10, 12, 32, 33, 35, 38, 42
Burnand, F.C., 57, 79
Burnett, Carol, 378, 397, 414
Burns, David, 394, 406
Burns, Karla, 173
Burrows, Abe, 350, 361, 386
Burt, Clare, 493
Burt, David, 490

Burton, Margaret, 180
Burton, Richard, 229
Byatt, Irene, 321
Bye Bye Birdie, 370, 383
By Jupiter, 206, 213
Byrne, Debbie, 478, 496
By the Beautiful Sea, 381

Cabaret, 410–11, 429
Cabaret Girl, The, 175, 212
Cabayo, Ena, 171, 211
Caesar, Sid, 400
Caffi, Jean-Paul, 232
Cage aux Folles, La, 503, 517
Cagliostro in Wien, 102
Caillavet, Gaston de, 129
Caine, Rebecca, 495
Caire, Réda, 129, 246
Cairncross, James, 435, 437
Calès, Claude, 49
Callaway, Liz, 510
Call Me Madam, 348–50, 383
Calloway, Cab, 407
Calon, Jean-Claude, 420
Calvin, Henry, 362
Camargo, La, 34
Camelot, 333–5, 382
Cameron, John, 54, 56, 60, 64, 66, 71, 74, 77, 148
Campbell, Judy, 441
Can-Can, 361
Cancion del amor mio, 261
Candide, 335–8, 382
Canterbury Tales, 459, 475
Cantor, Eddie, 191
Capote, Truman, 373
Capri, Nadine, 260
Caravelle d'or, La, 261
Caravelli, 407
Carbo, Edmond, 253
Card, The, 470
Carder, Tom, 467
Cardinale, Roberto, 234
Careless Rapture, 223, 224, 225, 226, 227, 239, 240
Carey, Macdonald, 209
Carey, Thomas, 171
Cariou, Len, 397, 398, 399, 506
Cariven, Marcel, 20, 26, 44, 243, 254
Carlès, Roméo, 248, 274
Carlisle, Kitty, 127, 337
Carlyle, Louise, 185
Carmen Jones, 210, 213
Carmichael, Ian, 414
Carnaval aux Caraïbes, 262
Carne, Judy, 439
Carnival, 392, 429
Carousel, 314–18, 382

Carpentier, Marcel, 46, 245
Carr, Charmian, 325
Carreras, José, 23, 321, 360, 386
Carroll, David James, 490
Carroll, Diahann, 373, 385
Carson, Danielle, 201, 492
Carson, Jeannie, 238, 344
Carte, Bridget D'Oyly, 54
Carte, Rupert D'Oyly, 54
Carter, Jack, 376
Carton, Pauline, 42, 251
Caryll, Ivan, 85, 159
Casa delle tre ragazze, La, see *Dreimäderlhaus, Das*
Casadesus, Mathilde, 36
Casanova, 100, 104
Case, Allen, 185
Case, John Carol, 74
Casey, Warren, 418
Cassidy, Jack, 177, 185, 202, 203, 205, 333, 375
Castets, Maryse, 27
Castle, Joyce, 357
Castle, Roy, 492
Cat and the Fiddle, The, 176, 212
Cats, 477–80, 516, 517
Cauchard, Denise, 41
Cavalcade, 220
Cavalieri, Deena, 128
Caznoff, Philip, 490
Cecil, Sylvia, 230
Cent Vièrges, Les, 34
Chabrier, Emmanuel, 44
Chakiris, George, 359
Challan, René, 9
Channing, Carol, 406, 347
Channing, Stockard, 421
Chanson d'amour, see *Dreimäderlhaus, Das*
Chanson de Fortunio, Le, 31, 52
Chanson gitane, 248, 309
Chant du desert, Le, see *Desert Song, The*
Chant du Tzigane, Le, see *Forbidden Melody*
Chantel, Viviane, 262
Chanteur de Mexico, Le, 257–8
Chaplin, Sidney, 355, 364, 392, 402
Chappell, Eddie, 185
Chapuis, Gérard, 232
Charisse, Cyd, 446, 447
Charles, Maria, 439, 440, 441
Charles, Pamela, 460
Charlie Girl, 446–7, 475
Charlotte Sweet, 516, 517
Château, Christiane, 43
Château à Toto, Le, 4
Chatel, Liliane, 25
Chauve-souris, La, see *Fledermaus, Die*
Chee-Chee, 198
Chess, 488, 516
Chevalier, Maurice, 244, 247, 248, 361
Chicago, 412–13, 430

Chicot, Etienne, 499
Chieftain, The, 79
Chivot, Henri, 24
Chocolate Soldier, The, see *tapfere Soldat, Der*
Chorus Line, A, 415–16
Christ, Rudolf, 89, 110, 135, 281, 284, 286, 296
Christie, Tony, 468
Christiné, Henri, 241, 242–6
Christmas, David, 423
Christmas in King Street, 438
Christopher Columbus, 34
Christy, Eileen, 316
Chrysanthemum, 453, 474
Chryst, Dorothea, 20, 125, 132, 142, 279, 324
Chu Chin Chow, 215, 239
Church, Sandra, 365
Ciboulette, 248, 249, 309
Cilento, Wayne, 415
Circus, Martin, 265
Claret, Jack, 292
Clark, Petula, 326, 345
Clarke, Morris, 332
Clarkson, Paul, 493
Claudia, 469
Claverie, Michèle, 162
Clay, Frederic, 53
Clayburgh, Jill, 417
Clayton, Jan, 316
Clement, Maris, 357
Clément, Willy, 8, 20, 37
Clements, Sir John, 316
Clervanne, Madeleine, 251
Cliff, Laddie, 218
Clifford, Veronica, 420
Clin, Serge, 39, 254
Clivia, 303
Cloches de Corneville, Les, 37–9, 51, 52
Clo-Clo, 268, 269
Clooney, Rosemary, 344
Close, Glenn, 404
Clutsam, G.H., 148
Clyde, Gordon, 217
Coca, Imogen, 404
Cocarde de Mimi-Pinson, La, 250–1
Coertse, Mimi, 141
Coeur et la main, Le, 34
Cohan, George M., 159
Cohen, Albert, 497
Cohenour, Patti, 509, 510
Cohn, Marc, 483
Cole, Andy, 84, 169, 176, 177, 226, 293
Cole, Kay, 415
Coleman, Cy, 400–5
Coles, Charles 'Honi', 184
Coles, Priti, 486
Colette, 470, 490
Colicos, Nick, 355
Colker, Jerry, 513

Collart, Claudine, 4, 36, 271
Collins, Dorothy, 396
Collins, José, 217
Collins, Michael, 81
Colman, Robert, 167
Colson, Kevin, 487
Comden, Betty, 338, 354, 364, 396, 403
Comedy of Errors, The, 438
Come Spy with Me, 461, 475
Command, Michèle, 42
Comment réussir dans les affaires . . ., see *How to Succeed in Business . . .*
Company, 394, 430
Connecticut Yankee, A, 199
Connell, Jane, 236, 379, 408
Connelli, Judy, 412
Connors, Ursula, 215
Constantine, Eddie, 262
Conti, Tom, 416
Contrabandista, The, 79
Conversation Piece, 220, 228, 229, 239
Conway, Shirl, 378
Cook, Barbara, 172, 317, 323, 356, 369, 378, 387, 396
Cooke, Charles, 439
Cookson, Peter, 361
Cooper, Marilyn, 359
Cooper, Terence, 379, 452
Coote, Robert, 330
Corazza, Rémy, 10, 25, 27
Corbett, Ronnie, 202
Cordier, Noëlle, 265
Cordy, Annie, 260, 261, 262, 407
Cormon, 33
Corsair, The, 154
Coslow, Sam, 433
Costigan, George, 491
Cott, Thomas, 192
Coulon, René, 38
Coulter, Kay, 203
Country Girl, The, 85
Coupland, Diana, 444
Courtneidge, Cicely, 215, 225, 238
Covington, Julie, 417, 467
Coward, Noël, 220, 228–31
Cox, Catherine, 510
Cox, Jean, 305
Cox and Box, 53, 57, 76, 85, 86
Coyne, Joseph, 178
Cradle Will Rock, The, 211
Craig, Charles, 269, 272
Crane, Norma, 389
Craven, Gemma, 321, 416, 438, 455
Crawford, Michael, 405, 471, 484
Crémieux, Hector, 33
Créole, La, 26, 52
Crespin, Régine, 11, 19, 21
Crest of the Wave, The, 224, 227, 240

Cribbins, Bernard, 194, 471
Criswell, Kim, 154, 196
Crockett, Gene, 209
Crofoot, Alan, 6, 419
Croft, David, 293
Croisset, Francis de, 249
Cronyn, Hume, 208
Croquefer, 28
Crosby, Bing, 192, 321, 352
Crosby, Kim, 503
Crucke, Koen, 168
Crumb, Anne, 487
Csap, Eva, 16
Csárdásfürstin, Die, 1, 139–42, 151
Cullum, John, 403, 427
Cumia, Lyne, 36, 38, 43
Cunitz, Maud, 296
Curry, Tim, 472, 473
Curzi, Cesare, 99, 100
Cuvillier, Charles, 146, 147

Dachary, Lina, 14, 17, 20, 24, 26, 28, 31, 36, 39,
    43, 129, 162, 180, 258
Dahlberg, Monika, 147, 303, 305
d'Alba, Julia, 220
Dale, Grover, 432
Dale, Jim, 404, 470
Dallapozza, Adolf, 7, 91, 104, 108, 115, 117,
    147, 149, 277, 305
Dallas, Lorna, 171
Daltrey, David, 466
Daltys, Claude, 283
Dame, Donald, 165
Dames at Sea, 423, 429
Damn Yankees, 368, 383
Damon, Stuart, 202, 263, 446
Damone, Vic, 181, 363
Damonte, Magali, 45
Dance a Little Closer, 506
Dancing Years, The, 223–7, 239, 240
Dandry, Evelyne, 387
Daneman, Paul, 334
d'Angelo, Beverly, 428
Daniels, Barbara, 327
Daniels, David, 184
Daniels, Jeff, 482
Danner, Blythe, 422
Darian, Anita, 165, 323
Darling, Edward, 215
Darling, Jean, 316
Dary, René, 282
d'Attili, Maria, 234
Dautin, Yves, 494
Dassary, André, 162, 168, 248, 254, 258, 280
Dassy, Déva, 5, 8, 20
David, Anne-Marie, 464
David, Clifford, 202, 422
David, Hal, 422

Davies, Aileen, 76
Davies, Harry Parr, 217
Davies, Irving, 340
Davis, Buster, 364
Davis, Charles K., 128
Davis, Sammy, jr, 321, 344, 346, 352, 376, 456
Dawn, Julie, 168
Dawson, Anna, 34, 436
Dawson, Peter, 61
Day, Doris, 341, 367
Day, Edith, 161, 167, 187, 189, 432
Day, Frances, 232
Dayan, Tiki, 498
Day in Hollywood . . ., A, 472, 475
Dean, Yvonne, 59, 76
Dear Anyone, 490
Dearest Enemy, 198
Dear World, 408, 430
Debus Allen G., 155
de Carlo, Yvonne, 396
Decaux, Alain, 22
Dédé, 244, 309
Dee, Kiki, 491
Deems, Mickey, 193
Deilhes, Suzy, 39
de Jong, Jasperina, 402
de Koven, Reginald, 154
Delage, Roger, 45
Delair, Suzy, 19, 283
Delance, Georges, 26
Delange, Pierrette, 23, 407
de Laurentiis, Semina, 514
della Casa, Lisa, 20, 128, 276
dell'Isola, Salvatore, 21, 203, 320
de Lon, Jack, 353
Delpech, Michel, 494
Delysia, Alice, 147, 282
Demas, Carole, 420
Demigny, Bernard, 5
Denain, Pierre, 252
Dench, Judi, 410
Denes, Oskar, 301
Denever, see *Fledermaus, Die*
Denise, Gita, 379
Dennen, Barry, 410, 463, 464
Dennis, Carol, 509
Dennis, Patrick, 400, 407
Dens, Michel, 2, 9, 25, 35, 36, 38, 39, 41, 43, 46,
    47, 49, 51, 105, 129, 135, 149, 271, 274, 293
Denyer, Jay, 454
de Paul, Gene, 372, 381
Derfflinger, 121
de Rieux, Max, 46, 243, 247
Dermota, Anton, 88, 90
Derricks, Cleavant, 507
Desailly, Jean, 26, 283
Desert Song, The, 1, 166–8, 212
de Shields, André, 425

Desmond, Florence, 232
Desmoutiers, Gisèle, 48
Destry Rides Again, 375, 383
De Sylva, B.G., 190
Deux Aveugles, Les, 30
Deux Pêcheurs, Les, 30
Devine, Loretta, 507
Devos, Claude, 5, 8, 9, 41, 44, 47, 48, 129, 135, 271
Dewitte, Richard, 495
Dhéry, Robert, 32
Diary of Adam, The, 390
Dickson, Barbara, 468, 489, 491
Dickson, Dorothy, 175, 224
Dickson, Muriel, 67
Didrichs, Ursula, 299
Diedrich, John, 198, 508
Diener, Joan, 419, 420
Dishy, Bob, 206
Disney, Agnès, 17
di Stefano, Giuseppe, 90, 272, 279
Divorce Me, Darling, 442, 474
Dixon, Beryl, 71
Dixon, Lee, 312
Dohm, Ernst, 10, 16
Do I Hear a Waltz?, 385, 429
Dollarprinzessin, Die, 117, 137, 151
Domingo, Placido, 92, 94, 386
Donaldson, Walter, 190
Donath, Helen, 124, 269, 270, 277
Dönch, Karl, 99, 110, 125, 292
Doniat, Aimé, 5, 8, 14, 15, 17, 24, 26, 28, 39, 44, 47, 129, 141, 280
Donna Juanita, 109
Donnelly, Dorothy, 149
Dorak, Martina, 497
Dorelli, Johnny, 423
Do Re Mi, 372, 391
Dorf ohne Glock, Das, 294
Doria, Renée, 43
Dostal, Nico, 303
Douchka, 262
Douglas, Nigel, 97, 129, 286
Douglass, Stephen, 172, 176, 177, 368, 380
Doussard, Jean, 15
Dowling, Denis, 67, 73, 74
Dragonette, Jessica, 160
Drake, Alfred, 162, 312, 317, 345, 362
Drake's Dream, 470
Dran, André, 5, 8, 11
Dranem, 247, 248
Dreamgirls, 506, 517
Dreigroschenoper, Die, 297–301, 308
Dreimäderlhaus, Das, 1, 147–9, 151
Drei Walzer, 1, 102, 104, 105, 282, 308, 309
Drew, Eleanor, 435, 436, 437, 438
Drummond-Grant, Ann, 54, 59, 63, 66, 68, 69, 71, 74

Dubarry, Die, 113–14, 151
Dubarry Was a Lady, 193, 196, 197
Dubin, Al, 504
Dubois, Claude, 498
Duby, Jacques, 387
Ducros, Jacques, 32
Duenna, The, 438
Dufresne, Diane, 499
Dulizkaya, Lya, 390, 411
Dumas, Roger, 250
Duncan, Sandy, 440, 460
Dunn, Don, 179
Dunn, Geoffrey, 5, 7, 10, 20, 97, 441
Dunne, Irene, 172
Dupuy, René, 263
Duru, Alfred, 24
Duval, Denise, 129
Duvaleix, 3, 5, 8, 10, 41, 43, 44, 48, 162, 180, 257

Earl and the Girl, The, 154
Ebb, Fred, 410–13, 505
Ebersole, Christine, 313
Ebert, Elizabeth, 94
Ebnet, Liselotte, 308, 324
Eddington, Paul, 447
Eddy, Jennifer, 97
Eddy, Nelson, 136, 156, 161, 165, 167, 168, 169, 204, 220, 231, 314
Edwards, Alan, 441
Edwards, Jimmy, 217
Edwards, Sherman, 421
Egan, Peter, 84
Eine Frau, die weiss was sie will, 282
Eine Nacht in Venedig, 92, 99–101, 151
Eisler, David, 357
Eklund, Gunnel, 130
Elg, Taina, 508
Eliot, T.S., 477
Elizondo, Evangelina, 237
Elliman, Yvonne, 463, 464
Elliott, Victoria, 93, 337
Ellis, Chris, 161, 182
Ellis, Mary, 223, 224, 225, 432
Ellis, Vivian, 218, 232–5
Elmes, Edgar, 225
Elmore, Steve, 423
Emerald Isle, The, 53, 79, 86
Emmanuel, Ivor, 227
Emmanuel, Jacques, 21
Emney, Joan, 367
Engel, Lehman, 136, 162, 185, 202–3, 229, 333
English, Jon, 464
Erminie, 53
Ervil, Janine, 105, 246, 293
Esquiluz, Kurt, 96, 109
Essex, David, 417, 468
Estan toccando . . ., see *They're Playing our Song*

Etcheverry, Jésus, 36, 38
Etoile, L', 44, 52
Etting, Ruth, 191
Eva, 133
Evanko, Ed, 460
Evans, Sir Geraint, 54, 71, 77
Evans, Jessie, 189, 460
Evans, Kathryn, 194
Evans, Maurice, 377
Evans, Wilbur, 170, 321, 491
Evita, 467–70, 474, 475
Ewen, Trudi, 200
Expresso Bongo, 443, 474
Eysler, Edmund, 297

Fagan, J.B., 234
Fahey, Brian, 168
Fain, Sammy, 189, 231
Fairbanks, Douglas, 244
Faith, Adam, 452
Fall, Leo, 136, 241, 265–8
Fancourt, Darrell, 60
Fandango, 262
Fanny, 375
Fantasticks, The, 371, 383
Farguès, Philippe, 252, 253
Faris, Alexander, 5, 72
Farkas, Katalin, 146
Farley, J.J., 516
Farnham, Johnny, 446
Farran, Merrick, 217
Farrar, John, 421
Farrell, Eileen, 327
Fassbänder, Brigitte, 91, 134
Fatinitza, 109, 151
Favorit, Der, 305
Fawdon, Michelle, 464
Faye, Alice, 190
Fehringer, Franz, 83, 120, 268, 307
Feiffer, Jules, 390
Felbermayer, Anny, 299
Felder, Linda, 8, 14, 24
Fellowes, Susannah, 236
Felsenstein, Christoph, 138
Felton, Felix, 344
Femme du Boulanger, La, 418
Fenholt, Jeff, 464
Fenn, Jean, 163
Ferenz, Willy, 95
Ferland, Danielle, 503
Fernandel, 44, 250, 251
Fernandel, Frank, 263
Ferrari, Violetta, 411
Ferrer, José, 433
Fête en Camargue, La, 262
Feuerwerk, 308
Fiander, Lewis, 422
Fiddler on the Roof, 1, 388–90, 429

fidele Bauer, Der, 137, 151
Fidelio, 7
Field, Pamela, 77
Fielding, Fenella, 440, 441
Fielding, Henry, 452
Fields, Dorothy, 339, 378, 381, 401
Fields, Gracie, 220
Fields, Herbert, 339
Fields, Joseph, 347
Fiesta, 261
Filistad, Aldo, 256
Fille de Madame Angot, La, 34–6, 51, 52
Fille du Tambour-Major, La, 25, 51
Fings Ain't Wot They Used T'Be, 452
Finian's Rainbow, 343, 431
Finke, Martin, 97, 113, 149, 270, 277, 279
Finn, William, 512
Fiorello!, 376
Firbank, Ronald, 440
Firefly, The, 160, 163, 212
Firth, David, 485
Fisch-ton-kan, 46
Fischer-Dieskau, Dietrich, 91, 97
Fisher, Dudu, 497
Fisher, Eddie, 503
Fitzgerald, Ella, 187
Fitzgibbon, Maggie, 176, 177, 184, 202, 327
Fledermaus, Die, 87–94, 150
Flers, Robert de, 129, 249
Flora the Red Menace, 410
Florence, Marina, 243
Florodora, 85
Flower Drum Song, 372
Flynn, Eric, 189, 341, 469
Flynn, Radley, 56
Follies, 395–7, 430
Follow a Star, 232
Follow That Girl, 437, 474
Fontagnère, Guy, 162, 180, 293
Foran, Dick, 199
Forbidden Melody, 170
Forli, Andrine, 274, 293
Forrest, Robert, 337, 362
Forrester, Maureen, 317
Förster, Jürgen, 116
Försterchristel, Die, 306
Forsyth, Bruce, 168, 401, 457
Forsyth, Henderson, 425
Forsythe, Robyn, 478
For the Love of Mike, 218, 240
Fortune Teller, The, 155, 158
Fortunio, 46
Forty-Five Minutes from Broadway, 159, 212
42nd Street, 504, 516
Four Musketeers, The, 460
Foy, Eddie, jr, 365, 367
Franchi, Sergio, 386
Francks, Don, 344

Frankowski, Hans, 290
Fraser, Al, 515
Fraser-Simson, Harold, 215
Frasquita, 280
Frau Luna, 119–20
Fredrick, Richard, 149
Free as Air, 436
Fremdenführer, Der, 118
French, Harold, 184
French, Percy, 448
Fresnay, Pierre, 282
Fretwell, Elizabeth, 272
Friedauer, Harry, 137, 266, 271, 272, 275, 302, 305
Friederike, 276–7, 294
Friedman, Shraga, 450
Friml, Rudolf, 147, 160–3, 217
Froboess, Conny, 302
Fröhlich, Peter, 297
Frohman, Jane, 200
Frühjahrsparade, 306, 310
Fryatt, John, 20
Fuchs, Gabriele, 104, 113, 277
Fuentes, Reuben, 323
Funicello, Annette, 158
Funny Face, 183
Funny Girl, 391–2, 429
Funny Thing Happened on the Way to the Forum, A, 393, 429
Fyffe, Jane, 163
Fyson, Leslie, 127, 234

Gage, Roger, 454
Galemba, S., 23
Gall, France, 499
Gallagher, Helen, 179, 200, 401
Gallo, Inigo, 308
Gangsters du Château d'If, Les, 252
Ganne, Louis, 49–51
Garber, Victor, 399
Garcisanz, Isabelle, 44
Gardener, Rita, 372
Gardiner, John Eliot, 45
Gardner, Geraldine, 478
Garland, Judy, 341, 374, 451
Garner, Jay, 425
Garrett, Betty, 197
Garrett, Lesley, 72
Garrison, David, 173, 472
Gascoigne, Jill, 376
Gasparone, 111–13, 151
Gauchos de Marseille, Les, 252
Gaudin, Philippe, 105
Gautier, Dick, 370
Gautier, Georges, 45
Gay, Noel, 235
Gay Divorce, 196
Gay Hussar, The, 231

Gaynes, George, 354
Gaynor, Gloria, 503
Gaynor, Mitzi, 192, 319
Gayson, Eunice, 326
Gay's the Word, 224, 225, 240
Gedda, Nicolai, 10, 89, 91, 94, 95, 98, 99, 100, 104, 111, 123, 124, 126, 130, 134, 139, 250, 269, 270, 271, 273, 274, 275, 278, 284, 285, 318
Geese, Heinz, 294
Geisen, Erik, 166
Geisha, The, 82–4, 86
Geld, Gary, 426
Gemignani, Paul, 396
Genée, Richard, 91
Gènes, Henri, 243, 261
Geneviève de Brabant, 13, 51
Gentlemen Prefer Blondes, 346, 383
Genton, Samantha, 157
Gentry, Bobbie, 422
George, Tricia, 435
George M, 159
Georges, Trevor Michael, 484
Gerbault, Alain, 283
Germain, Pierre, 5, 38, 135, 283, 293
German, Sir Edward, 80–2
Gerron, Kurt, 300
Gershwin, George, 182–7, 218
geschiedene Frau, Die, 138
Gesner, Clarke, 418
Geszty, Sylvia, 278, 279, 303
Gibb, Maurice, 459
Gielgud, Sir John, 331
Gilbert, James, 454
Gilbert, Jean, 121
Gilbert, Olive, 223, 224, 225, 226, 419
Gilbert, Robert, 293
Gilbert, Sir William S., 53–78
Gilboe, Gerda, 331
Gildo, Rex, 302
Gilford, Jack, 179, 180, 187, 196, 394, 419
Gill, Dorothy, 61, 68
Gillan, Ian, 463
Gillette, Priscilla, 380
Gillmer, Caroline, 508
Gilmore, Peter, 371, 437, 441
Gingold, Hermione, 397
Ginivan, Gary, 478
Giono, Jean, 418
Gipsy, 261
Gipsy Baron, The, see *Zigeunerbaron, Der*
Girardi, Alexander, 287
Giraudeau, Jean, 37, 38
Giraudoux, Jean, 408
Girerd, Raymond, 245
Girl Crazy, 185
Girl Friend, The, 198
Girl in Pink Tights, The, 170, 372

Girl in the Spotlight, 158
Girl Who Came to Supper, The, 433
Giroflé-Girofla, 34
Giuditta, 277–80, 309
Glada änken, see *lustige Witwe, Die*
Glamorous Night, 223, 225, 226, 227, 239, 240
Glawitsch, Rupert, 284, 286
Gleason, Joanna, 503
Gleeson, Colette, 471
Glossop, Peter, 80
Glover, Cynthia, 81, 85
Glückliche Reise, 295, 309
Glynn, Carlin, 424
Glynne, Howell, 80, 127
Goblin Market, 513, 517
Goddard, Willoughby, 447, 450
Godfrey, Isidore, 63, 68, 76
Godin, Guy, 50
Godspell, 417, 430
Goebel, Alexander, 469, 486
Goggi, Laura, 416
Goggin, Dan, 514
Gold, Louise, 515
Golden Apple, The, 380, 383
Golden Boy, 413
Gold'ne Meisterin, Die, 297
Gondoliers, The, 75–7, 86
Goodall, Valorie, 272
Goodbye Mr Chips, 457, 490
Goodier, Harry, 76
Goodman, Al, 149, 161, 176, 450
Goodman, John, 509
Good News, 190
Good Old Bad Old Days, The, 457
Görner, Christine 100, 137, 266, 184, 314
Gospel at Colonus, The, 515
Goss, Julia, 58
Gottlieb, Peter, 251
Goublier, Gustave, 250
Goulding, Charles, 60, 68
Goulet, Robert, 317, 332, 334, 341, 346, 401
Grab Me a Gondola, 454, 475
Grace, Nicolas, 358
Gräfin Mariza, 284–6, 309
Graf von Luxemburg, Der, 130–1, 151
Graham, Deborah, 515
Graham, Harry, 269, 293
Grahame, Gloria, 312
Grainer, Ron, 457
Gramatzki, Ilse, 97
Grand Duke, The, 78
Grande-Duchesse de Gérolstein, La, 10–13, 52, 282, 309
Grandjean, Andrée, 5, 245
Grand Tour, The, 409
Granger, Claudine, 29, 32, 168, 232, 243, 252, 253, 301
Granichstädten, Bruno, 290

Grant, Deborah, 405
Grant, Gogi, 172
Grant, Peter, 167
Granzer, Robert, 92
Granzow, Beate, 119
Grassi, André, 44
Graves, Peter, 225, 432
Gray, Dolores, 363, 375
Gray, Lissa, 163
Gray, Margery, 193
Grayson, Kathryn, 172, 346
Grease, 420, 430
Great Waltz, The, see *Walzer aus Wien*
Green, Adolf, 209, 338, 354, 364, 396, 403
Green, Lois, 432
Green, Marion, 48
Green, Martyn, 54, 60, 61, 63, 66, 69, 70, 74, 76, 460
Green, Stanley, 237, 318, 380
Green, Teddy, 179, 438, 457
Greene, Ellen, 511, 512
Greene, Herbert, 364
Greene, Leon, 67
Greene, Milton, 388
Greener, Dorothy, 175
Greenwillow, 372
Greer, Frances, 162
Greer, Jo Ann, 200
Gregg, Hubert, 453
Gressier, Jules, 5, 36, 41, 47, 48, 50
Grey, Joel, 410
Grifasi, Joe, 511
Griffin, Elsie, 59
Griffiths, Andy, 375
Grimaldi, Marion, 176, 177, 215, 227, 294, 432, 437, 439
Grimandi, Cristina, 480
Grimes, Tammy, 159, 504
Grimm, Barbara, 198
Grimm, Hans-Gunther, 100
Grist, Reri, 359
Grobe, Donald, 284
Groenendaal, Cris, 196, 400
Groener, Harry, 313
Groh, Herbert Ernst, 103, 132, 133, 275, 301
Gross, Erwin, 291
grosse Sünderin, Die, 296, 309
Grosskurth, Kurt, 107
Grossmith, George, jr, 178
Grout, James, 446
Gruber, Ferry, 7, 21, 106, 107, 142, 146, 279, 287, 303, 304
Gruberova, Edita, 93
Grüezi, 305
Grün, Bernard, 231
Grund, Bert, 137
Grunden, Per, 124, 130, 291
Guard, Philip, 437

Guardino, Harry, 505
Güden, Hilde, 88, 94, 96, 104, 110, 117, 122, 124, 125, 278
Guétary, Georges, 254, 258, 259, 260, 262
Guitry, Sacha, 250, 282
Guittard, Laurence, 313, 397
Gül Baba, 145
Gunton, Bob, 468
Gustafson, John, 332
Guy, Jacqueline, 260
Guylás, Dénes, 146
Guyon, Fabienne, 12, 494, 512
Guys and Dolls, 350–2, 383
Gwyther, Geoffrey, 189
Gypsy, 265–6, 383
Gyurkovics, Mária, 144

Haas, Waltraut, 291
Hackett, Buddy, 370
Haddon Hall, 79
Hagara, Willi, 302
Hagen, Hans, 142
Hague, Albert, 372, 377
Hahn, Reynaldo, 248, 282
Haigh, Kenneth, 451
Hair, 427, 429
Hale, Binnie, 178, 218
Halévy, Ludwig, 21
Haley, Jack, 374
Half a Sixpence, 445, 474
Hall, Adelaide, 238
Hall, Carol, 424
Hall, Irlin, 443
Hall, Juanita, 319
Hallelujah Baby, 391
Hallstein, Ingeborg, 21, 119, 284, 291, 296
Halman, Ella, 54, 63, 71, 74, 76
Hamel, Michel, 9, 15, 17, 20, 26, 32, 33, 43
Hamilton, Margaret, 374
Hamlisch, Marvin, 414–17
Hammerstein, Oscar, 210, 312–27
Hammond–Stroud, Derek, 97
Hamóri, Ildikó, 143, 497
Hampshire, Susan, 220, 437
Hamshere, Keith, 450
Hanan, Stephen, 478
Hancock, Sheila, 444
Haney, Carol, 367
Hanley, Ellen, 202
Hans Andersen, 471, 475
Hans le joueur de flûte, 50, 52, 156
Hanson, John, 163, 165, 167, 227, 460
Happy Day, The, 217
Happy End, 301
Happy Time, The, 413
Harburg, E.Y., 343
Harding, Muriel, 54, 56, 59, 60, 61, 74, 76
Hare, Doris, 440

Harger, Gary, 427
Harman, Barry, 514, 515
Harmon, Peggy, 513
Harmsworth, Sir Geoffrey, 218
Harney, Ben, 507
Harnick, Sheldon, 129, 376, 387–91
Harnoncourt, Nikolas, 93
Harom a kislány see Dreimäderlhaus, Das
Harper, Heather, 64
Harrington, Leslie, 156
Harris, Barbara, 390
Harris, Holly, 202
Harris, Richard, 334
Harrison, Rex, 328, 329, 330
Hart, Ann, 347, 447
Hart, Dunstan, 224
Hart, Linda, 194
Hart, Lorenz, 191, 198–201
Hart, Moss, 500
Hartemann, Jean-Claude, 39, 46
Hartley-Morris, Jan, 221
Hartung, Gretl, 267
Hartwig, Anke, 198
Hartwig, Hildegard, 147
Harvey, Frederick, 81, 161
Harvey, Laurence, 334
Harwood, Elizabeth, 64, 67, 68, 75, 125
Haskins, Virginia, 314
Hassall, Christopher, 127, 128, 272
Hatch, Tony, 470
Hauck, Walther, 148
Hauksson, Leifur, 512
Havens, Richie, 483
Hawkins, John, 459
Hawkins, June, 374
Haworth, Jill, 410
Hawthorne, James, 97
Hawtrey, Charles, 238
Hay, Patricia, 128
Hayes, Marvin, 211
Hayes, Nancye, 412, 508
Haymes, Dick, 349
Haynes, Tiger, 425
Hazel Flagg, 372
Hazell, Hy, 443, 446, 453
Házy, Erszébet, 94, 96, 97, 141, 284, 287
Head, Murray, 463, 489
Heal, Joan, 442, 452, 454
Heald, Anthony, 194
Healy, David, 352, 396
Hearn, George, 396, 410, 503
Heath, Eira, 434
Hell Can Be Heaven, 490
Hellman, Lillian, 355
Hello, Dolly!, 1, 406–7, 429
Helmuth, Osvald, 331
Helpmann, Sir Robert, 442
Heming, Percy, 182

Hemsley, Sherman, 426
Hemsley, Thomas, 426
Henderson, Florence, 314, 320, 375, 433
Henderson, Ray, 190
Hendrix, Paula, 202
Heneker, David, 443–8
Hennetier, Huguette, 13
Henson, Leslie, 182, 183, 218, 234
Henson, Nicky, 460
Herbert, A.P., 232, 234
Herbert, Victor, 155–9
Here Comes the Bride, 218
Hérent, Colette, 293
Hérent, René, 36
Herman, Jerry, 405–10, 503
Herrera, Mauricio, 416
Herrmann, Keith, 515
Hervé, 1, 3, 17–18, 43, 53
Herzogin von Chicago, Die, 287
Herz über Bord, 294
Heuberger, Richard, 118
Hewer, John, 433, 493
Hewett, Peggy, 472
Hewlett, Donald, 454
Hewlett, Peter, 483
Hibbert, Geoffrey, 442
Hide and Seek, 218, 219, 240
Hiégel, Pierre, 49, 243, 248
High Button Shoes, 372
High Jinks, 163
High Society, 193
High, Wide and Handsome, 178
Hildegarde, 196
Hilgenberg, Katherine, 316
Hill, Richard, 459
Hill, Rose, 455
Hill, Ruby, 374
Hill, Vince, 227
Hillman, David, 128
Hills, Julia, 493
Hill Smith, Marilyn, 34, 70, 131, 286, 358
Himmelblaue Träume, 305
Hindmarsh, Jean, 61, 63, 69, 71
Hinton, Pip, 344, 515
Hired Man, The, 493
Hirigoyen, Rudy, 254, 255, 256, 257, 259, 261
His Monkey Wife, 442, 474
Hit the Deck, 198, 212
HMS Pinafore, 59–61, 86
Hoadly, Graham, 219
Hobson, Valerie, 322
Hochzeit am Bodensee, see *Himmelblaue Träume*
Hochzeitsnacht im Paradies, 307
Hockridge, Edmund, 167, 367
Hodges, Eddie, 369
Hoffmann, Lore, 284, 286
Hoffmann, Willi, 83, 102, 112, 268
Holgate, Danny, 351

Holgate, Ron, 394, 422
Holland, Lyndsie, 77
Hollandweibchen, Das, 284, 286
Holliday, David, 359, 433
Holliday, Jennifer, 364
Holliday, Melanie, 92
Holloway, Stanley, 73, 181, 329
Hollreiser, Heinrich, 96
Hollweg, Werner, 93, 125, 276
Holm, Celeste, 312, 373
Holm, Renate, 90, 91, 104, 107, 108, 111, 116,
    117, 130, 135, 147, 271, 276, 303, 305, 307
Holmes, Christine, 446
Holmes, John, 73
Holmes, Richard, 442
Holmes, Rupert, 510
Hönig, Dieter, 166
Honthy, Hanna, 140
Hood, Ann, 57, 68
Hood, Basil, 78, 80
Hooray for Daisy, 436
Hopkins, Linda, 426
Hoppe, Heinz, 131, 137, 138, 267, 302
Hopperger, Hannerl, 293
Horne, Lena, 373
Horne, Marilyn, 211, 419
Horsey, Martin, 450
Horton, Robert, 414
Horusitzky, Adrienne, 420
Hoshour, Robert, 515
Hosking, Arthur, 76
Hoskins, Basil, 461
Hossack, Grant, 201
Hotine, Marina, 243, 245, 248, 255, 256, 293
Houp-La, 218
House of Flowers, 373
Howard, Ann, 84, 97, 127, 227, 385, 461
Howard, Ken, 402
Howard, Natalie, 484
Howard, Sydney, 192
Howe, Michael, 480
Howerd, Frankie, 394
Howes, Bobby, 215, 218
Howes, Sally Ann, 239, 336, 471
Howland, Beth, 395
Howlett, Neil, 81
How to Succeed in Business . . ., 386–7, 429
Hubbard, Bruce, 173
Hübener, Ilse, 83
Hubert, Michel, 27
Huberty, Lucien, 43
Hübner, Karin, 299
Hudson, Travis, 174
Hughes, David, 127, 135, 161
Hughes, Rhetta, 506
Hulbert, Claude, 184
Hulbert, Jack, 161, 238
Hull, Lisa, 447

Hume, Doreen, 176, 181, 199
Humphries, Barry, 449, 451
110 in the Shade, 414
Hunt, Jan, 171
Hunter, Tab, 368
Hurley, Laurel, 128
Hurt, Jo, 200
Husmann, Ron, 377
Huston, Walter, 208
Huszka, Jenö, 145
Hutcheson, LaVern, 211
Hutton, Betty, 341
Hutton, Bruce, 467
Hyde, Bruce, 460
Hyde, Maria Jane, 483, 484

I Am a Camera, 410
I and Albert, 413, 470
ideale Geliebte, Die, 308
Idle, Eric, 72
I Do, I Do, 414
Ignace, 250–1
Ile de Tulipatan, L', 29, 51
Illes, Marie, 480
Ilosfálvy, Róbert, 126, 142, 144, 145
I Love my Wife, 403, 430
I Married an Angel, 204
Im Reiche des Indras, 120
Im weissen Rössl, 1, 290–4, 308
Indien, 262
Indigo und die vierzig Räuber, 103
Ingham, Barrie, 461
Ingham, Winefride, 230
In Pursuit of Love, 438
Instant Marriage, 460
Into the Woods, 502, 517
Iolanthe, 65–7, 86
Irene, 187
Irma la douce, 262–4, 309
Irons, Jeremy, 417
Irosch, Mirjana, 92, 118, 122, 126
Irving, George S., 188, 204, 263, 347
Isherwood, Christopher, 410
It Happened in Nordland, 158
It's a Bird, It's a Plane, It's Superman, 413
Ivanovsky, V., 133
Iwanow, Tatjana, 137

Jackman, Hope, 449, 450
Jacobi, Viktor, 142–4, 217
Jacobowsky and the Colonel, 409
Jacobs, Arthur, 56, 80
Jacobs, Jim, 418
Jacobsen, Irving, 419
Jacott, Ruth, 479
Jaeger, Frederick, 453
Jakobowski, Edward, 53

Jamaica, 373
Jambel, Lisette, 257
James, Barry, 496
James, Graham, 452
James, Olga, 211, 376
James, Polly, 446
James, Sid, 345, 371, 452
János vitéz, 144, 152
Janowitz, Gundula, 90
Jansen, Jacques, 129, 247
Jarno, Georg, 306
Jason, Neville, 220
Jeanmaire, Zizi, 262
Jeffreys, Anne, 342, 362
Jeffreys, Celia, 166
Jenbach, Béla, 140
Jenkins, Daniel, 509
Jenkins, Neil, 131
Jenn, Myvanwy, 442
Jennings, Jerry J., 125
Jennings, Ken, 399
Jerome, Timothy, 236
Jerusalem, Siegfried, 124, 269, 270
Jessel, Leon, 146, 149
Jessop, Sharon, 508
Jesus Christ Superstar, 462–5, 474
Jewell, Derek, 466
Jill Darling, 232, 240
Jobin, André, 36, 171
John, Elton, 473
Johnny Johnson, 207
Johnny the Priest, 453
Johns, Glynis, 397
Johnson, Bill, 197, 345
Johnson, Christine, 316
Johnson, Darlene, 201
Johnson, Laurie, 452, 460
Johnson, Patricia, 227, 327
Johnson, Susan, 353
Johnson, Van, 369
Jonas, Emil, 53
Jones, Allan, 163, 172
Jones, Davy, 450
Jones, Dean, 395
Jones, Gareth, 57, 459
Jones, Neil, 327
Jones, Paul, 466
Jones, Shirley, 312, 315, 333, 370
Jones, Sidney, 82–4, 217
Jones, Tom, 371, 414
Jones, Trefor, 223, 234, 454
Jorrocks, 447, 475
Joseph and the Amazing Technicolor Dreamcoat, 465, 474
Josephs, Julia, 219
Josephs, William, 460
Joslyn, Betsy, 400
Jourdan, Louis, 361

Jour et la nuit, Le, 34
Joye, Jean-Marie, 168, 243
Joy of Living, The, 178
Jubilee, 196
Juhnke, Harald, 119
Julia, Raul, 507
Jumbo, 205
Jysor, Robert 50

Kacsóh, Pongrác, 144
Kaga, Takeshi, 464
Kahn, Gus, 190
Kahn, Madeleine, 404
Kaiserin, Die, 267, 294, 309
Kaiserin Josephine, 287, 294
Kaiserin Katharina, 294
Kalès, Elizabeth, 292
Kálmán, Emmerich, 138–42, 241, 284–94
Kander, John, 410–13, 505
Karajan, Herbert von, 89, 90, 125
Karczykowski, Ryszard, 92, 129
Karlin, Miriam, 388
Karner, Peter, 147
Karneval in Rom, 100, 102
Karnilova, Maria, 388, 422
Kasper, Eva, 135
Kassir, John, 513
Katinka, 163
Kattnigg, Rudolf, 306
Kaufman, George, 500
Kay, Hershy, 165, 356, 404
Kaye, Danny, 196, 208, 471
Kaye, Davy, 455
Kaye, Robert R., 206
Kaye, Stubby, 351, 381
Keaton, Diane, 428
Kedrova, Lila, 410, 411
Keel, Howard, 171, 172, 314, 341, 346, 363
Keeler, Ruby, 179
Kelemen, Zoltan, 125
Keith, Brian, 463
Keller, Jeff, 506
Kellogg, Lynne, 428
Kelly, Gene, 332
Kelly, Patsy, 188
Kelly, Paula, 402
Kelton, Pert, 369
Kemmer, Joachim, 292, 480
Kennedy, Cheryl, 439, 442, 447
Kennedy, Michael, 161, 182
Kenney, James, 443
Kennington, Lynne, 202, 217
Kent, Barry, 159, 334
Kent, William, 183
Kerker, Gustave, 159
Kern, Jerome, 170–8, 218, 231
Kern, Patricia, 67, 73, 80
Kert, Larry, 359

Kiley, Richard, 362, 378, 385, 419
King, Dennis, 73
King, John Michael, 330
King, Mabel, 425
King and I, The, 322–4, 382
Kings and Clowns, 457
King's Rhapsody, 223–7, 239
Kipps, 445
Kirk, Lisa, 345, 366, 409
Kirkwood, Pat, 355, 453
Kirsten, Dorothy, 157, 158, 165, 169
Kismet, 362–4, 382
Kiss Me, Kate, 192, 345–6, 382
Klausner, Terri Ann, 513
Kleban, Edward, 415
Klein, Peter, 99
Klein, Robert, 416
Kline, Kevin, 62
Klug, Hedi, 291
Klugman, Jack, 366
Kmentt, Waldemar, 90, 92, 94, 108, 124, 125, 278
Knepler, Paul, 112
Knickerbocker Holiday, 208, 213
Knight, Gillian, 54, 65, 66, 75
Knittel, Sonja, 292, 302
Knoblock, Edward, 362
Kobart, Ruth, 394
Koch, Martin, 496
Koller, Dagmar, 92, 126, 139, 149, 272, 276, 292, 297, 402, 412, 420
Kollo, Rene, 106, 120, 121, 122, 125, 139, 276, 284, 295, 296
Kollo, Walter, 118, 120
Kollo, Willi, 120
Koltai, Valéria (Vali), 143, 287
König, Günther, 504
Kopyc, Frank, 514
Korberg, Tommy, 489
Korngold, Erich Wolfgang, 98, 103
Korondi, György, 141
Korte, Hans, 299
Köth, Erika, 90, 95, 104, 114, 117, 125, 131, 148, 265, 295, 305
Kovacs, Joszef, 145
Kováts, Kriszta, 469, 497
Kraus, Herold, 303
Krauss, Clemens, 88
Krebs, Helmut, 89
Kretzmer, Herbert, 494
Kreuder, Peter, 308
Kreuger, Miles, 171, 175
Kreuzberger, Rudi, 102
Krieger, Henry, 506, 509
Kriff, Jean, 15, 28, 30, 31
Kuchar, Erich, 292, 306
Kuhlman, Charles, 93, 160
Kuhn, Judy, 490, 496

Kühn, Rudolf, 341
Kulp, Nancy, 173
Künneke, Eduard, 294
Künneke, Evelyn, 16, 295
Kunz, Erich, 89, 90, 94, 95, 96, 98, 99, 122, 123, 124, 148, 270
Kusche, Benno, 7, 94, 96, 112, 117, 124, 125, 138, 147, 150, 274, 295, 314
Kuster, Herbert, 106
Kutschera, Franz, 299

Lacoste, Mireille, 42
Ladd, Johnny, 454
Lady and the Tiger, 390
Lady Be Good!, 183
Lady Hamilton, 294
Lady in the Dark, 208, 213
Lady Mary, 218
Lady May, 438
Lady Windermere's Fan, 431
Lafaye, Suzanne, 10, 21, 25, 35, 246, 247
Laffont, Jean, 243
Lafont, Jean-Philippe, 10, 32, 33
Là-haut, 247, 309, 315
Lahr, Bert, 192
Laine, Cleo, 171, 440, 511
Laird, Marvin, 471
Lambert, Mark, 397
Lambert, Patricia, 226, 369
Lamla, Norbert, 497
Land des Lächelns, Das, 1, 269–73, 309
Landis, Jessie Royce, 235
Landstreicher, Der, 118
Lane, Burton, 343
Lane, Lupino, 235
Lang, Barbara, 193
Lang, Harold, 199, 345
Lang, Philip, 330, 341
Langford, Bonnie, 478
Langton, Diane, 455, 506
Lankston, John, 357
Lansbury, Angela, 366, 399, 400, 408
Lanza, Mario, 163, 164, 220
Larner, Elizabeth, 169, 344
la Rue, Danny, 461
Last, James, 299
Latouche, John, 356, 380
Laurence, Paula, 197
Laurens, Rose, 494, 498
Laurents, Arthur, 365
Laverne, Henri, 50
Lavie, Aric, 324
Lawford, Peter, 190
Lawrence, Carol, 359
Lawrence, Eddie, 364
Lawrence, Gertrude, 184, 208, 222, 231, 322
Lawrence, Stephanie, 482
Lawrenson, Jon, 226

Lawson, Dennis, 201, 219
Lawson, Winifred, 54, 56, 63, 65
Laye, Dilys, 444
Laye, Evelyn, 169, 218, 220, 238, 433, 448
Leachman, Cloris, 186
Leányvásár, 143, 151
Lear, Evelyn, 207
Leave it to Jane, 174, 212
Leave it to Me, 196, 213
Leblanc, Gyözo, 279, 286
Lebowsky, Stanley, 237, 412
Le Bris, Michèle, 141
Lecocq, Charles, 1, 3, 34–7
Leçon de Chant, Le, 31
Ledoux, Fernand, 38
Ledry, Jack, 232
Lee, Bill, 320, 325
Lee, Margo, 447
Lee, Michelle, 186, 402
Lee, Vanessa, 220, 224, 227, 432
Lee-Hill, Sharon, 478, 490
Legay, Henri, 14, 36, 141
Legge, Walter, 89, 270
Legrand, Jacques, 29
Legrand, Raymond, 168, 263
Lehár, Franz, 87, 121–34, 241, 268–80
Leibowitz, René, 5, 8, 11
Leicht Kavallerie, 29
Leigh, Adele, 90, 220, 327, 359, 363, 396
Leigh, Barbara, 161, 216, 294
Leigh, Carolyn, 400
Leigh, Janet, 371
Leigh, Mitch, 418
Lemnitz, Tiana, 296
Lemper, Ute, 480, 483, 484
Lennart, Isobel, 391
Lenoty, René, 49, 283
Lenya, Lotte, 207, 290, 300, 301, 410
Lerner, Alan Jay, 328–36, 506
Lester, Edwin, 128
Let 'em Eat Cake, 186, 213
Leterrier, Eugene, 45
Let's Face It, 196, 213
letzte Walzer, Der, 217, 281, 309
Levene, Sam, 351
Leventon, Annabel, 428
Lewis, Bertha, 54, 60, 63, 65, 67, 76
Lewis, Brenda, 337
Lewis, Richard, 54, 56, 60, 62, 69, 71, 74, 77
Liane, 299
Libellentanz, 268–9
Lido Lady, 198
liebe Augustin, Der, 138, 151, 166, 309
Lieberson, Goddard, 165, 184, 185, 201, 203, 205, 209, 228, 333
Liebesberg, Else, 114, 135, 138, 286
L'il Abner, 381
Lilac Time, see Dreimäderlhaus, Das

lila Domino, Der, 147, 152
Lili Bárónö, 145, 152
Lillie, Beatrice, 456
Lilo, 361
Lincke, Paul, 118
Lind, Eva, 92
Linden, Hal, 193, 391
Lindner, Brigitte, 7, 97, 150, 270, 279
Lindsay, Robert, 236
Lingen, Theo, 7
Lins, Hans Maria, 112, 117, 137, 266, 314
Linval, Monique, 22, 40, 129
Lipman, Maureen, 355
Lipp, Wilma, 88, 90, 110, 116
Lisbon Story, The, 217
Lischen et Fritzchen, 31, 52
Listen to the Wind, 235
Lister, Eve, 177
Little, Caryl, 448
Little, Cleavon, 426
Little Johnny Jones, 154
Little Mary Sunshine, 379
Little Me, 400, 429
Little Night Music, A, 397, 429
Littler, Emile, 217
Little Shop of Horrors, 511, 516
Litz, Gisela, 7, 108, 111
Livermore, Reg, 405, 473
Liza of Lambeth, 470
Lloyd, Jeremy, 458
Lloyd Webber, Andrew, 462, 476–88
Lobasa, Monique, 148
lockende Flamme, Die, 294
Locke, Robert, 492
Locke, Shamus, 432
Lock up your Daughters, 452, 475
Loesser, Frank, 344, 350–3, 386–7
Loewe, Frederick, 328–36
Löffler, Hans, 118
Logan, Ella, 343
Logan, Jenny, 189
Lohe, Jean, 83
Lom, Herbert, 322
Long, Shorty, 353
Long, Tamara, 423
Lonsdale, Frederic, 48
Look Ma, I'm Dancin', 238
Loor, Friedl, 131, 141, 284
Loos, Anita, 346
Loose, Emmy, 98, 99, 104, 123, 124, 270
Lopez, Francis, 242, 248, 253, 254–62
Lopez, Maria, 258
Lopez, Priscilla, 415, 472
Loren, Sophia, 420
Lorca, Francis, 253
Loreau, Jacques, 293
Lorraine, Guido, 454
Losch, Liselotte, 102

Lost in the Stars, 372
Lotis, Dennis, 461
Loudon, Dorothy, 413
Louise, Merle, 399
Louisiana Purchase, 350
Lovano, Lucien, 48
Love from Judy, 238
Love Life, 372
Lowe, Marion, 127
Löwinger, Guggi, 287, 306
Lublin, Eliane, 12, 50
Lucas, Veronica, 226
Luders, Gustav, 154, 159
Ludwig, Christa, 90
Ludwig, Hanna, 99
Luguet, André, 387
Lund, Art, 353
Lupi, Lucien, 258, 259
LuPone, Patti, 194, 418, 468, 495
lustige Krieg, Der, 101–2, 151
lustige Witwe, Die, 1, 7, 88, 122–30, 150
Lutz, Meyer, 53
Luz, Franc, 511
Lynn, Carol, 238
Lynn, Vera, 452
Lynne, Gillian, 477
Lynton, Bobby, 447
Lysistrata, 118
Lytton, Henry, 54, 59, 67, 76

Mabit, Alain, 27
McAlpine, William, 80, 127
McArdle, Andrea, 413
Macaria, 416
McBain, Robert, 437
McCarty, Mary, 412
McCarthy, Joseph, 187–9
McCarthy, Siobhan, 468
McCauley, Jack, 347
McCollum, Sadie, 136
McCracken, Joan, 347
McCue, William, 215
McCutcheon, Bill, 194
MacDermott, Galt, 418
McDonald, Grace, 178
MacDonald, Jeanette, 156, 158, 161, 168, 169, 189, 204, 220
Macfarlane, Gaye, 405
McGillin, Howard, 194, 510
McGlinn, John, 173, 195
McGovern, Maureen, 187
Mack and Mabel, 409, 430
McKay, Don, 339, 359
McKay, Margery, 325, 327
Mackeben, Theo, 300
McKechnie, Donna, 415
McKeever, Jacqueline, 355
McKellar, Kenneth, 363

McKenzie, Julia, 352, 396, 403
Mackie, Lesley, 332
Mackintosh, Cameron, 193, 437, 494
MacLaine, Shirley, 361, 402
McLeerie, Allyn Ann, 172
McNally, John, 167
MacRae, Gordon, 156, 157, 162, 165, 167, 169, 177, 204, 312, 315
Madame Favart, 18, 24–5, 52
Madame Pompadour, 138, 267, 294
Madame Scandaleuse, 308
Maddern, Jeanne, 208
Madeleine, 155
Madwoman of Chaillot, The, 408
Maggie May, 451, 474
Maguire, Michael, 496
Magyar Melody, 218, 240
Mahoney, Janet, 189
Mahoney-Bennett, Kathleen, 194
Maid of the Mountains, The, 215, 216–18, 232, 239
Maikl, Liselotte, 141
Majkut, Erich, 116, 137
Makarova, Natalia, 203
Make Me an Offer, 444, 474
Makrai, Pál, 497
Malcolm, Christopher, 472
Mallabrera, André, 7, 25, 31, 51, 93
Mallory, Victoria
Malmsjö, Jan, 504
Malnick, Michael, 447
Malten, William, 207
Mame, 407–8
Mam'zelle Nitouche, 43–4, 52
Manchet, Eliane, 16
Mango, Angelo, 175
Manina, 303
Mankowitz, Wolf, 443, 444, 455
Mann, Terrence V., 478, 496
Man of La Mancha, 419–20, 429
Man of Magic, 460
Mansur, Susan, 425
Mantovani, 363
Manuel, Robert, 15
Manzetti, Gérard, 512
Marcel, Alain, 512
March of the Falsettos, 512
Mardi Gras, 470
Mareuil, Jean, 407
Margret, Ann, 371
Maria, Teresa, 327
Mária Föhadnagy, 145
Mariage aux lanternes, Le, 1, 33
Mariano, Luis, 254, 255, 256, 257, 260
Marie, 494
Mariette, 121, 282, 309
Marietti, Jean, 271
Marin, Sophie, 12

Marischka, Ernst, 99
Markevitch, Igor, 22
Marks, Alfred, 452
Marmont, Pam, 432
Marquet, Mary, 46, 283
Marseillaise, La, 259, 262
Marshall, Pat, 376
Marshall, Peter, 371
Marszalek, Franz, 102, 112, 296, 303
Martial, Jacques, 512
Martikke, Sigrid, 104
Martin, Barney, 412
Martin, Barry, 435
Martin, Dean, 346, 352, 364
Martin, Denis, 224
Martin, Diana, 219
Martin, Hugh, 238
Martin, Jill, 359
Martin, Mary, 196, 209, 229, 230, 320, 326, 338, 340, 406, 414
Martin, Millicent, 443, 456, 470
Martin, Steve, 512
Martin, Tony, 178, 181, 324
Martin, Virginia, 400
Martos, Ferenc, 145
Marty, Jean-Pierre, 9, 51
Marx, Groucho, 73
Maschwitz, Eric, 131, 231, 238
Mascotte, La, 40–1, 52
Marvin, Lee, 336
Maske in Blau, 307
Mason, Marlyn, 317
Massard, Robert, 12, 39, 40, 49, 273, 274, 300, 318
Massari, Silvia, 469
Massary, Fritzi, 267, 282, 287
Massey, Daniel, 396, 444
Masson, Luis, 9
Masterson, Valerie, 59, 62, 68, 71, 221
Mattes, Willy, 140, 149, 275, 284, 290
Matthews, Carmen, 408
Matthews, Christina, 219, 436
Matthews, Jessie, 446
Mattson, Eric, 316
Mauceri, John, 356, 357, 358
Maurane, Camille, 24, 47, 48
Maurer, Serge, 33
May, Hans, 433
Mayer, Frederic, 291
Meadmore, Robert, 441
Me and Juliet, 372
Me and My Girl, 215, 235–8, 239
Meat Loaf, 473
Mecker, Karl-Ernst, 150, 267, 276
Medford, Kay, 366, 392
Méditerranée, 256–7, 308
Meehan, Danny, 392
Meilhac, Henri, 21

Melchior, Lauritz, 165
Mella, Michel, 465
Melville, Alan, 224, 225, 239
Memma, Stefano, 30
Mendonca, Mauro, 469
Menke, Jeanne, 327
Menken, Alan, 511
Mentzel, Ilse, 103, 133
Mercedes, Maria, 508
Mercer, Frances, 178
Mercer, Johnny, 374, 381
Mercer, Marian, 456
Mercier, Jacques, 45
Mercier, Jean-Daniel, 245
Meredith, Burgess, 207
Merkès, Alain, 141
Merkès, Marcel, 38, 47, 129, 141, 162, 253, 293
Merlino, Gene, 334
Merman, Ethel, 180, 192, 196, 197, 339, 340, 348, 349, 350, 365, 366
Merri, Judi, 77
Merrie England, 80–1, 86
Merrill, Dina, 204
Merrill, Robert, 136, 170, 172, 317, 318, 336, 390, 391, 392
Merrill, Scott, 300
Merrily We Roll Along, 500, 517
Merry Gentleman, The, 438
Merry Widow, The, see *lustige Witwe, Die*
Merson, Billy, 161
Mertz, Yerry, 29, 30
Merval, Paulette, 38, 47, 129, 141, 162, 180, 253, 254, 293
Mesdames de la Halle, 31–2, 52
Mesplé, Mady, 6, 12, 19, 32, 35, 38, 42, 46, 47, 105, 250
Messager, André, 1, 3, 46–9, 241, 282
Mestral, Armand, 249
Metropolis, 491
Mexican Hayride, 197
Mey, Anita, 299
Mey, Gise, 243, 249, 255, 256
Michael, Patricia, 334, 386, 442, 448
Michalksi, Carl, 112, 117, 266, 291
Micheau, Janine, 38, 50
Michel, Solange, 36, 135
Michell, Keith, 234, 263, 458, 504
Middleton, Ray, 340
Midgely, Marietta and Vernon, 227
Migenes, Julia, 388
Mikado, The, 70–3, 86
Miles, Gaynor, 458
Milford, Penelope, 427
Miljakovic, Olivera, 140, 274, 285
Milk and Honey, 405–6
Millar, Gertie, 218
Millar, Mary, 234
Millar, Sir Ronald, 458

Mille, Jacqueline, 387
Mille et une nuits, Les, 262
Miller, Ann, 181, 345
Miller, Jonathan, 72, 358
Miller, Kevin, 6, 10
Miller, Robin, 423
Miller, Roger, 509
Miller, Valerie, 434
Millet, Danièle, 72
Millöcker, Carl, 87, 109–15
Mills, Erie, 357
Mills, John, 232
Mills, Stephanie, 425
Milster, Angelika, 480, 481
Minnelli, Liza, 410, 413, 505, 506
Minich, Peter, 110, 117, 122, 126, 135, 148, 284, 285, 290, 291, 303, 306
Minty, Shirley, 81
Mira, Brigitte, 120, 308
Mireille, 494
Misérables, Les, 493–8, 516, 517
Miss Liberty, 372
Mitchell, James, 393
Mitchell, Margaret, 54, 63, 66, 69, 76
Mitchell, Terry, 398
Mitchell, Warren, 331
Mlle Modiste, 155, 157
Mödl, Martha, 16, 117
Moffat, John, 461
Moffo, Anna, 106
Mogg, Herbert, 118
Möhler, Hubert, 16
Moïzan, Geneviève, 41, 46, 50
Moksyakov, A., 289
Molina, Alfred, 376
Mollet, Pierre, 129
Mollien, Jean, 4, 8, 11
Monckton, Lionel, 84
Monié, Bernard, 265
Monika, 303
Monkhouse, Bob, 202
Monnot, Marguerite, 262
Monsieur Beaucaire, 48, 52
Monsieur Carnaval, 262
Monsieur Choufleuri . . ., 31, 32, 33, 52
Monteil, Denise, 22
Montevecchi, Liliane, 397, 508
Montgomery, James, 187
Moody, Ron, 449
Moore, Ada, 373
Moore, Grace, 169
Moore, Melba, 426, 428
Moorefield, Olive, 346
Moranis, Rick, 512
More, Julian, 263, 443, 454
Moreau, Jean-Luc, 405
Moreno, Rita, 323, 360
Morgan, Helen, 170

Morin, Amélie, 414
Morison, Elsie, 54, 56, 60, 62, 64, 69, 71, 75, 77
Morison, Patricia, 345
Moross, Jerome, 372, 380
Morris, Anita, 508
Morris, Gary, 496
Morris, James R., 156
Morris, Libby, 366
Morrison, Ann, 513
Morrison, Diana, 488
Morrow, Doretta, 167, 362
Morrow, Geraldene, 447
Morrow, Karen, 202
Morse, Robert, 386
Morton, David, 438
Moser, Edda, 124, 134, 279, 285
Mosier, Enid, 373
Moss, Kathi, 508
Mostel, Zero, 388, 394
Most Happy Fella, The, 352, 382
Mount, Peggy, 234
Mourruau, Daniel, 15
Mousquetaires au couvent, Les, 41–3, 51
Moutet, Jo, 260
Mozart, Wolfgang Amadeus, 250, 309
Mr and Mrs, 460
Mr Cinders, 215, 218–19, 239, 240
Mr Whittington, 222
Mr Wonderful, 376
Muliar, Fritz 148
Munsel, Patrice, 21, 128, 172, 324
Murano, Maria, 249, 280, 390
Murray, Kathleen, 175
Murray, Wynn, 204
Murphy, Jennifer, 469
Musgrave, Frank, 53
Music in the Air, 176, 212
Music Man, The, 368–70, 382
Musy, Louis, 37, 42
Muszely, Melitta, 114, 266, 267, 276
Mutiny, 491
My Fair Lady, 328–31, 382
My One and Only, 183
Mystery of Edwin Drood, The, 510–11, 517

Nabors, Jim, 419
Nagy, Anikó, 469, 497
Nagy, Robert, 157
Nancel, Nicky, 10
Nash, Ogden, 209
Nash, Royston, 58
Natel, Jean-Marc, 493
Natoma, 155
Naughty Marietta, 155, 212
Navarre, Louis, 420
Neagle, Anna, 179, 446
Nedbal, Oskar, 146
Neely, Ted, 463

Nelson, Gene, 312, 396
Nelson, Kenneth, 171, 372
Nelson, Portia, 202, 203, 380
Németh, Marika, 142, 143, 284, 285, 288
Nesbitt, Cathleen, 229
Neville, John, 438
Neway, Patricia, 176, 217, 323, 326
Newell, Norman, 6, 20, 81, 84, 167, 226,
Newell, Raymond, 454
Newley, Anthony, 456, 457
Newman, Greatrex, 219
Newman, Yvonne, 66
Newton-John, Olivia, 421
New Moon, The, 168–70, 212
Nicholas, Harold, 374
Nicholas, Paul, 428, 446, 447, 464, 477, 490
Nichols, Joy, 367
Nichols, Robert, 173
Niessner, Anton, 123
Night Boat, The, 174
Nightingale, The, 413
Nijenhuis, Nancy, 479
Nina Rosa, 170
Nine, 507–8, 517
Nini la Chance, 262
Nistler, Luzia, 486
Nixon, Marni, 323, 330, 360
Noël, Magali, 402
Noguera, Louis, 22, 271
No, No, Nanette, 1, 178–80, 212, 240, 241
Norman, Jessye, 9
Norman, Lucille, 162, 167, 177, 204
Norman, Monty, 263, 443, 455
Normand, Mabel, 244
Norris, Harry, 76
Norton, Frederic, 215
Novello, Ivor, 175, 218, 222–7
Nugent, Moya, 228
Nunn, Trevor 477
Nunsense, 514, 517
Nuovolone, Félix, 26
Nymph Errant, 192, 196, 222
Nype, Russell, 159, 349

Obersteiger, Der, 114, 177–8, 151
Ochmann, Wieslaw, 276
O'Connor, Bill, 434
O'Connor, Des, 445
O'Connor, Donald, 192, 350
Oeggl, Georg, 102
Offenbach, Jacques, 1, 3–34, 53
Of Thee I Sing, 186, 212, 213
O'Hara, Jill, 413
O'Hara, John, 199
O'Hara, Paige, 173, 187, 410
O'Haughey, M., 412
Oh, Boy!, 175
Oh, I Say!, 174

Oh, Joy!, 175, 212
Oh, Kay!, 184
Ohringer, Jane, 468
Oklahoma!, 311, 312–14, 382
Okley, Pierre, 407
Old Chelsea, 238
Oldham, Derek, 6, 61, 65, 70, 76, 161
Olegario, Frank, 263
Ollendorf, Fritz, 146, 150
Oliver!, 449, 474
Oliver, Thelma, 401
Olsen, George, 191
Olvis, William, 337
Olympus on my Mind, 514
O'May, John, 469
O'Neill, Con, 492
O'Neill, Maire, 238
Once Upon a Mattress, 378–9, 382
One Touch of Venus, 209, 213
Only Girl, The, 158
On the Level, 459
On the Town, 338–9, 382
On the Twentieth Century, 403, 429
Opawsky, Margit, 281
Operette, 220, 228, 229, 239
Opernball, Der, 118
Opie, Alan, 34
Orbach, Jerry, 372, 393, 412, 422, 504
Oreste, 163
Orphée aux enfers, 3, 12, 47, 51, 52
Orpheus in the Underworld, see *Orphée aux enfers*
Orth, Norbert, 290
O'Shea, Tessie, 433
Osborn, Leonard, 54, 56, 60, 61, 69, 71, 74, 76
Ossola, Charles , 33
Osterwald, Bibi, 202, 380
Oszvald, Marika, 145
Ott, Horace, 351
Our Man Crichton, 460
Out of This World, 197, 372, 398

Pacific 1860, 229–30, 240
Pacific Overtures, 398
Paganini, 273, 309
Page, Ken, 478
Page, Veronica, 398
Pagnol, Marcel, 375, 418
Paige, Elaine, 194, 428, 468, 470, 471, 478, 489
Paige, Janis, 367
Paint Your Wagon, 335, 382
Pajama Game, The, 366–7, 382
Pal Joey, 199, 212
Palmer, Christene, 58, 68
Palmer, David, 59, 68
Palmer, Felicity, 72
Pallenberg, Max, 267
Palmer, Peter, 381
Palócoz, László, 141

Pampel, Wolfgang, 486
Panama Hattie, 197
Parsons, Estelle, 205
Parton, Dolly, 425
Pascual, Carmen, 414
Passionella, 390
Passion Flower Hotel, 460
Pas sur la bouche, 246
Patch, Wally, 444
Patience, 63–5, 86
Patinkin, Mandy, 321, 397, 468, 502
Patzak, Julius, 88, 94, 95, 115
Paul, Alan, 421
Paule, Sylvia, 9
Paulik, Anton, 98, 110
Paulsen, Harald, 298, 300
Payn, Graham, 230, 432
Payne, Laurie, 135, 163
Payne, Sarah, 405, 492
Payol, André, 32
Pays de sourire, Le, see *Land des Lächelns, Das*
Pearse, James, 220
Peerce, Jan, 165, 336
Peg, 448
Peggy Ann, 198
Pen, Polly, 513
Pennafort, Kleuza de, 280
Perchance to Dream, 223, 225, 226, 240
Perelman, S. J., 209
Peres, Michal, 324
Périchole, La, 3, 12, 18, 21–4, 52
Perilli, Maria, 230
Perkins, Anthony, 205
Perles des Antilles, La, 261
Perriers, Danièle, 15
Pert, Jill, 459
Pertwee, Jon, 84, 189, 471
Peter Pan, 372
Peters, Bernadette, 409, 423, 481, 502, 503
Peters, Roberta, 165, 317, 318
Peterson, Kurt, 418
Petina, Irra, 337, 356, 358
Petit, Roland, 262
Petit Duc, Le, 36–7, 51
Petite boutique d'horreurs, see *Little Shop of Horrors*
Petite Lily, La, 262
P'tites Michu, Les, 47, 51
Petit Faust, Le, 17, 51
Peyron, Joseph, 24, 31
Peyron, Thierry, 26
Pezzaro, Jo-Ann, 264, 469
Pezzino, Léonard, 32
Pfeifer, Alfred, 486
Phantom of the Opéra, The, 484–6, 516, 517
Phillips, Eddie, 184
Phillips, Jeff, 478
Phillips, Neville, 453
Phillips, Sîan, 201

Phil the Fluter, 448
Phi-Phi, 242–4, 308
Piaf, Edith, 252
Pic et Pioche, 262
Pickens, Jane, 176
Pickwick, 457
Picon, Molly, 390, 406
Pierangeli, Carlo, 84, 280
Pierjac, 251, 258, 283
Piervil, Jacky, 257, 261
Pietri, Michaël, 16
Pinal, Silvia, 408
Pinero, Sir Arthur, 79, 437
Pink Lady, The, 85, 159
Pinza, Ezio, 319, 375
Pipe Dream, 372
Pipistrello, Il, see *Fledermaus, Die*
Pippin, 417
Pippin, Donald, 503
Piquet, Robert, 283
Pirates of Penzance, The, 61–3, 85, 96
Pisani, Robert, 283
Pitti, Katalin, 279, 286
Pixley, Frank, 159
Plain and Fancy, 377
Plamondon, Luc, 498
Planquette, Robert, 1, 3, 37–40, 53
Plantey, Bernard, 13, 24, 141, 292
Plasson, Michel, 19, 22
Please, Teacher!, 218, 240
Plumes rouges, Les, 262
Plunkett, Maryann, 237
Poell, Alfred, 89
Poiret, Jean, 503
Poirier, Arlette, 105
Polenblut, 146–7, 152
Polka des lampions, La, 262
Pollak, Anna, 20
Polyakov, G., 23
Pomarez, André, 263
Pondeau, Monique, 25
Pons, Lily, 228
Pont des Soupirs, Le, 13, 14–15, 52
Ponto, Erich, 300
Popp, André, 263
Popp, Lucia, 92, 117, 130, 276
Poppell, Jack, 486
Poppy, 455–6, 490
Poretta, Frank, 128, 323, 324, 333
Port du soleil, Le, 252
Porte, Pierre, 21
Porter, Cole, 191–8, 222, 231, 345, 361
Posford, George, 231
Potopovskaya, D., 133
Potter, Philip, 62, 64, 68, 75
Pourcel, Frank, 283
Pour Don Carlos, 258
Powell, Jane, 181, 336

Powell, Susan, 514
Power, Elizabeth, 438
Pracht, Mary Ellen, 149, 158
Prado, Hilton, 469
Pratt, Peter, 54, 59, 63, 68, 71
Preger, Kurt, 89, 94, 106, 109, 110, 116, 282, 298
Premiere in Mailand, 308
Presnell, Harve, 336
Preston, Robert, 369, 370, 408, 409, 414
Previn, André, 336, 364
Prey, Hermann, 92, 95, 99, 100, 108, 110, 113, 122, 124
Pridan, Ariel, 512
Prikoba, Herbert, 285, 286
Primrose, 182, 218
Prince, Jack, 375
Prince and the Showgirl, The, 433
Prince de Madrid, Le, 261
Prince of Pilsen, The, 159, 160, 212
Princesse Czardas, see *Csárdásfürstin, Die*
Princess Ida, 67–8, 86
Princess Pat, The, 158
Pringle, Bryan, 471
Printemps, Yvonne, 105, 196, 228, 250, 282–3
Prior, Marina, 195, 478
Private Lives, 240
Prochnik, Bruce, 450
Proetti, Luigi, 416
Promises, Promises, 422
Prophet, Johnny, 346
Protschka, Josef, 93, 94, 97
Prowse, Juliet, 402
Prudhon, Huguette, 4
Pruvost, Jacques, 22
Pufferl, Merl, 128
Pull Both Ends, 470
Pump Boys and Dinettes, 513, 517
Purlie, 426, 429
Putz, Hans, 290, 324

Quaker Girl, The, 85, 218
Quast, Philip, 496
Quatre Barbus, les, 262
Quatre Jours à Paris, 260
Quatro, Suzi, 341
Quayle, Anna, 456
Quilley, Denis, 176, 181, 202, 410, 454
Quinn, Anthony, 411
Quinn, Patricia, 473
Quiseekay, Diana, 451

Radd, Ronald, 422
Rado, James, 428
Rae, Charlotte, 300
Rae, Jacqui, 195
Rafael, Jorge, 405

Ragni, Gerome, 428
Rainmaker, The, 414
Raisbeck, Rosina, 326
Raitt, John, 172, 314, 315, 316, 340, 367
Rall, Tommy, 405
Ralph, Sheryl Lee, 507
Ramey, Samuel, 317
Ramsay, Robin, 464
Ramsey, Bill, 302
Randolph, Elsie, 222
Randolph, James, 351
Rands, Leslie, 56, 60, 65
Ranieri, Massimo, 405
Rape upon Rape, 452
Raphanel, Ghyslaine, 45
Rathburn, Roger, 179
Rátonyi, Róbert, 141, 143, 144, 287
Rattigan, Terence, 433
Raymond, Fred, 305
Raymond, Gary, 263
Raynaud, Michèle, 11
Raz, Rivka, 324, 451
Reading, Bertice, 321, 440, 441
Reams, Lee Roy, 504
Reardon, John, 129, 209, 337, 338
Rebroff, Ivan, 276, 390
Redgrave, Vanessa, 334
Redhead, 378
Red, Hot and Blue, 193, 196, 213
Red Mill, The, 155, 157, 212
Reece, Brian, 239
Reed, John, 54, 57, 59, 61, 63, 64, 66, 68, 69, 75, 76, 77
Reed, Michael, 219, 221
Rees, Jackie, 508
Rees, Terence, 78
Reeve, Scott, 357, 358
Reeves, Peter, 466
Regan, Peter, 447
Reid, Meston, 58, 78
Reid, William, 127
Reilly, Charles Nelson, 406
Renard, Colette, 262, 263
Renard, Jules, 515
Renaud, Madeleine, 19
Renaux, Nadine, 20, 37, 38, 41, 43, 47
Rendall, David, 222, 317
Rennie, Malcolm, 435
Resnik, Regina, 90, 318, 363
Réthy, Esther, 110
Rêve de Vienne, 262
Revill, Clive, 73, 263, 450
Revoil, Fanély, 246, 247, 248
Revolution française, La, 264, 309
Rey, Gaston, 17, 26, 244, 280
Reynolds, Burt, 425
Reynolds, Debbie, 181, 188, 322, 352
Reynolds, Dorothy, 436,437

Rhodes, Jane, 7, 10, 12
Ribot, Janine, 256, 257
Rice, Sarah, 399
Rice, Tim, 462–70, 488–90
Richard, Cliff, 444
Richards, Angela, 458
Richards, Carole, 332, 350
Richards, Donald, 343
Richardson, Ian, 330, 438
Richardson, Mark, 72
Richardson, Ron, 509
Richert, Wanda, 504
Richter, Traute, 303
Riddle, Nelson, 361
Ride, Ride!, 470
Riedinger, Colette, 35, 37, 42, 105, 129, 131, 243, 249, 274, 283, 292
Rieu, Marcelle, 30
Rigby, Harry, 188, 190
Rigby, Jean, 72
Rigg, Diana, 396
Righetti, Romana, 280, 286
Rika, Dominique, 256
Rink, The, 413, 505–6
Riordan, Joseph 58
Rio Rita, 189
Rip!, 39–40, 52
Ristori, Gabrielle, 42
Ritchard, Cyril, 24
Ritzmann, Martin, 94, 284
Rivera, Chita, 210, 359, 370, 376, 402, 412, 505
Roar of the Greasepaint . . ., The, 457
Robert, Gisèle, 256
Robert, Marcel, 11
Roberta, 177, 212
Robert and Elizabeth, 457–9, 474
Roberts, Joan, 177, 312
Roberts, Rachel, 451
Robertson, Liz, 506
Robeson, Paul, 170
Robin, Leo, 347
Robin, Mado, 105, 135
Robin Hood, 154, 212
Robinson, Elisabeth, 226
Robinson, Richard, 169
Robinson Crusoe, 33
Rocky Horror Show, The, 472, 474
Rodgers, Anton, 457
Rodgers, Eileen, 193, 377
Rodgers, Mary, 372, 378
Rodgers, Richard, 191, 198–206, 385–6
Roegg, Nicolette, 455
Roffmann, Frederick, 156
Rogati, E., 114
Roger, Germaine, 44, 244
Rogers, 244, 249
Rogers, Anne, 179, 226, 439, 440
Röhr, Rosi, 305

Roi des Galéjeurs, Le, 252
Roi du Pacifique, Le, 262
Rökk, Marika, 307, 407
Romaguera, Joaquin, 399
Romance by Candlelight, 433
Romance, Romance, 515
Romberg, Sigmund, 164–70, 231
Rome, Harold, 372, 374–6
Ronstadt, Linda, 62
Roon, Elisabeth, 102, 106, 108, 109, 118
Rose, Arthur, 235
Rose, George, 62, 330, 460, 511
Rose de Saint-Flour, La, 30
Rose Marie, 1, 161–2, 163, 212, 241
Rosen, Michaela, 416
Rosenthal, Manuel, 32
Rose of Persia, The, 53, 78
Rose of the Auvergne, The, see *Rose de Saint-Flour, La*
Rosetti, Christina, 513
Rose von Stambul, Die, 151, 266, 309
Ross, Adrian, 48, 126
Ross, Jerry, 366–8
Ross, Ted, 425
Rossi, Tino, 254, 256
Rössl-Majdan, Hilde, 96
Roswaenge, Helge, 276, 296, 299
Rothenberger, Anneliese, 7, 10, 90, 91, 96, 99, 100, 104, 108, 113, 116, 126, 134, 139, 140, 269, 271, 274, 284, 285, 290
Rothschilds, The, 391
Rouleau, Joseph, 69
Round, Thomas, 54, 57, 61, 63, 66, 68, 69, 71, 76, 126, 127, 148
Rounseville, Robert, 73, 165, 315, 356, 391, 419
Roussel, Marie-France, 494
Route fleurie, La, 260, 308
Routledge, Patricia, 379, 437, 461
Roux, Michel, 5, 8, 20, 47, 49
Rowe McAllen, Kathleen, 488
Rowland, Patsy, 441
Royal, Ted, 206, 332, 351, 439
Rubens, Paul, 217
Rubenstein, John, 417
Rubin, Arthur, 157, 396
Ruby, Thelma, 447
Ruddigore, 68–70, 85
Rudensky, Shmuel, 390
Rudiferia, Milena, 139, 140
Ruffelle, Frances, 409, 483, 495
Ruick, Barbara, 185, 315
Runyon, Damon, 350
Rupert, Michael, 513
Russell, Rosalind, 354, 355, 366
Rutland, John, 439, 440
Ryan, Irene, 417
Ryan, Mark, 468
Rydell, Bobby, 371

Rydl, Kurt, 93
Rysanek, Lotte, 114, 186, 284

Sager, Carol Bayer, 416
Sail Away, 432–3, 474
Saison in Salzburg, 307, 310
Salad Days, 434–6, 474
Salez, François, 30
Sally, 175, 212
Saltimbanques, Les, 49, 50, 52
San Basilio, Paloma, 469
Sanders, Jean, 207
Sanders, George, 350
Sandford, Kenneth, 58, 64, 66, 68, 69, 77
Sands, Tommy, 158
Sands, Robert, 165
Sanial, Anne-Marie, 27
San Juan, Olga, 335
Sansom, Mary, 64, 66, 76
Sarandon, Susan, 473
Sardou, Michel, 494, 495
Sargent, Sir Malcolm, 53–4, 55, 62, 68, 69, 74, 75
Sarvil, René, 251, 252
Sasvári, Sándor, 465, 497
Satton, Lon, 482, 483
Saunders, Terry, 323
Sautereau, Nadine, 25
Savage, John, 428
Savident, John, 459, 485
Saxon, Luther, 210
Say Darling, 372
Schädle, Lotte, 150, 305
Schatzmeister, Der, 118
Schellow, Eric, 298
Schenk, Otto, 91
Scheyrer, Gisela, 90, 94, 102, 108
Schlemm, Anny, 102, 268
Schmid, Patric, 33
Schmidinger, Josef, 95
Schmidt, Harvey, 371
Schmidt-Bolcke, Werner, 150
Schneider, Willy, 120, 268
Schock, Rudolf, 21, 90, 96, 100, 104, 108, 110, 114, 117, 118, 122, 125, 131, 132, 135, 138, 141, 142, 146, 147, 148, 149, 287–8
Schofield, Andrew, 491
Schönberg, Claude-Michel, 264, 493
Schöne, Rainer, 463
schöne Galathee, Die, 106, 107, 151
Schöner, Sonja, 83, 131, 138, 276, 284
Schönherr, Max, 281
Schön ist die Welt, 269
Schorg, Gretl, 83, 268
Schramm, Margit, 20, 118, 120, 122, 125, 131, 132, 135, 138, 141, 142, 146, 147, 149, 267, 271, 284, 287, 303, 304, 305, 306, 307
Schröder, Friedrich, 306, 307

Schubert, Franz, 147
Schultes, Jean, 265
Schütz, Ernst, 112, 148
Schwaiger, Rosl, 83
Schwartz, Arthur, 218, 372, 381
Schwarz, Hanna, 97
schwarze Hecht, Der, 308
Schwartz, Stephen, 417, 418
Schwarzkopf, Elisabeth, 89, 94, 95, 98, 99, 104,
    269, 270
Schwarzwaldmädel, 149–50, 152
Scofield, Paul, 443
Scott, Bonnie, 387
Scott, Helena, 337, 353
Scott, Maureen, 341
Scotto, Vincent, 251–4
Scovotti, Jeannette, 97, 101, 157, 323
Seal, Elizabeth, 263, 367, 435
Secombe, Harry, 450, 457, 460
Secret de Marco Polo, Le, 261
Secret Diary of Adrian Mole, The, 491
Seegers, Rosl, 103, 132, 133
See-Saw, 402, 430
Segal, Vivienne, 199
Seidl, Lea, 96
Seiffert, Peter, 92
S. E. La Embajadora, 261
Sell, Janie, 188
Sellers, Georges, 252
Sendin, Ashleigh, 194
Sénéchal, Michel, 6, 19, 23, 38, 44, 45, 105
Serabian, Lorraine, 411
Serafin, Harald, 118, 292
Serenade, 158
Serenella, 414
Serpette, Gaston, 53
Serrador, Pastor, 414
Sesto, Camillo, 464
Seven Lively Arts, The, 197
1776, 421–2, 430
70, Girls, 70, 413
Sewell, Danny, 450
Shacklock, Constance, 326
Shafer, Robert, 337
Shankley, Jeff, 483
Shapiro, Debbie, 412
Shapiro, Ted, 233
Sharkey, Anna, 442, 515
Shaw, Hollace, 178
Shaw, John, 64
Shaw, Reta, 367
Shayne, Tracy, 496
Sheffield, Leo, 56, 76
Shelby, Laurel, 203
Shell, Ray, 482, 483
She Loves Me, 387
Shelton, Reid, 316, 413
Shenandoah, 426–7, 430

Shepherd, Thomas Z., 209
Sherman, Alan, 352
Sherman, Hiram, 207
Sherrin, Ned, 457
Shilling, Eric, 6, 20, 66
Shimada, Kaho, 496
Shoemaker's Holiday, The, 438
Shore, Dinah, 324, 346, 349
Short, John, 509
Shovelton, Geoffrey, 57
Show Boat, 170–4, 212, 431
Shuard, Amy, 12
Shutta, Ethel, 396
Sie spielen unser Lied, see *They're Playing Our Song*,
Silk Stockings, 372
Sills, Beverley, 129, 158
Silver, Johnny, 351
Simionato, Giulietta, 90
Simmons, Jean, 398
Simon, Annick, 13
Simon, Neil, 400
Sinatra, Frank, 192, 200, 321, 344, 346, 352, 361
Sinclair, Belinda, 472
Sinclair, Bernard, 9, 35, 38, 105, 302
Sinclair, Monica, 54, 60, 62, 64, 66, 69, 71, 75,
    77, 80, 226
Singer, Gideon, 420
Singin' in the Rain, 492–3, 517
Skeels, Steven Michael, 483
Skitch, Jeffrey, 60, 68, 76
Slade, Julian, 434–8
Sladen, Victoria, 68
Slyper, Jacques, 40
Smalls, Charlie, 425
Smigra, Tamara, 289
Smith, Grant, 478
Smith, Harry Bache, 154
Smith, Kenneth, 157
Smith, Loring, 406
Smith, Martin, 221
Smith, Muriel, 210, 319, 322, 323, 324
Smith, Rex, 62
Smith, Rufus, 335
Söhnker, Hans, 275
Soleil d'Espagne, 262
Solomon, Edward, 53
Some Like it Hot, 262
Something for the Boys, 197
Sondheim, Stephen, 356, 365, 385, 393–400,
    499–503
Sone, Roy, 445
Song and Dance, 481–2, 517
Songbook, 455, 474
Song of Norway, 336–8, 382
Sont, Gerry, 504
Soper, Gay, 460, 471, 496
Sorano, Daniel, 39
Sorcerer, The, 58–9, 86

Sorvino, Paul, 418
Sothern, Ann, 209
Sound of Music, The, 115, 324–7
Souris, 246
Sousa, Jean Philip, 154
Southern Maid, A, 217
South Pacific, 318–22, 382
Spaak, Catherine, 423
Spanellys, Georgette, 35
Sparrow, James, 245
Spear, Bernard, 406, 419
Spearman, Rawn, 373
Spewack, Sam and Bella, 345
Spialek, Hans, 195
Spierenburg, Christine, 114
St Denis, Teddie, 235
St Helier, Ivy, 220
St Louis, Louis, 421
St Louis Woman, 373–4, 382
Staal, Herta, 114
Stafford, Jo, 346
Staiger, Libi, 353
Stand Up and Sing, 222
Stange, Stanislaus, 136
Staniforth, Michael, 482, 483
Stanno suonando la nostra canzone, see *They're Playing Our Song*
Starkie, Martin, 460
Starlight Express, 482–4, 517
Starmania, 498–9, 517
Steafel, Sheila, 435
Steber, Eleanor, 158, 169
Steele, Suzanne, 6
Steele, Tommy, 344, 445, 492
Steffan, Ernst, 112
Steffe, Edwin, 112, 163, 460
Steffek, Hanny, 124
Stein, Joseph, 388
Stein, Leo, 140
Steinberg, Pinchas, 16
Stephens, Madge, 217
Stephenson, B. C., 57
Sternquist, Sonia, 130
Stevens, Marti, 184
Stevens, Risë, 136, 171, 172, 207, 323
Stewardson, Joe, 366
Stewart, Michael, 403, 409
Stewart, Robb, 453
Stewart, Thomas, 207
Stiot, Monique, 13, 15
Stockton, Frank, 390
Stolz, Robert, 110, 124, 125, 132, 142, 232, 241, 290, 291, 304–6
Stop the World, I Want to Get Off, 456–7, 474
Storch, Eberhard, 314
Storm, Rebecca, 492
Stoska, Polyna, 342
Stoss, Franz, 292

Straker, Peter, 428
Stratas, Teresa, 117, 125, 173, 276
Stratton, Chester, 199
Straus, Oscar, 102, 104, 134–6, 217, 241, 281–4
Strauss, Johann, 87–105
Strazzer, Carlos Augusto, 469
Streamline, 232
Street Scene, 342–3, 382
Streich, Rita, 98, 99, 100, 104, 110, 275
Streisand, Barbra, 391, 407
Stritch, Elaine, 200, 203, 395, 397, 432
Strohbauer, Hans, 114, 141, 284
Strouse, Charles, 413–14, 506
Stuart, Ralph, 178
Stubbs, Levi, 512
Student Prince, The, 164–6, 212
Studholme, Marion, 73, 93
Sturial, Grant, 514
Stutzmann, Christiane, 35, 38
Styler, Alan, 58, 66, 76
Styne, Jule, 313, 347, 364, 391–2
Sugar, 391
Suka, Sándor, 145
Sullivan, Sir Arthur, 53–80
Sullivan, Jo, 300, 332, 342, 353
Sullivan, Joseph, 342
Sullivan, Sheila, 206
Summer, Donna, 428
Summerhays, Jane, 236
Summers, Michelle, 198
Sunday in the Park with George, 501–2, 517
Supervia, Conchita, 280
Suppé, Franz von, 87, 106–9
Sutherland, Joan, 128, 220, 228
Swan Esther, 490
Swanson, Gloria, 177
Sweeney Todd, 398–400, 430
Sweet Adeline, 178
Sweet Charity, 401–2, 429
Sweethearts, 155
Swerling, Jo, 350
Syers, Mark, 468
Sylvia, Simone, 251
Symington, Eve, 204
Szakácsi, Sándor, 469
Szemere, László, 109
Szibill, 142–3, 171, 212
Szirmai, Albert, 218

Tabbert, William, 320, 375
Ta bouche, 246, 247, 309
Talbot, Howard, 84
Talmar, Herta, 112, 120, 307
Talva, Galina, 349
Tamblyn, Russ, 181
Tanner, Susan Jane, 478, 495
Tanner, Tony, 452, 456

Tänzerin Fanny Elssler, Die, 104, 294
Tap Dance Kid, The, 509
tapfere Soldat, Der, 135
Tarrès, Enriqueta, 12
Tate, Stephen, 478, 490
Tauber, Richard, 110, 220, 238, 287
Tausky, Vilem, 84
Tayles, Jacques, 302
Taylor, Elizabeth, 398
Taylor, Femi, 441
Taylor, John, 446
Taylor, Ron, 511
Tchenko, Katia, 260
Tebaldi, Renata, 11, 89
Teeter, Lara, 204
Teichmann, Edith, 299
te Kanawa, Kiri, 187, 321, 331, 360
Telson, Bob 516
Temps des guitares, Les, 261
Tenderloin, 377
Terada, Minoru, 464
Teresina, 282
Terkal, Karl, 90, 94, 96, 114, 116, 117, 131, 138, 141
Terrasson, René, 11, 13, 27, 28
Tête de linotte, 261
te Wiata, Inia, 172, 215, 324, 353
Teyte, Maggie, 48, 228
Thatcher, Heather, 228
That's a Good Girl, 218
Theodore, Donna, 427
Theodore & Co, 175, 212, 218
They're Playing our Song, 416–17, 430
Thibault, Eliane, 36, 44, 390
Thibeault, Françoise, 499
Thomas, Marjorie, 66, 77
Thomas, Mary, 159, 234, 293
Thomas, Robert, 226
Thompson, Alexander M., 81
Thompson, Emma, 236
Thornton, Eric, 66
Thornton, Frank, 236
Thornton, John, 478
1001 Nacht, 103, 151
Three Guys Naked from the Waist Down, 513
Three Musketeers, The, 163
Threepenny Opera, see *Dreigroschenoper, Die*
Three Sisters, The, 178
Tibbett, Lawrence, 169
Tierney, Harry, 187–9
Tierney, Vivienne, 131
Time, 491
Timmons, Mary, 79
Tinkler, Mark, 358
Tip-Toes, 185
Tirmont, Dominique, 25, 250, 283, 402
Tobias, Oliver, 428, 463
Todd, Diane, 395

Toison d'or, La, 258–9
Toledano, Avi, 498
Tom Brown's Schooldays, 470
Tom Jones, 81–2, 86
Tommy, 473
Toni, 218
Tonight at 8.30, 231, 240
Too Many Girls, 204, 213
Topol, 388, 389
Toppano, Peta, 508
Torelli, Inès, 308
Tough at the Top, 234, 240
Towb, Harry, 194
Towers, Constance, 172
Toye, Jennifer, 71, 76
Toye, Wendy, 340
Tozzi, Giorgio, 161, 165, 234,319, 320, 321
Traubel, Helen, 73
Traubner, Richard, 298
Trauminsel, 305, 306
Traumland, 296
Travelling Music Show, The, 457
Travolta, John, 421
Traxel, Josef, 276
Treasure Girl, 198
Tree Grows in Brooklyn, A, 381
Tréhy, Robert, 341
Trelawny, 437–8, 474
Trempont, Michel, 7, 19, 23, 32, 33, 42
Trent, Bruce, 199, 375
Trent, Jackie, 470
Tresmand, Ivy, 181
Trial by Jury, 55–7, 86
Triola, Ann, 177
Trois de la Marine, 251, 252, 253
Trois Mousquetaires, Les, 261
Trois Valses, see *Drei Walzer*
Tromb-al-ca-zar, 29, 51
Troyanos, Tatiana, 360
Truhitte, Dan, 325
Tucker, Richard, 419
Tucker, Sophie, 232
Tunbridge, Joe, 434
Tune, Tommy, 183, 402, 410
Tunick, Jonathan, 395, 423
Turner, Claramae, 315
Turner, Geraldine, 195, 412
Turner, Martin, 194
Twain, Mark, 390
Twenty Minutes South, 453
Twiggy, 183
Two Cities, 460
Two Gentlemen of Verona (Slade), 438
Two Gentlemen of Verona (McDermott), 428–9
Tyne, George, 300
Tysick, Sylvia, 370
Tzelniker, Meier, 161, 444

Udell, Peter, 426
Udvardy, Tibor, 93, 97, 143, 287, 288
Uglebjerg, Preben, 331
Ukelele Ike (Cliff Edwards), 183
Ullett, Nick, 236
Ullrich, Luise, 412
Ulvaeus, Bjorn, 488
Un de la Canebière, 251, 252, 309
Ungarische Hochzeit, Die, 303
Unger, Gerhard, 21, 110, 116
Unsinkable Molly Brown, The, 372
Up in Central Park, 170
Uppman, Theodore, 24
Usmanov, A., 133
Utopia (Limited), 77–8, 86

Vagabond King, The, 49, 162, 163, 217
Vagabond tzigane, Le, 262
Valdarnini, Loly, 8
Vallee, Rudy, 387
Valmouth, 440, 474
Valses de Vienne, see *Walzer aus Wien*
Van, Bobby, 179, 203
van Allan, Richard, 72
Vandair, Maurice, 253
van Dam, José, 250
van Druten, John, 410
van Dyke, Dick, 370, 371
van Jüten, Grit, 295
Vanloo, Albert, 45
van Ree, Jean, 16
Vanzo, Alain, 12, 22
Varady, Julia, 94, 97
Varlan, Nick, 232
Varney, Louis, 41–3
Varon, Eliane, 250, 259, 260, 292
Vaughan, Sarah, 321
Vedova allegra, La, see *lustige Witwe, Die*
Veilchen vom Montmartre, Das, 139, 286, 289–90
Velvet Lady, The, 158
Venora, Lee, 323, 324, 362
Venus in Seide, 304, 310
Vera-Ellen, 199
Verdon, Gwen, 368, 378, 401, 402, 412
Vereen, Ben, 417, 464
Verlen, Arta, 105
Vernon, Virginia, 455
Véronique, 46–7, 52, 309
Very Good, Eddie, 174
Very Warm for May, 178
Vespermann, Gerd, 16
Vestoff, Virginia, 422
Vetter aus Dingsda, Das, 294, 309
Veuve joyeuse, La, see *lustige Witwe, Die*
Vidnovic, Martin, 313, 510, 514
Vielgeliebte, Die, 303
Vie parisienne, La, 3, 12, 18, 19–21, 52
Vigna, Elisabeth, 265

Vig Özvegy, see *lustige Witwe, Die*
Vikidal, Gyula, 497
Viktoria und ihr Husar, 301–2, 310
Villamor, José, 261
Vincy, Raymond, 241, 253, 260
Vinter, Gilbert, 82
Violettes impériales, 253–4
Violoneux, Le, 30
Violon sur le toit, Un, see *Fiddler on the Roof*
Virtue in Danger, 460, 461, 474
Viti, Geraldine, 380
Vittoz, Vincent, 27, 512
Vivalda, Janette, 22, 129
Viva Mexico, 261
Viva Napoli, 309
Vogelhändler, Der, 115–17, 150, 151
Volga, 261
Voli, Albert, 29
Voltaire, 355
von Stade, Frederica, 173, 196, 318, 327
Voss, Stephanie, 135, 163, 452

Wächter, Eberhard, 90, 110, 116, 122, 124
Wächter, Franz, 139, 140
Wadsworth, Andrew C., 491
Wagemann, Rose, 106
Wagner, Chuck, 503
Wagner, Jeannine, 169
Wagner, Sieglinde, 89
Wakefield, Ann, 439
Wakefield, John, 73, 215
Wakeham, Michael, 217
Walbrook, Anton, 349, 433
Walker, Don, 317, 388
Walker, Nancy, 338
Wall, Max, 367
Wallace, Ian, 66, 71, 215, 363
Wallace, Paul, 365
Wallberg, Heinz, 276, 277
Waller, Gordon, 466
Waller, Jack, 434
Wallis, Shani, 355, 450
Walsh, Mary Jane, 196
Walsh, Richard, 493
Walton, Ray, 368
Waltzes from Vienna, see *Walzer aus Wien*
Walzer aus Wien, 1, 103, 105, 151
Walzertraum, Ein, 1, 134–5, 151
Wann, Jim, 513
Warfield, William, 172
Waring, Derek, 439
Warner, John, 435
Warren, Colette, 341
Warren, Harry, 504
Warren, Julie, 199
Warwick, Ruth, 188
Water Gipsies, The, 233, 235
Waters, John, 416

Watson, Richard, 56, 68, 69, 70, 74, 76
Watson, Susan, 179, 316, 370
Watters, Marlys, 359
Wattis, Richard, 461
Wayne, David, 343
Weaver, Jackie, 416
Weaving, Jon, 6, 20
Webb, George, 211
Webb, Lizbeth, 225, 233, 234
Webb, Marti, 417, 446, 470, 481
Wedding in Paris, A, 433, 444, 474
Wedding-Mary, 308
Weede, Robert, 337, 352, 353, 405
Weill, Kurt, 206–10, 297–301
Weir, Leonard, 168, 294, 330
Weismann, Elya, 302
Welch, Elisabeth, 211, 222, 223, 225
Welchman, Harry, 167
Weldon, Joan, 128
Welitch, Ljuba, 93
Wellman, Jane, 439
Wells, H. G., 445
Wenham, Jane, 438, 441, 454, 461
Wenn die kleinen Veilchen blühen, 306
Werfel, Franz, 142
Westenberg, Robert, 503
West Side Story, 358–61, 382
Wewel, Günter, 113
What a Way to Run a Revolution, 470
Wheeler, Hugh, 197, 356
When You're Young, 460
Where's Charley?, 344
White, Don, 33, 34
White, Jane, 379
White, Roger, 185
White, Sheila, 423, 448, 459
White T. H., 333
White, Terri, 404
White, Trevor, 464
Whiteman, Paul, 171
Whitfield, June, 238
Whitford, Peter, 195
Whiting, Jack, 178, 192, 380
Whiting, Richard, 472
Whitsun-Jones, Paul, 449
Whoopee!, 190
Wiecken, Isabel, 469
Wie einst im Mai, 120–1, 152
Wiener, John, 503
Wiener Blut, 104, 151
Wieth, Mogens, 331
Wilbur, Richard, 356
Wilcox, Larry, 374, 492
Wild, Jack, 450
Wildcat, 400
Wilde, Marty, 371, 445
Wilde, Oscar, 431
Wildflower, 181

Wild Grows the Heather, 431, 434
Wildest Dreams, 436
Wilhelm, Horst, 114
Wilkinson Colm (C. T.), 467, 470, 495
Wilkof, Lee, 511
Willemetz, Albert, 26, 241, 242, 244, 248
Williams, Kenneth, 442
Williams, Neil, 218, 231
Williams, Rita, 293
Williams, Treat, 428
Willson, Meredith, 368
Wilson, Catherine, 128
Wilson, Julie, 239, 345
Wilson, Sandy, 438–43
Wilson, Snoo, 7
Wilson-Hyde, Eric, 81
Winckler, Gerhard, 308
Windsor, Barbara, 459, 461
Windsor Castle, 53
Windy City, 490
Winnie the Pooh, 438
Winter, Edward, 422
Wisdom, Norman, 344, 457
Wise, Jim, 418
Wish You Were Here, 374–5
Wisniewska, Helga, 276, 305
Wiz, The, 425, 430
Wizard of Oz, The, 374
Wodehouse, P. G., 184
Wodka Cola, see *Leave it to Me*
Wolff, Angelika, 295
Wolfington, Iggie, 269
Wolfson, Martin, 300
Woman of the Year, 505
Wonderful Town, 353–5, 382
Wood, Peggy, 202
Woodland, Rae, 226
Woods, John, 478
Woods, Kerry, 478
Wordsworth, Richard, 452, 461
Worster, Howett, 169
Worth, Billie, 349
Wren, Jenny, 442
Wright, Bob, 128
Wright, Colin, 71
Wright, Joyce, 76
Wright, Robert, 337, 362
Wrightson, Earl, 162
Wunderlich, Fritz, 100, 110, 266, 267, 269, 276, 284
Wynn, Ed, 158
Wynter, Mark, 441, 447, 448, 459

Yadin, Yossi, 390, 412
Yakovenko, A., 133
Yakushev, Y., 133
Yarnell, Bruce, 340
Yeini, Elior, 497

Yellen, Jack, 233
Yeomen of the Guard, The, 73–5, 86
Yes, Madam, 218, 222, 240
Yeston, Maury, 507
Yo y mi chica, see *Me and My Girl*
Youmans, Vincent, 178–81
Young, Alexander, 66, 74, 77, 93
Young, Charles, 81, 216, 234
Young, Ronald, 439
Young-Schmidt, Alexandra, 486
Young Visiters, The, 460
You're a Good Man, Charlie Brown, 423, 429
Yvain, Maurice, 241, 246–9, 282

Zadek, Hilde, 94, 116
Zampieri, Giuseppe, 90

Zanetti, Jacomo, 31
Zareska, Eugenia, 11
Zarewitsch, Der, 275–6, 309
Zauberin Lola, 294
Zednik, Heinz, 274
Zell (Camillo Walzel), 91
Zeller, Carl, 87, 115–17
Zentay, Anna, 144, 288
Ziehrer, Carl Michael, 118, 151
Zien, Chip, 513
Zigeunerbaron, Der, 1, 92, 93, 94–7, 150, 151
Zigeunerliebe, 131–3, 151
Zillger, Ruth, 102
Zirkusprinzessen, Die, 286, 309
Zoo, The, 57, 85
Zorina, Vera, 203
Zsadon, Andrea, 145